BLACK

CHICAGO'S

FIRST

CENTURY

BLACK
CHICAGO'S
FIRST
CENTURY

Volume 1, 1833–1900

CHRISTOPHER ROBERT REED

University of Missouri Press
Columbia and London

Library of Congress Cataloging-in-Publication Data

Reed, Christopher Robert.
    Black Chicago's first century / Christopher Robert Reed.
        p. cm.
    Summary: "Examines the first one hundred years of African American
settlement and achievements in Chicago. It spans the antebellum, Civil
War, Reconstruction, and post-Reconstruction periods"—Provided by
publisher.
    Includes bibliographical references and index.
    ISBN 0-8262-1570-X (v. 1 : alk. paper)
    1. African Americans—Illinois—Chicago—History—19th century.
2. African Americans—Illinois—Chicago—History—20th century.
3. Chicago (Ill.)—History—19th century. 4. Chicago (Ill.)—History—
20th century. 5. Chicago (Ill.)—Race relations. I. Title: Black Chicago's
1st century. II. Title.
F548.9.N4R437   2005
977.3'1100496073—dc22

                                                              2005006294

∞™ This paper meets the requirements of the
American National Standard for Permanence of Paper
for Printed Library Materials, Z39.48, 1984.

Designer: Stephanie Foley
Typesetter: Foley Design
Printer and binder: Thomson-Shore, Inc.
Typefaces: Goudy and Ottomat

Jacket photos: Center, *Quinn Chapel A.M.E. Church (courtesy of Quinn
Chapel A.M.E.)*; Left to right, *Mary Richardson Jones, Dr. A. M. Curtis,
and Mary Davenport (Vivian G. Harsh Research Collection of Afro-American
History and Literature, Chicago Public Library)*, and *A. D. E. Jackson
(Special Collections and Preservation Division, Chicago Public Library.*

to six phenomenal women

JOSEPHINE PEAY SLAUGHTER

RUSSIE SLAUGHTER BERRY

MELINDA DEE SLAUGHTER GREEN

BERYL TRIMBLE SLAUGHTER

EVA LEWIS REID

JOSEPHINE SLAUGHTER REED RHODES

Contents

Part II.

Harbor of Opportunity for New Citizens, 1866–1900

Chapter 3. Freedom and Fire during the Reconstruction Era, 1866–1879

Illustrations

Acknowledgments

T HIS PROJECT could never have been completed in the form it finally assumed without the personal interest and cooperation, along with the professional commitment, of a score or more of individuals and institutions. Direct bloodline descendants of several of the oldest African American settler families of Chicago as well as the spiritual and intellectual heirs of the Old Settlers' shared memories, written material, photographs, and other memorabilia contributed mightily to the production of *Black Chicago's First Century, 1833–1933*. This roll of major contributors includes the following: Grace Mason and Michelle Madison of the Atkinson family, Leota Johnson from the Taylor family, Jeanne Boger Jones from the Hall family, and Lloyd C. Wheeler, III, from the Jones and Wheeler families.

For their professional assistance over the last decade, I wish to thank Michael Missick and the staff at the National Archives in Washington, D.C.; Mark Sorenson, Greg Cox, and Kim Efrid at the Illinois State Archives in Springfield; Anita Haskell at the Murray-Green Library at Roosevelt University, along with technical assistance from Ronald Elms and Len Redmond in Office Services; Robert Miller and Michael Flug and staff at the Vivian G. Harsh Collection at the Carter G. Woodson Center of the Chicago Public Library, as well as Teresa Yoder and other staff at the Harold Washington Center of the Chicago Public Library; John Hoffman and James Cornelius at the Illinois Historical Survey and Lincoln Room at the University of Illinois at Urbana-Champaign; Emeritus Professor William Andrews of SUNY-Brockport; Elaine Schwanekamp at the Chautauqua County Historical Society in Westfield, New York; Linda Evans and the staff of the Chicago Historical Society; and the staff of the Regenstein Library at the University of Chicago.

For the unbridled enthusiasm and critical review of all or parts of the book from and beyond the academy, I wish to thank Lynn Y. Weiner, Brigitte M. Erbe, Robert T. Starks, Dennis Dickerson, Suellen Hoy, Laura Janota, John Bracey, Jr., Deirdra Ann Lucas, Vinton Thompson, and Dr. Adelaide Cromwell of Brookline, Massachusetts, as well as Lerone Bennett, Jr., Sharon Vaughn, Jerolyn Croswell, Marionette C. Phelps, Muriel Wilson, Elizabeth Glasco, Lynn Von Dreele, Cherie Pleau, Lynnett Davis, and the home-schooled family of Jonathan and LaShone Kelly.

The local clergy informed and contributed also in reconstructing this saga of a spirit-driven people. I extend my appreciation to Rev. Anthony Vinson, Sr., along with Luster and Olavenia Jackson of Bethel A.M.E. Church; Rev. James A. Missick of the Original Providence Baptist Church; Rev. James M. Moody of the Quinn Chapel A.M.E. Church; Rev. A. Lincoln James of the Greater Bethesda Baptist Church; and Father Martini Shaw of the St. James Episcopal Church.

Captain DeKalb Wolcott, II, of the Chicago Fire Department, and fire department historians Ken Little and Father John McNalis, along with Patti Thomas, president of the African American Film and TV Makers, helped shape the story of black firefighters.

The role of the sergeant in the military hierarchy gained greater importance in my way of thinking as I examined the content of Civil War records and conferred with Tech. Sgt. Albert A. Burns, Seventh U.S. Army (a veteran of World War II) and Sgt. Malcolm M. Reed, Fourth Marine Division (a veteran of Gulf War I).

Graduate students at Roosevelt University deserve mention for their insightful views and inquiries. Those who participated in lively discussions both inside and outside the classroom of History 465 (The History of Black Chicago) about the validity of ideas and interpretations presented in *Black Chicago's First Century* included Clinton P. Walker, Janice Collier, Curtis Keyes, Jr., Nick McCormick, Ronald T. Jones, Eve Bady, Susan Bova, and Terrence Henderson.

Special thanks to my wife, Marva P. Reed, who spent many hours at the National Archives scouring veterans' records for possible useful data on Chicago's black Civil War heroes. Of course, all errors in interpretation and presentation rest on my shoulders alone.

Extra-special thanks go to my editor at the University of Missouri Press, Julie Schroeder, who personified acuity of mind and eye as she elevated copyediting to a fine art form. In her perseverance in this task, she demonstrated a bonding with the author that will not be forgotten. Further, I also wish to thank the press's director and editor-in-chief, Beverly Jarrett, and acquisitions editor Clair Willcox, for considering this manuscript, for at times it must have appeared an impossible burden rather than a blessing.

The late nineteenth century in black history is indeed a stretch of undiscovered territory, and from it this project will surely bear productive fruit.

Abbreviations

ATA   A. T. Andreas, *A History of Chicago,* in three volumes

AWT   Albion W. Tourgee Papers, Chautaugua County Historical Society, Westfield, New York

BLP   Bessie Louise Pierce, *History of Chicago,* in three volumes

BM   St. Clair Drake and Horace R. Cayton, *Black Metropolis*

BTW   Booker T. Washington Papers, Library of Congress, Washington, D.C.

CD   *Chicago Defender*

CHS   Chicago Historical Society

CIO   *Chicago Inter Ocean*

CT   *Chicago Tribune*

CVA   St. Clair Drake, *Churches and Voluntary Associations in the Chicago Negro Community*

CWPR   Federal Pension Records of Soldiers of the 29th Infantry, Illinois, USCT, National Archives, Washington, D.C.

IWP   Illinois Writers Project/"Negro in Illinois" Papers, Vivian G. Harsh Research Collection of Afro-American History and Literature, Chicago Public Library, Carter G. Woodson Regional Library

SOS   "Story of Old Settlers Reads Like Fiction," *Chicago Defender,* May 3, 1930, 23

OT   "Chicago in 1843: A Real 'Oldtimer' on the Life of Early Colored Settlers," *Springfield Illinois Record,* July 9, 1898, 1.

PN   W. E. B. Du Bois, *The Philadelphia Negro*

BLACK

CHICAGO'S

FIRST

CENTURY

Introduction

The American Negro must remake his past in order to make his future. Though it is orthodox to think of America as the one country where it is unnecessary to have a past, what is a luxury for a nation as a whole becomes a prime social necessity for the Negro. For him, a group tradition must supply compensation for persecution, and pride of race the antidote for prejudice. History must restore what slavery took away, for it is the social damage of slavery that the present generation must repair and offset. So among the rising democratic millions we find the Negro thinking more collectively, more retrospectively than the rest, and apt out of the very pressure of the present to become the most enthusiastic antiquarian of them all.

— ARTHUR A. SCHOMBURG, "The Negro Digs Up His Past"

T HIS BOOK resulted from my efforts to meet an academic need to expand knowledge and to provide a long-awaited glimpse into the history of the earliest phases of African American life in Chicago. The twenty-first-century reader *might* assume that a comprehensive history of early Chicago's African American population exists; its current social mass of more than one million persons makes it a force that warrants attention of the nation's scholars, politicians, and policy makers for generations. A priori reasoning would lead one to presume that such a written history does exist. Since it does not, it is natural to wish for one: After all, the Chicago African American population of the previous century experienced a multifaceted involvement within the city's political economy and maintained a highly visible municipal presence. Thus, with the publication of this first volume of *Black Chicago's First Century*, this history is finally available.

In 1973, I introduced at Northern Illinois University what I believe to be the first comprehensive course ever conceived on black Chicago history. I wanted to create a usable classroom reference exploring life in the nineteenth and early twentieth centuries, for the absence of such had critically impeded both teaching and learning. Scholarly and lay reading audiences who struggled with an understanding of black life in Chicago during the antebellum and Civil War periods as well as in later periods often resorted to discussing imagined incidents and exaggerating meanings about what had actually transpired historically. Simply put, the *facts* had not been presented, let alone proffered accurately. In terms of historical authenticity, many of the more dynamic features of life were quite overlooked. Usable theory, of course, remained nonexistent.

Notably missing in essays, scholarly articles, and conversation were acknowledgments of the immediate black interests evinced in business and its growth and development and in a military tradition. Both fed into the emerging ethos and organizational life, which included political involvement. Yet throughout the nineteenth and twentieth centuries, knowledge of these economic and martial phenomena lay embedded in a transgenerational self-awareness of an invigorated African American identity even before the end of slavery. Significantly, this self-awareness was one that originated in the early formation of community life, and its viable appearance made Chicago and its frontier existence unique in some respects among northern antebellum and Reconstruction-era cities.

Emerging in the early nineteenth century, the intersection of agency, opportunity, and an acquired sense of place yielded the rudimentary elements of a fledgling African American community in Chicago with its own culture, and therefore a legitimate history. James Oliver Horton provided a partial template as he pioneered generally in the effort to establish a foundation and to spur an interest in the *interior* life of the antebellum, northern African American community. In the case of New York City, Nell Irvin Painter has further shown that mere documentation of a written tradition and the presence of an educated cohort only validated the existence of a civilizing feature of urban life and an exceptional human presence, not that of a full-fledged community.[1]

Indisputably, Chicago had a fledgling African American community in formation by the eighteen-forties. This was a period that, because of Chicago's infinitesimally small black population, was overlooked by the major, twentieth-century historical studies on free populations in northern cities. Nonetheless, the lives, travails, and triumphs of what thrived as a small community throughout the nineteenth century emerged as a social mass representing a demographic laboratory in its own right in the early twentieth century. By the time St. Clair Drake and Horace R. Cayton's *Black Metropo-*

lis was published in 1945, black Chicago had become the template for the entirety of black urban America, and New York and Philadelphia had lost their primacy as national models.[2]

Meeting the challenge from black America's preeminent bibliophile of the 1920s, Arthur Schomburg, who noted his generation's responsibility to tell the story of its times and origins, this study attempts the same for Chicagoans and persons interested in this neglected and uncovered history. An examination of the situation reveals that because of monumental problems previously encountered in mind-set and research, there was neither an attempt at writing a comprehensive history of black Chicago nor any clear footsteps to follow—that is, a study extending over a substantial period of time and encompassing the various distinctive features of this group's place in the origins, growth, and development of Chicago, or a viable scholarly or lay approach that could stand scrutiny through posterity. Part of the historical gap was filled in 1940 with St. Clair Drake's *Churches and Voluntary Associations in the Chicago Negro Community*. Written in collaboration with budding University of Chicago–trained historian Lawrence D. Reddick (who coincidentally was destined to serve as curator of the famed Schomburg Collection of the New York Pubic Library), this sociological study also presented a historical template on black Chicago. Supplementing this work by 1967 was historian Allan H. Spear's important period work, *Black Chicago: The Making of a Negro Ghetto, 1890–1920*. Spear emphasized how the Great Migration of 1915–1918 and urban pathology produced the Negro ghetto. However, a long-term, comprehensive saga of continuous African American *community life*, including both setbacks and accomplishments, with its struggle to establish relevant being, participation, and contribution to Chicago's development, has until now eluded exposition.[3]

In order to construct a comprehensive history, data were essential, along with a workable framework. Raw data, from which information could be extracted after gleaning, sifting, and interpreting, was crucial to this study. Meanwhile, it was important to have a master paradigm (or a set of smaller paradigms) through which data could be interpreted for narrative, analysis, and theory.

The data arose from recollective, associational, and, importantly, written evidence. These sources substantiated a transgenerational awareness of who and what the African Americans were. For example, roughly a hundred years after the permanent settlement of Chicago by increasing numbers of whites and blacks, Joanna Hudlin Snowden pondered why the earliest history of the city seemed to be of so little importance to the present generation of the 1930s. The past had assumed an extraordinary importance to Snowden because she had been a child of the pioneer generation; she had been born in 1863 and was a survivor of the Great Fire of 1871. She possessed a sense of the usable past at a time when the present conferred upon Chicagoans a message of ordeal and turmoil. Nevertheless, the distresses of the decade of the Great Depression did not and could not overwhelm Snowden, who had experienced so much in the way of trials and counterbalancing triumph. She was especially proud of her African American heritage and of her group's contribution to the making of Chicago. Further, it was her hope that memory could be translated into usable written history.

Assuming the challenge of such a large historical project as the current volume was formidable. In the absence of expansive manuscript collections and bulging archives, and with only scattered copies of the first black newspapers available, the task of reconstructing the earliest portion of this history seemed initially too daunting to be undertaken, much less completed. Yet other sources indeed existed. While to some they might or might not have the equivalency of contemporary observation, recording, and analysis, these alternatives included various uses of memory.[4]

The basis for the first written records on life in early black Chicago resulted from tapping into memory by interviewing longtime residents. Their memories connected recollections of the past in a manner that allowed invaluable historical reconstruction and a clearer understanding of motives and actions. The interviewing efforts of both lay and academic researchers enabled me to extract history from memory. At the community level, Frederick H. H. Robb pioneered oral history interviews in compiling data for *The Negro in Chicago, 1779–1929*. Another exemplary effort in this regard was the Saturday, May 30, 1930, issue of the *Chicago Defender*, which relied on the collective memory of the oldest residents, called affectionately the "Old Settlers," to outline the saga of an emerging and transformed group. As the newspaper celebrated its twenty-fifth anniversary in a self-congratulatory manner, it included a major feature article on the history of African Americans in Chicago since Jean Baptiste Pointe Du Sable's residency around 1770. It proudly printed that "while there are old settlers who recall the days when Abraham Lincoln's body lay in state at the Federal building, yet the social, economic, political and religious life of early Chicago has never been chronicled and presented to the people of today."[5]

This readily identifiable page twenty-three appropriately carried the title, "Story of Old Settlers Reads Like Fiction." It nearly filled the entire sixteen-by-twenty-six-inch page and was displayed in six wide columns. In order for the newspaper to claim a major role in the city's unfolding history, the *Defender* demarcated black Chicago history into a formative period that commenced before the paper began publishing in 1905 and the quarter century that followed. Its stake in the development and growth of African American life was defined as its efforts aimed at helping the group achieve its fullest potential. The paper declared that it was in the twentieth century—when the *Chicago Defender* began reporting on the progress attained—that "the Race was beginning to find itself and to seek advantages to forge ahead in every respect."

To its eternal credit, the *Chicago Defender*'s contribution to establishing a historical base for the African American claim to place, role, and accomplishment did not end in this solitary, pioneering effort. Beginning in 1932, the paper also printed a series on life in old Chicago in 1932 and 1933. Columnist A. N. Fields's forty-part series, "Chicago Yesterday, Today, and Tomorrow," began its weekly run on October 1, 1932, with a story of Republican political powerhouse Edward H. Wright and ended with a photographic study on June 24, 1933. With interviews of important political figures as well as historical personages (such as "Fred Douglass at 1893 World's Fair," published on June 10, 1933), Fields, with the assistance of fellow columnist Nahum Daniel Brascher on at least one, and possibly two, occasions, provided a chronicle of a previous unrecorded history. Lacking a truly chronological framework at times, and omitting key historical episodes such Du Sable's residency and black participation in the Civil War, the series nonetheless has value. Fields explained on October 29, 1932, that his essays aimed at being "not only authentic but informative as well." He proffered temporal boundaries, however, that indicated a limited historical net into which he would collect information. The series, he wrote "will cover a period of 50 years, dealing with political facts largely unknown by the present generation." In addition, Fields observed that "out of the memory and from the limited history of recorded events, interesting details are being brought to light of Chicago early settlers—stories of hope and ambition and the courage of a people who were endeavoring to seek a place for themselves and for their posterity. The history of early Chicago reads like a romance to one who attempts to make a mental journey through the stirring events of the past 50 years or more of Race life in this great cosmopolitan center."

In claiming it was the first to chronicle the African American's history in Chicago, the *Defender* was inaccurate by thirty-two years, for memory also played an important role in one earlier effort by an African American newspaper. On July 9, 1898, the *Illinois Record*, published in Springfield, printed "Chicago in 1843: A Real 'Oldtimer' on the Life of Early Colored Settlers." This multicolumn account and the several that followed it (as well as previous recollections on special topics such as past social life) qualify as uniquely fitting the bill of chronicling. The data presented were based on memory and interviews conducted by Robert Hall, the son of a Chicago pioneer, Rev. Abram T. Hall of the Quinn Chapel A.M.E. Church. Because of its contemporary nature and its power to inform, the account of the

"Oldtimer" serve as a major template for the first chapter of this book, which deals with the antebellum period, 1833–1860.[6]

Significantly, in the twentieth century, a rarely mentioned grassroots effort of monumental importance, which extended throughout the length of the previous century, attempted to reconstruct a formal history. Initiated by descendants of the pioneer generation of African Americans of the 1830s, 1840s, and 1850s, this partially successful effort resulted in the accumulation of written as well as photographic data.[7]

The primary effort to reconstruct and to formally write black Chicago history belonged to the previously mentioned Joanna Hudlin Snowden, who in 1918 conceived of and undertook to reconstruct a history based on written documentation as well as memory. Yet as she described the situation in 1938, encountering so little encouragement for the project caused her to delay recording this history. The ultimate incentive convincing her to act rested in her disappointment with both the lack of a community-based plan to absorb and socialize World War I migrants and their subsequent exploitation by both whites and blacks. At the juncture where these social problems seemed finally to have the potential to overwhelm her, she experienced rejuvenation as a septuagenarian. Once again motivated to pursue the project, she embarked on a twofold mission. First, she endeavored to inform key constituencies within the black community of their collective heritage in order to engender social change in her community. These clusters included the newcomers from the Great Migration of 1915–1918, the young people already in residence before that period but who were unimpressed with the past as they embraced the titillations of the twentieth century, and the latter's silent parents, who were residents with several decades' residence and experience in Chicago. As a group, Snowden wished them to know the "difference between those years [of the nineteenth century] back there and these years and find out whether they [were] living up to their opportunities." Second, and just as important and obviously intertwined, she wanted to establish her claim to the pioneer heritage of her parents and of her own identity as an "early Chicagoan." Her latter attempt in 1938 to interest the *Chicago Defender* in her project proved unsuccessful as either lagging interest in her plan or the diversions of the times overshadowed any formal writing.[8]

Simultaneously during the nineteen thirties, Franklyn Henderson, a member of the pioneer Atkinson family, began his quest to protect the heritage of the first generation of Atkinsons in Chicago while he instilled in his family a sense of pride in their place in the city's history. He collected and stored photographs along with other documents in his pursuits. Notably, a figurine of a dog with a nose missing as a result of damage from the Great

Fire of 1871 remains a prized family possession as well as a reminder of the Atkinson family's *place* in the city's history. Two of Henderson's grandnieces, reminiscing about him to a newspaper reporter in the last decade of the twentieth century, felt inspired enough to continue the efforts of their beloved "Uncle Petey" to disseminate information about this history. As one in a line of official historians of the Old Settlers Club, which had been organized in 1904, Henderson played a singular role in promoting black Chicago history.[9]

Significantly, descendants from other families, such as the Halls, the Joneses, the Wheelers, and the Johnsons, have carried on a tradition of keeping this history alive through the retention of family records, including photographs. Some have begun advanced research into their family's place in the general history of the black community and the city. With the organization of the Chicago Afro-American Genealogical and Historical Society and the Patricia Liddell Genealogical Researchers in the 1980s, to which some of them belong, the process of historical preservation, research, writing, and dissemination has advanced impressively.

Early in the twentieth century, Chicago's academic community tapped into this database of memory and extrapolated important objective characteristics of the black population from it through the technique of interviewing. Social scientists at the University of Chicago pioneered the process, using it extensively to reconstruct segments of the history (presumably subjective) of the African American population in Chicago. In 1903, Monroe Nathan Work utilized this technique to complete his master's thesis, "Negro Real Estate Holders of Chicago." As he attempted to determine the extent to which African Americans controlled real estate in the city, which for his generation was a sign of evolving citizenship, he engaged in a personal canvass with "investigations concerning past property ownership" (which out of necessity indicated verbal interchanges to extract oral evidence of historical patterns).

In what became a standard introduction to the "Chicago School's" sociological studies, the history of any given group preceded the actual sociological analysis of that community. Thus, E. Franklin Frazier used interviews to reconstruct history from memory for his 1931 doctoral study that became *The Negro Family in Chicago* (1932). In addition, in 1940 St. Clair Drake produced *Churches and Voluntary Associations in the Chicago Negro Community* under the auspices of the New Deal's Works Project Administration—a project that provided a partial template for this study. Most importantly, the tome produced by Drake and Cayton, *Black Metropolis*, relied on interviewing "Old Settlers" to establish the patterns of community life. Interestingly, the authors' introductory historical sketch rested on the work of their colleague Lawrence D. Reddick, who departed solely from a reliance on human memory to an examination of contemporary white newspaper accounts and other written sources that complemented memory as a research approach.[10] In doing so, he steered history away from perhaps the most important element that memory could have brought into historical writing, the collective identity that African Americans had been forging as a result of their repeated transformations from slavery to citizenship.

As could be expected, the contemporary academy played an essential role in providing conceptualization for this history. Young black scholars trained at the University of Chicago and engaging in social science research even before the advent of the "Chicago School" contributed their collective scholarship.[11] Supplementing this work outside the intellectual confines of the University of Chicago, but nonetheless influenced by the academy, the writings, research insights, and social service activities of publicists Fannie Barrier Williams and Ida B. Wells-Barnett, along with Revs. Reverdy Ransom and Richard R. Wright Jr., made an important contribution to understanding the black community along the lines of pioneering social science standards.[12] Their collective findings are now being considered seriously as part of an African American pioneer effort at social science research.[13]

The associational activities of black Chicago were more than adequately reflected in the linkage between group effort and the rise of news coverage. Primarily, early localized black newspapers such as the *Conservator*, *Appeal*, and *Broad Ax* (and later the *Defender*, *Whip*, and *Bee*) chronicled activities of the church, fraternal order, and social club. Coupled with this channel of information, which strategically placed items of interest to an African American reading public, were the *Springfield (Ill.) Record*, the *Minneapolis Western Appeal*, the *Indianapolis Freeman*, and the *Cleveland Gazette*, along with the white *Chicago Inter Ocean*, *Chicago Tribune*, and *Chicago Daily News*. The Civil War veterans complemented this effort as they used the media to inform black Chicagoans of their tradition, sacrifice, and accomplishments through the activities of John Brown Post #50. Apprehensive of fading from memory, they willed themselves into the civic and community consciousness of the city through their highly visible associational presence.

The sustenance of historical reconstruction remained the written account; thus my search for information on the activities of ordinary black Chicagoans led to the National Archives in Washington, D.C. When I began this project, it was apparent that I was embarking on an exhausting research effort. Part of this daunting challenge involved determining just how well or how poorly an unsung and invisible "poverty-stricken group," as Drake and Cayton described the bulk of the African American population at the end of the Civil War, had adjusted and competed in industrializing Chicago. Equally clear was the fact that I was embarking on a tortuous journey into the unknown, where neither theory nor data might exist. Cautious in relying on the a priori approach, I procrastinated over its use until I turned to the empirical procedures inherent in the a posteriori line of reasoning. W. E. B. Du Bois's cautionary notes in *Souls of Black Folk* seemed just as sensible a century after its introduction as they did in 1903: "We must not forget that most Americans answer all queries regarding the Negro *a priori,* and that the least that human courtesy can do is to listen to evidence"; and "We seldom study the condition of the Negro to-day honestly and carefully. It is so much easier to assume that we know it all. Or perhaps, having reached conclusions in our own minds, we are loth to have them disturbed by facts."[14] Thus, I decided to let the data lead me to conceptualization. For the rank and file, no thorough data base appeared to exist despite a thorough examination of books, journals, diaries, and newspapers. At this point, fortuitous circumstances led me to a trove of long-sought information on the African American human condition.

As I investigated the extent to which Chicago's African Americans participated in the Civil War (1861–1865), I found that there was almost no mention at all of the existence, let alone the meaningful participation, of African Americans in the local war effort or in the city's growth and development in this period at all. The same held true for battlefield participation. Only scant references existed in Drake and Cayton's *Black Metropolis* or in Reddick's lost historical account.[15] Of course, as sociologists, these researchers presented a historical sketch, not a full chronicle of African American life in Chicago. They did mention the uncertain social position blacks held in Chicago with both purported friend and foe, along with labor strife, and community development.

In a renewed search for social data, I felt pressure from the disturbing possibility that data might not exist at all. Where should I look for such data? Two recent histories on the military service of black Illinoisans, not specifically Chicagoans, had referred to the soldiers' federal pension records stored at the U.S. National Archives and Records Agency in Washington, D.C., so I began what became an extensive search at that repository. These efforts produced almost immediate rewards. To paraphrase historian Ralph A. Austen, "the value of these documents [lay] not only in their scope but also in their provenance. They [were] the working records of the very phenomenon we wish[ed] to understand, created for the purpose of managing the immediate [task of compensating veterans for meritable service] rather than shaping [the] image [of African Americans troops] among contemporary or future critics."[16] I not only found additional military information about the Twenty-ninth Infantry, USCT, Illinois's only black regiment on the field of battle, but also discovered information on other important social aspects of the soldiers' lives. Included were intimate circumstances of life under bondage, from the physical and health problems they acquired both during civilian and military life to the type of family structures that existed before, during, and after the war. Moreover, information was obtainable on their adjustment to civilian life in Chicago, their connection to quasi-military organizations after the war, their associations with former comrades and with the new leadership of black Chicago, and, importantly, their place in the Chicago labor scene during and after the war. As a group, who better represented the rank and file than former slaves molded into soldiers, who were further transformed into veterans, then into civilian workers and the heads of families?

These data required a framework that facilitated a fuller understanding of the meaning of black life. The instrument of choice was a longitudinal research model, informally constructed but still useful as the means of studying a large number of individuals with initially similar yet sometimes disparate backgrounds over an extended period of time. Next, selecting and then following a sample analytically over a prescribed period of time, when illuminated with collective biographical sketches, led to a better comprehension of the character of this important segment of the African American population.

Importantly, generality and comparability had to be weighed against specificity and uniqueness. The value of comparative history necessitated examination of the local experience through extended lenses in space and time. Other northern cities and some outside the region held populations that experienced both similar as well as disparate aspects of what black Chicago encountered.[17] While less than unique in many instances, the particular experience of Chicago still warranted full study because it defied generalization. One other recurring problem stood out when the particular (local) was placed against the general (national): Conclusions reached about particular dynamics at work in Chicago blur, weaken, or invalidate accepted interpretations of a general situation or condition among African Americans.

Several exceptions to the results of this deductive approach stood out. Full participation in the antebellum black convention movement eluded Chicagoans, and what they experienced was only somewhat reflective of the general trend. Local, or particular, aspects of life linked to very low literacy and, accordingly, no local newspaper, the lack of a corps of orators, and the city's extreme distance from the epicenter of eastern seaboard activism made Chicago seemingly unique and shaped a more particularistic course than that associated with easterners from Boston, New York, and Philadelphia. Also, education that was routinely denied African American children and required special schools nationally was provided to them in Chicago through a blend of New England morality and municipal fiat.[18]

Later, while post-Reconstruction labor relations between whites and blacks followed a similar course to that found in the more heavily populated cities in the East, the perception of the black worker nationally differed from that held of Chicago and in the city itself. While relegated primarily to the service sector, no complete exclusion of blacks from cooperation with whites inside or outside of that sector ever resulted. Elsewhere in the economic sphere, in business endeavors, August Meier noted that constructing a national model for the development of a post–Civil War nexus between black businesses and an emerging bourgeoisie worked best when Chicago and Boston were excluded. This correctly implies Chicago's specific or local features prevent illustrative generalizations. Later, self-consciousness and pride in being African Americans led black Chicagoans to successfully demand that blacks be given a chance to participate in the Spanish-American War, but only under their own leadership.[19] They won that concession by playing power politics and set a national precedent during the conflict.

The combined value of both very old and somewhat recent scholarship informed conceptual and factual understanding in this study. Sometimes consulting the older works consigned to the dustheap revealed the most relevant theoretical bases from which understanding flowed. Crossing interdisciplinary lines, the works of sociologists Charles S. Johnson, E. Franklin Frazier, Horace R. Cayton, and St. Clair Drake proved especially helpful since they demonstrated scholarly concern and intimate familiarity with the nuances of thinking, motives, and behavior of the African Americans in Chicago; their works have withstood decades of scrutiny. Outside of the city, W. E. B. Du Bois's *The Philadelphia Negro,* a century after its initial publication, continued to provide insight into the character of nineteenth-century, northern, urban life and served as another model for this study.[20] More recent scholarship on nineteenth-century life was incorporated into this study inasmuch as its theoretical and narrative relevancies allowed. Highly theoretical, too often it loses coherence as to the core history it purports to examine and explain. As to what the data offered, they appeared usable only if I developed another framework, one capable of retrieving maximum information from the records while being able to interpret their meanings centrally, contextually, holistically, and—always—accurately. At this point, the necessity of a paradigm proved essential in the study.

Paradigmatic solutions, as I envisioned them, appeared through a framework that included five elements: racial self-identification and affirmation, internal social structure, culture and race relations, political and associational participation, and economic activities. First, a recognition of uninterrupted instances of demonstrated human agency among African Americans is imperative in order to understand the dynamics of black Chicago's history. Evidence of independent action occurred constantly, whether in the life of the bondsman, the free person, the person without national status, or the citizen. The will of the African American was perpetually juxtaposed with externally induced actions or reactions, the result of the subordinate status assigned and implied because of race. So the unending challenge at hand required validation of the very *being* of African Americans. The transition from chattel to contraband and finally to citizen illustrated this odyssey only too well. This meant showing, in effect, that the African American existed as part of a global humanity, an idea challenged during the time of slavery and just as aggressively once the tenets of Social Darwinism gained widespread acceptance during the Gilded Age of the 1880s and 1890s. Without question, the descent from being to acknowledged nonexistence was painful for the victim. Yet this prejudice also affected the national fabric as its nefarious influence became pervasive. Constitutionally, it had a root in the three-fifths clause. In the nation's earliest proprietary affairs, it appeared in the economic transition from bonded human servitude to chattel slavery.

By the nineteenth century, when Chicago emerged as a frontier settlement, the locus of race prejudice and dehumanization was found in the antebellum South's need to validate the subordination of Africans under the "peculiar institution." Joel Williamson described these efforts: "Whereas New England was giving rise to Hawthorne [and] Longfellow . . . the South was bending more and more of its intelligence toward the creation of an elaborate argument for slavery. Drawing upon literature, history, theology, law . . . and the incipient disciplines of economics, political science and sociology, the South in and after the 1830s was generating and preaching a whole system of thought dedicated to the principle that Afro-American slavery was right because God had made the Negro to be a natural slave. *The key object was to unlink the Negro from the great chain of humanity, to make him a different creature somehow subhuman and specifically fitted to slavery.*"[21] In this context, the estrangement that slavery wrought came in the response of a slave worker to an inquiry into his actions of the moment, which revealed much more about his concept of self, humanity, and *being*. He answered: "Han't got no self."[22]

In a literary context, Huckleberry Finn's famed antebellum river mishap resounded with this conversation: "We blowed out a cylinder-head. Good gracious! Anybody hurt? No'm. *Killed* a nigger. Well, it's lucky, because sometimes people do get hurt." In the context of labor and economic worthiness in the late nineteenth century, in the northern mind the African American laborer became the "disaffected worker," a clear threat to free labor and a danger to civil order.[23]

Perhaps Ralph Ellison said it best fifty years ago: "I am an invisible man . . . I am a man of substance, of flesh and bone, fiber and liquids,—and I might even be said to possess a mind. I am invisible, understand, simply because people refuse to see me. . . . That invisibility to which I refer occurs because of a peculiar disposition of those with whom I come into contact. A matter of the construction of their *inner* eyes, those eyes with which they look through their physical eyes upon reality. . . . You often doubt if you really exist."[24]

Second, the evolving nature of the social structure of black Chicago required focusing on those changing internal group characteristics that authenticated any claim of social differentiation related to class as well as to heterogeneity.[25] Of significance, constant, not intermittent, migration fueled the process as new arrivals journeyed from the eastern seaboard, from the Midwest, and from the Deep South to reside in Chicago. Since this movement of African Americans preceded the "Great Migration" of the twentieth century, an examination of the process served to increase an understanding of the dynamics of the group.[26] Demographic analysis afforded recognition of social segmentation and provided insight into the composition, attitudes, and motivations of the heterogeneous African American community. This unveiling was usually overshadowed by a supposed homogeneity that outside observers anticipated as an accepted truth for generations. Internal group differences entailing provenance, occupation, skin complexion, education, gender, ideology, political belief, and class, along with changing external conditions such as racism and egalitarianism, produced views, interests, and activities that undergirded a collective sense of agency on the part of African Americans. Recognition and subsequent examination of these elements contributing to social segmentation also revealed facets of African American life that hitherto were unexplored patterns of adjustment in freedom. Transformation in thinking, lifestyles, and activities demonstrated a dynamism in life: African Americans evolved from free persons of color and refugees/fugitives to partial societal participants during the antebellum period; from former slaves to freedmen and freedwomen to citizens in the Civil War and during Reconstruction; and from various levels of assimilating persons into members of the "Top Tenth," the laboring class, or the poverty-stricken "Submerged Tenth" during the Gilded Age of the 1880s and 1890s.

Further, understanding the dynamics of black Chicago's societal configurations allows for interpretation of the demeanor and thinking of its members, along with presenting an accurate description of stratification. Before a class structure based on economic differentiation emerged, internal group distinctions among these sojourners initially appeared as legal, racial, and social dissimilarities.[27] During the post-emancipation period, they appeared as differences that were sociocultural in character. As Chicago entered into a period of industrial and commercial potency during the 1880s and 1890s, more formalized lines of distinction based on wealth, prestige, and status began appearing within the African American community because of a growing professional coterie and expansion within the business sector. While still somewhat elastic by the turn of the century, the lines of distinction were becoming more rigid, notwithstanding the lack of wealth in black Chicago when compared to the city's white captains of industry and commerce. At the close of the century, social differences manifested themselves as socioeconomic disparities linked to popularity as well as to some confusing notions associated with class.

Establishing the character of social stratification required an approach recognizing diversity between hierarchical layers as well as within them. In *Churches and Voluntary Associations in the Chicago Negro Community*, St. Clair Drake saw the international celebration of 1893, the World's Columbian Exposition, as accentuating the more salutary side of American race relations. Drake suggested the need to examine thoroughly the complex nature of the city's African American population, seeing the world's fair as significantly affecting black life externally, in race relations, and internally, in the quality of African American religious and associational life, which by implication and his analytical predisposition, included class.[28]

The extremely disparate nature of the interests among this expanding group of citizens produced further problems for an urbanizing group undergoing social change well in advance of the twentieth century's "Great Migration." While conventional academic reasoning might have dictated analyzing the nature of a preconceived class system based on fanciful economic influences, Drake resisted this tendency in determining its nonexistence altogether during this era. He found neither a social grouping nor a system linked primarily to the means of accumulating wealth. Instead, he uncovered a level of differentiation at this incipient stage of its evolution that developed along cultural and social lines, producing three sociocultural clusters comprising the basic configuration of African American society during this era. The elite, or *refined* element, represented the status to which African Americans with high mainstream expectations could aspire. The *respectables* constituted the largest portion of the social arrangement and was a group composed of the solid working-class element. The *riffraff* made up the third group, the economically and socially dispossessed who conformed to W. E. B. Du Bois's "Submerged Tenth." Throughout each stratum, family life remained an important feature of life, varying from resilient to less than resilient, and overwhelmingly headed by two parents.[29]

The work of another University of Chicago student, Richard R. Wright Jr., provided contemporary analysis of the city's African American community at the turn of the century. In 1901 he modeled his work on the pattern of Du Bois's recently published *The Philadelphia Negro* (1899), in that he used close observation and interviewing to collect data on African Americans. His approach and work, no doubt, further served to influence Drake's writings. Wright, after applying Du Bois's model from Philadelphia to the Chicago scene, concluded that "social grades" rather than classes had formed. He uncovered the existence of four of these social grades that ordinarily would escape notice "by those who do not mingle closely with the race." First, professional persons, large entrepreneurs, and skilled artisans constituted one group; next, permanently employed domestics and laborers made up another cluster; then, unskilled workers and those chronically plagued by irregular employment formed another group; and last, a socially undesirable set of "idlers and gamblers" belonged to a fourth segment.[30] As to the status elevation of professionals into a discernible class, as late as 1910 it remained inchoate. The number of college-trained professionals (excluding the U.S. Census's inclusion of showmen, artists, musicians, and actors in this category) rested at approximately 20 percent of the total number of professionals.[31] Nonetheless, the rudimentary lines of a bifurcated middle class (composed of the elite and high-income *respectables*), a working class, and an underclass moved steadily toward solidification.

In 1909, the observation of erudite attorney Edward E. Wilson, in responding to the question "are there signs of class distinction among Negroes?" assumes salience. He observed: "[T]here are gradually emerging classes among us. They are not yet well-defined; social discipline and the acquirement of culture and wealth have not gone on long enough."[32]

Last, and most significantly, historical examination of nineteenth-century black Chicago reveals that objective conditions within that community belied the validity of the *assertion* that service workers, such as Pullman porters, waiters, and maids, belonged to the elite, or upper class.[33] Any acceptance being given to the assertion (but not factual analysis) of E. Franklin Frazier that was absorbed into Drake and Cayton's *Black Metropolis* merely perpetuates myth. In particular, Frazier's use of a manuscript entitled "Autobiography of a Physician" became the basis for understanding, or as argued here, misunderstanding, social class formation before the end of the nineteenth century. How little did Frazier realize the extent to which the "physician's" comments would be accepted as truth by generations of scholars in the twentieth century as to economic and social relations, leadership, and the possibility of the development of a self-sustaining African American market.

The nature of the relationship between those who purportedly direct the affairs of a society based on their wealth, prestige, or status *and* the rank and file leads to the search for the presumed linkage between class and leadership.[34] Yet in black Chicago, direction and guidance over the activities and thoughts of the ordinary stratum often rested within its own ranks. This increased the possibility of a multifaceted character to the concept of leadership that constantly changed over time. Interestingly, it has frequently been overlooked in favor of applying one model of monolithic leadership dominant over all spheres of life for one span of time.[35] In this case, the late nineteenth and early twentieth centuries provided the temporal setting for this template to work itself out. However, its application to earlier periods depended on supposed static conditions of life, when in fact dynamism reigned.

Frontier Chicago, for example, offered almost no choices for guidance for an indigenous set of leaderships to emerge outside of the economic and religious spheres. However, these proved viable channels for years to come and as soon as an organizational base formed, even with a small population, options and prerogatives for a true African American leadership were to prove themselves unlimited. The fear of reenslavement of refugees or possible enslavement of certificated free people of color stimulated other types of action; soon, activism as a requisite for leadership developed. This choice appeared in the alliance of able spokesmen such as John Jones and others who formed a sizeable, activist abolitionist coterie which rendered assistance in helping runaway slaves and challenging the Illinois Black Laws.

The wartime and postwar periods brought a transformation through social change as well as a proliferation of institutions with variegated sets of leadership reflective of prevailing circumstances and the needs of their specialized memberships. During the war, the black civilian population relied on a more independent set of spokesmen than previously to promote their interests, while the black military population on the battlefield recognized a leadership in the personage of a newly created position of authority: the African American sergeant. Leadership was bestowed within a democratic setting, not inherited or assumed, because of the direction provided in pursuing the group's acknowledged interests. It therefore becomes implausible to have expected the social elite to garner either recognition or support from the masses based on any inherent privilege or elevated status. The indispensable link between leadership and followers became the relevance of the former's actions to the latter's needs. This continued increase in associational life further engendered a belief and reliance on indigenous direction and guidance to sustain community life that has not been reversed to this day.

Third, Chicago should be viewed as a prism through which distorted racial beams flowed. For the most part, both internal and external race relations were fluid. Externally, with this important emphasis on race (no matter how artificial a construct), its linkage to culture cannot be overstressed, and the evolution of both must be viewed historically, in this case with a backward glance. Significantly, the character of race relations as viewed through twenty-first-century eyes has been shaped by a national policy of only fifty years' duration. The monumental U.S. Supreme Court decision in 1954 in *Brown v. Topeka, Kansas, Board of Education* directed the nation on a new course in race relations that promoted racial integration in all areas of interaction and endeavors for the first time in American history. Earlier historical instances of racial fluidity never included this aspect of total inclusion and at a level of genuinely embraced national public policy. Life before the pivotal year 1954 included a half century of earnestness by neoabolitionists, primarily within the NAACP, to transform the theory of racial equality into a practical and accepted blueprint for living.[36] Previous to this period, from 1865 to 1909, when mass emancipation freed four million souls from legalized oppression and racial subordination in the name of national economic benefit and recognition of a God-ordained racial hierarchy, the possibility of equal access to opportunity pervaded northern thought and dominated some segments of public policy. Previous to these developments, slavery and near racial caste were permanent fixtures throughout the entirety of American society.

At the same time the nation was forming and reinforcing its views and institutions on race, and further imbedding them deeper into the culture, among persons of African descent an internal, parallel world of race and culture was evolving. The former even assumed a life of its own as exemplified by the internal color line among African Americans. For the mass of this population, persons of unmixed African descent at the mass level unequivocally identified themselves exclusively by the construct of race and affinity for the perpetuation of their way of life. St. Clair Drake wrote on the historical bases from which this identity derived: "The people of the Diaspora in North America never developed an African-American culture in the sense that the people of the Caribbean and South America did. Rather what might be called an *Afro*-American sub-culture evolved."[37] This was not a culture independently constructed away from the indigenous African homeland with an authentic core clearly intact, but it was one quite similar to the garden variety found in America among immigrants from Europe, Asia, South America, and the indigenous peoples of North America. Within this subculture, persons sought an internally produced affirmation for their being, rather than one that was externally developed and requiring a hegemonic sanction from a dominant, outside group. This permitted them to develop a consciousness free from wondering what whites thought about them during their every waking moment.

Ira B. Berlin, Marc Favreau, and Steven F. Miller explored this concept of a black parallel world and found that it evolved from the mainland North American slave experience.[38] Another important effort to illuminate the character of this subculture was defined throughout a series of interviews in the 1970s that revolved around a core black culture for its urban, northern component. John Langston Gwaltney's *Drylongso: A Self-Portrait of Black America* defined Drake's *Afro*-American subculture at several levels. According to Gwaltney, an ethnologist, "Core black culture is more than ad hoc synchronic adaptive survival. Its values, systems of logic and world view are rooted in a lengthy peasant tradition and clandestine theology. It is the notion of sacrifice for kin, the belief in the natural sequence of cause and effect. . . . The expectations and canons of core black culture are arbiters of black intra-communal status and style. . . . In black culture there is a durable, general tolerance, amazingly free of condescension, for the individual's right to follow the truth where it leads. . . . [And, not surprisingly], the sense of nationhood among blacks is as old as [blacks'] abhorrence of slavery. Black nationhood is not rooted in territoriality so much as it is in a profound belief in the fitness of core black culture and in the solidarity born of a transgenerational detestation of [black] subordination [to whites]. The tradition which is so vital in shaping black culture was founded and fostered by those slave foreparents who are so widely respected for their refusal to accept, in their hearts, the Euro-American definition of them as things."[39]

In dramatic contrast, however important the influence of core black culture was over the many, a sentiment toward a countervailing national identity as Americans, or Colored Americans, grew stronger among the few. These were members of the educated, articulate, national elite of both mixed and unmixed parentage. As white Americans slowly began to recognize their claim to the benefits of citizenship—the likes of which were tested by the level of inclusion or exclusion from American competitive, professional life, such as legal, health, and educational groups—this group's hopes of inclusion into the American mainstream were buoyed. From this source, the Afro-Saxon mentality sprang, one that comported itself antithetically to that of the Afro-American, so the worldviews of the elite and of the masses grew dialectically disparate.

When these two worldviews and cultures intersected, the results were uniquely American, or in the case locally, unique to Chicago. Interracial relations in Chicago ranged from amiability to indifference to antagonism. White southerners in residence in the city during the antebellum era supported slavery and the notion of racial inferiority, in contrast to the beliefs and actions of the egalitarian New Englanders. Immigrant groups uncertain about their status either contested with African Americans as impediments to their advancement or cooperated with them as fellow subalterns. One important factor in Chicago that made life more comfortable for blacks of all legal statuses was the supportive humanistic thrust from abolitionists during Chicago's frontier years. This feature also proved effective despite rising Negrophobia during the Civil War. With emancipation, under indigenous African American direction, the struggle to end racial proscription continually built in intensity even with a decline in abolitionist efforts—equality of opportunity—fought for and buttressed by the protection of the Fourteenth Amendment.

Later in the nineteenth century, the African American community produced articulate spokesmen in attorneys Edward H. Morris and Ferdinand L. Barnett, who distinguished themselves in behalf of equality of opportunity and equal protection under the law. Once in debate, Morris argued that the solution to the purported race problem could be solved by "let[ting] us alone in the enjoyment of the rights and privileges you have guaranteed to all by your organic law."[40] At the same time, blacks eschewed any fascination for the implied social intimacy that whites envisioned with the phrase *social equality*. By the end of the nineteenth century, when speaking before the Parliament of Representative Women at the World's Columbian Exposition, assimilationist Fannie Barrier Williams referred to the debate among whites on the topic as nonsense.[41] The bane of white social separatists, interracial marriage, produced an uneasiness among most African Americans as much as it did whites, and sometimes for the same reasons. Yet, among the latter, the practice and parties were never denounced because of an understanding of white America's hypocrisy and foibles on this issue.[42]

Moreover, differences existed among African Americans as to racial goals. The racial duality W. E. B. Du Bois described so eloquently in *Souls of Black Folk* (1903), a model he did not expect to be promulgated as it has, fit the experiences of the assimilationist elite perfectly.[43] The African American, according to Du Bois, was aware that he was both a Negro and an American, meaning that he sought refuge in the black world among African Americans and their institutions while concurrently pursuing the full enjoyment of his citizenship rights among the dominant, majority white American citizenry.

However, the members of this group must have felt that they were

perennially swimming upstream in a society that made them forever distinguish between a possibly attainable racial equality of opportunity and an
equally threatening social equality. The former popular, but often misunderstood, phrase stood for openness and a chance to compete in an unfettered environment. Always a minority within a minority, with external and
internal opposition to their aspirations, African Americans persevered
nonetheless as they sought fulfillment of a diluted version of the American
Dream. Among the elite, they resisted any attempt to limit their right to
engage in a variety of interracial activities in the private domain as well as
the public sphere if circumstances warranted. A visit to Chicago's famed
Auditorium Theater to view opera or to hear a leading singer of high culture
necessarily fulfilled their aesthetic interests. A high level of participation at
the World's Columbian Exposition, popularly referred to as the Chicago
World's Fair of 1893, further met the requirements of citizenship.[44] In 1895,
the fair-minded women of the Chicago Woman's Club overcame the barriers
of racial prejudice and accepted the sophisticated and erudite Fannie Barrier
Williams into membership. At the turn of the century, a radical departure
from limitations on open social interaction occurred when Unitarian minister Celia Parker Woolley opened the Frederick Douglass Center on the
fringe of the Black Belt community and extended an invitation of members
of the black elite to join with their white counterparts in purely social activities. This was followed by organization in 1912 of a branch of the newly
formed NAACP as a group committed to broaching the barrier of racial
separation even further.

Occasionally, social distinctions (based on class) among African Americans were used tactically in order to facilitate from whites the right to access
public accommodations.[45] However, this emphasis on individual accomplishments and a differential in income level at no time indicated a devia-
tion from the strategic adherence to building collective racial pride and
solidarity that made up the grand blueprint for eventual racial equity.
Importantly, as to personal or family wealth, the black elite were anything
but "to the manor born." Overall, they excelled in the acquisition of knowledge and cultural appreciation, but not in property and money.

The masses of the African American community continued, however, to
eschew close social contact with most whites. While it has been fashionable
to assume that African Americans aggressively sought racial equality from
their earliest arrival in the New World, Drake and Cayton point out that
they could not believe en masse in the theoretical possibility of attaining
racial equality *along social lines* until the twentieth century. The factors contributing to this sentiment and rejectionist attitude were predicated on the
strong influence that certain remnants of their West African cultures had

on their self-perception, the attractiveness of an *Afro*-American subculture that assumed a powerful insularity, and the pervasiveness of racism despite white denial to reality. Significantly, the 1920s introduced pervasive economic prosperity that benefited blacks nationally from Durham to Tulsa to Chicago, a factor that made social contact with whites a matter of marginal importance. Chicago specifically promised fulfillment of the "Dream of the Black Metropolis," which had the power to virtually displace the elusive American Dream. This decade of economic progress was short-lived, however, and the Great Depression crushed economic hope. But it did open up the possibility of cordial interracial relations on a social basis, as the Left and the unions proved that the NAACP's belief in attaining the American Dream was more than fantasy. The epochal Second World War then brought such massive change as to alter African American thinking on race relations forever. Once the theoretical became the possible, through experience and observation, the notion of sharing in the American Dream resulted in an adjustment to black thinking and action.[46]

Finally, the African American community's acceptance or rejection of separate development—as manifested through thought, institutions, and activities—depended on the point of origination of the concept or plan. If white liberals, radicals, conservatives, or racists made any suggestion affecting black life, as in the case of a 1889 idea to build an all-black YMCA on the South Side, rejection could routinely be expected.[47] It was viewed as a step backward in racial progress and as another imposition by the dominant society. Had the notion sprung from black minds, addressing the needs of the community, discussion might not have generated an automatic rejection. This was the case in 1898 when Armour Institute planned to open a kindergarten for the children of working African American mothers. Ida B. Wells-Barnett's consternation with the opposition boiled to a point of eruption at what she saw as a need based on practicality. The kindergarten was opened eventually.[48]

Fourth, institutional development (including activities within the spheres of religion and of politics) revealed a great deal about the internal dynamics of black life as they encountered change through associational activities. Church life passed through several phases, the first occurring during the antebellum period, which found issues existing in black and white, with interracial worship yielding to pressures of internal black life and resulting in the formation of black churches of the Methodist and Baptist persuasions. Then, the Civil War acted as a stimulant to social change, and the result was an increase in black-led churches based on demographic expansion. Moreover, the post-Reconstruction era saw a proliferation of denominations, with five bodies in existence and a population choosing freely among all of them—Baptist, Methodist, Episcopalian, Presbyterian, and Roman Catholic. Last, at the end of the century, two phenomena appeared that had long-term effects on African American life far into the next century and beyond: Tensions among congregants about the essence of worship produced a division between an elite-based church and a mass-based institution, giving rise to the mission church and an invigorating style of worship. Further, changing social conditions warranted the emergence of a more activist, world-oriented church with appropriate social services to meet the more mundane needs of congregants. Significantly, throughout the nineteenth century, as important as the form of worship was, sacramental expressions such as baptisms, marriages, and funerals also became immensely important as indices of the meaning of black life. Baptism expanded the church body, marriage promoted family formation, and funerary rites announced the end of the cycle of physical church membership with an exalted membership into the Church Triumphant.

Fraternal organizations of the city's black males were highly visible to the generations living through the nineteenth century because of their influence over so many facets of African American life, but less so for researchers who had been misleadingly trained to ignore this component of the social order. Fraternal organizations should be seen as part of a demonstration of human agency by highly assertive males. Contemporarily on the local scene, Fannie Barrier Williams could write: "50 percent of the best men belonged to fraternal orders." Scholars separated from Chicago by time and distance agreed with W. E. B. Du Bois, who noted that the secret society provided two services: social intercourse and insurance. They also "furnish[ed] pastime from the monotony of work, a field for ambition and intrigue, a chance for parade, and insurance against misfortune." Lawrence Levine observed that "In a society geared to deny the potency and maturity of Negroes, these institutions offered them surrogates for what the larger society tended to withhold."[49] Meanwhile, although led by males, influential women's auxiliaries provided a voice for females. However, these organizations were supportive in character and therefore not *the* voice of female agency that would mark their most significant contributions to black Chicago.

By the time the largest national bodies of black women organized formally as the National Association of Colored Women in 1896, the African American women of Chicago had distinguished themselves with an enviable record of leadership and achievement in both the domestic and civic spheres.[50] For six decades, organized women's activities in Chicago contributed to the remarkable progress evident by 1900. Antebellum activities consisted of courageous efforts in behalf of fleeing slaves and laying the groundwork for a recognizable community. Quinn Chapel A.M.E Church's "Big Four" was a major force of abolitionism.[51] Helping the destitute during the Great Fire of Chicago has always been a discernible footnote. Postwar endeavors revolved around the church, literary club, and charitable organization. The announcement to the nation in 1891 that Chicago would host the World's Columbian Exposition spurred women nationally to organize to advocate a positive black presence. In Chicago, two bodies emerged to insure that an exemplary exhibit as well as overall representation in decision-making about matters affecting African Americans would be realized. The Woman's Columbian Auxiliary Association and the Woman's Columbian Association organized immediately. Further, they organized domestically in support of the troops of the all-black Eighth Infantry Regiment that served in Cuba.

As a sign of womanly involvement, small clubs grew in number. Highlighting these diverse efforts with their commitment to racial betterment was the formation of the Ida B. Wells Club in 1893. Organized before the antilynching crusader's residence in Chicago, it honored her well-known courageous work in behalf of black women's reputations and the endangered lives in the South of both men and women. Reform of society and meeting the mounting social welfare needs of blacks were the primary motivators of their activities.[52]

The martial tradition among the African Americans of Chicago represented another institutional channel that has been ignored by researchers, who through insular periodization have assigned the post–Civil War era in the North a position subsumed under the eras of Reconstruction and of industrialism. As Stuart McConnell has written, "the late nineteenth century was a postwar era."[53] The conspicuous presence and activities of the war veteran—affectionately referred to as "old soldier" and "soldier"—along with two military publications in 1888 by African American veterans, *A History of the Negro Troops in the War of the Rebellion, 1861–1865*, by George Washington Williams, and *The Black Phalanx: A History of the Negro Soldiers of the United States in the Wars of 1775–1912, 1861-'65*, by James T. Wilson, more than adequately informed the people of the period.[54] For black males, the veteran had a role with an importance that cannot be underestimated because military service was an experience that is usually considered essential in establishing manhood in most societies.[55] Appropriate in a (white) society promoting the very ignominious feature of human depravity (slavery and subordination) that it despised in its own pre-revolutionary experience, this expression of militancy by blacks would be overshadowed historically by an emphasis on attempts at systemic change through nonconfrontational means.

The development of manhood appearing along a continuum can be seen in various episodes that warrant inclusion as part of the incubation of the martial tradition among black Chicagoans. The dauntless activities of the conductors of the Underground Railroad initially illustrated the transcendence of courage and righteousness over danger and injustice. The Civil War service of black Chicagoans as members of the Twenty-ninth Infantry, USCT, as well as other units, replete with fatalities *in combat* and triumph *on the battlefield,* presented the nation with a new view of the African American as a man, and therefore, a human with true *being.* Desires for citizenship and social inclusion in the postwar world led to the formation of militia units such as the Hannibal Guard, the Cadets, the Ninth Battalion, and finally the Eighth Regiment of the Illinois National Guard by 1894. The completion of the circle was realized with battlefield service in the Spanish American War and the First World War.

Finally, the value that white citizens placed on political participation was presumed to have carried a similar weight in the lives of black Chicagoans even at a time when full participation was impossible. With different roots, interest in and the level of actual participation in the process of governing and partisan party activities evolved gradually over time. Scholars have been consumed by the debate as to whether these origins rested in a civic consciousness consistent with the mythical Yankee reasons for political involvement—in a quest for power to offset this domination by a marginalized group, such as was the case with the Irish, in accordance with a protest tradition that seemed the most advantageous route to fulfillment of citizenship rights—or in changing social conditions that promised greater opportunities over time.[56] Evidence found in this study supports the latter interpretative category.

Quasi-political involvement through alliances with white abolitionists, mass meetings, and petition-writing predated legal political participation. Extension of the electoral franchise to African American males in 1870 resulted in limited job patronage and office holding. Patron-clientage politics was the order of the day, with whites completely in control over the political apparatus. Awaiting a time when viable organization could develop, African Americans inched along looking for opportunities. Greater political involvement led African Americans to the precipice of shifting from clientage politics to independent politics in the next century.[57] Advanced thinking within the ranks of politicians, such as those who joined Edward H. Wright, aimed at independence, something Wright partially accomplished when he formed his Appomattox Club in 1900. This organization paved the way toward twentieth-century successes as it acted as a springboard for black political power in the 1920s. Partisanism had Republicanism ruling the day in national matters with occasional interruptions locally of Democratic involvement.

Fifth, as we will see, the entrepreneurial and business spirit manifested in African American life is related to Chicago, which acted as the economic engine for a region as well as a significant cog in the nineteenth-century national and global economies. Despite its highly publicized political image today, Chicago has continually generated immense wealth both over space and in time. Recognition of this facet of life is important. Within this book, the economic sphere is examined in relation to the disparate character of how income was derived—from labor, business, and the professions. Work is examined as being more than the molder of the laborer, so attention is focused on the ability of the black worker to flourish in a life that existed beyond the bounds of labor. Although the struggles of the post-Civil War industrial workforce usually garners almost all of the attention accorded labor relations, the focus here is on labor in nonindustrial settings, for it also contributed to the city's economic health. Next, consideration is given to continuous entrepreneurial and business interest and activities of African Americans, tendencies that manifested themselves before slavery ended and citizenship was granted. The nineteenth century produced a business tradition among African Americans, one that was recorded as early as 1885 in a black-produced business directory. Professional interest and advancement marked the nineteenth century as both native-born talent and migrating members of the "Talented Tenth" adhered to a national standard of competence. The culmination of the activities in this area, coupled with those in other areas, came with the realization of the "Dream of the Black Metropolis," the self-contained black city within a city by the 1920s.

This history of the lives of the African American citizens of Chicago during their first hundred years of residency represents a story told from their collective points of view, inclusive of the elite as well as the less well known. Through the point of view of the participating subject of this saga, or that of his or her surrogate who reconstructed history from memory, the African American man, woman, and child live again as they did nearly one to two centuries ago. Their stilled, anonymous voices are represented by their previously overlooked words, recollections, and photographs. The African American point of view is thus facilitated through the existence of the spoken word as written down unceremoniously by observers as well as by trained interviewers. The result is a recorded account that amounts to articulation through mostly contemporaneous utterances. First-person accounts based on memory are herein accorded special treatment as representative of particularized, valued experience. What this contributes is the subjective element of life, a component that sociologist E. Franklin Frazier stated is so often missing in explorations conducted in purely objective terms.[58] Complementing these sources and written accounts is the record of participation and presentation of an event as played out through camera lenses.

In an effort to resurrect the unsung and the unseen, I have intentionally mentioned names of persons whose lives and possible achievements will never be fully uncovered. *Details* normally subsumed into and by larger themes are given deliberate prominence in this study, and I believe a general readership, upon reflection, will appreciate this approach. Examination of the federal pension records of Civil War soldiers held at the National Archives and Records Agency in Washington, D.C., introduced me to soldiers and their families and associates whose lives were destined for perpetual obscurity. Their stories opened the doors to understanding how the rank and file lived, failed, and prospered. Respect for the sacrifice of these Civil War soldiers compelled me, in traditional African American religious fervor, literally to "call the roll" of the previous unknowns. Personal consideration for my maternal great-grandfather, Private Henry Slaughter (a Kentuckian who became a Chicagoan at the end of his eight decades of life) of Company K, 116th Infantry, USCT, played its part also.[59] In the first two chapters, which cover the period before the general emancipation of 1865, I felt an ancestral obligation to include names. Further, in Chapters 3 through 5, which are devoted to sharing a part of their lives, I included, of course, more names. To further delve into their lives, Appendix E was constructed to explain how I made use of these federal records of Chicago's black Civil War soldiers.

Scholarly examination of this phenomenon conducted as part of the new social history of a generation ago buttressed the approach employed in this study. The historian Lawrence W. Levine argued that "it is time for historians to expand their own consciousness by examining the consciousness of those they have hitherto ignored or neglected. It is time that the study of human intellect be broadened to embrace Joseph Levenson's admirable definition of intellectual history as the 'history not of thought, but of men thinking.'" William M. Tuttle Jr., another distinguished historian, pointed out that "of all the scholarly disciplines, history at least should honor the commitment to study the individual as well as the unique in history; and this should be more than a commitment to study more than the educated, articulate, quotable individuals representative of the governing elite. It should be to study members of the bottom and middle strata of society as well."[60] By demonstrating ceaseless change over time in uncovering this remarkable story in all of its complexity, one of the historian's basic criteria is satisfied. In presenting new interpretations to old and new data even others are broached.

Prologue

The Birth of Black Chicago

The election came; Lincoln was president, then the war. The Race played its part. . . . Then freedom came and the end of the war, and with the first real history that bears any semblance of authenticity since DeSaible begins.

— "Story of Old Settlers Reads Like Fiction,"
Chicago Defender, 1930

WHILE LISTENING to the radio one summer day in 1985, I was surprised to hear an advertisement over Chicago's largest classical station read live by a well-known, professional voice with baritone qualities that acknowledged Jean Baptiste Pointe Du Sable (or DeSaible) not only as the city's founder, but also as the embodiment of its entrepreneurial and business spirit.[1] From this announcement, it appeared that Du Sable, and by extension, the African Americans of Chicago, had received historical recognition of their being an integral part of the city's history. Indisputably, Chicago's history involved an important black presence at its beginning as a trading settlement in the late eighteenth century, during its growth as a town and as a fledgling city in the early nineteenth century, throughout its development as a metropolis in the Reconstruction era and in the American Industrial Age, and into the twentieth century.

DU SABLE: A MODEL FOR ALL TIMES

At the time I heard the radio ad, Du Sable's claim to being the first permanent, historically recognized, nonindigenous settler, was already well documented.[2] Its being revived was nothing unprecedented, because this had been the case for Du Sable's legacy on numerous occasions previously.[3] Significantly, Du Sable's residency was considered as both the beginning of continuous community life and an acknowledgment of the African American foundation for Chicago's inspiring, commercial spirit.[4]

Jean Baptiste Pointe Du Sable's presence at Chicago for approximately twenty-five years (ca. 1775–1800) heralded some of the best features that life in a future Americanized Chicago would produce. He represented a model for all times in that his life embodied a humanistic concern for intergroup coexistence balanced against the eighteenth century's avaricious commercial spirit. Moreover, this man of the eighteenth century embodied the requisite strains of cosmopolitanism needed for the emergence of metropolitan Chicago in the twentieth and twenty-first centuries. All the same, with his initial entry into the area, Du Sable had planted the seeds for the demise of indigenous lake cultures that were economically subsistent, but basically self-sufficient, at the time he and previous French colonials encountered them.

In 1800, Du Sable, the city's first permanent, nonindigenous settler, voluntarily sold his extensive holdings and moved with his family to French-controlled St. Charles, Missouri. With his departure, a major impetus for commercial dynamism disappeared temporarily. The sentiment in the pages of the Chicago Defender, expressed in the epigraph above, represented a most salient feature of African American life in Chicago during its first historical century. It continued a tradition among some blacks that acknowledged Du Sable's historical status as laudatory and authentic rather than one considered legendary or mythical.

The vital statistics of Jean Baptiste Pointe Du Sable are inexact. Du Sable was either born sometime around 1845 in St. Marc, Haiti, to a mother of West African ancestry and a father of French blood, or born to a free black woman and an unknown Frenchman near Montreal, Canada.[5] Born outside of the regimen of slavery that made life profitable for the French and Spanish authorities and planters on the island of Santo Domingo as well as in French America, and correspondingly miserable for persons of African descent, who were consigned to a lifetime of economic exploitation and physical degradation, his world was presumably separate from this ongoing tragedy. One history has him arriving in the territory of Louisiana in 1765 after an education in France, filled with the ambition to use his skills and test his mettle on the fabled, fortune-beckoning, North American mainland. Within two years, he traveled up the Mississippi River to St. Charles (in the future state of Missouri). By 1769, it appeared that he lived in Canada, and after a while he decided to travel southward to Chicago, the geographical trading pivot the Native Americans had exploited commercially for generations, where "the river meets the lake."[6]

For Du Sable's contemporary Euro-American world, his residency at

Chicago marked the beginning of continuous community life in the western tradition as it highlighted successful economic exchange and peaceful intergroup relations in a region where Potawatomi resistance against British and American incursions had produced decades of warfare.[7] Sometime around 1775, Du Sable settled in the area and began to build a permanent trading establishment from which he could personally control the fur trade and related commercial activities. Here at Chicago, he actively sought and gained financial success over the next quarter century, as evidenced by his extensive homestead and trading complex located at what was Pine (Michigan Avenue) and Water streets. The physically imposing, large-framed, "handsome Negro, [who was] well-educated," chose a wife from among the Potawatomi people, whose hegemony was recognized over the area. She was his beloved Kittiwaha (Catherine). Along with two children, Jean Baptiste *fils* and Suzanne, they enjoyed life in a major dwelling, a "frame-house" that measured forty by twenty-two feet. It bore absolutely no resemblance to the "rude cabin" described by racial detractors and was surrounded by a bake house, a milk house, a smokehouse, a chicken house with "44 big hens," a workhouse, a cow house, and a barn that housed "30 Big horned beasts."[8] The house was graced with the appropriate accoutrements for this type of dwelling and for a man described as holding "a commission for some office," from some unidentified political or governmental entity, either Native American or European. The Du Sable family's material possessions were substantial, and at the time of their departure, they left behind for sale a desk, at least two paintings, two mirrors, "20 large wooden plates," and a "coffee-grinder from France."[9] They obviously carried with them many more items of a personal and valuable nature at the time they left Chicago.

Du Sable's economic involvement in this trading sphere depended on maintaining good political relations with the dominant ethnic force in the Chicago Plain, the Potawatomi. His fluency in language, his marriage into the group, and his positive attitude toward non-European peoples no doubt contributed to his success. The scope of his economic activities ranged from merchandising pork, flour, and bread to hunters, fur trappers, and settlers to trading in furs to selling manufactured items resulting from his skill as a cooper and carpenter.[10] He benefited also from the monopoly he held in the absence of competition.

Speculation as to the character of any political or military office he held in the 1790s has linked him to the Potawatomi and his possibly holding a subchieftaincy. With this possibility, once the Potawatomi and other groups signed a peace agreement with the U.S. government in 1795 at Greenville (near Toledo, Ohio), Du Sable's future at Chicago would have certainly dimmed. Before the century ended, word of American control over a six-square-mile plot that eventually became American Chicago found specula-tors concocting various schemes for the newly acquired area. This supplies the reason for Du Sable's decision in 1800 to leave and return southward into an area governed under alternating Spanish and French authority along the western bank of the Mississippi River. If he had a British or French com-mission of some sort, the treaty would also have ended his plans for contin-ued commercial activities at Chicago because of American condescending, and even hostile, racial attitudes toward persons of African descent.[11] It is unimaginable that he could have lived in peace with American whites after the Greenville treaty.

When frontier America (in its physicality, Fort Dearborn) encountered Potawatomi-French Chicago (in its commercial and cultural syncretism) in 1803–1804, neither overwhelmed the other immediately. Cooperation, rather than conflict, marked the initial character of relations consistent with the shape of Du Sable's intralacustrine diplomacy. In the wake of Du Sable's departure in 1800, American expansionism took only three decades to expel the Potawatomi and other resident native peoples—economically, physically, and culturally. Consistent with American public sentiment on race it can be well imagined that the memory of this successful and "hand-some Negro" was deliberately allowed to fade by both civilian and military authorities.

The departure of the Du Sable family left a void that was soon to be filled by an equally dynamic American presence after 1816, when Fort Dearborn was rebuilt following its destruction in 1812. Jean Baptiste Pointe Du Sable left an imprint on the land that has had him credited authoritatively as Chicago's "first landed proprietor," effective peacemaker, and economic visionary. Significantly, his experience proved to be the opposite of all per-sons of African descent who followed in his wake. Chicago's African Americans perpetually confronted the social damage wrought by slavery and racism in every generation after Du Sable's residency. Frederick Douglass even raised its specter as late as the World's Columbian Exposition in 1893.[12] The horrific nature of life under bondage demanded from each vic-tim a level of perseverance and resolve that is admirable in itself. Given the constant level of racism, discrimination, and prejudice they faced sans slav-ery, they were forced to revitalize themselves continually. They accom-plished this repeatedly during the antebellum period, which they perceived as a livable present, no matter the obstacles, and during the post-emanci-pation period, when they envisioned a promising future especially when viewed from a religious bent.

Sometime in the nineteenth century, perhaps as early as the 1830s, African Americans recognized in Jean Baptiste Pointe Du Sable's accomplishments a model of what could be achieved through agency without the impediment of slavery obstructing their advancement. Then, there is the probability that Du Sable's success was known popularly by blacks through-out the sprawling frontier network where freedom was limited but not mem-ory. It is not too difficult to imagine that stories or references to Du Sable remained pervasive among the French traders and mixed-bloods of French and Native American heritage for some time after his departure.[13] The *Chicago Defender*'s reference indicated the extent to which blacks had developed a consciousness that the opportunity for real change had finally begun with their liberation in 1865. Traditional acceptance of a "real his-tory" linked to Du Sable reasonably could have established a partial basis for the push for commercial advancement and extensions of freedoms apparent since 1865. In any event, future decades would bring both a formal histori-cal recognition of Du Sable's contributions, such as occurred with A. T. Andreas's work on Chicago in 1885, and an actualization of Du Sable's dream through a black-controlled venue—the city within a city—found in the South Side enclave later referred to as the "Black Belt" or the "Black Metropolis" by the 1920s.

Between the period of Du Sable's departure and sometime around Chi-cago's frontier condition being raised to town status by the Illinois General Assembly in 1833, the muted, sometimes latent, influence of persons of West African descent rose again. There was, of course, a woman of African descent who was held in bondage by an American military officer at Fort Dearborn. This unknown soul died with approximately one-half of the ninety-four persons who evacuated the fort before the Potawatomi attack of 1812. More likely than not, there must have been among the "half-breeds, quarter-breeds and men of no breed at all," more sons and daughters of Africa. In any event, the saga of Du Sable culminated in entrepreneurial and business success over a vast continuum of time.

The noted Chicago historian Bessie Louise Pierce observed that, follow-ing in the footsteps of this enterprising business pioneer, African Americans operated two of the three frontier town's bathhouses during the 1830s. One resident whose name played prominently in early Chicago history was Lewis Isbel, a dweller in the state of Illinois since 1824 and in the city since 1837 as a prospering barber.[14] Isbel intermingled within the dominant white American settlement and, by the time of the Civil War, proved his worth as a citizen by recruiting black soldiers to fight in the cause to preserve the dignity of African humanity and the Union. Historically rooted, a tendency toward independence of action accompanied the attainment of freedom and the thrust for the enjoyment of the rights and privileges of citizenship.

The famed John Jones arrived in the late 1840s and succeeded not only as a tailor to the wealthy, but also as a merchant-tailor who built his own downtown structure before the Civil War. However, it took the mass emancipation of all persons of African descent in 1865 to provide the most opportune channel through which their true creative economic abilities could flow. Near the end of the century, and with the boisterous promotion of the World's Columbian Exposition of 1893, black Chicago provided services in barbering, saloon keeping, and the restaurant trade. Enthusiasm for entrepreneurship and business led to plans to build new hotels to accommodate an expansive multiracial patronage at the fair.[15] This period represented an incipient stage of growth for black businesspersons as well as for the African American market. It further validated Professor Abram L. Harris's analysis that a spirit of business enterprise grew throughout the nation shortly after the Emancipation: "From the '80s on, the Negro masses, urged by their leaders, were led to place increasing faith in business and property as a means of escaping poverty and achieving economic independence."[16] Anthony Overton's relocation of his Hygienic Manufacturing Company from Kansas City in 1911 helped lead another surge.

African American confidence in using economic advancement as a major channel of racial progress reached fruition in the twentieth century when the first full-blown generation of black entrepreneurs and businesspersons appeared. With national postwar prosperity in the 1920s, the "Black Metropolis" emerged. This attempt by blacks to bring to fruition the realization of the concept of *imperio en imperio*, the creation of a self-contained city within the city, was scoffed at by some but endorsed by so many more. The Black Metropolis claim of maintaining black control over an extensive amount of space grew to rest on the potential of a solid political and economic base. While some black businesses depended on a limited white clientele, the arrival of an additional fifty thousand new workers/citizens as part of the Great Migration between 1915 and 1918 dramatically expanded the black consumer base, allowing for the growth and development of even more African American businesses. Drake and Cayton contended that it was this dramatic wartime arrival that provided the final base of support for the businesses of the Black Metropolis.[17] With economic prosperity, the theoretical possibility of racial equality assumed a lesser importance than continued, unfettered economic advancement.

Benefiting from an inelasticity in demand within the economic sphere, namely the evolution of a captive African American market willing to accept whatever level of goods and services were offered them regardless of price, these halcyon days of the 1920s generated phenomenal instances of economic advancement for black businesses. The maturation of the Binga State Bank in 1921 and the emergence of Anthony Overton's Douglass

National Bank in 1923 led to these two banks controlling one-third of all black bank assets nationally. Just as impressively, black Chicagoans organized these insurance companies on the modern corporate model: Supreme Liberty Life Insurance, Metropolitan Mutual Assurance, and Victory Life Insurance. In transportation, one enterprising gentleman organized a cab company that put a fleet of seventy vehicles on the streets daily, each driven by a uniformed chauffeur. In manufacturing, Parker House Sausage Company and Walter Johnson's Therapeutic Light Company emerged.

The dream of a Black Metropolis unfortunately foundered during the Great Depression, with the failure of the two banking giants and of many smaller businesses. Supreme and Metropolitan did manage to survive the economic disaster, and there were some other financial bright spots. Notably, in 1935, a new financial institution, Illinois Federal Savings and Loan, and a business association, the Cosmopolitan Chamber of Commerce, appeared. Then, the Johnson Publishing Company was created in the middle of the Second World War. The post–World War Two era heralded another opportunity for the nation to experience peace accompanied by prosperity. Aided by continued migration as part of the second phase of the Great Migration, a proliferation of businesses resulted that offered an expanded range of goods and services relevant for new tastes in a more sophisticated and growing market.

PART I

HAVEN OF
LIBERTY
FOR FORMER
CHATTEL
AND
CONTRABAND
1833–1865

Introduction to Part I

BETWEEN 1833 and 1865, black Chicago partially fulfilled famed bibliophile Arthur Schomburg's preconditions for a workable history geared to meet the demands of African Americans throughout the African diasporan world. Among the indispensable elements in remaking their past in order to build a secure future, Schomburg cited the development of a group tradition, pride in race, and, importantly, a restoration of the confidence that the slave experience had extracted from so many of their minds and personalities. Even without a direct link to the successes of Du Sable, habits, traditions, and positive linkages of the past formed a nexus that constituted *real history* in contradiction to what the *Chicago Defender* had printed. The antebellum and Civil War periods bore witness to a favorable African American response to the simultaneous interaction between internal impulse and self-interest, which meant doing what they wanted, and external racial constraints, which found them responding to the more powerful will of others. Social conditions imposed or influenced by whites, then, shaped only a portion of their lives. Their desires as *they* perceived them allowed for a semblance of happiness. This demonstration of agency was especially true in the African American enthusiasm for worship and for recreation, which demonstrated the extent to which the racially driven dynamics of their internal world acted. In the workplace, they acceded more readily to what the outside work dictated. Black Chicagoans, indeed, were sufficiently motivated to transform themselves into *subjects* making history, rather than being the *objects* of policy decisions enacted by others. Moreover, they felt linked by a common thread of what they perceived to be racial destiny, one several generations in the future realized in the dream of the Black Metropolis.

The city's historically recognized founder, Jean Baptiste Pointe Du Sable, personified the concept of agency or the exertion of personal power or influence. In succeeding decades, persons of African descent who followed in Du Sable's footsteps encountered a different and variegated racial setting. Some whites refused to recognize even the possibility of African American human potential. Nonetheless, with the presence of abolitionists of all persuasions, Chicago, in relative terms in the North, stood as a haven of liberty and opportunity.

At this point, Arthur Schomburg's blueprint seemed accurate as to the necessity of building a group tradition for racial advancement. One could imagine the African American outlook over time as they bonded into one group: experiencing passive liberation in the North during the antebellum period; embracing active liberation as combatants during the Civil War; developing "New Negro" sentiments early in the emancipation phase, which yielded to self-determination that was, at first, expectant until the 1920s, when it was finally brought into realization. Remarkably, all of these sentiments were reinforced by almost constant linear successes.

Within the mass of refugees from Southern slavery, heterogeneity counterbalanced homogeneity. Feelings, attitudes, perceptions, and dreams differed based on experience and mind-set. Some feelings and attitudes were also held in common. While there were differences among African Americans depending on their time of arrival to Chicago before the Civil War, a number of them shared the same sense of fatalism. This was also the case with some of the later migrants from the Upper South, namely from Virginia and Kentucky. They all possessed a personal set of views of the redeemable as well as dispensable features of their past lives as slaves. A significant end in this cycle of fatalistic thinking came with the break between the past, in the person of the former slave who became an abolitionist or a camp follower, or the slave man or woman who became a compensated wage worker, or who *by choice* assumed the status of husband, wife, father, or mother.

They exercised their freedom through unfettered movement to reach Chicago—by lake shipping, as Abram T. Hall did; by stagecoach, as was case with John and Mary Richardson Jones; or by traveling on foot, as innumerable runaways successfully showed on the Underground Railroad, the mechanism set up to help refugees escape to the north and onward sometimes to slave-free Canada. Complementing this prized mobility, the men of the Twenty-ninth Infantry left Chicago by rail to protect this newly won freedom on Civil War battlefields.

The associational activities of Chicagoans included organizing churches, initiating fraternal life, and participating in the black convention movement, even if it was of a limited nature. What they experienced was reflective of the general trend even as some aspects of life in Chicago seemed to be unique to the city.

During the wartime period, personal transformation resulted from contact in a physician's office as men, not chattel, *volunteered* to be examined for military service. In houses of worship and on the streets of Chicago, men were enlisted by their fellow kinsmen to join in a cause much greater than themselves—the liberation of an entire people numbering four million. Pride also built upon personal contact with fellow African Americans who

exuded success, such as that found in the personage of the professional practitioner in medicine and the prosperous citizen in business. Residence in
Chicago brought the refugee face-to-face with aspiring, northern-oriented
and -educated African Americans such as Dr. C. H. Hutchinson and lecturer H. Ford Douglas, along with the successful businessmen John Jones and
Lewis Isbel (or Isabel). Because of the inauguration of a federal bureaucratic
enlistment process, members of the black elite began providing leadership
to an independent body of citizens.

Chicago, seen as an arena of economic opportunity, proved a proper choice.
From laborer to domestic servant to businessperson, compensated production sustained African American life and provided hope that a better life
awaited in the future, once slavery ended in the South and racial restrictions eased in the North. This accounted for the roots of African American
entrepreneurial and business action. A future observer, Charles S. Johnson,
found it the very character of frontier-period, wartime, and industrial-era
Chicago. "Cities have personalities. . . . Similar differences between cities
account for the curiously varied directions of growth which the Negro populations take. They help to explain the furious striving after commercial
glory in Chicago."[1]

Hope increased, moreover, with the coming of the Civil War and the
signing of the Emancipation Proclamation. Despite its shortcomings, it had
transcended all expectations in 1863 just with its issuance. Later, in March
1865, successful pressure by African Americans, along with that of their
white allies, resulted in the repeal of the formal instrument of legalized
Illinois bigotry, the Illinois Black Laws. Then, of the several momentous
events affecting the status and conditions under which the African Americans in Chicago lived, the most significant was the legal end of bondage
through the ratification of the Thirteenth Amendment in December 1865.
While emancipation generated hope of a better life, it delivered a tumultuous one. The mettle of the African American would be tested repeatedly,
but despite obstacles, progress was evident.

At this same time, emancipation was won on Civil War battlefields, and
an attachment to the martial spirit pervaded African American thinking.
Especially among soldiers, combat experience in 1864 and 1865 grew to be
valued for a generation or so until memory faded against the daily vicissitudes of urban survival in the industrializing world. The Grand Army of the
Republic's John Brown Post Number 50 showed the away. Still, the emergence of the Hannibal Guard in 1872 showed that the martial spirit was still
in the air. By 1897, the formation of the Eighth Regiment, Illinois National
Guard, began another tradition, which rested on valor in the Spanish-American War and then was reforged in World War I.

A proliferation of institutional life, a sure sign of social change, was evidenced in the formation of churches, families, and fraternal and cultural bodies. The first church experience centered around biracialism, with white Protestants opening their doors to their Colored brethren. However, it yielded to a more powerful impulse from within African American ranks centering around a sense of black racial destiny in religious affairs. Beginning a precedent with the establishment of the first African American church in 1847, three more were formed by the advent of the Civil War. Through consolidation and independent formation, the city housed four African American Protestant churches by the end of the war. All chose black pastoral leadership and worshiped along liturgical lines that conformed to African American wishes and traditions.

Migration to Chicago and fulfillment in the longevity of settlement produced another tradition. It contained elements of courage, disregard for the unknown, curiosity about the different, and confidence in the inevitability of individual and group triumph. In focusing on migration and place, the noted sociologist Charles S. Johnson once dubbed the entirety of Illinois, and, in particular, Chicago, as the "Mecca of the Migrant Mob."[2] The migrants came from far and near, sojourning over space but also over time in the seventeenth, eighteenth, and nineteenth centuries. Whether or not their ethnic roots were from West Africa, as remnants of the Ibo, Mandingo, Yoruba, or other societies in the earliest days of the African diaspora, these African Americans came as sojourners, arriving during slavery under French, Spanish, and American periods of hegemony. Tennessee, Kansas, Virginia, North Carolina, Mississippi, and Alabama sent their residents at a much later time.

Acknowledgment of an existing preoccupation with and sense of place rested on the presence of the "Old Settlers." The oldest settlers, the pioneers of the antebellum period, 1833–1860, and their offspring, would refer to themselves with this sobriquet.[3] They resided in the city before the Civil War, and therefore also before the Great Fire of 1871, and they interacted with whites in ways distinctive to those eras. Many were persons who had certificates of freedom. Some did not have such paperwork and were refugees, or fugitives, as they were derisively designated by the laws of the land. Yet, all African Americans commonly shared the same experience of the city with its countervailing offerings of social proscription and unbridled hope. The formation of the "Old Settlers," the result of a mind-set requiring group status, confirmed the uniqueness of place and a corresponding sense of belonging in the "Windy City," had Du Sablean roots into which literally each generation could tap. For Chicago, it took on a very special quality that elevated it to the ethereal. Tuttle wrote of this phenomenon: "Chicago was not only a city; it was a state of mind."[4]

To a much lesser extent, the small number of Civil War veterans formed a part of this group. Place, time, circumstance, and *being* were marked by significant events and the triumph over adversity associated with them. This was particularly true of the Emancipation of 1865 and the fires of 1871 and 1874. Figuratively, for a people rooted in biblical imagery, 1865 saw the black Lazarus rise from the living death of bondage, and thus ended three decades of life that began the African American saga.

Chapter 1

Antebellum Frontier Town and "City of Refuge," 1833–1860

The kidnaping of fugitive slaves by slave owners, assisted by some of the low whites and officers of the city, was the chief conversation among our people. That the Negroes might not become paupers the laws of the state demanded $2,000 security from each and every one who came in the city or state, but to the honor of Chicago, the law was never enforced and the setting of every sun marked the arrival of a strange Negro.

— "A Real Oldtimer on the Life of Early Colored Settlers"

Were any Negroes ever sold in Chicago? Yes, a free Negro was one day arrested [in 1842] and put up to auction to be sold to the highest bidder. [But] it would have been hazardous for any man to buy him to keep in slavery or to sell him again. . . . Mr. Ogden bought the Negro for 25 cents and again set him at liberty.

— ATTORNEY LEMUEL C. FREER

Then came the passage of the fugitive slave law [in 1850], and many of the poor colored people were so frightened at what it portended that they fled to Canada.

— MARSHA FREEMAN EDMOND

WHATEVER ELSE it was during its initial, antebellum phase—a frontier town that in 1833 could be described demographically as a place where the population was filled with "rogues of every description, white, black, brown and red—half breeds,

42

quarter breeds and men of no breed at all," or that, in 1853, was said to be so primitive physically that "only years ago the prairie grass was scarcely trodden down"—Chicago represented a "City of Refuge" for African Americans seeking freedom from slavery and racial subordination.[1] This circumstance of urban transformation, along with several other active factors, such as economic opportunity, humanitarianism, and demographic increase, molded African American life between 1833 and 1860. As a result of those collective influences, the first phase of sustained community life among African Americans occurred.

Continual, salutary demographic changes affected African Americans, influencing them individually, in the aggregate, in family formation, and in their residency patterns. Then, a complex, multifaceted ethos governing internal dynamics authenticated a unique side of life existing within an incipient, heterogeneous African American population. The ensuing cultural base turned healthy population growth into vital institutional development within a parallel world incubating in the heart of frontier Chicago.

Just as important, in a nation committed to white racial supremacy, pervasive societal constraints kept the lives of blacks in a state of perpetual flux as they existed in mainstream America. At no time, however, were these debilitating influences so overwhelming that they could stymie the indomitable spirit of African Americans to end their existence under racial proscription immediately and in bondage eventually.[2] The significance of these local experiences reveals uniqueness when compared to the national scene.

I. THE DEMOGRAPHY OF A PEOPLE

The statistical base for the demographic profile of black Chicago during the antebellum period originates from three census sources—the U.S. censuses of 1840, 1850, and 1860, the Illinois state census of 1845, and the Chicago city censuses of 1837, 1843, and 1848. Relegated into a special category as "Colored" persons, their status as exceptional persons was never doubted. Complementing these numerical data are narratives, chronicles, and remembrances that give a social dimension to the lives of the people involved. In Chicago of the 1830s, a small group of persons of West African descent, never amounting to more than 1 to 2 percent of the fledgling frontier town's total population, struggled initially to maintain its existence. This group grew to constitute a body comprising 77 persons out of 4,066 residents in 1837. Within their ranks were 41 males and 36 females, probably mostly adults because of the frontier nature of this setting. Elsewhere in the free states of the north, this ratio appeared in opposite fashion.[3]

As to the states of origins for these free people of color and refugees (usually referred to pejoratively as "fugitives," as though escape from forced bondage could lack moral legitimacy),[4] they emigrated from nearby Missouri and Kentucky and throughout the Old Northwest, as well as from faraway Pennsylvania, Virginia, and North Carolina. Regarding the last, its highest court could rule that anyone suffering enslavement was "doomed in his own person, and his posterity, to live without knowledge, and without the capacity to make anything his own, and to toil that another may reap the fruits. . . . [S]uch services can only be expected from one who has no will of his own."[5] Pennsylvania, long regarded as the haven of liberty for refugees from slavery, took many steps to restrict its African American citizens also. Pennsylvania, especially Philadelphia, had abandoned its progressive stance on race during the aftermath of the War of 1812. By the 1830s, Philadelphia dishonored itself with Negrophobia and mob violence.[6] The Old Dominion, long majestic in its own eyes, proved itself as mean as any other state in the antebellum Union when it came to the status of free persons able to liberate themselves from bondage. The Virginia legislature passed the infamous Law of 1806 to curtail the number of free persons of color living in the state, relegating them to the precarious position of having to leave Virginia within twelve months or face reenslavement.[7]

By 1840, the sixth census of the United States showed a decline in Chicago's African American population as it plunged to 53 persons. This presented a problem when focusing on increases and decreases and determining net in-migration without information as to gross in-migration over specific periods, for example, U.S. census years. Whether those who left were persons who migrated elsewhere because of coercion, either occasioned by peripatetic slave catchers, or the lure of a more permanent freedom in British Canada (which abolished slavery late in the previous century), is unknown. Then, the dire economic influence of the Panic of 1837 could have caused the migration of labor-seeking individuals elsewhere. However, there can be no doubt that Chicago's status as a major terminus on the Underground Railroad played a major role in any fluctuations in population.[8]

Significantly, the likelihood of the emergence of family life within this smaller population seemed reasonable, something unusual for a frontier environment such as this, but indicative of the rapidity at which development was occurring in various facets of town life. Among whites, ready-made institutions, such as churches, fraternal associations, businesses, and schools, were quickly replicated in their New England and New York forms. In particular, the 1840 ranks of the fifty-three African Americans included fourteen children under the age of ten (nine boys and five girls), along with nine males and females between the ages of ten through twenty-four. Only three persons more than fifty-five years of age lived among them, with the bulk of the group being the twenty-seven individuals who ranged from twenty-four to fifty-five years of age. Prominently positioned in the midst of the latter were fifteen males and seven females between the ages of twenty-four and thirty-six.

By the time of the second Chicago census, completed three years later in 1843, the African American population had risen again, now to sixty-five persons. With the city's total increasing slightly, the black numbers contained a glimmer of hope for the future establishment of a community, for there were twenty-two persons in the youngest age category, those who were less than twenty-one years of age. The remaining forty-three members of this band of free people and refugees included thirty men and thirteen women. The populational glimmer was transformed into a sunburst within months, as the Illinois state census of 1845 shows a near-doubling of the black population of 1837, counting 140 African Americans.[9] Overall, this was an increase of 115 percent over the 1843 population that occurred in the midst of an explosion of the white population, which nearly trebled its size to 11,948.

Possibly missed in that census was the November birth of James Stewart, the newest member of the city's small African American community. He would attend public school, live as other youngsters of his circumstances did, and, importantly, in 1864 enlist as an eighteen-year-old in the Illinois all-black Twenty-ninth Infantry Regiment, to fight for family, friends, and nation.[10]

The power of the influence of these trying times and burdensome experiences resulted in an important wellspring of memories that would be used to reinvigorate life in future days. As an index to this momentous era, the records of the Old Settlers Social Club, organized in 1904, testify poignantly to the importance of arrival in the City of Refuge. Strong historical memories served to link dreamed-of freedom with its realization. In a gesture to humanity, the names of some of the *historically unseen* and *usually overlooked* African American settlers who arrived in the city during these early days are herein listed as they appeared in the *Membership Rolls of the Old Settlers Social Club.* In 1845, Lavinia Lee arrived; in 1846, Rachel Collins Grant and James Early Powell reached the city; in 1849, Clinton Artist, Ella Randall Lewis, and George Walker Mead took up residence.[11] Coincidentally, in March of that same year, future community leader John Jones and his wife, Mary, and infant daughter, Lavinia, headed northward from Alton with their freedom papers in hand.

Moreover, certain composite recollections of African Americans who either lived through this period or heard from their parents about this period were printed in this group's most powerful voice, the *Chicago Defender,* in 1930.

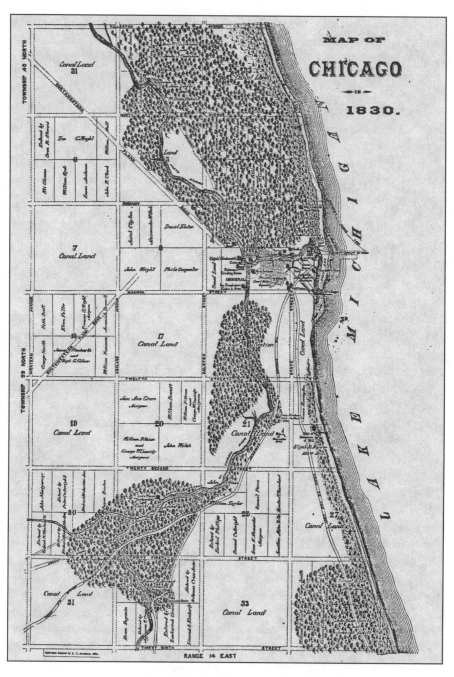

Fig. 1. Map of Chicago, 1830.
From A. T. Andreas, History of Chicago *(1884).*

They make interesting reading and hint at another set of reasons for the flux in population. In the development of Chicago, "the Race member was playing his part. In the late '40s he was with the westbound pioneers who left the East for the exploration of the Oregon country. Many of them took the trail to the gold fields and many of them stopped in or returned to the Chicago region. They helped fight the Indians when necessary and traded with them when the redskins were friendly. They helped carve out a metropolis which we now look upon with pride."[12]

With impressive speed, the frontier atmosphere receded, allowing family life to form upon a base of urban stability (Figure 1). Chicago historian Bessie Louise Pierce found that the necessary conditions for such a metamorphosis had occurred by the city's second decade of existence. For African Americans, a favorable population mix as to males to females had also emerged. The sexual ratio in the Illinois state census of 1845 was nearly balanced by this time, with 73 males and 67 females, implying the possibility of a suitable mix between marriageable males and females for family formation. Two individuals who serve as examples were Pennsylvanian Abram Thompson (A. T.) Hall and another recent arrival, Joanna Huss, who had come to the city in the company of her mother, Adelphia Stewart, of North Carolina. As chronicled by their son, Hall and Huss fell in love; they "met, loved, wooed and [were] united in marriage in 1846."[13] The groom was twenty-four years of age and the bride was sixteen, the typical ages for marriage on the frontier. By 1848, the couple welcomed their first child, Amy, as a resident of Chicago. These social interactions made Chicago comparably consistent with the pattern of two-parent, independent households that dominated the early-nineteenth-century social landscape of other northern cities.[14]

However, little Amy Hall did not hold the distinction of being the first African American child born in Chicago. That signal event took place earlier in 1845 as Amy's parents were arriving in Chicago. Mr. and Mrs. Henry King became parents to a son, Cassius.[15] This baby boy was the first black child born within a family structure since Jean Baptiste and Catherine Du Sable's daughter, who was born late in the eighteenth century in the period preceding American military occupation and civilian settlement. Soon, Joseph and Mary Hudlin also welcomed their daughter, Joanna, to the new community. An increasing number of births were recorded as family life flourished. Among these pioneers, the presence of children already born must also be factored, as shown in the arrival of little Lavinia Jones with her parents, John and Mary. In Chicago, the trend of growing families, now a pattern, stood in contrast to what urban historian Leonard Curry found for the north in general among African Americans. No high percentage of children was being born to African Americans, even with the pool of free women increasing. In addition, he found that African Americans had a lower fertility rate coupled with a higher mortality rate. Out-of-wedlock births appeared rare for both slaves and free females of color.[16] Last, families in the north, and probably in Chicago, who lived with their white employers, must also be factored into this scenario along with independent black households.[17]

The local census of 1848 listed 288 persons of African descent out of a total population of 20,028. By virtue of their transient status, refugees consistently missed being included in the censuses. One group of five adults and an infant passed through town around the time the 1848 tally was taken. Having fled from the Kentucky farm or plantation of a master named Tyler, they were anxious to move farther northward, away from any pursuers. Among their ranks was future Chicago Civil War soldier James Green, who, along with his Kentucky slave companions, reached Whitehall, Michigan, after a journey made safe by abolitionists in the Chicago Underground Railroad. They carried a letter of introduction and support from Chicago abolitionists that they delivered to their new benefactors, including African American stationmaster Walter Duke. The latter aided them in their adjustment and displayed the soundness of judgment and action that would win him the praise of his white neighbors over the next several decades. Once they settled in, they attempted to move beyond their marks and memories of Southern bondage—with James, the stripes on his back from beatings, and with Mariah, the infant she brought with her that was her former master Tyler's son. After establishing themselves in the workforce, James Green married his fellow escapee Mariah and adopted her infant son, John Tyler. The Greens established a family that numbered six within a decade, and then dwindled to three with the deaths of two of the children and Mariah. By 1857, James Green returned to Chicago as a permanent resident until his service in the Twenty-ninth Regiment, Illinois, United States Colored Troops (USCT).[18]

Meanwhile, far to the south in North Carolina, little Edward Maybin was born under the most difficult circumstances imaginable. Three years after his birth, he and his mother, Jane, were sold to a new slave master in Tennessee. Hating her condition and that imposed on little Edward, and possessed with the strength of spirit, mind, and body to resist slavery even though caring for a very young child, Jane escaped with her toddler. Unfortunately, the pace of their escape and the physical needs of Edward prevented a safe flight. As Edward recalled, "she had tried to escape taking me with her, but after about 4 days, we were captured & taken back. I remember that very distinctly, for I had got tired out & had laid down by the side of the road, and when they came after us on horses, they took me first. After we were taken back, our master John Maybin sold my mother to a man in Kentucky."[19] This is one story that resulted in a happy ending, although one of long duration, for mother and child were reunited in the City of Refuge after the war.

Consistent with the pattern of continuing increase, the federal government's census of 1850 showed another leap in Chicago's growth, astoundingly placing the city's overall population at 29,963 denizens in a town laying claim to the sobriquet of the "Queen City of the North West."[20] The African American population now reached 323 persons, with the gender ratio standing at 181 males and 142 females. These African Americans now accounted for 1.08 percent of the total population. Moreover, these data represented an increase for blacks of 131 percent over the 1845 figure. Two factors of consequence affecting this figure were mortality and migration. The cholera epidemic of 1849 caused the deaths of over nine hundred inhabitants. Its devastation was such that a contemporary noted in retrospect that "from that same gate in the cholera year I watched eight funerals in one afternoon in half a square. It was a dreadful time. Everyone left the city who could, even some of the doctors fled."[21] The direct effect on African Americans is unknown at this time, but some members of their community were obviously also victims of this tragedy. Other urban diseases that threatened all Chicagoans included typhoid fever and dysentery.

Migration from within the Old Northwest continued as the five-member Easley family from Terre Haute, Indiana, moved into rental housing in the Third Ward at the northwest corner of Madison and La Salle streets. Composed of parents Samuel and Lydia, sons Willis and David, and daughter, Lydia, the family adjusted quickly to Chicago's environs. Within several years, they moved southward to Clark and Harrison. The children availed themselves of a free public education, as the signatures of the boys on federal documents from later decades attest.[22]

The local records of the *Membership Rolls of the Old Settlers Social Club* show the following arrivals: In 1850, Julia Anne Dawson; in 1851, Kate Hunt and Anna Simpson; in 1853, the future Mrs. Dave McGowan and Louisa L. Washington; in 1854, C. C. Carey, Anna Nelson, W. C. Hawkins, Albert Pettit, Robert C. Waring Sr., and Melinda Porter (who would never forget the exact day and month she reached the City of Refuge, September 24, 1854); in 1855, Julia Marshall Fowler and Allen Hawley; in 1856, Mary E. Henderson, Edmond Johnson, Samuel H. Bond, Charlie Bond, Josephine Stiles, William C. Dawson, and Sophia Long; in 1857, Elisha Winslow and Nancy Holman (who decades later remembered the month, if not the date of her arrival, September 1857); in 1858, Henry Bartlett, William Brown Sr., Dora Crummel Brown, William H. Bond, and an A. Hardin; in 1859, Mary Walker, Caroline Cole Curtiss, Lizzie Hall Dyer, John J. Grant, Martha Gray,

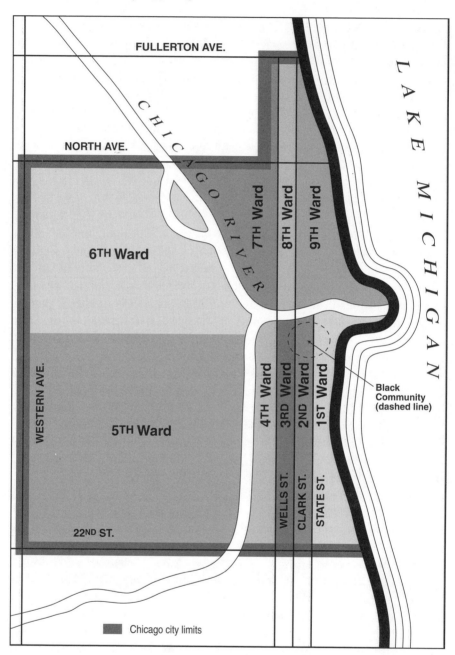

Fig. 2. Ward Boundaries of Chicago, 1847.
Based on map in *Bessie Louise Pierce, A History of Chicago, 1:323.*

Charlie Jackson, and Margaret Pierce. Two more new arrivals could recall with exactness their reaching their "land of hope" in 1859: Hattie Warner, who arrived on July 6, 1859, and James H. Lewis, who arrived on September 1, 1859. In 1860, Georgana Stallcup, Carrie Jenkins Skinner, and Thornton Buckner placed their feet on the muddy streets of the lakefront city. A youngster from Washington, D.C., also appeared; sixteen-year-old Charles B. Taylor arrived in the city where he would spend his next seventy-eight years in continuous residency. As impressive as this longevity seems, his granddaughter, Annetta Oglesby, exceeded the family mark, with 101 years of uninterrupted residency.[23]

Spatially, according to Bessie Louise Pierce, "the Negro population though small was fairly well concentrated, for 82 percent, in 1850, lived in the South Division, particularly in the First and Second wards" (Figure 2). The boundaries of the First Ward extended from Lake Michigan to State Street, and from Twenty-second Street on the south to the Chicago River on the north; it included seventy-four persons (forty-eight males and twenty-six females). The Second Ward's boundaries extended from State to Clark Street, and Twenty-second to the Chicago River. Included in its boundaries were seventy-three blacks (thirty-two male and forty-one female). The Third Ward was located between Clark, Twenty-second, and Wells streets and the Chicago River. There were fifty-eight inhabitants (thirty-two males and twenty-six females). Then, in the Fourth Ward, located between Wells and Twenty-second streets and the South Branch of the Chicago River, there were sixty persons (twenty-seven males and thirty-three females). The total for the area was 265 residents, divided somewhat evenly with 139 males and 126 females. Fifty-eight persons lived elsewhere in the West or North Divisions.[24]

Despite this demographic concentration, this clustering was not the equivalent to a twentieth-century ghetto. Neither could it be called an African American neighborhood, as "the Negro and white population lived side by side. The Negro people were integrally related to the white society; both work and worship, and to some extent, play, brought many of them into face to face contacts with their white neighbors."[25] Rather, this apparent gregariousness represented several natural inclinations such as defensive living in a racially and legally hostile environment, the need for nurturing and shelter among kin and friends, and the importance attached by all Chicagoans to lakefront and riverbank habitations near work. This residential choice, after all, lay in the town's most popular section, which was basically a residential area located one-half mile south of the main commercial and service thoroughfares of Lake and Water streets.

Evidence that the African American family miraculously had emerged, alive and well, came in the figures that showed that, by 1850, there were 8 infants awaiting their first birthday, a fact with significance in the family-oriented world of the nineteenth century. A total of 93 youngsters under the age of fifteen years composed nearly a third of the total African American population, approximating the ratio of age groups to the total white population in Chicago and the United States. As for the gender ratio among African Americans, it showed signs of stabilization, with 181 males and 142 females. During this period of two-parent, or "double-headed," households, the balance between the sexes of marriageable spouses served an indispensable role in family formation and community advancement.[26]

By 1860, on the eve of the Civil War, the African American population reached 955 souls, an increase of 195 percent over the 1850 population but a mere .87 percent of the total population of 109,260. As to their spatial location, Pierce stated that "about 72 per cent (of the black population) was concentrated in the First, Second, and Third Wards." Sharing the same fear that Frederick Douglass expressed about the constant possibility of being spirited off to the oppression of Southern slavery, or worried about the "continual kidnaping[s] which so excited our people," or fearing other, real possibilities of reenslavement, three hundred of this number fled to Canada, and approximately forty-seven migrated to Haiti.[27]

Nationally, Leonard F. Curry's comprehensive view of fifteen northern and southern cities with substantial African American populations showed that overall the first half of the nineteenth century brought a dramatic pattern of growth to America's urban populations. Whites increased their numbers by natural births over deaths and immigration, while free people of color augmented their ranks through manumission and natural increase. For frontier Chicago, manumission was not an important channel to consider while slavery was illegal in the state of Illinois. Outside immigration from Santo Domingo, Canada, or elsewhere to Chicago, despite Du Sable's pioneering sojourn in the late eighteenth century and its becoming an important lake port, no doubt resulted in the few black sailors who arrived during the antebellum period. The refugees from slavery expanded their numbers continuously through the courageous act of flight.

Beyond the interpretations possible from statistics, an examination of the social dimensions of this group seems fundamental to reconstructing a history such as this. Reliance on social memory along with oral traditions add tremendously to historical understanding. With the nexus of time and written recollection some of this history has been preserved for posterity. The extracted memory of one self-described "Oldtimer" at the century's end has immeasurable value. In contrast, the *Chicago Defender* printed an account of the historic African American past in 1930 that devalued the period from 1800 to 1865. Its "Story of [an] Old Settler" read: "The election [of 1860]

came; Lincoln was president, then the war. The Race played its part. . . .
Then freedom came and the end of the war, and with it the first *real* history
that bears any semblance of authenticity since De Saible [Du Sable] begins."[28]
The existence and accomplishments of a generation of pioneers arriving
before the end of the war were cast aside unceremoniously.

Framing the social history benefited from intellectual parameters set at
opposite ends of the twentieth century. W. E. B. Du Bois's admonishment in
his classic *The Souls of Black Folk* (1903) and Leon F. Litwack's endorsement
of exploring the historical experiences of ordinary folk in *Trouble in Mind*
(1998) help immensely in recovering the history of African Americans. So
in these pages, the "Oldtimer" is allowed to recount the following: "The city
limits were Harrison street on the south, Superior on the north and Union
on the west.[29] The reason the limits embraced no more territory was because
of the marshes, which covered nearly all of the South and West Sides. At
that time railroad corporations did not control Chicago; in fact[,] there
were none in the state and our only means of transportation was by wagon
trains to the north, south and west and by steamboat and vessels east. During
the winter our city was entirely shut in and the only means of communication with the outside world was through the medium of Frink & Walker's
stage line. Following that came the Chicago and La Salle canal, which connected with the Illinois River." Among the colored citizens of Chicago in
1843 were John and Rachel Day, Oliver C. Henson, John Johnson, the
Artises, Daniel Lipiscomb, Maria Williams Parker, John Dixon, Anna
Williams Fulton, Abram Taylor, Henry Knight, Williams Smith, known as
"Tremont Smith," and William Winder.[30] A. T. Hall, who was a barber on
the *Missouri,* which traveled between Buffalo and Chicago, "frequently visited the city."

His journey through time continued: "In 1844 came an exodus of people
headed by Henry King . . . and Wm. Styles. There were others, but their
names I have forgotten. Following them came Clayburn Bunch and family
and Isaiah Parker. [John] Jones established his clothes cleaning business and
from the start met with success. Everybody worked and not much time was
given in forming a 400 [a social elite] or in the discussion of whom should
be the Ward McAllister [an arbiter of societal protocol]. The kidnaping of
fugitive slaves by slave owners, assisted by some of the low whites and the
officers of the city, was the chief conversation among our people. That the
Negroes might not become paupers the laws of the state demanded $2,000
security from each and every one who came in the city or state, but to the
honor of Chicago, the law was never enforced and the setting of every sun
marked the arrival of a strange Negro."[31]

Indeed, there were others, whose names and existence the Oldtimer would never have known, let alone forgotten. Alexander Garrett was born in 1844 in Chicago, as he was led to believe by his parents. Destined for military service in the impending Civil War, Garrett stated later, "I am unable to furnish any record of my birth as I was born during the slave period and no record was made at the time, but I remember distinctly that my parents gave the date of my birth as Feb[ruary] 7, 1844, the family bible being burned up in [the Great Fire of] 1871, but there was no record either in the bible or otherwise."[32]

At mid-decade, the Oldtimer again filled in the dynamics of life. "In 1845 came A. T. Hall, Douglas N. Davidson, Alexander Lewis and Henry Wells and family. Two new arrivees, who described themselves as coming from 'British North America' [i.e., slavery-free Canada], took residence in 1846. They were Henry O. Wagoner and his wife of two years who set up their home in a 'little domicile on Dearborn Street.'"[33]

"Eighteen forty-seven marked the establishment of our first colored church, Quinn Chapel, and the first colored saloon," the Oldtimer continued. Chicago, while on the western fringes of American settlement during the early nineteenth century, was never without extensive social contact, with foreign and domestic visitors, transients, and migrants being found in abundance. The "Oldtimer" could remember when one peripatetic guest began to make his mark. He recalled,

> About this time appeared a young man who was determined to be a great leader, a man whose ardor, eloquence and intelligent efforts [did] much to bring about a sentiment that eventually stirred the hearts of the Northern people. He had been a slave and when he pictured the horrors of that cruel institution and appealed to the people in behalf of his race a mighty activity was apparent that showed that the days of slavery were numbered. This man was Frederick Douglass, whose name is dear to every Negro and whose fame will endure till the end of time. We all worked in harmony then and although there were no society lions nor political leaders our progress was rapid. It was the ambition of each and every one to own his home and assist in the advancement of his people along all lines.[34]

However, another young man, Isaac Atkinson, appeared in Chicago in 1847, accompanied by his young wife, Emma Jane. By their reckoning they constituted the thirteenth black family to reach Chicago with plans to settle permanently (Figures 3 and 4).[35]

Among those who in the future would later be considered pioneering notables, the names of John and Mary Richardson Jones, Abram T. and Joanna Hall, and Joseph and Anna Elizabeth Hudlin were most prominently

Fig. 3. Isaac Atkinson.
*Vivian G. Harsh Research Collection
of Afro-American History and
Literature, Chicago Public Library.*

Fig. 4. Emma Jane Atkinson.
*Vivian G. Harsh Research Collection
of Afro-American History and
Literature, Chicago Public Library.*

recorded. The Hudlins married in 1855, within a year after their separate arrivals in the city from St. Louis.[36] Joseph Hudlin had been born into slavery in Culpepper Court House, Virginia, in 1830, arriving in the Midwest while working as a steward on a Mississippi River steamboat. Anna Elizabeth Hudlin was born free in Uniontown, Pennsylvania, in 1840 to a mother freed by the Quakers and who moved westward to experience a newer freedom.[37] Their marriage ages of twenty-five and possibly fifteen might indicate a discrepancy in their birth dates, something not uncommon in the nation.

Others also arrived during this period, including George De Baptiste and Lloyd G. Wheeler. The latter arrived in the city during the mid-1850s. Wheeler's birthplace was Ohio, where his family planted firm roots in abolitionism. White resentment of the Wheelers' efforts in behalf of aiding fugitive slaves forced them to flee to Canada after the passage of the Fugitive Slave Act of 1850. There, and in Detroit, young Wheeler spent his adolescence and early adult years. Arriving in Chicago before the end of the Civil War, he quickly associated with the legendary John Jones, forming a lifelong relationship approximating that of surrogate father and son. Wheeler became Jones's business partner shortly before the latter's death in 1879. In his own right, Wheeler earned the distinction of becoming the first black person to pass the Illinois Bar, an honor he achieved in 1869.[38] Others who appeared in the city were a grocer, O. G. Hanson, already in the city before 1845, and a William Johnson.[39]

In whatever space African Americans occupied as they assisted other Chicagoans in claiming the land for extensive settlement, they confirmed the perceptions of the "Oldtimer" in seeking eventual home ownership. But before ownership came urban tenancy, and more often than not, discrimination. Regarding housing opportunities for African Americans, Pierce wrote that "the owners of property found it undesirable to rent to them." According to the Hortons, by midcentury, Chicago was nevertheless included among several northern cities where African American adult lodgers, or boarders, composed one-third of the group's population. "Available evidence indicates that boarding was one way of coping with hardship and unfortunate circumstance. . . . Beset by economic problems and limited by discrimination . . . [they] created expanded household structures." Males tended to live in boarding houses; females chose to live with families as lodgers. The black abolitionist H. Ford Douglas and his wife, Stella, lived with her parents in a household that also contained nonrelated boarders.[40]

On new city thoroughfares on which "now may be seen rows of buildings, and streets crowded with a mass of living and moving humanity," these black pioneers sought to establish themselves as part of Chicago's lifeblood.[41] Most housing was single story; by the 1850s, "a two story building was heralded as (a sign of) urban maturity." Homes were wooden, but not cabins except across the river in the Western Division, and those made of brick and stone had wooden interiors. Chicago was a city "made of pine, a city of board and shingles."[42] At no time could the Eastern residential pattern of alley life, garrets, cellars, and lofts be found in this newly constructed frontier town, where no basements existed and one-story houses dominated.

Property owning assumed an importance as a symbol of economic freedom. Pioneer research using canvassing and reliance on the memory of Old Settlers allowed budding sociologist Monroe Nathan Work around 1900 to reconstruct a pattern of evolving property ownership from as early as 1837. In that year, only one property owner existed, and that was purportedly of

Fig. 5. Hudlin family and their house.
From Frederick H. Robb, The Negro in Chicago, 1779-1929.
University of Illinois at Chicago, the University Library,
Department of Special Collections Rare Book Collection.

commercial property. However, by 1844, there were five owners of real estate, and ten by 1847.[43] These properties were located in the old First and Second wards of the city, in the area immediately south of as well as west of the Chicago River. With so few property owners, most African Americans rented homes and rooms, or resided as lodgers in the homes of others and in rooming houses.

These residences rested on streets that were rarely paved, and the drainage system was poor; the future Loop area was sitting at lake level. Adding to the possibility of pestilence was the custom of leaving dead animal carcasses in the streets. This Southern Division was typical for Chicago with streets that "passed from mud to dust, in the season, and reverted to mud. 'Sidewalks' were merely more mud. Even women wore boots."[44]

Purportedly, in 1850, a resident named Honey Hall, who resided at Fifth Avenue (now Wells) and Harrison, "inherited much property and was reputed for many years to be Chicago's wealthiest Negro."[45] Joseph Henry Hudlin and his wife, Anna, were the first African Americans to build their own home, which was located at 239 Third Avenue (now Plymouth Court), near Medinah Place. Construction of this five-room cottage was completed in 1857. The accompanying photograph of the Hudlin family in front of their home shows clearly its clapboard construction and utilitarian lines (Figure 5). Modest yet comfortable, this domicile would serve as a refuge for both races after the fire of 1871. When John Jones, his wife, Mary Richardson Jones, and their infant daughter, Lavinia, arrived in Chicago in 1845, they rented a one-room cottage located on the northwest corner of Madison and Fifth Street (now Wells Street). Within a decade or so, they moved to a more commodious, comfortable, yet unpretentious home, which they owned.[46]

After the Fugitive Slave Act of 1850, many escaped to Canada, a decision that stymied some ambitions and dashed the hopes of a number of property owners. Work wrote that "it appears from the best sources of information that the majority of the property owners who fled, disposed of their holdings at great sacrifice."[47] Despite this setback, by 1854 there were fifteen homes and stores, along with two pieces of church property, owned by African Americans. This property ownership represented a territory extending as far south as Thirty-third Street.

Demographically positioned in the city's center, and a numerical near-anomaly with such small numbers, African Americans nonetheless posed no threat to white hegemony. Nor did they seem poised to replace the departing Potawatomi and other Native Americans, who had left the city and state in 1836, as public nuisance "number one," for that inglorious position was immediately presented to Irish immigrants, who were employed in building the canal. Instead, the role that African Americans assumed was the one that Drake and Cayton described as being "protagonist of the abolitionist drama."[48]

II. THE ETHOS OF A PEOPLE: FOUNDATIONS OF CULTURE AND COMMUNITY

A. Culture

Incontestably, Chicago witnessed the birth of an incipient African American community in its second decade as a permanent urban settlement. The preconditions of demographic significance, spatial proximity of members of the group, institutional development involving family, church, and social organization, and the emergence of a sustaining Afro-American subculture paved the way for a settlement of note. Moreover, a cultural like-mindedness among African Americans provided the group with a cohesive base for unified action against external constraints. The existence of a functional, unifying culture proved essential to the establishment of a viable community in Chicago. This network of kin, friends, and associations, comprising persons with certificated freedom as well as commandeered emancipation, and intermingled with lineages that derived from both racially unmixed and mixed roots, represented heterogeneity in its essence. The fugitive slave emigrated surreptitiously to Chicago initially as an outsider and then faced absorption into the broader community. Chicago presented nothing like an idealized example of a full-fledged community—it was real in every aspect. Unlike Du Sable's unitary world of social equals, frontier black Chicago existed racially as sometimes both overlapping (biracial) and parallel (black) worlds, the latter being one in which the most important public discourse was that conducted among only African Americans. This is something that the city's white abolitionists clearly understood in its sincerity and moral-rootedness, and without language geared specifically for their ears. Most important, this incipient community would sustain itself dynamically into the twentieth century, where it would be known by the sobriquet of "Black Metropolis."[49]

According to sociologist St. Clair Drake, in the case of the United States, a distinctive Afro-American subculture evolved as an alternative to the commonly recognized African American cultures of Haiti, Jamaica, Cuba, and Brazil. Historian Herbert G. Gutman found its locus in the South among slaves, and far earlier in time than Genovese's date of origination in the 1830s. Serving the same purpose as these more fully developed African-based variations, this Afro-American subculture still produced in-group cohesion, and Chicago conformed to this national pattern. Professors James Oliver Horton and Lois E. Horton added another dimension: "Though after the mid-eighteenth century the vast majority of blacks had been born in America, Africa retained its importance as the ancestral home. Even in the most optimistic times, black people were ambivalent about America, and by the nineteenth century most black Americans had a dual identity, recognizing their American and their African heritage." Further, as E. Franklin Frazier would have applied it to any refugee in Chicago, "sometimes the slave's conception of himself and his relationship to others were built upon the lingering memories of his status in Africa."[50]

In this vein, discussion of emigration to Africa filled the African American imagination as much as securing a permanent home in America, or the long-sought goal of eliminating slavery. During this frontier period, the downstate-based, black-led Wood River Baptist Association sent a missionary to Liberia in 1847 to report back on conditions in Africa. He returned and the next year delivered a favorable assessment. Later, Quinn Chapel A.M.E. Church hosted a mass meeting that dealt with the issue of emigration on August 10, 1858, a notion that the majority considered but summarily rejected. To be sure, a consideration of Caucasian sensitivities to differences between the races led to unrelenting linkages of non-Caucasians (excluding Native Americans) to Africa.[51]

Unequivocally, persons of unmixed African descent at the mass level identified themselves exclusively by the construct of race and affinity for the perpetuation of their way of life.[52] This was not a subculture independently constructed away from the indigenous African homeland with an authentic core clearly intact, but it was one quite similar to the garden variety to be found later in America among European immigrants. Within this subculture, persons sought an internally produced affirmation for their being, rather than one that was externally developed and requiring a hegemonic sanction from a dominant, outside group. This permitted them to develop a consciousness free from wondering what whites thought about them during their every waking moment. Empowered by religious conviction, they suffered no disillusionment with themselves or life, nor did they ever let despair descend into hopelessness. Their lives and the totality of their being rested on their will to survive, to eradicate slavery in some way, and, at some point in time, to advance in society beyond mere secure survival.

Refugees in Chicago, as former African slaves in various stages of acculturation to mainstream American life, found themselves in a transformative phase as they experienced quasi-freedom. Evolving from the general mainland North American slave experience, and "owing to the African heritage of their forebears and their experience in bondage," as Ira Berlin, Marc Favreau, and Steven Miller describe,

> slaves developed a distinctive set of beliefs and practices that were manifested in art, cuisine, dance, music, religion, and patterns of work and leisure. This cultural repertoire—articulated in ethical imperatives and conceptions of appropriate social relations—was both a resource for coping with a world they could not control and a product of their ongoing conflict with their owners. . . . Out of lives marked by hard work and oppression, Southern slaves developed a culture that prized the joyful moments to be found in even the most mundane existence, steadfastness in the face of worldly trial, and faith in the ultimate triumph of the right. It helped sustain slaves through their long captivity and prepared them to strive for a better life when freedom came at last.[53]

One such joyous moment (among many) was captured in a local newspaper's exposé on African American saloon life in 1860, where social convention was disregarded and pleasurable abandonment reigned supreme. The reporter recounted: "The fiddler saws and dances with his head and feet and arms. . . . The fiddler redoubles his efforts . . . barrel hoops split, double shuffles and pigeon wings of the most extraordinary character are described, some on their heads, some on their heels, until wearied out, the fiddler closes with a flourish and with an extra pigeon wing and a crash of the boot heels, revolving Africa ceases to spin."[54]

Beside the refugees, the other half of the African American residents of the city belonged to a pool of persons who comprised the free people of color, whose emancipation through self-purchase was both representative and exemplary. Illinois's prototype was Free Frank McWorter, a native of Kentucky who personified the vitality and will that represented the best in African American agency in the North. He therefore served as a flesh-and-blood model of what heights could be attained through personal desire irrespective of the odds. He purchased his freedom, then that of his family, and then he started a town in central-western Illinois—New Philadelphia. There he ran successful commercial farm activities and served as town proprietor over this small, racially integrated urban cluster. Unique in the fulfillment of his dreams and therefore similar to Du Sable, he was not unique in his personal dynamism, for he had counterparts in Chicago with such men as Henry O. Wagoner, H. Ford Douglas, and John Jones, the merchant-tailor.[55]

Without a doubt, for Chicago history specifically, the saga of John Jones and his family bears repeating. In his life's story, the fears and expectations of all persons who had experienced bondage recognized the precariousness of their existence. He was born on a plantation near the Tidewater, in Greene County, North Carolina, on or about November 3, 1816. His early life was shaped primarily by both his precarious legal status as a free person of color and his biracial heritage, his mother being a free mulatto and his father a man of German stock named Bromfield, who had been residing in the area for a lengthy period. While Jones began life legally outside the oppressiveness of slavery, he was similarly outside the protective ring that afforded the personal liberty and economic opportunity enjoyed by white Americans by virtue of their skin color. Known early by both the surnames of Bromfield and Jones, the precariousness of John's future was immediately apparent to his mother, who feared that his father or his father's relatives might attempt to enslave the youngster. To insure for him any economic advantages that might be available as he matured, she apprenticed John to a white man named Sheppard, who took responsibility over Jones's early training. This act, in effect, relegated Jones to a life more reminiscent of indentured servitude than the quasi-freedom that free people of color experienced. Sheppard moved to Tennessee and bound the young Jones over to a tailor named Richard Clere until the youngster reached the age of twenty-one in 1837. Clere lived fifty miles from Memphis, in Somerville, so Jones's life was one of further social isolation. Evidently applying himself with the seriousness that would mark his late adult life, John developed the skills necessary for self-sufficiency under Clere's training. As was the custom of the period for a skilled worker with market demand, he was soon hired out by his employer to a tailor in a town of some size on a major trade route, Memphis, on the Mississippi River.

There in Memphis, Jones tasted of the refreshing fruits of liberty and social stability through his association with a free African American family headed by a blacksmith, Mr. Richardson. The Richardsons were also of mixed racial heritage, facilitating a union that evolved based on common roots, or perhaps a shared sense of rootlessness. As Richardson tired of limited opportunities for himself and his family in Tennessee, he planned and subsequently moved his family to free Illinois. This unit included his daughter, Mary, with whom the young Jones had fallen in love. For a destination, Richardson chose Alton, the home of abolitionist martyr Elijah Lovejoy, as well as a major stop on the Underground Railroad.

Jones, meanwhile, who had lost a mentor and a family, remained in the South to complete his term of service. Besides his apparent loneliness once the Richardsons departed, Jones soon encountered other problems, occasioned first by his return to Somerville, and second by the impending death of his sickly master in trade, Clere. Once again, the uncertainty of life in America for any person of African descent, bond or quasi-free, enveloped Jones. He had reason to believe that the heirs of his master were preparing to claim ownership of him, the apprentice, as part of their inheritance once the master tailor died. They planned to sell him into slavery, possibly into the Deep South to the independent republic of Texas, from which escape was almost impossible.

A false affidavit had been filed alleging Jones was a slave and much younger than he actually was. This affidavit claimed that he was nine years of age in 1837, which would cause him to lose six years toward his date with quasi-freedom that he had actually accrued. Thus, before Clere died, Jones acted with alacrity to obtain a certificate attesting to his free status. Having been given permission to return to North Carolina to obtain the evidence to support his claim, in early January 1838 Jones filed a petition before a Somerville judge, setting forth his claim to freedom under both his mother's surname, Jones, and his alternative, paternal surname, Bromfield. His claim rested on his mother's status and the apprenticeship of his services (and not the sale of his person) to Clere. Perceptively requesting that he be brought into court and discharged on a writ of habeas corpus, he protected his status as a matter of certitude and legal record. By January 16, 1838, he had secured his certificate of freedom, with the court ordering his release from Clere's service and custody. The newly freed tailor returned to Memphis, worked diligently with a purpose in mind for his ultimate move to freedom outside the slave South, saving his earnings for his anticipated departure. In 1841, his goal accomplished, John Jones headed north across the Mason-Dixon Line to freedom and a reuniting with Mary Richardson.

With only a hundred dollars in his pocket, John Jones had reached a new phase in his search for permanent freedom and in his intent to marry his beloved Mary. However, he arrived in Illinois only to encounter the exclusionary Black Laws, which aimed at restricting the residency of free people of color. Earning the additional money necessary to post a bond of $250 in 1844, he registered in accordance with law in the office of the clerk of Madison County. With an official description (five feet, six inches tall, with a scar over the left eyebrow, a scratch over the cheekbone, a scar over the left shinbone, and a complexion that was listed as mulatto), with an official designation as a tailor in trade, with an affirmation of good character, having pledged that he would not become a public charge of that jurisdiction, and with his certificate of freedom from North Carolina in hand, John Jones finally had entered the realm of the free in accordance with standing law.[56]

B. The Possibility of Internal Group Distinctions

Within the emerging Chicago African American community, the likelihood of the emergence of contentious differences and stratification could reasonably be predicted at some point in its evolution. However, they were not sufficiently developed during this time period to appear as serious threats to the unity that bound the community into a solid antislavery phalanx. Distinctions based on racial origin, legal distinctions between the enslaved and the emancipated, social status, gender, economic well-being, interracial contact and skin color, and chosen cultural affinity (Anglo-American or Afro-American) loomed ominously, if Chicago followed the national pattern of the nineteenth century.[57] But Chicago did not. "The small Negro community of the pre Civil War era seems to have been homogeneous, socially," wrote Drake. Of greatest significance, the power of shared oppression bonded disparate personages together whether they desired it or not.[58]

Rhetoric from one of the annual national conventions informed black America of its inexorable link to African-based kin in bondage and under oppression everywhere. In 1848, Frederick Douglass described the situation:

In the Northern states, we are not slaves to individuals, not personal slaves, yet in many respects we are the slaves of the community. We are, however, far enough removed from the actual condition of the slave, to make us largely responsible for their continued enslavement, or their speedy deliverance from chains. For in the proportion which we shall rise in the scale of human improvement, in that proportion do we augment the probabilities of a speedy emancipation of our enslaved fellow-countrymen. *It is more than a figure of speech to say, that we are as a people, chained together.* We are one people—one in general complexion, one in a common degradation, one in popular estimation.—As one rises, all must rise, and as one falls all must fall.[59]

The earliest point of contention among northern blacks, according to historian Ira Berlin, would have existed between the American-born and African-born as well as the ethnic distinctions among the latter:

The American Revolution submerged such differences among black people in the cause of freedom [nationally]. As distinctions between Africans and African Americans disappeared, new differences—between free and slave—emerged, creating new fissures within the black community along new points of alliance. And as separate worlds of freedom and slavery solidified, legal standing mattered more and more. By the beginning of the nineteenth century, legal distinctions between slave and free had become an important basis of social standing in black society. With such distinctions, a new politics emerged, for free and slave had different aspirations and strategies for achieving their goals. Their competing agendas complicated alliances and divisions within black society.[60]

The general trend on the national scene, however, gave little or no insight into the unique experiences of black Chicagoans during the frontier, antebellum phase of their historical development. Theirs was a unifying, rather than a divisive, experience built upon commonality of purpose: to protect themselves from the ravages of racial proscription on an immediate basis and eliminate bondage as soon as feasible on a permanent basis.[61] As the *Illinois Record's* "Oldtimer" had said, "it was the ambition of each and every one to . . . assist in the advancement of his people along all lines." Comparatively across the chasm of race, their social condition approximated that of the white settlers of Illinois and the other parts of the Old Northwest; they experienced a kind of social equality within the economic sphere as they were both resisting and succumbing to the enervating and transformative influences of the market economy.[62]

Meaningfully, a shared bond of *fear* neutralized any social pretensions because of either painful personal experiences or knowledge of relatives and friends still suffering in bondage. The African American aggregate's fears of illegal enslavement of people of color and legally sanctioned reenslavement of fugitives being heartfelt, both real and artificial gregariousness seemed a rational posture. John and Mary Jones experienced this dread in their journey from Alton to Chicago in 1845. They were challenged by a stage driver on their northward trek, but they quickly convinced him of their legal status and right to travel freely. This personal link to slavery molded the Joneses into "Everyman and Everywoman."[63] Their temporary plight during travel in a free state reenforced their commitment to embrace as many persons of African descent as they could who faced this uncertain future. Not too long after the Joneses' journey, three young female refugees from Missouri successfully negotiated the hazardous route from St. Louis to Chicago. Hiding them under straw in a wagon, it was the Joneses who helped conceal them from "late in the fall . . . until navigation opened [in the area's waterways in the spring], and then they were sent to Canada." Years later, the generosity that marked antebellum relations among African Americans continued as one of the young women, who had subsequently married, sent one of her daughters to live with the Joneses until she finished school and began teaching in Chicago.[64] Conclusively, shared fears and common hopes marked the group beneficence of the period.

Further, social status partially depended on the time of arrival in Chicago. The emergence of the *first generation* of black Chicagoan families, such as the Hudlins, the Joneses, the Halls, and the Atkinsons, who arrived in the 1840s and 1850s accounted partially for a sense of belonging, or an affinity for experience in a common physical place. Later, it gave birth to the twentieth century's "Old Settler" mentality.[65] In later decades, these original pioneers would express their uneasiness and sometimes their displeasure with the arrival of newcomers in future migratory waves, from those entering the city during the Civil War to those who arrived during World War I, occasioning the "Great Migration."[66]

Eventually, social status became linked with a sense of acceptance as bona fide Chicagoans and the rate of adapting socially to Anglo-Saxon Protestant standards of public deportment, manners, and achievement. The *Illinois Record*'s Oldtimer vividly remembered that "With the establishment of the church and the saloon [in 1847,] social distinctions appeared, but the line was not drawn to such an extent as to interfere with our unity of action in all cases where the interests of each or any of us were at issue." Importantly, a line appeared that would grow more influential as time passed, the population expanded, and opportunities became more available and manipulated by persons possessing the keenest level of agency. A century later, E. Franklin Frazier found that "it was in the memory of the ancestors who were pioneers in some field or activity or had succeeded in winning recognition and a place in the community that formed the link between the successive generations. Among this class, whatever distinction in the Negro group has been acquired by occupation, wealth, and other achievement has become a slender, but important, social heritage that has been transmitted from generation to generation and gives stability to life."[67]

The collective adjustment among African American women to life in the North would have paralleled in part the sagas of women such as Sojourner Truth, who spent her earliest days in slavery in New York state, antislavery journalist Mary Ann Shadd Cary of Ontario, Canada, and Helen Murray Douglass, devoted wife of Frederick Douglass, a resident of New England and later upper New York state. Just like Helen Murray Douglass, women of African descent in Chicago found themselves relegated to a collateral role in an American scenario in which the patriarch ruled family life to near totality. James Oliver Horton has written that "men dominated leadership but women played key roles." At the same time, many women accommodated themselves to a situation in which they controlled home life. Gender conflict related to domicile or societal hegemony, then, assumed no appreciable role for women "told that they must provide a subtle guidance for their husbands and all black men. Care must be taken, however, that guidance did not becoming nagging annoyance."[68]

For Emma Atkinson, Joanna Hall, Anna Elizabeth Hudlin, Mary Richardson Jones, and many others, racial constraints, constant fears of reenslavement, a demanding work regimen necessary to sustain life and being, and a resignation to social convention that allowed little opportunity for gender contention, further promoted a *seeming* acceptance of subordination in status. Horton has written that, for this period, "all women were expected to defer to men, but for black women deference was a racial imperative. Slavery and racism intended to emasculate black men; black men sought to counter the effects of such an intention. Part of the responsibility of black men was to 'act like a man,' and part of the responsibility of black women was to 'encourage and support the manhood of our men.'"[69]

Significantly, these women were not totally invisible and voiceless ciphers by any means. Horton continues, pointing out that "For black women, no less than black men, freedom and dignity were tied to assertiveness, even to the point of violence." When Mary Richardson Jones recalled her husband's contribution to the advancement of her race, she also spoke of her thoughts on the matter. In particular, she remembered how she challenged their frequent household guest John Brown about the means he envisioned would bring emancipation. Initially employing indirection, she spoke to her husband about her misgivings. "I told Mr. Jones I thought [Brown] was a little off on the slavery question, and I did not think he was right, and I did not believe he could ever do what he wanted to do, and that somebody would have to give up his life before it was done." The next morning, indirection yielded to direct communication on the issue: "I asked [Brown] if he had any family. He said; 'Yes, madam, I have quite a large family, besides over a million other people I am looking out for, and some of these days I am going to free them, if I live long enough.' I thought to myself, how are you going to free them?"[70] Brown's ultimate answer came in 1859 at Harper's Ferry, Virginia.

On another occasion, Mary Richardson Jones displayed apprehension and annoyance at harboring militant antislavery fighters like Brown and his cohorts. She told her husband that she was always willing to assist any refugees, and Brown personally, but not his entourage. "I said to my husband: 'I do not want John Brown's fighters. I am willing to take care of him, but not his fighters,' and told him that he would lay himself liable, but he said: 'They are here, and I am going to let them in.'" They entered the house, and Mrs. Jones remembered: "I don't know how many, but [they were] four or five of the roughest looking men I ever saw"; they enjoyed the meal she prepared and "behaved very nicely." Mary Richardson Jones also opened her home to Allan Pinkerton and other abolitionists over the course of the antebellum era, thereby sharing in the danger and dread her husband faced. Her granddaughter, Theodora Lee Purnell, assessed Jones's role posthumously: "Mary Jones was at [her husband's] side in his every endeavor and accomplishment. . . . In her own field she made Chicago history."[71] And that expansive field covered her being a totally supportive companion for over thirty years, having a willingness to commit to militant resistance in protection of refugees in her home, fulfilling the role as mistress over the Joneses' household tasks, and, last but not least, being a suffragist.

Quinn Chapel A.M.E. Church took particular pride in the courage of its women, especially those champions who bravely served as conductors on the Underground Railroad. Several women in particular distinguished themselves to earn the sobriquet of "The Big Four."[72] These women included Emma Jane Atkinson (Figure 5), probably Mary Richardson Jones, Joanna Hall, and a certain "Aunt Charlotte," who distinguished herself as the equal to men as a champion of freedom. Hiding sixteen refugees until they could move in safety to Canada, this courageous figure darkened her house one night and avoided all contact with outsiders until two white visitors stopped by to ask a favor. Responding to entreaties to open her door, Aunt Charlotte whispered, "I sure thought you was them catchers 'till you spoke." As to her prized "passengers," she sighed, "poor things, I must wake them at two in the morning and start them on their way."[73]

Overall, Mary Richardson Jones and the others showed themselves to be remarkably strong-willed and savvy. As scholars have recently pointed out, these women were

> phenomenal in the courage demonstrated in their involvement in the activities of the Underground Railroad, the institution-building skills exhibited in organizing churches, and the internal fortitude exhibited in working, raising children, maintaining homes in a time when their freedom and lives, and those of their husbands, brothers, sisters, and children were always in jeopardy. Moreover, while it is probable that most were unable to read, they made sure that their children learned to read and go to school. They acted as negotiators for goods and services, along with being providers of same. Being African American and female developed into a double jeopardy, the likes of which were counterbalanced by the strength of soul and spirit which these women exemplified and passed on, making that notion a glaring contradiction.[74]

For women, work accompanied all of the other demands made upon them. Receiving even fewer options than the men, black women generally were forced to take on domestic work, which usually took the form of steady employment. This contrasted greatly with the seasonal employment that black men acquired—outdoor work, for example, that was forced to shut down in wintertime. Women often engaged in domestic work that took place in the homes of their employers; however, another alternative was "taking in" laundry or sewing work that was performed in their own homes. This latter arrangement was especially practical, as it enabled women to care for their own children at the same time.[75]

At this point in the city's history, the absence of normative class distinctions usually found along socioeconomic lines was explainable by the incipient and limited nature of African American wealth. One notable and isolated case deviated from this absence of pronounced social differentiation. E. Franklin Frazier wrote of a Chicago pioneer family whose patriarch wished something better socially in life for his family. He found indiscriminate, defensive clustering of African American families and individuals in the South Division of the city as unacceptable. His response was to move to "his own place on the [western] outskirts of the city."[76] Spatially, this was a rather isolated area, sparse in population and attractive for cattle keeping.

A future search for economic differentiation, based on its being perceived as an obstacle to group cohesion, offered no viable explanation for the shape of their social structure, nor did it give great insight into the meaning of their lives. Economic exclusion based on race accompanying social proscription merely strengthened their sense of group. Comparatively, in other northern communities, Leonard Curry found that economic opportunities, or a lack thereof, grew to become a major problem. Charles Wesley found that during the 1850s competition for employment from newly arrived immigrants became a problem throughout the northeastern United States, and Tommy Bogger wrote that even in Norfolk, Virginia, free people of color faced a similar problem. In Chicago, despite the notable but limited entrée by African Americans into the world of the market economy, most engaged for the most part without competition in common labor, personal service, and domestic service in homes, restaurants, taverns, and hotels such as the Lake House and Sherman House. As the Oldtimer reminisced, "our employment was chiefly barbering, cooking and waiting, while a few were hostlers at the hotels." Economist Abram Harris noted that the hostler Harry Knight, for example, "ran one of the largest stables in the city."[77]

Yet there were always exceptions. For example, William Baker, who came to Chicago in 1855, worked as calciminer, or whitewasher.[78] John Ellis Clark, better known as "Old Jack," earned his living as a town crier and finder of lost children. With so many wooded areas and swampy depressions in and around the city, it was common for young children to become separated from their parents, and "Old Jack" often received a fee for his role in numerous family reconciliations.[79]

In 1846, four years before it passed the nefarious Fugitive Slave Act, the U.S. Congress approved legislation that designated Chicago as an official port of entry. Economically significant, the act translated into widening opportunities for employment on the docks and wharves along the Chicago River, the city's first water lifeblood. Interlacustrine cargo from around the Great Lakes and the St. Lawrence River system was regularly unloaded on the riverbanks amid an environment of rapid growth and the labor scarcity common to frontier areas. African American and diasporan sailors on lake-bound shipping lent not only color to the Chicago labor scene but also another element to the African American employment mix. African American labor appeared prominently as cooks, barbers, dockhands, watchmen, and sailors. Black sailors could be found manning vessels like the Lowell, a two-masted, square-rigged brig that was approximately fifty feet in length (Figure 6). Always working in a precarious environment, it was an unusual event when, in 1853, the captain hired an all-black crew to sail the brig with its cargo to its next port. White resentment, presumably from the Irish, grew, and a mob assembled nearby, requiring the presence of the sheriff and a police guard to protect the ship, its cargo, and its labor contingent as they departed the brig's mooring on the Chicago River.[80] Labor tension fit into

Fig. 6. Ships in the Chicago River; the SS *Lowell* is at right.
From A. T. Andreas, History of Chicago *(1884).*

an employment pattern in the North where African Americans were some-times feared by white employers and employees because of the competitive threat they represented to white racial hegemony—yet at the same time, they were criticized as being undesirable workers. Obviously, African Americans developed no labor consciousness or affinity as fellow workers with white laborers as they encountered constant discrimination in this expansive yet volatile economic setting.

Business operations in this profitable frontier setting somewhat forecast the twentieth-century Black Metropolis filled with extensive entrepreneurial and business operations. The number of businesses rose from three in 1837 to eighty-four by 1860. Chicago's economy during this period thrived in an early stage of development; Pierce described it as a *town economy*, which flourished until the coming of the railroads at midcentury. One unfortunate feature of the early economic success involved increased trade between the Midwest and the slaveholding South. Increased commerce over the rails included transporting slave-produced products such as cotton. The Illinois Central Railroad alone carried over 5 million pounds of cotton (and wool) to the city in 1859. Soon it became a place noted nationally where commerce and industry bloomed.[81]

Success in any locale depends on the human factor; Chicago's experience was consistent with historian Arthur M. Schlesinger Jr.'s assessment that the frontier's social inequality—in this case racial as much as class-oriented—bred a drive toward egalitarianism, and African Americans proved themselves as assertive as other Chicagoans in their drive toward economic equality. This notion is supported by Henry O. Wagoner, who recalled, "In many, many hours of quietude, I ruminate over the earliest days of Chicago and of the ambitious, restless, go-a-head, intelligent business men of the times."[82] Possible success or failure awaited the adventurous in spirit with their daring, creativity, and accumulated capital as the city moved into a new economic phase on the eve of the Civil War, with its developing *economy of the city*.

The possibility of blacks exerting even a modicum of influence over white policy makers through the accumulation of wealth made economic exertion equally attractive. Appeals for morality in public policy matters had their place, but in an economically dynamic environment, a contemporary in St. Louis wrote, "every one knows that money, in whose hands soever it may be found, has an influence proportioned to its amount." As to the selfishness wealth could engender, the Missourian credited race pride with overcoming self-interest: "Wealth is power, and there is not a Colored man in our midst who would not cheerfully part with his last dollar to effect the elevation of this race."[83] John Jones and others certainly must have harbored these same sentiments, even if they were unrecorded on parchment.

With African Americans inspired by the entrepreneurial spirit and business energy pervading the nation,[84] white hostility sometimes seemed almost surmountable in this sphere as compared to the area of wage employment. A pattern of business involvement was emerging, not limited to scattered examples such as John Johnson, who owned the first barbershop by 1837, or the grocer O. G. Hanson, who amicably extended the John Jones family credit of two dollars to ensure their survival when they arrived in the city in 1845. J. B. Davis replicated Hanson's feat in 1857 as he operated his own grocery store. African Americans operated (and owned, in the case of Lewis Isbel) two of the three bathhouses in the city by 1842. The advent of saloon ownership, a lucrative pursuit in a frontier setting, materialized by 1847. The "Oldtimer" quoted in the *Illinois Record* vividly remembered the importance of business and also of another source of division: "The first saloon was established by a tall, slim, dark man on Randolph street next to the Sherman House, and with him, business appeared to be good."[85] Israel Bunch was supposedly the group's first drayman (or teamster) in 1858. John Collins became the first decorator.

Early cattle-keeping on the city's periphery, at Thirty-first Street on the south, and Fifth Avenue and Crawford on the far west, foretold of an interest in the small, but lucrative, livestock industry. As noted, one African American demonstrated his business acumen in the early 1850s in the city's West Division. In the vicinity of Racine (then Ann Street) and Lake, this ambitious African American herded perhaps several dozen head of cattle. The unnamed patriarch of the family had lived an unusual life under bondage in Kentucky, him being trusted to drive his master's cattle alone into free territory, negotiate the sale, and return to his wife and children with the master's portion of the sale. He eventually bought his and his family's freedom and settled in 1854 on the western boundary of the city, deliberately away from the central city African American enclave.[86] Jacob F. Platt, a native of New York state, arrived in Chicago in 1852 with a desire to continue in the lucrative business field of lumbering and tanning in which he had experienced only success in the East. His first entry into those areas in Chicago came in the partnership of Kaidder, Platt, and Huntington. Located at Van Buren and the Chicago River, the enterprise fulfilled Platt's dream to the fullest and propelled him into future economic prominence as a single proprietor.[87]

The most thoroughly documented, successful African American businessman, though, was John Jones. This businessman conducted his affairs so well that he located at 119 Dearborn Street for greater access to the city's well-to-do. In a newspaper ad, he listed his establishment in the *Chicago Press* and *Tribune*, giving notice to his upscale customers of his new and favorable location:

> JOHN JONES. Clothes, Dresses and Repairer. Gentlemen, I take this method of informing you that I may be found at all business hours at my shop, 119 Dearborn Street, east side between Washington and Madison, ready and willing to do all work in my home that you may think proper to favor me with, in the best manner possible. I have all kinds of trimming for repairing gentlemen's clothes. Bring on your clothes, gents, and have them cleaned and repaired. . . . Remember, garments left with me are in responsible hands. I am permanently located at 119 Dearborn Street. Yours for work, J. JONES.[88]

Barbering especially proved to be an exciting and lucrative business endeavor. Being independent through self-employment, without a modern "craft master," or the market period's "boss" to whom to answer, was appealing to the self-reliant. Barbering also provided an opportunity to associate with the town's "movers and shakers." This inducement encouraged Lewis Isbel to pursue this occupation with vigor. At the time, barbering was considered an important trade among African Americans, who assigned it a high status. It was furthermore associated with mastery of some reading and writing skills.[89] And if a man wished to improve his mental abilities while performing in a such a setting, he could easily do so exposed as he was to constant enhancement by influential whites.

Purportedly, Lewis Isbel reigned as the city's premier barber, or "chin scraper." Along with his free parents, Isbel departed from Kentucky in 1824 and arrived in Paris, Illinois. As the Isbel family established itself in town, another child was born, and this daughter laid claim to being the first free African American born in the state. By 1838, Lewis Isbel headed north and arrived in fledgling Chicago, where he worked under the tutelage of John Johnson as the city's second black barber. In later years, when Isbel disclaimed the title that belonged to Johnson as the pioneer of the trade, he recalled with anything but modesty that he soon became Chicago's best barber. His clientele included regulars such as Fernando Jones, William B. Ogden, and the Beaubien brothers as well as infrequent customers such as the luminaries Stephen Douglas, Abraham Lincoln, and U. S. Grant. Late in his life, during a period of reflection and self-assessment, he recalled, "They were all great men, too." As a septuagenarian reliving his experiences, he seemed "content with the reflected greatness which shone on the blade of his razor and [was] now settled on him for having performed the tonsorial service on men of such prominence."[90]

One aspect of Isbel's personality and business approach seemed obvious—he was the type of barber who controlled his tongue while at work. Some barbers gained notoriety as tattlers, gossips, and incessant talkers while their customers were virtually held hostage under the razor. Others engendered respect by performing their jobs well, remembering their place as providers of a service, and speaking when appropriate around power brokers. When they did verbalize, they exercised the liberty to act as "the only men in the community who enjoyed, at all times, the privilege of free speech."[91] Wise utterances also played their part.

Isbel's journey from obscurity to celebrity mirrored the possibilities of the age. When he first arrived, he worked in primitive conditions with Johnson on Clark Street between Lake and Randolph. Soon he struck out on his own and established a shop in Frink and Walker's stage office at Lake and Dearborn streets, opposite the popular accommodations offered at the Tremont House. Early in the 1840s he moved again, this time to an alley location north of the Sherman House hotel. With a growing clientele in regular need of shaving, trimming, and bleeding, Isbel secured space within the Sherman House itself, offering what he described as the town's first combination barbershop and bathhouse.

As a barber, Isbel saw himself as more than a mere servant of the wealthy— he was a secondary confidant. He became the keeper of a place where the personalities who wielded power assembled once, twice, or maybe three times a week. "Sometimes they came to talk over the live topics of the day, and at other times came out of necessity. But whether it was that they wanted to learn the latest village gossip, or to transact matters of business with him or whom he called, they all came."[92]

Several other men made their living in this pursuit, such as Abram Harris and other barbers, including Oliver C. Henson, John Dixon, and Henry Knight, who were listed in Norris's *General Directory*. Pioneer barber John Johnson gained notice for owning his barbershop in a two-story building that housed the city's first YMCA reading room on the second floor. That these individuals were listed at all in the *General Directory* with full names, addresses, and occupation, and within the ranks of fully recognized white citizens, established their status as part of humanity. In contrast, Southern record keeping accorded African Americans no such recognition.[93]

Just as barbers excelled because of their manual dexterity, future professionals would recall how Chicago supported two African American physicians with equal nimbleness of hands immediately before the advent of the Civil War. Contemporaries availed themselves of the services of Dr. C. H. Hutchinson and Dr. Charles H. McCallister. The state of the medical profession at that time required no licensing and evidently cared little about color.[94]

The horse and its man-made appendage, whether the wagon, cart, carriage, or stage, kept Chicago moving, both inside its borders and outside. Primitively conquering space and time, these conveyances prevented complete social isolation and afforded the operator a sense of economic independence. The *Illinois Record's* "Oldtimer" described that during the winter months, Chicago faced near physical isolation, with stage traffic being the only means of communication to the outside world. Inside the city, Isaac Atkinson began operating his own carriage business by 1858, carrying passengers over fewer and fewer muddy streets and ground-level debris, as plank roads miraculously made their appearance. As to Atkinson's success, one late-nineteenth-century recollection claimed that "in the early 50's Isaac Atkinson ran a bus which was a rival of [Frank] Parmelee."[95] Constituting an essential cog in the fledgling town's transportation network, one could imagine his commitment to service and business prosperity amid this scene: "Hackmen at the railroad depots and at street corners barked at strangers, 'Hack, sir, hack, sir.'"[96]

Hauling and distributing lake water to the city's residents afforded Isom Artis a comfortable livelihood.[97] Lake water provided Chicagoans a healthier supply than the polluted water from the Chicago River. Artis and other men became known as watermen, taking their two-wheeled carts to the lake, at the foot of Randolph Street, and filling barrels with the precious resource.

Perhaps it was Artis who provided the water to residents living past Adams Street, "where one was dependent upon a water man who called three times a week and filled the family water barrel from his cart, a large barrel on two wheels."[98] In this competitive economic setting, the watermen faced their first major competition as the Chicago Hydraulic Company began its operations in 1842 and then in the 1850s from a hydraulically supplied water flow that coursed through street hydrants.[99]

The scope of the African American experience in Chicago extended beyond having legal or appropriated freedom, or facing gender contention, or possessing mixed racial origins. How whites defined social acceptability among persons of African descent, the special relationships certain African Americans had with whites, and how whites related to differences in skin color did offer another source of distinction.[100] Another telling phenomenon is how the state of Illinois, through its legal division of individuals of varying degrees of African descent into two categories, Negroes and Mulattoes, represented a social reality among African Americans as well as a convenient, inclusive instrument of racial exclusion (see Appendix A). Similarly, the Illinois state law on Negroes and mulattoes that was updated in 1853 to advance control on a state level over the activities of these proscribed persons revealed more about Illinois society than might be readily apparent. By legal definition and social distinction, Negroes were persons of unmixed African parentage. Mulattoes, according to Section 10 of the law of 1853, were persons who had an ancestry containing "one-fourth Negro blood." Originating from a biracial union, they could range in complexion from the darkest hue to the most fair, and in some cases they were mistaken for Caucasian. As the major legal constraint controlling African American activities, the Black Laws regulated the lives of all persons of African descent with malicious equanimity.

In this slap at humanity, Illinois simply conformed to a national trend. In Chicago, "the sheriff one morning received a letter with orders to arrest a woman quite white, who was both beautiful and educated, who, having been purchased by someone in New Orleans, had run away."[101] The young woman was fortunate to be warned and aided in fleeing the city for safety elsewhere. The message for African Americans was clear: A pale complexion alone offered no safety in color-conscious America.

Not unexpectedly, there existed no evidence of a fissure in Chicago between "Negroes and mulattoes."[102] Given the high level of external pressure just to survive even in a somewhat racially hospitable milieu, and with Northern views on race as basically inclusionary for all persons of African descent, distinctions of this type failed to thrive. But Frazier did find a latent social distance as he reviewed the nineteenth century from a vantage point in the early twentieth. With findings based on the memories of persons born after the antebellum period, he wrote: "This has been the case since the beginning of the Negro community. The small group of Negroes, mostly mulattoes, who represented the vanguard of the race and thrift and attempts to acquire some degree of [Anglo-Saxon] culture, had continually attempted to escape from the less energetic and the lower elements of the Negro population."[103] His example of Chicago's first African American cattle keeper, who moved away from the heavily black neighborhoods, illustrated his point. However, no other recorded cases manifested themselves. In contradistinction, John Jones emerged as the community spokesman and representative Everyman. He spearheaded the fight against both the Illinois Black Laws and Southern slavery and also was a member of Chicago's first African American church and Masonic lodge.

Yet, in public deportment, what historian Gary B. Nash found in Philadelphia might possibly have applied also to Chicago several decades later, in the 1840s and 1850s. He wrote that while members of one segment of the black population concerned themselves seriously with how they behaved in public, in their churches, and on the work site, others were more attuned to their Southern behavioral patterns, which disturbed whites of all classes. In the case of the former, respectable behavior became the norm. In the case of the latter, "some of them spoke in southern dialect, drank and gambled, dressed flamboyantly, sometimes ran afoul of the law, and affected a body language—the sauntering gait, unrestrained singing and laughter, and exuberant dancing—that set them apart from 'respectable' black society." Undoubtedly, African Americans drew a line in regard to their behavior around whites.[104]

In addition, for the North in general, Leon F. Litwack noted that Negroes themselves sometimes drew a color line. He wrote, "equally significant in determining a Negro's place in the social order was the relative darkness of his skin. . . . Although a light color did not automatically secure a Negro's place in the hierarchy, it often afforded him greater economic opportunities, which, in turn, assumed him a high rank in Negro society. In many cases, whites simply preferred to hire mulattoes, feeling that their closer proximity to Caucasian features also made them more intelligent and physically attractive."[105] The extent to which internal race relations revolved around lightness of skin and a biracial lineage could have affected the worldview of persons of mixed racial lineage as well as their individual status. However, at no time did color gradations escape the wary whites, the social critics and creators of this human rainbow. One example of this curiosity occurred at a saloon as a white reporter surveyed a different segment of humanity: "They are all shades of color. Some so black, that a bottle of ink, spilled in their faces, would stain them white; here, one with a polished ebony countenance and glittering pearly white teeth, which would be death to a hen roost; . . . some with the rich tint of the olive, and so on through the various gradations of color until you come to an octoroon, evidently the belle of the room. Her sanguine one eighth, has lent a rich, transparent, wine tinge to her face, and a gentle wave to her hair, by which alone the close observer would discover that she was under the ban [of social proscription for being considered a Negro]."[106] What is certain is that in Chicago, African Americans united beyond internal color distinctions in a milieu where only two races were recognized, and triracialism was an anomaly considered solely Southern in nature.[107] Hence, the reason behind the bonding together of all hues seemed clear enough. It facilitated the struggle in behalf of the twin goals of eliminating Illinois's laws of racial proscription and the Southern system of enslavement that consigned their relatives to a living hell.

As to their relations to whites, since a continuing American racial protocol dictated that African American advancement rest on the patronage of prominent whites, in Chicago, a patron-client relationship developed between a smattering of white egalitarians and biracial African Americans. Either motivated by a sincere religious commitment to extending respect based on a shared humanity, out of a sense of noblesse oblige, or out of what historian Leon F. Litwack saw as an affinity among whites for light-complexioned African Americans, certain important links evolved.[108] The good reception enjoyed by John Jones, Henry O. Wagoner, and their close friend, the peripatetic Frederick Douglass, might just have had to do with skin color and its acceptability to Caucasians as much as it had to do with their accomplishments. As late as 1956, in a major scholarly contribution on the history of American slavery, in order to humanize African Americans to a less-than-receptive white audience, a liberal scholar resorted to a clever analogy that troubled him as much as it offended some blacks and enlightened many whites. Kenneth M. Stampp wrote, "I have assumed that the slaves were merely ordinary human beings, that innately Negroes are, after all, only white men with black skins, nothing more, nothing less."[109] Whatever restrictions were in place, Jones and Wagoner appeared to be respected as *men* by white men as well as by black men. Jones enjoyed a close relationship with attorney Lemuel C. Freer, who befriended him from the outset of his arrival in the city. Freer authored Jones's earliest writings, but "one day he told him that he would do it no longer,—that he must learn to write himself. To this Jones attributed his first efforts in that direction."[110] Interestingly, one of Jones's obituaries in 1879, cognizant of his father's heritage and in disregard of his mother's, referred to him in this manner: "An Old German Resident Gathered to His Fathers." When the abolitionist Zebina Eastman began to prepare notes for posterity on his role in advancing the cause of humanity through the abolition of slavery, he found it easy to distinguish John Jones as "a well known mulatto in Chicago."[111]

Henry O. Wagoner had also descended from a biracial lineage. His physiognomy and orientation helped him move in white circles as well as obtain a job as "compositor in a newspaper office, the 'Western Citizen,' an antislavery paper, edited by Z. Eastman." He once referred to one of his kin as "my *white* relative, Mr. Wagoner Kennedy."[112] Isaac Atkinson's mixed lineage included a Scottish father, Richard, and a full-blooded Cherokee mother, Cecilia. His wife, Emma Jane, had biracial parents with Cherokee and African American bloodlines.[113] H. Ford Douglas used his mixed heritage and resulting complexion to his advantage as he served with an all-white Illinois regiment during the Civil War.[114]

Once again, the "Oldtimer" narrated the importance of place and of time and, in doing so, uncovered the possibilities of different social aspirations and strategies for achieving goals. "With the establishment of the church and the saloon social distinctions appeared, but the line was not drawn to such an extent as to interfere with our unity of action in all cases where the interests of each or any of us were at issue. Often when a fugitive was captured and taken into court by his owner, all of the colored people would unite, and with the assistance of their white friends of the city and surrounding villages, determine upon a plan that would create consternation among the Southern whites and result in the liberation of the captured black. These were stirring times," he reiterated, "times that caused all hearts to beat in sympathy and act as one in a common purpose. Plain, but true, unacquainted with extravagances, ignorant of politics and other things which enter so largely into the lives of men who today struggle for success; we were pleased our efforts resulted in partial success and deep within our hearts we believed that God, in his own good time and in his own good way would blot out this cruel slavery and raise us to the dignity of American citizenship."[115]

Assuming the Oldtimer accurately depicted the Chicago scene, the most serious areas of contention were avoided because of a unified commitment to a single goal, advancing the interests of the group in the aggregate. Obviously, an acceptance of the Afro-American cultural affinities emanating from within the group would have produced differences. Depending on the level of exposure either to an African-based subculture as well as to an Anglo-American base, various identities could have been embraced. The African cultural base was gradually eroding; the various religious, philosophical, and social aspects of West

African cultures of the Yoruba, Mandingo, Ashanti, Ibo, Wolof, Temne, and others, faded with each passing year without reinforcing elements from these societies. This process is in keeping with St. Clair Drake's thesis, in that what he termed an "*Afro*-American" subculture was growing. In slaveholding societies to the south, whether Jamaica, Cuba, or Brazil, Drake contended that a full-blown African American culture existed. However, in looking at church and associational activities, the unity of the whole was reinforced by support of commonly respected institutions. Above all in this parallel world, African Americans ignored the white concept of cultural hierarchies.[116]

Far beyond the antebellum period, somewhere in the post-Reconstruction era, African American life more clearly reflected discernible social distinctions. The most prominent groups were the *refined*, the *respectables*, and the *riffraff*. Economic standing played its part, but more importantly all aspects of life were linked to the level of adherence to church life and, of course, some choice of cultural expression.[117] Unlike the South, African Americans in Chicago had neither blood nor marital ties to prominent whites. Any prospective member of an elite seeking acquired status based on race would require a link to whites through humanitarian or ideological affiliations. These channels were reserved for support in keeping the spirit of neo-abolitionism alive as well as a commitment to a creed of civic virtue. Very late in the nineteenth century, an interracial bond, for better or for worse, in the Machiavellian sphere of politics would be forged.

C. Religion, Church Formation, and Recreation

In establishing the groundwork for a religious tradition, Chicago's African Americans confirmed the contention about the attraction of African-based religion to the people of the diaspora. As Berlin wrote, "drawn by the promise of salvation and the prospect of controlling their own destiny, black people rushed to joined the new [black-controlled] churches."[118] While whites wrestled and split in Chicago over the issue of slavery, blacks split with them over that issue as well as autonomy, manner of worship (or liturgy), and freedom of personal expression.

For historian Leonard Curry, the existence of the northern African American community came only with the separation of African Americans from white-initiated church life and perception of an ethnic community. This corresponded slightly with Drake's thesis that a fully African-based culture did not exist independently in America, only the variant in the form of an Afro-American subculture that was somewhat weak and in need of nurturing. To Curry, community formation paved the way for church life, and it was white exclusion that created in African Americans the awareness that they had to create something for themselves. His thesis read, in effect: White culture opened the possibility of African American agency. In contrast, Drake's thesis defined the vast boundaries of the wellspring of this agency.[119] Chicago, however, represented a case where African Americans slowly fashioned the institutional life of their own community in a manner consistent with their own unique historical experiences and interests as they received moral support and financial assistance from amiable whites in many areas. Importantly, every new immigrant carried the germ of human agency within his or her consciousness, expectations, and experiences.

Originally, blacks worshiped with whites in the predominant Methodist, and then the Baptist, churches of the city.[120] In fulfilling their sacramental obligations of baptism, marriage, and funerary rites, African Americans sought peace with their God along with the cooperation of their white co-religionists. When Cassius King was born, his baptism could only have been performed at a white church. When Abraham and Joanna Hall married, the religious procedure preceded the advent of the black church. No doubt, a white Methodist minister performed the rites. The same had to be true for funerals. With the varying degrees of openness of the white Methodists, Baptists, and Presbyterians, the question arises as to why they failed to satisfy their fellow black Christians, preventing them from leaving white churches and forming African American religious bodies.

The answer is to be found in understanding that the ultimate expression of institutional independence among the African Americans of Chicago materialized itself in the black American church. And any understanding of this institution requires examination of both its raison d'être and its mission. The former was rooted in the spirituality that forged the West African character, gave meaning to life and circumstances, and manifested itself throughout ritualistic activities such as godly praise, prayer, and preaching. The religious task at hand was realizable through the myriad institutional dimensions so closely associated with African American church life, such as Sabbath observance, family formation, temperance, and abolitionism, among others.

Examining the roles of theology and ritualistic worship in African American life is essential to understanding how the black church emerged. Primarily, the church as an institution emerged from a system of Africanized Christian belief that linked African Americans with the spiritual world of their ancestors. African Americans required and worshiped a liberating God who both met their immediate and long-term needs, and they found him in the Christian religion but not in all of its churches. They recognized in God and his divine son, Jesus Christ, many of the familiar ingredients found in their

African religious roots: transcendence and ultimate authority, along with immanence and unconditional caring. Whether their Southern masters or Northern "social betters" wanted them to accept this religion ranked secondary to their need for this type of religion, which placed them at the center of God's creations. In the face of continuous adversity, they believed, as the Oldtimer expounded, in a "God, [who] in his own good time and in his own good way would blot out this cruel slavery."

The message of salvation that the Apostle Paul offered to the oppressed in the beginning of the Common Era was also offered by religious Americans in the nineteenth century: love, hope, and charity. This inspiration originated in the Holy Bible, which was believed literally as accurate history and not considered allegory. Nonetheless, the African Americans' ability to express themselves while in the presence of this ubiquitous loving God was stifled by man-made convention. In their theological experiences, they encountered a Calvinistic-influenced approach in bonding with their immanent God, through Jesus Christ, who was kept at a spiritual distance by a refusal by whites to always publicly acknowledge Him with zeal. With the finite nature of American slavery counterbalanced through this uncompromising religious belief, an anticipated eschatological fulfillment made even daily trials more bearable.

Meanwhile, liturgical expression had to keep pace with theological commitment and promise, or there would not be African American support for that particular church or denomination. White Methodists and Baptists in Chicago demanded controlled, emotionless behavior in church. Listening to a scriptural commandment to "Make a joyful noise unto the Lord" fit into the African collective memory, which they often tapped as they sought to survive in a hostile America. Attempting to match this theological need with a liturgical mode more consistent to their lives, they demonstrated human agency to create churches of their own in which they could worship God properly.

In the preaching of their minsters, African Americans sought both an oral and aural satisfaction. The *Word* as preached had to ring a sincerity impossible without a complete surrender to the Spirit of the Lord. This required a voice of ringing, extemporaneous fervor that was delivered to receptive ears. Carol George wrote in *Segregated Sabbaths:* "Some sermons were written down and subsequently printed, but they offered a literary version of what was essentially an aural expression. As such, they fail to describe a man's preaching talents, but they do point out what his theological interests were." Additionally, preachers made no distinctions between secular and religious matters, with them abandoning both white substance and white form.[121]

The emergence of the black church as an institution represented as clear an example of agency at the collective level as could be presented among this population. It existed as the center of the parallel world that African Americans inhabited while they lived among both friendly and hostile whites. It authenticated, moreover, the realization of the African American vision in its fullest physical expression. One of the first attempts at writing a portion of black Chicago history described the situation thus: "As the Negro population grew, there was felt a need for some kind of organization among themselves to meet *their* religious, social, civic and economic needs. . . . There came a desire for a church separate from the whites."[122] At the apex of its worldly involvement, it was the center of protest activism. More importantly, it nurtured a flock that sought a complete liberation of spirit, mind, and body attainable only through religious faith. It was a place where transcendence loomed beyond possibility and became probability.

Activities in the East among black Methodists of the African Methodist Episcopal (A.M.E.) denomination partially emerged because of racism. Recruitment among blacks ensued nationally. Notably, no evidence has been found to substantiate any notion that racism spurred African Americans to form Baptist churches. Elsewhere in Illinois, in Evanston and in Aurora, Baptist cooperation between the races ostensibly produced a church life that appeared idyllic on the surface. Yet a stirring among persons of African descent caused a movement toward autonomy in religious worship in Chicago and elsewhere throughout the nineteenth century.[123]

The Oldtimer reminiscing in the *Illinois Record* article stated that Quinn Chapel A.M.E. Church "originated in the house of Madison Patterson on State St., between Madison and Monroe, and the first gospel sermon was preached by a colored Missionary named Philip Ward in the old Madison Street school house."[124] Clarifying historical memory, Chicago African American church history began undramatically in 1844 when a prayer band of from four to seven persons met in Abram T. Hall's barbershop at Canal and Lake to worship and discuss his group's religious needs. By these actions, they laid the foundation for the Quinn Chapel A.M.E. So, based on necessity, but spurred with deep religiosity, the Chicagoans met continually in the homes of members—in John Day's home, located at Lake and Randolph, at the home of member Maria Parker, located at La Salle and Washington, and later in other residences. Also, lacking the formal means to meet all of their liturgical needs, humanitarian and fellow white Methodists rendered assistance to the fledgling Quinn Chapel.

By 1847, "Hall and his little band of praying people," meeting under the spiritual leadership of exhorter Madison Washington (or Patterson) and the missionary organizer Philip Ward, formally organized and chartered the body. The church was named after William Paul Quinn, a leading African American minister of the faith who converted them to the A.M.E. cause in his extensive and successful missionary work in the Old Northwest. Abram T. Hall, who was the first African American licensed to preach in Illinois, and who was destined for decades to come to bring spiritual life to blacks through his vigorous religious efforts, served at Quinn Chapel as the first steward, trustee, and Scriptures "class-leader."[125] Shortly after its founding, Quinn Chapel occupied its first permanent church structure on the southwest corner of Fourth Avenue (now Custom House Place) and Jackson Boulevard (the current site of the Union League Club). Then, A.M.E. bishops in the East sent Rev. George Johnson to lead this congregation, which now was housed in a formal structure at Washington and La Salle streets.[126] Quinn Chapel also served as an important station on the Underground Railroad. This resistance to slavery remained a proud part of Quinn Chapel's heritage throughout the nineteenth century and beyond.

Abram T. Hall, who was likened by his son and namesake to the Jason of Greek mythology, began life as a son of free people of color in western Pennsylvania and became a groundbreaking spiritual liberator and church builder. He organized churches in Chicago, in far-western Chicagoland's Fox River Valley, in Iowa, and in Wisconsin. However, the "golden fleece" that Hall sought was salvation from sin for himself and for all to whom he preached the Gospel. As a young man, he had been influenced by his father, who was an itinerant exhorter and perhaps even a preacher. He is reported to have organized churches in Lewiston and Erie, Pennsylvania, before he embarked on a trip westward through the Great Lakes to Chicago. Employment as a barber on the lake schooner *Missouri* allowed him to meet his earthly needs. Permanent residence on shore at Chicago promised a better life in pursuit of his divine mission. As a barber, he met with fellow Christians, white and black, settling in with a small group of like-minded worshipers until Quinn Chapel emerged as a formal body (Figure 7).

A second church, Zoar Baptist, was organized in 1850 among religious folk who either abandoned their white coreligionists, or else chose to have their own institution for worship, seeking "to serve God freely under their own vine and fig tree." They began worship under the spiritual leadership of Rev. R. J. Robinson, who journeyed from Alton, Illinois, for this purpose. Once the pastor established stability, he returned to the southern part of the state and was succeeded by Rev. H. H. Hawkins as Zoar's first permanent pastor. The church was located at Buffalo and Taylor and had a congregation that attracted 120 members, fueled by "the influx of numerous refugees from the Southern States."

In 1858, under the reconciling pastoral leadership of Rev. D. G. Lett, the

Fig. 7. Rev. and Mrs. Abram T. Hall.
Courtesy of Jeanne Boger Jones.

fate of Zoar Baptist was sealed as it sought to accommodate the ritualistic requests of recent migrants with those of more urbanized, northern congregants. Historians of Chicago describe the friction that resulted. A. T. Andreas referred to "trouble in reference to the governance of the church," and Miles Fisher wrote that "some few of the recent migrants from the South were neither good citizens nor useful church members. The Zoar Church had a few of this class. They brought with them their own ideas of church worship and government which retarded the progress of the Zoar congregation."[127] The problem could have revolved around any number of factors such as the ritualistic washing of feet in accordance to Jesus Christ's act during the Last Supper, adult baptism, or emotive responses during services.

Andreas found that "in consequence of this difficulty about fifty to sixty members in 1858 seceded." Rev. Wallace Shelton, a member of the congregation, was evidently part of the dissenting group. Church historian Fisher, in contrast, wrote that the internal rift resulted in the exclusion of twenty-one members, which reduced the congregation's size to fifty-seven. In any event, those who left were allowed to reenter the fold the following year. For his part, Rev. Shelton aided in the establishment of the new Mount Zion Baptist Church shortly after the departure of the dissident members in 1858.[128]

Mount Zion Baptist suffered no such internal strife but lacked the drawing power to attract a congregation large enough to sustain the church. A Canadian, a Rev. Tansbury, led this new flock as its first permanent minister at rental property on Clark Street near Harrison. Tansbury returned to Canada within a short span of time as the church languished without public support. With the advent of war and weaknesses apparent at both Zoar and Mount Zion, a sense of Christian charity (or spirit-based love) provided unity, and the two bodies merged in 1862 to form the Olivet Baptist Church.

Beyond its nurturing spiritual core, the African American church in Chicago demonstrably fostered democracy and individual freedom within its structure. Unlike the rigidly hierarchical white Protestant churches, social grades were nonexistent among a people who lacked them internally and who had suffered from their existence externally. Separate pews, balconies, and other special recognition found no place in these churches. Ministers served at the approval of God and at the sufferance of the congregants. As twice-chosen leaders, they represented the first wave of institutionally produced leaders, as opposed to the type of individual leader that John Jones represented. Importantly, every church member had an equal voice, and church dissent could become quite disquieting and disruptive when stirred. Church-splitting was the deleterious feature of this influence.

Furthermore, consistent with changing circumstances and the rising needs of its congregants, the African American church adapted itself to meet whatever emergent secular challenges arose. The church served as a meeting place for protest, an incubator for courageous leadership and stalwart fellowship, and a distribution point for information, goods, and services. The activism as expressed in its participation in the Underground Railroad as well as support for an active posture against injustice and bondage is covered throughout this chapter.

The probability of the appearance of certain aspects of social distinction between the congregants of these churches and the denizens of the saloon was somewhat obscured in the recollections of the "Oldtimer." He failed to convey another glaring reality, no doubt clouded by his youthful unawareness during that period, the religious home environment in which he reached maturity, and the selectivity of memory in matters of assessing group frailties. His comment that "Champagne tastes and beer pockets had not been developed; cigarette fiends were unknown qualities and men who lived on the earnings of others were not tolerated," paled in comparison to the unfriendly observations of the reporter for the *Chicago Daily Journal*.[129]

On the eve of the Civil War, the newspaper headline featured the following: "Negro Dive In Full Blast." Granted that the saloon was not to be equated with the "dive"—disreputable, bawdy conduct at this site was described in glaring details approximating indignation (or perhaps latent envy):

> Our readers may often have noticed in police reports and elsewhere, the term "Negro dive," without fully appreciating its meaning, or being cognizant of the elements which make up this colored institution existing in our midst. . . . The "dive" is usually a one story building, with only two rooms. The windows are glazed as to the lower sash, that the orgies within may be invisible to eavesdroppers. . . . [Food, drink, camaraderie, and dance prevail.] The fiddler saws and dances. . . . The fiddler redoubles his efforts . . . [then there is momentary exhaustion]. Then all hands pass into the front room, where the males partake of the stronger fluids and the females indulge in pop and the pale pigs feet, until the fiddler shall again summon them to the crazy dance. . . . Thus it goes on all night.[130]

The dichotomy in acceptable and expected behavior between respectable citizens and pleasure seekers surely, and quickly, resulted in social distinction and mutual hostility. Accordingly in Philadelphia, these pronounced differences in public behavior delineated the desires of the respectable blacks to be considered such in the eyes of whites and at the same time the disregard unassimilated African Americans had for white social convention.[131]

The influence of economic deprivation on deportment was so deleterious that Douglass "argued that the want of money was the root of all evil to the colored people. They were shut out. . . . Their poverty kept them ignorant, and their ignorance kept them degraded."[132] The examples of degraded or morally unacceptable behavior related to social debasement ranged from the lascivious to the criminal. Not unexpectedly, on the eve of the Civil War, the incipient phase of a distinct criminal culture was evident. This blight represented the bane of order found desirable within the sphere of the religious and family oriented.

Despite the proscribed social status of African Americans in Chicago, it did not constitute a condition resulting in dependency and earning civic stigma. As to the status of blacks within the welfare reform system, it was the Irish who represented the first problem of this sort. With destitute Irish canal workers, the city faced its "first problem of poor relief."[133]

D. Community-Based Initiatives, Associations, and Secular Interests

Intragroup cooperation and institution building, according to the Hortons, rested on "the communal ethic of mutual responsibility that was a part of black Africa's heritage, and for many part of their Native American heritage"; therefore, it "made such cooperative organization a cultural imperative." From churches to literary activities to quasi-politics, black Chicagoans actively built an institutional framework from which they could enrich their lives as they protected themselves from racist policies and practices. According to Drake, "associations also represent the formal crystallization of many of the values of the society." So, in pursuit of recognition of the humanity of the group, manhood (or citizenship rights), abolition, social commitment, and a need for camaraderie to boost morale, the number of organizations of every type increased. Fraternal organizations included the Knights of Tabor, formed in 1855, a Masonic lodge that eventually bore John Jones's name, a lodge in the Order of Good Samaritanism in 1859, and sometime during this period, a lodge of the Order of Odd Fellows, headed by Dr. C. H. Hutchinson.[134]

In addition, "there was a growing consciousness of the need for provision to take care of the sick and bury the dead among the women, in addition to what the secret orders were doing. The Daughters of Union was organized in 1854 by Mrs. Anna Simpson as a benevolent order."[135] Other groups promoted literacy and intellectual inquiry, except that in the latter case, with such a great deficiency in literacy, the scope of discussion was limited. Within a generation of Emancipation, this would not be the case as a coterie of well-educated African Americans along with a truly inquisitive group of ordinary citizens would fill the churches whenever discourse was offered.

Racial exclusion prevented full participation in political matters, whether voting or office holding; consequently, institutional involvement took unusual paths. The Oldtimer vividly recalled the relationship: "Political matters were handled entirely by white people and so we had no voice in the shaping of policy of parties; there were no leaders, ward heelers or tricksters." This African American exclusion within the public arena ironically took place despite the fact that the city's first "town crier of auctions and lost children was a Negro"—John Ellis Clark.[136] This minor appointment indicated that at least a modicum of recognition of responsibility for some type of appointed governmental position had been made. More importantly though, male white America in general considered the political arena as the private preserve of Anglo-Saxons, considering blacks too deficient in thought and unrestrained in passion to engage in serious governmental matters. It was, in effect, the realm of men, where the power-oriented rituals of manhood were manifested.

Despite exclusion, a number of activities generated by African Americans took on a political tone despite the prohibition against African American participation in shaping public policy through decision making in the public arena. In this instance, Chicago was more similar to Detroit, in that its small black community had gotten deeply involved in quasi-politics despite outright prohibitions on voting and office holding. Specifically, the more activist of the men preoccupied themselves with lobbying friendly politicians to support a campaign for equal rights and participating on two occasions in abolitionist political campaigns.[137]

Participation in political matters followed two paths: It tended to be either conducted behind the screen of white patronage or as part of the seemingly invisible (to whites) national convention network, but one highly visible to certain blacks. First, white patrons who were avowed abolitionists were sought, and through their actions petitions, memorials, and opinions found the light the day. The tone of all petitions smacked of deference to the power of white America and bordered on obsequiousness, with blacks' appeals couched in language acceptable to white America.[138] The Declaration of Independence and the Constitution were cited most frequently in an attempt to link white action with the highest authority they respected. Demands were never made. But resentment built against the easy manner with which recent German and Irish arrivals to the nation and city received the franchise.

With allies among the whites, blacks sought to have the voice of the free serve as their voice. Abolitionism thrived in Chicago. With Presbyterians in the lead, the major Protestant denominations, including the Methodists, Congregationalists, and Baptists, allied to fight what they viewed as a national abomination. Black churches benefited from working closely with whites within and outside religious institutions, for this collaboration even extended to newspapers such as the *Western Citizen* and sometimes the *Chicago Tribune*. By 1840, the Chicago Anti-slavery Society was organized. As early as 1842, a candidate for mayor, Henry Smith, ran on a platform of destroying slavery and repealing the Illinois Black Laws (see Appendix A). Despite this abolitionist activism, the Age of Jackson and the Common Man proved just as much to be an age of hypocrisy and incongruities.

Contradictions produced a split between white and black abolitionists as well as among the black abolitionists. Frederick Douglass separated from

William Lloyd Garrison and his abolitionist cohorts, who supported Garrison's nonpolitical approach to emancipation and his interpretation of the U.S. Constitution as a proslavery document. Garrison's refrain, which had gained popularity, resounded thus: The Constitution was "a covenant with death and an agreement with hell." There were obvious ramifications in Chicago, for despite Garrison's popularity and heroic status, black Chicagoans preferred political means directed toward liberation, along with other related tactics. At a meeting held on December 26, 1853, African Americans supported Douglass's new opinion that the Constitution was an antislavery document with the power to end slavery. They resolved to "promote their true interest by giving to his efforts as an editor and a lecturer their active sympathy and approval, and to his paper their generous support."[139]

Meanwhile, as for African American participation in black quasi-political activities, the "Negro convention movement" beckoned. Dozens of local, state, and national meetings in the thirty years from 1830 to the beginning of the Civil War. None were held in Chicago, apparently because of the small population, the late formation of a mature community life, and the city's location on the fringe of western settlement.[140] In addition, geographical and ideological rivalries from the eastern states and Ohio brought a level of turmoil that Chicagoans could never have hoped to understand or accommodate to their needs.[141] Nevertheless, black Chicagoans attended meetings, although sporadically, and formed opinions based on an examination of issues and democratic discussion. Although African Americans were excluded by law from direct participation in the mainstream's political process, they did manage to express their desires to see slavery abolished and personal liberty made a reality. As early as 1843, a black representative left Chicago for Buffalo, New York, and a militant political convention called by the Liberty party.

Historically, in what might have represented the city's first interregional involvement by African Americans in trans-associational life, locally, on August 7, 1848, a meeting was held at Quinn Chapel A.M.E. Church to appoint two delegates for the "Great National Convention of Colored Freemen of the United States" (mainly living in the Old Northwest) to be held in Cleveland, Ohio. John Jones and Abram T. Hall were the delegates chosen to associate with some of the major spokesmen who formed the leadership of the northern protest ranks. While dominated by members of the elite from older, eastern cities, the rhetoric would have resounded as familiar to the two Chicagoans. Emphases on race pride, unity, increased agency, upgrading the occupational statuses of black workers, and creating more autonomous interregional black institutions had all been heard before

Fig. 8. John Jones.
Chicago Historical Society,
ICHi-22362, photographer—Sommer.

Fig. 9. Henry O. Wagoner.
From Simmons, Men of Mark *(1887).*

at home. A plea for independent racial associations that were not racially exclusive would have seemed impractical and too theoretical.[142]

Several years later, with African American political awareness building and quasi-political activities heightening, Jones assumed a vice presidency at an abolitionist meeting held at the Zion Baptist Church, which urged affiliation with the Free Soil party and formulated plans for more agitation in Springfield in behalf of ending the Black Laws. In direct pursuit of the vote to remedy the disfranchisement dictated under the Illinois Black Laws, Jones, Wagoner, and James D. Bonner journeyed to Springfield to lobby for relief.[143]

As important as the counsel of and association with friendly whites grew, another influential, unifying force emerged from among the ranks of a leadership found within the network of northern African American communities. The indomitable Frederick Douglass personified the best of that coterie and appeared frequently in Chicago as he proved himself ubiquitous in the fight against Southern slavery and Northern injustice. Douglass, the amazing ex-slave orator, worked actively with John Jones, Henry O. Wagoner, and others, usually staying at Jones's home when in town. His stature was such that he was considered *the* "prominent leader, advocate, and exponent of the wrongs and demands of the Colored people of the U.S."[144] Importantly, it was he who exposed Jones to a world in which human rights were enjoyed to the fullest extent. In his autobiography, Douglass recalled with belated irritation a trip he and Chicagoans H. Ford Douglas and John Jones made to a hotel in Janesville, Wisconsin, where they were accepted as guests but seated apart from whites at mealtime. "Thus seated, I took occasion to say loud enough for the crowd to hear me, that I had been out to the stable, and made a great discovery. Asked by Mr. Jones what my discovery was, I said that I saw black horses and white horses eating together in peace from the same trough, from which I inferred that the horses of Janesville were more civilized than its people. The crowd saw the hit, and broke out into a good-natured laugh. We were afterward entertained at the same table with the other guests" (Figures 8 and 9).[145]

The *Illinois Record's* Oldtimer also remembered the scope of social life as it included recreation and education. "Social functions of the day consisted of quilting and dancing," he recounted. "The old style fiddles with plantation airs was the music of the times, but the dancers would have done credit to modern 'rag time,'[146] so supple were they. There was no society, consequently no sombre hued, Lord Chesterfields, 'Only Me's,' 'Real Things,' etc. . . . The first literary society or debating club was organized in the school on Clark Street, between Madison and Monroe[,] and John Jones was made president. Among the weighty questions were 'Who was the mother of the chickens, the hen that laid the eggs or the one that hatched them?' and resolved that the African had more cause than the Indian to complain of the treatment received from the white men. Debate often waxed warm and the discussions of our society was the only intelligent amusement we had."[147] Intelligent discussion, then, was not the sole preserve of white Chicagoans.

Interest in education ranked high among the free people, and they made every attempt to avail themselves of both private and public opportunities for advancement. While Pierce has written that there was a practice "of segregating the races in the common schools," this is conjectural before the Civil War, since there were attempts by Democrats to institute de jure segregation in the schools only after they assumed political control of the city in 1862. And both Herrick and Homel found otherwise. In particular, Homel wrote that "local ordinances adopted in 1849 and 1851 removed [any] earlier racial restriction and conferred the right to public education on all children."[148] By definition, public education at this time meant elementary-level instruction only.[149] In addition, the presence of Massachusetts-born abolitionist Philo Carpenter on the first school board worked no doubt to the benefit of African American enrollment.

In 1850, there were fifty-eight children between the ages of five and four-teen in the African American population, and they appeared to be wel-comed in the schools, with many attending School No. 1 near Washington and Dearborn streets. E. Franklin Frazier found that twenty-nine African American youngsters attended school by the 1850s, when the black popu-lation had reached 323 persons.[150] One of these was Alexander Garrett, who later served in the Twenty-ninth Regiment, Illinois, USCT. Garrett's strong, legible signature on documents he signed later in the century stand as vigorous testimony to the value of a Chicago public school education. By 1860, there were 207 African American children of school age, represent-ing 1.6 percent of the total school population. Balanced against their over-all status in society, African Americans viewed having 20 percent of their children in public schools as an acceptable figure.

Chicago, in contrast to the East, afforded opportunities unknown in pub-lic education to black New Yorkers, Bostonians, and Philadelphians up to 1850. When African Americans attended public schools in other cities, it was on a limited and segregated basis. Primarily, they relied on various forms of nonpublic education to meet their intellectual and vocational needs.[151] The example in Chicago broke the rule governing public education in the North because these parents never had to establish private, church-run, or entrepreneurial schools. In New York, African Free Schools existed, and in Boston, African American youngsters attended a racially segregated public facility.

Community-based initiatives for educating adults also gained in impor-tance. Self-teaching became the rule for adults, followed by organized attempts to expand skills and knowledge. So John Jones learned on his own with the strong encouragement from his white abolitionist friend, Attorney L. C. P. Freer.[152] Abram T. Hall, who lacked formal education, combined his enthusiasm for religion with a strong interest in acquiring reading and writ-ing skills. Henry O. Wagoner, arriving in Chicago without the ability to read and write, later became literate and started a Literary and Debating Society in December 1852 at Quinn Chapel A.M.E. Church. Also, an entity named the Progressive Library Association was formed sometime during this period. Black Chicago needed persons capable of reading and sharing the printed word to facilitate the flow of needed information among free blacks in the North, so the importance of education was obvious. Black news-papers from near and far such as the *Provincial Freeman* (Chatham, Ontario, Canada), *Douglass' Monthly* (Rochester), and the weekly *Aliened American* (Cleveland) played a major part in supplying that information.[153]

At the professional level, Chicago's Rush Medical College opened its doors to African American students. Rush College graduated Philadelphian

David James Peck, who earned his M.D. in 1848.[154] Peck thereby had the distinction of becoming the first person of African descent to receive a medical diploma in the United States.

Beyond satisfying the needs of the mind, satisfaction that was physically challenging beckoned. Whites participated in horse racing, gambling, hunting, the throwing game of quoits, and a wide variety of other amusements. Their early attempts at supporting theater met with such moral opposition from churches that for several years performances of plays were taboo. For African Americans, occasionally some notable social interaction across racial lines did occur. For example, the well-known barber Lewis Isbel participated in a ten-mile footrace in 1847. With the alluring prize of three hundred dollars at stake, Isbel competed against the champion Native American runners of America and Canada before a thousand excited spectators. While not the winner, his participation raises interesting questions on the possibility of amiable social interaction beyond the near-intimate contacts he made as a barber to the wealthy and prominent. Physical isolation within Chicago's small boundaries seemed to severely restrict residents, so, as the "Oldtimer" recalled, "Picnics and excursions were unknown."[155]

III. WHITE RACIAL CONSTRAINTS AND INTERRACIAL COLLABORATION

The deleterious influence of racism extended beyond the Illinois Black Laws and was ingrained in the habits, customs, and stereotypes held by an overwhelming number of white Chicagoans. The African Americans in Chicago were fortunate because the sentiments of those citizens were counterbalanced by the many salutary racial relationships emanating from the influential white abolitionist minority. Chicago thus possessed a duality in moral purpose: It was both an abolitionist stronghold and a part of a state and nation where racial differences brought hardships for persons of African descent, no matter the percentage of racial admixture. As the abolitionist L. C. Freer recalled, the milieu was anything but conducive to African American advancement. He stated that African Americans "were free, but they were looked upon as beings who had no right to exist outside of slavery, by a very large part of the community." Part of the reason for the atmosphere of prejudice, according to historian Charles N. Zucker, stemmed from whites from the South, who initially filled Illinois in great numbers. They arrived first in the state's southern tier and then filtered into Chicago in significant numbers. They viewed free people of color as "an anomaly in a [national] caste system based on racial slavery. The free Negro was a member of a social group that in theory had no place in the social order." In the same vein, historian Pierce has written that "upon their black brethren Chicagoans, like many other Northerners, showered [both] kindliness and intolerance."[156]

When future Chicagoans John and Mary Jones and their infant daughter, Lavinia, headed northward through the state with their freedom papers in their luggage, they traveled under the watchful (and not always too friendly) eyes of white travelers who suspected that they might be fugitives. The travelers finally reached Chicago on March 11, 1845. Before their arrival in their City of Refuge, they were challenged by a sheriff near Ottawa, Illinois, who relented in his questioning only after the white stagecoach driver vouched for the Joneses and the origin of their journey.[157] Kidnapping and illegal enslavement did not seem far-fetched in the minds of this family. Nonetheless, such obstacles could not thwart the indomitable spirit of African Americans to eliminate their group's enslavement along with racial proscription.

A. The Illinois Black Laws

The town that the Joneses reached, even as a "City of Refuge," could not avoid national sentiment supporting racial proscription. The infamous Black Laws of Illinois restricted African American life, denying them the right to vote, to serve on juries, and to testify in court against whites. In 1854, charges in the police court against a white woman for adultery were dismissed because the witnesses were African Americans. Moreover, according to Pierce, "at the same time common carriers took into consideration what must have been the public will of the day and excluded Negroes from the accommodations provided others," and whites "seemed to see no inconsistencies in providing a separate section in the theaters for Negroes."[158]

At least Chicagoans did not sanction slavery, so despite violations of the state constitution in southern Illinois near the Missouri and Kentucky borders, Chicago and most other parts of the state remained slave-free. The nearest Chicago came to having a slave sale occurred in 1842. Edwin Heathcock entered the pages of the city's written history after he was arrested following a complaint by a hostile coworker that he did not possess a certificate of freedom attesting to his legal status. The person with whom this African American had quarreled on the docks of the Chicago River, and who was charged with assault by Heathcock after striking him with a club and knocking him to the ground, retaliated accordingly against one of Chicago's most vulnerable residents. Heathcock's inability to produce papers affirming his claim of freedom, or evidence that he had posted bond allowing him to live in Illinois, forced the sheriff under the law to initiate a sale of this refugee's services under a recent 1829 Illinois law. Under this enactment, the accused's services were to be sold, or hired out, on a monthly basis by the sheriff for up to one full year.

Indignation grew among African Americans, militant white abolitionists, and moderate, fair-minded whites who, ironically, objected both to the position of the militants and to African bondage. In an effort to garner support for protest action, posters were pasted early one Sunday morning along a thoroughfare leading to the churches of the city's wealthier citizens. Heathcock, a respectable workingman who held church membership, benefited from his status. One poster read: "The selling of a Methodist brother in good standing, as a piece of property, was not considered altogether proper by some, even though we were not regarded as the contemptible abolitionists."[159] As the proceeding unfolded, the prisoner was purchased by a member of the enraged assemblage as a last-minute effort to prevent his return to jail. The sale price was twenty-five cents; the action was his immediate release.[160]

For the refugee lacking legal sanction for his or her presence in Illinois, and deemed either subject to indenture or a slave fugitive under the highest law of the law, the U.S. Constitution, no measure of security was possible. The infamous Heathcock incident recounted several generations later further affirmed the seriousness of the situation. This sense of daily dread made the freeman or the refugee's attempt at living a normal life impossible. One family of refugees that reached Chicago previously, and who tried to acclimate themselves to the freedom of the North, still had reason to fear the specter of the ubiquitous slave catcher spiriting them away. What they feared most became a reality as they walked along Clark Street one day as a family unit. A federal marshal appeared, arrested them, and sent them back south. They were never heard of again.[161]

At the same time, the most wholesome influences of New England abolitionist sentiment permeated life throughout Chicago, and nowhere was it more pronounced than in its moral tenor. Bondage had passed from New England over two generations previous, and in its place there evolved an aversion that reached a fever pitch by the 1830s and 1840s. Many of that region's sons and daughters dominated early Chicago in all of the spheres that regulated life: religion, government, business, and education. Indeed, they all felt the moral contagion of slavery, so the turmoil over slavery affected all Christian denominations to varying degrees. Most serious was the example of the Presbyterians. Forty-eight members, all abolitionists, left the city's Third Presbyterian Church in 1851 because of disagreement on the extent to which active resistance should be mounted against slavery.[162] Led by Philo Carpenter, they organized the First Congregational Church on May 22, 1851. As a participant in the grand sectional struggle against slavery, First Congregational distinguished itself through its support for refugees as it became a major depot on the Underground Railroad. With honor accorded through derision, "the chapel was derogatorily known as 'Carpenter's Nigger Chapel.'"[163] Its location was on Washington Street between Halsted and Union. The attitudes that churches such as this exhibited insured that Chicago would become one of the nation's premier havens for the persecuted. While they did not advocate social equality, their propensity to support opportunity, albeit limited, and public order meant that as Chicago grew, so did the possibilities for African Americans to realize rewarding lives in its seemingly charmed future.

Yet the fear of being spirited off—literally recaptured on the streets of Chicago or in one's home, because of fugitive status—was dreadfully real.[164] In comparison to other Northern states such as New York, Pennsylvania, Ohio, Massachusetts, and Wisconsin, where the personal liberty of African Americans was protected by law, Illinois failed in its ethical responsibility, and Chicago still represented only a part of a morally rotten whole.[165] According to the historian Thomas D. Morris, personal liberty laws embodied the moral spirit needed in the nation, and followed in the North, that neutralized the Southern slave codes. The presumption that every African American person possessed the essence of humanity and therefore had value in his or her being was recognized in the courts. The spirit of these laws was seemingly dealt a deathblow with the Dred Scott decision of 1857, but it was resilient enough to help inspire the Civil Rights Act of 1866, which in turn became the foundation for the Fourteenth Amendment of 1868. By logical progression, the 1885 Illinois Civil Rights Act followed as another guarantee of basic human rights.

While Illinois never passed a personal liberty law, the act of 1833 served as a quasi-law to protect some of the rights that African Americans sought. In fact, when the 1833 enactment passed the Illinois legislature, the state was only fifteen years old, and the frontier settlement of Chicago had just received its status as a town from the legislature. However, if the nation and state did not openly support personal liberty protection for blacks, certain segments of the population of Chicago still actively pursued protection of the rights of their fellow Chicagoans.

B. Refuge and the Underground Railroad

The famed Underground Railroad, the system through which refugees moved through hostile territory to safe havens, and then on to freedom, ended at Chicago and, at other times, Detroit. Apprehension about one's personal safety in the United States might lead to a journey across the Detroit River to Canadian soil, where slavery had been abolished in 1833 under the Imperial Act. Detroit and Chicago were the most renowned terminuses of the Old Northwest. The local origins of this freedom network might be placed in 1839 when Dr. C. V. Dyer came to the rescue of a refugee. Accounts from the time reported that a "strange, famished, terrified Negro" had appeared outside the city limits on his way to freedom. Transported through the town's outskirts by friends and conductors, the man finally reached the home of Dyer, who arranged for the final leg of his ordeal to Canada.[166] To that large segment of Chicago's fair-minded citizenry, the evil of Southern slavery (even in southern Illinois) was the cause, symptom, and curse of the American economic exploitation of West Africans. Liberation, abolition, and emancipation provided the long-term cure; meanwhile, the Underground Railroad supplied temporary relief. Yet no majority opinion in the city itself formed to declare slavery as the ultimate abomination worthy only of total elimination. Meaningfully, recent scholarship shows that even white evangelicals who actively debated and opposed slavery, sometimes did the latter at a distance.[167] This was not the case for the predominately white First Baptist Church, which split over the issue of slavery in 1843. The Second Baptist Church emerged from this spiritual conflagration as an antislavery church and relocated in the Western Division of the city.[168]

It was almost predictable that some organized efforts would emanate from the ranks of Chicago's abolitionists. These principled activists translated a portion of their moral fervor into manning the Underground Railroad. Displaying courage and a seeming disregard for the dire consequences of challenging the racial status quo, these white stalwarts for emancipation suffered egregious insults, slights, and retaliations from their Negrophobic neighbors as well as from supposedly tolerant white citizens. If a desire to emancipate the enslaved Africans carried some logical weight, the fear of large numbers of emancipated blacks in the American body politic produced a psychological near panic.[169] In its foulest manifestation, it produced mob action throughout the North. Chicago, however, appeared immune. On the eve of a conclave reuniting antislavery whites in 1874, one participant could reminisce, "Am I mistaken, if not[,] Chicago is the only city of prominence that during the days of fiery trial did not disgrace her good name by mobbing anti[-]slavery meetings. All honor to Chicago."[170]

Among the activist leaders who arose from civic, religious, and professional arenas of the white community were Philo Carpenter, publisher Zebina Eastman of the *Western Citizen*, Calvin De Wolf, James H. Collins, Dr. C. V. Dyer, J. V. Smith, Lemuel C. Freer, James D. Walker, Orlando Davidson, and Allan Pinkerton.[171] From outside the formal city limits,

William Morris, who lived northwest along Milwaukee Avenue, and John Brown of "Bleeding Kansas," shared their commitment and the danger of being involved in this moral crusade. Brown arrived in Chicago in February 1859, on just one of his sojourns in the city, as he traveled to slave-free Canada with eleven refugees from slavery in Missouri. In this case, they had been liberated by Brown at gunpoint in December 1858 from three Missouri farms at the cost of the life of one resisting slaveholder, this event having transpired eighty-two days before their arrival in Chicago.[172] By December 1859, Brown would be dead and martyred.

Among the African American men who were active abolitionists were John Jones, Henry O. Wagoner, Abram Hall, H. Ford Douglas, James D. Bonner, Henry Bradford, Barney L. Ford, Alexander Smith, and Joseph H. Barquet—these men demonstrated their courageous commitment to the fullest degree.[173] Along with Quinn Chapel's "Big Four," in fact, members of both genders qualified as dauntless activists in pursuit of freedom.

Chicago contained at least seven readily identifiable stations on the Underground Railroad, with five in the immediate area of the combined residential and commercial section. Allan Pinkerton's house on Adams Street was frequently "besieged by prayerful Negroes, seeking his aid on behalf of some trembling and hunted fugitive."[174] Dr. Dyer's home at Dearborn and Monroe provided a safe haven, as did the house of John and Mary Jones, located north of Monroe Street at Dearborn. Quinn Chapel A.M.E. Church at Jackson and Dearborn was a very active station, and so was the Tremont House, a hotel located at Lake and Dearborn streets. Thus did Dearborn serve as a corridor to freedom; two generations later, and two miles southward, it would serve as an important corridor again—this time in cultural and economic advancement (Figure 10).

Philo Carpenter allowed his drugstore at La Salle and Wacker to serve as an Underground Railroad "depot."[175] West of the river, on Washington Street between Halsted and Union, stood the First Congregational Church, which distinguished itself as a valued station. Gardner House, on the city's far southern extremes, miles beyond the city limits, was another important station.[176] Additionally, friendly, assertive crowd action cleared the streets of Chicago of slave catchers, earning the city notoriety among slaveholders in the South, who labeled it "a sink hole of abolition" and a "nigger-loving town."[177]

Unlike other cities in the North, such as New York, Philadelphia, and Cincinnati, where whites rioted against the presence of African Americans as either refugees or workers, Chicago's citizenry chose an alternative path.[178] In Chicago, whites and blacks rioted together against slave catching. In 1857, when a refugee named Eliza was discovered by slave catchers as she

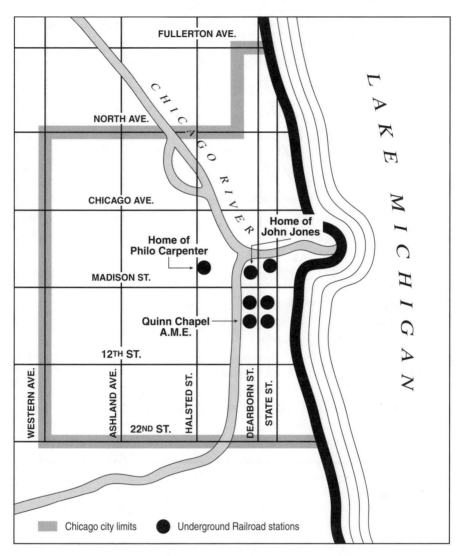

Fig. 10. Underground Railroad locations of Chicago.

worked as a domestic in a city brothel, abolitionists went to work and arrested the refugee under the pretense of her being "disorderly."[179] Eliza's release was immediate once she cleared the clutches of the Southern intruders. On another occasion, even the appearance of kidnapping motivated Chicagoans into action. One slaveholding Kentuckian, visiting the city sometime in the 1850s with a young man whom he considered chattel in tow, felt the wrath of morally indignant Chicago as a mob formed around the hotel to stop what they had misconstrued as a kidnapping.[180] As it happened, the Kentuckian *owned* the young man in question *legally,* a situation and relationship that Chicagoans regarded as a moral abomination.

C. The 1850s: A Decade Demanding Vigilance

The Oldtimer interviewed by the *Illinois Record* described the heightening anxiety of the decade preceding the Civil War: "The South had assumed the rebellious attitude. The Dred Scott decision had caused the nation to become alert" to the impending crisis, impasse, and war.[181] In his pathos he had captured the spirit of the period in all of its vindictiveness and oppressiveness. The passage of time did not bring an alleviation of the national blight of slavery as some apologists for slavery hoped. For example, the diffusionists felt that slavery would continually dissipate latitudinally southward until it collapsed under its own weight. With eighteenth-century abolition in the North and then the Upper South, supposedly the fate of the "peculiar institution" was inevitably being signaled.[182] Unfortunately, the change in tempo merely brought a continuation to the terror of bondage and the threat of reenslavement. Now, on a seemingly yearly basis, event after event exacerbated African American angst about their future in America. Chicago's opposition to slavery notwithstanding, the state of Illinois and the nation continued to create an unpleasant environment for African Americans in the 1850s.

The first shock wave among many during the tumultuous decade began with the passage and enforcement of the Fugitive Slave Act of 1850, which buttressed the original act of 1793 and was aimed at mollifying Southern fears and stultifying black escapes to the North. As part of the Compromise of 1850, the reach of slaveholders was expanded through federal fiat, forcing public participation in slave catching. This legislation was passed in order to placate Southern uneasiness about either an imagined Northern assault aimed directly against slavery, or an indifference to the decades-long need to maintain sectional happiness, by supporting Southern claims to property rights. This mandate had the effect of infuriating many Northern whites generally, and it was especially resented by Chicagoans. In response, the Chicago City Council passed denunciatory resolutions following the congressional passage of the Fugitive Slave Act. Even though the council had acted honorably, it also did so injudiciously, as it exceeded the scope of its powers. In response to this body's actions, and perhaps anticipating even more compromises of this sort in which he would be involved, Illinois's influential vote in the U.S. Senate, Stephen A. Douglas, excoriated the council in person for having assumed it could challenge national law.[183]

The responses from African Americans throughout the North escalated to a point where many were prepared to defend themselves and their families to the death, while others considered flight northward to Canada.[184] Not unexpectedly, the law elicited a militant, self-defensive response among many black Chicagoans. The small African American community gathered at Quinn Chapel A.M.E. Church in an evening meeting on September 30, 1850, after President Millard Fillmore signed the nefarious bill into law. Over three hundred persons, which obviously included a substantial number of supportive whites, decided to formally organize to confront the problem. First, a committee of seven developed a plan of action against the oppressive statute. With a sense of urgency fully warranted by the circumstances, a leadership committee formed to propose a course of action. Crossing any incipient class lines, it was led by Rev. I. S. C. Murray, who was joined by Richard L. Cooper, William Jackson, Alexander Smith, Rev. G. W. Johnson, John Jones, and one other man. They recommended: "Since we must abandon the hope of any protection from government, and cannot rely upon protection from the people, we are therefore left no alternative but a resort to self protection." That they did, and with a flourish. African Americans organized a Liberty Association to keep an eye out for strangers and empowered to meet violence with equal doses. They heartily endorsed the spirit of Patrick Henry's admonition to enemies that they preferred liberty even if it meant their deaths. In their opinion, "the tendency of the Fugitive Slave Bill . . . [was] to enslave every colored man in the United States."[185] Patrols of six persons each were formed to seek out the dreaded slave catchers when sighted. In searching for an answer to the Fugitive Slave Act, memory once again revived an alternative scenario in which the often-spurned choice of anti-American militancy regained some popular interest.

Flight to Canada offered only one of several migratory choices to counter the threat of reenslavement during the decade. Interest in, or at least discussion about, emigration to South America or West Africa permeated the North.[186] In Chicago, the *Western Citizen* reported on blacks who sold their possessions for less than actual worth as they fled north to Canada. Among the fugitives were long-established citizens "who ha[d] acquired a comfortable homestead in our midst by honest labor."[187] Years later, one black Chicagoan wrote about what she had witnessed: "Many of the poor colored people were so frightened at what it [the Fugitive Slave Act] portended they fled to Canada."[188] Their fear of persecution, recapture, and reenslavement was real, but in an ironic twist, it reenforced a sense of unified struggle among those choosing to remain under the protective umbrella of an aroused community. It was a trust that brought rewards.

Beyond militant resistance, there were several effective tactics used to elude a return to the South, including questioning the authenticity of documents and challenging the accuracy of physical identification; these strategies proved especially successful.[189] The latter maneuver came into play as soon as the cruelty of the Fugitive Slave Act came to the public's and press's attention on June 7, 1851, in what was probably not the first case heard. In dramatic fashion, it served notice of the nefariousness of the slave act. Five-feet, eight-inch William Johnson, a man with a dark complexion, was arrested as a fugitive and brought before U.S. magistrate George W. Meeker. Chicago attorney Samuel S. Martin acted in behalf of Missouri slaveholder Crawford E. Smith's interest in the case, which involved a fugitive who had escaped, appropriately, on July 4, 1850. A smiling and relieved Johnson won acquittal within a week by reason of a glaring discrepancy with the writ leading to his arrest, which described him as being five feet five inches in height and with a copper complexion.[190]

One of the city's leading spokesmen of African American abolitionism, John Jones, became active in a quagmire in 1852 with which he was only too personally familiar. He and the white abolitionist attorney L. C. Freer thwarted slave catchers in a remarkably famous episode. Endorsing the maxim that the end justified whatever means were necessary for success, Jones went door-to-door collecting money to buy gold in exchange for a man's freedom. Next, the law was applied with the following device to affirm the rescue:

> Whereas, on the 28th day of August, A.D. 1852, James Pettit, of Summervale, in the State of Tennessee, one of the Barbary States of the federal Union, commonly known as the "United States of America," by his attorney in fact George C. Gray, executed a paper purporting to be a "bill of sale," conveying to me, the undersigned, a certain slave *man*, named in the brief barbarous dialect of the said State of Tennessee, "Albert" and otherwise called "Albert Pettit" transferring to me all his interest in the bones and muscles, body and soul of said Albert.
>
> And, Whereas said bill of sale was not received by me for any purpose of private gain, for the fulfilling of any scriptural prophecy, or for the executing as the minister of God of any of his supposed vengeful decrees pronounced against the children of "Ham" on account of the crime and folly of one of the children of Noah, but for doubtful authority, that is to say, "All things whatsoever ye would that men should do unto you do ye even so do to them."
>
> And, Whereas the undersigned believes the voluntary holding [of] a man in bondage "is the sum of all villainies,"
>
> And Whereas, although the said slave man is legally free as the

undersigned is advised and believes, by reason of the undesigned having brought him from the said Barbary State to a nominally free State
to wit, Illinois, yet the undersigned desiring to divest himself of every
appearance of the detestable crime of slave-hunting declares by the
indenture following to wit: This indenture made this 15th day of
September, A.D. 1852, between John Jones, of the city of Chicago and
State of Illinois party of the first, and Albert Pettit, of the place aforesaid party of the second, part witnesseth, that said party of the first part
in consideration of a charitable contribution of the good citizens of
Chicago aforesaid which enabled him to redeem him the said Albert
Pettit, a subject of the said Barbary State, and in further consideration
of the love and affection I bear to the said Albert as a member of the
family of man, I hereby release, relinquish and discharge to the said
Albert any and every claim I may have on his body, soul and services
on the account of the said bill of sale and do in consideration as aforesaid declare him free from all personal obligations to me except such
obligations as are due from every man to his fellow by the common law
of humanity.

In witness whereof I, the said John Jones, do hereunto set my hand
and seal this 15th day of September, A.D. 1852.[191]

Despite this one victory, circumstances did not improve and in some
cases they only worsened. In 1853, the Illinois General Assembly updated
the Black Laws, prompting a pointed assessment of its venality by Frederick
Douglass. "In looking at the black law then recently enacted in Illinois," he
pondered, "one is struck dumb by its enormity." He sensed a pecuniary
motive along with the racist: "It would seem that the men who passed that
law had not only successfully banished from their minds all sense of justice,
but all sense of shame as well; these law codes propose to sell the bodies and
souls of the blacks to provide the means of intelligence and refinement for
the whites—to rob the black stranger who ventures among them to increase
their educational fund."[192]

Whatever its purpose beyond control and humiliation, it actuated a gathering in Chicago that resembled a convention, which met on October 6,
1853. While the meeting took place in Chicago, its scope was such that it
enjoyed statewide interest. The protest theme emphasized taxation without
representation. Jones spoke thus:

We will plant our trees in American soil, and repose under the shade
thereof. We do not wish to offer violence to any person unless driven
to the extreme, in which case we are determined to defend ourselves at
all hazards, even should it be to the shedding of human blood, and in

doing this, will appeal to the Supreme Judge of the Social World to support us in the justness of our cause. . . . We who have tasted freedom are ready to exclaim in the language of the brave Patrick Henry, "Give us Liberty or give us death!"[193]

This repetition of Patrick Henry's vehement proclamation provides a different glimpse of the communal intentions of Chicago's African Americans. They proposed anything but a revolutionary solution to eliminating their problem, however. Given extant circumstances, it would have been the prudent course to follow—an acceptable public defense of more volatile private thoughts. Advocating the values of the majority in accumulating property, educating their children, and deporting themselves properly in public places, these African Americans committed themselves to observing Anglo-Saxon standards and desired to convince white Americans that, indeed, they lived up to these standards. Whether their public protest was rooted in reality or existed as part of a strategic public demeanor to ameliorate white hostility and paternalism from foe and friend, respectively, is conjectural. One historian has recently proffered a view for the Northeast that equated the rhetoric of voices of protest as a legitimizing thrust by the elite undertaken in the interests of all African Americans.[194]

At the same time, African Americans were fighting a renewed racist thrust from the state of Illinois as the Black Laws were strengthened as a means of social control over free people of color. The climate of uneasiness continued as the Kansas-Nebraska Act of 1854 reopened a portion of the Missouri Compromise lands with the remote possibility of slavery establishing itself there. Tensions developed there as well as in Chicago. That same year, another of the period's annual conventions was called by the luminaries within emigrationist ranks (Martin R. Delany, James Theodore Holly, H. Ford Douglas, and others) to consider leaving the United States on a permanent basis. The National Emigration Convention of Colored People met in Cleveland and considered the future status of blacks. Whether any Chicagoans, other than the soon-to-be-resident H. Ford Douglas, attended is unknown, but the rhetoric would not have been uncommon to their ears. The lengthy, convincing statement was endorsed by several cosigners in whose ranks Douglas fit comfortably. They wrote: "Let it be understood, as a great principle of political economy, that no people can be free who themselves do not constitute an essential part of the *ruling element* of the country in which they live. . . . The liberty of no man is secure, who controls not his own political destiny."[195]

Importantly, as a newcomer to Chicago the next year, and sporadically after that until the war, H. Ford Douglas, spoke at the conference. Douglas, in many respects, had experienced a life similar to that of his mentor, Frederick Douglass. The younger man was born in 1831 in Virginia, the son of a slave owner and a slave woman. "He felt superb about his African blood; he was disdainful of his white blood, but not as much as he would had it been Saxon instead of Scottish." This free spirit escaped from bondage at the age of fifteen and embodied a burning desire to see the destruction of the peculiar institution as soon as possible. Strategically committed to improvement of the African American at home, or abroad if need be, at the Cleveland convention, Douglas proposed emigration "solely as a tactical measure to uproot slavery, refusing to conduct himself as an American citizen while the nation sheltered bondage." Canada looked inviting for this antislavery emigrationist, who eschewed advocating returning to Africa for any other than tactical abolitionist reasons, unlike "nationalist emigrationists" such as Delany and Holly.[196]

Once Douglas reached Chicago in 1855, he became active in antislavery activities and the distribution of the black emigrationist newspaper, the *Provincial Freeman*. He remained in the city for only two years before he spent a year in Canada, then returned to Chicago. Peripatetic like Douglass, he became a human conduit of information about African American agency and resistance to slavery elsewhere in the nation. Importantly, Douglas presented black Chicagoans with a contrast to its relatively more subdued activists and spokesmen. More charismatic and much more rhetorically volatile than John Jones, Douglas must have both frightened and awed his fellow Chicagoans. He was described as having "a physique so noble and a presence so attractive as to charm and interest the listener at once" and an oratorical ability that mesmerized. He was especially critical of Lincoln for his hypocrisy on slavery, his opposition to equality for blacks, and his support for white supremacy.[197]

Meanwhile, African Americans continued to live their lives under the odious Fugitive Slave Act. Also around 1855, three alleged fugitives were arrested and jailed in Chicago before their release in Springfield before a judge for lack of evidence. When they returned to Chicago, their apprehension of rearrest was realized as a U.S. marshal from Springfield sought them out. Chicago authorities refused to cooperate, and the federal official left the city empty-handed.[198] In another case, a married couple described as "almost white, industrious and happy" and with twin daughters born within eight months of her mother's manumission by her husband, faced the dread of losing their daughters to the mother's former slave master. Although the girls were legally the chattel property of the slave owner, the slave catchers were thwarted from taking them from their parents under a warrant. The girls fortunately were sent to Canada before they could be seized.[199]

In response to deteriorating conditions, the spirit of black militancy continued to build. In 1856, a second state convention took place in Alton, Illinois. The Illinois State Convention of free blacks stretched on for three days in November, during which time assertions of rights and entreaties to fairness dominated discussions. The convention's influence was broad, with statewide participation shown in the presence of delegates from five counties. Collaboration among John Jones, H. Ford Douglas, William Johnson, Lewis Isbel, and others produced a strong civil rights position that was enunciated in a the group's "Declaration of Sentiment and Plan of Action."[200]

The presence of H. Ford Douglas, a frequent participant in the national black convention movement, guaranteed that militant rhetoric aimed at producing positive action would be considered. Douglas was considered by historian Vincent Harding as one of the mainstays of the "Black Radical Tradition" of the middle nineteenth century, which pursued a rejectionist course in regard to complete belief in the American Promise.[201] He chaired committees on the Declaration of Sentiment, on drafting the organization's constitution and bylaws for the Repeal Association, and on the group's formal statement.[202] One accepted protest tactic of the conference involved preparing annual reports for the state legislature on African American progress and the impediments encountered while making progress. Colonization was denounced as the right of blacks to freedom in America was extolled.

The year 1857 only brought additional woes into the lives of America's most legally oppressed people. Economic disaster arrived on the wings of a national panic. Then, the fear of reenslavement and other lesser indignities directly at black humanity were exacerbated in 1857 by the U.S. Supreme Court's ruling in the Dred Scott case. The economic event proved a decisive and determining one for all the inhabitants of the city. Subsequently, the claims of freedom of the family of slave Dred Scott reached the national spotlight on March 1857 and signaled another threat to African American hopes for freedom and citizenship. The Chief Justice of the U.S. Supreme Court, Roger B. Taney of Maryland, declared that "a Negro had no rights which the white man was bound to respect; and that the Negro might justly and lawfully be reduced to slavery." Taney and the new, pro-slavery president, James Buchanan of Pennsylvania, had connived to placate the South once again in what could have been a routine rejection of a claim for freedom. But they had decided to quiet the slave powers' apprehension that slavery might end some day soon.

The thoughts of Frederick Douglass, to whom so many in Chicago looked for leadership, were telling on this matter. Douglass felt that slaveholders showed "no sign of a wish to quit their iron grasp upon the sable throats of their victims. Their motto is 'a firm hold and a tighter grip' for every new effort that is made to break their cruel power."[203] All claims to national citizenship disappeared with the dawning recognition that life under slavery seemed perpetual. For some whites and blacks, a foreboding sense of doom grew because, beyond freedom and citizenship, the possibility of extending slavery into the western territories was real. Following the Kansas-Nebraska Act by three years, this decision did more than placate the South—it made the specter of Southern domination more ominous.

Antislavery white Chicagoans demonstrated their dissatisfaction with the unsettling decision in church and in the press.[204] The sentiments of black Chicagoans corresponded with those of Frederick Douglass, and indignation festered. Douglass further enunciated his views on the linkage between an end to slavery and the hope of citizenship in America, stating:

> that slaves are, within the contemplation of the Constitution of the United States, property; that slaves are property in the same sense that horses, sheep, and swine are property; that the old doctrine that slavery is a creature of local law is false; that the right of the slaveholder to his slave does not depend upon the local law, but is secured wherever the Constitution of the United States extends; that the Congress has no right to prohibit slavery anywhere, that slavery may go in safety anywhere under the star-spangled banner.[205]

If the argument that the U.S. Constitution favors the sanctity of property rights over all else were carried to its logical conclusion, how could a territorial legislature, state constitution, or popular sentiment bar a slaveholder from any locale?[206]

The contest of the U.S. Senate seat of incumbent Stephen A. Douglas produced the famed Lincoln-Douglas debates of 1858 and also increased the worries associated with the Dred Scott decision of the previous year. Lincoln constantly raised the issue throughout the state of Illinois both in the company of Douglas and on those occasions when he followed the senator into a town immediately after Douglas had spoken.[207] At the time of the debates, Senator Douglas resorted to race-baiting involving a previous visit to the state by Frederick Douglass. The senator rhetorically transformed the cordial relationship the former slave enjoyed with a white couple into a situation in which the specter of interracial camaraderie and miscegenation was raised to frighten whites into turning against Lincoln.[208] Douglas prevailed in the senatorial selection process that took place in the Illinois General Assembly, but when the presidential election of 1860 was held, Lincoln bested Douglas.

As discouraging as circumstances were, many African Americans still felt that America existed as their only real home, such was their feeling about the only land mass with which they could identify after generations of toil. Yet the issue grew paramount to some African Americans because of past memory, shared heritage of memory, and contemporary pressures on African Americans. For some, it seemed natural to want to leave the United States, and a mass meeting was held to discuss the contentious subject. The leadership of Quinn Chapel A.M.E. hosted the event on August 10, 1858, and the discussion was spirited. Henry O. Wagoner argued in favor of remaining in America and seemed to echo the sentiment of the majority. So did Chicago's most famous African American visitor, Frederick Douglass, who usually opposed all forms of colonization and separatism and used his influence on all he encountered.[209] This placed him on a collision course ideologically with H. Ford Douglas, the rising star of Chicago and Illinois rhetoricians.

The fateful year 1859 brought sometimes contrasting rhetoric and action over slavery to a climax. H. Ford Douglas contributed his part. He attended a Chicago meeting of abolitionists held at Quinn Chapel A.M.E. Church early in the year, before the Harper's Ferry raid; Frederick Douglass was present. After the esteemed Easterner had spoken, H. Ford Douglas, who was known to express the most heartfelt militancy of Afro-America, was pressed by the audience into speaking. "As the gathering continued its clamor for him, Douglas relentingly requested a topic, and the crowd suggested he lecture on the Dred Scott Decision and Emigration, which he proceeded to deliver in his inimitable style."[210] Disagreement with Douglass followed immediately, but they still traveled together throughout in behalf of the antislavery cause.

By fall 1859, Mary Richardson Jones and her husband, John, sat and reflected on John Brown's reply to her inquiry several years previously about the use and effectiveness of violence to extract retribution from the South's slave masters. Brown, their friend and fellow abolitionist, had attempted to foment a slave revolution insurrection deep in Virginia's Shenandoah Valley from the federal arsenal at Harper's Ferry. Brown's impatience with the slow pace of emancipation, with the nation evincing only a lukewarm response to the crisis at hand, had led him to jump-start the day of Jubilee—the liberation of America's four million enslaved. Dauntlessly, Brown led a force of slightly over twenty men, including family members and fellow militant abolitionists, both black and white, into battle against the Slave Power and the national government that backed it.

While no Chicagoans were among Brown's tiny army of liberation, his actions won the approval of some black and white Chicagoans. Not unexpectedly, H. Ford Douglas was one such African American sympathizer who openly supported Brown's motives, tactics, and aims. After he had uttered his sentiments publicly, the Democratic party's *Times* obliquely accused him of being an avid Brown advocate who endorsed killing slave owners and inciting civil war. The Republican party's *Press and Tribune* defended him and whatever utterances he made because "whatever intemperate language [Douglas used was] caused by the brutal and debasing system which the *Times* uph[eld]."[211]

John Brown fired the imagination of African Americans and white anti-slavery advocates to consider, even if silently, the unthinkable—a direct war carried to the slaveholding South to end slavery once and for all. Openly, they expressed themselves differently about the raid, and just as the Joneses had eschewed the use of violence as a means of ending their people's plight, so did many other abolitionists. Frederick Douglass had earlier made it clear to Brown that he disapproved of the plan that called for an armed assault upon the federal government.[212] Nonetheless, as time went by and with the South's indignation building to a boiling point, some black and white Chicagoans, as well as Frederick Douglass, began to find Brown's motivations morally pure, even if his plan of action proved a repugnant choice.[213] Igniting the spark to civil war and the subsequent liberation of oppressed millions, Brown in deed and death proved himself a hero for the times and for generations to come. Within fourteen months, from Brown's martyrdom to Lincoln's electoral victory, the nation divided and war loomed imminent.

At the end of the antebellum period, black Chicago had become firmly ensconced as a feature of the city's landscape. With the establishment of community in the midst of white settlement in the south-central section of the city, the saga of transformation continued. This experience differed initially from the other African American urban clusters of the North because of Chicago's youthfulness, its having no historical ties to slavery, the small size of its black community with no press or elite, but with the church as a centralizing, democratic venue for leadership, and with parallel development of life within a burgeoning American town in a perpetual state of flux. Further, African American involvement in behalf of their own interests served a positive end; as C. Peter Ripley has observed, "Black abolitionism instilled optimism and confidence among free blacks and fugitive slaves."[214]

Chapter 2

The Civil War and "Jubilee,"
1861–1865

The election [of 1860] came; Lincoln was president, then the war. The Race played its part. In a number of the Illinois outfits members of the group were enlisted. Then freedom came and the end of the war.

— "Story of Old Settlers," *Chicago Defender*, May 3, 1930

[At Petersburg,] we were greatly exposed to rain and bad weather and Garrett contracted rheumatism and suffered from it a great deal. He was also disabled a part of the time by piles which was brought on by lifting in building breastworks. . . . I know he was a good soldier [even though] he was a musician, but he did duty with the rest of the boys.

— Affidavit from Federal Pension File of ALEXANDER GARRETT

[At Petersburg,] there is heavy firing of artillery and small arms every night from both sides, which sounds beautiful to us.

— SERGEANT WILLIAM MCCOSLIN, "Letter from the Front"

The blue lines grew longer and longer, and rank after rank came into view, as if there was no end to them.

— BRUCE CATTON, *A Stillness at Appomattox*

They looked like a blue checkerboard in the distance, with the white and black soldiers lined up together.

— CHRIS M. CALKINS, The Appomattox Campaign

110

THE CIVIL WAR, or, as Charles and Mary Beard described it, the Second American Revolution,[1] had a multifarious effect on the nation and directly affected Chicago in ways ranging from ordinary to momentous. While it produced economic change for white America, it also did so for black America, as many newcomers within its boundaries traded Southern chattel slavery for wage slavery in Chicago at its worst. Northern wage labor, whatever its limitations, still proved an improvement over its Southern precursor. Better known is how the city's economy expanded as it provided essential material items of war for Union troops in the field in the form of foodstuffs, horses, boots, and other supplies. Just as the first American revolution opened the door of choice and liberty as well as the pursuit of happiness for Anglo-Americans, the second slowly did the same for *all* former chattels and racially proscribed African Americans.

Furthermore, Chicago sent its men, black as well as white, to the battlefields on the eastern as well as the western front as "the Race played its part" in this monumental struggle. Chicago contributed manpower to more than one black regiment of the U.S. Colored Troops. But before Chicago sent its black men to battle, it received a flood of refugees from the fighting between Union and Confederate forces in the Deep South on the western front—from Alabama, Mississippi, and Louisiana, along with those from Arkansas, Tennessee, Missouri, and Kentucky in the Upper South and border region. As hundreds of African Americans reached the city from those states as well as from nearby Indiana and distant Virginia as the product of this massive upheaval, they in turn generated a change in Chicago's demographic composition and in its internal and external racial relationships.

I. THE DEMOGRAPHY OF AN EVOLVING PEOPLE

The hundreds of newly emancipated persons with African ancestry who entered Chicago midway through the war entered a city that regressed in its racial attitudes to the point of loathing their presence as much as it did the horrors of war. Along with at least six hundred persons already in residence at the advent of the war, these new refugees fortunately encountered an active and hospitable African American community with a sensitivity to newcomers that counterbalanced any racial hostility or slights. At the war's onset in 1861, the city's African American population of 955 quickly shrank as 300 persons, or one-third of the total population, left Chicago for safety in slave-free Canada. Significantly, another 47 blacks departed for permanent residency in black-run Haiti, which at that time could be just as frightening, foreboding, and unfriendly as the environment in Chicago.[2]

The major problem statistically with the population level by 1865 lay with the assessment of how many persons arrived during the war, as opposed to after the war, and up to the completion of the 1870 U.S. census. From the dwindling population of 1860, the African American population started to swell into a mass of 3,691 by the year 1870, the result of an increase of more than 600 percent over the year 1860 figure of some 600 residents. Net in-migration as assessed every ten years masked the dynamics undergirding gross in-migration, which took into account the transient nature of the overall general population, including African Americans. By weight of numbers, newcomers overwhelmed the resident black population. Even so, by virtue of the latter's earlier urban acclimation and assimilation, coupled with knowledge of the city's racial protocols, the newcomers' numerical edge would prove less than overwhelmingly significant as African Americans proceeded into the future.

The family of former slaves Elijah and Nancy Clary, now publicly considered refugees, personified the very essence of this crush of humanity that sought immediate freedom.[3] In 1862, when fighting ensued between Union and Confederate forces near Tuscumbria, Alabama, Nancy Clary and several of her children fled North with the assistance of a white Chicago minister who promised to help the family relocate in Chicago. The clergyman kept his word, and the family settled in, awaiting favorable news that husband and father, Elijah, and son and brother, Louis, had reached the safety of the North. Before that wish could materialize, however, the two men faced impressment into a labor battalion supporting military operations of the Union army. Whether it was the army of the Union or the Confederacy, black labor was considered invaluable in building fortifications and performing other essential military services. The father and his son were finally reunited with their family in Chicago in 1863. Louis, age twenty, immediately began work as a stevedore on the docks of the Chicago River until he enlisted in the U.S. Army as a private in 1864.

William Graves had an experience similar to Elijah and Louis Clary's impressment in that he was forced to serve in the Confederate army as a military laborer in Louisiana. As he recalled, "I was in the Southern army until the summer of 1862, then I went to Chicago, Il. Then I enlisted in the army at Chicago."[4] As a child, William Graves had been sold as a slave in Kentucky and was later sold again into Missouri, ending up in Louisiana, where his status as a slave led to his impressment. He escaped through the Underground Railroad, disembarking in the City of Refuge.

Around 1862 or 1863, Andrew Peter Jackson arrived in what would become, near the end of the century, the far western reaches of Chicago's boundary. For almost a century, in what was to be known as first Cicero

township, then Austinville, and finally the Village of Austin, four generations of the Jackson family settled and lived racially secluded, but not socially
isolated, from their white neighbors. Military service awaited Jackson; his
future life included a growing family that would soon be immersed in community service, work, recreation, and worship.[5]

The Clary family, William Graves, and Andrew Peter Jackson represented
the advance wave of wartime migrants, who reached Chicago both furtively
and openly, amid nighttime travel along the Underground Railroad and
daytime passage on the Illinois Central. This migratory influx was estimated
to have averaged at least twenty refugees arriving in the city daily. Supposedly, on one particular day eighty persons arrived, and sixty arrived on
another, much to the dismay of the city's pro-Southern Democrats.[6] This
wartime flight of former African slaves developed significantly into a pattern
of continuous postwar migration that would extend late into the twentieth
century.

The ranks of the newly arrived encountered the likes of current Chicago-
ans John and Mary Jones, Lewis Isbel, H. Ford Douglas, Henry O. Wagoner,
Abram and Joanna Hall, and others on the streets and churches within the
South Division of the city. These men and women represented established
African American life. Alexander Garrett, Moses Conley, William Armstrong,
William Chambers, and brothers Willis and David Easley also walked the
streets of Chicago, but they were younger and were destined for glory on distant battlefields as part of the all-black Twenty-ninth Infantry Regiment
organized in 1863.

Another important segment within the African American population
consisted of lesser-known individuals and families who had secured their freedom before the war began and who would not establish military connections,
thereby leaving no written records. Then there were youngsters recently
born in the city, or who were recently arrived and had yet to determine their
course in life, but their presence was noticeable because of future contributions. Among these was young Edward H. Morris, who was destined for
prominence in the legal profession in the latter part of the century. He and
his family had arrived in the city in 1863, and they took up residency at 537
Clark Street while attending St. Patrick's Catholic Church and its school.[7]
Another addition to the preadult population was Ida Platt, born to free parents in 1863. Platt was destined to be the first African American woman
admitted into legal practice before the Illinois Bar.[8] Along with other children in their age range, they constituted the *second generation* of pioneers
and would represent the leadership of the Old Settlers at the century's end.

• • •

II. CULTURE, COMMUNITY, AND PERSONALITIES

A. *The Adjustment to Life under Freedom*

Facing a steady dose of Northern racism in a city where neither African Americans nor their cause carried the overwhelming acceptance as they did in the period before the war, the pioneers and newcomers encountered immense obstacles. They would experience two major challenges in their lives related to demographic changes. First, as an expanding population with special needs, they would have to adjust to numerous social changes: to a new quality of sociability from white Chicago residents in general; to municipal services such as education and police protection of their rights as humans to travel and work in safety, even if not yet citizens; and to the fluid social dynamics within the African American community. Second, changing demographics affected black religious values and accompanying church life; also, associational activities would be more influential than ever in the lives of African Americans seeking success and respectability in thought, deportment, and basic quality of life.

Adjusting to life in Chicago was linked to other problems, such as understanding the implications of gross in-migration. Newly arrived African Americans faced challenges in adapting to city life and in ascertaining the extent to which freedom and their arrival in Chicago turned into an improvement over a life in bondage in the South. These challenges were accompanied by the fact that white abolitionist friends demanded a transformation of personality and strategy to accommodate the nation's state of belligerency. Assertiveness in embracing military service to destroy slavery in the South required a personal willingness to confront whites verbally and physically in an overt manner that was sanctioned by war and the opportunities it afforded at the moment. A more concerted challenge to existing vestiges of racism was encouraged, so the Illinois Black Laws and the influence of the Dred Scott decision on citizenship claim fell under more intense attack. White antagonists—among them members of the Democratic party, Southerners in the city, pro-slavery sympathizers, and the Irish—endeavored to enforce the status quo in regard to limiting civil rights.

Then, within the African American community, the interests of residents with future pioneer status, recent runaways, and so-called contrabands began to mesh out of necessity and cultural affinity, which facilitated a semblance of racial progress during the war. While the time proved itself more and more propitious to societal change, the road to unity and effective action placed strains on the community's culture as well as required adjustments in attitude, tactics, and strategies toward change. The pioneers, such as John Jones, Henry O. Wagoner, and others, led the struggle for the attainment of rights. Meanwhile, newcomers faced problems that were more basic as they made the adjustment to life in a milieu of freedom.

The historian Lawrence W. Levine explored two spheres of adjustment along the spectrum of cultural and social adaptation to life in post-Emancipation America. In the South, as would be the case in Chicago, he found that "freedom ultimately weakened the cultural self-containing characteristics among slaves and placed an increasing number of Negroes in a culturally marginal structure." Both concepts accommodated features of Drake's perception of the role of the Afro-American subculture. One, cultural self-containment, related to groups "whose cultural standards and world view [were] determined largely by the values of the group itself and [were] held with a relative lack of self-consciousness." The other, marginality, was linked to a "more obviously bi-cultural or multi-cultural situation in which a group, poised to some extent between two worlds, [found] its desire to absorb and emulate the culture of a dominant group, in an attempt to attain and enjoy the latter's privileges and status, in tension with its urge to continue to identify with many of its own central cultural traditions."[9] Cultural self-containment appeared as the dominant pattern in Chicago, with evidence showing that it strengthened rather than weakened in the urbanizing world of wartime Chicago. As to marginality in Chicago, based on limitations placed on avenues for advancement even for certain well-educated, Northern-born African Americans, it would not exist fully for at least three decades, at about the time of the World's Columbian Exposition of 1893.[10]

Three decades after the war, W. E. B. Du Bois provided a suitable framework from which to examine the Chicago population and the nature of the refugees' adjustment to the city as well as the influence of the city upon them. Du Bois suggested that investigation proceed from an assumption as to the population's heterogeneity in composition along with its collective hope and aspirations. "Judgement of the thousands of Negroes," the noted scholar advised, "must be in all cases considerably modified by a knowledge of their previous history and antecedents."[11] The experiential foundation of the Clarys and other former slave families rested on their having spent almost the entirety of their lives—childhood, adolescence, and early adulthood—smothered by the oppressive influences of slavery. In general, they knew neither freedom of action nor freedom of thought; they lacked both family and individual names; and they did not know their birth dates and birthplaces.[12] They did not know the fullness of childhood, parenthood, or family life; the exhilarating power of self-regulation in daily life; or the experience of choosing freely a marriageable mate. Social, psychological, and physiological damage reached a level of severity that found too many with permanent scars. Others, fortunately, adjusted more quickly to the change accompanying freedom.

Veteran William Graves's experiences paralleled those of the Clary family. He reflected:

> I was born on the Falconer plantation [in Kentucky], at the time of my birth the plantation belonged to Nelson Falconer. . . . [A]nd I lived on that plantation until shortly before the war when I was sold to a nigger trader and taken to Louisiana and sold down there to a man by the name of Kimper.[13]

His courageous transformation from slave to soldier spoke volumes of his mind-set and worldview. He sought and achieved freedom through flight in the midst of war.

Between bondage in the South and border states and the liberating experience of freedom in Chicago often lay the transitional experience of the contraband camp. Persons escaping of their own volition or liberated by Union troops were directed into encampments where they remained before heading north, if indeed, that was their destination. Chicagoan and Universalist missionary Mary A. Livermore provided a view of life during this transitional period:

> All ages, both sexes, every shade of complexion, and every variety of character, were found here. I had lived on a Southern plantation for two years . . . in my early life, and the people and scenes were not as novel to me as [to] my [fellow white] companions. They were overwhelmed with astonishment at the intelligence, good sense, and decorum manifested by all. They had expected to see a gathering of half-humanized baboons or gorillas, and were not certain that they ought not take with them an interpreter. All with whom we conversed gave an intelligent and graphic account of their escape from slavery, and their descriptions of "massa" and "missus" revealed a clear insight into character. They admitted that they were not in as good condition now as they had been "at home," but they expected to have better days by and by, and to earn money, and to keep house, and to "live like white folks." Not one regretted their change of circumstances.
>
> "Why, missus," said a very intelligent mulatto woman, with considerable pretensions to beauty, who had come from Point Lookout, laying her right forefinger in the broad palm of her left hand to give emphasis to her speech, "we'd ruther be jes' as po' as we can be, if we's only free, than ter b'long to anybody, an hab all de money ole massa's got, or is eber gwine ter hab."

Refugees such as these brought their stories and scars, along with their fears and hopes, to enrich their lives in Chicago. Lodged in federal archives, the story of Louis Clary's mother relates her family's journey with clarity and poignancy:

> Before the war I was a slave & lived at Tuscumbria, Alabama. I was raised by Capt. Travis who gave me to his daughter when she married John Dellahaust[.] When he died I was sold to Jack Adams and on his death I was sold to Bill Clary who lived about 5 miles from Tuscumbria[.] The first time I was married was while I lived with John Dellahaust to Berry Dellahaust and lived with him about five years and had four children by him, Sarah, Martha, Louis & Mary Francis. When Dellahaust's slaves were sold, Berry & I were sold apart and I never saw him again, & I do not know whatever became of him. I and my children were bought by Jack Adams and while I was living with Adams, I was married to Elijah and we all took the name of Adams. After Adams died his widow married Bill Clary and we all took the name of Clary. I had ten children[,] I think it was, by Elijah. I had fourteen children in all. All of my children were born in Alabama. My baby was two & a half months old when I left them to come north. It was between 1862 & 1863. I think when I left home two of my children had died there & when Elijah & I left we brought 12 children with us. We went first to Tuscumbria and then to Iuka & from there to Corinth, Miss[issippi,] and there Elijah & Louis were set to work with the [Union] Army. Louis was then 20 years of age. They were not regular soldiers [but military laborers], but were under Capt. Harper & worked with the guns and ammunition, unloading them & moving them about. The Army peoples would not let the men folks go any farther, but sent the women & children off to get them out of the way [of hostilities.] My daughter Martha was married & had children of her own & she was living up in town at Corinth & when I was ordered away I sent my boy Joe from the corral to tell her we were going, but he did not get back & I never saw or heard of either of them after that time. I was sent to Cairo Ill. I took with us 9 of my children[.] After being in Cairo about 3 weeks I was brought to Chicago by a minister who wanted to get places for my children who were old enough to do chores. Arrived here [and] I [rented housing.] And did washing & finally got my children all with me and after I had been here about 7 months, Elijah & Louis came here. They had been discharged from their work at Memphis[,] Tenn. & traced us to Chicago.[14]

The Clary family afterwards suffered constant disruption of family life. They were to lose six children while residing in Chicago to cholera, measles, tuberculosis, typhoid fever, and hemorrhaging of the lungs; face uncertainty as to their future; and suffer deprivation in meeting their economic needs, their being so impoverished. Unfortunately, their story assumed a repetitive character among the refugees.

Frank McAllister and his wife, Celia, must also be included among the newcomers. The latter was a former slave in Missouri, who arrived and married legally in the city in 1862. The McAllisters found housing and settled at 318 South Clark Street. Mrs. McAllister worked as a washerwoman, or laundress, and remained in the city until 1881, two years after her husband's death on May 1, 1879. Like others of these Chicagoans in transition, she moved west into the Fox River Valley—in her case, to the city of Aurora. The story of St. Louis, Missouri, refugee, Maria Simpson, rang just as true. A former slave before self-liberation, a wife to a free man, the mother to two small children, Maria Simpson escaped and came to Chicago during the war.[15]

Private Cato Flowers of Company C of the Twenty-ninth Regiment was the son of Edward, approximately age sixty, and Louise Flowers, approximately age forty-nine upon their arrival in Chicago. They came to Chicago after fleeing from slavery in Tennessee in November 1862. The family remained just as impoverished upon residing in the city as they had been in slavery—their combined personal worth was placed at less than twenty-five dollars. In itself, this was an indictment of slavery at its exploitative worst as well as grim testimony to the economic environment in which ordinary folk operated in the North. Private Flowers worked to support his family chopping wood for two dollars a day and was also a common laborer.[16] He enlisted in the service on January 3, 1864, at the age of nineteen, to help them financially. Sadly, the soldier died of smallpox while in service on August 12, 1864. His parents continued to fare poorly, living off their meager earnings of forty to fifty dollars per year between October 1863 and sometime in 1867; they also lived in dependency on the charity of neighbors. By 1873, Mr. Flowers had died, leaving Mrs. Flowers completely destitute.[17]

Logan Davis reached the city in 1862 at the age of thirteen, a year before his enlistment in the Twenty-ninth Infantry. This youthful refugee from Hopkins County, Kentucky, recounted his saga briefly: "First owner Mr Lobes Sold me when 5 yrs old to Mr Green Binam and got freedom by escape to north in 1862." Other Kentuckians reaching the city were Jerry M. Smith and Lewis T. Wood. They worked as cooks at the Sherman House Hotel for at least a year before Wood enlisted in the army in June 1864. For whatever reason, Smith delayed making that monumental decision like his friend's, waiting until January 1865.[18]

The wartime flight of former slaves was filled with difficulties, the most egregious being the need to smuggle refugees into Illinois and northward to Chicago because of the nefarious Black Laws. It was anything other than traveling to liberation in a purportedly "free" state. Mary A. Livermore related the saga:

> Past Milliken's Bend [in Union-occupied Mississippi] . . . I was standing on the upper deck [of a steamer], watching the Negroes roll the [cotton] bales up the plank, I espied in the crowd below [H.] Ford Douglas, a well-known Colored man of Chicago, who had no inconsiderable local reputation as an anti-slavery lecturer. . . . He uttered a cry of joy as he saw me, accompanying his salute with a gesture of delight. We had known each other for some years, and he rushed on board to meet me. Grasping my hand warmly, he said: "The Lord has sent you this time, sure! I have been praying that He would send along somebody that I could trust; but I [had not] thought He would answer by sending you. You will not refuse to do me a great favor?"
>
> "Certainly not, Ford; you know that without asking."
>
> "I have in my tent a little colored boy, six or eight years old, a slave child whom I have stolen. His mother was a slave living near New Orleans, but before the war she escaped to Chicago. Will you take the boy to his mother?"
>
> "It will not be safe, Mrs. Livermore," immediately imposed one of our company, a member of the Illinois Legislature. "You will run great risk in undertaking to carry a Negro boy through Illinois."
>
> The infamous "Black Laws" of Illinois were then in force, and anyone who took a Negro into the state was liable, under these statutes, to heavy fine and imprisonment. Under the stimulus of a most senseless and rabid Negrophobia, then at fever heat, the provost-marshal at Cairo searched every Northern-bound train for Negroes, as well as deserters. . . .
>
> "You cannot escape detection if you try to run this boy through Cairo," said the surgeon of our party. "You had better leave this child alone."[19]

Mrs. Livermore took the risk and safely delivered the child to his mother, Sarah Morris, but not without first endangering her own personal safety as she smuggled the youngster into Illinois. Locating the mother, she instinctively questioned her as to how the two had become separated. The mother's explanation was revealing. With the constant flights from the plantation by other women, the mistress kept a close eye on the mother's movements. The plantation owners, upon taking a trip to Rhode Island, brought the mother with them but left the child behind as a hostage. Once in the North, however, she remained. Tormented over her decision to achieve personal freedom while leaving her only child alone in the South, the mother ultimately decided to flee when she realized it was God's will. Her story is poignant, earnest, and filled with pathos; her anxiety, however, is counter-balanced by an enraptured religious conviction:

> When I left Lou's'anny I didn't tink not to go back agin. . . . But one Sabba' day massa and missis dey gone to ride on de beach, an' I set down o de doorstep an' tink o' my little chile; an' den I hear de Lor' speak to me out of de stillness. He say, "Sarah, go up stars, an' pack up your tings, an' go to Ch'cago!" But I say: "Oh, no Lor'! I want to go back to dat chile. What dat little chile do on dat big place widout his mammy? No, Lor', I don't want to go to Ch'cago."
>
> An de Lor' He speak agin in de stillness, an' dis time wid a great voice, and say: "Sarah, do as I tell yer! I'll take keer of that chile; you go to Ch'cago." So I go up stars, an' pick up my duds, a-cryin' all de time. I tell de Lor' on my two knees two, tree time: "If yer please, O Lor' King, lemme go back to my chile! I don't want to be free. What for shall I be free, an' my chile be lef' down on massa's ole place?" Ebery time de Lor' King He say loud, so it fill all de room, "Go to Ch'cago!" . . . "All aboard!" [While on the train] I was gwine to jump off, for I said: "O Lor' King, I don't want noffin widout my chile! I don't want heben widout my pickaninny! I can't go to Ch'cago!" An' de Lor' King ketched me back; an' he said, so loud and strong I 'spected all de folks would hear, "DAT CHILE'S MY CHILE; I'LL TAKE KEER O' HIM!" So I gin up to de Lor' den, honey; and all de big storm in my heart stop, an' I was dat happy I could ha' sung an' shouted, like I was in a praise-meetin'. . . .
>
> An' de Lor' King is jes' as good as His word; an' He's sent de pick-aninny, grown so peart an' so big that nobody but his mammy would eber ha' known him. So now I prommis' de Lor' King I'll neber mistrust Him no more, an dat dis chile shall be His chile.[20]

Once in the city, refugees were welcomed and absorbed into what was transforming into a resilient and expanding African American community. These newcomers were considered part of a racial family—whether real or fictive kin—who were reassembling as part of a reunited whole. For these children of another phase of the Exodus, Mount Sinai bore the name of Chicago. African Americans in general shared an ethos that relied heavily on those features of the Afro-American subculture embracing compassion, resolve, patience, comradeship leading to clustering, and the sharing of available resources, whether spatial, economic, or spiritual. The prominence of these qualities was most visible in the spheres of work, worship, and residence. Ironically, they benefited from the tendency of white Northerners, unlike whites in the South, to basically ignore a small populace of virtually powerless people. Essentially left to their own devices to facilitate the rate and mode of urban adjustment, they looked to their new community for leadership, support, and camaraderie.

Not to be overlooked, the newcomers also brought attitudes, values, and habits that reflected the lingering negative effects of life under bondage on plantations, farms, and villages in the South and the border states. Noted anthropologist Allison Davis observed that "the accustomed standard of living is a factor in studying social changes."[21] Those attributes held by newcomers could sufficiently hinder adjustment in an urban setting as much as racial hostility could. They unfortunately had the potential to stymie the fullest cooperation with their racial brethren also as they sought group advancement. If the experience of resident and urban-acclimated black Chicagoans was anything like that of their counterparts in Washington, D.C., the transition worked out somewhat satisfactorily to all parties.[22]

According to Herbert G. Gutman, humanity's and the African Americans' most important socializing institution, the family, proved its "adaptive capacities at critical moments." This was indeed such a time, and African Americans, especially the refugees, used familial bonding as that critical ingredient necessary for both survival and enhancement of their family's circumstances. It meant that they "clung to the notion of sacrifice for kin," adding to community life a "durable, general tolerance, amazingly free of condescension, for the individual's right to follow the truth where it leads."[23] Sacrifice for kin meant Civil War service with no guarantee of a safe return to home and family. In the cases of two soldiers, Louis Clary and Cato Flowers, it was a dual sacrifice, since these young men first cared for dependent parents in Chicago by engaging in arduous work in the North after escaping from bondage.

Group solidarity, manifested in a plethora of institutions abounding in the community, grew with more than just an immediate abhorrence of slavery and as a tradition of widespread refusal to accept, in their hearts, the Euro-American definition of them as inferiors and things. Even while accommodating realistically to their precarious position in society, a belief in the rejection of racial subordination also marked their lives. Enlistment into the Twenty-ninth Infantry Regiment confirmed this conviction among the younger men. Later, during the stress of combat and general service, some of these men developed a sense of enduring comradeship that would transcend time.

In the competitive North, former slaves were immediately confronted with learning to renegotiate their personal, social, and labor relationships with whites and their fellow blacks. Frazier wrote that "Emancipation was a crisis in the life of the Negro that tended to destroy all his traditional ways of thinking and acting. To some slaves who saw the old order collapse and heard the announcement that they were free, emancipation appeared 'like notin' but de judgement day.'"[24] Newcomers found extra incentives to transform themselves as they increasingly associated with the resident population, who more often than not absorbed them into a larger circle of social experiences. Just as in Washington, D.C., internal differences assumed a secondary importance to intragroup concerns and unity. Whether emancipation had been commandeered through escape or had been the result of fiats, such as the Emancipation Proclamation or the Thirteenth Amendment, the result was the same. Self-sufficiency and survival loomed as imperatives, as necessary, and as the indispensable means to an end.

Once ensconced in the atmosphere of liberty that the North afforded, the effects on personality development were dramatic. No longer considered chattel by influential others (meaning all whites), and free of the enforcement mechanisms of the South, the creative expression of an individual's will could begin. It was not as though all of life's limitations and restrictions disappeared, but enough did to produce an immensely liberating climate for the soul, mind, and body. Dreams could be conjured, hopes could be buoyed, and realization of the imaginable was always possible, even if not probable. Empowered by the additional thrust of agency just released, the refugee sometimes joined, or at least listened to, other, established blacks as they fought the oppressiveness of the Illinois Black Laws, portions of the U.S. Constitution, and the Dred Scott decision—because they wanted to and could. This enhanced their sense of agency, as it built self-worth for the individual and the group through struggle that sometimes produced victory.

What historian John W. Blassingame proposed as a viable model for effecting the development of personality on the Southern plantation had applicability in the city.[25] The "significant other" in the lives of Chicago's African Americans now entered their lives as leaders of their own group. By living in close proximity to each other in the Southern Division of the central city, they established and constantly reenforced the value of their culture and the potential power of their community. The existence of veterans' records containing social data covering the half century after the end of the Civil War illuminated this relationship. As free persons on their way to becoming citizens, African Americans enjoyed a change in status that also opened institutional channels, always accessible to whites, but of which blacks had only dreamt previously. These new experiences with a black professional class ranged from formalized marriages before officiating black clergy to attorney-client conferences involving the legal steps necessary to win approval of a pension claim.[26] Constant interaction in this setting among the group went a long way in producing a "new type of Negro" who sought greater control over his or her destiny.

Along personal lines, adjustment to life in the North meant confronting the traumas of realizing that bondage was over and freedom of choice was real; that Southern values had to be discarded in favor of more modern Northern values of individualism, personal accountability, material accumulation, self-improvement, reliability, thrift, deferral of immediate gratification, and competitiveness; and that wartime stresses required different powers of accommodation to circumstances than those needed to fulfill the civil requirements of peacetime. Wages could be negotiated; the same was true for housing space. The education of children was expected. Later, true state-recognized personhood appeared with the extension of state citizenship rights in 1865 (when the Illinois Black Laws were repealed), national citizenship rights in 1868 (with the passage of the Fourteenth Amendment), and the franchise in 1870.

Arrival in the North, of course, brought anxiety, as the refugee had to be constantly vigilant to protect his or her freedom. This produced an edginess that, among other factors, affected personality, because every sense had to be honed for constant danger. Sharpness of mind and of the senses were requisites to insure safety. Beyond individual adjustments to life in a new environment, and whether ingrained or not from previous experiences, a sociability among other African Americans also had to be cultivated to benefit from the group's strength of numbers, surveillance, and support. Whether noting a furtive glance from a white stranger, a noisy footstep behind, or a small group of travelers in the city's streets who looked suspiciously like slave catchers, the refugee's mind found no peace until slavery legally ended.

While it would be many decades before racial equality—interpreted by persons of this period as close personal, or intimate, interaction—was sought aggressively, African Americans still continued their struggle to achieve some semblance of equality of opportunity.[27] This dream, which had grown in the minds and hearts of some of the earliest settlers, was shared with the newcomers to their collective benefit. So, despite the deliberate efforts of contemporary apologists for slavery during the antebellum period to soft-pedal the oppressiveness of slavery, along with those of subsequent generations of inadvertent apologists to continue this reprehensible myth during the postwar era and the early twentieth century, the saga of the emancipated African continued in all of its indomitability when confronting racial adversity.

The places that provided temporary solace from this unrelenting tension were to be found in opposite ends of the social spectrum—the church and the saloon, or as its worse manifestation was referred to in previous times, the "dive." Self-affirmation and exuberance in prayer, sermon, and song produced relief as an individual succumbed to the power of otherworldliness through religion. Contrastingly, heavy drinking and furious dancing produced the numbness that allowed escape to the nether regions of the mind.

Without restrictions on religion and worship, the black church assumed a visibility and relevance to the former slave's interests that related primarily to liberation for all. Moreover, the church provided the first line of leadership and the first place of refuge. Overt manifestations of group solidarity through freedom of assembly and speech met encouragement in the North, where such expression was considered commonplace. Freedom in family formation would have affected personality positively because of the nurturing that the family brought. In an environment where private property set the basic limits on personal worth as well as economic worth, control over property had to have not only made the successful pioneer Hudlin family feel better about themselves, but also given the admiring, or even envious, blacks an example of the heightened possibilities achievable in freedom. Negotiating to rent would have provided some aspects of positive social interaction with whites as the owner entrusted the lessee with partial property responsibilities and an expectation of regular payment. Sharing rental space in homes as well as in boarding houses allowed blacks to congregate and perpetuated a sense of group worth apart from contact with the white world. Conforming to proper deportment served African Americans well because this limited restriction applied to all residents of the city and was sanctioned by religious leaders as well.

B. Emancipation

Early in the war, the hopes of African Americans already residing in the city were buoyed by news that Union generals were freeing the slaves they encountered. Under the cover of removing valuable contraband from the hands of the enemy, General Benjamin F. Butler of Massachusetts emancipated all slaves entering his lines in Virginia. He was followed in his action by Generals John C. Fremont in Missouri and David Hunter in South Carolina. Unfortunately by 1862, because of the continued resistance of Abraham Lincoln, the federal government's official policy mandated the return of slaves to their masters.[28]

If friendly and humane Union generals and soldiers were doing their part, African Americans did theirs, also. Their activism on their own behalf had them fighting a two-front war during a war—which was in effect a version of World War II's "Double-V" strategy, Civil War–style. Accordingly, it was a matter of repealing the Black Laws at home in Illinois and, at the same time, defeating the Confederacy and destroying slavery once and for all. The racial handicaps in Illinois were egregious. At an Emancipation Day celebration, Lewis Isbel fell victim to a white pickpocket. After catching the perpetrator, Isbel suffered insult after injury when his testimony against the white man was disallowed in court by the provisions of the Black Laws that forbade African American testimony against whites.[29]

As one might expect, given Chicago's reputation on the slavery issue, pressures from abolitionist circles mounted, urging President Abraham Lincoln to end slavery as soon as possible. From within congressional circles, Senator Lyman Trumbull of Illinois urged emancipation and acted legislatively to have the process protected through constitutional means as the Thirteenth Amendment. Emancipatory pressures continued to build as hostilities increased. Locally, John Jones distinguished himself as the leader among African Americans by writing, cajoling, and meeting constantly on the matter. He and the other black and white activists who believed in the ultimate triumph of justice had their day when, through concerted effort on March 3, 1865, the Illinois General Assembly rescinded the Black Laws.

National success came early in 1862 as the U.S. Congress acted in its own domain, voting to abolish slavery in the District of Columbia. Thus, emancipation of the total slave population of this city occurred on April 17, 1862. This congressional act continued to overshadow (and with good reason) the partial presidential emancipation of January 1, 1863, which is accorded so much more attention. For at least three decades after, on every seventeenth of April, the black population of the nation's capital paraded along Pennsylvania Avenue, passing the White House to a presidential review. For years every class and social grouping (highbrow, aspiring socialite, and rank and file) and racial mix (mulatto, quadroon, and pure blood) marched together. The perceptive assessment of one observer warrants a full recitation:

> It always puzzles strangers to Washington, who happen to be here on the 17th of April, to find that the colored people of the District of Columbia have an Emancipation Day of their own. . . . If they never knew it before, they will never forget it, if they are here on what is known as "Mancipation Day" by most of the old-time colored people in the District. . . . For on that day there is a procession of colored militia and other more or less uniformed citizens in the street and on either sidewalk. . . . With all their musical ability, the people in these processions are like children in their love of the drum, so that there is always noise enough to engage the ear even if there were not enough color to attract the eye.[30]

Finally, a decisive blow aimed directly against slavery seemed to be on the horizon. On September 7, 1862, a public meeting was held in the city to increase pressure on Lincoln to act decisively on the matter. Led by white abolitionists, a delegation was formed and met with him in Washington on September 13.[31] Turning back Lee's invasion at Antietam had given Lincoln the victory he needed to justify his action. A preliminary proclamation in September led to a final version on January 1, 1863. Once the proclamation was issued, elation ruled. John Hope Franklin wrote of every African American population in northern cities, including Chicago, celebrating its issuance.

It was not a case of the document solving the problem completely, but it sufficed in that it addressed it in its limited way. In Chicago, the ceremony surrounding the event was both solemn and celebratory. Held appropriately at Quinn Chapel A.M.E. Church, the enormity of the celebration required morning and evening services. For its part, the friendly *Chicago Tribune* reported on the observances as part of "the Jubilee." Aware of the limitations of the document and the previous reluctance of Lincoln to act decisively on the matter of emancipation, that morning, "Rev. Mr. Dare, the pastor, followed in a fervent prayer, filled with thanks to the Most High for the manifestations of Divine Interposition in behalf of the down-trodden and oppressed slaves, and closing with an affecting appeal in behalf of the Government." As to the importance of slavery as the root cause of the war, a visiting Canadian speaker at Quinn Chapel talked about slavery as "the first, great and only cause of the war, and that consequently the only way to end the war was to remove the cause."[32] The proclamation authorized the raising of a black army of liberation, and this message was not lost on African Americans. The best way to end slavery was by destroying its support apparatus found on the field of battle in the form of the Confederate army.

At the evening portion of the celebration, the participants passed a resolution that conveyed "the spirit of the meeting." The contents of the document follow:

> WHEREAS, The President of the United States of America has issued a proclamation of freedom to all States and parts of States in rebellion against the Government on this the 1st day of January, in the year of our Lord, 1863; and whereas it has pleased Almighty God to select Abraham Lincoln as his instrument through which His justice is to be rendered to all men in this country; therefore,
>
> Resolved, that we hail with deep emotion the auspicious event, and as good and loyal colored Americans we tender to Abraham Lincoln our sincerest thanks in the name of the republic, of God, and of humanity[;]
>
> Resolved, That in the President of the United States we recognize the Christian patriot and honest man, who, since his inauguration as chief magistrate, his acts have been blessed of God, and will be embalmed in

the hearts of his countrymen, and when some future historian, shall come
to write the history, they will find a document that will go down in posterity beside the immortal Declaration of Independence[;]

Resolved, We also congratulate all lovers of the rights of man upon
this auspicious and glorious result of our labors; they have secured for
themselves endearing immortality, viz: liberty to four millions of slaves,
privileges never heretofore enjoyed by 300,000 nominal freemen of the
North, and to untold thousands of the poorer whites in the States now
in rebellion[;]

Resolved, That we will ever hold this, the first day of January, 1863,
as abolishment day, the day that four millions of African-Americans
were redeemed from the thraldom of American slavery into the noon-
day of universal life, by the single shake of the pen of one man—
Abraham Lincoln[;]

Resolved, That, amidst our happiness, we reflect with sadness upon
the fact that so many soldiers of freedom have fallen in the struggle, but
their cenotaph will ever be in the hearts of a grateful people[;]

Resolved, That as heretofore, so hereafter we being loyal to the
Government, should they give us the rights of man, we will "pledge our
lives, our fortunes and our sacred honor" to sustain the true declaration
of Jefferson and Adams, recognizing as a self-evident truth the right of
all men to the pursuit of happiness, and to this end we will not sheath
the sword of truth until we have unfurled our banner, dipped in the
blood of millions, on the Gulf coast, and proclaim to the bondman, your
chains are severed, every yoke is broken; under the American sky
redeemed, regenerated and disenthalled by the sacred genius of universal
emancipation.[33]

However, in their jubilation, African Americans resisted confusing reality
with boundless hopes and expectations. Foolhardiness had no place in their
perpetual struggle for dignity and for full recognition of their humanity.
They understood exactly what the document meant and could achieve, so
their exuberance rested on achieving the possible.[34] In the depth of their
understanding of both the significance of the moment and the event, their
thoughts were articulated by Frederick Douglass, who explained: "It only
abolished slavery where it did not exist, and left it intact where it did exist.
. . . For my own part, I took the proclamation, first and last, *for a little more
than it purported*, and saw in its spirit a life and power far beyond its letter.
Its meaning to me was the entire abolition of slavery, wherever the evil could
be reached by the federal arm, and I saw that its moral power would extend
much farther."[35]

It was from this strategic perspective that John Jones and other African

Americans continued to busy themselves. They accomplished this goal by tactically encouraging whites to act in their behalf politically with the president and with Congress, especially regarding opposition to the proclamation in Illinois, where Democrats in the General Assembly voted resolutions against its enforcement.[36] At the same time, African Americans continued to pursue the destruction of the infamous Illinois Black Laws and to recruit African American males as combat soldiers.

C. Religion and Church Life

Black theology, which had been clandestine for generations in the South, played an influential role in formulating the values, systems of logic, and worldview of the Southern rural slave and his or her Southern urban counterpart. It now emerged in the North in the form of highly visible church participation and with the creation of two new churches and the reconstitution of two older and smaller churches that were faltering and facing extinction into a third religious body.

An acceleration of the pace of war directly influenced African American institutional development during the war, proving the adage that social change produces an expansion of institutions. Drake and Cayton acknowledged the process in their study of the growing black population. Indeed, the institution with the most pervasive influence over black life beyond that of the patriarchal family was the African American church. The church remained the rock of life as well as a source of spiritual empowerment for the individual and locus of collective action in behalf of group advancement. Over time, it underwent innumerable changes that saw it rise in stature as its relevance in the lives of worshipers increased. So did the external pressures of balancing racial self-expression and accommodation to the beliefs and practices of white Protestant bodies, mainly Methodist and Baptist, along with internal tensions within the black congregations between democratic and elitist tendencies in worship. The constant rise in the migrant population produced, for example, a corresponding need on the part of the church to remain consistent with the basic religious components of the Afro-American subculture. Meanwhile, an early reliance on a learned, or seminary-trained leadership, competed with a clergy and church leadership that relied primarily on experience within the church and a personalized, metaphysical bonding with God and the Gospel.

In religious life, both the Baptists and the African Methodists were active. The prewar Baptist churches, Zoar and Mount Zion, found they could not flourish as they proceeded on separate paths. Small memberships and a

Fig. 11. Rev. Richard De Baptiste.
From Simmons, Men of Mark *(1887).*

Fig. 12. Mother Harriett Coleman Moore.
Courtesy of Bethel A.M.E. Church.

recognition of the necessity to put aside manageable differences produced a realistic decision to merge. Thus, in December 1862, they reorganized in the south-central part of the city as the Olivet Baptist Church. Rev. Richard De Baptiste took the reins and impressively increased the church's membership and its financial standing (Figure 11). His administrative talents were widely recognized and were shared throughout the state as he was elected secretary to the Wood River Baptist Association in 1864.[37] The resolute De Baptiste led Olivet until 1883, and then he departed for the East.

At the same time, the African Methodists were also actively in the midst of social change. Quinn Chapel, the city's oldest African American church, located at Customs House Place and Jackson, faced overcrowding brought about by the influx of hundreds of fleeing slaves as Union armies overran the trans-Mississippi South. A small group of members, slightly over a dozen in number and including religious stalwart "Mother" Moore (Figure 12), met to discuss setting up a mission church in the same part of the city to provide another place of worship. In the spring of 1862, Bethel A.M.E. was organized with the approval and support of Quinn Chapel's board of trustees, along with the minister and bishop of the area.[38] With Bethel lacking a spiritual leader, Quinn Chapel lent one of its ministers, Rev. John B. Dawson, to tend to the spiritual needs of the flock until the A.M.E. bishopric could send a permanent leader. By June 1862, Rev. Aeons McIntosh assumed his duties as head of Bethel.

There were, however, monumental problems demanding immediate attention; these required the knowledge and resources of a biblical Solomon. One problem involved finding a suitable edifice for the mission; another was determining the best ways to aid former slaves in the adjustment to both physical and spiritual freedom. A building was rented at Griswold (now La Salle Place) and Jackson (on the block housing today's modern Board of Trade building), and its walls were promptly whitewashed and the interior properly cleaned. A small organ was purchased "just to give tone to the place," and plain pine benches were added to accommodate about 250 persons.[39]

Another problem was a greater impediment of establishing church life; it involved the lack of literacy among the incoming, expanding flock— McIntosh "was hard pressed for the assistance of men and women who could read and write." Coupled with illiteracy stood a limited understanding of American folkways and stateways. Basic constitutional guarantees of freedom of worship, assembly, expression, and movement had to be absorbed into the refugees' ways of thinking once the Illinois Black Laws were rescinded on March 15, 1865. Simple power over self through self-regulation and discipline had to be learned. Bethel pursued its spiritual mandate and soon celebrated with other religious bodies the end of slavery in 1865, as God spoke

Fig. 13. *Illustrated News* sketch of a Northern church service, ca. 1870.
*Photographs and Prints Division, Schomburg Center for Research in Black Culture,
The New York Public Library, Astor, Lenox, and Tilden Foundations.*

with finality to "let my people go" (Figure 13).[40]

The religious background of the refugees would challenge the more urbane among the residents of black Chicago, such as the families of John Jones, Abraham Hall, and others. Mary A. Livermore described the worship of these contraband, as it occurred aboard a northern-bound steamer on the Union-controlled Mississippi: "When they were awake, they were either cooking, or eating, or holding 'praise-meetings.' It would be difficult to say which they most enjoyed. The 'praise-meeting' was the usual occupation of the evening. Then they sang and prayed until their enthusiasm became tempestuous. They beat time with their feet, they whirled in dizzy gyrations, or vented their effervescence of spirit in quick convulsive leaps from the floor, accompanied by earsplitting shouts." Livermore also noted the religious meetings she saw on land in a contraband camp: "The prayer-meetings were held every evening as soon as supper was ended, and [this] was the great staple of their enjoyment. In them they found never-failing satisfaction."[41]

Livermore took careful notes on the structure, tone, and spirit of the service, as well as the music and prayer, observing the following:

The meeting commenced by the singing of a hymn. It was a song and chorus. The leader, a good singer, stood in the center of the room, and sang alone the first two lines:—

"I see de angel's beck'nin'—I hear dem call me 'way,

I see de golden city, an' de eberlastin' day!"

And then the whole congregation rose to their feet, and with a mighty rush of melody, and an astonishing enthusiasm, joined in the inspiring chorus:—

"Oh gwine home to glory—won't yer go along wid me,

Whar de blessed angels beckon, an' de Lor' my Savior be?"

The leader was a good improvisatore as well as singer, and long after the stock of ready-made verses was exhausted, he went on and on, adding impromptu and rough rhymes, and the congregation came in, promptly and with ever-rising enthusiasm, with the oft-repeated chorus. All sang with closed eyes, thus shutting out all external impressions, and abandoned themselves to the ecstasy of the hour. The leader gesticulated violently, swinging his arms around his head, uplifting his hands, and clasping them tightly and pointing into space; while his companions swayed slowly to and fro, beating time to the music with their feet.

At last the swaying became wild and dizzy gyrations, which were interspersed with quick, convulsive leaps from the floor. Accompanying all this was a general hand-shaking. . . . After this followed a prayer. Never have I heard a prayer of more pathos and earnestness. It appealed to God, as Infinite Justice, and with confidence that the wrongs of the slave would be redressed.

"You know, O Lor' King," said the kneeing supplicant, "how many a time we've been hongry, and had noffin to eat,—how we've worked all day and night in de cotton and 'bacca fields, and had no time to sleep and take care of our chillen, and how we've bin kep' out in de frost and de snow, and suffered many persecutions. But now, O King, you've brought us up hyar under de shadder o' de Linkum army, and we 'pend on Thee for de rest. We're gwine to wait for Thee, O King to show us de way."[42]

In describing this group of refugees, Livermore shows their indomitable faith in their Creator:

Subdued, impassive, solemn, hope and courage now and then lighting up their sable faces, they were a most interesting study. Mothers carried their piquant-faced babies on one arm, and led little woolly-headed toddlers by the other. Old men and women, gray, nearly blind, some of them bent almost double, bore on their hands and backs the small "plunder" they had "toted" from their homes, on the plantation, or the "bread and meat" furnished them by some friendly authorities. They were all going forth, like the Israelites, "from the land of bondage to the land they knew not."

Like the Hebrews, they trusted implicitly in God to guide them, and their common speech, as we spoke with them, had an Old Testament flavor. Never before had I witnessed such a spectacle. There were between three and four hundred of them. Half of the middle deck of the huge boat was assigned them, into which they filed, and began to arrange themselves in families and neighborhood groups.[43]

The former slaves also reserved a place for retribution against the wicked by a vengeful God. Mrs. Livermore told this story of how a normally calm, close-mouthed, and respected house slave reacted in private to the beating of her daughter for a serving accident that upset the master:

Later in the day "Aunt Aggy" came to my room on some household errand, when I expressed my indignation at the brutal treatment her daughter had received, uttering myself with the frankness of a New England girl of nineteen who had been trained to be true to her convictions. I was astonished at the change that came over the taciturn and dignified woman. Turning squarely about and facing me, with her large, lustrous eyes blazing with excitement, she spoke in a tone and manner that would have befitted a seer uttering a prophecy:—"Thar's a day a-comin'! Thar's a day a-comin'!" she said, with right hand uplifted; "I hear de rumblin' ob de chariots! I see the flashin' ob de guns! White folks' blood is a-runnin' on de ground like a riber, an' de dead's heaped up dat high!" measuring to the level of her shoulder. "Oh, Lor'! hasten the day when de blows, an' de bruises, an' de aches, an' de pains shall come to de white folks, an' de buzzards shall eat 'em as dey's dead in de streets. Oh, Lor'! roll on de chariots, an' gib de black people rest an' peace. Oh, Lor'! gib me de pleasure ob livin' till dat day, when I shall see white folks shot down like de wolves when dey come hongry out o' de woods!" . . . "I allers knowed it was a-comin'," she said. "I allers heerd de rumblin' o' de wheels. . . . An' de Lor', He's keept His promise, an' 'venged His people, jes' as I knowed He would."[44]

In the West Division, the Providence Baptist was organized in 1863 as the city's fourth African American church. An offshoot of the African Americans' quest for control over their spiritual lives, Providence Baptist became another of the several churches organized during the war to meet the spiritual needs of the burgeoning black community. Increasing pride in being African American and the issuance of the Emancipation Proclamation had resulted in efforts by blacks to build their own institutions; successes in these endeavors increased confidence even more. Providence Baptist Church exemplified this trend perfectly. After worshiping among the whites in the Union Baptist Church for a number of years, black congregants reached a point where their numbers, sentiments, resources, and determination to be autonomous from the white congregants spurred them to establish an independent church.[45] The first level of organization was that of the prayer band, in which one dozen hearty souls organized under a scriptural mandate in a member's living room. The next phase included the building of a church edifice with black hands.

The difference between the white Union church and black Providence church was substantive in nature. In the latter, there was a conscious recognition of the primacy of the spiritual over the liturgical. Emotive expression served as a vital component of religious commitment and was not viewed as a detriment. As Mary A. Livermore had observed, African Americans had mastered "shutting out all external impulses" in order to fully experience "the ecstasy of the hour." This ecstasy, or rapture, allowed the economically deprived to transcend the mundane and to embrace the eternal promise of Christianity. With this, one of the basic elements that brought dynamism to the Afro-American subculture had surfaced as a part of black urban life.[46] Another was the belief that the mistreatment of them as modern-day Israelites would bring retribution in this world or the next. The tendency toward vengefulness fed the mistrust many had of whites in general.

The emergence of Providence as the city's fourth black Protestant church was also directly related to the presence and influence of the Olivet Baptist.[47] Although it was only a year older, Olivet now stood proudly as the "Mother Church" among Chicago's African American Baptists, with its primary organizational roots dating back to 1853. Throughout the remainder of the nineteenth century, Providence and Olivet interacted closely in pursuit of their goal of establishing a religious-oriented pattern of life among black Chicagoans along Baptist lines. Not to be overlooked, a small number of black Catholics worshiped with fellow white congregants. With a mind-set similar to the black Protestants, as their ranks grew they longed for the day when their numbers and resources would allow for the formation of a church of their own. That dream would be realized within two decades.

D. Education

Preparation to fully benefit from freedom included many variables, one of the most important being education. The path proved itself slippery, however. In 1861, there was a controversy about admitting an African American youngster into the Normal department of the high school where she would be trained and qualified to teach, but she was finally admitted. In addition, the forces of racial supremacy were to have their day, temporarily, as a separate school for African American children was opened in accordance with an act of the state legislature. Affected were 207 children of school age, representing only 1.6 percent of the total school population. John Jones distinguished himself again as a champion of civil rights by leading a delegation to Springfield to challenge the legislation.[48] Meanwhile, indignant African American parents such as Joseph and Mary Hudlin marched on the offices of the school board and mayor, which brought them temporary success, for their children remained in an integrated setting.[49] The revised city charter of 1865 repealed the segregation law, however, and the separate school, which had been under a boycott, was abolished in April of that year.[50]

Chicago Public Schools pupils Alexander Garrett and Willis and David Easley enlisted in the army in January 1863 to lay claim to the rights of citizenship. Shortly thereafter, in an ironic twist, because of racism a mulatto girl with an average grade percentage of ninety-seven was prevented from receiving her diploma in the company of her classmates at the regular commencement exercises.

III. INTERRACIAL RELATIONS

A. Liberty and Distrust

Four score years after the event that historians Charles and Mary Beard described as the Second American Revolution ended, two University of Chicago–trained sociologists perceptively wrote about the Civil War and its transformative influences on race relations. St. Clair Drake and Horace R. Cayton declared the following in their tome, *Black Metropolis:* "Before the Civil War the Negro was the protagonist of the abolitionist drama. After Emancipation he was no longer a hero around whom stirring battles were fought in the city streets and the courts. He and his people had become just one more poverty-stricken group competing in a city where economic and political issues were being fought out behind the facade of racial, national, and religious alignments."[51]

Race mattered greatly to recently arrived refugees from the areas of combat in the South, who brought with them very few personal possessions (as if it were even possible to accumulate under chattel slavery). They did bring, however, a distrust of whites that was rooted in personal experience

extending over generations. Emigration from the Southern war zone provided the city with hundreds of new residents during the war. Even if there
had not been a buildup in white hostility against African Americans exceeding pre–Civil War levels, mistrust would still have existed.[52]

While some very religious African Americans could envision the day of
Jubilee on the horizon with the advent of the war, followed by the issuance
of the Emancipation Proclamation, more sober minds reflected on conditions in prewar Illinois and Chicago. Illinois had neither passed a personal
liberty law nor relented in its need to regulate African American life through
its Black Laws. Ironically, Chicago had proved itself most worthy of a claim
to civilized behavior by resorting to mob action to protect refugees and by
evading the law to escort refugees to Canada. Yet one year into the war, pro-
Confederate, anti-Negro, Democratic sentiments surfaced with an intensity that belied the city's reputation as a haven for freedom.

Pierce described the inconsistencies in the attitudes of white Chicagoans, who, while "politically Republican during the Civil War and generally
hostile to slavery expansion earlier, . . . wished to protect Negroes in their
rights, but not to the point of elevating them to the plane of equality.
Opposing the further extension of the 'Black Laws' of Illinois in 1848, dis-
approving of the law of 1853 which prevented the immigration of free
Negroes into the state, these protectors of fugitive slaves raised no objection
to the exclusion of Negro testimony against a white person in the courts of
law; they seemed to see no inconsistencies in providing a separate section in
the theaters for Negroes, and in segregating the races in the common schools.
. . . At the same time common carriers took into consideration what must
have been the public will of the day and excluded Negroes from the accommodations provided others, just as the owners of property found it undesirable to rent to them."[53]

While Pierce viewed Chicago politics as Republican-dominated, a more
contemporary perspective saw them as being Democratic and therefore
more hostile to both the humanity of African Americans and their potential for advancement. Frederick F. Cook, former reporter for the virulent
antiblack and anti-Lincoln *Chicago Times*, saw the period as one of Democratic hegemony, especially after 1862.[54] Increased antagonism toward blacks
now enjoyed formal political sanction.

Across the racial divide, old racist antagonisms on the part of native-born
Americans were enhanced by the enmity immigrants developed, especially
among the Irish. Strained race relations were exacerbated even more during
the war as the issue of emancipation loomed. In 1861, the *Chicago Evening
Journal* raised the question of social equality when it discussed the issue of
admitting a qualified African American Chicago school graduate into the

Normal (Education) department of the high school: "Is it our determination that the African shall, in all respects, be placed in the same social position as the whites? Are they to be the husbands of our daughters, the companions of our sons, the models of our children?"[55] As broadly defined by a certain segment of whites, equality between the races also encompassed restricting the right of blacks to use public accommodations and to seek work. They complained thus in these instances: "The doctrine of Negro equality was practically illustrated in this city . . . [when] two Negroes laboring under the impression that the good time equality had really come, entered one of the Clark street omnibuses [freely]"; and "a number of the [Irish] shoremen and other laborers waited upon [an employer of blacks] and requested him to discharge the Negroes, as it was degrading to them to see blacks working upon an equality with themselves."[56]

Racist hysteria during the heat of summer in July 1862 led to the infamous Omnibus Riot, which was followed in August by a riot on the riverbank. An Irish omnibus driver on the Clark Street line objected to the presence of an African American passenger, W. E. Walker, and assaulted him. The rider, described as an octoroon and lighter in complexion than the white driver who protested his presence, was a regular customer on the line and had never experienced trouble previously. After a scuffle initiated by the driver led to his defeat, the driver left the scene and the authorities, acting with dispatch, arrested the driver.[57] The next month, hundreds of Irish gathered on the riverfront to unload a schooner and beat African Americans who had shrewdly outbid them for the work. In this instance, overwhelming police force was needed to restore order.[58]

In January 1863, following the issuance of the Emancipation Proclamation, antiblack hysteria grew in intensity. One death was attributed to Negrophobia. The *Chicago Tribune* reported one such assault under the headline "Another Horrible Tragedy—A Man Murdered In His Bed." The victim was Robert Bailey, an African American from the city's West Division. Bailey served as watchman on the schooner *Barber* as it lay moored at Washington Street in the South Branch of the Chicago River. He was bludgeoned nearly to death in his bed and died there after struggling to his feet. Describing Bailey as a "sober, industrious, peaceable man," the newspaper, consistent with the temper of the times, immediately blamed "some devil in the malicious form of a Negro-hater" for the crime.[59]

While the intent of some African Americans was an expansion of opportunities commensurate with effort, many more were oblivious to the imagined fears of northern whites. Whites worried about social equality; African Americans either concerned themselves with relishing the feel of freedom from coercive, unremunerative work or concerned themselves with equality of opportunity. The hostility with which the Irish treated African Americans in the spheres of work, recreation, and personal contact is explainable by examining the Irish perception of their precarious status. Beyond the acute competition in labor that blacks represented, the Irish objected to the limited recognition of their whiteness, or racial belonging, by Protestants of English stock and sought relief through scapegoating and violence against a vulnerable target. What they saw everywhere in their own vulnerability in dealing with aggressive Anglo-Saxons, they transferred to African Americans nationally. In Massachusetts and New York, this was definitely the case. Several examples stand as testimonials to bigotry gone wild. In the 1850s, racial tensions in textile mills in Lynn, Massachusetts, led to one of the most dramatic court cases involving discrimination, and Irish hostility boiled over in 1863 during draft riots in New York City. Cincinnati, on the northern banks of the Ohio River, experienced strife as well, since it straddled abolitionist sentiment along with the rabid antiblack Southern sentiment of Kentuckians and the Irish.[60]

As a result of this volatile, racist mind-set, it was not surprising that in 1864, a mob estimated to be as large as four hundred to five hundred Irishmen assembled to attack any and all African Americans at the corner of Clark and Old (18th) streets. As reported, "the blacks had committed no offense whatsoever, except wanting to support themselves through honest labor."[61]

B. Employment, Business, and the Professions

With their most recent experience as slave laborers, African Americans newly arrived from Southern plantations and farms were obviously accustomed to working and performing hard, drudgery-filled labor. Accompanying their own positive attitude as to their own self-maintenance, they carried a misconception, related to their experiences with the Southern planter class, about work and whites. Mrs. Livermore, and others, found that "it surprises them to see white men work."[62] Obviously misinformed as to the attitude of Northern whites toward personal labor, African Americans seeking employment with fair compensation soon encountered difficulties in the competitive environment of the North, where virtually everyone worked and many were willing to seek unfair advantage to maintain a monopoly in their particular sphere of work. Not unexpectedly, domestic service and manual labor dominated as the primary work options pursued by black women and men. The bulk of the men labored as waiters in hotels, in taverns, and on boats moored alongside the Chicago River. Some performed transit and delivery work as teamsters. African American women fared little better as menial workers, many finding employment as laundresses.

On the docks and wharves of the Chicago River, black stevedores impatiently waited to be hired from a daily pool of workers vying for favored positions and waiting for orders to load or unload lake cargo; among the many eager workers, blacks were often chosen last.[63] Dock work nationally proved itself dangerous, and injuries were common. Contraband Elijah Clary and his son, Louis (who worked regularly until his enlistment in the U.S. Army in January 1864), depended on the strenuous dock work of loading and unloading ships to support their family. Louis Clary was five feet eleven inches tall, a "strong[,] rugged kind of man [who] worked steady."[64] Contradicting the image of the African American as a bad or unreliable worker (an ironic label for former slaves who produced so much wealth for others), the Clarys and others like them wanted to work, but like all members of their occupational group were subject to uncertainties of winter weather, which froze the lake and river and placed them at the caprice of sailing schedules bringing goods into port. Just as bad, wages for all workers in Chicago failed to keep pace with raising expenses despite the city's booming, wartime economy.[65]

The level of resistance to blacks working was high but not completely unexpected. The *Chicago Tribune* of July 15, 1864, reported a conflict between a mob of five hundred Irishmen and a dozen African American workmen laboring on a lumber dock on the Chicago River. Another element of danger on the docks appeared as gangs of Irish workers attempted to monopolize all loading and unloading of lake cargo for the benefit of their own group. In what they perceived to be a matter of survival for their group, Irish workers reacted violently to African Americans as competitors throughout the North, in New York, Boston, Cleveland, Detroit, Brooklyn, and Albany, as well as in Chicago.[66] Elijah Clary could possibly have been among that small group of African American men in July 1864 while his son was fighting his way to glory at Petersburg and the Battle of the Crater two weeks hence.

Yet even with violent resistance and subtle exclusions in employment, exceptions always existed. William Baker, who came to Chicago in 1855, drove an express wagon in 1863.[67] Joseph W. Moore, born in Virginia in 1840, accompanied his father to Chicago, where the patriarch established a restaurant in the West Division. Moore followed in his father's footsteps. The case of Richard Mason Hancock, who lived in the West Division, provided a welcomed exception to the prevailing labor pattern. Born into a free family in North Carolina in 1832, he had the advantage of securing a modicum of education despite the slave state's legal prohibition on such an undertaking. From his father he learned the skills of a carpenter and even served under him as an apprentice. Hancock left North Carolina in the 1850s and arrived in Lockport, New York, where he was fortunate enough to work in an area where his skills as a joiner were recognized. After building canal boats for two years, he mastered "pattern-making, a branch of the trade that require[d] . . . a complete mastery of carpentry . . . higher mathematics, a knowledge of drafting and the constant exercise of the very best judgement. For four years he worked and studied to make himself proficient, and at the end of that period had mastered all the theory and much of the practical details of that branch of the trade."[68]

Arriving in Chicago during the war in 1862, Hancock met the president of the Eagle Works Manufacturing Company, W. Gates, who hired him based on his skills and a belief in the equality of opportunity for all people. At this time, Eagle purportedly housed the largest machine and boiler shops in the region. As supervising foreman of the pattern department of fourteen workers, all white, he initially faced resentment and a three-day strike. With war orders piling up, company president Gates replaced the recalcitrants, and Hancock remained in his position for another decade. During this time, he taught essential machine skills to two other African Americans, who duplicated his feat elsewhere. Interestingly, working at that facility were two men who joined the Twenty-ninth Regiment, USCT.[69] Hancock remained with Eagle Works until the company closed during the depression of 1873–1877.

Later, at the Liberty Iron Works Pattern Shop, where intricate mining equipment was manufactured, Hancock continued to prove his mettle. Sometime during this period of industrial growth, he was identified with the Allis Chalmers Machine Shop.[70] By 1887, Hancock was serving his fifteenth year on the job and was joined by his son, George. Conscious of the need to help others move upward, Hancock successfully encouraged the employment of other black workers in skilled as well as semiskilled positions.

Early on the road to establishing the twentieth century's "Black Metropolis," which required a commercial base for its foundation, the number of African American businesses reached thirty-three, with three being in the area of retail and the remainder in the service sector.[71] This imbalance of highly undercapitalized efforts to those requiring an appreciable outlay of capital and managerial experience signaled a pattern that would continue as consistently as did interest in making money in any avenues that were open.

Astonishingly, African Americans also entered the professions, with the first of two African American physicians, Dr. C. H. Hutchinson, providing medical services at Harrison and Clark streets in the years immediately preceding the Civil War. While his birthplace and other details of his life are unknown, he earned recognition as a medical practitioner and was assigned by the U.S. Army to examine white and black men for their military fitness after hostilities began in 1861. Attesting to the success of his practice, when he died in 1899, he purportedly had amassed considerable wealth. Another professional was the first dentist, New Jersey native James H. Smith, who operated a lucrative practice at Clark and State streets. He studied dentistry in New York and migrated westward sometime during or after the war. He remained in Chicago until the Great Fire of 1871, which no doubt acted as a disincentive, so he then moved southward to Little Rock, Arkansas.[72]

C. Quasi-political Activities

Although still denied political involvement, African Americans adhered to clientage politics, which involved alignment with powerful whites who were sympathetic to repealing the Illinois Black Laws. In 1864, with the aid of the pro-black *Chicago Tribune*, John Jones published his pamphlet on reasons to repeal the Black Laws. *The Black Laws of Illinois and a Few Reasons Why They Should Be Repealed* was an eloquent plea for full citizenship rights. Jones addressed this among his adroit arguments to the lawmakers, most of whom were men of property: "You ought to, and must, repeal those Black Laws for the sake of your own interest, to mention no higher motives. As matters stand now, you cannot prove by us that this or that man ran into a valuable wagonload of merchandise and destroyed it; therefore you are liable to lose hundreds of dollars any day if your wagons are driven by colored men, and you know they are, in great numbers." Just as was the case with Lewis Isbel, an African American could not have testified in court against a white man to protect the property of another one because of the Black Laws. The written word carried weight but equally effective was pressure politicking. Under the auspices of the Repeal Association of Chicago, John Jones traveled to Springfield to lobby for the revocation of the Black Laws.[73]

As part of a well-conceived plan of action, Jones delivered speeches, distributed his pamphlet, and led in the organization of Negro and white groups in every part of the state. Jones was further emboldened by the fact that African American troops were in the field in defense of the nation.[74] Furthermore, he lobbied members of the General Assembly throughout the winter session while the proposed repeal was under consideration. The *Chicago Tribune* reported on his efforts:

> Petitions continue to pour into the General Assembly from all parts of the state for the repeal of the infamous Black Laws and of other laws upon our statute books placing disabilities upon the African American

race in the state. The petitions are signed by a large number of leading men of the state, very many of whom, four years ago, voted against their being stricken from the statute books of Illinois. These Black Laws will be repealed—there is no doubt of it.[75]

On March 3, 1865, triumph came as the final tally showed the Senate voted 13 to 10 for repeal, and the House, 49 to 30. There was more to be achieved, such as gaining voting rights, but this was an important victory, made all the more auspicious because it benefited from wartime protest.

Another form of protest, often overlooked, was the persistence of grass-roots and intellectual interest in emigration to Africa. Martin R. Delany appeared in Chicago in 1863 and lectured to white and black audiences about the benefits to African Americans of returning to Africa instead of remaining in America or giving any consideration to colonization in Haiti or Central America. Dressed resplendently in African attire, Delany looked the part of an African chief as he extolled the advantages of life in complete racial freedom away from whites.[76] Delany's spiritual and emotional attachment to his ancestral homeland complemented his recent on-the-scene visit to West Africa that had led him to produce his influential *Official Report of the Niger Valley Exploring Party*. When studied in conjunction with *The Condition, Elevation, Emigration, and Destiny of the Colored People of the United States Politically Considered* (1852), the case for emigrating to Africa would have appeared appealing to some segments of the city's black community.

IV. WARTIME CHICAGO

Chicago as the home front introduced a different view of the city. Horses galloped around the outskirts of the city on the way to railroad depots to be subsequently delivered to waiting cavalry units. Meat was prepared in abundance for shipment to training and battlefield units. Boots and uniforms were sewn by the hundreds. Enthusiasm was high among loyal Unionists, but this sentiment was not universally shared by all Chicagoans. Hostility toward the war, Lincoln, and all persons of African descent predominated among many Democrats and among white Southerners who had filed into the city during the war.

In response to the medical and dietary needs of wounded troops on the battlefields and in military hospitals, Chicago hosted the first of two Sanitary Fairs in 1863 (the second took place in 1865). Widely supported by all socioeconomic strata of the Unionist population from within Chicago and from environs hundreds of miles away, the fairs raised hundreds of thousands of dollars from private sources. Abraham Lincoln donated an original version of the Emancipation Proclamation for auction that brought in three thousand dollars. Yet, to what extent did African Americans participate in these civilian efforts to support the war? If the example of Boston presented any indication, there probably was involvement, first, by the black churches. Boston's Josephine St. Pierre Ruffin worked with distinction for her race for the U.S. Sanitary Commission in Massachusetts,[77] so it is reasonable to expect the same type of contribution by Mrs. Anna Hudlin, who would distinguish herself after the Great Fire of 1871 as "an angel of the fire," and by Mrs. John Jones, the wife of Chicago's wealthiest and most influential African American. Mary Jones's husband had already lent the use of his office space for recruiting soldiers for the (black) Fifty-fourth Massachusetts Regiment.

Of the thousand or more other black souls in Chicago, of which one half were women, and perhaps one half of that number were adult, some evidence of participation exists. Some non-Chicagoan newcomers also sent donated items. One refugee, a "contraband[,] sent a blanket," while another refugee, from the area around Lake Superior, sent some socks she had knitted for her deceased soldier son, who would no longer need them. Another woman, who had recently come to Chicago from Alabama, donated a white, hand-stitched sheet. She asked earnestly, "may dis yer sheet, what I got wi' my own money, and stitched wi' my own hands, be sold for Massa Linkum's sojers?" It was accepted and her horrendous story of bondage was attached to it; it sold for much more than its actual value.[78]

A. Organization of an African American Regiment

The road to recruitment, enlistment, and service proved long and tortuous. The beginning lay with the African American will to fight for freedom. As early as April 1861, African Americans found themselves rejected by whites who publicly declared that the conflict was an internal matter among members of a superior race—"a white man's war." Abolitionist agitation for black participation as combatants reached its peak in the summer of 1862 with Radical Republican congressional authorization to raise a black army. As the *Chicago Tribune* explained, "blacks are loyal and want to help us. But mean, blind, suicidal prejudice refuses them the privilege."[79] Lincoln then reacted to his party's action with supportive measures. Typically, President Lincoln's thoughts on the matter of African American military participation focused more on practical strategies than on matters of race and emancipation because he feared Northern and border-state hostility to black freedom. "I was in my best judgement," the president said, "driven to the alternative of either surrendering the Union, and with it, the Constitution, or laying strong hand upon the Colored element."[80]

H. Ford Douglas acted immediately with the news that the nation would raise a black army to help end slavery once and for all. Following his pattern of matching his rhetorical and ideological commitments with action, he joined the all-white Ninety-fifth Infantry Regiment from Illinois in July 1862, passing as a white man for several days until discovered and accepted by the white troops.[81] Douglas's desire to strike a blow directly against his race's tormentors came in combat in Tennessee and Louisiana. He wrote to his mentor, Frederick Douglass, that his enthusiasm desired fulfillment and that came with action on the field of battle. "I enlisted six months ago in order to be better prepared to play my part in the great drama of the Negro's redemption. I wanted its drill, its practical details, for mere theory does not make a good soldier. I have learned something of war, for I have seen war in its brightest as well as its bloodiest phase, and yet I have nothing to regret. For since the stern necessities of this struggle have laid bare the naked issue of freedom on one side and slavery on the other—freedom shall have, in the future of this conflict if necessary, my blood as it has in the past my earnest and best words."[82] When his enlistment ended, he recruited black troops on the streets and in the churches of Chicago in 1864. Then he departed Chicago to recruit soldiers from among the ranks of the enslaved in Louisiana and along the Mississippi River.[83]

In the parlance of the period, Africa literally had to save itself while it helped save the Union. In pledging their lives at Quinn Chapel on January 1, 1863, African Americans talked of their willingness "to sustain the true declaration of Jefferson and Adams, recognizing as a self-evident truth the right of all men to the pursuit of happiness." Furthermore, they had committed themselves to not sheathing "the sword of truth until [they had] unfurled [their] banner, dipped in the blood of millions, on the Gulf coast, and proclaim[ed] to the bondman, your chains are severed."[84] Now they were ready to make good on their promise. They wanted to fight and, if necessary, sacrifice their lives, in the cause of liberation. This was the prime motivating factor for many of the enlistees.

In 1863, Governor Richard Yates authorized the raising of a black regiment, to be known as the First Colored Regiment of Illinois Volunteers. Once officially absorbed as part of the U.S. Army, its formal designation became the Twenty-ninth Regiment Illinois Infantry Volunteers, USCT. Before it was organized, however, some potential recruits from Illinois and at least a half dozen from Chicago had already joined the famed Fifty-fourth Massachusetts Infantry.[85] John Jones's downtown establishment on Dearborn

Street served initially as a recruiting office for the Fifty-fourth Massachusetts and possibly also for the Fifth Massachusetts Cavalry and Fifty-fifth Massachusetts Infantry Regiments, before it provided the same function for the Twenty-ninth Illinois.[86] Other black Chicagoans who were eager to fight joined units in other states where they previously had resided, such as the Twenty-third Virginia Infantry, USCT, or the Twenty-sixth New York.

The national pattern in enlistment found state quotas being met by whomsoever the state could recruit in other places. Actively recruiting in Chicago were outsiders Martin R. Delany and John Mercer Langston, men destined for national prominence in the years following the conflict.[87] Once the state of Illinois decided to raise a black regiment, the *Chicago Tribune* preferred keeping outside recruiters from invading Illinois and taking its potential soldiers. One editorial read:

> We are informed that recruiting agents are still in the city picking up colored men for Rhode Island, Connecticut and Michigan regiments, and that from six to fourteen men are recruited daily and shipped East on the night trains. Now, this is clearly in violation of the Governor's proclamation, forbidding the recruiting of men in Illinois for other States, which applies to blacks just the same as whites. Every man thus inveigled out of the State is counted as a part of the quota of the State to which he is sent, and Illinois must make good the loss by taking some other man.[88]

The paper even suggested severe punishments for offenders by the office of the U.S. Provost Marshal. As to the reason for raising a regiment, blacks were advised, "Nothing will redound so much to their benefit thereunder as a race. Let them share in the glory of this great and patriotic State, which now leads the column in the war for the Union and universal Liberty."[89]

Until recently the Twenty-ninth was invisible to most Americans, black and white. As part of Chicago history, it was as though the regiment was swallowed up in time or had never existed.[90] Its existence, however, provided the wellspring of black Chicago's military tradition.[91] Still, of the 1,811 men named in the regiment's roster, less than one-half had an affiliation with Illinois and many fewer with Chicago. An even smaller percentage actually *came from* Chicago.[92] A review of the state roster, along with federal pension records, primarily reviewing the files of Companies B and C, indicate that the portion of Chicagoans was perhaps only 5 to 10 percent. In this study, Chicagoans are defined as persons falling into two categories: residents already in the city, and recent fugitives of several months' or a year's residence who were recruited after reaching the city in the middle of the war and who decided to return to Chicago at the conflict's conclusion.

Recruitment proceeded haphazardly throughout the state. Nearing the end of the fall of 1863, however, Illinois could finally lay claim to its own African American regiment of sorts in the Twenty-ninth Illinois. The first company (of nearly one hundred men) of the proposed thousand-man regiment, designated Company A of the Twenty-ninth, was organized among recruits residing in the southern and central portions of the state of Illinois. The ranks of the unit began to grow in November 1863. By the Christmas season, Companies B, C, and D—units with a heavy concentration of Chicagoans—were being formed.

Imbued with the immediate enthusiasm emanating from the recent issuance of the Emancipation Proclamation, and coupled with a lingering, generational hatred of slavery and racial proscription, the African American community actively recruited soldiers from within its own swelling population. Recruiters included black abolitionists Henry O. Wagoner, John Jones, Lewis Isbel, and lesser lights, such as Civil War veteran H. Ford Douglas, who had passed as a white man to fight for the emancipation of his people earlier in the war. An examination of the Muster-In Rolls of these latter companies indicate that H. Ford Douglas had successful face-to-face contacts with at least two dozen men.[93] One can imagine how persuasive he must have been, since he had announced himself rhetorically as an enemy of slavery before the war, then proven himself as its actual destroyer. To fill the ranks of Company B, he personally recruited the Easley brothers, Willis and David, as well as Rodney Long, William Alexander, James A. Brown, James H. Smith, William Brown, Jefferson Day, George Brown, Willis A. Bogart, James D. Hawkins, William McClanahan, Joseph Ross, Robert Gregory, Archibald M. Gaity, Charles Scott, and others. The same muster-in records show the success of middle-aged civic activist Lewis Isbel as he persuaded twenty-year-olds Arthur Johnson, Louis Lee, James Lowe, Henry Rosier, Richard Robertson, James Bird, James Hamlin, and others to join the crusade against slavery.

Typical of those with antebellum roots in Chicago were Private David Easley and Sergeant Willis Easley of Company C, who enlisted into the Twenty-ninth Regiment in December 1863. Upon his enlistment, Willis described himself as a "schoolboy."[94] Among those who arrived during the war from the war-torn South were Louis Clary and Frank McAllister. Charles Griffin, who was born in Cleveland, arrived from Canada and enlisted (Figure 14). There were basically young men in the regiment; their average age stood at twenty-two years.[95] War in all its vicissitudes awaited them, most likely in the forms of injury, hardship, and death. Occupationally, their talents and training (or lack thereof, because of the restrictions of the slave

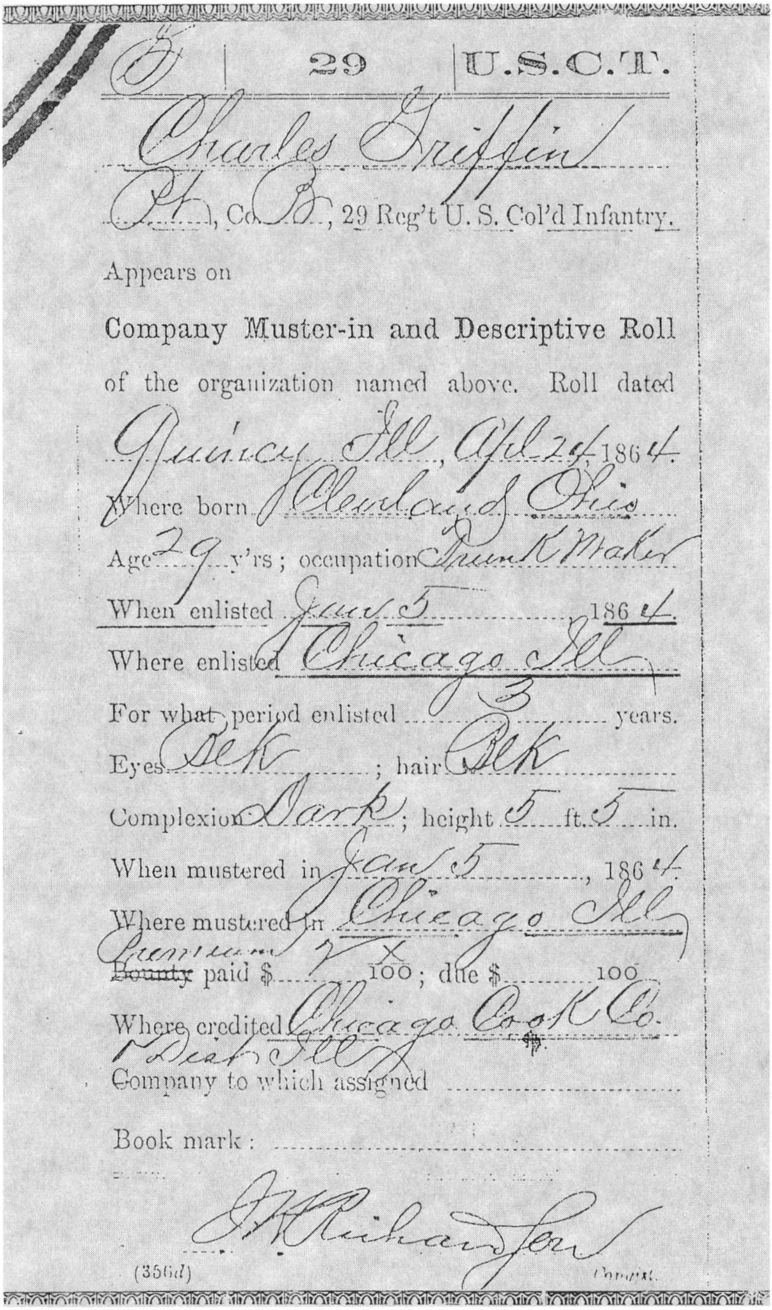

29 | U.S.C.T.

Charles Griffin

Pt., Co. B, 29 Reg't U. S. Col'd Infantry.

Appears on

Company Muster-in and Descriptive Roll

of the organization named above. Roll dated

Quincy Ill, Apl 24, 1864.

Where born Cleveland Ohio

Age 29 y'rs; occupation Trunk Maker

When enlisted Jan 5 1864.

Where enlisted Chicago Ill

For what period enlisted 3 years.

Eyes Blk; hair Blk

Complexion Dark; height 5 ft. 5 in.

When mustered in Jan 5, 1864.

Where mustered in Chicago Ill

Premium ~~Bounty~~ paid $ 100; due $ 100

Where credited Chicago Cook Co. 1 Dist Ill

Company to which assigned

Book mark:

J. H. Richardson

(356d) Copyist.

Fig. 14. Enlistment paper for Charles Griffin.
Courtesy of Alyce C. Griffin.

regimen) varied. In the main, they had been either slave laborers in bondage or manual laborers in quasi-freedom. Some had mastered the skills of barbering; some had been engaged in service activities; a few here and there had been cabinet makers, hostlers, a stone mason, boot makers, blacksmiths, teamsters, jockeys, and members of the maritime workforce on the Mississippi River system or on the Great Lakes. Almost none were well educated, and most lacked the rudiments of an education. Two remarkable exceptions were Sergeant William McCoslin and Willis A. Bogart—both men wrote articulately and with a depth of understanding beyond the ordinary. Nativity varied, with one man claiming England as his birthplace (Bogart) and another Mexico. Some escaped to freedom before the war, and others had escaped because of the war and the turmoil it brought to the slave regime. In each case, these men had exhibited courage beyond that which they demonstrated just to survive in bondage. Family ties might or might not have been existent.

One can only imagine the persuasive conversations of the day that the African American wing of abolitionist Chicago used to induce enlistments. As to motivation, what greater impulse than love of kin and hatred of the system that condemned them to perpetual bondage? Moreover, many of the enlistees remembered their personal humiliations and deprivations only too well. If whites, North and South, had fought for duty and honor, respectively, would not community pressure from the city's black churches and other associational influences have been just as strong an incentive for African Americans?

Yet there were many reasons for resisting enlistment.[96] The threat of immediate execution of any surrendering black in Northern blue obviously worked as a disincentive. In addition, the fact that Chicago's employers offered true remuneration rendered the city even more attractive to people who had previously labored at the master's will. Daily accommodation to Northern racism and slights, moreover, left a bitter taste in the black palate, translating in some individuals to an ambivalence for the Northern cause.

On the other hand, a recent study of an all-black Ohio regiment gives some insight as to nonmaterial incentives. The historian Versalle F. Washington has postulated that recent freedmen sought to test their freedom as well as to fight their old masters, while free people of color sought a chance to prove their worthiness for full citizenship rights.[97] Of those who answered the call, it is difficult to impossible to ascertain their sentiments precisely because of the absence of their recorded thoughts on the subject. No doubt, some were probably lured by the hundred-dollar county and local bounty that awaited enlistees as well as the promise of full pay, equal to that paid white soldiers.[98] Higher amounts attracted Henry Richardson, a former

Kentucky slave, whose actions in joining Company B led to his receiving a four-hundred-dollar bounty package.[99] Some would have been motivated simply by the opportunity to seek retribution against whites. Last, the desire in young men's hearts for adventure and for tackling a challenge also had to have played a part in inducing men to serve. As to whether they felt they were fulfilling a civic duty, these men lacked citizenship standing and were held in contempt by the majority of their fellow Illinoisans—thus the question assumes a certain absurdity. Beyond the unreasonableness of expecting them to discharge a civic obligation when their race was still in bondage, their motivation revolved around a racial commitment aimed at survival of self and kin.

Other active recruiters were the members of the officers' corps that would lead the black soldiers of the regiment into battle. Assuming commands that other white officers had scorned along racial grounds, the Twenty-ninth's white officers also faced the problem of extraordinary punishments from Confederate forces, ranging from personal humiliation to summary execution. Nonetheless, they wanted to serve both the cause of the Union and that of demonstrating the racial competence and bravery of African American troops in battle. Accomplishing the latter meant winning the trust of their black troops, not an easy task to accomplish given the hostility of most white Northerners to African Americans in general.[100]

The regiment's commander, Lieutenant Colonel Charles A. Bross, had a proven record as a combat veteran from his days on the battlefields of the western theater with the Eighty-eighth Illinois Infantry Regiment. Bross's politics belied his commitment to the abolition of slavery. Although a supporter of Democratic senator Stephen A. Douglas, who was lukewarm to emancipation, Bross allied himself with the city's abolitionist coterie during the war. That group included his brother, William, the editor of the pro-Union and staunchly Republican *Chicago Tribune*. Hector H. Aiken, age twenty-four, assumed command of Company B based on his wartime experience with Chicago's Board of Trade Battery. Illinois native James W. Brockaway assumed command over Company C.

Once these officers and other recruiters successfully recruited to the initially satisfactory level of six hundred men, the Twenty-ninth moved to Chicago on April 28, 1864, from its training base at Quincy, Illinois. There, the men received their issuance of military clothing, were drilled in squad- and company-level formations, and were introduced to military discipline as part of their daily routine. The half-filled regiment arrived in Chicago and remained at the Soldiers' Rest at the site of Camp Douglas on the city's southern stretch of lakefront for a day or so before it continued toward the eastern theater of battle. At a Chicago ceremony hailing the regiment's

Fig. 15. Illinois soldier, Union Army.
Illinois State Historical Library.

formation, abolitionists exhorted the troops to remember the Fort Pillow (Tennessee) massacre of surrendering black troops.[101] Presumably, black Chicago also turned out and spoke to the soldiers of sacrifice and reminded them about what needed destroying in order that their group could live in freedom. Step by step, the men of the Twenty-ninth were becoming more a part of America's army of liberation (Figure 15).

The men then traveled by train to the East and on May 1, 1864, arrived in Washington, D.C. In what had to represent the experience of a lifetime (up to that point), they confronted the exhilaration of freedom, technological thrills, speed and power defying that of nature, and of course, the impressive aura of wearing the uniform of the soldier. One African American soldier left a written record for posterity of the regiment's movement to the East and its battlefield activities. This simple action defied a priori reasoning in regard to African American ability in general, and these black Chicagoans in particular. Later published in an African American religious publication, his reflections on this journey into the unknown tell us much about the soldiers' experience:

> At 11 o'clock M., we started en route for the East, tolerably well rested, and in generally good spirits, feeling proud of the treatment we have received [from whites once they reached Pittsburgh] being the same if not better than some of the white troops received. Our trip over the mountains was a new thing to some of our Western boys, who had never been away from home. It seemed to interest them very much; crossing the mountains was quite an undertaking, especially when we went through the tunnels. Nothing of a great importance transpired until we arrived in Baltimore . . . [where] we were treated with respect by all the citizens.[102]

Baltimore's notorious and rabid pro-Southern street thugs such as the Plug Uglies and others must have been asleep or held at bay by the military authorities on this occasion.

Once in the Washington area, the regiment was able to reach its pre-scribed regimental strength, with a complement of one thousand men. In addition, recruits continued to arrive from Illinois and from the surrounding greater Washington area. Accordingly, most of the men who would make up the remaining companies, F, G, H, and I, were natives of Maryland and Virginia. Most important, training began and the men settled into camp life. Military organization required the appointment of sergeants from within the soldiers' ranks as noncommissioned officers. The authority for this selection fell to the white officers who themselves held commissions. Despite the racist character of the military, the noncommissioned officers possessed the same authority that white men held over black men. Designed to facilitate the decentralization of command authority throughout the Union army, the uniform role of the sergeant, whether black or white, cushioned conflict between the officers' corps and the men in the ranks. Sergeants assumed the responsibilities of training, disciplining, and providing for the welfare of the men. Additionally, acting as intermediaries between the African American soldiers and the white officers' corps, sergeants such as Easley, McCoslin, Brown, Long, and McKenney paved a new path for African American leadership.

As to what was expected of these soldiers, Colonel Thomas Wentworth Higginson wrote of the First South Carolina Volunteers he commanded:

> It needs but a few days to show the absurdity of distrusting the military availability of these people. They have quite as much average compre-

hension as whites of the need of the thing, as much courage (I doubt not), as much previous knowledge of the gun, and, above all, a readiness of ear and imitation, which, for purposes of drill, counterbalances any defect of mental training. To learn the drill, one does not need a set of college professors; one wants a squad of eager, active, pliant school boys; and the more childlike these pupils are the better. There is no trouble about the drill; they will surpass whites in that. As to camp-life, they have little to sacrifice; they are better fed, housed, and clothed than ever before in their lives . . . , and they appear to have few inconvenient vices.[103]

When Civil War historian Bruce Catton described General Ferrero's command, to which the Twenty-ninth belonged, he observed the unique qualities the African Americans introduced generally into camp life and soldiering. The white soldiers yearned of home, hearth, and the warmth of the past. In contrast, the black troops looked toward the future as they envisioned a freedom dreamed of and suddenly within their collective grasp. When reduced to musical expression, "His dreams were apocalyptic, not to be expressed in ordinary words," Catton wrote.

So when the colored troops met by the campfire to sing—and it was their favorite way to spend the evening—they sang made-up, spur-of-the-moment songs, which had never existed before either in words or in music, songs which grew out of the fire and the night and the dreams and hopes which hovered between fire and night forever. All of the colored troops were led by white men, and these white men listened, fascinated, to the campfire singing, and when they wrote about it they tried to tell why it moved them so deeply. . . . Most of these men were straight from the plantation. On many matters their ignorance was absolute. Yet they were men without doubts, and always their faith reached out to the future.[104]

These men, without doubt, were transforming themselves through their dreams, hopes, and personal will into men with power, the source of all human agency.

B. Battlefield Participation and Experience in Combat

The military service and combat history of any regiment can be viewed in many ways, one being the number of major battles, along with skirmishes, in which a unit participated. Regimental high points for the Twenty-ninth came in two major engagements, the first occurring on July 30, 1864, before Petersburg at the Crater, and the second on April 8 and 9, 1865, as part of the Appomattox Campaign. Casualty figures can be used as an indicator of the soldiers' contribution to the successful conclusion of a war. So can hard marches that maneuver troops in position to counter enemy movements and influence enemy strategy. "Although the Civil War has been portrayed as the first modern or industrial war in which machinery such as locomotives and rifled muskets or ironclad warships and naval torpedoes were engaged," wrote Eric T. Dean, "the infantryman in this war moved from one place to another mainly on foot. He sometimes covered ten and twenty miles a day, or even more in the case of a forced march when troops had to be maneuvered quickly to come to the aid of embattled and endangered comrades or to defend or seize key positions."[105] It was the Twenty-ninth's hard march after Richmond's fall that positioned it in front of the Army of Northern Virginia at Appomattox and propelled it into glory.

The importance to these various components of the war effort cannot be underestimated. Miller wrote in this vein: "Blacks deserved to be appreciated for their actual contributions to the war, not just their casualties or conduct under fire. Blacks were in the army because every man was needed in the routinely casualty-intensive operations, so their use in more than the secondary roles, mostly wagon guarding and hard labor, they had held before Petersburg was inevitable."[106] In evaluating the contributions of the Twenty-ninth Illinois, we should count as potentially important all engagements, sieges, wartime injuries, illnesses, and noncombat wounds of the soldiers. These personal costs demonstrated the extent to which the unit served in the nation's defense and ultimate triumph. Often the words of the combatants tell their stories more poignantly, for they display spirit, dedication, and courage in their sacrifice of health, body, and life.

The Twenty-ninth received its first training and drills with arms at Camp Casey, outside Washington, D.C., in May 1864 in the area around Union-controlled Alexandria, Virginia. The men of the Twenty-ninth were provided with their basic equipment and their main instrument of combat, the .58-caliber Springfield rifled musket. Some rifle training followed, but it was farther south in Virginia where the realities of war introduced the regiment to the conflict's fullest gore. General U. S. Grant and his Union forces had begun what was to be known as the bloody Battles of the Wilderness.[107] Promising to fight all summer if necessary to capture Richmond and thereby defeat the Confederacy, Grant continually moved his force of more than a hundred thousand men southeasterly as he sought a victory.

The Twenty-ninth Illinois's first engagement came on May 15, 1864, as part of the James River Campaign, which lasted from May 4, 1864, through

June 12, 1864. Confederate troops were encountered near Chancellorsville as the unit moved from the Rapidan River to the James River. At Cold Harbor, the regiment arrived while fighting was taking place but was held in reserve and never employed.

Having completed this phase of their military preparation, the regiment left Camp Casey permanently on May 31, 1864, and took water transport on the steamer *George Weems* to White House Landing, Virginia, arriving on June 2, 1864. Organized now as part of the Second Brigade, Fourth Division, Ninth Army Corps, they were placed under the leadership of General Ambrose E. Burnside, with General George G. Meade commanding the Army of the Potomac. The order of the day required the construction of fortifications, and it was in performing this work that Private Frank McAllister, Company C, injured his back when a section of timber fell on him. He suffered with bruised legs, leaving him with a limp. Continuously experiencing pain, rheumatism, and incontinence, he was discharged in March 1865.[108] Many more men of the Twenty-ninth would fall to injury and illness as they moved toward their rendezvous with destiny at the famous Battle of the Crater. Indeed, the effects of life under slavery had already extracted a price from some of the soldiers and would continue to do so on others after their service concluded. As to their tendencies to suffer from certain illnesses, such as those associated with their pulmonary systems, other African American soldiers in a similar situation were described thus:

> In speaking of the military qualities of the African Americans, I should add, that the only point where I am disappointed is one I have never seen raised by the most incredulous newspaper critics,—namely, their physical condition. To be sure they often look magnificently to my gymnasium-trained eye; and I always like to observe them when bathing,—such splendid muscular development, set off by that smooth coating of adipose tissue which makes them, like the South-Sea islanders, appear even more muscular than they are. Their skins are also of finer grain than those of whites, the surgeons say, and certainly are smoother and far more free from hair. But their weakness is pulmonary; pneumonia and pleurisy are their besetting ailments; they are easily made ill,—and easily cured. . . . Guard duty injures them more than whites, apparently; and double-quick movements, in choking dust, set them coughing badly. But then it is to be remembered that this is their sickly season, from January to March, and that their healthy season will come in summer, when the whites break down.[109]

Receiving new orders, the Twenty-ninth Illinois then marched from Old Church Tavern on June 12, 1864, and arrived at the headquarters of the

Army of the Potomac on June 18, 1864, and performed guard duties in a rear area. While they marched on, Private Cato Flowers, Company C, died on June 13, 1864, of smallpox at Claremont General Hospital in Alexandria, Virginia. The regiment manned positions around the Petersburg perimeter within rifle pits and endured static trench duty until June 27, 1864, when they moved five miles to the rear to Prince George Court House. They reached their destination on that same evening and then assumed readiness positions until a planned offensive to break through Confederate defenses on July 30.[110] Once again, Sergeant William McCoslin's description provided a firsthand account of what the men of the regiment were experiencing:

> Although the men were very tired, they were anxious to give fight to their enemies; but on arriving at the front, the programme being changed, we were ordered to rest until further orders, which was a godsend to us. We had two days' rest, and then were ordered to the front, to take a position in the rifle pits. Here we expected to see the rebels face to face, but in this we were disappointed.
>
> At daybreak the next morning we were relieved and marched to the rear to rest. We are and have been building forts and rifle pits which we consider healthier than going into the fight; but, when ordered, we are ready and willing to fight.
>
> Our regiment is not in good fighting trim at present, on account of an insufficiency of officers. In other respects they are all right. We are expecting every day to be sent to the front; but it is ordered otherwise, probably for the best. Our regiment has built two forts and about three miles of breastworks, which shows that we are not idle, and that we are learning to make fortifications, whether we learn to fight or not.
>
> We are now lying in camp, about a mile and a half from the city, resting a day or two. It is quite a treat for the boys to get a rest after working day and night, four hours on and four hours off. We have worked in that way for eight or ten days, without stopping. But my opinion now is, that the laboring work is nearly over, so that we will have nothing to do but watch the rebels.
>
> There is heavy firing of artillery and small arms every night from both sides, which sounds beautiful to us.[111]

In June 1864, the Union high command approved a daring plan for the Wilderness campaign that would involve the Twenty-ninth in the biggest battle of the regiment's young life. After weeks of static warfare around the strategic city of Petersburg, the plan called for digging an underground shaft, some 511 feet in length, under Confederate positions into which explosions would be ignited to blow a breach in the rebel lines. Grant's approval of the plan was tempered somewhat by his prior experience at Vicksburg, where a similar mine explosion had failed to produce the desired results.[112] Between June 25 and July 23, white troops from a Pennsylvania regiment that included many miners dug their tunnel. Then, for another four days, they planted their explosives, totaling eight thousand pounds of gunpowder. The date of July 30, 1864, was chosen for the explosion, combined with a full assault of Union troops including the Twenty-ninth. This "Battle of the Mine," or as it became better known, the Battle of the Crater, became famous, or infamous, because of the nature of the fighting and the defeat that occurred. The battle was of great importance, for once the Union troops could break through the enemy's lines, the possibility of moving on to the Confederate capital, Richmond, loomed.[113]

Initially, black soldiers of the Fourth Division, Ninth Army Corps, under the command of Brigadier General Edward Ferrero, were chosen to lead the assault because of their numbers, freshness, and perceived competence as fighting men. For his part, Ferrero's commander, Major General Burnside, had confidence in their abilities and wanted to use them. They eagerly began their training, although Drinkard has questioned whether they were actually being trained specifically for this assignment, properly or not. Hicken wrote that the soldiers' response to being chosen was translated into a triumphant song: "We-e looks li-ike me-en a-marchin' on—We looks li-ike men-er-war."[114]

Importantly, their role was diminished at this crucial point as General Meade introduced a mix of racial and military politics. The military hierarchy feared heavy casualties among the black troops, approximating Grant's other losses in recent weeks involving white troops. Abolitionists, they feared, might charge that African Americans were being used as cannon fodder. As a result, exhausted and untrained white troops from other regiments who were part of Brigadier General James Ledlie's Second Division won the honor by virtue of the draw of a straw.

Finally, the day of the explosion arrived. After a delay with a bad fuse, ignition came, and "the ground rumbled and shook as though angered in an earthquake. A mass of earth, shaped like an inverted cone, rose two hundred feet. Forked tongues of flame lifted through this earthen upheaval." The destructive force of the detonation created a crater that measured 30 feet in depth, 150 to 200 feet in length, and 60 feet in width. "As the dust cleared away, the troops stared at a frightful scene. . . . In the debris were men who were buried up to their necks, others to their waists, still others, with only their legs and arms protruding. To add to the hellishness came the roar of 110 federal cannon and 50 mortars."[115] When the battle commenced, the first white units became confused and entered the crater instead of moving around its perimeter. Entering this massive, devastated arena of death, they tasted the horrors of war at their worst. Confederates regrouped and counterattacked the Yankees trapped in the crater.

Although the Twenty-ninth did not join in the initial assault, the regiment did play a major role subsequently after it was committed to the battle. This occurred several hours after the attack began, around 9 a.m., when orders arrived for the all-black Twenty-third, Twenty-eighth, and Twenty-ninth to advance. Colonel Bross led the Twenty-ninth in the front of the column. As described by Andreas, "after the explosion of the mine beneath the principal fort . . . with Colonel Bross at their head, [he] gallantly led [his regiment forward]. Five color bearers were shot down, and then the Colonel, seizing the flag, carried it to the top of the works, and planted it on the parapet . . . and when striving to extricate his faithful and heroic men, who gallantly followed their beloved leader to the 'jaws of death,' he was stricken down by a ball, and died without a groan, leaving behind an unsullied name and a record of which his relatives and friends are deservedly proud."[116] At the peak of this phase of the battle, Bross had exalted his troops from the parapet with "forward, my brave boys." More Confederates troops arrived, swarming the Union troops who were trapped in the crater, and shooting and bayoneting the African Americans with alacrity and viciousness.

Many other acts of bravery were recalled by the veterans who fought at the Battle of the Crater. "Alabama soldiers who had fought their way to the lip of the crater, and were firing down into the center of the milling soldiers, were surprised to note that not all of the colored soldiers fell back. The Alabamians quickly concluded that the white Federal officers below must have been chosen upon the basis of courage, for both they and their colored subordinates fought 'with desperation.'"[117] Union soldier John Bird stated that he remembered the action of "that terrible charge." He recalled: "[I] was in the charge . . . at the mine explosion [surviving basically unscathed, and] saw [fellow combatant John Scott] fall." When Bird saw him after the battle, Scott "had his left arm taken off, or at least it was all shot to pieces and his right index finger had been shot and cut off, and he had a severe wound in the muscles and fleshy part of the right arm not far from the right shoulder." Sergeant Rodney Long of Company B received serious injuries to his left leg, the result of a shell exploding near him on July 30, 1864, at the crater. He was captured and imprisoned until February 1865, at which time he had to be hospitalized. He suffered a permanent disability. Private Peter Williams of Company C joined Long as a prisoner of war, being held at Libby and Andersonville prisons until his escape after the fall of Richmond in April 1865.[118]

Amidst powder, smoke, and fire the battle raged, and another sergeant, Jefferson Gash, led his men from Company D forward. He suffered a concussion and fell to the ground as a shell fragment and its force hit him squarely on his right side. While he was down but still fighting, he and a rebel soldier began "clubbing each other." The enemy soldier "jumped upon him, with his feet injuring his back, receiving such a strain, that he [never] recovered from it." The damage to the right side of his body included his eye and extended to his shoulder and elbow; subsequent years brought a shrinking of his arm as he aged. Private Richard Barbour also advanced up a hill and "was struck on the head by the rebels—some rebel struck him with the butt of a gun across his temple and knocked him senseless and he fell back in a ditch, and he was in Hosp., for a long time after that."[119]

Many other casualties resulted. The resistance of the Confederates continued to stiffen, and soon the Confederates were winning the day. With the ranks of the Union soldiers devastated, a retreat was ordered. Union losses totaled 540 lives in this failed assault, with 3,300 wounded or missing. From the Union's attacking forces, 9 officers and 275 enlisted men were listed as killed, wounded, or missing. As mentioned, the Twenty-ninth's commanding officer, popular Chicagoan Colonel Bross, was killed in action along with 36 of his men; 7 were missing in action. The historian Glatthaar summarized the losses of the African American troops: "In total, the black commands suffered more than 40 percent of the fatalities and 35 percent of the casualties despite a preponderance of white soldiers in the engagement."[120]

As General Burnside reported on the debacle, the standard charge arose that black troops could not execute their combat assignments with valor and thoroughness. The general wrote in response that "not all of the colored troops retired; some held the pits behind which they had advanced, severely checking the enemy until they were nearly killed." He spoke of the Twenty-ninth, but the fault lay with the command leadership, as posterity has shown.[121]

Back in Chicago, the city exhibited pride in the regiment. They focused not on the defeat, but in the courage the regiment displayed under fire. Bross, especially, was heralded for his sacrifice in the cause of equality and humanity. In a letter to Colonel Bross's widow, one soldier, English-born Willis A. Bogart of Company B, wrote:

> Respected Madam: You will excuse this letter, that I pen to you, but as I am one of the soldiers brought up under his discipline, I deem it my duty to address you. Allow me to say, that although a colored man, a private in the 29th, I found in Colonel Bross a friend, one in whom every member of the regiment placed the utmost confidence, for, and with whom, each one would help defend the country to the end. Yes, I can say with truth, they would willingly die by his side. . . . The 29th,

with its leader gone, feels there is no such commander under the sun, to lead it forward and cheer it up. He was loved by every one, because he was a friend to every one. . . . Weep not for him who was one of God's chosen ones, who tried to deliver his people out of Egypt.[122]

What followed was an additional eight months of siege after the Union failed again to defeat General Robert E. Lee's Army of Northern Virginia. Overall, siege operations around Petersburg, Virginia, translated into daily duty in the trenches between June 19, 1864, and April 3, 1865. This also meant dry, hot weather and malaria during the summer, and rain, cold, and cold-weather illnesses during the winter. For Sergeant William McKenney, it was a case of exaggerated misery. He recalled that "from the 27th M[ar]ch 1865 until Petersburg was taken and Lee surrendered it was raining most of the time and we were marching and fighting in that rain most of the time. I know I had rheumatism at that time—and have had it ever since." Another soldier, Moses Conley, recalled the siege: "We were greatly exposed to rain and bad weather and Garrett contracted rheumatism and suffered from it a great deal. He was also disabled a part of the time by piles which was brought on by lifting in building breastworks. . . . I know he was a good soldier [even though] he was a musician, but he did duty with the rest of the boys."[123]

The health of the men suffered, and the pension records indicate that warfare afflictions persisted long afterward, severely limiting their life chances after the war. The regimental surgeon wrote: "Many persons had died with lung diseases who might have lived longer if they had not been enlisted, and who might have given indication of their unfitness on a physical examination." Private Moses Nelson of Company D fit this medical profile. He suffered from lung problems, dying after the war and leaving five children and a widow who was unable to care for them. His employer and patron during the war, a Galesburg, Illinois, army officer who met him in Arkansas and brought him North, commented thus: "When he came north he would catch cold easily just as any other southern darkey would."[124]

Life in the army under siege conditions meant daily and nightly sniper fire from Confederate sharpshooters. The Union response was relentless artillery barrages into Petersburg, which brought much comfort to the Union troops. During the interludes, time was found for religion, educational instruction, and recreation, such as the new sport of baseball. General orders allowed the men of the Twenty-ninth to worship as they saw fit, consistent with their West African heritage and American experiences. Drinkard writes, "By order of Brigadier General William Birney, Commander of the Second Division, to which the 29th belonged as of December 1864, the men were not to be interfered with in their 'peculiar' modes of religious worship. Time was given them for their meetings before tattoo (at 8:00 p.m.) and on Sundays after inspection whenever possible."[125]

As to the spirit of black soldiers, the famed Union leader of black troops, Colonel Thomas Wentworth Higginson, observed, "I learned to think that we abolitionists had underrated the suffering produced by slavery among Negroes, but had overrated the demoralization. Or rather, we did not know the religious temperament of the Negroes had checked the demoralization." As to education, the rudiments of an elementary-level education purportedly were offered through reading, writing, and spelling. All of the Twenty-fifth Corps was to benefit from this opportunity. Yet realistically, under battle-field conditions, academic instruction ranked tertiary to combat duties and military training.[126] A random survey of the signatory skills of veterans of the Twenty-ninth on documents indicated that many of the Southern-born and recently emancipated troops had not mastered writing and, it can be assumed, reading.

Although siege activities often seemed to be filled with meaningless exertion and boredom, having a Union army numbering in the tens of thousands camped permanently within striking distance of the Confederate capital of Richmond marked a major turn in the war. Grant had forced the Confederacy to remain on the defensive on a daily basis instead of in a seasonal pattern, and Lee felt the stress immensely.[127] Of the combative engagements in which the Twenty-ninth was active, the regiment struggled in the middle of August 1864 to control the Weldon Railroad located south of Petersburg. Consistent with General Grant's strategy, all of the enemy's avenues of communication, transportation, and supply had to interdicted to bring the campaign and the war to a close. Thus, firefights were common. In the meantime, the struggle with the natural elements continued without abatement. The Twenty-ninth was near Oakland Station, Virginia, when Private Isaac Foster came upon his comrade, Hardin Harris, supine on the ground. He recalled:

> Near Oakland Station, Virginia while on a forced march he received a sunstroke while crossing on a pontoon bridge across the James River, I remember the circumstances well as I had been on a raid and was just returning to my command when I saw the claimant lying on the ground frothing at the mouth and the comrades told me he had received a sunstroke. I remember giving him a drink of water at the time. I remember the remainder of his service claimant suffered considerably with shortness of breath, pains in the heart and dizziness.[128]

The brigade's wagoner, James H. Rosell, also remembered Harris's sunstroke:

"I was 3rd duty Sergeant of the Co[mpany] and afterwards wagon master of the Brigade. I was with the command when the claimant was overcome by solar heat (sunstroke) we were on the march from Petersburg V[irgini]a about the month of August 1864."[129]

The regiment then fought at Poplar Grove Church on September 29 and 30 and October 1, 1864. There, Private William Watkins sustained serious right leg and ankle injuries after he was run over by Union artillerymen pulling a cannon out of position along a road. He was hospitalized, and the bodily damage he suffered contributed to "a shortened span of life." Also, while the regiment was halted at Poplar Grove Church, a three-hundred-pound, seventy-one-year-old soldier, Private Jesse Vaughn, physically broke down because of "scrupola" and rheumatism. His discharge from the service was immediate, but his health ills only increased in the five years before his death in 1869.[130]

Further action followed at Boydton Plank Road, and then the regiment prepared to settle in for the winter. While stationed at Hatcher's Run, between October 27 and 28 as well as in the spring of 1865, they sporadically encountered Confederate forces. Sergeant Jefferson Day of Company B remembered, "We had no fight [battle] at Hatcher's Run, only a slight skirmish, but there was considerable excitement about them [rebels] for a time—and we made all preparations for a battle." Regarding the regiment's performance up to this point, before the breakout in late March 1865, their commanding officer, Brigadier General Ferrero, saw fit to write: "I am very much pleased with the conduct of the colored troops."[131]

A major administrative reassignment in December 1864 placed the Twenty-ninth into the war's first all-black army corps—the Twenty-fifth. Between nine thousand and sixteen thousand African American fighting men in cavalry, artillery, and infantry units participated as part of this black phalanx, which was commanded by General Benjamin F. Butler.[132] This army of liberation combined with twenty-four thousand white troops; together, they formed the Twenty-fifth Corps—the reconstituted Army of the James.

By the end of the winter of 1864–1865, the nadir of the Confederacy was reached. Grant prepared his forces for an all-out assault to crush Lee's army once and for all. After enduring the hardships of the eight-month siege of Petersburg until March 28, 1865, the Twenty-ninth advanced to Varina Landing, Virginia. Joining other units of a large combined force, on March 28 the Twenty-ninth Illinois formed a skirmish line to push back the Confederates in the final assault against Petersburg. On the evening of March 29, the regiment advanced into the ranks of Confederate Battery Number Forty-five, and the Confederates fell back without firing a shot. The rout of the once-vaunted Army of Northern Virginia was now under way. Union forces within the Army of the Potomac and the Army of the James now poured past the siege lines and took Petersburg on April 3, 1865, officially at three o'clock in the morning.

Miles away, General Robert E. Lee abandoned the Confederate capital at Richmond within four hours, hoping or assuming that Grant and Meade's armies would follow a familiar Union pattern and remain in place in conquered real estate.[133] Such a static posture would afford Lee the opportunity to move the remnants of the Army of Northern Virginia westward to link up with Confederate forces under General Joseph Johnston. Instead, Grant ordered an unrelenting pursuit of Lee's retreating army. As an integral part of that force, the Twenty-ninth was on the verge of experiencing an event of historic proportions as it now pursued Lee as a detached part of the Twenty-fifth Corps, Army of the James. Now assigned to Woodward's Third Brigade, the regiment engaged in a forced march, covering the phenomenal distance of ninety-six miles in three days. Instead of moving directly behind Lee's forces, Union forces moved consistently forward but parallel in a flanking movement. Grant "pressed [his forces] forward relentlessly in two infantry columns and with Sheridan's cavalry harassing the retreating Confederates at every step,"[134] the strenuous drain of a forced march took its toll on the men of the Twenty-ninth. While forming their lines, Company C's wagoner, William Armstrong, received serious battlefield injuries. As described in one report: "While in pursuit of General Lee's army during the first days of April AD 1865 the said Armstrong was injured while in the line of duty as a soldier and as a wagoner by being caught between two wagons where his leg was crushed."[135]

The Union plan called for this amassed armed force to block Lee permanently and either engage his army or force its surrender. The Union cavalry under General Philip H. Sheridan's overall command intensified its pursuit to a point where the horse soldiers intercepted and frequently blocked portions of Lee's fleeing army until infantry could overtake the Confederates. At Farmville, fast-moving Union horsemen denied Lee's ragged and hungry band a trainload of food, shoes, and other supplies. Desperate, the Confederate general continued westward. Then, General George Armstrong Custer's cavalry beat Lee's forces to needed food at the Appomattox train station, capturing boxcars of supplies. As daring as Custer's movements were, his force would not be able to resist an infantry counterattack. According to Catton, in the overall upcoming battle, "cavalry alone could not bar the way very long, but if the blue infantry came up in time then it would be taps and dipped flags and good-by forever for Lee's army."[136]

Onward marched the Twenty-ninth and other infantry units until they reached Appomattox. Forming part of an early skirmish line at the sleepy

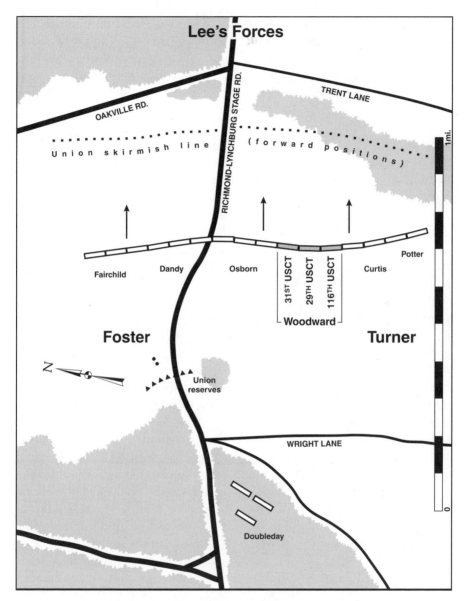

Fig. 16. Map of Appomattox Campaign, final formation;
note three USCT regiments under Woodward's command.

hamlet at the foothills of the Blue Ridge Mountains, the Twenty-ninth met the Confederates, advanced one mile following regimental skirmishers, and pushed the Confederates back until the two opposing forces faced off within one to two thousand feet. Regimental losses at this time were three men dead and three wounded.

The Union's final battlefield formation included in its center the Twenty-ninth Illinois, along with two other USCT regiments, the 116th from Kentucky and the Thirty-first from New York. On the right and left flanks, thousands of soldiers in the white regiments maneuvered into formation. As Lee looked forward from his position, he could feel only total futility, as "the blue lines grew longer and longer, and rank after rank came into view, as if there was no end to them."[137] Lee's final response was to send out four flags of surrender (Figure 16).

Significantly, the regiment's Civil War combat role ended on a most auspicious note. The Twenty-ninth had fulfilled its mission in its pursuit of Robert E. Lee's Army of Northern Virginia, although at Appomattox, they had made no full assault on his lines. Nonetheless, the Twenty-ninth had proven its mettle. What soldier would not have been proud to lay claim to having faced Lee down, in full battle formation, on that morning of April 9, 1865?[138] Although some white officers felt forced to constrain the cheers and shouts of their men, this exhilarating moment must have been a transformative one for the individual soldiers. Among the black troops, we can only assume that the experience affirmed self, group, and a future destined to be lived in freedom. In the ranks of the 116th Regiment, USCT, positioned immediately to the south of the Twenty-ninth's position, an officer recorded his views of the day: "Our brigade celebrated the event by firing volleys of musketry in the air. Officers hugged each other with joy. . . . [T]he men in that long line threw their caps upwards until they looked like a flock of crows. From wood and dale came the sound of cheers from thousands of throats. . . . [Then] the brigade moved forward a short distance and went into camp some three hundred yards from the Confederate camp."[139]

At this spot, which has become known through the years as the "surrender ground," Appomattox provided the climactic confrontation of the war, and within less than two months all Confederate resistance ceased. Invisible to those who wished it so at the time, and through much of posterity, the Twenty-ninth had stood tall in the middle of the line of battle as part of that long blue line. However, the regiment's service did not end at Appomattox. After Lee's surrender, the Twenty-ninth was reassigned to duty along the Rio Grande River as part of an American army positioned to fight any Texas remnants of the Confederate army and to deter French military action in Mexico.

V. AFTER APPOMATTOX: THE REALITY OF JUBILEE

At the end of 1865, African Americans in Chicago finally had time to reflect somberly upon the meaning not only of the last twelve months, but also of what probably seemed like an epoch. It began with the Southern response to Lincoln's election, which ignited a sectional crisis and ended with his death and the Union's unconditional victory on the battlefield. The "peculiar institution" of slavery collapsed as the Confederacy lay prostrate, and the anticipated day of Jubilee had been proven anything but illusory. Having triumphed over evil and achieved the possibility of finally shaping their own futures, African Americans were suddenly struck with a sense of purposelessness. Frederick Douglass experienced it; no doubt others did, also: "I felt that I had reached the end of the noblest and best part of my life," he reflected; the questions before him now were, "where should I go, and what should I do?" Another emancipated slave, Booker T. Washington, felt that "the North expected too much of [the former slave]. . . . It required more than the shock of four years of internecine war to change the solidarity of slavery into a society of organized self-helpfulness. A people who had been so long enslaved could not help being slavish in habits and instincts."[140]

The long-term residents of Chicago wrestled with these issues as well as with the unfinished business of securing citizenship, gaining the right to vote, expanding economic opportunities, and commanding the respect of others through deed, word, and deportment. Then, the death of Lincoln on April 15, 1865, sent shock waves throughout the North and in Chicago, resulting in sadness but also in a greater resolve to carry on in the midst of military victory. African Americans identified closely with the fallen president, so his death seemed a blow directed especially against them and their chances for a fair shake in America. When New York honored the fallen president, a crowd of supposedly one million showed up, but African Americans were initially denied a place in the funeral parade and assumed a position at the rear only after the friendly intervention by the New York police commissioner.[141] When Chicago venerated Lincoln, a funeral procession of thirty-seven thousand citizens followed his cortege, and "walking somberly together in the same division were the Sons of Erin, a deputation of 'Colored citizens,' the Chicago Board of Trade, and the Laborer's Benevolent Association."[142] While too young to march, a certain Mrs. Alice Matthews could recall over six decades later how she and her brother joined the throngs that visited the body of the president at the federal courthouse where it lay in state.[143]

Many African Americans held ambivalent feelings toward the fallen president while he vacillated between pursuing an all-out course to save the

Union at all costs and acting moralistically in behalf of humanity. The historian Vincent Harding captured the essence of these attitudes, writing,

> In spite of the difficulties they had had with him during the war, the children of Africa in America considered Lincoln a friend, an ally, a leader in their developing struggle to create the institution of freedom, to chart the new land. Now his death in a heroic, sacrificial mode made it possible for the emerging black community to avoid the harsh and certain clashes between their soaring visionary projections and the President's attempts to keep the future of black freedom in narrow bounds, to hold the rushing river within limits that he and other well-meaning whites could manage. So, after April 15, Abraham Lincoln could serve as a mythic symbol of Emancipation, a companion to John Brown, while black people tried to size up . . . Andrew Johnson.[144]

Months later, veterans of the war arrived in the city at the end of the year with their mission accomplished, the regiment having been mustered out in New Orleans and in Springfield, Illinois, between November and December 1865. The men of the Twenty-ninth Illinois had lost a total of 234 compatriots—officers and enlisted men—who had fallen to enemy fire, injuries, and disease.[145] With the end of hostilities and enlistments, some new faces could shine because of the regiment's impressive service on the field of battle. The noncommissioned officers of the Twenty-ninth Illinois—Sergeants Rodney Long, Willis Easley, James H. Brown, and others—had served in the front line of combat at the Battle of the Crater, in the siege lines ringing Petersburg's southern approaches, and in the pursuit of Robert E. Lee's fleeing and erstwhile vaunted Army of Northern Virginia. Now they would bond even closer with men with whom they had served with and led. A new indigenous leadership was emerging that in future years would assume a meaningful role in the lives of their families and communities.[146] The enlisted men formed or cemented extant links at this tumultuous point in their lives that in some cases would be everlasting.

Very positively, though, the veterans had reached the apogee of their young lives with freedom and a sense of what could be accomplished in life after they had emerged victors. In the middle of the war, H. Ford Douglas explained what they had endured and what the nation owed. "This mighty waste of manhood resulting from the dehumanizing character of slave institutions of America is now given back to the world through the patient toil and self-denial of this proud and haughty race. They must now pay back the Negro in Spiritual culture in opportunities for self-improvement what they have taken from him for two hundred years by the constant over-taxing of his physical nature. This law of supply and demand regulates itself." In the soldiers' mode of protest against injustice, they had successfully engaged in armed struggle on the battlefield and left an indelible imprint on the American psyche. More important, at the war's end, as Sergeant William McCoslin explained, was the African American combatant's frame of mind: "We, the Colored soldiers, have fairly won our rights by loyalty and bravery—shall we obtain them? If they are refused now, we shall *demand them*."[147] Now, in peacetime, new tactics were to be employed in their pursuit of life, liberty, and happiness.

For black Chicago, the Civil War, more than any other event in that century, proved the pivotal point for generations to come. But the past had to be overcome, and the pressing problem of the post-Emancipation period centered around making a living in a milieu in which occupational standing defined the individual and group and where racism relegated blacks to a subordinate economic rung. An adjustment to urbanization and industrialization was also necessary. African Americans would reunite with their sons and husbands and fathers who returned as veterans of the war and face the future united in freedom.

The wartime exodus of hundreds upon hundreds of African Americans set into motion a major migratory pattern that rivaled the significance of the "Great Migration" almost three generations hence. The migrants of this period joined with the pioneer generation to become the "Old Settlers" of the early twentieth century. The manner in which the small resident African American community considered refugees part of a unified racial family was paramount to understanding just who these newcomers were socially and culturally, and what they could be, based on their human potential. Equally important, the manner in which white Chicago accommodated them portended the future of interracial relations not only in this time but for generations to come. Refugees, excluding veterans, faced pressures of identity as they exerted themselves in a seemingly liberated, yet racist, environment. Collectively, black Chicago's youngsters—who were experiencing a lengthier acclimation to freedom in an urban setting and under more stable circumstances—were well situated socially and ideologically to benefit from a changing world. With their liberating expectations incubating, they represented a segment of the African American population whose future appeared unlimited, despite certain racial inhibitions.

PART II

HARBOR
OF
OPPORTUNITY
FOR
NEW CITIZENS
1866–1900

Introduction to Part II

L IFE FOR African Americans in the years following the end of the Civil War resonated differently in Chicago, as well as throughout the nonslave North, than it did for their kinsmen and friends residing in the South during the Reconstruction era. For black Chicago, the successful conclusion to the war brought an end to a precarious beginning, while in the South, vanquished white Southerners sought a continuation of the antebellum status quo, not only in terms of protecting the racial hierarchy, but in the all-important economic sphere. The Civil War thus acted as a pivot in the North, separating one span of time when there was the possibility of a better life for African Americans into one of probability. To white Southerners who were determined to have their own way, it represented a temporary impediment in the continuity of Southern life.

Although conditions in race relations in the North were not ideal, the promise of greater participation as bona fide persons and citizens did lead to economic involvement, albeit somewhat restricted, and importantly, enfranchisement. In greater contrast, at the end of the century, general circumstances in the South produced legalized segregation, sharecropping and peonage, an end to prominence in the trades, and disfranchisement. Constant emigration out of the South further stood as a testimony of that region's oppressive character.

Locally, black Chicago now entered its freedom phase with momentous signs of demographic change and economic progress. The internal social order, cultural expression, and associational activities took on new and significant forms. A truly heterogeneous African American community developed in contradistinction to one usually overshadowed in scholarly purview by one supposedly homogeneous. Internal group differences entailed class, occupation, gender, provenance, skin pigmentation, education, religion, ideology, and political belief. These differences were magnified by changing external conditions such as racism and egalitarianism that produced views, interests, and activities that undergirded the collective dynamism of African Americans. The roots of black social agency were deliberately overlooked within a national milieu that refused to recognize even the possibility of African American human potential for centuries, especially its ingrained, and now broadening, sense of agency. The transformative nature of this budding social order relegated professionals such as medical practitioners to the top of the social hierarchy while consigning service personnel such as porters and waiters to a lower rung.

Major events also greatly influenced the course of African American development and history. The Reconstruction era that followed the war ushered in an expansion of constitutional rights, a breath of freedom welcomed by blacks in both the North and the South. On the other hand, the Great Fire of 1871 and a subsequent devastating conflagration in 1874 adversely affected black Chicago. However, reflecting the pervasive spirit of Chicago, African Americans contributed to the city's rebirth. Then, as the nineteenth century closed, the famed World's Columbian Exposition of 1893 accentuated the more salutary side of American life. As St. Clair Drake has pointed out, this international celebration positively affected black life externally in race relations, and internally in the quality of African American religious and associational life.[1]

Residential patterns changed as part of demographic shifts, new interests, and broadened horizons. In fact, several black worlds were simultaneously in formation, and with a concentration of the black population in the South Division, black Chicago began its historic southward movement. The beginnings of the historic "Black Belt" took shape along Clark Street and on parallel thoroughfares, extending south of Twenty-second Street. North of this line of demarcation, the characteristics of the population assumed another identity as poverty marked life in this area. This northern tier, with its slumlike appearance, awash in poverty, crime, and despair, contrasted with the mix of opportunities and entrepreneurial creativity reflected in economic advancement in the southern tier, which was propelling itself into the future as the cosmopolitan Black Metropolis.

In employment, entrepreneurial pursuits, business, and the professions, progress was readily apparent. The Civil War had opened a door to an economic age that carried in its wake material change for all of the northern United States, despite the restraints placed on wage labor. Labor relations between whites and blacks followed a similar course to that found in the East, but the perception of the black worker in Chicago differed slightly from that held nationally. Despite the limitations of occupational choice, new or expanding job opportunities—such as Pullman porter, policeman, fireman, and laundress—allowed the laboring class to sustain itself until such time as incremental movement forward and upward could be made. These times especially provided business and professional opportunities that were laying the foundation for the future Black Metropolis. This was the time of "firsts." The Chicago's first black attorney passed the bar on April 20, 1869; the first African American newspaper appeared in 1878; the first business directory followed in 1885—all indicating the existence of a group large enough to be readily identifiable as a class of persons competing in the city's economic sphere. In addition, a small number of individuals began to accumulate wealth in amounts unimaginable previously.

The structure of black Chicago's social order highlighted the intricacies of the relationship between what was referred to in contemporary nineteenth-century black Chicago as *the classes* and *the masses*. The former group lent itself to an examination of the formation, evolution, size, and type of leadership provided by the elite. The latter concerned itself with the character, growth, and influence of the rank and file of black Chicago, who, by sheer numbers, have always dominated the demographic thrust of black Chicago, sometimes in virtual isolation from the elite. As the elite developed a sense of its uniqueness, the required reciprocal recognition did not necessarily emanate from supposed social lessers. This can be seen in the proliferation of leaderships over disparate groups within the greater African American community. Contrary to some beliefs and writings, no single, monolithic, linear pattern of leadership existed.

Drake and Cayton, the authors of *Black Metropolis*, perceptively analyzed the major transformation in the status of African Americans that became a significant element of this study. They wrote that "before the Civil War the Negro was the protagonist of the abolitionist drama. After Emancipation he was no longer a hero around whom stirring battles were fought in the city streets and the courts. He and his people had become just one more poverty-stricken group competing in a city where economic and political issues were being fought out behind the facade of racial, national, and religious alignments."[2] Some important data on this economically dispossessed group were found in the Civil War federal pension records held at the National Archives. Both the specifics and generalities associated with the character of the lives of these former soldiers in civilian life revealed a great deal about this small, yet integral, part of the total population. The veterans had families and children, and almost all had been slaves before the war.

But beyond the rank and file, internal group differences based on wealth and how it was accumulated yielded a better understanding of the dynamics of black Chicago's societal configurations. The aspirations of the elite were hampered by whites who failed to distinguish between a possibly attainable racial equality of opportunity, and an equally threatening social equality. The phrase "equality of opportunity," popular but often misunderstood, stood for openness and a chance to compete in an unfettered environment. Overall, always a minority within a minority, with external and internal opposition to their aspirations, the African American elite persevered nonetheless as they sought fulfillment of a diluted version of the American

Dream. Regarding their personal or family wealth, they were anything but "to the manor born." They excelled in the acquisition of knowledge and cultural appreciation, not in the acquisition of property and money.

Institutional development inclusive of the spheres of religion, military and fraternal life, and politics revealed a great deal about the internal dynamics of black life. Church life passed through new phases even more substantive than the shift from white to black worship patterns. Internal social and economic pressures within black life led to a proliferation of denominations, with five bodies in existence and a population choosing freely among them—Baptist, Methodist, Episcopalian, Presbyterian, and Roman Catholic. Significantly, at the end of the century, two phenomena appeared that had long-term effects on African American life far into the next century and beyond. Tensions among congregants about the essence of worship produced a division between an elite-based church and a mass-based institution, which led to the rise of the mission church and an invigorating style of worship. Further, changing social conditions warranted the emergence of a more activist, world-oriented church with appropriate social services to meet the more mundane needs of congregants. Significantly, throughout the nineteenth century, as important as the form of worship was, sacramental expressions such as baptism, marriage, and funerals also became immensely important as indices of the meaning of black life. Baptism expanded the church body, marriage promoted family formation, and funerary rites announced the end of the cycle of physical church membership with an exalted membership into the church triumphant.

Former military experience and fraternal life intersected and assumed new importance as an assertion of humanity in the development of a martial tradition among African Americans. This nexus nurtured the ultimate demonstration of protest against injustice through military service. The Civil War service of black Chicagoans, replete with fatalities *in combat* and triumph *on the battlefield* presented the nation with a new view of the African American as a man, and therefore, a human with true *being*. Desires for citizenship and social inclusion in the postwar world led to the formation of militia units such as the Hannibal Guard, the Cadets, the Ninth Battalion, and finally the Eighth Regiment of the Illinois National Guard. The completion of the circle of martial activism came with battlefield service in the Spanish-American War and in World War I.

Fraternal organizations, the ultimate in coping mechanisms for both the harshness and the vagaries of urban life, were highly visible to the generations living through the nineteenth century because of their influence over so many facets of African American life. This was less the case for so many researchers who ignored this facet of the social order. Fannie Barrier

Williams wrote that "50 percent of the best men belonged to fraternal orders." Lawrence Levine observed that "in a society geared to deny the potency and maturity of Negroes, these institutions offered them surrogates for what the larger society tended to withhold. Within their own black organizations, religious and secular, Negroes could run for office, vote, administer the expenditures of monies, wield power, surround themselves with the prerequisites and prestige forbidden to them outside their communities."[3]

As for political paramountcy, there was neither a unique political experience with an established goal nor an organization from which it could originate. Republicanism ruled the day with occasional interruptions locally of nocturnal Democratic involvement. Overall, for the nineteenth century, quasi-political involvement predated legal political participation. Limited job opportunities and office holding resulted from extension of the franchise in 1870, which brought fortuitous rewards to Northern blacks after they and their allies exerted pressure to pass the Fifteenth Amendment, aimed primarily at enfranchising Southern blacks. Locally, patron-client politics was the order of the day in the late nineteenth century, with whites completely in control over the political apparatus. Awaiting a time when viable organization could develop, African Americans inched along looking for future opportunities. At the same time, the more advanced thinkers within the ranks of the politicians joined Edward H. Wright as he formed his Appomattox Club in 1900. This organization paved the way toward twentieth-century successes as it acted as a springboard for black political power in the 1920s.

Chapter 3

Freedom and Fire during the
Reconstruction Era, 1866–1879

When the great heart of America shall become purged of the pollution of her long-existing conglomerate sin, when the chastisements of the Holy One shall have so purified the national conscience, resurrecting it from the tomb of ages, and so strengthened, extended and elevated the moral vision of the nation as to enable it to see God in ebony, in copper, or in bronze, as fully and as willingly as in Parian or alabaster or ivory, then and not until then, will she ascend into her true position among her sister nations of the earth.

— "Address of the Colored Citizens of Chicago to the
Congress of the United States," U.S. House of
Representatives, 39th Cong., 1st sess., May 10, 1866

The sky was redder than they [the Hudlin children] had ever seen it before. They were afraid and ran to awaken their father. Their young minds told them that "judgement day" was coming. [As their fear grew,] they went through the house screaming to the top of their voices.

— "Story of Old Settlers Reads Like Fiction,"
Chicago Defender, 1930

 NATIONAL TRANSFORMATION shaped by the compelling forces of the Reconstruction and accompanied locally by an epochal disaster, Chicago's Great Fire of 1871, profoundly influenced the transition of African Americans into a new way of life in triumphant, postwar Chicago. Significantly, the power of the twin legal evils of slavery and racial proscription was eliminated in the first instance and greatly dissipated in the second. Coming of age in a time when they could freely express themselves as bona fide residents and expectant citizens produced a radical social adjustment for four and one half million African Americans nationally, and for more than three thousand of that number locally, as they attempted to enjoy a hard-earned and well-deserved freedom. For the first time, the character of societal transformation accorded African Americans unfettered expressions of agency, choice, accountability, and respect.

When St. Clair Drake and Horace R. Cayton wrote of the Reconstruction era, they noted both a challenging social milieu and an unsettled status for Chicago's moral luminaries of abolitionist times. African Americans faced new problems that had to be overcome along with unfamiliar issues to which complex adjustments were required. The previous protagonists and "heroes around whom stirring battles were fought" were being absorbed into a mass of poverty-threatened workers who lived in an industrializing society in which there was little concern for the "conglomerate sin" of Southern slavery and national racial injustice. They were forced into economic and political competition in a city where major issues were being contested across the length of the Chicago landscape by forces with irresistible power. Nevertheless, outside the purview of Drake and Cayton, a small coterie of African Americans persisted in the economic sphere and revitalized the foundation of their business thrust, in effect facilitating growth and development for the entirety of their community.

To some degree, life in Chicago reflected change occurring at the national level, especially in Washington, D.C. The Radical Republican element within the party dominated overall Republican congressional control over a dynamic political economy and created an elastic system of race relations. Radical Republicanism in racial terms translated into a reality that allied African Americans with powerful friends at the pinnacle of their power. However, it was at the local level that a question of paramount importance has to be broached: How well or poorly did this "poverty-stricken group" fare as it contended with new challenges in politics and in the economy in industrializing Chicago?

Wartime and recent postwar arrivals to the city fared badly because of their newness to urban life, their lack of skills, and of course, their socially, although not legally, proscribed racial status. For one segment of the African American population in particular, Civil War veterans, military historian Edward A. Miller has written that "the history of the black soldier [was] in many ways a tragedy because the bright hope of freedom which brought many to the recruiting tables was not met in postwar America."[1] Yet the soldiers' experience was not a universal experience even among their own ranks, and this especially was not the case for that segment of the population that had achieved pioneer status. For those black Chicagoans who best understood and were prepared for the complexities of the day, these were expectant times.

I. DEMOGRAPHIC FEATURES OF LIFE

A dwindling African American population of less than one thousand in 1860 had swollen into a population of 3,691 by 1870, representing an increase of 286 percent over the previous decade's figure. This demographic phenomenon rested in the wartime flight of hundreds and hundreds of former slaves who were settling into a mode of continuous postwar migration. Included were a small number of Civil War veterans of the Twenty-ninth Infantry, Illinois, USCT, who mustered out of military service in Springfield, Illinois, during the months of November and December 1865 and headed for Chicago both as a new and old home. This small number of soldiers welcomed a short, two-hundred-mile trip northward to familiar hearth and home after surviving battlefield conditions a thousand miles from home during 1864 and 1865. Like fellow black and white veterans returning home, they would participate in general community building as well as in constructing an "imagined" community formed by those who shared the vicissitudes of life on the battlefield.[2]

By 1870, the geographical origins of the migrants represented a national dispersion with the Middle Atlantic states furnishing 7.50 percent of the population, and the New England states 1.26 percent of the city's African American population. Pierce analyzed this pattern:

> [A]lmost two thirds of the native-born blacks living in Chicago in 1870 came from the South, and of these not quite a third were from Kentucky, with the next largest number, or a little over one fifth, from Virginia. The Old Northwest sent 955, or almost 27 percent of the total native-born black population, and, as in the case of the white inhabitants, Illinois, with 606, furnished the most of any state in this region. To these were added 312 from the Middle Atlantic and New England states and the 22 Negroes who came from Iowa and Minnesota.[3]

One Texan arrived during the winter of 1873–1874 in the company of her white husband, Arthur. She was Lucy Parsons, or "Black Lucy," a person destined to play a major role in national labor history as an activist with an unswerving, revolutionary commitment to economic justice.[4]

Demographically, the minuscule size of the African American population affected its reception by whites, with African Americans representing slightly more than 1 percent of the city's total population. The city offered an alternating course of oversight and accommodation to a virtually unnoticeable population that represented only 1.2 percent and 1.1 percent of the city's total in 1870 and 1880, respectively. Being virtually invisible, Chicago offered African Americans neither the overt hostility that led to violence and riots elsewhere in the North nor the malignant neglect commonly associated with proscription in the workplace, schools, and church. It was this factor affecting the African American experience, along with the sense of agency associated with the pioneer generation, that readily influenced the shape of African American life in Chicago.

Spatially, the U.S. census of 1870 showed nearly 80 percent of the African American population lived in the area bordered by Sixteenth Street to the south, Lake Michigan to the east, and the Main and South branches of the Chicago River to the north and west; at the time, this area comprised the First, Second, and Third wards.[5] The housing stock they occupied authenticated their virtually imperceptible standing in that it was inconspicuous among other hardscrabble dwellings.

Property holdings in 1870 included thirty-nine residential and business structures and four church properties. In land-conscious Chicago, real estate purchases required perseverance as well as capital. When the members of the Bethel African Methodist Church entered into an agreement to buy land in 1865 in a better area at Taylor Street and Edison (now Plymouth Court), "the proposed sale of the property to Negroes for church purposes caused a great upheaval among the white aristocracy of that residence district; the question became so hot and serious that Mr. [Fernando] Jones [the white contractor], was forced to break the agreement. Later on the trustees bought fifty feet of ground on Third Avenue between Taylor and 12th streets from a colored lady, a member of Quinn Chapel, Mrs. Martha Blanks."[6] Based on his wealth at the time of the Great Fire, and indicative of future social tendencies, John Jones and his family could afford to and did live farther south and away from the masses on Ray Street. This placed the Jones family in future proximity to white Chicago's "Millionaire Row" along Grand Boulevard. By 1875, the Hudlin family moved to a larger home to better accommodate their family of eleven. They relocated outside the city limits at Fifty-first Street and Dearborn Avenue and established a new social circle also attractive to the purported elite of the period.[7]

Changes in population density were explainable because of constant in-migration, but also because of other circumstances. These included an increase in births, deaths, and out-migration. Arrivals included Ferdinand L. Barnett, who was born in Nashville but arrived in Chicago with his family in 1869 as a youngster from slavery-free Canada. Too young at this juncture to carry abolitionist credentials, he nonetheless carried a strong sense of the possibilities of personal agency when rendering his future decades of activism on behalf of civil rights. Barnett's parents had moved to Canada after his father, a blacksmith, purchased his freedom and then married a free woman of color.[8] The twentieth-century alderman Robert "Bob" Jackson was born in 1870, immediately before the Great Fire. He became a repository of his parents' memories of the conflagration as well as of dreams of a communal rebirth.

Veteran Louis Clary of the Twenty-ninth Illinois returned to Chicago after his unit was mustered out and resumed his duties as a laborer on the docks of the Chicago River in 1865. Representative of a new element in the demographics of black Chicago, veterans added immensely to urban life, but usually as part of a group with their own particular sense of community.[9] He remained fixed in that occupation until his death from consumption in 1875. Supplementing the arrival of the Civil War veterans of the Twenty-ninth Illinois, Charles Demond, a native of Ovid, New York, and a member of the Twenty-sixth Infantry Regiment, USCT, made his way to Chicago in 1872, but only after stops in his hometown and in Fremont, Ohio.[10] Robert Mitchell was born into slavery in 1853 in Alabama, and intrepidly escaped his plantation. During the Civil War he served as a combatant with various units, the last being the Twenty-second Ohio, USCT, in an artillery battery. Still in his teens, he must have viewed the future with some trepidation. Fortune smiled on him as he was taken in, reared, and educated by a wealthy white family in Ohio. Attracted to Chicago in 1873, he had difficulty in finding work, so he took on the job of waiter at the Palmer House.[11]

Factors other than death caused an out-migration. In 1866, Abram T. Hall, the inspired church builder who was associated with the rise of Quinn Chapel A.M.E. Church, led his family out of the city westward to Batavia to administer to African American families living along the Fox River who needed spiritual guidance.[12] With Hall's departure, an important cog in Chicago history was gone. Fortunately, the Hall family's influence was anything but impermanent, for his offspring returned to the city upon reaching adulthood. Regimental musician Logan Davis also returned to the city of his choice, earned wages as a laborer, and remained until 1870, when he decided to move to Racine, Wisconsin. Lloyd Wheeler left temporarily in the early 1870s in order to participate in politics in Reconstruction-era Arkansas. Overall, out-migration diminished in importance as advantages and opportunities increased in the city. Thus, population changes began to relate primarily to all other factors than those mentioned previously. Upward social mobility at home easily counterbalanced any semblance of a geographical drain as indicated in the high level of population increase throughout the rest of the century.[13] With this sense of satisfaction with *place*, the numbers of those who would consider themselves "Old Settlers" at the century's end continued to grow. This movement forward included maximizing use of the talents of an expanding population, comprising a steady stream of able, dynamic black newcomers and returning war veterans. Moreover, it was aided by progressive national legislation the likes of which had neither been imagined nor witnessed before.

II. THE RECONSTRUCTION AMENDMENTS

Contrary to popular imagination, which has associated the Reconstruction amendments enacted between 1865 and 1870 exclusively with the South, where more than four million freedmen and one quarter of a million of the former "free people of color" lived, these and other pieces of congressional legislation had a dramatic influence over life in Chicago for African Americans as well. To the credit of the state that would later be dubbed the "Land of Lincoln," Illinois became the first state to ratify the Thirteenth Amendment, one day after Congress voted to submit the resolution to the legislatures of the various states. The result was the legal end to slavery by national mandate on December 18, 1865, as three-fourths of the states yielded to military triumph and to moral rightness. Ratification of this constitutional amendment sent a shock wave throughout the African American community. As one might expect, it produced a feeling of euphoria along with a sense of closure—slavery was dead forever.

The year 1865 was a significant one indeed as it brought victory at Appomattox. However, it also shamed the nation with presidential assassination, legal sanctions allowing land reclamation by former masters from the freedmen's grasp, and amnesty and pardon for leading Confederates. While scholars far removed in time might someday envision some other view of slavery based on class analysis or personal paradigm, on a contemporary basis the death knell of this horrendous two-century experience was considered long overdue. The God of Redemption, always loving, also watching, had declared that the sable children of Israel had endured long enough. For all refugees residing in Chicago before 1865, the day of Jubilee had certainly arrived. Finally, there was no need to look over one's shoulder for the wretched slave catcher, who had become more of a scourge than ever before under the Fugitive Slave Act.

In addition, the ratification of the Thirteenth Amendment meant that freedmen could test their new freedom in a manner similar to their testing their mettle on the battlefield. More blacks traveled north and west to Chicago to join earlier sojourners. Yet emigration into a strange land could mean encountering a new form of hostility. The conflict with the socially uncertain Irish, who occupied the lowest rung of white America's social ladder, however, no longer could assume its past importance once the possibility of reenslavement was removed. No ethnic group could threaten exposure and thereby gain an advantage in labor competition along the wharves and docks of the Chicago River or in homes, hotels, and saloons.

The African American *residents* of Chicago earnestly sought to become the African American *citizens* of this city as soon as possible. To those of a religious bent, it was a miracle that occurred with the ratification of the Fourteenth Amendment to the U.S. Constitution on July 28, 1868, guaranteeing the permanency of the transformation from liberated commodity to free man and woman. For the first time, privileges beyond mere existence meant that African Americans could testify in the courts, carry the mails, sue and be sued, and act as corporate members of the American commonweal.

In the struggle for the passage of guarantees such as those later contained in the Fourteenth Amendment of 1868, blacks first supported congressional legislation like the Civil Rights Act of 1866. As the year unfolded, Senator Lyman Trumbull of Illinois, the chair of the Senate Judiciary Committee, introduced a civil rights bill to aid black Chicago's Southern kinsmen, numbering over four million. The legislation aimed to enlarge the powers of the Freedmen's Bureau to encompass meeting the complete needs of the former slaves—economic, humanitarian, educational, and judicial. When the Negrophobic president Andrew Johnson vetoed the bill, progressive white Chicago was incensed.[14] For its part, black Chicago was overwhelmingly livid.

Under their own leadership, African Americans met to challenge presidential perfidy. On Tuesday evening, April 10, 1866, they assembled at the Olivet Baptist Church to protest at a gathering described as a "largely attended and enthusiastic meeting." Their aim was to show "appreciation of the action of Congress in re-enacting the civil rights bill." With John Jones elected as chair and Lewis B. Waite as secretary, the assemblage discussed with indignation and clarity the threat to their rights from the Democrat Johnson's recalcitrance. To articulate their concerns, the body selected a committee of five to draft a set of resolutions to send to a friendly Republican Congress. What they returned to the full assemblage two weeks later was a petition showing that they as a group had evolved to a point where they could speak with a bold, united voice on this issue, and on any other matter. They declared that the Civil Rights Act, which they considered a racial Magna Carta, had been paid for by the sacrifice in blood made during the war that was fought under what they called a "fire-cleansed and blood-baptized flag." They resolved to support wholeheartedly the efforts of the Illinois senators, Trumbull and former war governor Yates, to promulgate "the grand idea that equality of rights for all men is the true, the safe, and the only reliable foundation possible to the support of American liberty." These future African American citizens fully understood the president's prerogative to exercise his veto, but the assemblage urged continued Republican congressional defiance. In the eyes of this gathering, the veto was "a shattered column of inextenuable iniquity" and one that left "defenceless in the presence of their selectest foes, and the enemies of the government of their country as well, millions of American citizens."[15]

With this challenge, their overall actions signaled that a new day had arrived in the political affairs of the city's disenfranchised citizens. African Americans now spoke on their own, in the most appropriate of moral and historical tones, to the locus of national government in the hopes of addressing their grievances. Their argument was genuinely American; their language for the time rang as euphonious. The message included the following:

> Loving our whole country with a devotion second to that of no other similar number of the American people—*always* her loyal children—it is yet but now that we are enabled to realize the brightness of the coming dawn of liberty's matin. Starting with and descending from the records of revolutionary battle-fields to the ensanguined contests of the late civil war, it is made manifest that in these blood stained periods of our country's history colored Americans have ever been found faithful to the flag, even while it but gave them the ignominy of its "stripes," and withheld from them the glory of its "stars."
>
> If, then, as is abundantly proven, they have thus, under every adversity of fortune, been true to the *republic* when she was *not* their *alma mater*, what shall they not be to her when, as now, she extends to them the right hand of her sacred fellowship?
>
> But giving her the whole heart, we ask from her the *whole hand!* . . .
>
> Constituting a part of the American nation, we possess it with a common destiny. Our record in the past, we think, warrants the belief that with it we will be found willing to do, to dare, to suffer, and, if need be, to die in defence of American constitutional liberty for the *entire* American people.[16]

Under relentless Radical Republican pressure, the presidential vetoes were overridden twice, much to the satisfaction of Chicago's African Americans and their white abolitionist allies.

The third of the Reconstruction amendments, the Fifteenth, addressed the political instability in the Southern states that was manifested through constant attempts to disfranchise the freedmen and restore white Democratic party rule. From the perspective of the national Republican leadership, they faced a threat to both the hegemony of the Republican party and the apparatus that insured needed African American voter support to keep the party in power nationally and in the South. The Republicans responded from the nation's capital by proposing legislation that protected the freedmen's right to vote under restored white Southern rule. Individual states were prevented from abusing their right to extend the franchise by resorting to restrictions along discriminatory racial lines.

Meanwhile, Illinois was experiencing its own crisis of conscience over whether to continue to exclude African American males from the political process or to enfranchise and empower them as both men and bona fide citizens. The matter came up at a specially convened session in which the Illinois Constitutional Convention considered possible changes in the state constitution of 1848. In debates over the reasons whether it should or should not pass legislation that would lead to a Fifteenth Amendment, the Illinois General Assembly faced the embarrassment of protecting the rights of citizens from afar when it denied its own citizens the right to vote. The issue was resolved in favor of blacks, as black men finally received the right to vote. Thus, at the time when the Southern black voter received his protection, the Illinois black voter received his first opportunity to exercise the franchise and could lay full claim to manhood in the fullest American sense.[17] Action on extending the franchise to women, unfortunately, was delayed indefinitely.[18] Ironies and other injustices aside, the right to the franchise was welcomed wholeheartedly by the mass of black Chicagoans.

As to the various states' decisions on the fate of the Fifteenth Amendment, the required three-fourths total was reached on March 30, 1870. The key, third ratification had taken place. If Chicago was anything like Detroit, it would have done as that city's citizens did. Katzman chronicled a celebration that was held on April 7, 1870, to commemorate the ratification of this amendment.[19] The successful ratification of the Fifteenth Amendment fortunately did not end the legislative initiative of the political abolitionists. Their concern for the protection of blacks' civil rights led to one last gesture to applaud the decades-long humanitarian struggles of Senator Charles Sumner of Massachusetts, whose health was failing.

As had become the custom among blacks throughout parts of the North, following the signing of Lincoln's Emancipation Proclamation on January 1, 1863, they commemorated this date as the advent of a dawning of a new life in America.[20] With the heralding of another new year on January 1, 1874, the eleventh anniversary of the Emancipation Proclamation, John Jones addressed the issue of black rights before the United Fellows, described as a "a workingmen's association." He argued:

> I will now attempt to show that we have made as good a record since our emancipation as any other class of citizens in this country. We have made our way from the cotton-patch and sugar-farm, to the legislative halls of both State and nation. . . . The hand of every man seemed to oppose us, and we had scarcely sufficient clothing or food to supply the natural wants of life. But with all these weights and limits what do we now behold? Everywhere the black man has sprung of his won free will and determination, in spite of Church and State, from the position of slavery and its consequences, to the bar, the pulpit, the lecture-room, the professorship, the degrees of M.D. and D.D. and to the bar of the Supreme Court of the United States. His eloquence electrifies thousands of listeners; his pen instructs the millions; his merchandise travels over sea and land; his property is reckoned by millions; his strong arm upholds the American Government; his patriotism cannot be made to blush, for there is no black treason.
>
> All that we ask, is to be paid the regular market price for our work. We work for what we get, and do not propose to quarrel with our neighbor because they may have more than we have.
>
> We must also have our civil rights; they must not be withheld from us any longer; they are essential to our complete freedom.[21]

Exactly how Jones defined civil rights might be explainable in congressional legislation enacted in 1875 as the Civil Rights Act. This paean to Senator Sumner appeared as legislation that was more significant morally than it was in actuality. It guaranteed access to public accommodations for all Americans, but its lasting importance lay in its signaling a conclusion to the Reconstruction legislative onslaught that lasted a decade. For their part, local African Americans clearly recognized that initiative emanating from their ranks would be the next step needed to protect the rights of citizenship.

III. THE GREAT CHICAGO FIRE

Chicago's Great Fire of October 1871 occupied a central role in the history, memory, and historical imagination not only of whites, but also of blacks. Chicago historian Frederick Francis Cook viewed the conflagration as a timeline of municipal demarcation. "As in our national life the old regime is divided by the Civil War of 1861, so in the mind of Chicagoans

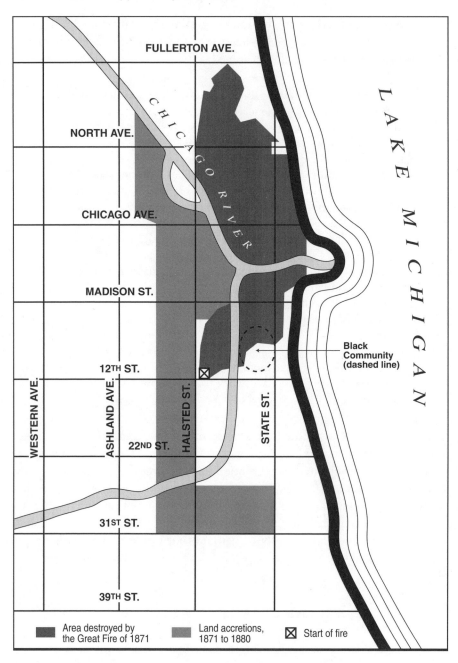

Fig. 17. Map of Chicago after the Great Fire of 1871.

the city's past is demarcated from the present by the great fire of 1871," he reminisced, as he methodically put memory into prose in order to inform posterity.[22] As an epochal event, the Great Fire of October 8, 1871, brought death to more than three hundred persons, homelessness to a third of the city's three hundred thousand residents, destruction to eighteen thousand structures, and property losses in the millions of dollars. In its physical scope, it destroyed a significant portion of the southwest side of the city, all of the north side, and the central city except for the area south of Harrison Street (Figure 17).

The African American community suffered, but in regard to physical damage, it suffered disproportionately less than the rest of the city. In terms of emotional trauma, African Americans viewed the tragedy from different perspectives, also. To white Chicagoans, the fiery holocaust that caused thousands to flee in all directions and drove them into the cool lake waters for safety and relief assumed a total importance that was lost on their fellow black citizens. Chaos, violence, destruction, uncertainty, and fear offered no new challenge to the collective black psyche. Compared to the traumas of bondage, liberation, combat, and postwar civilian adjustment, it took on the aura of being just another in a series of life's major tragedies and disappointments. Such a claim rests firmly with the historian's awareness that, as Conkin and Stromberg have noted, "the experiential past is largely hidden and lost. But one can infer, almost conclusively in some cases, the concepts and acts of people in the past, their articulated beliefs and the ends operative in their behavior. In fact, we can infer ends that they served without knowing they were doing so, or momentous events that they scarcely heeded, for we have the advantage of hindsight. Without it there could be no histories."[23]

E. Franklin Frazier acknowledged the fire's importance in people's memories when he interviewed Chicago blacks in 1927 as he prepared his monumental study *The Negro Family in Chicago*.[24] Families have remembered the fire in their own ways. A prized possession of the Atkinson family descendants, a century and a quarter later, is a burned, slightly damaged ceramic sculpture of a dog. It has served them both as a reminder of their family's presence at the end of the beginning of pioneer Chicago's history and of their family's resiliency under duress and triumph over adversity. Moreover, black veterans recognized this catastrophe as a pivotal event in their lives; many of them explained the absence of military service documentation in claims cases by referring to this fiery disaster. Most soldiers lost valuable documents such as marriage and birth certificates, the loss of which hindered verification of claims in the future. Adults, such as the Civil War veteran William Graves, lost loved ones. His stepson recalled, years later, "It seems that just after the Civil War [Graves] lived in Chicago and ran a bar-ber shop. He married some girl there and from what he said she was burned to death in the Chicago Fire."[25] First Sergeant Willis Easley of the Twenty-ninth Illinois, recounted on a pension form years later, in regard to a previous address on Pacific Street, "Burnt out there in Chicago Fire"; as for provid-ing evidentiary materials to substantiate his claim, he announced, "all papers lost Oct 1871 Chicago Fire."[26]

Several African American children who went on to become notable in the early twentieth century experienced the trauma of the event firsthand. Theirs was another perspective. These children of the fire included the future attorneys Edward H. Morris and Ferdinand Barnett, future alderman Robert Jackson, Mary Elizabeth Atkinson, and Joanna (Joan) Hudlin. Young Joan Hudlin and her siblings saw the fire directly, through the impression-able eyes of children. However, their perception could not have differed greatly from that of frightened adults: They noticed that the sky to the southwest was redder and darker than they had ever seen it. For these young members of Quinn Chapel A.M.E. Church, it appeared that "Judgment Day" had arrived.[27] For adult and youngster, believer or sinner, the confla-gration had the earmarkings of the End.

Joanna's family lived at 239 Third Avenue (now Plymouth Court), and her father, Joseph Hudlin, was head janitor at the Chicago Board of Trade. He saved its documents from the fire, running to his place of employment and removing all of the valuable papers from the vault. All others would be destroyed in the conflagration. His wife, Elizabeth, became one of the "angels of the fire" because of her humanitarian aid to whites and blacks alike in its aftermath.[28]

The response of the Hudlin family in the face of adversity no doubt typi-fied the actions of other church-going, respectable persons like themselves. The Hudlin home was not in the line of the fire and thus survived the disaster. So, just as other groups pitched in to help members of their own community as well as others,[29] the Hudlins opened their home, a five-room cottage, to both white and black neighbors. In fact, five families, white and black, were sheltered in their home, including the Atkinsons. That family had lost their home. Miraculously, a number of homes of other African Americans and the whites who lived around them were spared the flames.

Black institutional growth was stunted as this small, fledgling community faced substantial material losses, also. John Jones lost his first store on Dearborn Street; however, typical of him, he began rebuilding immediately.[30] Quinn Chapel A.M.E. suffered damage to its entire structure, causing it to temporarily relocate. "Bethel threw open its doors and invited the pastor and members of Quinn Chapel to occupy the lecture rooms of Bethel [while] Bethel would occupy the auditorium. The invitation was immediately accepted."[31]

As we have noted, those religiously inclined former slaves would likely have seen the fire as symbolizing a day of retribution brought by God against the many wicked whites. Excluding the tiny minority of abolitionists, God was punishing a race that had profited directly from the labors of their bondage in the South as well as that segment in the North that had acquiesced in this system of brutalization and exploitation. Already accustomed to assaults upon their spirit, minds, and bodies, when they experienced the Great Fire, it assumed the aura of just another of life's travails. Moreover, just as some blacks in reaching the North were surprised to see that white men actually *worked*, in contrast to what they had witnessed in the South, many were reluctant to concede that whites had developed a meaningful relationship with God; the evidence of the fire served to buttress this thinking, for, they reasoned, had whites lived more in tune with God's will, God might have held back this fiery catastrophe.

Recent research has uncovered the involvement of more urban-acclimated African Americans who, at this pivotal moment, demonstrated a high sense of civic awareness and commitment during the fire. Their efforts persisted in the aftermath of the conflagration and their concern for their fellow citizens and public and private property moved their recognized level of citizenship to a higher level than just being disinterested, self-absorbed citizens. Just as the Hudlin family and others challenged the fire on October 8, 1871, African Americans now proposed to more fully participate in civic affairs as part of their sense of civic duty. Not surprisingly, a militia company was formed to assist in preserving public order and to participate in defense of the city and the nation if need be. Further, as newly recognized citizens they expressed a desire to join the police and fire departments. In all of these ventures they realized success.

On July 14, 1874, another one of Chicago's perennial fires claimed homes and businesses that had previously survived the great catastrophe. This was the Second Great Fire, or the Black Fire, called so nowadays because so many of its victims were African American as opposed to those in the First. While church picnickers from Olivet, Quinn Chapel, and Bethel frolicked on the outskirts of the city as part of a scheduled Sunday School Union outing, their collective gaze cityward saw trouble. The city's first and only African American fire unit, Engine 21, saw its station house and equipment destroyed, but worse, one of its firemen was killed. Dislocation beckoned on a massive scale. As an example, the family of Charles B. Taylor suffered greatly, necessitating a temporary relocation by his wife and three children to Indianapolis, until Taylor could reestablish himself financially.[32]

Local historian Muriel Braxton Wilson examined the effects of this disaster on African Americans, after they had been spared three years previously, in light of real estate values and residential movement.[33] While white real estate speculators saw the removal of black homes and other hardscrabble dwellings as a blessing, African Americans lamented the loss of hearth and home. The area was viewed as impoverished, vice-ridden, but importantly, economically valuable. Some African Americans feared arson, but the source of the blaze was an abandoned oil factory once run by Polish Jews who quickly were scapegoated as had been the Irish Mrs. O'Leary. Other blacks resigned themselves to accepting the inevitable in a city still filled with many wooden houses, hot, dry summers, and repeated fire threats. With alacrity, assistance was forthcoming, with the Chicago Relief and Aid Society providing cash and other help. Significantly, the major result of this fire was to push the African American population southward into new territory, what would become the "Black Belt."

When the influence of freedom is contrasted with that of the two fires, the salutary nature of the former outdistances the deleterious effects of the latter. Freedom had meant negation of an inglorious chapter in their past, hope for a new beginning, and the actualization of dreams. With the city's future, indomitable "I Will" spirit, African Americans, along with their fellow white citizens, prepared to reclaim their lives from this physical disaster that was devastating, but not totally overwhelming. Bethel cooperated with and temporarily relocated to a white church, the Railroad Chapel, until early 1875, when a new structure was secured. The two fires represented only two more of life's obstacles to a group whose mind-set constantly anticipated and accommodated itself to life's adversities.

IV. THE ECONOMIC SPHERE: EMPLOYMENT, BUSINESS, AND THE PROFESSIONS

The advent of freedom introduced the black worker and self-employed individual into a world of contradictions. While American society measured human worth on the individual's ability to create products and service of value for the public good, it tolerated a playing field that reeked of exclusion. Competition, then, so highly regarded, was summarily removed as a viable channel for an African American demonstration of success. In the labor sphere, African Americans unfortunately were reintroduced into an environment in which a racial dimension remained a strong part of the division of labor. A racial hierarchy in labor that had been created nationally over centuries, and that was being fueled by rampant discrimination and prejudice, locally produced a structure of work manifesting the same nefarious practices and attitudes. Accordingly, the bulk of the African American population, which had always been relegated to the lower rung of the laboring ladder, remained in that position. And as such, one major starting point of the economic history of Chicago blacks was this group, who worked for others, who formed the bulk of the service sector of the city's labor force, and who suffered from economic proscription. Accustomed to struggle and disappointment, but buttressed by an ethos that relegated trials and tribulations into a pattern of expected and surmountable normality, African Americans could look to a future in which racial achievement always appeared imminent.

The other major starting point of the economic history of Chicago blacks was to be found in the business sphere. Persistence was yielding dividends for those who dared to pave a path of economic independence through self-employment and providing employment for others of their group. The market they served remained predominantly white, but with steady demographic increase among blacks, accompanied by a rising sense of group consciousness fueled by emancipation, the stage was set for a dramatic transformation within a few decades. Since none of this group, like their white counterparts in the laboring class, had ever experienced or benefited from privilege, they considered challenges and disappointments as part of the price to be paid for ultimate success. Religiously inspired optimism, not fatalism, pervaded their thinking and reinforced their sense that progress was always achievable. Meanwhile, the small but growing group of professionals prepared to emerge from economic invisibility.

Chicago at war's end presented the working class with a dire scenario. Bessie Louise Pierce described the situation thus:

> In late 1865, troops began to return home. Demobilization meant dislocation and readjustment. The winter of 1865-66 was hard; business houses retrenched; country boys looking for white-collar jobs were warned not to come to the city. . . . During this winter and the next, Chicago had many hungry, many cold, and many scantily clothed. A rainy autumn made it difficult to carry on outdoor work, so that carpenters, bricklayers, and outside painters, as well as common laborers, teamsters, and others were unable to save for what proved to be a time when the unemployed walked the streets. Credit from butchers and grocers occasionally saved the former wage earners from seeking public charity, and "odd jobs," such as cleaning sidewalks and sawing wood, sometimes kept formerly skilled and semiskilled, as well as common laborers, from the humiliation of begging.

To those in such dire straits, it must have been a bit tempting when, early in 1866, an employment agency advertised for three thousand men to go south to work for $50 a month besides board. At the same time good wages and transportation were offered for two hundred able-bodied Negroes who would labor as field hands on plantations near Vicksburg; and in the spring calls for men to become railroad laborers and farm hands again opened up a labor market for those willing to leave the city.[34]

When conditions improved at the decade's end, Chicago's employers discriminated in favor of the sons of Europe with their fairer skins. African Americans remained consistent, in that they met life's challenges head-on, no matter what their severity. Over the next three decades, a smattering of carpenters, plasterers, and other skilled craftsmen, as well as musicians, could be found but were almost invisible, immersed as they were in a citywide labor force numbering one-half million. Similar to conditions in Philadelphia, native-born and foreign-born whites divided the industrial jobs.[35]

Pierce continued her description of the time, saying, "By 1870, Chicago had about the average employment as had cities farther east, betokening a maturity in labor needs common to older communities. Of the total population of 298,977 in 1870, nearly 38 per cent or 112,960, worked in the service sector. Domestic and personal service claimed the time of about 14 per cent of those employed in 1870."[36] Extrapolation from this latter figure reveals that the domestic sphere accommodated roughly 12 percent of all persons employed within the entire workforce. At the conclusion of the decade of Emancipation, the class and occupational configuration of the African American population in Chicago rested primarily on this non-industrial, service-oriented base of approximately 2,800 to 3,000 workers, representing perhaps 80 percent of the 3,691 blacks in the city. Contemporary analysis depicted restaurant and hotel workers, domestic servants, and dockworkers as prevailing in the African American workforce.

For African Americans, who made up but 1.1 percent of the overall population, Drake and Cayton talked of limitations but also opportunities and success in the economic sphere.[37] One of the barriers to success and well-being African Americans encountered was the depression of 1873, which hit the nation savagely and lingered throughout the decade. Despite societal sanctions of racism, at no time did African Americans surrender en masse to this iniquity. Employment discrimination consistently thwarted ambition and aspiration but could not smother completely these qualities of human agency.

Ironically, disaster provided economic opportunity. As devastating as the Great Chicago Fire of 1871 was, it provided work for unskilled labor as debris had to be cleared to make way for the building of a physically new Chicago. Karen Sawislak described this work: "Thousands of pick-and-shovel-wielding men and boys and hundreds of teams and wagons . . . moved in to knock down crumbling walls, reclaim usable brick and scrap iron, and daily dump 5000 wagon loads of worthless rubble into Lake Michigan."[38] Ready with his "fleet" of wagons to aid in and prosper from removal of remnants of the damaged city was a "Mr. Bates"—and possibly others of African descent.[39] It can be assumed that the carpenters and brick masons who rebuilt the city were predominantly white, but it is also likely that there were a few African Americans included in their ranks.

Among the city's labor force, returning black Civil War soldiers found major obstacles to employment, the likes of which white carpenters, brick masons, ironworkers, and others would never encounter. The types of work open to returning veterans and their families in the aftermath of the conflict were limited, as occupational paths in unskilled and semiskilled work did not offer the soldier many opportunities. Having received no training for the future or for the use of their talents, and with a military background that trained them in such activities as building fortifications and honed their skills in survival and killing, it is no wonder that the lines of work they pursued in civilian life proved, essentially, to be dead ends.

The same limitations faced most former slaves who arrived in Chicago, but there were many exceptions. One bright spot appeared as wait service in the city's myriad restaurants and hotels beckoned African Americans seeking work. This sector was to become a mainstay of the black labor force for generations. Kentucky-born David McGowan arrived in the city in 1869 and settled in the West Division. He worked at the Schemp Winery, which later became a major restaurant. Through perseverance, McGowan earned the rank of maître d'hôtel and supervised the workforce later in the 1870s.[40] Robert Mitchell first worked as a waiter upon his arrival in Chicago in 1873 from Ohio. When George French Ecton reached the city in 1875 (also from Ohio, but, in his case, Cincinnati), he immediately sought and secured work in the area he knew best. Possessing an attitude common to many, that "no matter what his occupation, he prided himself on doing whatever he did well," his search proved successful. Just as the Great Fire had aroused a resurgence of energy among Chicagoans, Ecton, who arrived in town with equal vigor, "took charge of a dining room at the 'Hotel Woodruff.'"[41] Sergeant Rodney Long, a Civil War veteran, served as a waiter in restaurants and then on the railroads as well as working as a barber. When skyscrapers began to rise from the cityscape, veteran Alexander Garrett finally advanced beyond his occupation as a waiter to enter the industrial era as an elevator operator.[42]

Other soldiers returned to the limited occupational paths they had pursued before the war. Louis Clary worked on the docks of the Chicago River during times when wintertime ice did not block water traffic and impede work. John Abrams worked as a houseman late in this period and as a janitor in the new century. Others were teamsters, whitewashers, porters, cooks, and manual laborers.

Given Chicago's fluidity in race relations, exceptions did exist to counterbalance systemic job exclusion. Outside the domestic and service spheres, one example of the work experience in the exclusive industrial sector, into which few African Americans entered, was found in John Wesley Terry's introduction to urban life. He was born around 1846 into slave parentage in Tennessee and labored without remuneration until the war. Terry then tested his freedom of mobility, arriving in Chicago "in 1872—the year after 'the great fire.'" In 1873 he joined Olivet Baptist Church, led by Rev. Richard De Baptiste, and met and married Miss Catherine Brown of Nashville, Tennessee. Continuing to display the initiative that he exhibited even before the end of slavery, Terry made great strides despite racism in the industrial sphere. In 1875 this ambitious former slave went to work for the Chicago West Division Street Car Company in the car shops for two years, before the ministry beckoned. After formal religious training of four years, Terry was ordained by 1881 and began his religious sojourn. Unable to make ends meet, he returned to his previous employer while engaging in limited pastoral service. After one year, the part-time minister was promoted to a foreman over the iron and fitting department. Not only was Terry the only African American in this production unit, he dared to hold a management position despite the odds. He commanded such respect based on his performance that even the whites supported his claim to supervisor. The labor-conscious Terry joined the Knights of Labor in 1886 and was elected to the position of judge-advocate of the Charter Oak Assembly in March 1886.[43]

A. Occupational Paths: The Pullman Porter, Policeman, Washerwoman, and Fireman

Beginning around 1867, three new occupational outlets for males appeared, and another expanded for females, as the white population desiring its services also increased. First, for males, the position of Pullman porter was designed to meet the newest need of industrial magnate George M. Pullman as he sought to staff his earliest Palace Cars, which were, in effect, moving hotel suites. Then, in the aftermath of the Great Fire of 1871, the elevated municipal positions of policeman and fireman opened under a progressive city administration. Second, many black women, including the wives and widows of veterans, made an occupational choice (among the few available) that led them to become washerwomen. These laundresses assisted financially better-off women who would otherwise have faced "the dread of every well-regulated household, the washing and ironing" of dirty clothing.[44]

The industrialist Pullman sought workers with a particular personality capable of satisfying his white customers, both in the North and in the South. Racial and class deference bordering on obsequiousness, whether feigned or ingrained, fit the bill. Pullman even went so far as to demand that porters smile on all occasions when encountering white passengers. Matching previous disposition with a modern demand, his choice of a workforce caused him to recruit from persons who previously had held the status of slaves. In context, to this industrial magnate, who made millions manufacturing his Palace Cars, "which provided the needed link between the sumptuous hotels that met the traveler in all of our great cities," servility was demanded and expected from *all* of his employees, whether on the rails or at his model, all-white company town—appropriately named Pullman—located south of Chicago. As to whether racism was at the core of Pullman's demands when applied to African Americans, that point is problematical, since African American leaders from Frederick Douglass to Chicago's civic elite often spoke effusively about the industrialist's beneficence with apparent knowledge but indifference to his demands as an employer.

This first generation of workers that constituted the original pool of porters, almost all former slaves, had expectations that these employers could meet easily. To these workers, it seemed unrealistic to challenge the expected demeanor. So the image of the ubiquitous, sometimes overly courteous "George," with his obligatory smile, grew and soon dominated this new service by the end of the century. Chicagoan John Mitchell supposedly handled the first Pullman Car as it traveled on the C&A Railroad in 1867.[45] Many veterans from the Twenty-ninth Illinois entered the field, such as the former sergeants Willis Easley and Rodney Long, who worked for the Illinois Central and Michigan Central, respectively. The schedules were grueling; a federal pension examiner described his frustration in contacting Long for an interview about a war comrade: "For months past[,] his runs [to Denver] have been irregular and it has been impossible to tell in advance the days on which he will be in Chicago. I have made repeated trips to his boarding place to see him, and he has called on me at times when I was absent from my office. I have [also] communicated with him letter by letter and through acquaintances in relation to the [pension] case."[46] Significantly, over the next several decades and for generations into the future, Pullman porters would be typified by men with the attitudes and personality traits not only associated with bondage, but also linked to the "newer Negro" types who took on this work challenge because it was simply the best job available under the conditions of the day. That an individual emerged who would advance far beyond his employer's and society's initial expectations would account for the emergence of prospective leaders in the fields of law, finance, and government.

For this period in the nation's economic development, belying the sincerity of that smile, the Pullman porter work schedule was especially exhausting: it became all too common for porters to work a hundred hours per week on train runs. Long periods of standing and stooping, strenuous to the limbs in the extreme, took their toll over time. Veteran Willis Easley's postwar and late-age condition attested to that, with his having developed a debilitating case of varicose veins in his left leg. In addition, the chances for promotion were virtually nonexistent. "If [a porter] enters the service at 18[,] he will likely be receiving the same pay at 48 if he stays in the service," reported Wright.[47] However, when bolstered by tips, the wage level at times could exceed that enjoyed by a waiter or porter in private hotel service, so this benefit resulted in an attractiveness ordinarily unimaginable.

The work of the washerwoman was physically demanding, but it strangely represented an opportunity for survival in an even more hostile, exploitative work environment in which native-born white as well as European immigrant women moved up to other types of domestic service work. In the midst of such a challenging environment, African American women still brought dignity to themselves as they sought a modicum of economic self-sufficiency.[48] This type of work, menial as it was, provided basic sustenance. It was available, and the work ethic of these laborers was such that a willingness to pursue any semblance of independence always shone. Exemplifying the latter, Mrs. Delilia Watkins, widow of Private William Watkins, explained: "I am poor, a Colored woman, can neither read nor write, have five little ones at home yet to look out for, have to live over the washtub for a bare subsistence, have to ask for and accept help from my friends."[49] The historian Tera Hunter posited:

> Clearly the joy of freedom signified many things to black women, the full dimensions of which neither sympathetic Northerners nor erstwhile slaveholders fully understood or appreciated. . . . Their lives as field and house slaves . . . had been governed by rules and regulations over which they had no control. As freed people, however, they were committed to balancing the need to earn a living with needs for emotional sustenance, personal growth, and collective cultural expressions.[50]

The physical demands were obvious, and the difficulty surpassed that of other forms of service work. Their hands told a part of the story; their backs, arms, shoulders, and muscles relayed another. In general, they experienced what St. Louis emigrant Sarah Breedlove, later Madame C. J. Walker, had for two decades. Beginning early each Monday morning, they collected their day's work from two or three upwardly mobile white families in need of a steady supply of clean clothing befitting their social status. Madame C. J. Walker's biographer and descendant, A'Lelia Bundles, described this labor: "[T]he work, all done by hand in wooden washtubs and iron pots of boiling water, was study, strenuous and laborious. Wet sheets and tablecloths doubled in weight. Lye soap irritated hands and arms. Heated flatirons were heavy, cumbersome and dangerous."[51]

Whether they depended on a cart or their backs and shoulders to handle the bundle of a typical week's dirty laundry, these women maneuvered themselves along city streets to begin the arduous process necessary to complete their tasks. On other occasions, they might work in the homes of their customers, washing and ironing clothing. Mrs. Celia McAllister, the widow of veteran Frank McAllister, depended on "going out to work and for her daily labor at washing."[52] More often, with a weekend delivery date for outside work done within the friendlier confines of their humble abodes, the laundress's week was filled with the psychological stress associated with caring conscientiously for someone else's precious belongings and with the physical pressure to cleanse and press each item thoroughly—with kindling, soaking, scrubbing, lifting, rinsing, and ironing—performed with bodily precision.

Former slave Malinda Chappell, the wife of Civil War soldier Henry Chappell, found herself maligned by polite white society for her *choice* of work, as though she pursued this form of hard work as something elected. She was described thus: Malinda Chappell "impressed me fairly well and about as truthful as a colored woman in her walk of life usually is. She washes and irons for a living, is fairly intelligent, perhaps above the average colored woman who washes and irons." Mrs. Louisa Flowers, mother of soldier Cato Flowers, also took on this endeavor as a washerwoman to support herself and her invalid husband after their son died of disease during the war. Mrs. Nancy Clary, mother of Louis, repeated this personal saga in word and deed as she struggled to support herself and her family: "I have always done my part, and have earned my share to support the family. I have washed and ironed and done hard work."[53]

To counterbalance the demands of the work regimen, church life and family interaction provided the only acceptable avenues for relief from work's drudgery, providing them "emotional sustenance, personal growth, and collective cultural expressions." Malinda Chappell, for example, attended Quinn Chapel A.M.E. Church for her respite from distasteful exertion. Additionally, the advantages of this occupation materialized partially in a mother's ability to care for her children while working, the independence found in working away from the scrutinizing eyes of whites, the ability to set one's own schedule, and the low capital needed to undertake this endeavor.[54]

Governmental employment provided another option for black Chicagoans. Chicago's federal employees at the post office numbered seventy-eight, including the city's first African American letter carrier. Chicago's black municipal employees were scattered in offices and service capacities throughout the workforce, representing one of the more positive effects of political patronage. Some are listed in the next section on politics.

In the aftermath of the Great Fire of 1871, additional, unanticipated occupational paths opened. Municipal government now found a place for African American males in roles of civil protectors as they became firemen and policemen. The first black police officer was hired sometime between 1872 and 1875. Possibly he was M. V. French from the West Division, who lived at 819 Austin Avenue. Whoever was first, he was followed by a second policeman by 1875 or 1876.[55] The reputation of the Chicago Police Department varied and was not completely favorable. Pierce wrote the following of police demeanor in the late 1860s: "Not always, it was charged, were the police 'physically or morally brave.' To them . . . a drunken man was 'glorious subject for club practice,' a 'nigger' unless 'a brawny one,' was worth no more than 'an insult,' and women were often treated as if they were 'demons instead of human beings.' Prisoners were sometimes clubbed into submission by plain-clothes men, and women on the street, unable to pay for immunity, received the cruelest kind of treatment."[56] African American policemen, who, it must be presumed, were more professional and humane, were indeed welcomed.

Quite probably the Twenty-ninth Regiment's Rodney Long became the second Chicago policeman in 1875 or 1876. John Enders from the same regiment followed thereafter. Occupationally, the rise of the African American fireman and policeman, who composed part of the "respectables," significantly showed how the individual could rise, how the community could prove its worth, and how the knowledge and wherewithal to function within the system found use for individual and communal good. As part of purportedly the first wave of law officers, Rodney Long and John Enders's service as public guardians fit the character of men whose lives were built on the bedrock of assertiveness and courage. Both were lean and muscular at nearly six feet in height, tested in combat in Virginia, and willing to take on any form of civil disorder as well as Chicago's criminal element. They assertively took advantage of political opportunities and obtained appointments into the Chicago Police Department.

Notably, Long had fought at "the Crater," was captured by Confederate forces, and was sent to Libby Prison in Richmond, Virginia; he survived that six-month ordeal and then was paroled in February 1865, at which time he rejoined his regiment. The combination of the willingness of the Confederate forces to allow a black man to live in captivity as a prisoner of war rather than slaughter him on the battlefield or shortly thereafter, and importantly, Long's will to live under the adverse conditions of a Southern prison camp, showed something of his personality and fitness for the strenuous job of a city policeman. For his part, history has noted how Ender resisted Chicago Mayor Carter G. Harrison I's efforts to buy his political loyalty in 1883.[57]

The organization of Fire Engine Company 21 in December 1872 was especially significant. Although there is little evidence to explain why they were appointed, clearly the need for fire companies was felt after the city's great fires. Nonetheless, examination of extant circumstances and emerging political change provide reasonable explanations. Popular and political support for *Chicago Tribune* editor and publisher Joseph Medill led to his being drafted as a candidate for mayor in the wake of the fire crisis and his subsequent election. He demanded substantive changes in governmental powers for the mayor's office, especially control over the professional fire department (which was organized in 1857), freeing it from the spoils system of previous decades.[58] After involvement in fire rescue and defense as citizens, the respectable element of black society sought more meaningful participation. A door now opened, as the mayor's sense of fairness acknowledged African American assertiveness and their desire to participate more fully in municipal government. While representing only 1 percent of the city's population and a potential voting bloc with only two years of experience with the ballot, success came with the mayor's agreement to establish Fire Company 21.

The state of the African American community in Chicago before 1872 revealed a dynamism that presaged the coming of the black firemen. With active involvement in resisting and reacting to the devastating fire, community heroes such as the Hudlins and others not only assertively responded to dire circumstances in an advantageous way, but also gave momentum to what would soon be seen as an unquestionable fact that there would one day be black firemen. The character of the pool of African American men in the city by the time of the Great Fire of 1871 confirmed the existence of able-bodied, interested men of age. These men included both returning and migrating Civil War veterans, members of fraternal orders, and under-employed workers in the industrial and service sectors, all of whom were ready to fully participate in mainstream occupations once the opportunity afforded itself. Collectively, they exhibited the traits commonly associated with fire-men—courage under pressure, disciplined living, willingness to act on their own initiative when necessary, experience with organized effort, voluntary subordination to bureaucratic leadership, commitment to a prescribed mission, and dedication to a cause.

Some of the men had past military experience, and all were required to complete six months of probationary training before they formally joined the force. Accordingly, in June 1873, Martin Brown, Wilson Mankins, Stephen Paine, George Adams, James Porter, Thomas Sulphon, and Henry Pethybridge were the first men to form Engine Company 21. Their white captain, David Kenyon, had commanded black troops during the war, and this factor heavily influenced the departmental leadership's decision to appoint him. The first engineer was believed to have been a gentleman named "Watkins," or possibly an Adams, and the first lieutenant was named Mankins. Beginning a national tradition, they are believed to be the first municipally appointed firefighters in the United States, and at the local level, their firehouse was located in the basically African American neighborhood in which they all resided, on Twelfth Street near Third Avenue (now Plymouth Court). Impressive in their commitment to duty, their quick arrivals at all fires gained the attention of their superiors by the spring of 1878. One reason for their great speed was that they had created the first sliding pole at a fire station anywhere in the nation (Figures 18 and 19).[59]

B. The Business Sphere

In the commercial sphere, John Jones emerged from his strong pre–Civil War commercial base stronger financially than ever. Meantime, John W. E. Thomas, a grocer and owner of a private school, arrived in Chicago in 1865 from Alabama, where he had been reared by a white physician and his family.[60] Quite possibly it was a family to which he belonged by blood, given Southern racial etiquette. Drake and Cayton wrote of an active period of black commercial activity: "Reference has been made to John Jones, the tailor, in the Seventies. There were also barbers, hairdressers, masseurs and caterers. A few Negroes ran livery stables and served as draymen. . . . In the late Seventies, another Negro [named Platt] opened a large lumber yard from which he later made a small fortune. While most of these had a predominantly white clientele, there were also fewer lucrative restaurants, barber shops, and small stores in the small Negro area."[61]

The barbering profession continued to attract African Americans because of the lucrative market of white men who sought personal attention at

Fig. 18. Fire Engine Company 21.

Fig. 19. William Watkins, engineer, Company 21. *Vivian G. Harsh Research Collection of Afro-American History and Literature, Chicago Public Library.*

Fig. 20. Eliza Campbell-Taylor.
Chicago Historical Society, ICHi-22379.

Fig. 21. Joanna Cecilia Hudlin Snowden.
Chicago Historical Society, ICHi-22378.

grooming, for an increasing number of them held administrative jobs in a growing postwar economy. As self-employed persons, barbers enjoyed an economic status among fellow blacks that brought them both admiration and envy because of their place in an expanding economy.[62] Moreover, little in the area of extensive, formal skills was needed, and social status increased with this occupation. Private William Graves of Company B returned after the Civil War to his humble domicile and began a new life in his occupation as he "ran a barber shop."[63] He was joined in the same trade by James H. Brown, who reportedly also ran an employment bureau at Thirty-first Street and Cottage Grove Avenue.

Last, a predominantly male professional class, comprising well-trained physicians and attorneys, was slowly evolving. Edward H. Morris gained admission to the Illinois Bar in 1879, as did Franklin A. Denison. In medicine, Dr. C. H. Hutchinson and another unnamed physician remained active in their fields for some years. Among other professionals, Eliza Campbell-Taylor was appointed the first African American schoolteacher in Chicago (Figure 20). Quite possibly she taught at an integrated school such as the one that educated the children of former slaves like Eliza Jane Harris and Julia Simpson, who entered the Chicago school system after the war and attended the facility at Harrison and Clark streets, a racially mixed neighborhood. In contrast, in New York City, it was not until 1896 that a black teacher taught whites.[64]

The educational obstacles faced by both youngsters and their teachers had to be immense. The development of intellectual potential rested fundamentally on the ability of the pupil to first achieve a sense of his or her own personal worth. Yet simple matters like naming, birth date, and age—the beginning points for one's valuation of self—could be problematic. Later in life, one of the early public school pupils, Eliza Jane Harris, still exhibited the uncertainty of life and the confusion it posed, stating: "Like a good many colored people I don't know my age exactly but I think I was born between 1857 and 1859."[65] What effect this had on the learning process is conjectural, but it should be assumed that it was detrimental.

In contrast, other youngsters entered the city's schools from households more familiar with freedom and urban living. Joanna Hudlin and her eight siblings exemplified this component of the black population (Figure 21). She finished both elementary and high school, then studied secretarial services, mastering stenography and typing. With these skills she became the first black woman to work at a downtown bank.[66] Journalist Ferdinand L. Barnett enjoyed his free, racially mixed, public school education immensely and spent his adult life praising its benefits to all citizens.[67] Two of his life-long treasures were his high school graduation announcement and an invitation to his first class reunion. The benefits of a Chicago public school education received their final form of protection when the State of Illinois forbade discrimination by race in 1874 (see Appendix C).

V. A SENSE OF COMMUNITY

A. New and Revitalized Attitudes and Institutions

A healthy adjustment to city living required a changed attitude among this slowly urbanizing population. Least affected were the pioneers. They had experienced acclimation during the several decades since 1833, their racial pride (a sign of maturation) evincing itself in various self-defined celebrations such as their Emancipation Day festivities. For the bulk of African Americans, they now exercised the options newly made available in their lives. This meant they controlled their lives as much as free people could in a materialistic society such as the one that existed in Chicago. Especially impressive was their control over their inner selves as they rose above the bitterness that slavery engendered. Spurred by a spirituality that enabled

them to meet life's obstacles head-on, they moved beyond themselves despite
the horrors of bondage. Mary Livermore's observations of this ability during
the war amazed whites as to its empowering influence over blacks. They
found divine guidance and retribution in their spiritual beliefs. Livermore
recorded their prayers and utterances: "But now, O King, you've brought us
up hyar under de shadder o' de Linkum army, and we 'pend on Thee for de
rest," and "we're gwine to wait for Thee, O Kingy, to show us de way." Also,
Livermore recorded "a prayer of more pathos and earnestness [that followed].
It appealed to God, as Infinite Justice, and with confidence that the wrongs
of the slave would be redressed"; in this song, the emancipated individual
announces, "I allers knowed it was a-comin, I allers heerd de rumblin' o' de
wheels. . . . An' de Lor', He's keept His promise, an' venged His people, jes'
as I knowed He would."[68]

For blacks left behind deep in the plantation South, a different attitude
persisted that lingered into the future and oftentimes worked its way into
thinking in Chicago. Despite the assertiveness of many Southern blacks after
the war, there was an alternative mind-set that was given to resignation, an
acceptance of fate. Since African American success in Chicago demanded
a constant pattern of growth and development in all areas of endeavor, from
the social to the economic to the political, conflict between old and new
ways and attitudes plagued black Chicagoans constantly. As a young
Ferdinand L. Barnett assessed the situation, "But little has been done since
the emancipation to ameliorate their condition. Great efforts have been put
forth, but the harvest is great and the laborers comparatively so few, that the
results do not show to great advantage. As we have no past and only a poor
present, we must make a bright future. To do this we must acquire moral
greatness, intellectual excellence and wealth."[69] Accordingly, Barnett inaugurated a campaign in the pages of the *Conservator* to buttress the work of
the churches in transforming the slothful, the racially diffident, and the
nonassertive individual and family into a new people.

An all-important church life flourished, maintaining a communal stability
that extended beyond spiritual and moral guidance. Simply put, it anchored
the African American existence as it continued as a center of community
life. Quinn Chapel continued to exercise its influence over black life and
was joined by the wartime churches, Olivet Baptist and Bethel A.M.E. in
1862, and Providence Baptist in 1863. The first of the Reconstruction-era
churches appeared when African Americans in the West Division organized
St. Stephen A.M.E. in 1872 to meet the growing needs of African Methodists
in that part of town. Providence Baptist, born in the turmoil and exhilaration of war, already fulfilled that need for Christians who preferred the Baptist
tradition in that part of the city.

Changing times brought a new challenge to the prominence of Quinn Chapel A.M.E. as Olivet Baptist Church began its meteoric rise to institutional prominence. This Baptist congregation continued to be led by Virginia-born Richard De Baptiste, a man of mixed parentage, immense drive, and impressive administrative abilities. Worthy of note, just as De Baptiste arrived to stabilize the church, John Jones moved his membership from Olivet to a white Unitarian church.[70] Although this was an obvious sign of his rising stature within mainstream Chicago, it also raises the possibility that he and his wife had reached the peak of their dissatisfaction with the static character of church life that had to appeal to newly emancipated African Americans from the South. Jones's seemingly innocuous act amounted to the beginning of a pattern linking status and religious affiliation throughout the rest of the century.

At the time of Jones's defection, the few black churches provided physical settings for meeting, planning, and inaugurating new initiatives for their race in spheres that were professional, social, political, and recreational. These were all-purpose community linchpins with a value that was incalculable. Entertainment meant to enlighten and upgrade the race's appreciation of the finer things in American society was always important. As expected, the churches remained places that sponsored sundry activities geared to keeping church folk close to that institution and away from the pleasures of the world. One example occurred on February 4, 1878, when the Oriental Club performed a biblical pageant at the Turner Hall, Van Buren and Clark. All-day outings on Sunday began with worship at 11:00 a.m., Sunday School in the afternoon, dinner among the religious later, and conversation to end the day. Other, less-serious entertainment ranged from family dinners to musical recitals to attending black minstrel shows given by such groups as the Plantation Minstrels.

As inclusive as these churches were with their activities and memberships, they failed to meet another rising need for status differentiation. These churches were soon joined by the city's first black Episcopal church, St. Thomas, which was organized in 1878. Significantly, this emergence of a higher-status Protestant denomination represented another step toward diversified religious affiliation.

B. The First Newspaper

A desire to improve communication within the various elements of this growing black community induced Ferdinand L. Barnett to usher in the era of the black newspaper in 1878. It was an event in news publication, however, that coincided with a general growth pattern in the city, so it lacked

Fig. 22. Ferdinand L. Barnett.
Special Collections Research Center,
University of Chicago Library.

total uniqueness; the *Chicago Daily News* also began publication at this time. Out of a racial commitment to communicate with and to provide guidance to his race, Barnett started the *Chicago Conservator*.

After completing elementary and high school in the city, Barnett had attended college at Northwestern University, located in the adjacent northern suburb of Evanston. After successfully completing his studies in law, he passed the Illinois bar in 1878 and proceeded into both law and journalism. However, this fireball gave up active editorship of the paper and devoted his time entirely to law after four years at the joint effort.[71]

As the city's pioneer African American newspaper, the *Conservator*'s appearance marked a major institutional advance in black Chicago's communal maturity. Under the separate leaderships of Barnett and Rev. Richard De Baptiste, the *Conservator* demonstrated the influential role a newspaper could assume in guiding a community in transition. In and of itself, the paper's name seemed almost a statement of affirmation as to the salutary origins of the Chicago African American community and its cultural moorings, its continuous dignity under duress, and its ability to constantly move progressively forward as the African Americans enlarged their role in the life of Chicago. In contrast to earlier, antebellum institutions, which were insular, this newspaper assumed a pan-institutional influence over a broader course of urban behavior. While serving as editor, Barnett sought to establish a transcendent line of communication; in doing so, he applied a "method of presentation [that embodied] editorial discussion, interpretation, and comment rather than straight news presentation" (Figure 22).[72]

As a molder of African American image, thought, and behavior, Barnett crusaded in 1878 for change in the manner in which his race's title was presented. In his most notable campaign, "Spell It with a Capital," he fought to capitalize the first letter in *Negro:*

> We have noticed an error which all journalists seem to make. Whether from mistake or ill-intention, we are unable to say, but the profession universally begins Negro with a small letter. It is certainly improper, and as no one has ever given us a good reason for this breach of orthography, we will offer one. White men began printing long before Colored men dared read their works; had power to establish any rule they saw fit. As a mark of disrespect, as a stigma, as a badge of inferiority they tacitly agreed to spell his name without a capital. The French, German, Irish, Dutch, Japanese, and other nationalities are honored with a capital letter, but the sons of Ham must bear the burden of a small n.
>
> To our Colored journalistic brothers we present this as a matter of self interest. Spell it with a capital. To the Democratic journals we present this as a matter of good grammar. To the Republicans we present it as a matter of right. Spell it with a capital. To all persons who would take from our wearied shoulders a hair's weight of the burden of prejudice and ill will we bear, we present this as a matter of human charity and beg you SPELL IT WITH A CAPITAL.[73]

For his part, De Baptiste took equal pride in the paper's editorials, which ranged across the ideological spectrum in dealing with racism and economics, politics, nationalism versus integration, and interracial relations. Under such topics as "The Negro in Debt, but Who Owes Him?" "Colored votes and the Republican Party," "The Emigration Question," and "Social Equality," the cleric as journalist attempted to mold black thinking and behavior. In 1878, De Baptiste explained his journalistic goals thus:

> It will discuss in a fair and liberal spirit those questions that agitate and cause an honest difference of opinion among citizens, whose aims are alike patriotic; but will give special prominence to such matters as appertain to the intellectual, moral, and social development and business prosperity of the colored people, and at the same time, keep its columns open to a fair and courteous discussion of all important subjects. "Progress in all right directions," shall be its motto.[74]

Therefore, as a barometer and framer of thought, the *Conservator* began on a course that presaged the *Chicago Defender*'s early-twentieth-century campaign to identify with pride the African American people as the "Race" and its members as "Race men" and "Race women." Basically though, it not only battled racism in Chicago (of which the editor thought there was little), but also fought for the establishment of resilient, acceptable moral norms.

C. Traditional Family Formation

Families, of course, are important for community development, and twin strains of family formation emerged during this period. One involved the reconstruction of family life that had been disrupted by Southern slavery. The other included marriages and the birth of children resulting from the normal pattern of family life in Chicago. The quality of African American life obviously benefited through the perpetuation of the family. Analysis of the federal pension records of certain Civil War veterans from the Twenty-ninth Illinois revealed that members of this group strongly contributed to this pattern. Consistent with a post-Emancipation pattern that would extend throughout the nineteenth century, two-parent households typified community organization. Veterans entered a marriage pool that included many women twenty to thirty years their junior. Women married across the chasm of a generation of experience and life's travails because of a social convention within their community that recognized companionship over "spinsterhood," and mutual respect over romantic love. While the veteran, usually referred to as "soldier" in government documents, possessed little in the way of material possessions, or for that matter, a future promising pecuniary rewards, he was respected as a warrior who had actively participated in the liberation of his race. Chronologically older, he might just have approximated the image of what a father in bondage might have been, the ultimate protector. As a proven emancipator, bringing a successful conclusion to two generations of suffering under slavery, and accomplishing it at a risk to life and limb, he was respected within his own community. His wife, the product of the same experience, patiently toiled alongside him without any pretense to life in the manor. Often religiously fortified to expect little in Caesar's world but an ultimate reward in God's, life appeared tolerable while the present seemed bearable.

Willis Easley married Sarah and together they buried three children—Walter, Fred, and George—in less than two years, during 1872 and 1873. Other soldiers married or remained married and had children that survived the city's diseases and inclement weather. Civil War veteran Rodney Long of the Twenty-ninth Infantry Regiment married Louisa Clark in a Catholic service at St. Mary's Church, at Wabash and Eldredge Court. His bride had reached the marriageable age of eighteen on February 24, 1868. The ranks of African American Catholics, while small, continued to grow.

The children of the postwar unions grew and developed in an environment free of the vestiges of slavery and attended school on an equitable basis, transcending the limits imposed by the economic order, which relegated to the lowest rungs of the social ladder black adults, former slaves, and the children of slaves, who spent their hours working. So, just like the white masses, many, but not all, recognized the value of education. The ability to read a newspaper or the Bible was a luxury too valuable to let slip by, so skills in reading, writing, and elocution were encouraged for the young. For those parents who were indifferent to the opportunity at hand in the racially integrated schools of Chicago, Ferdinand L. Barnett had only words of scorn and warning.[75]

One story of family formation deserves historical reconstruction because of its pathos, courage, and triumph.[76] In some ways, the personages involved represented the new type of Everyman and Everywoman found on the streets of Chicago as former slaves entered the erstwhile City of Refuge, now transformed into the city of unbridled competition and opportunity. On February 1, 1866, the friends of Civil War veteran John Liter and Jane Hughes met in the home of Joseph and Catherine Wilson to witness and participate in a truly joyous event, one that dramatically heralded the arrival of freedom. As their courting ritual came to a close, the two, "somewhere around" thirty-seven years old, were married and remained so until death parted them two decades later. In a marriage where strength of character had to have played a dominant role, two individuals who had displayed courage under duress now formed a union at a time of change that would put this attribute as well as many others to constant testing. Postwar America and Chicago were hardly places for the fainthearted to thrive.

As former slaves, they knew neither their exact ages nor other vital statistics that shaped life and personality, but they responded to their hearts' desire at the moment. Church ritual followed, which would have been a Methodist Episcopal ceremony and thus obviously solemn, but which also would have included festive elements in accordance with Afro-American customs. Rev. Frederick Meyers from the nearby Bethel A.M.E. Church presided and blessed the union (Figure 23). The bride's two young daughters, Carrie and Anna, and son, Robert, ages eight, six, and four, respectively, were present and were no doubt as happy as their mother on this occasion where personal choice mattered and full family formation beckoned. They had a father and protection again in their lives.

Fig. 23. *Harper's Weekly* sketch of the marriage of an African American
soldier at Vicksburg by Chaplain Warren of the Freedmen's Bureau, 1866.
*Photographs and Prints Division, Schomburg Center for Research in Black Culture,
The New York Public Library, Astor, Lenox, and Tilden Foundations.*

After decades of bondage, this was John and Jane Hughes Liter's first marriage of choice, one conducted in a setting of freedom, and an event voluntarily assembled among supportive friends. Only the successful conclusion
of the war could have produced these conditions for these assembled former
slaves. Friends in attendance included Miss Frances Jones, Mrs. Mary Moore,
Miss Minerva Chase, and Mr. Thomas Hayden, whom friends also called
"Scipio." The latter was, no doubt, a slave name, indicative of a master who
enjoyed and admired the world of antiquity, and who took pleasure in
bestowing subordinates with names that bore no resemblance to their interests, abilities, sensitivities, or personal preferences.[77] Hayden worked as a
blacksmith in his own shop on Clark Street, and his choice of occupation
and decision to use a new first name revealed an independent streak that
would have put him in good company with the independent-minded Jane
Liter. Hayden, like the groom, worked with his hands and performed ardu-
ously to provide for himself.

As a new citizen of Chicago, Mrs. Liter's life before this moment had been
one in which she repeatedly demonstrated basic character traits that fit well
into the urban landscape, among them foresight, decisiveness, courage,
motherliness, amiability, and intelligence. In a claim made by an African

American veteran and his family, federal pension records contain an unusual assessment that attests to Jane Liter's intelligence: "She is a most intelligent woman, for one of her class, but without education and bears a good reputation for truth and veracity."[78] Of course, her deficiency in reading and writing skills and membership in "her class" related directly to her previous status as a chattel slave. Jane Liter's loathing of this intolerable status led her to end it through courageous flight. Franklin and Schweninger assessed such runaways, both women and men, and found in them similar personality traits:

> Here, too, then was diversity, but most runaways demonstrated self-confidence, self-assurance, self-possession, determination and self-reliance. They were resourceful, willful, focused, and purposeful. A number were quick-witted, wily and intelligent. . . . Among the most significant characteristics of runaways was their intelligence.[79]

But what was more remarkable about Jane Liter was that she was a member of that rare group of slave escapees who were female and whose children had accompanied them in flight. Of this circle, Franklin and Schweninger wrote:

> Young slave women were less likely to run away because they had often begun to raise families by their late teens and early twenties. With youngsters to care for, it became difficult to contemplate either leaving them behind or taking them in an escape attempt. Lying out in the woods or fleeing to more distant points would only mean suffering, danger, hardship for their children. As several historians have pointed out, although slave women desired freedom as much as slave men and were often as assertive and aggressive on the plantation as male slaves, the task of uprooting and carrying children in flight "was onerous, time-consuming, and exhaustive." As a result, a smaller proportion than among men decided to run away.[80]

Jane Liter admirably represented this group with her demonstrated courage. Further, she possessed an adaptability to marriage based on her experiences in slavery where open assertiveness was a dangerous attribute to exhibit. One wishes to deduce from this assumption that she fits this mold of the black woman emerging from slavery written by historian Eugene D. Genovese:

> A remarkable number of women did everything possible to strengthen their men's self-esteem and to defer to their leadership. What has been viewed as a debilitating female supremacy was in fact a closer approxi-

mation to a healthy sexual equality than was possible for whites and perhaps even for many postbellum blacks. . . . This female deference represented an effort by the women to support their men—an effort that could only have flowed from a judgement on what men ought to be and an awareness of the terrible ravages being wrought by slavery. On whatever level of consciousness, many women—perhaps a substantial majority—understood that the degradation of their men represented their own degradation as black women and that of their children. . . . The struggle of the women to define a feminine role for themselves and to strengthen their men's sense of their own masculinity came to fruition after the war when the women so readily deferred to their men without surrendering their own opinions and activities, which were often militant.[81]

Whatever Jane Liter thought on this occasion, it was tempered by an awareness of her past, which was filled with disappointments and probably despair at times but, more often than not, optimism related to her inherited temperament to never allow obstacles to permanently deter her from her plans for the future, for a life under her own control.

Her past life, of course, had revolved around slavery. While in bondage around 1845, Jane Liter gave birth to a son, Edward, and they entered a world totally unlike that of her West African ancestors. Considered chattel, or property, she and Edward lacked social status, or *being*, as members of humanity. Furthermore, under the system of American chattel slavery, Edward assumed his mother's status and was relegated to a life of bondage unless favorable circumstances changed their fate. Jane worked on a farm or plantation in North Carolina until around 1848 when, in an action that would prove to be characteristic for her, *she seized the time*.

If Jane Liter had possessed memories of West Africa, or had been privileged to have heard of the marriage and family customs of the Ashanti (Ghana), Bini (Nigeria), Fon (old Dahomey), or scores of other peoples, from whose ranks the enslaved of America originated in great numbers, Jane Liter would have known how abnormal her life's circumstances were.[82] If they were fortunate, the descendants of these Africans might possibly have had memories of what the Ashanti and others believed and practiced regarding the solemnity and social necessity of family life that originated with formal marriage. Regrettably, this was an experience of which Jane Liter was deprived until 1866.[83] Of course, just as simple, she could have observed quite closely how white masters lived as families, and how important marriage was to them, to view her condition as untenable.

With or without this knowledge of her cultural background, available evidence showed that sometime during Edward's third year in slavery, around

1848, Jane Liter and Edward were sold as a "family" unit to a new slave owner in Tennessee. Accurately credited with being intelligent, Jane knew that this was not the way she and Edward were meant to live. She decided she had to act decisively to make a break with the anomaly called "slavery." It was, in fact, a system so abominable and abnormal that even the whites themselves referred to it as the "peculiar institution." One day, when the opportunity presented itself, Jane courageously escaped with her son. Unfortunately, they were captured. As Edward later remembered, "she had tried to escape taking me with her, but after about four days, we were captured and taken back. I remember that very distinctly, for I had got tired out and had laid down by the side of the road, and when they came after us on horses, they took me first."[84] In the race for freedom, the quadruped and the slave catcher had easily overtaken the mother and her toddler.

Jane's punishment was separation from her beloved Edward and her sale to another slave owner in southern Kentucky. She did live to see her son again, but this reunion did not occur until twenty years after this traumatic breakup. Life on the Garner plantation near Concord, Kentucky, offered few of life's joys, but after a while the resilient Jane entered into a slave marriage with a fellow bondsman, Patrick Hughes. Historian John W. Blassingame reflected on this practice, writing that "the Southern plantation was unique in the New World because it permitted the development of a monogamous slave family." But this was marriage with a price. As Jane Liter matter-of-factly recalled the union, "there was a little ceremony and we became man and wife." Blassingame described the event thus: "[T]he marriage ceremony in most cases consisted of the slaves' simply getting the master's permission and moving into a cabin together. . . . [The masters would sometimes offer] a sumptuous feast in their own parlors to the slave guests. Afterwards, the slaves had long dances in the [slave] quarters in honor of the couple."[85]

Marital unions of this sort formed the pattern for plantation "marriages" and always required the approval of the slave master. Thus any attempt by masters to present this in light of solemnity, dignity, or permanency was illusory. These relationships existed solely at the pleasure of the slave owner. Frazier has written that, "in a world where patriarchal traditions were firmly established, probably even less consideration was shown for the preferences of slave women. When men of the servile race were ordered to mate, women, who on the whole played a more passive role, had little choice in the selection of mates . . . [yet] the masters either through necessity or because of their humanity showed some consideration for the wishes of the slaves in their mating."[86]

In the case of the intrepid Jane Liter, it might just be reasonable to assume that Patrick Hughes met some of her expectations as to what a husband should be and that she might have played some part in the arrangement of their union. Yet in the years following the end to slavery, the "slave marriage" was undeniably exposed for the farce that it was. In 1892, when Jane Hughes Liter was questioned about her marital status since entering adulthood, her response was candid and at the same time disheartening. She was asked why, in previous affidavits, she had stated that she was never married before her marriage in 1866 to John Liter. She responded in the same manner as other widows and mothers during the postwar period: "slave marriage was no marriage." They faced a social conundrum not of their own making. On one occasion, an African American attorney had counseled her previously on the ramifications of legal unions and the inherent fault in slave unions, telling her "that the pension office didn't call that any marriage."[87] Thus she had stated what white America wanted to hear, already knowing the response contained both truth and fiction.

Meanwhile, family life proved more formidable than might be expected under the circumstances. Under plantation conditions, three children were born to this union, Jane's first structured one—Robert, Anna, and Carrie. She demonstrated a motherliness of note, but maternity for African American women living under slavery faced a condemnation by slave masters and other apologists of the "peculiar institution." The sociologist Frazier contradicted the stereotype of the slave mother as uncaring and cold: "[I]t is not surprising, to find that slave mothers, instead of viewing with indifference the sale, the loss otherwise, of their children, often put up a stubborn resistance and suffered cruel punishments to prevent separation from them. The fact that slave families were often divided when it was to the economic advantage of the owners is too well established to take seriously the denials of those who have idealized slavery."[88]

Jane's adjustment to slavery for herself and her family amounted to little more than a temporary accommodation to harsh reality. Without immediate options, she would wait patiently until they appeared. As soon as a chance to strike out for freedom took place, once again she proved her courage by deciding and acting immediately. With her husband dead by the middle of 1862, she again relied solely on her own abilities—foresight, intelligence, and courage. Her long-awaited opportunity arrived with the Union assault on Forts Henry and Donelson on the Tennessee and Cumberland rivers, respectively, in the winter of 1862. Fighting began across the state border in northwestern Tennessee—notably near the Garner plantation in southern Kentucky. A well-coordinated Union offensive led by General U. S. Grant and U.S. Navy Flag Officer Andrew Foote commenced in early February 1862 and concluded in a swift Union victory. For Jane Liter, the results were

mixed. The military and naval victories over Confederate forces in seces-
sionist Tennessee had no legal effect on slavery on the north side of the
Tennessee-Kentucky border, for slave-state Kentucky was still in the Union.
Jane Hughes was left with the choice of remaining in slavery, with freedom
nearer than ever, or attempting for the second time an escape with children,
this time to safety with Northern military forces. "When the Union troops
took Fort Henry, my boy was just 3 weeks old," Jane Hughes Liter remembered. "That was in the spring[,] I think. The following fall[,] one night I
with my three children left the plantation and went to Fort Henry[,] where
the Union troops were[,] and the first boat that came along, all of the
women and children and old men who were not able to fight were put on a
boat and sent to Cairo, Ill.[,] where they said we were out of danger[,] and
after staying there about a month I went to Chicago."[89]

Life in Chicago with all its difficulties proved to be "no crystal stair."[90]
Nevertheless, the family's arrival in the City of Refuge meant an end to the
lash, to sales to other masters, to hard work, indignities, and humiliations—
it meant freedom of choice. It meant freedom over one's own body and fate.
With three children in her care, Jane Liter went to work and eventually
found some security with residency in the Wilson family home as a lodger.
Bethel A.M.E. Church was probably her church of choice, and her association with the Wilsons provided her with an opportunity to meet Joseph
Wilson's old comrade in arms, John Liter. Although she was in her thirties,
Jane was poor but striving for a semblance of economic independence, and
she was probably working in domestic service or as a washerwoman.

For his part, five-foot, five-inch, muscular John Liter had completed his
tour of duty in the Twenty-ninth Infantry Regiment in December 1865. He
had experienced the worst of war at the Battle of the Crater, where he had
engaged in hand-to-hand combat with the enemy. Liter was speared in the
groin by a Confederate soldier thrusting his bayonet during a charge up a
hill. He survived and took up residence in Chicago after the war and bonded
immediately with his close friend from his unit, Joseph Wilson. The relationship was especially strong because Wilson credited John Liter with saving his life in combat. They talked often and told stories of their "great
times in the army."[91] Liter settled into civilian life, apparently missing only
a permanent companion. Then he met Jane.

VI. POSTWAR MARTIAL SPIRIT

The postwar adjustment of another segment of Chicago's African American
community, the veterans, has so far been overlooked in local historical

inquiry. Their presence in communities throughout the country represented an important feature in African American life that accounted for the raised level of consciousness of the doable. Change, or its prospect, caused little consternation among the valiant men who had faced death daily. Those surrounding them often assumed attitudes related to this experience. Thus, in the midst of national exaltation of victory over the old order in the South and the triumph of modernization in all aspects of life, the spirit of the soldier proved a major stimulus for black advancement. The soldier's ultimate contribution rested not in any claim to leadership over various societal spheres, rather, it was rooted in his example of manhood that inspired both women and men to lead.

Making the soldiers into contributors to the vitality of their city and community required a certain set of "mental calibrations" to adjust to combat and then to readjust to a state of nonbelligerency that afforded the soldier emotional safety. Bonding became part of this process of personal rehabilitation. In addition, bonding with fellow veterans "was a refuge in a day when previously important links with others within or beyond the armies were weakening or disappearing. In reality, the soldier had nowhere to turn save to his friends in the ranks."[92]

Bonding among the veterans derived from their shared experiences of wartime service, along with associated personal interests and activities. As it affected white veterans, "they became convinced, quite accurately, that those at home did not understand the experience through which they [had] pass[ed], and they resented, with less justification, that civilian incomprehension." Civil War historian Gerald Linderman quoted a veteran's lament from the Virginia campaigns of 1864, the experience to which members of the Twenty-ninth could most relate: "I never knew before what campaigning was, I think, though that all [the Army of the Potomac] have a pretty fair idea of it now. We have had to march all day and all night, ford rivers, bivouac without blankets or any covering during rain and sunshine, and a good part of the time have been half-starved. . . . Any one who [got] through safely [should have] consider[ed] himself lucky."[93]

Among veterans of the Twenty-ninth, the close bond between John Wilson and John Liter has already been discussed. In addition, Charles Steele and Charles Smith, who enlisted and were examined the same day, March 1, 1864, bonded.[94] So did William Randall and William Collins, who were friends before the war and afterwards and who kept in contact, talking often. And in a case of soldiers with dissimilar first names, James Jones and Frank McAllister became close enough for the latter to allow Jones into his home to live when he needed help after the war.[95]

Another of the vexing problems confronting veterans during and after the war was their deteriorating health. Moreover, their health status to a great extent represented that of their community's. Poor health while in slavery was only compounded by the rigors of military service. The death rates in the city and state would bear grim witness to this situation as the years rolled on. Randall suffered in the company of comrades who acted as caregivers. He was one of a number of soldiers who "were badly used up on account of" the "terrible march" from Fort Harrison to Petersburg, during which time the regiment crossed the Rappahannock River over pontoon bridges. Randall had fallen into the river and had to be rescued. When William Randall became agonizingly ill during the 1870s with a diseased kidney and rheumatism, the result of the forced marching immediately before the surrender at Appomattox, "comrades would have to sit up with him at night to give him what comfort they could through his misery."[96]

For one soldier, Joseph Richardson, death awaited only days after his discharge from a wartime injury.[97] Another soldier, also named Joseph Richardson, had sustained an injury while building fortifications under continuous rifle assault at Petersburg. His comrades sought safety from rifle fire and, in doing so, allowed timber to fall on Richardson, injuring his back and legs.[98] The same scenario affected Frank McAllister of Company C. The full weight of a falling log crushed his back and legs as he built fortifications near the siege lines outside Petersburg at White House Landing in August 1864.[99]

McAllister had fled to the North during the war, thereby gaining his freedom. Working as a teamster and carrying trade over the streets of Chicago, he was adjusting to a new life and good fortune when circumstances improved even more. He met and chose Celia, also a former slave, as his wife in 1862. Almost as part of a tragic cycle—oppressive bondage to joyous liberty to preordained misfortune—at the age of thirty-eight he enlisted in the military, was discharged because of his injury at forty, and by the time he was forty-four he was described in medical records as "a broken down man."[100]

Once discharged from the military, he had suffered constantly from lameness and kidney problems resulting in urinary incontinence. His ability to make a living for his family obviously suffered, since the injury "incapacitat[ed] him from [performing] all kinds of manual labor" until his death.[101] Private McAllister's suffering ended with his well-documented, but inglorious, death on May 1, 1879, between the hours of eight and nine in the morning. It was noted "that he had become very poor and dissipated and but little attention was paid to him at the time of his death more than to get rid of his corpse about like a dead dog."[102]

The leadership pool of the black community benefited immensely from the experience of these veterans, especially those who exhibited leadership during the war years. While only whites could hold commissioned offices in the U.S. Army because of the racist practices of the time, the Twenty-ninth had its black leaders. For those men who were promoted to the rank of sergeant—whether first, commissary, or master—an overwhelming sense of pride abounded in their chests as well as in the men they were sworn to train, drill, and discipline and whose welfare they were to protect. In the restrictive world that whites dominated, blacks rarely found themselves in a position to command men, even men of their own group. Under the military code, sergeants received the recognition accorded all persons of superior rank, so the bulk of any company, composed primarily of privates and corporals, had to show their respect. While neither a salute nor a mandatory "Sir" was appropriate, authority existed nonetheless. As to the basis of their authority, it was to be found in Article I of the U.S. Army's regulations:

> 1. All inferiors are required to obey strictly, and to execute with alacrity and good faith, the lawful orders of the superiors appointed over them.
> 2. Military authority is to be exercised with firmness, but with kindness and justice to inferiors. Punishments should be strictly conformable to military law.[103]

The sergeant bridged the gap between the enlisted men and the commissioned officers. They had daily contact with the average soldier, and thus became better acquainted with the men on a more human level; for their part, the soldiers, while admiring and respecting the officers, admitted their sergeants into a more intimate place in their lives.

Edward Miller has written that a man's perceived intelligence played a major role in the selection of these noncommissioned officers. In the case of Willis Easley, "he was also a barber and probably literate, which may explain why he was immediately made a noncommissioned officer." Because of his mental acuity, William McKenney, a mulatto, rose in the ranks to become a sergeant but was mustered out as a corporal; he claimed that white officers grew to dislike his intelligence. He later alleged that race played a part in the delay in his being awarded a pension: "I do not think that my case as a Colored soldier has been looked into and considered with the amount of interest as half of the white soldiers have."[104]

Once the men and officers had fulfilled their tour of duty and the government decided that their military service was at an end, the regiment was mustered out in Springfield, Illinois, in December 1865. This began phase two in the soldier's life, for now he had earned the status of veteran. He had the option of terminating an enforced group membership that might have lost its relevance in peacetime civilian life. Yet there was bonding among the veterans derived from wartime service and associated interests and activities. Memories of military service could either endanger or reinvigorate a veteran's reintroduction to civilian life. There could be good memories to revive, as we have seen in the case of John Wilson and John Liter, who left the service with many good times about which to converse in later days. Yet there would often be the need to reshape memories in order to survive. This need likely aided the bonding process among fellow veterans upon encountering one another on the streets of Chicago. Without the company of fellow veterans, these men must have felt isolated in a hostile, industrial, overcrowded urban environment. Unfortunately, this was a world that no longer needed the soldier, black or white.

Late-nineteenth-century black Chicago had significant safety nets for those in need of social, economic, and psychological support: family and kin, friends, church, fraternal orders, and a veterans' post. In this milieu, the veteran sank or swam under his own as well as his community's effort. For persons who had been free for an extended time in the North before military service, their world showed even more immediate promise since the Illinois Black Laws had been rescinded in March 1865. With limitations on testimony, movement, and other features of humanity and citizenship removed, they could engage in the five-year fight to secure the franchise. Although one could wonder whether the camaraderie and network of the veterans were a "retrospective distortion of the Civil War experience, influenced perhaps by boredom with civilian life and part of a general tendency to look at the past through rose-colored glasses," Eric Dean has argued in favor of its genuineness.[105]

For many men, those who had enlisted several weeks or months after attaining their freedom, or even a year or two after reaching the North, this period after service constituted their first taste of real freedom. Freedom had to be experienced over time and beyond periods of duress to be fully enjoyed. The sergeants continued to play an important role at this stage of the veteran's life. When federal pension examiners needed assistance in locating witnesses in completing claims, it was the noncommissioned officers who were contacted to either give depositions on a given issue or help locate knowledgeable persons formerly belonging to the regiment. The sergeant's role was thus elevated in civilian life by the U.S. government's reliance on them as conduits in the claims process.

The need to bond with other African American men—to affirm manhood (by assuming civic duty), to establish a sense of fraternity, to render mutual assistance, and to inculcate group pride—found realization in the formation of disparate military organizations during the 1870s. Civil War

Fig. 24. Richard E. Moore.
Courtesy of Bethel A.M.E. Church.

veterans, in particular, pursued one such course that developed into a tradition. Nearby, to the east, the citizens of Detroit watched fifty reunited veterans of the 102nd Regiment, USCT, march when that city celebrated the
ratification of the Fifteenth Amendment in April 1870.[106] In that locale,
both civilian and soldier saw the link between the victors and the spoils—
in this case the vote. To insure that the veterans were not forgotten by the
public or by their own comrades, late in the decade Chicago soldiers reunited
and organized a veterans' post. In April 1879, just weeks before Frank
McAllister's death, African American veterans officially chartered John
Brown Post No. 50 under the auspices of the Grand Army of the Republic
(GAR). The post was committed to a creed of "Fraternity, Charity, and
Loyalty," and veteran William Smith was chosen as its first commander.[107]

Somewhat earlier, in 1872, that same quest for manhood and fraternity
prompted the organizing of the city's first peacetime African American militia
unit, the Hannibal Guard. Sometime thereafter, the Chicago Light Infantry
was formed at company strength with eighty-six men as part of the Seventh
Infantry, Illinois National Guard. A directory of the day noted that "Among
the members are to be found many ex-soldiers who were in the late war."
Befitting the experience of the men, the unit was known for its precision
drilling.[108] Then, by 1875, the Sixteenth Battalion was formed; it was composed of two companies, with a total of approximately two hundred men.[109]

Two sentiments merged. Northern society lavished great attention on the postwar victors in politics and other spheres, and the spark for acceptance of the rudiments of a martial tradition received resounding support. Thus the deeds of the veterans of the Civil War proved to former abolitionists that the black male was indeed a man and worthy of total societal recognition, and they touted this heroism to the whole of white society.[110]

Accordingly, a documented exuberance for the martial reigned among many segments of the black community, often fueled by veterans. When Bethel A.M.E. laid its cornerstone for a new church in 1875, the Hannibal Guard, under the leadership of Captain Richard E. Moore, along with a contingent of Masons, proudly stood by as community guardians (Figure 24).[111]

Interestingly, what one segment of the male community considered a reflection of true manhood might just have found little acceptance from another, for some veterans of Civil War combat units apparently disdained joining these organizations. The reasons for their reticence remain unknown. However, it is understandable that the discomforts of wartime service, combined with the vagaries of adjusting to civilian life had tested their mettle just as service in Virginia and Texas had. Some probably wanted to forget military life with its regimentation and deprivations.

W. E. B. Du Bois and Fannie Barrier Williams ranked the civilian version of the martial organization, the fraternal order, as second only to the church in organizational importance. The secret society, according to Du Bois, provided two services: positive social interaction and insurance—they "furnish[ed] pastime from the monotony of work, a field for ambition and intrigue, a chance for parade, and insurance against misfortune." According to Williams, they "affected[ed] every phase of their social life and represent[ed] the best achievements of the race in the matter of organization." Into the ranks of these associations flowed members of the "better class of Negro men," added Williams.[112] Had either Du Bois or Williams been alive during the war or had experience as a combatant, they would have added military élan into their observations.[113]

Exhibiting an inclusiveness either bordering on organizational genius or a high level of appreciation for cross-gender collaboration, "nearly all" of the secret orders had "auxiliary associations composed of women."[114] Cooperating across gender boundaries had immense, positive implications for family life, because the children of the membership were included in their various public activities. Indicative of the constant pressure produced by social change, proliferated organizations to include the Knights of Pythias, the True Reformers, the United Brotherhood, the Ancient Order of Foresters, the Elks, and the well-known Masons and Odd Fellows.

One of the leaders of the Masons and Odd Fellows was the prominent merchant-tailor John Jones. This community leader, who had risen to prominence before the Civil War, died in 1879, twenty days after Frank McAllister. Like McAllister, Jones spent his last days in the agony of poor health, having suffered from Bright's disease, a kidney disorder, for over a year. The similarities of their deaths ended when the preparations for celebrating Jones's life began. The well-documented life and death of Jones received major newspaper coverage in the *Chicago Tribune*. While unheard of for a "Colored man," even one of "prominence," Jones the Mason (who had a lodge named in his honor) and Odd Fellow in death rated the following call as a sign of comradeship: "An invitation is extended to all Masons, Odd-Fellows, and military and civic societies to attend his funeral. All bodies intending to participate are requested to report to the room at John Jones Lodge, A. F. and A. M., No. 326 Clark, 9:00 a.m. sharp."[115] Foreshadowing an increasingly rigid class structure by the new century, one man's death in obscurity was counterbalanced by another's in glory.

VII. POLITICS

The phenomenon that marked the entrance of Chicago African Americans into the city's political life and governmental operations represented nothing short of an upward climb from oblivion—manifested by political exclusion and civic marginality—to involvement in a participatory democracy. Furthermore, it required the confluence of several internal and external conditions. Externally, nineteenth-century Reconstruction-era politics in the North initially rested on the opening of a channel through which aspirations for involvement could be met. The end of the Illinois Black Laws in 1865 and subsequent enfranchisement of African American adult males in 1870 provided this opportunity. Further, external cooperation of progressive whites of the abolitionist stripe meant that the playing field would be leveled slightly more than it had ever been. Last, opposition from racist or recalcitrant whites had to be surmountable once it encountered the previous three factors, which could be formidable when found in unison.

The internal impulse to actively participate in politics required a willingness, combined with the strength of African Americans, to plunge into this competitive arena. A voting bloc of African Americans, coalescing with friendly white allies, with both acting in support of a determined black candidate in a free and open election, provided the formula for electoral triumph. Once in office, however, the African American still had to work for political relevancy.

John Jones had inaugurated the era of black participation in politics through office holding in the aftermath of the disastrous fire of 1871. However, in a city that hitched its Phoenix-marked star primarily to economic recovery and progress, municipal, state, and national politics assumed a lesser role in the political economy than can be imagined through hindsight in the early twenty-first century. Moreover, municipal machinations took on a lesser aura than did state and national politics. John Jones's success in light of the times carried great significance in the way of personal triumph and in assessing racial fluidity, but it provided no real glimpse into the formation of twentieth-century black machine politics. The incipient beginnings of a racial consciousness emanating from the mass level did, however, portend solidarity in voting patterns and thereby some semblance of future successes in politics.

While Illinois as a whole could appear unfriendly to African Americans, Chicago offered a different reception. As the erstwhile "sink hole of abolition," Chicago as a mecca had provided John Jones with an opportunity that he maximized through his opposition to the Illinois Black Laws and his election to county office in 1871. For Chicago, the context partially revolves around an exploration of the fluidity of racial interaction. It seemed that almost nothing was impossible in Chicago. John Jones's election in 1871 to municipal government set the stage for race-neutral involvement in the city's mainstream.

In the aftermath of the Great Fire, a combined surge of civic concern, indignation, and resolve demanded governmental reform as the city was rebuilt.[116] John Jones, respected by the city's civic and business leaders as a member of their circle, ran for office with approval from both Republican and Democratic parties, and he easily won election as a county commissioner on the Union Fire Proof ticket. The next year, he won a three-year term that ran from 1872 to 1875.[117] An attempt at a second three-year term failed and signaled a break that would last until 1894. Significantly, his election indicated the beginning of a pattern in which black candidates could win election in predominantly white voting districts. This interracial cooperation illustrated a unique character of the emerging black-white relationship.

Jones's defeat also marked the end of his political influence, as he was refused the support of blacks to run for a third term.[118] It is not absolutely clear how this came about; perhaps it was the charge of his leading a dictatorial "bed-room ring."[119] In any event, other names in the political sphere, such as Robert Hancock and William M. Baker, were soon heard as these men emerged as worthy political competitors. Meanwhile, in contrast to Chicago, which sought responsible government in the wake of the fire, nine hundred miles eastward in New York City, the notorious Democratic Tweed

Ring extended its hand to African Americans to join in their "Great Barbecue" of corrupt politics.[120]

Within five years of John Jones's initial political victory at the county level in November 1876, John W. E. Thomas, who had arrived in the city in 1865, was sworn in as the first African American member of the lower house of the Illinois General Assembly.[121] Determining to what extent Thomas's election conveyed value beyond its importance as a racial "first," which in itself often carries significance, rests on retrospective interpretation. The convergence of personal and party motivation, contextual political circumstances, and the electoral process all seemed to have played a pivotal role.

Thomas demonstrated his motivation to raise his status with his departure from his native Alabama in 1865 and association with a white benefactor. He arrived in Chicago prepared to take advantage of all the opportunities he encountered, whether in law, business, education, or politics.[122] His Southern experience with racial etiquette would work just as well for him in the Garden City once he entered politics and needed white sponsorships. Ambitious, he started out as a grocer and soon opened his own private school. John Jones's success had to have influenced him as to the possibility as to what he could achieve. When he spoke on the issue of African American participation as an inherent right, the strength of his political convictions became manifest. In 1878, when he sought reelection to a second term in the General Assembly, he said "permit me to say that my own people are solidly with me. It is their battle more than mine. I am in earnest in asking that the same consideration which is shown to white Republicans, to Irish and German and Scandinavian Republicans, be shown to colored Republicans."[123]

Further, in the volatile political year of 1876, the Hayes-Tilden election foretold the eventual likelihood of Democratic victory and a Democratic-controlled national government. Republican Chicago had every incentive to court and win every Republican vote. Thus, in the name of fairness and with a slot open for a third candidate to win a state representative's post from the Second District, the Republican party opened a door through which the ambitious Thomas entered. Originally opposed by individuals such as those belonging to the Municipal Reform Club, including Abraham Lincoln's sole surviving son, Robert Todd Lincoln, Thomas eventually got enough support to be placed on the Republican ticket. A Mr. Simeon W. King entered a motion to have Thomas's name placed on the ballot and "supported his motion through lengthy remarks."[124]

The nature of King's remarks has not been preserved, but if those remarks approximated the sentiments of former mayor John Wentworth, who spoke about how he had been mistaken to think that the issues that precipitated the Civil War had abated, they were a rallying cry of the abolitionist. Waving the "bloody shirt" of Northern and Union wartime loyalty, Wentworth stated that if voters wanted another war, they could choose to vote the Democratic ticket. If they wanted to betray the African Americans who proved themselves allies in the war and then afterward at Southern ballot boxes, they could support the return of Democratic party rule through a Tilden victory. On the other hand, Wentworth hailed the Republican ticket as one that was ready for reform and one that would stand by the Negro, who "helped us during the war."[125] Moreover, the Republicans claimed that Democratic presidential candidate Samuel J. Tilden promoted talk in the South of an assumption of Confederate war debts despite the Fourteenth Amendment prohibition of such a move.

According to the historian Harold F. Gosnell, black consciousness and solidarity contributed to Thomas's win because of "plumping," a part of the electoral process that allowed one voter to cast either one vote, one and one-half vote, or three votes for one or multiple candidates. Racially conscious African Americans would have only been too exuberant to match the election successes of their Southern brethren in placing one of their group into the state legislature. Thomas referred to this solidarity in stating that his motivation rested on his group's strength and solidarity. "Urged by large numbers of my fellow colored Republicans in Chicago, who claimed that numbering as they did some twelve hundred to 1,500 voters, they were entitled by every consideration of political fairness to representation in the Legislature, I consented to be a candidate."[126] However, that could have played only a part in Thomas's victory, because in amassing a total of 11,532 votes, and with only 7,000 blacks in the city and 1,200–1,500 voting, Thomas had obviously won with strong biracial and partisan Republican support.[127]

Thomas's experiences should be assumed to be based on cross-racial acceptance that enabled him to win black votes along with white support among the electorate when essential. The most relevant focus, then, is not on the whites who did not vote for Thomas, but on those who showed a willingness to vote for him. Even the benefit of the bullet vote, or "plumping," leaves another story to be told. Chicagoans had the capacity to be color-blind during this period while at the same time being very color-conscious, as exemplified by the need for a civil rights law.

Moreover, the need for white allies, mentors, and patrons, as encapsulated in political scientist Martin L. Kilson's concept of clientage politics, shaped the period. Within these often-friendly political confines, the ability to win as allies these racial outsiders opened all doors in early African American politics.[128] The relationship between attorney Kirk Hawes and Thomas seemed essential to his political success and might very well have replicated John Jones's relationship with influential whites. It might also explain Thomas's financial success. He would run again but not win reelection until 1882. In total, he served three terms for six years. The year 1882 marked a point of departure in state politics, because beginning that year, there would be continuous black representation in the lower house of the Illinois General Assembly.

Charles R. Branham has noted that during the period of Thomas's service, a diversified set of leaderships emerged to represent the interests of both black and white district constituents. With the increase in the black population through constant in-migration, "significant growth and diversification" was evident. From 3,600 in 1870, to 6,480 in 1880, to 14,000 in 1890, the black community became distinguishable as a bona fide, contributing segment of the general population. Simultaneously, Branham described the emergence, by the 1880s, of "a new category of community leadership . . . shaped and contoured to the rigors and discipline of urban politics." He placed Thomas in this scenario as an individual who steered clear of civic life while he devoted himself to the building of a political career. To wit, Thomas exemplified the professional politician, a category that will be explored later when in its fullest, future phase.[129]

Black politics had not emerged as a viable force providing a large number of jobs, so whenever an opportunity occurred, it was pursued with alacrity. Joseph W. Moore was the first South Town clerk, serving several terms. He also was active in fraternal orders in the 1890s.[130] Robert Mitchell, who as previously mentioned reached Chicago in 1873, began studying law in his spare time in the offices of T. B. Wakeman while he still was a waiter. He did not complete his studies but instead became a carpenter by having the right connections. His interest in the law remained, so when an opportunity to resume studying appeared, he did so in the offices of Mitchell (no relation), Baldwin, and Sheridan. Ambitious and undaunted, when the legal sphere closed to him, he entered the political arena. He was a delegate to the Cook County Republican convention in 1875 and had the opportunity to nominate John Jones for his second term in office. He worked in the office of the Cook County Recorder of Deeds until 1877, when election results forced him out. His return to the private sector as a steward at the Illinois Club proved short-lived as he traveled to southern Illinois to work for the Republican party. His reward upon returning to Chicago was the position of deputy clerk of the Criminal Court and then a second clerkship in the County Recorder of Deeds office, a position he held throughout the 1880s.[131]

After the war, Joseph W. Moore worked as a janitor with the American

Express Company, remaining there until 1876. Subsequently, he attended Fisk University in Nashville and returned to Chicago in 1879. Mixing public- and private-sector employment, he worked as a shipping clerk, then clerk of the South Chicago township and assessor of South Chicago. In 1883, he returned to the employ of the American Express Company, where he took on the responsibility of delivering money. William Baker, who came to Chicago in 1855, literally took the law into his own hands as he arrested and testified against a white horse thief, successfully sending the man to the penitentiary. By 1877, he moved to Springfield, assuming a new position as doorkeeper for the House of Representatives in the Illinois General Assembly.[132]

In the Reconstruction-era South, Lloyd Wheeler participated in Arkansas politics but returned to Chicago, where he took work at the post office and was on the government payroll. "A heavy mail bag on his back, loaded with letters and papers collected from various mail boxes was," as a newspaper gossip reported, "a haven of rest to the troubled times he left behind in the Brooks, Baxter 'mix-up' in Arkansas."[133]

The generation of the 1870s remade the civic and social thrust of black Chicago. John Jones died in 1879, and a "New Negro" mentality was apparent as manifested through new institutional breakthroughs. These included the establishment of a newspaper, the formation of martial organizations, the expansion of churches, business growth, and increased political involvement. Yet the employment pattern of a century's duration became fixed, as blacks found themselves relegated to the bottom rung of the occupational ladder in primarily service and menial labor positions. When exceptions materialized, they did little to alter the overall dismal earning pattern of black Chicagoans. On a brighter note, the political arena now offered democracy and full participation in place of civic marginality. Voting and office holding resulted in a first step toward fuller involvement as life in freedom continued. African Americans were more assertive and more independent of white assistance, even if they were still not completely free of the reliance on clientage. Notably, this period represented an initial stage of group development that would lead to a fuller African American civic, political, and institutional presence.

Chapter 4

Gilded Age Chicago, 1880–1892

Dawn has come for the Negro here. When I hear people complain because their progress economically is slow, I feel rather impatient, for it seems to me that, on the contrary, they have accomplished a great deal in the twenty-five years since emancipation. In spite of the heavy handicap of poverty and lack of education, there are many of the race who are property owners. Some of the Negroes of the city are quite prosperous.

— MARSHA FREEMAN EDMOND to JULIA BOYD of
New York, June 20, 1887 (Herma Clark, "When Chicago Was
Young: The Elegant Eighties," *Chicago Sunday Tribune,* June 28,
1936, in the Atkinson Family Collection)

[On social status,] the great mistake which white people make is to judge the whole Colored race by the sleeping-car porter, . . . by the newsboys and by roustabouts.

— DR. DANIEL HALE WILLIAMS, 1888
("Chicago: Doings of the week in the Great Western
Metropolis," *Western Appeal,* February 11, 1888)

[T]o the interrogatory, "what shall we do with the black brother?" this was early answered, "Let us alone in the enjoyment of the rights and privileges you have guaranteed to all by your organic law."

— EDWARD H. MORRIS, in debate, 1890
("Will Not Be Ignored: Rights of Colored People
Reviewed at Central Music Hall")

T HE RENOWNED sociologist Charles S. Johnson once described Illinois as the "Mecca of the Migrant Mob." While acknowledging the historical relevance of this unremitting migrant rush of the 1880s, his analysis neglected to explore comprehensively the meanings of this migratory trend, both in general and in particular for Chicago. Extremely favorable economic conditions and a social milieu free of oppressive racial restrictions afforded the answers. According to Mayer and Wade, the 1880s stood as a period of unparalleled prosperity and growth, encouraging a restlessness in those seeking their fortunes and new lives. "In these years, Chicago created a distinctive urban form in the skyscraper, adopted radical innovations in mass transit, became the nation's 'second city' with the addition of 120 square miles and 200,000 people, solidified its industrial and commercial leadership of the midcontinent, and dazzled millions with its Columbian Exposition in 1893."[1]

Both industrialization and energetic commercialization drove Chicago's growth, and with this phenomenal development emerged opportunities, directly for most white workers and sometimes even for African Americans. A channel of opportunity widened, nonetheless, for segments within the mass of black workers, businesspersons, and professionals. Furthermore, the emphasis on personal liberty of the antebellum period had evolved into custom in Chicago during the postwar decades, totally unlike the urban as well as the rural South.[2] In and of itself, this factor greatly stimulated entrepreneurship and professionalization.

The major focus of the present inquiry into black life in this era of economic expansion and near freedom of action continues to be determining the extent to which Drake and Cayton were accurate in assessing the meaning of life for the African American who was "no longer a hero around whom stirring battles were fought" and who had become part of a "poverty-stricken group competing in a city where economic and political issues were being fought out behind the facade of racial, national, and religious alignments."[3] Not unexpectedly, African American agency and the tenacious ability to transcend adversity prevented discouragement to the extent that they could not avail themselves of any peripheral benefits available in Chicago to advance individually and collectively. Exclusion from the industrial workforce and, concomitantly, relegation to the service and domestic spheres merely appeared as more of life's expected, and yet, for the secularly optimistic as well as the religiously devoted, momentary difficulties.

• • •

I. DEMOGRAPHICS

The demographic image of Chicago in this decade was of a city flooded with European immigrants. In contrast, in the African American mind's eye, it was a city of migrants, some descendants of the prewar free people of color coming from around the nation, but mostly former slaves. At the same time, a smaller number of northern-born, -acclimated, and -educated young adults arrived, destined to influence the quality of African American life through example and leadership from the pulpit, through the professions, and by personally interacting with the masses. This movement of humanity increased the city's African American population from its total of 3,600 residents in 1870 to 6,480 in 1880. While only 1.1 percent of the city's burgeoning total population, it represented a substantial 75 percent increase over the 1870 level nevertheless. By 1885, the ranks of the African Americans had swollen to 10,376.[4] Five years later, in census year 1890, this number had risen to 14,852, significantly representing a 225 percent increase over the 1880 total.[5] Despite this doubling in size, African Americans still accounted for only 1.3 percent of the city's total population that now exceeded one million persons.

Family formation and re-formation remained a constant factor in the demographics of black Chicago. Within this population in 1890 the sexual breakdown was 8,502 males and 6,350 females. The number of persons within the marriageable ages, fifteen years through sixty-four years, reached 12,016. School-age children between the ages of five through fourteen totaled 1,586. These youngsters lived within families that historian Herbert G. Gutman referred to as "double headed households," which became part of a continuing wave of families who socially dominated the landscape of black Chicago.[6] E. Franklin Frazier's examination of census data for the last two decades of the century continued to present a view of actual conditions and the overall influence of demographic change. He wrote:

> When the migrations, coming chiefly from the border states during the decade 1890 to 1900, caused the population to double itself, there was a decrease in the percentages of married and single males and females, which was compensated for by the increase in the percentage of widowed. During the first decade of the present century, when the tide of migration slowed down, there was a substantial decrease in the percentage of single Negroes and a corresponding increase in the proportion of married, widowed and divorced.[7]

In the last two decades of the nineteenth century, the absence of large numbers of children and older people provided an ample explanation of the character of the population with its high level of vigor, competitiveness, and restlessness. As a group in flux and full of ambition, it was freed of many of life's obligations that a later generation would encounter. In the 1890 census, children under fifteen years of age and the elderly (those over sixty-five) accounted for 1,436 of the 14,852 persons within the black communities. At 10 percent, they were nearly as invisible as the total black population was within the city's all-inclusive melting pot.

The state of the city's health, or its unhealthiness, plainly affected African Americans, who were as susceptible to diseases and the scourge of epidemic as any other segment of the Chicago population. In 1885, eighty thousand Chicagoans died of cholera, dysentery, and typhoid caused by bacteria in the polluted drinking water supply. Among African Americans, exact figures as to those infected are unknown. However, at least one Civil War family suffered its share of sorrow because of diseases. The Clary siblings, relatives of Private Louis Clary, appear to have been some of its prime victims. Mrs. Nancy Clary, their mother, explained the family's plight: "Six of my children have died since I came to Chicago, including Louis (in 1875). Henrietta and Eliza died with consumption. Mary Frances had cholera. Claybourn had typhoid fever. And Mason died with measles. I have four children left, all married and living in Chicago."[8] Another family, that of Charles B. Taylor, endured the loss of so many of their twelve children that it had family members repeating this haunting refrain: "They could keep only five children alive at one time."[9]

From this point of view, the Chicago story is just as much the saga of the transformation from mobile to urban life for African Americans as it is of industrial rise, financial growth, and spatial expansion. In addition to persons who became luminaries in later years, the swelling of black Chicago's population was occasioned by the movement of hundreds of ordinary folk into the city. Their story is intriguing to tell because those who flocked to Chicago in search of opportunities came from so many different parts of the South. From Kentucky's Bluegrass country to its bituminous mines, hundreds came for economic opportunity. From nearby Missouri they came, and they flocked in from Tennessee. Some journeyed afar from Virginia. Many were sojourners from areas on the fringe of the Deep South of cotton-producing, Black Belt fame.

The migratory flood that Charles S. Johnson described comprised names that are rarely mentioned in historical references. These individuals' place in history surfaced in the late 1930s when University of Chicago researcher David Nelson pointed out the compatriots of publisher Ferdinand L. Barnett as important figures of this day. Dr. J. E. Henderson was a physician trained initially in academics at Fisk and in medicine at Northwestern University's College of Medicine. Alexander Clark "was a leader in the Masonic Lodge," a frequent traveler throughout the Midwest, and "reported to be the best known and most influential man in the Midwest," with immense influence over the thinking and actions of both the laboring class and the elite. A. T. Hall (of the pioneer, antebellum Hall family, which had returned to the city) was another friend of Barnett's and a person with newspaper experience, who served as city editor.[10]

William R. Cowan of Danville, Kentucky, arrived as part of another part of this wave, reaching the city in 1880. Described as being "typical of Chicago's spirit of opportunity and faith in the possibilities of ultimate success," he entered the workforce as a porter but moved steadily upward. Soon, "by diligence and dependability, he became trustee and manager of a vast estate in the Loop."[11]

Housepainter Oscar De Priest, municipal payroller Edward Wright, and newspaper publisher Julius F. Taylor followed. De Priest came from Kansas as a youngster, the child of refugees of Alabama's racism. He began work as a calciminer. Wright arrived penniless in 1884 from New York City and secured a low-level patronage job in the Cook County Clerk's office. Taylor came from Virginia, arriving in Chicago in 1888, staying for a short period and leaving for Salt Lake City, Utah, where he started the *Broad Ax* newspaper. He returned to Chicago in 1899 to publish there until his death later during the next century. These three men were to advance socially far beyond their initial levels of entry to become important molders of political opinion and partisan participation.

Moreover, a professional coterie assembled during this decade, marking a level of occupational attainment that boded well for future generations of ambitious and able African Americans seeking a home in Chicago. Entry into the professions in the North was seen by African Americans as status recognition based solely on merit. It also represented a maturity of accomplishment, rather than age, because most of these achievers were in their late twenties to middle thirties by the time of the world's fair of 1893. The most well-known among this group was the transplanted Janesville, Wisconsin, resident Daniel Hale Williams, who distinguished himself through his medical skills and his founding of Provident Hospital in 1891. His résumé included successful surgery on the human heart in 1893, service as chief surgeon at the Freedmen's Hospital in Washington, D.C., from 1893 to 1898, and founding efforts at more than forty African American hospitals throughout the nation. From his founding of Provident, he personally led a virtual crusade of national scope to establish other black hospitals and nursing schools (Figure 25).[12]

Fig. 25. Dr. Daniel Hale Williams.
Vivian G. Harsh Research Collection of
Afro-American History and Literature,
Chicago Public Library.

Fig. 26. Dr. Charles E. Bentley.
From Appeal.

The child of free parents from Hollidaysburg, Pennsylvania, he was born in 1856 (or 1858). He received his secondary-education training in racially progressive Janesville, Wisconsin, and was graduated from the Janesville Classical Academy in 1878. Following his apprenticeship under Wisconsin's renowned surgeon general, Dr. Henry Palmer, Williams arrived in Chicago in fall 1880 to enroll at the rigorous medical program of the nationally regarded Chicago Medical School (now a part of Northwestern University).[13] Upon successfully completing his medical training, he received his M.D. in 1883. Moving freely in Chicago medical circles, he received an appointment as an attending physician at the Protestant Orphan Asylum and was on the surgical staff at the South Side Dispensary. He later joined the Chicago Medical College as a clinical instructor. Further, the recognition he earned as a medical practitioner led to his being on the Illinois State Board of Health, from 1887 to 1891.[14] His discouragement with the dearth of training facilities and positions for other African Americans, especially nurses, motivated him to lead a group of African American Chicagoans in organizing the racially integrated Provident Hospital in 1891.

Dr. Charles Edwin Bentley was perhaps Williams's closest friend in the city. He, too, was born of free parents, in 1859, but his birthplace was in the neighboring state of Ohio, in Cincinnati. After having shared their early adult years in Janesville in social and professional preparation, Bentley married their avuncular landlord's daughter, Traviata, and the newlyweds settled in Chicago shortly after Williams had arrived. Here, Bentley began an impressive career in dentistry after having graduated from the Chicago College of Dental Surgery (later the Loyola School of Dentistry) in 1887. Within two years, he was elected president of the Odontographic Society. At the same time, he rose to the rank of Clinician in Oral Surgery at the Rush Medical College and demonstrated his surgical skills before hundreds of Southern and Northern white dental students. A year later, he achieved faculty status at the Chicago College of Dental Surgery.[15] Once in private practice, Bentley quickly developed a lucrative practice in the Loop, built around a mostly white clientele (Figure 26).

Others prospered in the medical profession. Dr. A. Wilberforce Williams, born in 1864, was a native of Monroe, Louisiana. He lived in Springfield, Missouri, and reached Chicago in 1882 or 1883. Having graduated from Lincoln Institute in Missouri in 1881 or 1882, he taught school but still dreamed of a career in medicine. He next entered the Chicago Medical College, from which he graduated in 1884 and "soon became identified with Provident Hospital."[16] Dr. Austin Maurice Curtis (Figure 27), born in Raleigh in 1868, arrived in Chicago to attend Northwestern University for medical training, which he completed in 1891. He held the position of attending surgeon at Provident in 1892; four years later, he was on staff as an attending physician at the Cook County Hospital. He remained in the city until 1898, when he decided there were even greater career opportunities in Washington, D.C. Another colleague, Dr. George Cleveland Hall (Figure 28), reached the city late in the 1880s and started a practice in medicine by the time the world fair's gates opened. A graduate of eclectic training at the downtown Bennett College, he supposedly lacked Williams's respect as a practitioner because of the questionable rigor of Bennett's curriculum and competency of its training staff. Despite Williams's apprehensions, Hall joined the staff of Provident and established a creditable medical record for himself as the new century dawned.

Other professions beyond medicine beckoned. The story of journalist Fannie Barrier Williams, who exercised her prerogatives and entered the world of letters, is one of the most interesting because of its atypicality (Figure 29).[17] She was born in Brockport, New York, in 1854, to free parents who themselves were children of the freeborn. Her father, Anthony J. Barrier, listed his parentage as mixed, the result of a union between a com-

Fig. 27. Dr. Austin M. Curtis.
*Vivian G. Harsh Research Collection
of Afro-American History and
Literature, Chicago Public Library.*

Fig. 28. George Cleveland Hall.
*Chicago Historical Society, ICHi-22352,
photographer—Stevens.*

Fig. 29. Fannie Barrier Williams.
*Moorland-Spingarn Research Center,
Howard University.*

Fig. 30. S. Laing Williams.
*From H. J. Kletzing and W. H. Crogman,
Progress of a Race (New York:
Negro Universities Press, 1897).*

bination of a French father and a Pennsylvania-born African American mother. Within this Erie Canal town in the famous "burned over" district of evangelical Protestant America, the family lived well, with Mr. Barrier owning property worth eighteen hundred dollars in 1855 and being registered as a native-born qualified voter. The property holdings of the Barriers increased constantly through time, therefore expanding the world of opportunities available to Fannie Barrier. She lived her formative years in the less racially oppressive milieu of upper New York state, in a setting where African Americans were rarely seen and were palpably invisible demographically, their numbers being so infinitesimally small. In 1820, Brockport (formerly Sweden) had only a single, childless black family living in town. The doors of the schoolhouse were open to all children, so Barrier attended the local school; later, she was graduated from the State Normal School in Brockport in 1870. Her initiation into the world of race relations, acceptance, and place came as the family circle grew to include her young adult, single maternal aunt and an African American couple who were lodgers, the Hornbecks. Mr. Hornbeck, who was a barber by trade, was twenty-four years of age, and his wife was presumably within the same range. One can imagine the young Fannie easily becoming the center of attention to these additional members of the now-extended Barrier family.

Character formation, of necessity, in the "burned over" district evolved around morality, personal accountability, and civic virtue. Fannie Barrier breathed in the air of abolitionism and egalitarianism and considered herself a full-fledged citizen in this version of the American nation. Individual success appeared achievable, but her awareness of the possibility of group success depended on her encounters during adulthood. Fannie Barrier's full initiation into the complicated world of American race relations came later as she traveled to the East Coast and then into the Deep South. Teaching and travel in the South exposed her to the worst of America. However, she had never been so shielded from racism or oblivious to social realities that she could not fix conclusively the limits of her access to the American Dream. Pragmatism counterbalanced unbridled optimism. When Williams contemplated marriage, it was to another African American, a sure indication of her awareness of that part of the nation's unwritten racial protocol that forbade marriage between the races. (In contrast, Frederick Douglass took as his second wife a Caucasian, Helen Pitts, who originated from nearby Honeoye in upstate New York. This union created turmoil of a scandalous nature and split the newlyweds' families along with white and black America.) Fannie Barrier married black attorney S. Laing Williams in 1887 in Brockport, and the couple moved to Chicago before the decade had ended. Civically and socially prominent in Chicago, she and her husband founded the Prudence Crandall Club, an organization that promoted the highest appreciation of American mainstream ideals and values among the few highly educated African Americans in Chicago. Once her activities and the nature of her cultural orientation gained the attention of the city's white women's elite, she was selected to join the exclusive Chicago Woman's Club in 1895, thus becoming the first and only African American member.[18] In the next century, she joined the Chicago Library Board as its first and only African American member for over a decade. Moreover, for the next half century, among the African American women of Chicago, only Williams gained entrée into the upper level of civic service dominated by polite white society. Treated by twentieth-century historians with almost as much scorn as her husband, because of his close twentieth-century affiliation with Booker T. Washington, she is only recently being given the respect her life warranted.[19]

Native-born Georgian S. Laing Williams spent his formative years before marriage to Fannie Barrier training for a legal career (Figure 30). After his graduation from the University of Michigan, he attended the Columbian Law School in Washington, D.C. (later George Washington University Law School) and entered practice in Chicago in 1885 at the age of twenty-six. His intellectual interests as well as his desire to expand the cultural scope and activities of other college-educated persons such as his wife and himself led to his founding the Prudence Crandall Club in 1887. In this vein, Williams accepted an invitation to join the intellectually exclusive American Negro Academy in the late 1890s. This membership accorded him the opportunity to interact with the likes of Alexander Crummell, W. E. B. Du Bois, John Wesley Cromwell, and others. As to Williams's reputation historically, it has suffered unfairly because of his later association with Booker T. Washington early in the twentieth century. The portrait painted of him by his detractors is that of a sycophant, lacking professional integrity and competence in his chosen field.[20] Interestingly, the same charge grew about George Cleveland Hall's skill after he developed a close association with Washington, opening the door to speculation as to why twentieth-century scholars have accepted without investigation what appear to be ad hominem attacks lacking the substance to be considered as factual.

II. THE CHANGING HUMAN LANDSCAPE: POPULATION AND PROPERTY OWNERSHIP

Spatially, as the African Americans in this expanding group either resettled or were in the process of initial arrival in Chicago, they settled into a section of the city different than the one their predecessors had previously occupied. In doing so, their mind-set on "place" changed in this city they considered the "Great Western Metropolis." For the first time, they would be able to lay claim to an area that would become their neighborhood exclusively and with permanency.[21] In this, they would contribute to the description of Chicago as being "a city of neighborhoods." Whether or not they owned the property in which they resided was of little importance, as their claim was based on a spiritual connection to the land on which they lived and the cultural imprint they imposed on the area. In addition, they had developed a sense of place in regard to the growing city as a whole that led them to claim a stronger attraction to their being "Chicagoans."

A heavy concentration of African Americans now lived south of the central business district, known as downtown and later the Loop, instead of primarily in it. The formation of the segregated Black Belt had begun as African Americans were relocating into an area two miles south of downtown along Clark Street. This shift in residency occurred because the decade of the 1880s was a period of economic upswing nationally and of a real estate boom locally. Monroe Nathan Work wrote that "after 1884 the best families and the churches disposed of their property and with few exceptions Negro property owners in this section ceased."[22] In addition, 1889 brought the annexation of towns and villages on the periphery of Chicago, making better housing and house lots available for those able to move from the overcrowded city.

From Sixteenth Street southward to Twenty-sixth Street, along Clark Street, and for a distance of a quarter of a mile in either direction east and west, this black tide of humanity moved. The family of Elijah and Nancy Clary and the parents of veteran Louis Clary moved frequently throughout this area during this period. As to the accessibility of property and housing for blacks, race-conscious white Chicago could be hostile and resistant. When the congregation of Quinn Chapel sought better surroundings for a new church, it had to enlist the aid of a white friend to purchase property on its behalf. This location, the southeast corner of Wabash and Twenty-fourth Street, became a historical monument to African American self-sufficiency for over a century.[23]

Race-conscious white Chicago could be brutally helpful at times. The Chicago Tribune advertised the following in 1890: "To rent—1907 Butterfield st., a 3-room flat, colored people only; rent $9."[24] That same realtor offered other flats, at the same or higher prices, but none with a racial designation. By inference, all housing stock was reserved for whites, unless otherwise noted. The black Western Appeal advertised housing also, however it was geared to lodgers and offered with graciousness. Mrs. J. C. Plummer of 2974

Dearborn Street offered the following: FOR RENT—One nice furnished room for two gentlemen."[25] Nonrelated tenants were being invited to join in a pseudo-familial relationship as lodgers to solve both Mrs. Plummer's economic needs and the renters' desire for family-style accommodations.

The beginning of a new trend emerged as African Americans moved farther and farther south of Thirty-first Street, only a mile from the city's southernmost boundary (which until 1889 was Thirty-ninth Street). Previously considered the suburbs when John and Mary Jones moved to 43 Ray Street (around Twenty-ninth Street) into a "substantial white frame structure of dignified classical lines," the neighborhood was now being transformed into an area of "fantastic stone mansions" being built for the white elite and was earning the sobriquet of "Millionaire's Row." The Atkinson family moved in, becoming either the first, or one of the first, black families to reside in the area south of Thirty-first Street, and between State Street and Lake Michigan. Also, during this same span of time, Civil War veteran Sergeant James H. Brown of the Twenty-ninth Illinois moved from 221 East Thirty-first Street to 3121 Cottage Grove Avenue in 1883. Prominent businessman and society leader Lloyd G. Wheeler abandoned the dense Dearborn Corridor in 1888 and moved to Hyde Park. In 1892, the Kentuckian William R. Cowan, who arrived in Chicago in 1880, purchased property at 3352 Giles Avenue, into which he moved after improvements and his marriage in 1896.[26]

Along with length of residence, which Drake and Cayton delineated as a major characteristic of those belonging to Chicago's elite, *choice* of residence was another option open to the respectable element, reflecting the opportunities available to persons with ample resources. Many of the white-collar or professional class listed earlier chose to live outside the predominantly black corridor encompassing Dearborn, Clark, Armour, Butterfield, and other north-south streets. Notable were the Lloyd Garrison Wheelers, whose residence was now located at 4344 South Langley Avenue. The S. Laing Williamses selected a residence on Forty-second Place off of Grand Boulevard, a thoroughfare named appropriately for its actual appearance and on which some of the wealthier Anglo-Saxon, Irish, and German Jewish families of the city lived in magnificent mansions.

Considering its intermittent shabbiness and elegance, poorly paved streets, wooden sidewalks, and rising population density, the Dearborn Street Corridor paled in comparison with the areas to the south and east of it. With these vast differences in living conditions, the few members of the WASP-identified "Afro-Saxon" refined element and the demographically preponderant respectables moved as two ships passing in a fog-laden night. They glided past, often oblivious to one another's presence, and wished to stay that way so as to avoid the possibility of a social collision.

Contemporary analysis of census data from 1890 by Monroe Nathan Work corroborated the extensive character of property ownership. There were 247 African Americans listed on the tax rolls as homeowners, a dramatic increase over the 39 property owners in 1870. The positive correlation between homeownership and family life also demonstrated racial progress. Over on the West Side, within the Lake Street Corridor, John Wesley Terry and his wife lived in a "a cozy home on Fulton Street." Richard Mason Hancock and his wife lived in what was described as a comfortable home on West Fulton Street; their social lives included membership at St. Thomas Episcopal Church, in the Masons, and in the elite Prudence Crandall Circle. Meanwhile, their neighbors, Mr. and Mrs. John French, moved far to the city's western extremities into a "new and elegant residence" at 1002 West Walnut, one filled with "spacious double parlors." It was a setting fit to entertain a former governor and putative U.S. senator, the Honorable B. S. Pinchback of Louisiana. Inside of the city overall, 28.73 percent of all families owned their own homes; among African American families, the figure had climbed to a relatively impressive 8 percent.[27]

There was another dimension to African American affinity to the land. It had a proud history and formed an integral part of the Old Settlers' claim to status within two decades, along with the importance of time of arrival in Chicago. African Americans envisioned themselves as being citizens of the entirety of the city, particularly beyond the Dearborn Corridor and within close proximity to the most attractive parts of the city. Litwack had written: "Living in largely separate worlds, the two races [still] interacted in conformity to custom, law, and 'place.'" This observation was affirmed in the attitude taken through black boosterism, treating "place" as both related to social status as perceived by whites and blacks, along with a sensitivity to the ambience of physical location.

When in 1887 Ferdinand L. Barnett sought to convince curious and potential out-of-town members of his Masonic order to come to Chicago as their next convention site, he swelled with pride in his description of the city of his *civic* birth:

> The season of the year strikingly commends the convention and celebration to all who desire to take a short vacation, the countless inducements and attractions of Chicago will more than repay all visitors at this time of year. The unequaled system of magnificent parks and boulevards which surrounds *our city,* the handsome palatial eight to thirteen story office buildings, residences unsurpassed by any city in America, if by any city in the world; the great inland sea at our door with its cool evening breezes, the water works, cable cars, magnificent depots, hotels and theatres, all tend to interest and please the visitor.[28]

Similar rhetorical flourish abounded several years later when the announcement was made that the city would act as the nation's host for the proposed World's Columbian Exposition, with the Congress's approval and financial support. Besides the African American fraternal groups that adjusted their plans accordingly to avail themselves of a trip to Chicago, the leading civil rights organization, the largest educational association, and the major churches made plans to come to the city that their African American kin found so attractive and in which they had become so interested.

III. THE ECONOMIC SPHERE

African Americans perceived the economic dynamics of the city in much the same manner as other groups. In pursuit of wealth, either they labored as employees of others seeking to sustain their daily existence, or they strove to amass capital and prosper as self-employed entrepreneurs or businessmen. Of these 14,271 Chicago residents in 1890, 8,080 held employment in the following areas, followed by their percentage as part of the city's total working population: domestic and personal service, 4,972 (34 percent); manufacturing and mechanical, 1,376 (1.9 percent); trade, 474 (1.3 percent); transportation and communication, 395 (2.2 percent); clerical services, 133 (0.4 percent); the professional services (which included musicians as well as physicians and lawyers), 115 (1.3 percent); public services, 48 (1.6 percent); and agriculture, 7 (2.2 percent). In addition, the U.S. census for 1890 enumerated 560 African Americans as unclassified workers.[29]

While industrial Chicago struggled in the city's factories and streets, 61.5 percent of the total black workforce earned their living in the racially proscribed, parallel world of the domestic and personal services. Within the manufacturing sector, African Americans faced nearly total exclusion. "According to local tradition," wrote Drake and Cayton, "the first Negroes to work in the packing industry were a beef-boner and a butcher, who secured jobs in 1881. . . . Between 1881 and 1894, a few Negroes filtered into the stockyards and packing plants without any apparent opposition from the foreign-born white workers who predominated in the industry."[30] The epochal Haymarket Riot of 1886, which featured white labor and capital in a contest for survival, understandingly meant little to a black workforce whose future in the industrial arena had to wait a generation.

Contemporary narrative and analysis depicted restaurant and hotel workers, domestic servants, Pullman porters, foundry men, and dockworkers as prevailing in the African American workforce.[31] For example, a summary of a pension application for one of the Chicago's veterans from the Twenty-ninth Regiment reported that "many of his old comrades are still here, but they are scattered around the city, many of them doing menial work."[32] On the other hand, the idyllic view that Marsha Freeman Edmond held in 1887 that *some* African Americans were prosperous downplayed the fact that they were *too few* among the fourteen thousand black citizens. The bulk of the population sought and obtained work in common labor, which proved itself all too common for African American males who lacked the opportunities to enter the industrial workforce where wages were higher.

A smattering of carpenters, plasterers, musicians, and other skilled craftsmen could be found but were almost invisible, immersed as they were in a citywide labor force of nearly a quarter million. Except for a handful who strategically existed in situations where a needed skill overshadowed racist preference, clerical positions remained outside the pale to competent African Americans of both genders.[33] In a post–Civil War rarity, veteran John Enders worked as a detective for the Chicago Police Department and Enos Bond as a detective for the adjacent government of the Town of Lake.[34]

Females in particular faced their own kind of discrimination because of gender, with three-fourths of them being relegated into the domestic and service sectors. Washing and ironing clothes both at home and outside the home continued to provide many women the needed income to sustain themselves at the level of bare subsistence. In 1892, Katherine Chappell, the wife of Civil War veteran Henry Chappell, struggled to support her disabled husband when she could barely work. A federal pension examiner reported that Private Chappell would have been "a charge upon the public charity, if it were not for the hard daily labor, working out in service, washing and ironing, and such kind of work, which his wife does to make a living. His wife is an aged woman and liable at any time to become incapacitated by the hard labor she is compelled to do."[35] In another instance, one worker's efforts produced the fruits of success in the next century. The child of a washerwoman who struggled to survive and dared to dream about her family's future on Dearborn Street would later reflect on how he eventually became a physician and came to reside on palatial Grand Boulevard.[36]

The anticipated world's fair of 1893 affected employment as it both acted as an economic stimulant and as a magnet for prospective laborers. St. Clair Drake attributed significant growth within the working class to the fair, describing how African Americans migrated to the city to find work and subsequently decided to remain permanently because of job opportunities.[37] Yet most of the employed workers in the city on the eve of the world's fair of 1893 appear to have been residents of the city already. Thus, Chicago's black laboring force before and during the fair basically would have remained a workforce residentially and remuneratively peripheral to the mass of the city's labor force. Nevertheless, *Scribner's Magazine* found it could correctly describe the black working class in positive terms, which, although it might appear cryptic outside the period in which the essayist wrote it, nevertheless resonated with clarity to both its working-class resident and its cosmopolitan readership: "The colored people have done and are doing remarkably well, considering the disadvantages and discouragements under which they live. . . . They are industrious rather than hard working. . . . And economical rather than acquisitive."[38]

Notwithstanding the documented, indispensable role of the African slave laborer as a major factor in the growth of the American economy between the late seventeenth and middle nineteenth centuries, the fair was held at a time when the free white industrial laborer could best exert himself following the labor upheaval surrounding the Haymarket Riot in 1886. Realistically, it was not a case in which white labor enjoyed unfettered access to work, reasonable hours of labor, and adequate compensation. But whites were able to engage in a struggle to protect their interests and test their mettle to organize, remain united, and press their demands to a successful conclusion.[39]

Sadly, at the same time, racism on the part of organized labor in the North had excluded African Americans from that economic sector except for a peripheral involvement. One historian has examined the exclusion of the black worker in regard to the general perception of the group and concluded that, by this period, the group had been seen as either worthy of mainstream acceptance or not. In the latter instance, black labor was prone to be disregarded or dreaded as "disaffected workers." The definition of true workers and producers in the North was thus reserved for white males. Throughout the nation, excluding that portion of "hardworking and successful black individuals in mainstream thought," there existed belief in the canard describing other African Americans as "a mass of lazy black ne'er-do-wells who appeared to want government to provide for and elevate their social status."[40] Notwithstanding the earlier black belief in white laziness,[41] more likely the most appropriate description in Chicago was a combination of *Scribner's* assessment and what Du Bois proposed comparatively as an explanation for the plight of Philadelphia's black labor force.

Du Bois studied economic conditions in Philadelphia during this decade and concluded that while racism played a part in the exclusion of the African American worker from industry, "possibly a more potent part, [was] the natural spirit of monopoly and desire to keep up wages. So long as the cry against 'Irish' or 'foreigners' was able to marshal race prejudice in the service of those who desired to keep those people out of some employments, that cry was sedulously used. So to-day the workmen plainly [saw] that a large amount of competition [could] be shut off by taking advantage of public opinion and drawing the color line." Critical in his observation and thought, Du Bois did not let capital off the hook cleanly. Employers had to share a portion of the blame for racial exclusion, also. One exceptional experiment in fair play was instituted at the Midvale Steel Works by Frederick W. Taylor, hailed as the "father of scientific management." Taylor proved conclusively that race differences played no part in the push for efficiency that he so fervently and successfully pursued.[42]

Yet, the presence of African Americans in organized labor activities, including strikes, however marginal to the core of industrial workers' solidarity and union organization, did represent that first step needed to progress toward the center of labor involvement. Avoiding oversimplification, the Knights of Labor and the United Labor party did incorporate certain African American individuals and groups, such as waiters and barbers, into their efforts and with some success.[43]

However, as early as the spring of 1891, when five white labor organizations, including the Knights of Labor, met to discuss the control of work at the proposed fairgrounds in anticipation of ground breaking, white racial advantage was in the back of their minds. Despite the image of the Knights as a conglomeration of organizations that embraced inclusiveness in employment even in regard to African Americans, the matter of color-blind economic opportunity was never mentioned. The most important issues were the eight-hour day, the employment of native-born white Americans who were primarily local residents, and the institution of a minimum wage to allay the invasion of low-priced, nonunion labor. Without insuring a guarantee of the right of nonwhites to work, in Chicago at least, the Knights, as champions of the rights of the African American worker, failed in their mission.[44] This setback occurred at a time when African Americans composed at least 10 percent of the Knights' national membership and were especially active among waiters in Chicago.[45]

Not unexpectedly, in 1892 friction between African American workers and the city's organized labor movement was exacerbated nearly beyond repair as members of the Knights in Chicago endorsed the deportation of African Americans to Africa. The city's African American workers responded by staging a protest meeting, the members of which produced in its aftermath a circulating letter of indignation that attracted sizeable coverage in the white press. Sadly, within six months of the fair's closing, the Knights again raised the ire of African American workers when the idea of lessening job competition by deporting black labor to Central Africa was announced. Soundly patriotic American to the core, the women of the Chicago Colored Women's Club reacted with words of indignation and a suggestion that "if

Fig. 31. Mary Davenport.
*Vivian G. Harsh Research Collection of
Afro-American History and Literature,
Chicago Public Library.*

Figs. 32 and 33. Black policemen
of Chicago, late 1800s.
*Special Collections and Preservation
Division, Chicago Public Library.*

this country is too small for the Knights of Labor and the Negro, then let the Knights leave."[46] While nothing beyond these nonviolent actions by blacks took place, if the interests of the dominant immigrant groups in the city, the Germans and the Irish, had been involved they might have resorted to physical confrontation. African Americans engaged in limited, usually solitary or isolated demonstrations in defiance to labor injustices. Given the strength of unions in the city and the exclusion they practiced against African Americans, union memberships guaranteed work for whites and only a greater sense of isolation for African Americans.[47]

During the same period, in 1891, an abiding faith in the ultimate equity of the American labor system saw African American expectations of work rise by the very fact that the world fair's grounds of canals, lagoons, walkways, and buildings had to be constructed by the spring of 1893. Both skilled and unskilled labor was in demand for all, but only for a limited number of African Americans. This work deadline auspiciously resulted in work for seven thousand to eight thousand men who constituted, appropriate to the pervasiveness of the fair's pronounced martial air, a virtual "army of laborers with a staff of artists and architects . . . under the command of D. H. Burnham, . . . a man born for generalship."[48]

Within the city's municipal workforce, black government employees were scattered in offices and service capacities throughout Chicago. One library clerk, a female, was on the city's payroll by 1892, and another would be added as a political gesture by Mayor Carter Harrison during the world's fair. The Chicago Fire Department still carried its single black fire company, Engine 21.

By 1886, there were four African American members of the Chicago Police Department; by 1894, the department expanded its force to include twenty-three men in uniform because of the "liberal political administration of Mayor Washburne." One of the policemen was a former Baltimorean, Philip Greene, who arrived in Chicago in 1881 at the age of twenty-five. Greene worked as a Pullman porter until he joined the force in 1887. Interestingly, Patrolman Greene performed his duties at the Illinois Central train station in civilian clothes. The first matron was hired, and Mrs. Mary Davenport assumed that post (Figures 31, 32, 33).[49]

Federal employees at the post office numbered seventy-eight. Accurately or not, Robert Mitchell, a press source for information on the activities of the African American community, reported in 1884 that "there are forty-eight clerks holding [federal] government and city clerkships in Chicago, and their salaries aggregate[d] between $45,000 and $50,000 yearly." While this employment seemed a major step upward for blacks, providing security and good pay, it was considered only a stepping-stone to better work by whites.[50]

As described to this point, the thrust of any major, discernible African American economic advancement occurred in the nonindustrial, service-oriented spheres and not in the industrial, business, and wider governmental arenas. Submerged in the statistics were stories of achievement that could only have resulted when assertive, talented, hardworking individuals received the "fair chance" that racial spokesman Edward H. Morris spoke about publicly in 1890. Chicago provided that fair chance to architect George W. Browne, a former slave from Kentucky who designed and built extensively in the city, evidently in white areas, also. A former Mississippi slave, Lemuel Moore, was another individual who benefited from the Chicago milieu, and he manufactured a patented mop, which, along with his investments in bonds and real estate, provided a comfortable life.[51]

West Sider James G. Gordon also represented the infrequently found, but evident still, anomaly in employment among African American workers. He arrived in the city in 1881 from Virginia and began work as a coachman. He became a machinist after three years, working at the Caldwell Machine shops at Eighteenth and Western avenues. Later, Gordon started his own trucking business and allegedly built an "independent fortune" before retirement.[52]

Lewis W. Cummins also belonged to the group of achievers who made Chicago function efficiently and made the African American community conscious of the possibilities of success. Born in 1857 in Alabama, he benefited from the interest of a supportive white family who sent him to nearby Talladega College to prepare for his future. Following an early career in teaching in the South, he headed north, arrived in Chicago in 1887, and accepted work in the service sector until he could advance occupationally. Soon he was city editor of the *Conservator*, reading law in his spare moments, and continuing to look ambitiously upward. In January 1890, the dry goods firm of Siegel, Cooper, and Company contacted him about assuming a supervisory position in the downtown section of the city. He was appointed general salesman, or "floor walker," over an entire floor in the store, with full authority in that position, a first for an African American.[53]

No matter how impressive the achievements of a small number of African Americans outside the domestic and service domains, an underside existed in contradiction to various examples of economic progress typifying the Gilded Age. From Haymarket in 1886, to the lure of jobs occasioned by the upcoming World's Columbian Exposition, to the devastating Panic of 1893 and beyond, the economic order created an army of unemployed and underemployed workers, black as well as white.[54] Most were economically dispossessed because of the tendency of monopoly capitalism to produce an excess of laborers at any given time. Others suffered due to physical infirmity and disabilities related to employment or peripheral activities, such as military service undertaken to protect the Union and its flowering economic system. Among those falling into the latter category were veterans such as William Randall of the Twenty-ninth Illinois.

Work was as central to Randall's being as his desire for complete freedom. Arriving in Chicago during the war, he immediately began hauling coal and other items as a teamster as well as cutting wood for fuel. He boasted of his prowess in the latter activity, which was interrupted only by military service: "He used to say he then could cut and put up his two cords of wood a day." His strength of body provided enough in wages for his family of three to sustain itself until his enlistment in the Union army in February 1864. The rigors of the Petersburg campaign drained him, though, as he succumbed to exhaustion and damage to his kidney. His body broke during a hard march (the bane of the infantryman) from Fort Harrison to the outskirts of Petersburg.[55] His fall and near-drowning in the Rappahannock River had been caused by total exhaustion, the result of the weight of his heavy knapsack and the ammunition he was hauling. Immediate hospitalization resulted, followed by light work in the hospital and cooking duties once he returned to camp with his comrades.

After the regiment was demobilized in November 1865, Randall had returned home "a sickly looking man [who] did not seem to have strength to do any kind of labor." Yet pride and an inner sense that he would get better drove him to do whatever work he could. When comrades in arms and friends counseled a request for a disability pension, he ignored them. Dreading his descent into infirmity and loss of strength, he was now fully aware "that the war . . . had used him up." With his income diminished by frequent bodily immobilization from kidney disease, Randall also refrained from regular visits to the doctor's office for relief and medication. He resorted instead to long bouts at home in a fixed bodily position while he waited for his wartime comrades to stop by and turn his body. His wife's skills were used to prepare plasters (wrappings) composed of resin and hog's lard. Meanwhile, as his health deteriorated, he still sought to work at whatever task his body would allow, while growing more aware that he was not going to improve. His last attempt at work ended with his becoming ill on a streetcar and being returned to his home. For his eventual widow, Mary Jane, his sickness was draining, as he required constant bed care. So was his screaming "when he would attempt to urinate . . . [and as] he passed quantities of blood instead of urine." This hemorrhaging of the kidney became the ultimate cause of death for a man who had been described as "a robust able bodied man [who] did nothing but heavy work" before his military service. Death from a diseased kidney finally ended his commitment to labor.[56] Unfortunately, other veterans suffered similarly.

A. Wait Service: "Commanders of the Dining Room"

Among the members of the service sector, perhaps no occupational group approached their work with the sense of "industriousness" that *Scribner's* noted more than did waitpersons, both male and female, the former sometimes referred to as the "Commanders of the Dining Room." Ordinarily, more than fifteen hundred male waiters earned livable to barely livable wages while working in a competitive and stressful workplace.[57] Taking advantage of work opportunities in the inexpensive restaurants of Herman H. Kohlsaat built throughout the downtown section, along with elegant hotels such as Potter Palmer's Palmer House Hotel, hundreds of African Americans found steady, but exacting, employment. Whether in private homes, working also as butlers, or in public in restaurants, they performed with agility, charm, skill, strength, and pride in calling. Their demeanor commonly was reminiscent to whites of the group's previous condition of forced obsequiousness just three decades before. This perceived acceptance of racial subordination demonstrated more an ability to give the customer, paraphrasing the words of Marshall Field, what he or she wanted at the moment. An effective waiter conferred on the diner an elevation in social status, even if just for an hour and even if undeserved by actual social rank. An ability to interact amicably with diners produced bigger tips along with a sense of satisfaction with a job well done.

Male wait staff developed a unique system of ranking within their culture of work. Headwaiters directed a hierarchy that included assistants to their position, a captain, and various grades of lieutenancy. The position of headwaiter also produced greater benefits. The family of Palmer House headwaiter Charles Jordan received one such benefit when, upon Jordan's death in Arkansas, Chicago hotel magnate Potter Palmer assumed the expenses of embalming and shipping Jordan's remains home to Chicago for burial. C. C. Lewis exhibited another trait associated with his status when, in May 1893, he challenged a strike called by the Colored Waiters' Alliance against at least three hotels, no doubt aware of the fact that his personal relationship carried a level of security with ownership that waiters could only envy in an owner-dominated workplace. His sentiment, that of siding with capital against labor, probably represented the standard feeling of persons in control who gained the most from labor's output of energy in the workplace.[58] In addition, since Lewis's name was often associated with the organizations to which the African American elite belonged—meaning the more than two dozen attorneys who had passed the Illinois Bar and the smattering of physicians trained in white, northern institutions—he considered himself a small part of the city's embryonic black establishment.

Wait service showed a downside that was dismal and sometimes a dead end. Richard R. Wright Jr. found that monotony plagued this occupation, resulting in constant moving from workplace to workplace. Chicago historian Perry R. Duis wrote of "owners [who] routinely responded to slack times by reducing their staff size with little or no notice. This meant that some waiters in effect worked on a day-to-day basis." Comparatively, Katzman wrote that in Detroit waiters faced a constant apprehension about a reduction in force, long hours, and uncertain pay. These conditions were probably not unique to any specific locale and help explain the basis of African American protest in the workplace in Chicago. Differentiation in grades of service, responsibility, and remuneration often extended to what Wright called "10 grades and pay runs."[59] At one hotel, the Lexington, the distinctive ranks among waiters corresponded directly to internal authority and pay. At the bottom of the work pyramid were the rank and file, who reported to second and first lieutenants, the captain, and two assistants to the workforce's leader, the headwaiter.

According to what we know from research findings and anecdotes, which often have been estimated and thus lack precision, the earnings of waiters varied. For example, earnings could climb as high as seventy-five dollars a month for a headwaiter, which would explain why, as Frazier put it, "a man would pride himself on being able to tell you" of his pecuniary achievement. Civil War veteran Lewis T. Wood reached this position. Yet wages could also fall as low as fifteen dollars per month for a water boy and climb to a hundred dollars per month for a well-skilled headwaiter, according to Wright. And Drake and Cayton relate the story of one Old Settler, a son of slave parents, who came to the city in 1887 from Missouri at the age of nineteen. He mentioned the prevalence of miscegenation as one index to the freedom existing at the time, but he does not point to high wages as such an index: "In those days Chicago was in its youth. I was a young man and soon got a job waiting tables in various restaurants and working in hotels. I made eighteen dollars a month." Young Paul Lawrence Dunbar found work as a waiter in a hotel and met another aspiring poet, James Corrothers, "who eked out his earnings as space writer for Chicago newspapers by waiting on table during the evening rush hours. This 'dinner waiting' brought three dollars a week and dinner."[60]

Because of blatant racism, black workers earned their living outside the more remunerative industrial sphere, so a sense of industrially based labor consciousness and workers' solidarity was less likely to be nurtured. On the other hand, instances of cooperative action among black waiters as well as collaboration with white waiters did take place. Importantly, both individually and generally, the Knights of Labor stretched out their hands in workers' fraternity (in contrast to their stance in 1892). To reiterate, John Wesley

Terry of the Chicago West Division Street Car Company joined the Knights and was elected judge-advocate of the Charter Oaks Assembly in 1886.[61] That same year, the Knights appealed to black service-sector workers, organizing a local composed of African American waiters. The assignation of status within a division of labor necessitated the establishment of separate locals within the national union movement effort if blacks were to be included. This insulting feature of union organization did not sit well with African American labor and evolved into a hostility toward the white-dominated labor movement, a hostility that continued into the next century.[62]

As a result of the Knights' early efforts, notwithstanding racism, three hundred to four hundred waiters and restaurant porters formed the William Lloyd Garrison Colored Waiters Local Assembly 8286. This group represented the first black entry into organized labor in Chicago and was followed within two years by a second black local, the Charles Sumner Waiters' Union, which organized after separating from 8286. Perhaps the apex of organizing came in 1890 when a group of black waiters, either from the two extant locals or independent, joined the short-lived, German-led Culinary Alliance, which was composed of eight separate labor organizations. Dissatisfaction with wages and working conditions led African American waiters to join the alliance in striking in late spring and early summer of 1890. Demanding a raise to $10.00 from their starvation level of $7.50 a week, fifty waiters left Brockway and McKey's Restaurant on Clark Street and won acceptance of their demands. Strikes at other restaurants ensued, and many restaurateurs agreed to the strikers' demands. To guard against strikebreakers, a cordon was placed around restaurants being struck. Regular meetings were held to keep morale high and discipline within the ranks at the union headquarters, along with assemblages at Quinn Chapel A.M.E. Church. These measures appear to have been successful, and the job action spread to the Tremont House, Commercial Hotel, and the Palmer House. Many of the actions resulted in workers' victories.[63]

Other instances of organized action followed. When a customer leveled a charge of theft at the Hyde Park Hotel (located on the South Side lake front), the wait staff of thirty men was detained, questioned, and searched. In protest, the entire workforce left their work site.[64] Again, in May 1893, several strikes took place that this time were led by African Americans. Loop restaurants were crippled and some concessions were won, indicating a labor consciousness in advance of black entry into the industrial workforce.[65] By 1892, an organization named the Chicago Waiters' Alliance was in existence, with an uncertain date of origin, that called for what appeared to be another in a series of meetings at a local church promoting organization to fight for higher wages and better working conditions.[66]

Even though workers were carving their own niches in the workplace, compensation, whether adequate or inadequate, did not have the power to dictate the sum of a worker's attitudes. The same applied to purported shows of workers' consciousness and organized action. Defying convention about the nexus of work and life, African American women workers in the domestic sector held attitudes toward work that could be applied to their male racial counterparts.[67] Several generations removed in time, historian Sharon Harley described them, citing May Anna Madison:

> I don't know any black woman who is too proud to get out here and work. . . . [But] working for other people can't be but so good for you because you are working for them and not for yourself. See, the best work is work that you want to do that you do for yourself. . . . One very important difference between white people and black people is that white people think that you *are* your work. Now, a black person has more sense than that because he knows that what I am doing doesn't have anything to do with what I want to do or what I do when I am doing for myself. Now, black people think that work is just what I have to do to get what I want.[68]

In the same vein, for the twentieth-century southern worker, Robin D. G. Kelley described and analyzed variations and continuities as African Americans molded the sphere of work as much as it shaped their thinking, behavior, and lives.[69]

This predisposition to see work as the slave saw it for centuries—as the expenditure of energy for the benefit of persons engaging in calculated exploitation—had also dramatically affected the thinking of black labor. With a fatalistic view toward life and, by extension, work for others, this activity was to be endured but relieved by a higher power at a time of reckoning, divine or otherwise. Another aspect that influenced the thinking of black laborers involved a sense of personal mastery over a challenging task, which offered rewards on a daily basis, with each job done well. This approach approximated the skilled craftsman's attitude about his finished product.

B. Transportation: Pullman Porters, the "Ambassadors of Hospitality"

Another major segment within the service-oriented workforce was the group of Pullman porters, who provided hotel-type service on railroad coaches and in the luxurious Pullman Palace Cars. Because of their effectiveness in their service, they earned the sobriquet of "Ambassadors of Hospitality." This occupational group symbolized a labor segment with a unique status among African Americans. This was explained by their rising above their previous work experience, playing an essential role in the burgeoning railroad industry, and having an expected workplace demeanor that required the utmost in personal discipline around whites. As the era of industrialism went forward and performed its unique transformation of American society, a new economic opportunity evolved for a nation becoming dependent on the rails for long-distance transportation and the expectation of luxury as its nonmaterial by-product. Blacks were barred nationally as conductors and engineers, and outside the South as trainmen and firemen; however, the job of porter assumed the status of an opportunity beyond farmwork. William H. Harris wrote: "The Pullman Palace Car Company of Chicago employed many African Americans as porters and maids on sleeping cars to perform personal services for the increasing number of passengers who traveled across the country."[70] But Pullman did even more than this. African Americans virtually monopolized this entire service sector.[71]

Nevertheless, Pullman porters received poor wages, worked long hours on trains, and were rarely in one location very long. Dependent on the public's willingness to tip to supplement his inadequate wage base, the porter smiled and "consequently, [had to] stoop to conquer."[72] Moreover, the Pullman Company could be ruthless in its control over the work and lives of porters. One recalcitrant porter released from rail wait service sued the company for a $22.50 balance on his wages. The company filed a counter claim amounting to $22.62 for shortages in beverages, fruits, and alcohol drinks. A judge disregarded the Pullman Company claim and ruled in the former porter's favor.[73] Remaining porters had to worry about shortages of towels and linen, often considered by travelers as legitimate pelf at the end of their journey. Porters who were deemed responsible for this loss had their wages docked at a rate between two and three dollars a month.[74]

The porters responded ultimately by organizing. As members of the United Brotherhood of Railway Porters, they encouraged thrift and the maintenance of high standards in deportment. They adopted the stance that "the position of porter, though lowly, should be filled by a gentleman."[75] Instances of porters stealing or cooperating with white passengers to conceal the latter's lewd activities on trains incurred the ire of these honest and moral porters. When some in the group raised the idea of using the strike as a tactic to improve their work conditions, they yielded to the counterargument that strikebreakers would flock to take their jobs.[76]

By the end of the century, as a newer generation of workers succeeded the original pool of former slaves, the expectations of these employees rose without any appreciable change occurring in the employer's expected work demeanor. The image of the ubiquitous, sometimes overly courteous "George," with his obligatory smile, still dominated this service by the end of the century. Yet, for the later generation of porters coming into service around and after 1893, their public image belied their antithetical one of elevated status among African Americans of all classes, who knew all too well the intricacies of wearing the mask in a white-dominated society.[77] To confirm this disparity between perception and actuality, one only has to reflect on the careers and successes of erstwhile porters Jesse Binga and Edward "Ed" Wright, who in the next century became the personification of African American assertiveness and success in entrepreneurial and business endeavors, as well as in politics.[78]

In order to compensate for the drudgery and the sometimes excessive demands on their labor, the "Daddy Joe" stories evolved. While based on a real person, the exploits of this extraordinary figure outgrew reality and seemed appropriate remedies for all occasions when members of his race needed relief from the worst aspects of their economic and psychological oppression. According to these stories, which were told in private in off-hours around the Baker heating stoves, Daddy Joe's stature was Bunyanesque. Not surprisingly, his height and hands were so imposing that he could "walk flat-footed down the aisle and let the upper berths down on each other."[79] Whether encountering hostile red men on the Plains or malicious white men in the palace cars, Daddy Joe proved himself master of the situation. Through it all, his demeanor established the standard to which all Pullman porters aspired: loyalty and dedication to the job, regardless of the impediments.

Renowned sociologist E. Franklin Frazier incidentally both legitimized and elevated the status of these workers to legend when, in 1932, his doctoral dissertation of the previous year was published. He maintained that "the occupational organization of the Negro community conform[ed] to the distribution of Pullman porters, who at one time represented on the whole the group that had a comparable good income and a high conception of his place in the community. 'Once in Chicago,' said a former Pullman porter, 'you weren't anybody unless you were a Pullman porter. We handled more money than most of the colored people, and led all the social life.'"[80] This commentary had indicated a significance beyond the sphere of work and extended into the social realms of recreation and leadership. Over time, however, what has grown into urban myth and been recognized nationally, never has been substantiated in fact, while being contradicted by contemporary evidence.

C. Women Inside and Outside the Service Domain

African American women in the racially restrictive Chicago work scene faced reinforced levels of discrimination. As women, they encountered the glass ceiling, and as black women they faced conditions of work more restrictive and less remunerative than the men. Even more devastating, "There [was] this difference however, that while a Negro man [might] always feel that there is a chance to reach the top, the Negro woman does not have that chance except very rarely."[81] Women who worked in homes or hotels labored as "scrub girls" who could advance to head housekeepers. Competition existed within households with white workers, particularly Swedish girls, which always relegated African Americans to the lowest rung. Blacks often served as cooks. Wages were always low, with some workers earning only twelve to twenty dollars per month, plus lodging and meals, and with just one half-day off every week. Meanwhile, the economic plight of washerwomen remained static.

The door of economic opportunity, which occasionally stood ajar, allowed some black Chicagoans to enter the modern world of the clerical worker. Young Joanna Cecilia Snowden of the Hudlin family became the first African American bank clerk in the city. At the time of the world's fair, Fannie Barrier Williams found, however, that there was a deliberate and systematized exclusion of African American women from opportunities in the clerical sphere at a time when the city was touting its economic vitality; the claims were contradictory and hypocritical. Except for a handful of workers strategically existing in venues where needed skill overshadowed racist preference, clerical positions remained outside the pale to competent African Americans of both genders.[82] To an audience of fairgoers, Williams defiantly recounted one telling episode of this period:

> Not long ago I presented the case of a bright young woman to a well-known bank president of Chicago, who was in need of a thoroughly competent stenographer and typewriter. The president was fully satisfied with the young woman as exceptionally qualified for the position, and manifested much pleasure in commending her to the directors for appointment, and at the same time disclaimed that there could be any opposition on account of the slight tinge of African blood that identified her as a colored woman. Yet, when the matter was brought before the directors for action, these mighty men of money and business, these men whose prominence in all great things of the city would seem to lift them above all narrowness and foolishness, scented the African taint, and at once bravely came to the rescue of the bank and society by dash-

ing the hopes of this capable yet helpless young woman. No other question but that of color determined the action of these men, many of the foremost members of the humane society and heavy contributors to foreign missions and church extension work.[83]

D. Business Growth and Development

By 1880, black Chicago was entering its sixth decade of business development. What historian August Meier described generally as a "shift in the economic basis of the Negro bourgeoisie [that] proceeded at an uneven rate, earlier and more rapidly in some cities than in others," fit circumstances in Chicago absolutely. It was left to business historian Juliet E. K. Walker, however, to focus primarily on the local level with the origins, formation, evolution, and accomplishments of African American entrepreneurship and business development. Walker declared that "historically, businesses have provided African Americans with their greatest economic successes" as she "illustrate[d] the historic continuity of black business in America since the colonial era to the post civil rights era."[84]

The growth and financial successes of black businesses appeared diminutive to be sure when contrasted with the city's economic big four: Marshall Field, Philip D. Armour, George M. Pullman, and Potter Palmer. Nevertheless, this recent growth was significant when compared to the progress made since Appomattox, and their success clearly attested to African American entrepreneurial and business vigor, perseverance, and acumen. This awareness prompted Marsha Freeman Edmond to write contemporarily that "some of the Negroes of the city are quite prosperous."

In a city basking in the reflected glory of its industrial might and prosperity, the nearly total exclusion of African Americans from the manufacturing sector as late as the 1890s relegated them to an economic venue of both circumscribed opportunity and limited expectations. The commercial sphere appeared almost as forbidding. Amassing a fortune through meat packing, steel production, transportation, real estate, or merchandising existed only in the realm of the impossible. While white Chicago developed its upper class, a group from which its civic leadership emerged, black Chicago was prevented from building a comparable wellspring. Undeterred, black Chicago achieved to the highest extent possible under the circumstances. To its credit, black Chicago counted 111 businesses that had been established by 1885, with 46 located in the retail sector and 64 in service-related areas (Figure 34).[85]

Proud of what had been accomplished, businessman Isaac Counsellor

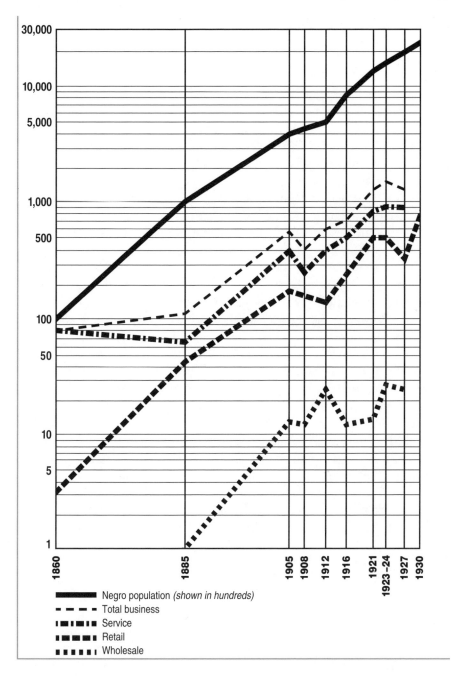

Fig. 34. Growth of black-owned businesses, 1860-1930.
Redrawn from St. Clair Drake and Horace R. Cayton, Black Metropolis
(Chicago: University of Chicago Press, 1993 [1945]).

Harris compiled and published black Chicago's first business directory in 1885, *The Colored Men's Professional and Business Directory*. The most significant publication since the *Conservator* was launched in 1878, it was representative of a newer, more energized mood toward entrepreneurial and business success as well as of the cadre of economic pioneers that possessed that materialist sentiment. Thus, when Harris compiled his directory, he wrote accurately of the role of initiative in that Chicago's most assertive, enterprising, and successful African Americans achieved success because none were "to the manor born."[86]

This absence of a lineage to wealth pervaded African American thought and effort in Chicago, influencing attitudes and shaping values that resulted in an extremely realistic view of the linkage among business success, status, and class. As the nineteenth-century resident, the "Old-timer," recalled, "no one dreamed that a member of our Race would [ever] be wealthy."[87] Few were. There were the exceptions, however, and Isaac C. Harris had begun to document their existence. Nathaniel Jones purportedly made $120,000 in a single sales transaction involving Pullman Company stock.[88]

Some even made money outside the business sphere, in law and medicine. Notable were Edward H. Morris and Dr. Daniel Hale Williams, who had struggled against economic and racial odds to amass wealth. Stories abound about the two and their climb from poverty. "When he was admitted to the bar, in 1879, he [Morris] was unable to purchase a suit of clothes to make himself presentable, and so kept on his long overcoat, and during the examination had it buttoned up so as not to show the fractures which time and wear had made in his antiquated pants."[89] During this period, Morris's wealth from dealings in real estate would exceed $50,000 (Figure 35).

Williams's fine medical education had been achieved "through his personal exertions, his parents being unable to render financial assistance." He also accumulated wealth because of his profitable practice. While one man of medicine accumulated wealth in spite of his outward appearance and desires, another acquired it from an unusual source. As chronicled by Rayford W. Logan, "Dr. Charles H. McCallister, a practicing physician, received a substantial inheritance at the time of his Kentucky slave-owning father's death in 1886."[90]

Harris's *Directory* represented the major extant guidepost of the late nineteenth century on African American economic life in Chicago, having its value predicated on the combination of its comprehensiveness, objectivity, and accuracy. Even though the *Directory* promoted a cause, that of African American commercial advancement, its raison d'être never blurred the comprehensive glimpse of life it presented. It established, moreover, the existence of a variety of related recreational, cultural, and associational

Fig. 35. Edward H. Morris.
Chicago Historical Society, ICHi-22371.

activities and organizations that enriched black life. Contemporary to the period, based on direct observation and survey, and recognized as the primary document on the makeup of African American society nearing the end of the century, it has enjoyed far too limited use as a source of knowledge about black Chicago.[91]

Consistent with a national pattern among African Americans in which they embraced the virtues of a group economy,[92] Harris established that businessmen were proud to show how far African Americans had progressed less than a generation since Emancipation, and that these individuals wanted to tap into an already existing African American market. Harris wrote:

> I have frequently consulted with many of our leading citizens and well-thinking people upon the great need of a work of this kind, and they have earnestly admitted with one accord that a directory of the business, professions and prominent occupations of the enterprising colored people in the city of Chicago would be a work of vast importance, and a reliable medium of authoritative information, while its

many advantages would be highly appreciated by all lovers of our race progress. . . . The unjust discrimination made on the account of color, by many writers, and their biased ideas, will not allow them to view and treat our industrial, educational and financial progress in the true light of merit, justice and reason; therefore, being actuated by a sensibility of race pride, and the great love and admiration which I have for the exemplary enterprise demonstrated by the colored people of Chicago, I have felt it to be an imperative duty to collect, with great care and discretion, a few facts and figures, in order to show to others of our race what the colored people in the great metropolis of the west are doing towards an honest accumulation of wealth, establishment of business, and acquiring that experience in the various professions and the branches of industry necessary to make life a grand success and the elevation of our race a true and constant aim.

There seems to be a great degree of race pride, inspiring the better class with an inordinate desire to see each other succeed in whatever pursuit they may perchance engage in. This fact is demonstrated in many instances by the large patronage and co-operation which they received from one another, it being occasionally sufficient enough to support different branches of business where the trade is entirely colored.[93]

Support for black business by either the "better class" or other segments of the African American community did not appear without effort from within the ranks of the black business community itself. African Americans in Chicago shopped where and as they pleased, limited primarily by income and their right to choice. Accordingly, the *Conservator* responded to what it perceived to be lagging racial support for businesses and self-employed skilled contractors with constant appeals to "buy black." One editorial comment printed evidently in its own behalf read: "We have type, press and materials to do all kinds of printing. Shall they rust while you take your tickets, circulars and invitations to white people, or shall we be kept busy and made prosperous by your patronage? We believe that Chicago colored people will help their own people first." The appeal ended with the anticipatory, "We shall see."[94]

Retrospectively, to the generation of the "Era of the Black Metropolis," in the 1920s, the accomplishments in business of this generation were inspiring. Robb observed, in 1927, that

up until recent years there was no record kept of Negro fortunes as separate and distinct from fortunes accumulated by individuals identified with the other groups. It is impossible, therefore, to account for all of the fortunes that should be credited to the Negro group. While the fortunes of the present-day Negro are larger and there are more of them,

Fig. 36. Lloyd G. Wheeler.
Chicago Historical Society,
ICHi-22386, photographer—Stevens.

it must be remembered and understood that in the age of the pioneers there were fewer opportunities to acquire fortunes, and the fortunes of that day were in many instances made in competition with other racial groups for business. Some of the early fortunes may have been modest ones but the fact that they were wrung from the community after bitterly fought competition with their peers makes all of the more creditable their achievements.[95]

The few growing wealthy included Lloyd G. Wheeler, a lawyer by professional training but also a merchant-tailor by vocation (Figure 36). As John Jones's successor of the Jones-Wheeler tailoring enterprise, Wheeler employed a workforce of fifteen to twenty workers repairing and dyeing men's clothing in his downtown location. Another business demonstrating an appreciable amount of success was the firm of Platt and Goode. The partnership was run by the son of J. F. Platt, a man who had prospered in the lumber business and later combined his talents with those of a carpenter to prosper in the furniture and lumber business.[96] In previous years, Platt Place existed on the West Side and was named for this successful businessman.[97]

The Colored Men's Professional and Business Directory of 1885 listed forty barbershops, fifteen restaurants, and twenty saloons. Investment in saloons that catered to a white clientele was prevalent. One interviewee answered a question about black business progress thus: "You may be surprised to hear that in the liquor business alone upward of $200,000 worth of stock and saloon fixtures are owned by colored men."[98] The wealth of saloon keepers reached levels equal to or surpassing members of the "refined" element, or elite, with saloon owners Andrew H. Scott, John Hunter, Frank G. Rollins, Emmanuel Jackson, and John Smith respectively being worth $350,000, $175,000, $90,000, $75,000, and $65,000. Around the same time, physician Daniel Hale Williams, attorney Edward E. Wilson, and dentist Charles E. Bentley attained levels of wealth respectively of $150,000, $50,000, and $25,000. The wealth of the grand dame Mrs. Mary Richardson Jones was estimated at $210,000.[99]

Undertaking became an important business endeavor, too. George T. Kersey, a native of Chatham, Ontario, Canada, reached the city in 1888. Within several years he was in business with Daniel Jackson, the son of the prosperous saloon keeper Emmanuel Jackson. Then, David McGowan joined them for a brief time before Kersey and McGowan withdrew to form a partnership with another young enterpriser named Morsell.[100]

Yet another lucrative business avenue was catering. Charles J. Smiley, the French Company, and D. H. Weir enjoyed prosperity as they provided to the needs of the city's white elite. Business historian Juliet E. K. Walker has described C. J. Smiley's operation:

> [He] provided a full range of services. For weddings, he furnished not only the cake, floral arrangements, and church decorations but also male and female security people to safeguard the wedding gifts. By the turn of the century, Smiley's catering enterprise was so extensive he owned 16 horses to pull his delivery wagons and was said to be the largest employer of blacks in Chicago.[101]

At least one enterprising veteran of dubious character operated an employment, or intelligence, bureau located at 3121 Cottage Grove Avenue.[102] A popular labor-related activity of the decade, these bureaus catered to a job-hungry market that existed in the middle of an opportunity-driven economy. Unfortunately, just as immigrants were constantly being misled and swindled of their money, it appeared that former Sergeant James H. Brown might have set up a similar scheme to defraud fellow veterans along with trusting civilians. At his office, which probably shared space with his barbershop, Brown enjoyed the company of civilian and veteran customers. Charges for the service of job location and placement ran from two to five dollars for illegitimate operations, and double those amounts at legitimate enterprises.[103] Brown's intentions arouse suspicions nationally because of his being accused of defrauding the U.S. government of a pension amounting to two dollars per month for an alleged injury incurred during the Battle of the Crater. Eventually, the government terminated Brown's pension, amid charges of deception in the pension process brought by an honest comrade in arms, Sergeant Willis Easley, who accused Brown of offering him a fifty-dollar bribe for a deceptive affidavit.[104]

More common were the smaller concerns requiring limited capital, such as Ed Washington's coffee shop, at the foot of the Chicago River at Fifth Avenue. Once, to his amazement upon returning to his store late one night, Washington found his food supplies being eaten by a brazen burglar. To his chagrin, the culprit was Michael Welch, a white man.[105] Another store owner appealed to persons out on the South Side on Sunday nights after church services ended. For anyone desiring that delightful and popular confection, ice cream, Mr. I. B. Walters advertised that "if you wish to be in the swim[,] go to Walters."[106]

The thinking of African American businessmen proved too complex to be categorized into a single racial ideology. They enjoyed a mixed relationship between what historian August Meier described as the militant wing of integrationism and group economic chauvinism. Accordingly, Ferdinand L. Barnett combined a racial appeal with a push for things mainstream American in the *Conservator*. Ralph Nelson Davis assessed Barnett in this manner: "The editor . . . was a force as a person—a reflection of what is referred to as personal journalism. . . . Mr. Barnett . . . stated that the uplift and advancement of the Negro constituted a major feature of the paper's program." As Nell Irvin Painter has pointed out, when it came to segregated education, he was also recognized as an ardent supporter of having the future of African American youngsters being placed in the hands of teachers of their own group. Barnett was civic-minded and positively affected the entirety of the small African American population; his social standing was "associated with his position as a lawyer, and with the estimate and appraisal of his character as an educated person of culture and refinement. This was not only true of the community's conception of the editor, but, to a degree, the editor's notion of his mission was affected by this idea."[107]

Beyond racial constraints, African Americans desired to participate fully in the expanding, urban market economy, understanding that if they could not fully enter it during the world's fair decade, then it would happen sometime in the future. As an informed voice for an urban population, the *Conservator* had not fully distinguished itself at this point.[108] Competition from other regional papers, such as the *Cleveland Gazette*, the *Indianapolis Freeman*, and the *St. Paul Western Appeal*, which circulated weekly in Chicago and with as much if not more news about black Chicagoans, steadily challenged the *Conservator*. Davis found that, in its limited focus, the *Conservator* emphasized "editorial discussion, interpretation, and comment rather than straight news presentation."[109] He did not comment as to its quality.

E. The Professions

Growth within the professions of medicine and law was impressive and resulted in a small but well-trained professional class. The legal corps was described as the largest in the country, including "not only graduates of law colleges, but of universities as well . . . [and] the record they have made at the bar is an honor to the race, and well may their example be held up to the colored men and women of other cities as worthy of imitation."[110] These attorneys included Lloyd Garrison Wheeler, Ferdinand L. Barnett, Edward H. Morris, S. Laing Williams, and Franklin Denison. These five achieved vanguard status, ranking as the first, third, fifth, eleventh, and twelfth African Americans to succeed in passing the Illinois bar. Wheeler's later, close association with Booker T. Washington was obviously influenced by their shared perception of how best to achieve racial advancement in the peculiar venue of the post-Emancipation South. Back in Chicago, Wheeler soon achieved the same prominence Jones held as merchant-tailor. Marriage to Jones's niece, Renae Petit, followed. Established financially by the 1890s, and known for his free spending at a time when University of Chicago professor Thorstein Veblen was excoriating the practice of conspicuous consumption among persons of his class, Wheeler assumed the mantle of "Ward McAllister (or social leader) of black Chicago." A devout capitalist, he adopted the same economic mode of thought that mesmerized the nation, and he soon embraced Booker T. Washington as a friend.

The ambitious Edward H. Morris displayed a new interest beyond the law and decided on electoral politics. He ran for and won a seat in the Thirty-seventh session of the Illinois General Assembly, serving between 1891 and 1893. Franklin Denison distinguished himself in both law and the military, becoming an officer in the famed Eighth Illinois Regiment in future years. Another notable was Edward H. Wright, who was born in New York City, attended its public schools, and graduated from the City College of New York at the age of sixteen. Arriving in Chicago in 1888, he would become the preeminent leader of early-twentieth-century black politics (Figure 37).

Three other noteworthy attorneys deserve mention. J. W. E. Thomas gained recognition in politics and in the struggle to gain civil rights legisla-

Fig. 37. Edward H. Wright.

Fig. 38. Hale G. Parker.
From Appeal.

tion. Another attorney was John G. Jones, then the most irascible member of the bar, who was known as "Indignation Jones" because of his acerbic, contrarian style. Whenever controversy stirred over issues real or imagined, Jones was always present, if not in the middle of the fray. On one occasion, a slight at a downstate Illinois hotel spurred Jones and his friends into action with the resulting product being the Illinois Civil Rights Act of 1885. In another, far less substantial controversy, Jones challenged the character of Dr. Daniel Hale Williams after he had made a remark about the social strati- fication of black Chicago. To clarify the issue to whites, who had a tendency to classify African Americans into a homogeneous grouping, Williams had told a white reporter that "the great mistake which white people make is to judge the whole Colored race by the sleeping-car porter (who is not half so black as he has been painted), by the newsboys and roustabouts." Jones took immediate offense on the grounds that the physician was denigrating the first two occupation holders based on their labor while elevating his esteemed position. After calling a meeting to express his indignation on behalf of his race, Jones found himself being criticized for becoming overzealous. "Brother Jones means well and is on the alert to discover attacks on the race," stated another attorney present, "but he has made a mistake [and] I am here for justice." The matter was resolved with no action taken, to the complete dis- satisfaction of Jones, but with the approval of the assemblage.[111]

The last of the three was one of the outstanding and accomplished figures of the period and was the twenty-third African American to pass the Illinois bar. He was Hale Giddings Parker, who proudly claimed Ohio as his birthplace. There, his family had lived a comfortable life, the result of the business and scientific achievements of his father, John Percival Parker. The elder Parker owned and managed the Phoenix Foundry and Machine Works in Ripley, located in southeastern Ohio.[112] A resident of St. Louis for sixteen years, he was soon to call Chicago his home as a result of his participation in the world's fair as commissioner-at-large representing Missouri. Since he was the sole African American to gain an appointment to the National Board of Commissioners, the fair's governing board, he became the representative of black America, something he considered an honor (Figure 38).[113]

His credentials in education, in the professions, and in the industrial sphere were quite impressive. Parker graduated from Oberlin College in 1873, where he studied the liberal arts; then he turned his attention to law and attended the St. Louis Law School, from which he was graduated in 1882. He subsequently passed the bar in both Missouri and Illinois. At the time of his national appointment, he served as principal of the Alexandre Dumas school in St. Louis, where he was highly regarded as an administrator. He gained practical, scientific, and managerial experience from his association with his father's foundry in Ripley, where he worked as a machinist, a supervisor, a legal consultant, and finally as the business promoter of the family's patented machines throughout the South and West.

Placed on a path of success early in life, Parker developed a mind-set that locked on high achievement as the only acceptable standard for African Americans. From his father, young Parker inherited an attitude of intrepid directness based on a childhood upbringing in a household that had gained renown in complete defiance of the slave regime. His father had gained prominence for his solitary forays across the Ohio River into slaveholding Kentucky and his ultimate return with rescued and frightened slaves in tow. Always armed and ready for a fight on the Ohio side of the river, John Percival Parker provided a model of achievement that could not have escaped young Hale during his formative years. In his successful entrepreneurial, business, and scientific pursuits, Hale was further exposed to the possibilities of what could be achieved in America despite the odds.[114] In the light of extant circumstances nationally, Parker was led to engage in provocative rhetoric in behalf of racial advancement and he might have sometimes appeared isolated from the realities of the day. In the aftermath of the world's fair, he chose the black ideological epicenter of Chicago as his permanent home.

IV. THE FABRIC OF SOCIETY

Just as John Jones had represented "Everyman" during the antebellum period, the Gilded Age produced fresh faces to qualify for this honor. The postwar era brought distinctions based on more complex linkages of wealth, work, culture, and public deportment. Now a multiple "Everyman" and an "Everywoman" represented a variegated set of groups with disparate images. They conformed roughly to the three sociocultural clusters St. Clair Drake described as composing African American society during the 1890s. The elite or "refined" element represented the status to which African Americans with high mainstream expectations could aspire. The "respectables" constituted the largest portion of the social arrangement and was a group composed of the solid working-class element, who were mainly domestic, service, skilled, and unskilled workers. Other respectables included the handful of part-time politicians and political appointees as well as the operators of barber shops, restaurants, and saloons.

Drake's third segment of black society, condescendingly labeled as "riffraff," did, in fact, constitute the African American contribution to the nation's and city's lumpen proletariat. In 1896, three years after the fair, this group included perhaps 5,700 persons (25 percent) out of a total city population of 22,742 African Americans.[115] Only extensive extrapolation allows us to create a figure for the population of the early eighteen-nineties. Because of the onset of economic depression in 1893, which lasted for four years and increased the pool of the unemployed, the 1896 total might be both ephemeral and inflated. This segment of society included the noncriminal poor as well as wealthy criminals. Living varied lifestyles across this portion of the social spectrum, the dispossessed were nevertheless considered homogeneous in the eyes of outsiders with respectable social credentials mainly because of their lack of them. Many of the Civil War veterans fell within the expansive ranks of this group.

One need only look at the contemporary record to see which of Drake's three variegated social groups dominated African American society and spoke authoritatively about matters of public decorum and group needs. Nineteenth-century public utterance (such as Daniel H. Williams's socially controversial comments in February 1888), civic involvement (such as the heralded Charity Ball of March 1892), and legal challenges (exemplified in the case of *Baylies v. Curry*, which began in March 1888), along with this chapter's survey of the accomplishments and activities of the "refined," clearly outweigh the value of twentieth-century sociological interpretation by Charles S. Johnson, E. Franklin Frazier, and St. Clair Drake of the "Chicago School."

A. The Respectables, or Ordinary People

The respectables best typified black Chicago because of their numbers and their influence over each other through their conjoined but at times disparate leaderships. They were church affiliated, morally upright, but less culturally anchored than the refined in the dominant Anglo-Saxon world. In the case of whites, this was both because of less black interest in that group with its attraction to high culture, and a lack of socialization or educational training that promoted an appreciation of supposedly superior WASP values. The respectables felt comfort in their enjoyment of the best components of Afro-American subculture. Many Civil War veterans and their families were representative of the respectable segment of the African American population. Of this group, Civil War Sergeant Willis Easley worked his way up the occupational ladder to become either a special aide or messenger to railroad management at the general offices of the Illinois Central Railroad. Likewise, Sergeant Rodney Long fulfilled a dream of exercising authority by becoming a member, perhaps the first or second, of the Chicago Police Department.

As a younger, up-and-coming individual, Robert R. Jackson epitomized this group as politician, soldier, and community leader. He was born in 1870 in Malta, Illinois, and attended the public schools in Chicago before graduation in 1885. He obtained a job in the Chicago Post Office as a clerk and by 1909 had risen to the rank of assistant superintendent at the Armour Station. He served in the Spanish-American War as an officer and with distinction; in 1917, he was elected the second African American alderman to sit in the Chicago City Council.

Across the chasm of gender, the schoolteacher Lettie Trent represented Jackson's counterpart. Because of her involvement in civic or community activities before 1891, and her occupational success, demeanor, and utterances, she seemed to embody a rugged belief in her group's destiny as she defined it. Trent demonstrated an assertiveness in racial matters heretofore unseen since H. Ford Douglas's wartime agitation for citizenship rights and not replicated until Ida B. Wells's arrival in 1895 as a permanent resident.

Businessmen within the ranks of the respectables saw economic opportunities and acted quickly to their advantage. Operating enterprises that had grown considerably in a milieu conducive to risk taking, hard work, and visions of wealth, they were able to advertise for the planned world's fair entertainment and housing in an impressive fashion. The *Indianapolis Freeman* reported that vacant lots stood ready for construction, and "several of our leading citizens have erected flat buildings for the exclusive use, if so desired, of Afro-Americans."[116] In addition, Dr. Charles E. Bentley from the elite joined with certain respectables, along with politician George F. Ecton and the *Appeal's* managing editor, Charles F. Adams, to propose the building of the Union Club for African American gentlemen.[117]

Drake's description of a functioning Afro-American subculture seemed especially appropriate for life within the world of the respectables. Family formation revolved around a kinship network composed of real and fictive kin but also around the monogamous family. As to the latter's newness in national African American life, Du Bois maintained in 1897 thus: "Among the masses of the Negro people in America the monogamic home is comparatively a new institution, not more than two or three generations old."[118] Consistent with his time frame, the monogamous family had evidenced its importance in the formation of black Chicago as early as the pioneer generation. Frazier found that in Chicago, monogamy occurred more often among persons with greater financial and educational attainments by the time of his twentieth-century study *The Negro Family in Chicago*. Importantly, his targeted study group was made up of descendants of the pioneers.

A generation after bondage ended and the cultural isolation of the mass of African Americans had ceased, persons of unmixed African descent still identified themselves in racial terms that reiterated their affinity for the perpetuation of their chosen, particular way of life. The question of establishing a racial identity for those persons of unmixed blood and loyalties has rarely been addressed, but the attempt here is to give it the attention it deserves. Despite the importance of racial duality in the lives and mind-sets of *some* African Americans, David Levering Lewis has indicated that it should never have been considered the only choice of persons of African descent in America, Chicago, or anywhere else on the globe. Further, Gwaltney postulated that "to the prudent black American masses, however, core black culture *is* the mainstream [culture]."[119]

In the spheres of work, family, and friends, employment in wait service in restaurants and on the rails could carry a heightened status unachievable by the worker whose work regimen was more routine. Association with the nation's elite in the grand hotels and restaurants in the nation's second-largest metropolis placed the waiter, even if only in his hidden thoughts, in close proximity to individuals at the pinnacle of economic power. For the few who were college graduates or with partial college training, serving their supposed racial and social "betters" probably allowed the opportunity for some internal group version of racial one-upmanship. At the turn of the century, a researcher from the University of Chicago evaluated them after personal contact and found that "most of the *headwaiters* [were] very clever men."[120] Their rank in society belied their intelligence and potential. Their trademark of an effervescent smile might have been a grin after all.

The experiences of one such waiter on the dining cars of the Chicago, Burlington, and Quincy Railroad illustrated several of these points. John M. Washington started to work for the CB&Q in 1881 at the age of twenty-two, wishing to join the wait staff. Without experience and skills, he was relegated to managing and cleaning the gas lamps in dining cars, an area in which he excelled, until such time that an apprenticeship of observing was offered. Once in the service, Washington distinguished himself for being able to take and serve twelve full orders at one time. Over time, company officials recognized his value to the railroad, and he was promoted to mail messenger and bank liaison, which "brought him in[to] contact with many of the country's leading railroad magnates."[121]

Moreover, wearing their uniforms as symbols of their knightly authority, Pullman porters assumed unto themselves a power never envisioned by their employers and customers and recognizable all too clearly in the black community. On occasions, these men could be masters of any given situation. These "ambassadors" also expanded their horizons individually as well as collectively, gaining knowledge of how the nation and the world operated through travel, eavesdropping on the discussions of the nation's movers and shakers, and reflecting on what they said and heard in dialogues with sympathetic whites.[122] In 1883, one Pullman porter, Floyd Thornhill, initially engaged in an informal conversation with a U.S. senator that soon transformed itself into a formal interview used in a senate hearing on labor conditions in the South.[123] Perhaps with knowledge of the aforementioned, or of a similar episode on the rails, historian J. A. Rogers illustrated this newly emerging personality among the Pullman porters through his use of a composite character, Dixon, who bettered his Southern "better" intellectually on a transcontinental train ride.[124]

Once home within a family setting, anecdotes and reenactments of white posturing and pretense surely attracted willing ears.[125] Seen by men and women alike as part of labor's nobility, and sometimes suave and handsome, the Pullman porter often failed in family life. One joke aptly described the situation and its effect on family stability: "Mrs. Jones—'Do you find married life lonesome and monotonous?' Mrs. Brown—'Oh no. My husband is a railroad man, you know.'"[126] Often, constant travel could produce in the porter a sense of rootlessness and subsequent irresponsible behavior in a given locale. One case of the later involved an out-of-wedlock relationship and disaster for parenting within family boundaries. A certain peripatetic Mr. Byers, or Bias, who was charming, obviously attractive in various aspects of his deportment, and presumably handsome in the eyes of some of the younger women at Olivet Baptist Church, met a young churchgoer who was considered "wild" or promiscuous by her more moralistic peers. The young woman in question matched his biological proclivities with hers, and their union produced a young female child sometime after the Great Fire of 1871. The young mother recounted later in life how "we were engaged to get married but he went off and never came back any more."[127]

The education of the race in the 1890s would be placed partially in the hands of perhaps a half dozen African American teachers in the city. African American families eagerly availed themselves of the advantages of free public education, and the participation of the young increased along with the population. As a result, the value associated with formal learning pervaded the ranks of the respectables. Success stories of children educated in the Chicago Public Schools were reported in the black press. Featured were the musically gifted James H. Johnson, and William G. Anderson, the skilled stenographer and typewriter who was assigned to the probate court, where he earned a hundred dollars per month. Johnson had attended the old Jones School and afterwards Haven Elementary; Anderson attended Scammon Elementary and West Chicago evening High School.[128]

The first black teacher purportedly hired in the city system, Eliza Campbell-Taylor, was joined by another woman, perhaps Mary E. Mann.[129] These pioneering educators entered a system, which, when headed by the iconoclastic superintendent Ella Flagg Young during the 1880s, committed itself to educating all children to their fullest potential, whether native white, European immigrant, or black migrant. Promoting a policy of preparing the city's young for productive citizenship rather than inglorious roles as cogs within Chicago's industrial colossus, Young supported the living concept of democracy and civic strength through diversity.

Mrs. Lettie Trent, a schoolteacher whose name would figure prominently in protest at the world's fair in 1893, served in that decade and beyond. Not to be overlooked was the untapped teaching experience of Fannie Barrier Williams and Ida B. Wells, both of whom had college training and used it initially in behalf of black youngsters in the South. Unfortunately, neither woman did so in behalf of those in Chicago.

Literacy supposedly increased among adults to a point where "less than one half of one per cent of the total Colored population" could not read and write, and that small segment of illiterates was composed of "old people[,] formerly slaves who had no chance to get an education."[130] This figure is both conjectural and suspect, given the constant in-migration of adults from areas and from circumstances where educational opportunities were still limited after the end of slavery. Two news items in the black press showing contention in churches illustrate this point. At Olivet Baptist Church, a reporter recorded this comment: "You see . . . [our director of music] conducts her own business and will not be dictated to by some members of the

church who are here from Kentucky and other Southern states that can neither read nor write, and don't know when a note is sounded on the organ."
At Bethel A.M.E. Church, the following conversation was recorded:
"Three thirds of us have petitioned for Bro. Reed [to remain as head of this
church]. 'What's that?' asked the Bishop. Three thirds have petitioned for
Bro. Reed. 'My good brother, you are a little mixed in your arithmetic; three
thirds is all,' said Bishop Brown. Well, most of us want him back."[131]

In the sphere of recreation within African American society, dominated
as it was by the working class, the replication of what the white nouveaux
riches experienced allowed headwaiters to join Pullman porters, valets, and
personal messengers to the millionaires in acting as the arbiters of working-
class standards of conduct. This explains the description and role of Julius
Avendorph, a personal messenger to financial magnate and civic giant
Ferdinand W. Peck, and later, to Robert Todd Lincoln, as the "social arbiter
of black Chicago." The cakewalk—the African American dance caricature
of Nordic pretense and arrogance—originated from this group and spread
from the plantation to the black theater. An embarrassment to the black
elite, it fit the needs of working-class African Americans as it provided relief
from the tensions of laboring in a hostile white world and as a vehicle
through which to sometimes challenge white authority covertly.[132]

On the other hand, having fun in and of itself often reigned as the prime
motivation behind some of these activities. Paul Lawrence Dunbar witnessed this ability of the worker to transform drudgery and downtime into
an exciting recreational episode. He wrote about young waiters in a hotel:

> When they were not busy they would gather around and talk, usually
> about girls. In order to keep an eye out for prospective customers, they
> always stood near the dining-room door, much to the annoyance of the
> busy waiters who had to pass through with heavy trays.
> "Jump back!" would come the warning, and then with a teasing grin
> for the romantic topic, "Jump back, *honey*, jump back!"
> The boys jumped, and then went on with their gossip—
> "I seen my lady home las' night!"
> "Uh-oh! An' then what?"
> "I raise' huh lips an' took a li'l taste. M-m-m!"
> In between came the repeated warning, "Jump back!"
> It echoed in Paul's mind like a refrain. Soon, he turned it into the poem
> entitled "A Negro Love Song."[133]

Bolstering the popular belief held first by Chicagoans of successive generations, which now has gained currency as to its authenticity nationally,

was the demonstrated ability of Pullman porters, waiters, and others to translate their experience in fine living into one that the greater community could enjoy with them. In a social realm dominated by camaraderie and an escape into leisure activities, food and social interaction had the power to transform a people, especially members of the working class in the service areas. To see how a supposedly dispirited group could use a menu to affirm self-esteem among persons accustomed to social and racial proscription requires only a scan of the serving list at the third annual banquet of the Newport Hunting and Fishing Club on January 22, 1885. The menu featured fillet of beef larded aux champignon, rabbit braise, stewed bear with jelly, squirrel larded, quail on toast, roast venison, baked red snapper, and other delicacies.[134]

The plethora of social clubs and fraternal orders that pervaded the city depended on such annual functions to ease the tensions of living in an increasingly hostile society. The desire to be left alone, free from white interference, to have "good times"—much the same thing that the European immigrant groups wanted—makes too much sense not to have been accepted and examined by earlier social analysts on African American behavior. The associational activities of this group also revolved around fraternal orders such as the Order of Elks, the Masons, Odd Fellows, and the Knights of Pythias. The Gilded Age witnessed an expansion in their influence and representation within the African American population. Veterans and nonveterans alike joined, finding another important niche in society for members of a proscribed group. Its functional role was apparent: "Blacks found a way to bring order out of the chaos of white indifference, abuse, and neglect through the structure, ceremony, and ritual in a fraternal lodge of their own making. The lodge was a place where a common man of small economic means could be exalted to a position of high esteem and honor through his own efforts and his moral standing among his peers. . . . [It] strengthened racial solidarity among like-minded, self-respecting blacks who considered themselves exemplars of the community."[135] One veteran and fraternal leader's funeral in New England in 1885 brought out thousands to pay their respects. Occupationally, however, he had performed janitorial services.

Even members of the elite joined to enhance their standing in the black community and solidify their professional interests. Exemplifying the importance of fraternal life in personal and professional advancement, Edward H. Morris joined the United Grand Order of Odd Fellows in 1882 and rose to the rank of deputy grand marshal a year later. Within six years of initial membership, he had moved up to become Grand Master, an office he retained for fifteen years. Ferdinand L. Barnett was a member of the Masons and actively promoted their coming to Chicago for a national conference.

The entertainment and leisure activities of this group reflected the effectiveness with which blacks adopted coping mechanisms to deal with pervasive racism. In elaborate ritualized balls, dinners, and picnics, African Americans carried an enjoyment of life to its ultimate levels. Newspapers were filled with accounts of these activities that were so variegated in scope as to include dinners with menus rivaling those of the people of high social rank whom they served regularly in ballrooms, restaurants, and homes. Their varied aesthetic interests filled newspaper pages, also. When postal clerks, for example, honored one of their coworkers with a reception held at 1728 Indiana Avenue, the entertainment consisted of two separate piano solos, a flute solo, one vocal presentation, a larger, choral arrangement by the Parks Quintette Club, and two separate recitations. After an elaborately catered dinner, Professor Neely's Orchestra provided music for dancing.[136]

Movement through space for both fun and profit, provided by the nation's extensive rail system and its equestrian gaming enterprises, brought added enjoyment into everyday life for ordinary people. Seasonal travel with overloaded trunks to visit friends and relatives in faraway cities became commonplace.[137] Horse racing appealed to the respectables, who often behaved in a manner that was contrary to their professed religious morality when it came to their public conduct. It was fun-filled, however, and popular, and attracted black South Siders to the Washington Park Race Track, and South Siders and West Siders to the latter's Garfield Park Track.[138]

B. The Refined Element

The black elite, or refined element, stood separate from the respectables, developing its own way of thinking and behavior. It included professionals in the fields of medicine, law, and journalism, and their rise was a phenomenon of the post-Reconstruction era.[139] Frazier wrote that "originally, the small group of Negroes who because of superior culture emerged from the mass of the population and constituted the upper class did not represent primarily the occupational differentiation of the population."[140] Similar to his fellow researcher at the University of Chicago, Charles S. Johnson, Frazier was correct in his general assessment but was inaccurate with the particulars of the situation. At a time when mainstream America was setting higher standards within the professions, several dozen African Americans sought to, and indeed, met them. In Chicago, the 1880s introduced conditions that opened the door of opportunities, even if only slightly.

While the elite towered above African American society in terms of status, its members' role was tenuous at best in regard to any unqualified influence

over the entirety of the black population. Infinitesimally small, they numbered about 20 among 6,480 persons in 1880, and perhaps 50 among 14,271
residents in 1890. Indeed, if this group is considered to have occupied the
apex of a social pyramid, it was an almost indistinguishable tip. Claiming
group hegemony at the apex of a social pyramid reflective of Anglo-Saxon
values, and needing constant legitimization from outside the African American masses to sustain this position, they headed Richard R. Wright Jr.'s contemporary hierarchy of extant "social grades" in Chicago. As they extolled
their educational training, rigid moral codes, interest in the beaux arts, and
close identification with the dominant WASP power structure, they assumed
their right to pursue and share in the American Dream to the fullest. These
persons have recently been referred to in scholarship as "Afro-Saxons." As
to their position in America, Gatewood wrote that the black elite "constituted, on their own terms, an 'aristocracy,' that is, an aristocracy relative to
other blacks . . . but it scarcely conforms to customary usage of the term."[141]

The oldest embodiment of this culture at the beginning of the period was
Mrs. Mary Richardson Jones, John Jones's widow. She was heir to what was
believed to be the largest fortune accumulated by an African American at
the time of her husband's death in 1879. Purportedly, "Negro society in Chicago from the sixties to the mid-nineties revolved largely around her. She
was a stern dictator, quite austere in her leadership." Mrs. Jones held court
in her home on then-suburban Ray Avenue and Twenty-ninth Street in a
"substantial white frame structure of dignified classical lines." There she
received, in her "walnut and horsehair parlor," a young Daniel Hale Williams
upon his arrival to the city. When the two met, apart from age and experience, they met as social equals. Sitting under a portrait of her late husband,
the pair talked about personalities, events, and circumstances that predated
Williams's firsthand knowledge, but of which he had some familiarity based
on his family's long association with, and social standing among, the antebellum northern elite. In actuality, the younger newcomer to Chicago possessed all of the advantages of status. Williams's stature rested firmly on his
mother having claimed fictive kinship with Frederick Douglass along with
familial freedom dating back to the American Revolution.[142] Moreover, he
was well educated, professionally trained, moved in white circles as well as
black ones, and was soon to prove himself a man of national destiny in the
health field.

Skin color, personal decorum, occupation, and professional pursuits held
prominence among desired characteristics. Mary Richardson Jones, for her
part, had "ideas and ideals [that] were largely of the lily white type. It is said
that Dunbar, the poet, courted her grand-daughter, but that Mrs. Jones
objected to him because of his complexion." As the scion of one old family

assessed the historical pattern, "until the Great Migration Chicago Negro society was excruciating in its decorum and exclusiveness. The old families and the professional and business element ruled. Actors and saloonkeepers, no matter how much money they might have, were barred. Butlers and waiters, even though they might be employed on the Gold Coast, were not considered by the Chicago Negro 400."[143] Even Mrs. Jones's seemingly exalted status would be challenged within a decade by professionals both male and female.

This group's perennial swim upstream to attain full recognition of its citizenship rights continued throughout the decade of the 1880s and into the next, perpetually made more difficult as whites persisted in refusing to distinguish between a possibly attainable civil equality between the races and, in the eyes of whites, an equally threatening social equality involving intimate interpersonal contact. The former was the popular, but often misunderstood, black term for openness of opportunity in an unfettered competitive environment. The latter served whites as a device to justify discrimination and exclusion. Richard R. Wright Jr. once wrote an apt description: "The doctrine of social equality . . . assumed (not proved) that [African Americans] wanted to marry whites and thus 'pollute' the sacred stream of white superiority, and that would be a great crime against humanity . . . [as part of a strategy] the cry of 'social equality' was made to bar [African Americans] from every line of progress they endeavored to enter."[144]

Before hundreds at the world's fair of 1893, Fannie Barrier Williams clearly enunciated her position on the issue of social equality by lambasting whites and explaining that blacks did not seek involuntary social contact. When the Kentucky-born, northern-educated, and urban-oriented attorney Edward H. Morris debated a champion of protecting the racial status quo at the downtown Central Hall before a mixed audience in 1890, he spoke along lines that were "dignified and well delivered, [and] upon generally accepted lines of thought." Emphasizing the need for a "fair chance," Morris spoke of how "Afro-Americans are no longer the wards of the nation. They want now a chance [to compete] with the rest. They will work out their own salvation." This willingness to face a Social Darwinian world with neither handicap nor special advantage was something that Morris felt obligated to point out to whites. "To all white men in this country the Negro's face is the mirror of the past. Looking upon it, they are reminded of the shameful slavery, servitude, and debasement of the Afro-American race and hence they look upon it with contempt." In order to advance an argument that African Americans deserved the same rights as other Chicagoans, it was necessary to emphasize the heterogeneity found among the city's African Americans along socioeconomic lines. Simply, African Americans of the middling class and above desired and deserved a difference in recognition for their status achievement as opposed to those in the laboring class.[145]

Partly because of his articulation of his sociocultural group's position as well as his acknowledged legal acumen, Morris earned the mantle of dean of African American lawyers in the next century. His impressive demeanor and self-confidence in the midst of a debate on race, indicative of the "New Negro" of the last decade at the close of the century, impressed a white journalist enough to ascribe to him characteristics acceptable to most whites: "Mr. Morris is a tall, finely built man, with an intelligent, earnest face, and in every respect a creditable specimen of the race whose cause he was there to champion." In contrast, his white counterpart descriptively appeared in the newspaper as "stout, bald-headed, [and] jovial."[146] In the legal sphere, it was Morris who embodied elite professionalism.

Fannie Barrier Williams's life offered an example of another experience uncommon in America at a time when racial segregation and subordination pervaded American society. Until age eighteen, this native of Brockport, New York, experienced an innocence in interracial relationships even more remarkable than that of W. E. B. Du Bois's well-documented life in Great Barrington, Massachusetts. Her parents enjoyed themselves and were recognized as fellow citizens and respected as humans. Of her earliest years, she recalled to a national audience the following vision of what America could be if truly color blind:

> We three children were sent to school as soon as we were old enough, and remained there until we graduated. During our school days our associates, schoolmates and companions were all white boys and girls. These relationships were natural, spontaneous and free from all restraint. We went freely to each other's houses, to parties, socials, and joined on equal terms in all school entertainments with perfect comradeship. We suffered from no discriminations on account of color or "previous condition," and lived in blissful ignorance of the fact that we were practicing the damnable sin of "social equality." Indeed until I became a young woman and went South to teach I had never been reminded that I belonged to an "inferior race."

When she planned to marry, she arranged for it to take place in Brockport. She recalled the situation:

> After teaching a few years in the South, I went back to my home in New York State. . . . After the buffetings, discouragements and discourtesies that I had been compelled to endure, it was almost as in a dream that I

saw my schoolmates gather around me, making my home beautiful with flowers, managing every detail of preparation for my wedding, showering me with gifts, and joining in the ceremony with tears and blessings. My own family and husband were the only persons to lend color to the occasion. Minister, attendants, friends, flowers and hearts were of purest white. If this be social equality it was not of my own seeking and no one seemed harmed by it.[147]

One must wonder, though, what type of reception she would have been accorded had her spouse been someone other than an African American. In any event, Mrs. Williams's experience in Chicago failed to replicate these halcyon days in western New York, but she did enjoy a measure of life somewhat similar.

Culturally, the twenty-five-member Prudence Crandall Study Club typified the kind of organization that nurtured the elite when it committed itself to intellectual enlightenment and perfecting social decorum. Under the alternating leadership of Lloyd G. Wheeler and S. Laing and Fannie Williams, this organization set the standard for cultural interests. They probed intellectual matters and listened to lecturers invited to speak on their areas of expertise. At the club's last session of the season in 1888, at Mrs. Mary Richardson Jones's home on Ray Avenue, Rev. Jenkin Lloyd Jones lectured on "The Great Paintings of the World."[148] Mastering conversational German became the rage for the elite in 1888, and one of language specialist Professor C. F. Adams's prized students was Fannie Barrier Williams.[149] The elite also savored the rise of talented African American violinist, James H. Johnson, which further showed how far blacks had advanced since Emancipation. Accomplished, and recognized as such by whites, Johnson studied in the East as well as abroad in Europe as he perfected his skills.[150]

There was one event in particular, however, in late winter of 1891–1892, that marked how far African Americans had risen in the civic and cultural spheres. The great Charity Ball of March 3, 1892, combined cultural enjoyment with civic obligation to inaugurate charitable giving into a new and impressive tradition. The *Appeal* devoted a full page to this cultural breakthrough, as black Chicago announced its coming of age:

It was the first time that the graceful and the fascinating muse, Terpsichore, had been made to do duty in the glorious cause of humanity among the Afro-Americans of Chicago. This was the first time that wealth and culture had publicly recognized that the highest purpose of individual happiness is to make happier and more comfortable the lot of an unfortunate fellow creature. Never before had the great people, blessed with an abundance of this world's goods, been willing to indulge in the frivolity of the dance for the sake of sweet charity. It was a public testimonial to the fact that goodness predominates and that even that folly, the mazy waltz, which many theologians and church members abhor, can be turned to the service of right, and act as a ministering angel in the hour of gloom and misery.

The issue of social status and the absence of obvious social friction did not escape the reporter's attention:

There was an air of gentility about it which has never heretofore pervaded a public ball in this city. While all of those who attended were not of the aristocracy[,] yet they were people of intelligence and good breeding, and were just as much at home and had just as good a time as those who have a great deal more money and are supposed to belong to the select circle whose sacred portals are guarded from the many who do not move in their particular set. The absence of restraint and snobbishness was one of the most commendable features of the evening. While it is true that the leaders of society confined their attentions to the friends with whom they are accustomed to associate in society, they did not carry their exclusiveness to the extent of rudeness. Every one was made to feel at ease, and the reception committee performed its duties with rare tact and cleverness.[151]

The Charity Ball represented another milestone in that it revealed between the sociocultural groups a widening gap that was within a decade of being transformed into formal socioeconomic divisions, that is, social classes. Further, the divisions that existed and were readily recognized now within black Chicago serve to refute the notion that all occupational and economic groups had an equal opportunity to belong to "society." The list of sponsors and attendees included almost all of the refined element, and the clothing worn, especially by the ladies, indicated an expenditure beyond the wages of service personnel. "Probably the most interesting part of the ball to the ladies was the variety and beauty of the costumes," and this presentation of finery, coupled with the performance on the dance floor, served notice on who belonged to society and who did not.[152] The actions of the elite negated the physical law that proposed that two objects could not occupy the same physical space simultaneously. It was accomplished annually in the Dearborn Corridor until such time as the elite had completely moved away. In the meantime, social distance sufficed.

Playing an integral role in African American cultural life was church participation, which involved active involvement in the nine major, and several new and rising churches. Now sitting in formal edifices, these churches reflected the permanency and aspirations of the congregations. Inside each, the required demeanor often appeared foreign to Southern migrants who were accustomed to different church traditions, which embraced emotional and personal responses to the Spirit.[153] Newcomers either conformed, as hundreds had done before them, or ignored this variant form of black church life to join smaller, mission churches. For a few African Americans, such as S. Laing and Fannie Barrier Williams and Dr. Charles E. Bentley, membership in predominantly white churches beckoned. By 1887, the white Unitarian minister Rev. Jenkin Lloyd Jones opened All Souls to African Americans just as a black Baptist minister, Rev. Bird Wilkins, planned his own Liberty Temple that aimed to attract the elite of both races.[154] For other blacks interested in raising their status through a proper church affiliation, new faiths beckoned as the Episcopalians, Presbyterians, and Roman Catholics organized churches.

Moreover, contact with whites in relationships other than providing services attested to this group's prominence. One example included Mayor John Roche's selection of Dr. Daniel Hale Williams to join the official city welcoming committee for President Grover Cleveland. Another included Mayor DeWitt Cregier's appointment of Lloyd G. Wheeler and Edward H. Morris to the city's World's Columbian Exposition committee. Then, Dr. Charles E. Bentley could be seen "roam[ing] the [World's Columbian Exposition's] fairgrounds after methodically taking notes at the Congress of Dentistry as his profession's official observer."[155]

As an embodiment of the times, Hale G. Parker represented the elite's "Everyman" par excellence. Here was an individual whose interests and life's associations in the professions, education, the arts, and the world of industrial capitalism, albeit on a small scale, substantiated true claims to elite status. He emerged publicly in late 1892 and to his credit lobbied the management of the upcoming world's fair for inclusion on terms most African Americans could accept. Nevertheless, even with his appointment as an alternate member of the Board of Commissioners for the state of Missouri, certain African Americans remained dissatisfied with the role their group had at the fair. Eschewing the idea of being swallowed up into a melting pot, they envisioned an identification extolling their racial and cultural distinctiveness. This notion appeared as anathema to Afro-Saxons, who saw their future insured best in a color-blind yet egalitarian nation. For his part, Parker lambasted his fellow blacks about extolling racial pride and a racial destiny as viable means to achieve the end of full recognition as American citizens.

Parker tapped into the deepest feelings and sentiments of the elite toward this nation that had led them to embrace a hope that someday they would become part of the American mainstream. During the Reconstruction era, this hope evolved into a strategy. It was a strategy, however, that embraced methods and means linked paradoxically to distinctiveness and racial isolation. The appearance of inconsistency began with the widespread exaltation of "race pride," "race consciousness," and "race solidarity" as the fundamental means to achieve the strategy of full recognition of citizenship rights and black humanity. Parker, embodying the national spirit of assimilationist racial advancement, looked askance at these means as counterproductive, if not altogether destructive of strategic value. The evolution of Dr. Charles E. Bentley's thoughts would prove to be remarkably similar, as he emerged from the obscurity of his young adult life on the eve of the fair to reach the pinnacle of professional and civic prominence in the next century.[156]

The growing numbers of assimilationists, encompassing more than just Afro-Saxons, also included persons willing to counterbalance the desired end of enjoying full citizenship rights and respect as persons with means that were contradictory to that end. Nonetheless, even if these cultural pluralists were, by degree, somewhat less than "true believers," they considered themselves just as correct and logical in their choice of alternative means to promote their strategy. The means of race solidarity embracing some semblance of voluntary separation still seemed practical in a world filled with so many paradoxes and ambiguities related to race. Wilson J. Moses, in his historical examination of the time between 1850 and 1925, considered this period one in which "some of the best educated and most gifted black men and women were associated with institutional separation."[157]

Hale G. Parker's denunciation of race pride, race history, and race destiny clearly illustrated his concern when he attempted to check what he considered excesses in divergent African American thinking. When the full text of Parker's pronouncement is examined closely in light of extant circumstances, it is evident that he was only addressing one of several sets of ideological exchanges pervading both the nation and Chicago at this time. He was not placing himself "above" the rest of his fellow African Americans, as one historian has imagined.[158] Parker was clarifying his position to those with whom he identified both racially and ideologically, while seeking to restrain those actions and principles that he felt jeopardized racial advancement. Basically, like Washington, his ideological opposite, he sought a strategic advantage from which to ensure maximum black participation in the fair, and on a broader scale, the American nation. When necessary, Parker could exert himself fully and in public to protect the dignity of his race. When he headed the Dumas School in St. Louis, white teachers serving under a separate supervision but still under his general jurisdiction refused to be seen in a public celebration with black kindergarteners who were taught in a facility attached to the Dumas facility. Parker ordered an end to participation altogether unless the white teachers accompanied their charges.[159]

Commissioner Parker's awareness of these tendencies convinced him of the necessity to address them in his message calling for full participation in the nation's affairs despite pervasive racism. He opposed withdrawal in the face of injustice and exclusion, accommodation to unjust conditions, and separate development whether advocated by nationalist strategists or integrationist tacticians. But what he opposed carried little influence beyond the circle of those persons sharing his beliefs on race, so he earned the scorn of many envious and less capable persons than himself. Within diverse black America, "Parker [did] not claim to belong to all these elements, nor [did] he claim or wish to claim the honor of association with—well [under] one half of the whole and probably not one-third."[160]

Parker was soon to be prominent at the upcoming world's fair, his being one of only three African Americans holding official positions, so the ideological sentiments of Commissioner Parker along with those of Haitian Commissioner Frederick Douglass carried special importance. Both men held a strong belief in the inevitability of African American triumph over racism in a competitive, Darwinian environment. Involvement in that arena was a requisite, and a demonstration of competence remained a continuous responsibility. If the major problem of the late nineteenth century was the color line, the solution required a maximum commitment to improve self and nation along with a stronger dose of faith in American ideals and institutions. Parker and Charles E. Bentley, as well as the temporally ubiquitous Frederick Douglass, consistently challenged any form of compromise to the national promise of equal opportunity for all and to inequality both in thought and practice, whether it manifested itself in social isolation, voluntary separation, or emigration. In their minds and over the long haul, it was a matter involving the immovable object of white racial supremacy being somehow unable to withstand the irresistible force of the American Dream as encompassed in the promise of equal opportunity for all citizens.

Seven years after Isaac C. Harris penned his views in support of timeliness of promoting race pride, Parker heaped scorn on the advocates of group economy and self-help. "The 'Colored merchant' is getting to be a numerous article and is lavishly applied to any citizen of color engaged in any pursuit," he wrote sardonically, speaking from his successful, competitive experience in the business sphere. "Tried by the ordinary tests of a legitimate commercial business he becomes less numerous and rises to the level of *merchant*, just as 'our Colored leaders' when tried by the tests of leadership dwindle to a few who can be *called leaders of men*. And this is the consummation we insist on. . . . Out of this arises the imperative duty of all men to become patrons of the World's Fair."[161]

As to the fair and those alternatives to the full participation espoused by Parker, withdrawal symbolized anything but "a judicious method of redressing or reforming a wrong, nor of enforcing a right." He continued that it amounted to "a desertion of the field in the hour of actual engagement, in which public and private interests are ruthlessly sacrificed. . . . In an hour like this, when the great forces and agencies which have unfolded the life of the world are to be exposed to modern thought, to advise contempt of the opportunity to show identification with those forces will certainly be construed to the disparagement of the colored people." But such was the frustration in the heat of this battle that Chicago's Lettie Trent and Memphis's Ida B. Wells considered this approach rather than experience any more racial slights. And of course every emigrationist gravitated to the position that physical withdrawal by the mass of African Americans represented the only true solution to continued oppression in America.[162]

Voluntary separatism resulting in all-black institutions, relationships, communities, and towns fared little better in Parker's eyes. He considered "the dangerous mistake of sacrificing great opportunities for advancement on a mistaken 'race pride,' in the vain attempt to build a 'race history' and to work out a 'separate and distinct destiny' in this democratic country, must be defeated. There is nothing more incompatible with the manifest destiny of the republic. It is resistance to the logical current of *our* history and to the noble efforts consecrated to the cause of freedom and humanity by the bravest souls of the century."[163]

The racial duality associated with W. E. B. Du Bois, of contending loyalties to a concomitant "Negroness" and an "Americanness," opened the possibility that African Americans would often act in contradiction to any "true believer's" commitment, such as Hale G. Parker's. The latter's purist concept of integration rejected any voluntary grouping, voluntary separation, or drawing of the color line among African Americans themselves.[164] The danger of duality could be seen in the elite black community, according to Arna Bontemps and Jack Conroy, as even a seemingly socially accepted mulatto like Chicago's legendary John Jones "never lost his identity as a Colored American." Chicago dentist Charles E. Bentley, originally a native of Cincinnati of mixed racial ancestry, promoted the American Union Club, an all-black investment and mutual aid club capitalized at $100,000. Significantly, it advertised itself as "a valuable enterprise to the Colored people of the city, and something that no young man who has the interest of the race at heart and desires elevation of society should fail to cooperate with."[165]

However, even within occupational groupings, cultural interests differed because of contrary views of the racial world. A physician such as Daniel Hale Williams, and his dentist friend, Charles Edwin Bentley, lived in a disparate world from that enjoyed by an anonymous doctor cited by E. Franklin Frazier in his famous study *The Negro Family in Chicago*. The account of this physician's view of the city's black social makeup contrasted greatly with the picture of the city's culture and glamour described by Gatewood in *Aristocrats of Color* and, importantly, as actually experienced by the refined element.[166]

The world that the Afro-Saxons dominated existed parallel to that inhabited by the masses. Sometimes their worlds overlapped, but not with such regularity as to form a pattern of contact requiring a code of conduct. Both groups worried about the state of race relations, though the Afro-Saxons worried more than the rank and file. When the issue of equality came up, it was a matter of the elite feeling secure through their ability to enjoy not social equality with whites or even the benefit of equal equality with all other blacks, but an equality of opportunity related to their achievements and attainments. In the white world, this challenged their view of what best suited blacks, which amounted to one as being too many, none as being too much.

The accumulation of wealth did not necessarily confer elite status. Politician John W. E. Thomas left an estate of more than $100,000 at the time of his death in 1899. In another case, historian Rayford W. Logan reported on a certain Mr. Lewis Bates, a former slave from North Carolina who, although unlettered, left an estate of $500,000 at the time of his death. Bates owned valuable property with white tenants and amassed his fortune from shrewd real estate deals.[167]

Overall, social distance existed, but never at a level where interaction totally ceased between the three groups that Drake described. Attorneys such as Ferdinand Barnett and Edward H. Morris provided legal services to Civil War veterans seeking compensation for wartime injuries and infirmities. The renowned dentist Dr. Charles E. Bentley served his predominantly white clientele in a Loop suite, but he never neglected his African American patients. Physicians such as Dr. Daniel Hale Williams, A. Wilberforce Williams, and others stood ready to help heal the sick and build community bridges through the efforts of Provident Hospital, which was located in the heart of the expanding South Side African American community.

C. The Economically Dispossessed

The plight of the Civil War veterans, their wives, and their widows is a picture of urban despair and deprivation on a scale that is usually associated with newly arrived European immigrants. Lacking the economic resources to live among the respectables in many instances, they were forced to reside socially among the riffraff and faced the stigma of shameful living through association. Like their counterparts in the South, where many former slaves were transformed into sharecroppers and lived under the most abject of conditions, the northern economically dispossessed similarly lived their lives adrift in a sea of economic and social despair. Now that they were reaching middle age, they became more prone to illnesses and injuries and often lost the capacity to sustain themselves economically. The veterans, many of whom had suffered from health problems contracted during slavery—problems that were exacerbated by the hardships of military life—were often physically and mentally broken by this period. In 1890, a bright spot appeared when Congress passed the Dependent Pension Act. This legislation was the result of GAR pressure politics and guaranteed more veterans an opportunity to relieve their economic plight based solely on service and inability to work.[168] The benefit nonetheless exposed another sore spot in American life for the former slave, as many were bereft of the educational training needed to sign their names on governmental forms as well as to read and understand the pension process to which they had committed themselves. In their frequency of movement from one inexpensive dwelling to another, they further revealed the precariousness of their situation.[169]

The case of Hardin Harris was especially heart-wrenching. During his active days of military service, he suffered ill health on the battlefield. Forever after, Harris's health was broken; when he reached the 1890s, he suffered from a life of economic deprivation. Described as "a fit subject for the poor house" by one physician, and as being "filthy in his person and rather poorly nourished" by another, this veteran lived his last days in a slum.[170] To complete a claim for a pension, a rather compassionate federal pension examiner personally escorted him around the city seeking out his former comrades to obtain as many favorable depositions as possible that related to his military-related illness. For any veteran who questioned his importance as he eked out a living in a fast-paced industrial society in which he seemed to have no place, humane, personal attention of this type had to be welcomed.

The case of James Jones was just as poignant. Here was another instance where a federal bureaucrat extended himself beyond normal practices for a veteran, probably out of a sense of honor due to the nation's war heroes. Examiner and Chicagoan J. H. Stibbs handled many cases, but one in particular affected him most deeply. He described it as "one of the most trying I have ever handled." He wrote in his summary:

> Claimant . . . has been aptly said by Dr. Davis . . . to be "constitutionally tired," [the soldier is] a thick headed lout of a fellow without sense or judgement enough to assist an examiner in the least in the matter of examining his own claim and for this reason I have taken especial pains to do for him all that any examiner could have. Have spent hours traveling about the city with him and did all that could be done to secure the facts relating to this case. He never had a settled habitation, or employment here. Did odd jobs about town and it is impossible to find any one having full knowledge of his physical condition from the date of his discharge until he left here in 1871.[171]

When expedient, the African American community itself could evoke particular elements of stereotypical racial imagery if it deemed it necessary to elicit sympathy from whites. One claimant wrote that "I am poor, a Colored woman, can neither read nor write. . . . I feel as though my case was fairly proven and that the color line should now be no bar to my widow's pension." The widow's attorney, Ferdinand L. Barnett, adhered to this tactic by referring to her as a "poor old Colored woman."[172]

The case of mothers was no more encouraging than that of the men, their wives, and their widows. After evaluating the claim of the family of Private Louis Clary, whose death in 1877 led to his mother filing a dependent's claim in 1892, five years after the death of her husband, Elijah, an examiner wrote a most telling summation of the impoverished side of life in black Chicago. As we encounter Mrs. Clary a second time, perhaps we see even more of the meaning of her life:

> The witnesses to origin are of the best of their class, and I think it may safely be conceded that soldier's death was due to disease contracted in the service. The claimant is a thoroughly honest old woman [of seventy years], who tells her story just as she remembers it. As she states, she and her family lived as the average of their class and it is difficult to say wherein she was a dependent, but the family were all workers. Soldier the most important of the lot and his steady and certain earnings were counted on to meet current expenses. In an ordinary "white case" there would be no doubt as to the mother's dependence, or as I view it we must consider that claimant was a dependent under the law.[173]

Life among the dispossessed produced its own social dynamics. Interpersonal dislocation and disorganization among the soldiers paralleled the attitudes many of the "riffraff" held toward the institution of marriage. While the respectable and refined segments of black society exalted its place in society as stabilizing and honorable, others treated its sanctity with disdain and contempt. The attitude of Nancy Clary exemplified the former. A dependent mother of a veteran, Mrs. Nancy Clary could state with pride in her deposition in 1892: "I have four children left [and they are] all married & living in Chicago."[174] And the importance of marriage was such that Rev. Thomas W. Henderson of the Quinn Chapel A.M.E. Church could reverently proclaim pride in the fact that he had officiated at the weddings of 269 couples between the middle of 1885 and 1887.[175]

Certainly, the positive dynamics of family life were embraced among all segments of society, including the very poor. One included sacrifice for kin. Several Civil War soldiers cared for dependent parents while all lived in abject poverty. This also required disregarding one's own thoughts of personal happiness with a wife and children.

For those persons committed to family stability, beyond sickness and marital fidelity still lay death. No respecter of age, race, class, or gender, death visited the ranks of the veterans as it did all other groups. What is interesting was the attention a seemingly unimportant, anonymous soul received in a city of now over one million persons. One major daily newspaper saw fit to carry a story on the death of veteran Isaac Foster of Company C, Twenty-ninth Illinois. "Foster was over 80 years old, and had for years been a character on the levee." The soldier had not prospered, for at the time of his death "an old stove and an old blanket constituted the furnishings of his dingy hovel." His dwelling was no more than a shed he had rented at the rear of 111 Harrison Street. A former slave without financial recompense, a former warrior without popular recognition beyond pension papers on his person and a reputation for eccentricity, Foster the old soldier had just faded away.[176]

Veteran Richard Barbour chose an attitude toward life and a corresponding course of conduct that appeared as anathema to churchgoing respectables, but it was one that was not totally unrepresentative of one segment of the population. In his early life in Chicago, marriage and family formation assumed prominent places. Yet, after growing up in a two-parent household in Chicago in which the sanctity of the bonds of matrimony were emphasized, he set out on a course in his adult years that led to him breaking the rules for respectable living among church folk in the city. His sister Florence was married legally in what appeared to be a stable relationship with her husband of some years. In contrast, Barbour developed a penchant for finding, pursuing, and winning the favor of what appears to have been an abundant quantity of marriageable females, at least three with the name Lizzie, or with some other derivation of his mother's name, Eliza. After the war ended, this master philanderer and prevaricator met and possibly married the first of as many as four wives.[177]

In Barbour's amorous affairs, he constantly sought to convince those around him—family and friends—that his companions were his legal spouses or at least persons living under respectable circumstances. In his twenties, he married the first of the three wives named Lizzie. He never appeared to have had any children by any of these women. To differentiate between the wives and widows in their records, the federal pension examiners resorted to numbering the women and describing their physical attributes. There was Lizzie number one, whom Barbour met and married around 1866 or 1867 at St. Louis as he traveled the Mississippi River system as a steamboat cook. As a result of this occupation, he moved constantly along the Red, Missouri, and Ohio rivers, and other parts of the greater Mississippi River system. He married Lizzie number two sometime in the 1870s. She was described as "a very dark fat colored woman" and "a hard woman." His next union was to Lizzie number three, whom Barbour married sometime around 1880. She was a free New Yorker who was reared by a white family, the Dorseys, who took her in as an orphan. She worked throughout New York state and eventually labored as a service worker in the oil fields of Titusville, Pennsylvania, after the war. Described as a "light brown skin woman of medium size" and a "settled woman," she left for Chicago following the Great Fire of 1871, motivated by the sense of excitement that a big, bustling city offered. While working in a white-operated brothel, she met Barbour, who was employed there as a porter. Lizzie left him temporarily to work for a white madam who had desperately beseeched her to work in building up her establishment in Sioux City, Iowa. Occasionally, the third Mrs. Barbour sent her husband money to induce him to join her outside Chicago, but he never left the city. The charade supposedly concluded when Lizzie received news through a Pullman porter that Barbour had died, leaving her to assume that she was his legal widow.

However, this was not quite the case. The very live Barbour now broke precedence in spousal names and began another of his nefarious affairs with a non-Lizzie as wife number four, a woman named Carrie Reynolds. They were married in Chicago in 1890. Carrie Reynolds Barbour was another New Yorker of mixed blood, who was described in her appearance as being "rather slim and nearly white." In his four marriages, this gentleman seems never to have divorced. When two widows, Elizabeth "Lizzie" Dorsey Barbour and Carrie Reynolds Barbour, applied for pensions several years after his death in September 1890, the conflicting claims eventually revealed so much about the soldier that neither widow was entitled to a pension in her own right under federal provisions. For his part, the soldier appears possibly to have died of a disability linked to his military service. He suffered from rheumatism, then kidney problems. While under the medical care of Dr. Daniel Hale Williams, after a two-year bout with dropsy, an ailment that had left Barbour badly swollen and bedridden, he passed away, calling on his fellow veterans to visit him.[178]

What this veteran attempted in marital craftiness, a civilian duplicated. J. Bight, a Pullman porter, married at least three times legally and entered into at least two casual relationships before his last wife discovered his philanderings. Morality in Victorian-era Chicago had taken a major step backward, so the episode was presented in the news as a subject deserving of public rebuke.[179]

D. The Riffraff, or Underclass

At the far end of the city's social spectrum were Chicago's human jetsam and flotsam, the denizens of the underworld of gambling, theft, prostitution, and other forms of criminal behavior. The physical dimensions of those portions of Chicago where vice flourished and the denizens of the criminal underworld resided in extensive numbers were staggering for the times. The area surely met the appellation of being "Wicked City," as Paul Lawrence Dunbar's mother imagined it in warning her son of big-city life as he left Dayton for the world's fair. During the 1890s, Mrs. Dunbar had heard Chicago spoken of in both glowing and alarming terms. As to the realization of just what Chicago could be as a threat to spirit, body, and mind, Paul Lawrence Dunbar confided his apprehensions to his mother, saying, "Oh, Ma, I don't want to go to Chicago. Chicago's such a big city. And wicked." Maternally, and with assurance, she quietly replied, "Now, Son, if you have faith in yourself, wicked folks can't hurt you. You just go along."[180]

The worst, or the "wicked" part of town, stretched from Van Buren or Harrison in the north to Twenty-second street in the south, and from Michigan or Dearborn in the east to Clark or the meandering Chicago River in the west, encompassing almost a full square mile of the city's South Side heartland. This was a part of the notorious "Levee" section, where within its boundaries murders were common but dismissed by Mayor Carter G. Harrison as political slander. "As for gambling, it flourished almost undisturbed. . . . And the social evil [of prostitution], fenced into segregated districts, was a miasma from which rose disease, police corruption, and disaster."[181]

In its northern extremities, from Van Buren to Twelfth, the immorality of the Levee red-light district flourished unabated; thus, this area represented Chicago's number one social problem. The group of African Americans living in this slum was dwarfed by the foreign population. The small enclave dominated by African Americans took on the nickname of "Cheyenne" because of the section's resemblance to that wild city of the Far West. One guide to pleasure spots for the wicked recommended that "if this locality is visited at all, it should be in broad daylight and in good company. 'Cheyenne' might fitly be termed the Whitechapel of Chicago."[182]

The frivolity associated with the decade contributed to its sobriquet as the "Gay Nineties" and provided employment beyond the pale of legality and accepted morality. A menagerie of individuals willing to engage in nefarious activities was arriving constantly in the city with plans to ensnare weak and temptable world's fair visitors. For the white "swells" and "sports" who sought anonymous entertainment away from their normally sedate milieu of Victorian morality, the fun to be had proved irresistible.

The stratum referred to by Drake as the "riffraff" of Chicago's African American community, and which Du Bois referred to as the "Submerged Tenth" when he encountered its members in Philadelphia's Seventh Ward, made its contribution to this bacchanalian and sybaritic atmosphere by virtue of its undisciplined social behavior and blindness to the responsibilities of home, community, and self. These persons were often unemployed and sometimes criminal in character; many had come to the city during and after 1892 because of both the legitimate and illegitimate opportunities the fair afforded. Sometimes the equivalent of part of today's "underclass," they frequented and operated gambling dens, working as card sharks, bouncers, enforcers, or thieves. They contributed to the economic crimes of larceny, robbery, and burglary that Monroe Nathan Work documented in his 1896 study on the nature and causes of crime among African Americans in Chicago.[183]

While the Irish held the ignominious distinction of being the city's most dangerous group, the white public's association of African Americans with crime led to a stereotyped image that convinced one white man that by blackening his face, he could both commit and get away with theft. He nonetheless failed in his attempt.[184]

A much more serious criminal offense took place in 1888, following the Haymarket Riot executions by only six months. Race, gender, occupation, media propaganda, and recently transformed codified law all came into play in this brutal murder of a teenage sweatshop worker. The victim was a fourteen-year-old Irish girl, and the accused was her seventeen-year-old African American male supervisor; both worked on State Street at a shoe factory. A rather rapid guilty verdict by an all-white jury resulted from a combination of latent racism and a determination that the accused not escape his just punishment. In this case, it was a hanging that satisfied the popular will. The defense presented an insanity plea along with a challenge to conflicting circumstantial evidence. Within the African American community, there was initial interest but a subsequent absence of assertive protest in support of the defendant.[185] Part of the explanation stemmed from an

African American community of fourteen thousand predominantly working-class individuals who valued respectability and morality as much as the Victorian era's WASP establishment.

Du Bois's perception of Philadelphia's contagion of antisocial thought and behavior can be applied to the black denizens of Chicago's Cheyenne section of the Levee in order to present a view of the internal dynamics of the criminal class. This early pioneer in sociology wrote:

> The size of the more desperate class of criminals and their shrewd abettors is of course comparatively small, but it is large enough to characterize the slum districts. Around this central body lies a large crowd of satellites and feeders: young idlers attracted by the excitement, shiftless and lazy ne'er-do-wells, who have sunk from better things, and a rough crowd of pleasure seekers and libertines. These are the fellows who figure in the police courts for larceny and fighting, and drift thus into graver crime or shrewder dissoluteness. They are usually far more ignorant than their leaders, and rapidly die out from disease and excess. . . . Their environment in this city makes it easier for them to live by crime or the results of crime than by work, and being without ambition—or perhaps having lost ambition and grown bitter with the world—they drift with the stream.[186]

Most notorious of the male black leaders of the Chicago underworld was Dan Webster. Born into slavery in 1812, his resistance to and contempt for white society with its hypocritical protocols led him to escape on the Mississippi River around 1832 at the age of twenty. He took his owner's flatboat and sold it so he could marry a young woman he met in St. Louis. They fled to freedom in the North and arrived in Detroit, where they were married. From there they crossed the Detroit River into Canada and permanent freedom. Described as giantlike, his form was impressive, as he stood six feet two inches tall and weighed over two hundred pounds. He also had a "glassy eye," thin lips, and high cheekbones to go with his "woolly skull and speck of yellow forehead."[187]

Working on lake shipping, Webster arrived in Chicago in 1849 and stayed after his ship sank to the bottom during a storm. His legitimate business was selling pig's feet at the freight depot of the Rock Island Railway Station, while his illegitimate activities involved him in the corrupt world of frontier politics and street crime. Eventually he was sent to the penitentiary for counterfeiting currency, and upon his release he headed for his home on Pacific Avenue between Polk and Harrison. There, he emerged as a criminal boss, with his domain being located in the roughest section of the Levee.

With the sale of pig's feet as a cover, and through a combination of intimidation and good cooking, he turned the operation into a very lucrative one. When a young white traveler or visitor would enter his store, "Dan would glare at him like a fiend and pick up his favorite weapon—an axe—and like as not the young fellow out seeing the sights would throw his pocket-book at the colossal African rather than provoke him."[188]

In an era when deference to whites marked interracial protocol, Dan Webster showed no such extraordinary respect. "Dese white people dun run this yearth long nuff," he was reported to have said. He also made money by having his corrupt police friends arrest the patrons of his saloon, whom he would then charge to get them bailed out of jail. As a thief and leader of criminals in burglary, mugging, extortion, and foot-pads (pickpockets), he was a genius and was recognized as such by the police. As a master criminal, he was lionized by young black criminals.[189]

Physically Webster's female counterpart was "Big Mag," who became the bane of police officers who dared to arrest her. Described as "nearly six feet in height, as straight as an arrow and of such marvelous strength that no officer on the force would take to arrest her singlehanded [because] she had a record with the pistol, too."[190] Along with this female perpetrator, other women of this type openly engaged in street-level violence in broad daylight.

As to dens of prostitution and other nefarious venues, "it was also understood by those knowledgeable in such matters that some 'boarding houses' catered to the more private and intimate recreational needs of their clientele," one writer found.[191] The Levee district housed the city's red-light district, and within its boundaries were located three African American brothels featuring Colored "Gay Ladies of the Night" who availed themselves to free-spending Caucasian customers. Several madams of color, such as Diddie Briggs, Big Maude and "Black Susan" Winslow (who purportedly weighed 449 pounds), maintained lucrative establishments and anticipated healthy profits from the clientele of the fair.[192] The city's second "best known" madam, Vina Fields, planned to meet the increased demand of the next year's fair by doubling her labor force to sixty women. This large number was especially disheartening because it probably equaled the number Du Bois listed for the entire area he canvassed in Philadelphia, which had a population twice the size of Chicago's.[193]

Intelligent, perceptive, resourceful, and focused on her desire to make money, Vina Fields demanded a commitment from her prostitutes that approximated the number of work hours required in the equally exploitative legitimate world. She posted rules and regulations in the rooms of her brothel that enforced decorum and adherence to a basically demoralizing protocol for the women. This madam also knew empirically that "girls [did] not take to the life from love of vice, neither [did] they remain in it from any taste of debauchery. It [was] an easy lazy way to make a living, and once they [were] started either by force, fraud or ill-luck there [was] no way of getting back." Her reputation among persons associated with the moral netherworld ranked high. "The police have nothing to say against her," Stead wrote in his timeless jeremiad, *If Christ Came to Chicago.* "An old experienced police matron emphatically declared that 'Vina is a good woman' and I think it will be admitted by all who know her, that she is probably as good as any woman can be who conducts so bad a business."[194]

As for her exploitation of black women in this field of dead-end, demoralizing labor, Fields justified the situation thus: "What brings [the] girls here? . . . Misery . . . Always misery. Unhappy homes, cruel parents, bad husbands . . . I don't know one exception." Fields envisioned herself as providing a haven for the abused. And she was known to feed the hungry and homeless. Yet, as Stead observed firsthand, "in the brothel as in the factory the person at the top carries off most of the booty." As for her own child, Fields's daughter attended a convent, far away from the source of her parent's ill-gotten tuition payments.[195] The dispossessed members of the netherworld, self-stigmatized as well as branded by their contemporaries as immoral, also shaped their sphere of existence as much as they could. However, as the ultimate victims of economic deprivation and labor proscription, they fared no better than exploited creatures in the gilded cages of the era.

The African American presence in police reports and in the prison population was disproportionate to its size in the city's population.[196] In part, it was reflective of the group's proscribed status in the American economic order. Comparatively, Du Bois's description of their counterparts in Philadelphia is relevant because in its social genesis, these populations both originated in the aftermath of economic isolation in the workplace and in the social disorganization inherent in the legacy of slavery. Both males and females engaged in crimes such as larceny, robbery, and burglary. Also, incidences of arrest for disorderly conduct were frequent.

E. The Complexities of Race Relations: The Black Desire for Equality of Opportunity and the White Fear of Social Equality

Race as a cultural construct as well as a determinant of social status and privilege still persisted as America's Achilles' heel and the bane of black Chicago's claim to being an equal heir to the national legacy of opportunity for all. While progressive thinking in the twenty-first century has relieved many Caucasians of the burden of supporting the notion of white privilege and its counterpart—the belief that nonwhites clamored for the approval of whites in their daily lives—the world of the nineteenth century retained its own unique beliefs. Accordingly, an evolution in African American thinking and behavior about race resulted in some African Americans remaking the civic and social ideal of black Chicago after John Jones died in 1879. A "newer Negro" mentality was appearing in competition with an almost total reliance on whites for paternalistic guidance and protection. The former featured a more assertive posture and was more independent of white assistance, even if, at times, the difference was hard to distinguish. Changes dictated by the pervasive economic and social transformation of American society brought to the forefront more educated, professionally trained African Americans to assist in the advancement of their group. Nowhere was this more evident than in an emerging metropolis such as Chicago. This was at a time, however, when the black masses of Chicago lived their lives in a world almost parallel to whites and somewhat in seeming oblivion as to considerations of race. These attitudes represented neither ignorance of the gravity of their situation nor a denial of reality, but a conscious, rational accommodation to circumstances beyond their control along an indeterminate timeline.

There were several levels at which black Chicago adjusted to a world filled with racial ambiguities. When an individual or group encountered the various elements of white Chicago society's views on race, the response was influenced strongly by previous personal experiences. In order to understand what African Americans felt and thought, we must examine the perceptions they held of themselves and the emphasis they placed on self worth. Collectively, theirs being a world of the possible and the real, they more often than not eschewed intellectual niceties such as linguistically differentuating between the white and black meanings of words such as *equality*, *social equality*, and *civil equality*. This arcane exercise would be the domain of twentieth- and twenty-first-century academicians.[197]

In the main, African Americans avoided both excessive talk about the subject and monitored their behavior in the type of social equality that whites referred to as "forced" social mixing. Yet *equality*, to African Americans, signified unfettered access to the rights and privileges every native-born person of European stock and every foreign-born white Chicagoan enjoyed. It also meant freedom from white interference in black affairs and the bedrock of Afro-American culture that undergirded black life. Most African Americans sought only a semblance of civil equality. Frederick Douglass spoke for many as he described the differences between whites and blacks on this issue: "Social equality and civil equality rest upon an entirely different basis [of thought], and well enough the American people know it.

... [S]ocial equality is a matter between individuals. It is a reciprocal under-standing. I don't think when I ride with an educated polished rascal, that he is thereby made my equal, or when I ride with a numbskull that it makes me his equal, or makes him my equal. Social equality does not necessarily follow from civil equality." In the labor sphere, rather than endorse interra-cial solidarity, whites substituted the concept of industrial equality. It inferred that economic self-preservation superceded white racial concerns, so cooperation with blacks was desirable.[198]

As constructed by whites, the world of race was as complicated as the complexions and family ties African Americans both claimed and dis-avowed. It affected their view of racial conditions and their expectations of racial harmony or voluntary isolation. While Henry O. Wagoner, who had moved to Denver, Colorado, could reminisce about the excellent relations he had enjoyed with whites in Chicago, this cordiality was no longer emphasized the way it once had been. However, that is not to say it had lost its importance altogether. There were some who could reiterate that view of the eighties as a golden age of race relations. Attorney Edward H. Morris recounted that "before the fair in 1893 there was very little prejudice with-in or between the races." Ferdinand L. Barnett recalled circumstances sim-ilarly.[199] Middling to good relations existed, but this was accomplished without the nearly total reliance on white patrons that existed during the antebellum period.

In contrast, one man who had lived during this period remembered cir-cumstances differently: "The white man has given us freedom, the right to vote, to live on terms of equality with him, to be paid well for our work, and to receive many other benefits. . . . If the white man should decide that the black man has proved he is not fit to have the right to vote, that right may be taken away. We might also find it difficult to receive other favors to which we have been accustomed, and then what would happen to us? We must remember that this is a white man's country. Without his help we can do nothing. When we fight the white man we fight ourselves."[200]

Regardless of whether black Chicagoans favored assimilation into the American mainstream or racial insularity to remain free from white inter-ference to the greatest extent possible, examples of positive change had a salutary effect on their community. This included legislation protecting the civil rights of African Americans, as was the case with the Illinois Civil Rights Act of 1885. Also, the city's white newspapers had begun to recog-nize the humanity of black citizens, which mitigated against mistrust and suspicion.[201] Especially beneficial was the direct contact with the more racially enlightened and fair-minded Chicago whites, whether the wealthy from Millionaire's Row, or the middle-class evangelical Methodists, such as

Mr. and Mrs. Edward Knapp, or the white poor and downtrodden from the Levee. The heretofore unknown Knapp family broke racial protocol with their kindness toward Civil War widow Malinda Chappell and earned the condemnation of a white federal pension examiner, who wrote that Mrs. Chappell lived in "social equality" with "two degenerate white people," Edward Knapp and his wife, who themselves attended "a colored church" and had "sunk to the level of colored people."[202]

The mass of African Americans had never lived during a golden age of race relations and they had no realistic expectations of experiencing one soon or in the near future. To many African Americans, just daily living and survival, or perhaps prospering within racially prescribed limits, seemed acceptable. Others articulated a view such as this one espoused by black women in 1891: "One fact it holds to be self-evident, that the race must for itself exemplify THE WORK OF ITS HANDS. It cannot expect for the American white people to expend their energy and tax their best efforts to help any one class of American citizens; still less can this be expected when we consider that toward the Colored race there exists a well defined prejudice which in almost every avenue of action tends to work against us. We must be satisfied if we are allowed a fair field in which to direct our efforts."[203] These African Americans asked for no special favors, just unfettered access to compete fairly.

Finally, a newer tendency among black Chicagoans gained paramountcy in their thinking, life choices, and actions: It was to seek an indigenous set of leaders for most of their life's endeavors. Black church memberships demanded a leadership from their group as a matter of unchallengeable practice. The same preference held true for fraternal orders and their auxiliaries. The most striking display of racial chauvinism appeared in the demand that officers for a state militia (national guard) unit be African Americans throughout the commissioned ranks.

Many African Americans still considered the South as a secondary home, but they tempered their sentimentality with hostility to the heinous treatment meted out to black Americans in the region. Because of the casual to indifferent nature with which lynchings were carried out, they were considered a threat to African Americans everywhere. Further, along with memories of the South and old values that were difficult to discard, some black Chicagoans adapted to the process of northern urbanization very slowly. Those features appeared in the counterbalance found among recent Southern migrants that delineated race relations along lines that were extremely deferential to whites. The hypnotic hold that Kentucky-born Mayor Carter Harrison held over African American voters attested to that relationship.[204] Even the attorney Ferdinand L. Barnett could succumb to the use of this tactic of racial deference when necessary to benefit a client. As we have seen, in writing in behalf of a Civil War widow, he saw fit to refer to her as "this poor old Colored woman." Other African Americans exhibited fewer deferential qualities but still recognized that, in addition to the social and physical distance that whites maintained from less-well-off whites, there existed a prejudice that would forever have them acting to constrain African Americans in their expectations.

1. White Philanthropy and Black-White Bonding

For the refined and respectable segments of the black community, interracial relations were marked by the strong ties, sometimes personal, that they maintained in the philanthropic and social welfare spheres with white industrial and commercial magnates such as George M. Pullman, Potter Palmer, Phillip D. Armour, and Marshall Field as well as social workers Jane Addams of Hull House, Graham Taylor of Chicago Commons, and Mary McDowell of the University of Chicago Settlement. Some whites, such as the Unitarian ministers Jenkin Lloyd Jones and Celia Parker Woolley, enjoyed an exalted position because of their commitment to social justice. A variety of organizations routinely carried the names of exalted Caucasians: There was the Charles Sumner Waiters Association, the Albion W. Tourgee Club, the William L. Garrison Waiters' Unit of the Knights of Labor, the John A. Logan Colored Republican Club, the Prudence Crandall Study Club, and the GAR John Brown Post No. 10.

Of these relationships, the one that developed between former judge Albion W. Tourgee and Chicago's black elite represented one of the more remarkable linkages of the time. It qualifies, in fact, as being somewhat unique in the annals of race relations because it embraced a mutual awareness of intellectual and ideological dependency of the members of one group on the mind of a sole member of another. It was also illustrative of the complex nature of biracial interaction in the quarter century since Emancipation, and it was a relationship that continued into the 1960s, to the chagrin of some black racial militants.[205] Without a doubt, Fannie Barrier and S. Laing Williams, Ferdinand and Ida B. Wells Barnett, Lloyd G. Wheeler, Hale Giddings Parker, and others constituted the vanguard of black social, civic, and intellectual leadership, which by its very existence and composition bespoke of agency, progress, and independence. They were also people in search of powerful, influential, knowledgeable, and sensitive white friends to validate their thinking, behavior, and status. In their dealings with Tourgee, they were overwhelmingly deferential, sometimes to the point of near obsequiousness. This was all the more remarkable because it occurred in the period declared by historians to be the era of Frederick Douglass. The *overwhelming* influence of the old sage's utterances and strategies did not end until his death in 1895, and even then most were still considered relevant. Whether defensive, hyperbolic racial posturing or a sincerely felt sentiment, George E. Taylor, president of the National Colored Men's Protective Association, wrote: "As a race we owe more to Albion W. Tourgee, than to any man living."[206]

For his part, Tourgee embodied all of the attributes of an equal-rights advocate par excellence. He was, in effect, a composite of Garrison, Brown, Sumner, and Thaddeus Stevens. Although he lacked abolitionist stripes emanating from the antebellum period, his exemplary level of commitment to racial equality during the Civil War, Reconstruction, and post-Reconstruction periods earned him the respect and admiration of African Americans nationally, and remarkably from all social strata of black Chicagoans. An Albion W. Tourgee Club was organized to publicly recognize his leadership and service to this cause of placing humanity into interracial contact. Tourgee was described by a biographer as pompous, and his family background as a French Huguenot no doubt contributed to this trait, which fed into a distrust of Anglo-Saxon arrogance and self-centeredness, which he saw as the root of racial injustice. Emancipation had eliminated slavery, but it could not dislodge racial prejudice, which Tourgee envisioned as flowing from the Anglo-Saxon's preoccupation with himself and his bid for glory.[207]

When from his vantage point in western New York, Judge Tourgee observed that "Colored people have lost friends—true friends . . . very rapidly during a few years past," he attributed the phenomenon to African Americans failing to show gratitude to their white friends in the struggle for racial justice. "The *people* of the North do not regard them as kindly as they did. I am almost the only one except [for] a few teachers and agents of societies, who keep on fighting their battles for them."[208] Further, Tourgee had chastised African Americans for this oversight in his "Bystander's Notes," which caused Barnett to respond in this manner:

> I have long considered you one of our best friends, and most fortunately for us, a friend with power to do what his heart wills. Your letters are read by my people and all that you say, is by them, most thoughtfully considered. Your notes of this day's issue of the *Inter-Ocean* treat with friendly severity, a failing which is a matter of regret to every thoughtful Colored man. I do not concede that the race is entirely devoid of gratitude, although I must admit that our evidences of gratitude are too few. In your kindness of heart you make the best of excuses that can be offered, and at the same time remind us of a duty in which, I am sorry

to say, we have been remiss. . . . Let me thank you again for the invaluable aid you are rendering my race. Please do not conclude that gratitude finds no abiding place in our hearts. If you could know how gratefully we regard your interest in us and how we appreciate your efforts in our behalf, you would be slow to write us down as a race of ingrates.[209]

A postscript by Barnett informed Tourgee that he could be vouched for in terms of integrity by H. H. Kohlsaat and Mr. Nixon, editor of the *Inter Ocean*—both were recognized whites who championed racial fairness and who themselves had reputations of high repute.

Tourgee's purpose was clear-cut. He wanted to "stem the rising tide of repression, retrocession, denial, and deprivation of equal right[s] to the Colored man." His determination was herculean but not totally unwavering. He could write that "I might as well have tried to stem Niagara with a straw." The latter reference clearly identified him as a resident of western New York state, his closest physical contact with Chicagoans coming from his outspoken "Bystander's Notes" column in the *Chicago Inter Ocean* and his occasional visits to the city to lecture in black and white churches and meeting halls. Physical distance notwithstanding, the strength of his will, pen, and organizing abilities made him a champion of black Chicago's thirst for accelerated progress through better race relations. In his choice of methods for reaching racial justice, he did not eliminate violence as a tactic, if undertaken in self-defense, but did prefer to see African Americans organize themselves peacefully into a vanguard opposing injustice directly and openly at all times. As for education and proper public deportment, Tourgee saw them as useless until whites were forced to change their ways. "The fallacy that it is the ignorance of the Colored man that inspires the denial of personal rights and inflames the white man to a murderous frenzy against him, or that wealth and intelligence would appease his thirst for Colored blood is so absurd that I can hardly believe that [earlier] . . . I gave it my unqualified support."[210]

From the point of view of six members of the elite, genuflecting to Judge Tourgee in the days preceding either an effective black think tank such as Crummell's American Negro Academy or a national organization proactively fighting for equal protection under the law, such as Du Bois's Niagara Movement or Trotter's National Equal Rights League no doubt conformed to the etiquette of politeness of the day and made perfect sense. Their own words conjure up a picture of intelligence, however, without independence of thought or action. That this marked their written posture throughout the decade of the 1890s explains why the activities and thinking of the twentieth century appear so cataclysmic in regard to race relations. Ferdinand L.

Barnett, S. Laing Williams, Ida B. Wells, and Fannie Barrier Williams wrote consistently in a similar vein.

In 1891, perhaps being urged by his law partner and friend, Barnett, to demonstrate the abundance of the appreciation of which Barnett had already alluded, S. Laing Williams wrote to Tourgee. Williams's tone was revealing for its tactical posturing:

> I have for a long time been a student of your teachings in various forms. Being a Colored man, I am prompted by a special impulse of growing interest and gratitude to acknowledge the helpful influence in your writing in behalf of a more righteous public opinion relative to the Negro's status. . . . Nothing since the days of Garrison and Phillips contain[s] in our behalf so much that is heroic, unselfish, righteous, patriotic and effective as the Phillipics from Mayville.

Williams also pledged his support for Tourgee's idea for a national civil rights organization, the Citizens Equal Rights Association. Even the president of the extant National Colored Men's Protective Association of America exercised this grand gesture of gratitude.[211]

Ida B. Wells consulted Tourgee frequently on matters of race but also on several occasions to ask his opinion on how to proceed on choosing proper legal representation in a libel suit she considered. After discounting the black attorneys she had reasons to distrust in her native Memphis, she inquired as to better or appropriate representation among other black attorneys, explaining:

> I thank you for your suggestions. My reason for consulting you was that I wanted the opinion of one who was not a member of the race. The manhood of my race as lawyers is too partisan to give cool unbiased counsel. . . . I do not like to expose the weaknesses of my race but I do wish a clear, impartial opinion as to the prospects of winning the suit I have in contemplation. It is necessary to know the facts. If you will do this, I will try not [to] intrude on your time and patience again. Both have been severely tried in the affliction under which you now labor and for which you have my sincere sympathy. It is my earnest wish, and I know I voice the sentiments of thousands of my race, that the Bystander may live long to speak with clarion voice against wrong and injustice.[212]

Meanwhile—unknown to his future and fellow journalists on the *Chicago Conservator,* and also to his future bride—Barnett, along with his law partner, Williams, was in consultation with Tourgee as to whether they should take up Wells's libel case.[213]

Several years later, Ferdinand L. Barnett's admiration for Tourgee reached such a level that he considered the white judge's ambassadorial appointment to France a racial triumph for African Americans. Barnett enthusiastically wrote of his "extreme satisfaction" to Tourgee and ranked the judge's accomplishment with his own: "[W]hile I have my full share of race patriotism and am anxiously hoping for a generous recognition of my own race's, still I am free to confess that no appointment accorded to the Colored people will give me more pleasure than this deserved recognition of your own."[214]

At the time of the World's Columbian Exposition, Fannie Barrier Williams felt comfortable enough with Tourgee's wisdom to ask him how to proceed to document her upcoming world's fair presentation on the progress and present status of African American women, explaining to him:

> You are so accustomed to be appealed to for all kinds of information, suggestions, and advice from American Negroes, that you perhaps now ask no apology from those who still persist in troubling you. My only justification in writing this letter to you is that such information and suggestions as you can furnish me will be used in a way that will meet with your approval. . . . Your utterances so abound in startling facts, figures, and reasonings relative to the American Negro and his varied relations to every thing and every body that I do not feel like commencing my work without some word of advice or suggestion from you in this matter.[215]

Reflecting on Tourgee's creation of the periodical *Basis: A Journal of Citizenship,* Hale G. Parker wrote to the judge:

> Soon after the *Basis* made its appearance it occurred to me that an opportunity had been offered to the Colored people, indeed to all who have been beneficiaries of your patriotic devotion to the cause of justice and law, to make a partial payment on the debt they owe you by aiding to promote this new venture in fearless journalism which is no less their friend and benefactor.[216]

In another letter to Tourgee a few weeks later, Parker described his optimism for his race, when combined with the helpful efforts of whites:

> Be charitable enough not to ascribe my conservatism to any belief or expectation on my part that the success of the venture must depend upon patronage of the Colored people. I confess that the history of

their rallying to the support of kindred efforts has some discouraging pages. Yet I do not despair of their being taught to do their duty in this behalf. Like mankind everywhere they have yet to learn to do their duty to the living.[217]

Further, Parker considered Tourgee as the chief benefactor to whom he credited his winning his world's fair post.[218]

Lloyd G. Wheeler also expressed gratitude to Tourgee—while also displaying a tendency to confide group criticism—during the preparation for the world's fair, when the issue of a separate day for African Americans was being discussed, writing, "I am so gratified at the 'turning over' you gave this jubilee business that I cannot refrain from boring you with a note of thanks. Of course were the Colored people not burthened with the weaknesses as well as the strengths of human nature theirs would indeed be a pronounced case of arrested development but it does seem sometimes that an able bodied and determined fool killer could be used to great advantage in the race."[219]

With the purported elite thinking along these lines, it might appear somewhat easier to understand why disparate circles of leadership would develop to meet particular needs as well as to determine what type of relations African Americans should adopt with the white world—friendly as well as hostile. And there would be other voices than these heard. However, one member of the respectables, obviously friendly and a member of Quinn Chapel A.M.E. Church, wrote to the judge, "I think every black man in the world loves you." To the writer, a J. H. Jenkins, this appeared most apparent after the mere mention of Tourgee's name had produced a stomping of feet and a clapping of hands at his church that was reminiscent of Emancipation celebrations.[220]

Herman H. Kohlsaat, restaurateur and part owner of the *Inter Ocean*, was recognized as another humanitarian notable on the local scene. Kohlsaat's name appeared prominently in the establishment of Provident Hospital, with the first black library, and in Bethel A.M.E. Church history. His relationship appeared quite different from Tourgee's in that blacks developed only a material dependency on their part. This is traceable to the group involved, with more of Bethel's members belonging to the African American rank and file. Kohlsaat's most prominent intervention occurred sometime around 1885, when the value of Bethel A.M.E.'s property was fixed at $15,000. At the point that the church was pressured by the expansionist real estate plans of a railroad to purchase Bethel's land and building for that sum, Kohlsaat intervened and persuaded the church to hold out for a larger amount. The philanthropist even guaranteed $20,000 of his own funds to protect the church and a higher price. Negotiations ensued, all favoring the church. Railroad offers of $20,000 and $25,000 were refused, following Kohlsaat's lead. Bethel now sought an even higher sum for the valuable land. "These supposedly 'ignorant soft-headed' Colored persons, trustees of a 'darkey church,' as they were called, politely informed the affable representative of the railroad people that they would not take less than $35,000 for the property. Eventually, continually negotiating over fifteen months with Kohlsaat's backing, they received $41,500 and a gift to the church of an additional $3,500."[221]

2. Interracial Marriages

Jolts against assuming too sanguine an attitude toward race progress appeared constantly. In 1883, the U.S. Supreme Court invalidated portions of the Civil Rights Act of 1875, obviously shocking those black Chicagoans who had seen its passage as a sign of upcoming halcyon days in race relations. Within months, another uproar tore at the possibility of better race relations when news of Frederick Douglass's marriage to a white woman made national news. Intermarriage between the races as well as innumerable interracial matings throughout the nation was nothing new. Its influence had even produced the internal color line of preferred and despised complexions drawn so frequently among African Americans. Yet the widowed Douglass's marriage in January 1884—after a year and a half of mourning—to forty-six-year-old Helen Pitts immediately stirred controversy. Throughout the nation, blacks and whites expressed intense displeasure and resentment, and this occurred even within the Douglass and Pitts families.

The thoughts of some black Chicagoans were expressed in a widely printed interview that appeared in the *Chicago Daily News*. Robert M. Mitchell presented his opinion: "It is rather hard to explain the case to white people, for they have no idea of the 'caste' which exists among the Negro people. It is, of course, exaggerated. Understand that there are in Chicago and all over the country, a class of exceedingly well-educated Colored people. The ladies of this class are absolutely opposed to marrying a white man. They look upon it as degrading, and such colored ladies hesitate to associate with a white woman who has married a Negro."[222] When Mitchell referred to "caste" among African Americans, he was addressing the issue of social class and how, within the black community, strong social differences with related preferences existed. To the refined group and to many of the respectables, marrying across racial lines implied a desire to be like whites, with an inordinate desire to separate oneself from black culture and community. African Americans knew all too well about intergroup mating, as evidenced by the high incidence of births of mulattos, quadroons, and octoroons since colonial days. Mitchell's response addressed the issue of white fantasy.

To some African Americans, interracial matings and marriages appeared natural and salutary; consideration of Cupid's influence was not be denied. One Old Settler who arrived in Chicago in 1887 at the age of nineteen probed his memory to comment on the situation: "Well, all the Negroes lived down round the Loop. Those were the old days. There w[ere] some Colored men that had white wives and they lived good and w[ere] respectable. My aunt lived on Twenty-second and Cottage—I lived with her. There was a white family lived there and we all got along fine." As for Douglass, he further enjoyed the luxury of having such an extensive network of friends both among whites and blacks of higher status that he could easily avoid contact with the mass of African Americans.[223] This variety of social independence typified the social distance between the Afro-Saxon and the rank-and-file African American.

3. Biracialism and "Passing" for White

The character of life of persons whose ties were linked to interracial matings, unknown during this period by its twentieth-century label "miscegenation," has recently revived the interests of academicians. However, to the contemporary mind, especially that perspective associated with unmixed Colored people, "passing" and claims to high status based on skin color routinely evoked criticism or raised eyebrows.[224] This struggle over identity grew to be recognized as the problem of the "internal color line." The issue of color distinction within the group was as real after the antebellum period as it was during that era. William R. Cowan supposedly "passed" for fun and told his friends about the foibles of whites with their preoccupation with skin color.[225] It was a serious problem for others who passed just to secure work, or who actually felt distinct and therefore acted differently from and toward their darker-hued African American brethren.

Race, whether its construct is artificial or substantive, biological or cultural, does not concern us here as much as the pervasive adoption and use of the construct in daily living. In Chicago, the editor of the Broad Ax accused Dr. Bentley of being uncomfortable with his color and establishing a pattern of aloofness toward other blacks during this period. He was supposedly "willing to give up his little white Jesus, and all the goods things in the world, if he could be a little whiter." The fair-skinned Fannie Barrier Williams would, at another time in her life, protect her claim to first-class railroad accommodations in the South by claiming French blood, a claim the overwhelming number of rank-and-file African Americans could not make.[226] Dr. Daniel Hale Williams's reddish hair and Caucasian complexion became the subjects of whispers whenever African Americans were not touting his accomplishments. Captain Charles R. Marshall of the Eighth Illinois passed for white in La Salle, Illinois, to keep a position as bricklayer and supposedly evinced antiblack attitudes to curry favor and also protect his identity.[227] It would seem that, in addition to the need to distance oneself from the criminal element of black America, some members of the elite and respectable elements found the need to distance themselves from African Americans who simply looked too Negroid.

Along with others of their race, the refined often articulated a view that showed they wanted a speedy realization of the American Dream that today's African Americans still demand on an immediate basis. While this lent support to historian Allan H. Spear's thesis of an abolitionist, integrationist tradition being influential among blacks in Chicago, by no stretch of the imagination did they maintain any hegemony over popular belief and accepted practice.[228]

4. Interracial Amicability amid Black Distrust of White Intentions

Antebellum experiences of distrust of white intentions still persisted in the minds of many black residents, but such distrust was often mitigated by the kind of positive, incremental change to which blacks had become so accustomed in Chicago. On a national basis, America simply had not established a positive track record in dealing fairly in racial matters at this point in its history. No single incident pointed to this issue more than the lynching by gunshots of three prosperous African American grocers in Memphis on March 9, 1892. Owners of the successful People's Grocery on the outskirts of the city, the three men ran afoul of the South's racial code that rejected both black economic competition and defense of black citizenship rights.[229] Black Chicago's militant response was as immediate as it was dramatic. A meeting of over one thousand persons convened on Sunday evening, March 27, 1892, at the newly constructed Bethel A.M.E. Church, located in the heart of Chicago's Black Belt. Their aim was clear, and their tone grew combative as they protested the outrage at Memphis. Lynchings had become all too common, but the indignity was worsened by the fact that the victims were members of the urban bourgeoisie—men who had been expected to lead black America into the future. The pastor of Bethel, Rev. George W. Gaines, called for Christian forbearance, the supplies of which were dwindling, given the wave of reversals affecting black America. He was startled to find the normally patriotic assemblage so angered that it refused to sing the unofficial national anthem, "My Country 'Tis of Thee." "He did not at first comprehend the situation and asked, 'Don't you want to sing America?'

to which question a dozen voices answered 'No.' One man in the audience rose and said, 'I don't want to sing that song until this country is what it claims to be, 'Sweet land of Liberty.' The preacher then led 'John Brown's Body,' which the entire audience joined in singing."[230] White reaction to this meeting bordered on the hysterical. Local and national newspapers were alerted to this act of black assertiveness, and one white daily even called the meeting an example of anarchy.

Within forty-eight hours, Judge Albion W. Tourgee had journeyed to Chicago from his home in western New York state to lend his support to the protest. Speaking at Bethel, he praised the overflowing crowd for its patriotism in past years and shared how he challenged a white man to imagine "that he was dark, that his mother had been a slave, and then sing that song. . . . [The white man] declared . . . that he could not do it."[231]

Meanwhile, a newer sphere had emerged in which positive interracial contact took place: the realm of organized leisure activities. At the center of this realm was the sport destined to become the national pastime—baseball. Chicago had four all-white teams when the Civil War started, so some military men had gained exposure to the sport predating the highly touted wartime interest.[232] Accordingly, when troops introduced the game into Union camps in Virginia and elsewhere during the conflict to relieve the daily boredom the troops experienced when there was a lull in combat, they found willing participants and supporters. Members of the Twenty-ninth Illinois, USCT, most likely witnessed, participated in, or in some other manner experienced the thrill of the game with other black troops. Those infected with fever of the sport quite possibly were the enthusiastic importers of the game when they returned to Chicago. Interracial play existed in the major and minor leagues throughout the North until it was formally eliminated in 1887, spurred by racism in general and, in particular, by the popular white manager, the legendary Cap Anson, of the Chicago White Stockings.[233]

By 1886, if not earlier, the South Side boasted of an African American amateur team, organized by W. S. Peters, named the Unions. They played their games in uncrowded areas at Sixty-seventh and Langley and Thirty-seventh and Butler.[234] The Unions regularly competed against other amateur white teams who were unaffected by the decision in the more organized ranks of baseball. The Unions were on their way to becoming "the leading amateur Colored team . . . against all kinds of odds, the umpires and crowds in general being against them."[235] On one occasion, in the fall of 1887, playing before a crowd of thirty-five hundred baseball enthusiasts, the Unions defeated the Dreadnaughts for a fifty-dollar prize. The next week they repeated the feat against a collection of white all-stars.[236] By 1896, the Chicago Unions, having adopted their name in 1888, began to accept challenges exclusively for monetary reward and thereby opened the door to black professional baseball in Chicago.[237]

Interest in baseball grew to a level where black Chicago could support two teams by 1899. Formed from a defunct company squad from Adrian, Michigan, named the Page Fence Giants, the bulk of the team moved to Chicago in 1899 to become the nucleus of the Chicago Columbia Giants. From 1899 to 1900, the Chicago Columbia Giants competed with the Unions for fan support as both played against white teams. By 1901, former Unions outfielder Frank Leland took control of the two teams and organized them into the Chicago Union Giants.[238] From these organizations emerged the famous pitchers George Wilson and Joe Miller, along with right fielder Willis "Willie" Jones and catcher George "Chappie" Johnson, said to be one of the greatest catchers in black baseball. Pitcher and future manager Rube Foster and organizer Frank Leland would appear on the diamonds at the turn of the century to transform recreation into both fun and profit.

Cycling became a popular sport among all Americans during this period. Athletic and competitive African Americans organized as the Chicago Colored Bicyclists; their attempt at interracial competition unfortunately failed when they were denied entry into a long-distance race solely because they were African Americans.

5. Varied Responses to Issues of Race

African American reaction to prejudice, discrimination, and racism in general produced various responses—law-oriented (either in regard to its enactment or its interpretation), associational, and celebratory—all of which contributed to both understanding and confusion. Black Chicago's legislative, legal, associational, and celebratory remedies aimed at improving conditions of interracial contact were just as proactive as they were responsive. African Americans aggressively continued to use the law and the courts to protect their civil rights as they had done for a generation. Black Chicago, for example, felt threatened and responded with alacrity when the statutory protection of citizenship affirmed under the Civil Rights Act of 1875 was being gutted in 1883; the U.S. Supreme Court declared the first and second sections of the act unconstitutional and thereby eviscerated the legislation. Even though the act has been described as more significant morally than it was in actuality, the need for legal protection against discrimination seemed an absolute necessity. Another strategy was to seek relief in the courts. Another black remedy was legislative, seeking protection through replication of the law at the state level. Among legislative solutions, one arose that was similar to what had been tried in twelve other northern states between 1884 and 1887, and as five others would in and after 1890. In this instance, an affront to Chicago attorney John G. "Indignation" Jones in downstate Illinois spurred the head of the quasi-military Hannibal Guard, B. G. Johnson, to act to legally protect the rights of blacks against hotel discrimination. With no course of legal redress available on the books, a committee of nine, led by attorney Jones and with Johnson as secretary, set about to write a civil rights bill. Johnson claimed he drafted it and encouragingly received both subcommittee and committee approval of his work. It was then submitted to State Representative John W. E. Thomas for introduction into the Illinois General Assembly, where it passed in 1885.[239]

As to the effectiveness and relevance of the Civil Rights Act of 1885, African Americans might hope for the best results but were acclimated to less than desirable action. When, in a highly publicized case in 1888, *Baylies v. Curry*, victory came based on the principle of fairness in public places, many blacks felt elated. On a very practical level, the decision and the levying of a $100.00 fine for violation of the law had to have heartened the most skeptical of African Americans. As late as 1969, black lawyers of the Cook County Bar Association heralded Edward H. Morris's courtroom victory as a landmark triumph.[240] Upon closer examination, skeptics had their points, as the case set no precedents or failed to prevent further such violations of the law by changing white behavior, buttressed by an egregious example in 2003 to support their contention.[241] A recent legal analysis of *Baylies v. Curry* showed it to be a complicated case that extended far beyond civil rights to involve the changing black and white attitudes about class and what treatment blacks could expect once they met white standards of decorum and income.[242]

An African American theater party of four persons, led by John and Josephine Curry, objected to being denied the preferred first-balcony seating for which they had paid at the downtown People's Theater. The rejection was based on race and their being African Americans. The case quickly moved through the legal system and in one day attorney Edward H. Morris argued strategically that this denial violated the Illinois Civil Rights Act of 1885, which forbade discriminatory practices based solely on prescribed group membership, that is, membership in the Negro race. What the case exposed was a series of different perceptions of race, class, and the meaning of the law from both sides of the dispute, plaintiff as well as defendant. Yet despite victory under the 1885 law, no precedent was set. Morris, a legal traditionalist who believed deeply in the inherent rights of all humankind, argued the case as a violation of inalienable rights and privileges as guaranteed in the Declaration of Independence, the Constitution, and other pieces of formal law. Significantly, adhering to the aphorism that "the law is what the judges say it is," Morris correctly argued along lines that he knew would resonate to the ears and thinking of jurists in Chicago.

Josephine Curry—in whose name the suit was solely filed for some unknown reason, her husband being relegated to the sidelines—envisioned the offense as her being grouped into a racial caste that was made up exclusively of a mass of socially undifferentiated blacks. In her mind, she had paid for a first-class ticket as an individual and deserved the benefits of that act. Meanwhile, Curry's social status as a member of the "middle class," as a legal historian referred to her in support of an economic point of view, should have been the point of legal discussion. In emphasizing this fact, Curry relied on an economic tactic that ultimately did little harm, as it did not affect the positive verdict secured by her attorney, who followed a more traditional approach. The theater owner, Mr. Baylies, viewing Mrs. Curry as part of a proscribed group whose presence adversely affected other patrons of the theater if not kept separate from them, also used an economic approach. Coming from an opposite pole, Baylies rested his case on the grounds of the possible economic harm that would be inflicted on his business unless he was allowed the right to discriminate among his customers to avoid interracial conflict.[243]

Regardless of the sentiments of the defendant and plaintiff, the case was argued by legal practitioners who were unwilling to create new law, something Morris surmised, so he pursued it along basic legal grounds upon which the judges from the local through the appellate levels could agree.[244] Economic considerations were cast aside without having harmed the plaintiff's cause. Importantly, the spirit of the law and of the times precluded discrimination by group categorization. The Plessy case in 1896 notwithstanding, the judges rendered a decision that could have been expected in modernizing Chicago in the late 1880s. To them, the law clearly extended protection against exclusion based on race and narrowly restricted their decisions to avoid support for social equality, or racial integration. Given the context of the times, and in historical perspective, to black Chicagoans and other Illinoisans, this could not be considered anything other than an important, incremental victory on the path to greater, future, more comprehensive legal victories.[245]

The successful strategy built upon an African American reliance on and reverence for the law by a new cadre of racial spokesmen and protectors of civil rights within the ranks of the respectables and the refined. They expressively reiterated a full commitment to the principle of freedom won in 1865 and the exercise of fundamental political and civil rights all other Chicagoans enjoyed, whether of native Anglo-Saxon stock or recently arrived foreign-born stock. By January 1892, these spokesmen focused on celebrating the finality of slavery and emergence of their rights as citizens. In emphasizing the importance of the Emancipation Proclamation, they joined other African Americans in focusing on dates associated with freedom.[246] Their decision was to commemorate Emancipation Day on the first Sunday of each new year. "For many months this idea has been gaining headway," reported the *Chicago Inter Ocean*, and "a number of the leading clubs of Colored people having been agitating in its favor in all parts of the country. Yesterday the first attempt at giving the day due observance was made in this city."[247] Notable among the male speakers that assembled at Quinn Chapel A.M.E. Church were Dr. Charles E. Bentley, attorneys S. Laing Williams, Lloyd G. Wheeler, James A. Madden, and Ferdinand L. Barnett, and Revs. J. T. Jenifer and J. M. Townsend.

The general theme of the ceremony pertained to abolitionism and the courage of the few outstanding white Americans who broke with a worldwide tradition embracing enslavement and framed a new one embracing universal freedom. On behalf of a grateful African American population, S. Laing Williams read a resolution to "set apart that day for special services, commemorative of the labors of those who battled in the cause of freedom and political equality of all men." Speaking on parts of the theme, Lloyd G. Wheeler "considered abolition as an inspiration to humane questions," while Rev. Jenifer referred to it as "an inspiration to moral advancement." It was left to Ferdinand L. Barnett, however, to deliver the major address of the afternoon. He began his speech by reflecting on the statesmanship that brought about abolitionism: "Statesmanship is the product of high civilization." After chronicling human history from before antiquity until the nineteenth century, Barnett concluded by addressing the virtues of whites and the responsibility of blacks to address and emulate those attributes. "Great causes produce great men; small causes little ones. . . . The political records are full of the names of forgotten politicians, who tried to handle this question on side issues. On the other hand are the heroes who viewed it as the supreme question of the century . . . Phillips . . . Garrison . . . Whittier . . . Sumner, and Abraham Lincoln." For blacks he issued this challenge: "If, then, the white race, through this inspiring unselfishness, could reach out across race lines and do so much for us, how much more through that same influence ought we now be able to do for ourselves. Abolition was the supreme question of the past; citizenship is the question of the present. The white man solved the one, the Negro must help to solve the other."[248] For these racial stalwarts, it was opportunity under law and meeting citizenship obligations—not concern with interracial social issues (social equality)—that should dominate African American thinking.

At the associational or organizational level, civil rights activism manifested itself in actions that foreshadowed the more publicized activities of the early twentieth century. A postbellum initiative, not unlike the antebellum convention movement, produced organized action appropriate for the times, yet sometimes hinging on the radical. Chicago's strategic location within the eastern half of the U.S. rail network no doubt played an important role in its being selected in 1889 to host the inaugural conference leading to the birth of the Afro-American League of the United States, an event that occurred on January 15, 1890. The presence of attorneys Ferdinand L. Barnett and Edward H. Morris as hosts, two longtime Chicagoans with reputations for assertiveness on behalf of the rights of African Americans, moreover would have played a major role. The setting thus chosen was in a locale known for its constrained racist tendencies, and the timing seemed advantageous. By 1889, repeated African American entreaties for justice—from delegations throughout the nation, made to successive presidents from both parties and to various Congresses—had won no concessions. Yet the times demanded "an organized effort of some character upon the part of the Afro-American to maintain and defend his rights [as] a necessity."[249] This action, reflective of other forces, further became significant in its own right, for as John Hope Franklin and Alfred A. Moss Jr. have described the event, "black self-help efforts reached an important critical juncture" with its founding.[250]

The Afro-American League was conceived of as early as 1884 by journalist and publisher T. Thomas Fortune of New York, and it emerged in final form as a result of a call by Fortune, Chicagoan Ferdinand L. Barnett, and sixteen other racial spokespersons. Fortune's presence and support were essential for success in getting the organization off the ground. Accordingly, he has been described by some historians as the most influential spokesman for African Americans following Frederick Douglass's death up to the ascendancy of Booker T. Washington.[251] With 135 delegates representing twenty-three states, the league put forth an aggressive, proactive organization agenda to protect the citizenship rights of African Americans. A sense of permanence marked its organizational structure, which befitted the hopes for its posterity and success against entrenched racism and terrorism. Structurally, the league built from the top down, with state and local organizing units expected to act in cooperative deference to operating components situated at a higher level. A.M.E. Rev. Joseph Charles Price, D.D., of Livingstone College of North Carolina, who was described as "a full-blooded Negro, six-feet-two inches tall," was elected president; Fortune assumed the office of secretary; George H. Jackson served as treasurer; and Chicago's Edward H. Morris took on duties as attorney for the league.[252]

Its composition was entirely African American, even though its constitution called for an open membership. This was the result of its mission, which had to be carried out by the persons most affected by its outcome. Unilateral racial action by a black leadership also advantageously conveyed the message that its race was coming of age in producing leaders from within its own ranks that could advance a civil rights agenda beyond the biracial, patron-client relationship of the previous several generations. In the age of Social Darwinism, biracialism would have served only to undermine the African American's claim to fitness. As Fortune explained, America already had a color line in every aspect of life from education to religion to moral reform movements, so "if the white man cannot rescue our drunkards and evangelize our sinners except by insulting us, let him keep away from us." As it was, the league was accused by whites of fostering a movement seeking special treatment, or preferential "class legislation."[253]

The league's agenda resounded with the militancy of the earliest wave of the "New Negro" type, who at this juncture was labeled the "Afro-American Agitator." The times dictated a more intense effort than ever before and moreover required a change in the mind-set of African Americans. Fortune happily accepted the label for a new man and woman whose appearance heralded "the death knell of the shuffling, cringing creature in black who for two centuries and a half had given the right of way to the white man . . . [now yielding to] a new man in black, a freeman every inch, standing erect and undaunted, an American from head to foot, [who] had taken the place of the miserable creature."[254]

The plan of action also called for a protest against lynch law and a demand for punishment of the white terrorists who perpetrated these atrocities, and protests against taxation without representation, the inequitable distribution of school funds in the South, unfair jury trials, discrimination in public conveyances, and exploitative convict labor. In a concession to the realistic horror of facing unredemptive, violence-prone whites, working-class blacks were supported in their efforts to cast their buckets elsewhere, so "healthy emigration from terror-ridden sections to other and more law-abiding sections" of the country was endorsed.[255] Finally, in order to protect the integrity of their organization from political operatives and major party agendas, the league described itself as operating separately from partisan politics.

Promoted by the black press, and filled throughout its organizational structure by men of this medium, a clarion call reverberated throughout black America and was recognized by white America. Irvine Garland Penn wrote a review on the state of the African American press in 1891 and its role in fomenting concerted action:

> It seems the intention of the press to lay before every Afro-American this effort, which, in their judgement, is the best road to the goal. It is their intention that not an Afro-American shall be ignorant of the league and its purposes. . . . This aggressive, yet peaceable manner of

agitating is a commendable step, for the best sentiment of the people may be relied on to take the side of right; and since this side of right is the complete emancipation of the race from social, moral and political injustice, it is safe to say that the Anglo-Saxon, with whom we live and move, will some day, *en masse*, get on that side.

Then it is the business of the Afro-American to contend, to agitate; and it can be done in no more effectual way than through the league system. The press is determined; let the people rally.[256]

Ultimate success depended upon the maintenance of organizational stability over the years, which in turn depended upon winning the ideological support of the African American masses. Whereas the refined element in Chicago and elsewhere could be counted on to understand the possibilities of attaining the American Dream, enthusiasm from other strata could not be assured. Even in the post–John Jones era, where supposedly the white patron–black client relationship was diminishing, embarking on major projects such as these still demanded the support of the respectable element, and that remained elusive until midway through the next century.

In February 1890, a month after the formation of the Afro-American League, Edward H. Morris, its national attorney and one of the strongest advocates of black rights among Chicago's elite, addressed an interracial, downtown audience on the issue of rights that were being frequently denied even in Chicago. When a white member of the audience asked him what black citizens wanted, Morris replied in this manner: "Let us alone in the enjoyment of the rights and privileges you have guaranteed to all by your organic law."

Criticism of what was perceived to be the league's inactivity in 1892 might explain why a new organization, the National Colored Men's Protective Association, was formed during the same time period. As a matter of fact, the formation of rival and duplicate organizations was common throughout the period.[257] For its part, the National Colored Men's Protective Association was organized in the Windy City in 1891 and aimed to fight against Southern outrages such as lynchings, peonage, and disfranchisement, basically the same as the league. When the U.S. Congress showed interest in the killing of seventeen white workers by the Pinkerton Agency at the Carnegie Works at Homestead, Pennsylvania, Protective Association president George E. Taylor could only bemoan the blind eye it presented to African Americans. "No one deplores this situation worse than we," wrote Taylor, "and I yield to no one in my contempt for the Pinkerton system [of violence-prone strikebreaking], but it awakens new thoughts of surprise within us to note that Congress is more concerned with the shootings of these seventeen people than in the killing of the whole 10,091 Negroes during the past 27 years, or the killing and burning at the stake of the 178 Negroes for alleged crime during the past nine months."[258] National in membership, representatives came from every state in the Union. Chicagoans were present in small numbers, interspersed among several hundreds of supporters or more. When the group returned to the city in 1893, the ubiquitous attorney Edward H. Morris temporarily presided over the 1893 conference.

In the meantime, there was an abundance of efforts that were not organized enough to be considered associational, but that represented important responses to racial problems. A coterie of dissidents who mistrusted the intentions of whites emerged. Educated, sometimes with professional status, they found very little in the actions or thinking of white Chicagoans with which they found favor. Prominently carrying the torch of racial circumspection were attorney John G. "Indignation" Jones and schoolteacher Lettie Trent. Trent was active in social and community affairs and would figure prominently in another perceived affront to African Americans, the scheduled world's fair to be held in 1893.

Organized protest mounted nationally between 1890 and 1892 against the proposed World's Columbian Exposition. Alert to the need for a timeliness to organization and protest, African American women planned and acted immediately. Impressively, this effort mirrored a national mood against continued racial slights, real and imagined, confirming that dissatisfaction existed beyond local activities. Less impressive, though, was the infighting among the women along loosely held class lines. Opposition to the appointment of Fannie Barrier Williams of the refined element as a low- to middle-level spokesperson for African American interests became especially vicious, with black women denouncing Williams to Mrs. Bertha Honore Palmer, the grand dame over all women's interests at the fair. Ferdinand L. Barnett sprang into action in defense of his friend and wrote to Mrs. Palmer that the root causes of opposition to Williams were "jealousy and envy." Tellingly, he wrote that "the best of every race is the prey of its moral banditti, and we are no exception."[259]

As general opposition grew locally, one of the city's half-dozen schoolteachers, Lettie A. Trent, called for a boycott of the fair to call attention to and correct injustices in employment, representation, and administration of the affairs of the exposition. Formalized involvement and protest by women took place under the auspices of two groups—the Woman's Columbian Association and its rival, the Woman's Columbian Auxiliary Association, which combined the support of both women and men, but with the former in leadership roles. As one world's fair researcher has written, "the unceasing, embattled flow of ideas and activities from these women made as effective a display of race pride and talent as any static exhibit in the Fair's pavilions might have provided."[260]

At the same time, the African American insistence in military matters that black troops should be led by black officers should not be overlooked. The Eighth Infantry Regiment stood unique in American military history for nearly half a century in this regard. This racial assertiveness, which extended through individual, community, and military ranks, demonstrated conclusively how completely the transformation in personality and group thinking along racial lines had advanced in Chicago.

V. INSTITUTIONAL LIFE: CHURCH LIFE, RELIGION, AND SECULAR ASSOCIATIONS

A. Church Life and Religion

When Du Bois in 1893 assessed organizational life among Philadelphia's African Americans, he found as much deficient as he found beneficial within its boundaries. Among the latter features he found that after Emancipation, African Americans had "to organize before they knew the meaning of organization; to co-operate with those of their fellows to whom co-operation was an unknown term; to fix and fasten ideas of leadership and authority among those who had always looked to others for guidance and command. For these reasons the representative efforts of Negroes in working together along various lines [were] peculiarly promising for the future of both races."[261] Chicagoans seemed to have had that same advantage and more. No doubt, it related to their cohesion and the quality of their early leadership in a milieu where civic virtue existed without its being held in contempt as it would be by some future critics.

In Chicago, religious life seemed to be taken seriously; it was not taken for granted or given short shrift. In those instances where skepticism occurred, it was assumed that church and clergy had failed to meet the needs of the time, and in the last quarter of the nineteenth century this meant bringing a social emphasis, such as the Social Gospel, into the sanctuary and beyond. It also meant responding to a higher criticism in understanding human behavior and thought, including Social Darwinism with its ideas on evolution, survival, and competition. Just as the earliest formation of a black community originated from a spiritual base, so did the influence of the church in the post-Emancipation period. And just as sin flourished, so did religiosity.

The majority of the black Christian faithful worshiped at three Baptist churches (Olivet, Providence, and Bethesda, the last being organized in

1882); at three African Methodist Episcopal (A.M.E.) churches (Quinn, Bethel, and St. Stephen); at St. Thomas Episcopal Church; at Grace Presbyterian Church; and at St. Monica's Catholic Church. There was also a growing underground church movement of sorts, particularly among migrants, which manifested itself in the formation of missions or in small religious gatherings held in homes. Home worshipers sought a Southern folk-based setting and corresponding assemblage free of the Northern-based constraints that seemed to stymie full religious expression (Figures 39 and 40).

Yet the nine major churches in particular offered both variety and choice to African Americans, a clear reflection of the proliferation of institutions accompanying social change. Collectively, the clergy administered to the needs of religious African Americans in this Protestant-led city and influenced daily behavior immensely, so influential was the church as a social agent. The spiritual leadership of black Chicago grew and was to rest prominently in the hands of a learned clergy. At Olivet, Rev. Richard De Baptiste, pastor of the oldest African American church in the city, served until 1884 at Harmon Court and Holden Place in the downtown section. Rev. J. F. Thomas succeeded him and ministered to the needs of two thousand members in a new edifice at Dearborn and Twenty-sixth Street. He was described as a "pulpit orator of much power."

At the city's second-oldest black Baptist church, Providence, trained clergy—called through the Wood River Baptist Association and screened at Olivet—continued their ministry, tending to the needs of West Siders. During this period, Rev. Abraham L. Harris presided over the Christian faithful. Providence Baptist Church was located at 26 North Irving Place (now 314 North Bell Avenue) on the city's West Side, a division of the city experiencing impressive growth and development as it was transformed from prairie to residential neighborhoods. Under the leadership of the youthful Harris, a native of Xenia, Ohio, the church initiated programs aimed at broadening the membership through numerous faith-based activities. The formation ensued of a Sunday church school, a Baptist Young People's Union, a missionary society with very strong on-site ties with West Africans, a choir, and a Young People's Forum that was aimed at fostering intellectual inquiry and moral training in daily living. Secular activities included cantatas, plays, quilting parties, bazaars, and discussion groups.[262]

Freedom of choice in religion led to the organization of Bethesda in 1882, after ten members (eight women and two men) of Olivet separated from the church with the expressed intent of organizing a new one. Differences over the blessing of infants, the washing of feet, and the use of Sunday School literature from non-Baptist denominations spurred their departure.[263] The original members of Bethesda met in the home of Mrs. Nellie Johnson in

Fig. 39. Gathering at Providence Baptist Church.
Courtesy of Providence Baptist Church.

Fig. 40. Sketch of Providence Baptist Church.
From Appeal.

the 2800 block of Armour (now Federal) Street as a "house church," until such time as their numbers grew and resources increased. "After about three months of spiritual prayer meetings with Bible study, the initial group of ten persons grew to thirty-one."[264] The authorization to start a new church arrived from the Council of Baptist Ministers of Chicago and Vicinity, buoying the hopes of these Christian faithful and spurring them on to find a permanent structure in which to worship. They chose the name Bethesda, signifying rejuvenation such as that found at the pools of Bethesda mentioned in John 5:1-9. Full of hope, the congregation soon rented a wooden building at Twenty-ninth and Indiana Avenue and began worship with seventy-five members in the assemblage. Resources grew and, with them, the desire for a more fitting church structure in a better location. Although they considered building a new structure on a lot they had purchased in the 3400 block of Butterfield Street, they resolved in 1885 in favor of economy; thus, they moved the frame edifice, which had already been remodeled substantially, to the new lot, a process that consumed four days.

Continuous growth, influence, and effectiveness in church formation did not come without major disturbances and adjustments. The Baptists at Olivet and Bethesda experienced problems inside their churches as did the African Methodists at Bethel. The *Western Appeal*, obviously partial to the African Methodist Church with its higher prestige and superior organization, lambasted Olivet's membership as it battled over leadership within their choir and over the replacement of an old organist with a new one.[265] Under the disturbing and insulting headline, "Trubble in De Church," the *Western Appeal* again ridiculed the Baptist congregants at Bethesda for another debacle, after Rev. Bird Wilkins's conversion to Unitarianism in 1888: again, they sought to change their pastoral leadership. The *Appeal* mentioned that this amounted to ten pastors in the pulpit over a seven-year span. No doubt, their problems stemmed in part from their latest minister's previous denominational affiliation with African Methodism. Rev. Goosley had converted to the Baptist faith and seemed to satisfy the church's requirements for leadership as well as meeting the church's other needs during his first year in the pulpit. Then a dispute over his salary arose, and contention led to a nasty physical confrontation.[266] Meanwhile, in the case of Bethel A.M.E., the refusal of the pastor and congregation to follow church policy and accede to a regular rotation in pastors ended amicably and orderly—and was reported in the news as such.[267]

The attraction of mainstream American religion in the Gilded Age proved magnetic to better-educated African Americans, who tired of the old folk-based ways. So it was not surprising that in 1887, under the leadership of Rev. Bird Wilkins, a case of apostasy arose from behind the Baptist pulpit.

Wilkins began to espouse the Unitarian doctrine and an interest in modern themes that frightened his flock. Educated in his native Nashville in theological studies and an acknowledged church organizer, he soon introduced the progressive ideas of the day, which proved to be more than these churchgoers could tolerate. In a provocative interview published in the *Tribune,* he enunciated his views. That his views flew in the face of black religious convention is an understatement. Wilkins stated:

> I believe in the fatherly kindness of God. The old idea of a God of vengeance, ready to burn up the world in hell-fire, is opposed to reason and common sense and abhorrent to me. I no longer endorse the doctrine of the trinity, nor can I swallow the three persons in one and all omnipotent. My belief is that the Bible has a divine and human line of thought running through it; that there is much good in the Bible and a great deal that is the entire opposite. I preached a sermon which caused a great fuss in the congregation in which I showed that slavery, polygamy, Communism, murder, intemperance, and Socialism were not only taught by precept in the Bible, but also by example. I am also a free believer in open communion: that a Methodist, Presbyterian, Catholic, or a member of any denomination is entitled to the sacrament at my hands as well as the Baptist. I have acted on this belief, and this has been a constant cause of dissatisfaction to a minority of my flock.
>
> I came to Chicago with the idea of founding a large liberal church. I find it will be best to sunder my connection entirely with the Baptists before I can carry out my ideal. My congregation now numbers 185, most of which will follow me. A small portion of them are the old-style Baptists and chronic kickers. They have found fault right along and wanted to restrict me to sermons on orthodox subjects. I preached a sermon on Socialism some three weeks ago which caused a great stir in my church. I have received scores of letters applauding that sermon and I have received an offer from a New York lecture bureau of $100 per night to deliver a series of lectures, which I refused.
>
> REPORTER'S QUESTION: What is your present belief?
>
> I am a liberal Christian, with a leaning towards Unitarianism.
>
> REPORTER'S QUESTION: What is your program for the future?
>
> I cannot leave the Bethesda Church before the first of the year unless they consent. I am going to stay in Chicago and build a large church, to be known as Liberty Temple. I have already collected subscriptions amounting to $3,000, and any necessary amount can be obtained from my sympathizers. Here the liberal-minded colored people of all denominations will be gathered, and I intend to show Chicago and the world a new sight—an advancing and progressing colored congregation.[268]

Rev. Bird Wilkins's provocatively announced transfiguration challenged the essence of African American theology in the late nineteenth century. The need of these Chicagoans for an immanent God who, through his Son, Jesus Christ, could protect them individually, daily, and unswervingly, precluded the acceptance of the God of the Unitarians. The masses at Bethesda Baptist Church viewed Jesus as an all-empowering force in the face of constant adversity. When trouble arose, Jesus was nearby, as part of the Trinity. Moreover, a people who had lived through two great conflagrations in four years—the Great Fire of 1871 and the destruction of their Loop community in 1874—could not doubt the wrath of an Old Testament God who punished the wicked. Their unswerving loyalty to their traditional readings of the Scriptures neutralized any attempt to modernize their interpretation. Their isolationist religious views that protected them from a hostile white world could not allow the ecumenicalism Wilkins espoused, including openness in communal worship to groups whom they considered nonbelievers.

Wilkins's plans to build a Liberty Temple materialized as he organized and presided over the first black Unitarian church in Chicago. It became known as the Fifth Unitarian during its brief life of perhaps a year.[269] The choice of a meeting place presented a major problem. At first, Freiberg's Opera House, at Twenty-second Street and Wabash Avenue, provided a home. No doubt financial pressures to rent or purchase property hampered the church's growth. For that handful of black Christians who embraced Unitarianism outside the circle of Wilkins's supporters, Rev. Jenkin Lloyd Jones had already opened the doors of the formerly all-white All Souls Church. Only a few, however, such as Edward H. Morris and the Williamses—S. Laing and Fannie—joined All Souls. Meanwhile, Wilkins was succeeded at Bethesda sometime thereafter by Rev. J. E. Pond, who led the church back to the track of Christian Trinitarian orthodoxy and church stability.[270]

Meanwhile, the African Methodists continued to share their religious leaders from a rotating, national pool of educated clergy. Quinn Chapel A.M.E. had the distinction of being built from the ground up on a site it purchased at Wabash Avenue and Twenty-fourth Street. Designed by black architect Henry F. Starbuck and using only the resources of the congregation, the land was acquired at a cost of $29,000, and $60,000 was spent on the structure. Construction began in 1891 for the congregation of reportedly one thousand. Proving the wisdom and vision of its builders, it still stands majestically today (Figure 41). Quinn Chapel's pastors during this period were Rev. J. H. Shaefer in 1884 and the highly respected Rev. John T. Jenifer, who ministered to this African Methodist congregation after Shaefer's tenure ended in 1893. Building on this leadership, the church claimed, along with Olivet Baptist, to be the largest colored denomination

Fig. 41. Quinn Chapel A.M.E. Church.
Courtesy of Quinn Chapel A.M.E.

in the city.[271] In June 1887, the church's choir was described as having the ability to stir the hearts of all listeners whose hearts were capable of being touched by sensation. "There were some good voices in the choir," Chicagoan Marsha Freeman Edmond wrote to her friend Julia Boyd of New York, "and we enjoyed hearing the songs whose origins are shrouded in mystery, but which were born of a sublime faith that could see through the black night of oppression, the dawn of a glorious day."[272]

On the city's West Side, St. Stephen was the major denominational institution serving African Americans who embraced African Methodism. A variety of ministers were regularly appointed and then reassigned, as part of A.M.E. tradition. In 1881, Rev. C. S. Jacobs presided over the congregation when it relocated to a new church home at 682 Austin Avenue, near Damen Avenue. In order to increase the level of Christian training among the congregation, the first Sunday School was established by Miss Tillie Hubbard. Following a break after the regular morning service, during which families

Fig. 42. Bethel A.M.E. Church.
From Appeal

ate dinners prepared at home, they reassembled for more Christian education under the auspices of the new format. Jacobs was succeeded by Rev.
Ollie Knight in 1885, who served for three years. More change loomed, this
time in the secular world. Under Rev. L. H. Reynolds (1888–1891), the
church played a pivotal role in establishing the first black-led medical training facility in Chicago in 1891, Provident Hospital.[273] There, the famed
Dr. Daniel Hale Williams led an interracial staff of physicians and nurses
who attended to an integrated clientele. By 1892, Rev. S. R. Hardison took
the helm.

Over on the South Side, Bethel A.M.E. was led by Rev. J. W. Law during
the 1880s, who then was succeeded by Rev. George W. Gaines. Under Gaines,
Bethel A.M.E. moved deeper into the heart of the Black Belt, building
another magnificent structure designed by a black architect, a Mr. J. Turnock,
on the northeastern corner of Twenty-ninth and Dearborn (Figure 42). The
cornerstone was laid on August 17, 1890, amid pageantry provided by the fra-

ternal community. The Most Masterful Grand Master of Masons of Illinois performed the task and was accompanied by Corinthian Commandery, Knights Templar No. 1, St. George No. 4, and Godfrey No. 5. This celebration was described as "the most imposing Masonic demonstration ever made by the masonic order in the Northwest."[274]

The new Bethel Church was situated in a better residential neighborhood, among a host of respectables and the refined, and was surrounded by high-status whites to the south and east. The new building was described in the *Chicago Tribune* as being "a handsome church edifice."[275] Its seating capacity must also have been larger than most other black churches, given the fact that several were in the process of moving into larger quarters or would in the near future. A thirty-two-year-old pastor, Rev. D. A. Graham, who had been an ardent prohibitionist in Michigan, assumed the mantle of leadership in the spring of 1892. This youthful minister provided a dynamic leadership that witnessed an expanding church membership and retirement of the church's debt by 1893.

Despite the long-standing dominance of the African Methodists and Baptists over black religious life, other African Americans sought religious succor elsewhere, in smaller churches, some representing other denominations. It was in 1888 that Hermon Baptist was organized as a mission church on the North Side.[276] Then, nineteen sturdy Christian souls from Kentucky, Tennessee, Ohio, and Canada realized their dream after a year's existence in mission status as the Presbyterian Club by formally organizing Grace Presbyterian on July 19, 1888. They found leadership in a Lincoln University (Pennsylvania) graduate, the Virginia-born Reverend Moses H. Jackson. Housed in the inauspicious edifice of a storefront for years, the congregation triumphantly moved to Thirty-sixth Street and Vincennes Avenue in 1917.[277]

Episcopalians had organized earlier under the pastoral leadership of Dr. James E. Thompson, a graduate of St. Paul's College (New York), who presided over St. Thomas Episcopal Church (Figure 43). Although they began their church with only ten members and as a "house church" like Bethesda Baptist, by 1882 they were able to lay a cornerstone on the structure that would become their first church at Dearborn, near Thirtieth Street. Finally, the number of black Catholics reached sufficient strength in the decade of the 1890s to justify organizing St. Monica Catholic Church, located at 2251 Indiana Avenue. The nation's first Catholic priest of African ancestry, Father Augustin Tolton, who had studied at St. Francis College in Illinois and in Rome, came to the city in 1890 to head the congregation (Figure 44). Initially overshadowed by the older churches within the African Methodist and Baptist traditions, the future for all of these institutions continued to look promising as they materialized over time.[278]

Fig. 43. Father J. E. Thompson.
*Vivian G. Harsh Research Collection
of Afro-American History and
Literature, Chicago Public Library.*

Fig. 44. Father Augustin Tolton of
St. Monica's Catholic Church.
*Tolton Collection, University Archives,
Special Collections, Brenner Library,
Quincy University.*

At the core of these evolving church histories were differences in style and content of worship that were becoming more noticeable during this period. These variations, however, had more to do with usefulness and meaning in daily life while coping with northern, urban situations than with any factors based in class orientation. Certain segments of the respectables joined with the elite in distancing themselves from emotionalistic religious practices, with the African Methodists, Episcopalians, Presbyterians, and Catholics choosing this path. In doing so, they separated themselves from other respectables, who adhered to religious practices steeped in heavily southern-based, black core culture. While emotional release helped some Christian congregants negotiate through the day and transcend life's vicissitudes, others found that a reasoned, disciplined approach to everyday difficulties placed hardships in a perspective for them that was more remediable.

Meanwhile, in addition to sermons and songs, rituals such as marriages and funerals continued to act as major channels of religious expression. Black newspapers regularly featured these activities and thereby illustrated the importance of these ceremonies. Church-sponsored basket suppers were a way of promoting courtship among church members; if all went well, a success-ful basket supper led to engagement and then to marriage: "Each lady pre-pare[d] enough supper for two in a basket; each basket [was] sold at auction, the gentlemen being the bidders and the lady who prepared the supper help[ed] the purchaser eat it."[279]

Weddings themselves became more elaborate, as material prosperity increased among the respectables and the elite. In this vein, Mrs. Lettie Trent of 3731 Stanton Avenue hosted a bridal tea on December 3, 1886. It was described as "the most fashionable of the season and highly enjoyed by all present. The host and hostess spared no pains to make the occasion a pleasant one." Prominent persons who attended the event were always listed to insure the reader that the event was of great significance. Present during this marriage ceremony were Dr. D. H. Williams, Mr. E. H. Morris, Rev. J. E. Thompson, Mr. F. Waring, Miss Emma Douglas, and others. When the daughter of Mr. and Mrs. R. L. Plummer wed, over three hundred guests attended a reception held at 2454 South State in what were described as the family's "spacious parlors" (a phrase that became a common description by reporters of the period).

Funerals assumed sacramental importance. Rev. A. T. Hall returned to Chicago from the Fox River Valley and officiated at the funeral of Mrs. Florence E. Dorsey, an Erie, Pennsylvania, native whom Hall had united with Allen Dorsey earlier in her life. Describing the deceased, "She con-fessed the Christian religion in youth, and became a member of Bethel A.M.E. Church [when she arrived in the city in 1864], remaining a consis-tent member to the day of her death, dying in full triumph of living faith." Hall preached the funeral obsequies at Quinn Chapel, "taking for a text John 11th cha[p.,] 26th verse . . . [delivering a] discourse [that] was able, learned and eloquent, in which the speaker portrayed the beauties of the Christian hope, setting forth many of her Christian virtues. The remains then were taken in charge by Ester Court . . . and buried at Graceland."[280] The accessibility of grave sites in predominantly white cemeteries, such as Graceland on the far North Side, indicated that race relations had retained a level of fluidity consistent with Chicago's most humane folkways during this period.[281]

B. Reporting the News

The *Conservator* continued its publications with Olivet Baptist Church's pastor, Rev. Richard De Baptiste, acting as coeditor with Rev. G. C. Booth, until the former left the city in February 1882. At this point, Ferdinand L. Barnett's name appeared as the sole editor.[282] (The city's other African American newspaper, the *Observer*, had its rise and subsequent demise also sometime during this period.) By the time that De Baptiste left Chicago, he was credited with extending the *Conservator*'s readership "into the homes of the masses and satisfying the thirsty intellects of the intelligent Afro-Americans." Yet the paper's management changed constantly, and it appeared to be a less than lucrative enterprise. In 1887, Alexander Clark, who was listed as the proprietor, sold his interests in the newspaper to a "company of gentlemen," who promised to provide the public with a "newsy sheet."[283] Through the next decade it was challenged and eventually was surpassed in news coverage of the Chicago scene. Competition came from approximately 450 rail miles away. The appearance of the *Western Appeal*, operating from St. Paul, Minnesota, and distributed on Chicago newsstands and in restaurants in 1885, severely limited the extent to which the *Conservator* could expect any increase in revenues. Within four years, the *Western Appeal* proclaimed that it had captured the bulk of the Chicago market with a circulation that reached 2,100 copies per week.[284] Moreover, for a period it had surpassed the *Conservator* in comprehensive reporting, being inclusive of all groups, of myriad religious activities, and in various classes of social commentary. A deterioration in quality, however, unfortunately accompanied an increase of readership, with sensationalism, gossip, and crime reporting dominating the news. After reaching its circulation peak, news on Chicago became sporadic and incomplete, with the crime blotter occupying space previously devoted to the activities of the elite at their social affairs and the respectables within the churches.

It is important to note that the actual progress of these newspapers in general had not reached the level of journalistic accomplishment that the pioneer journalist and writer Frederick Douglass had desired. He foresaw the black press moving beyond its calls for race solidarity and recognition to explore issues that related to upgrading black status in such areas as justice, liberty, and citizenship, the latter in regard to self-reliance.[285] But at this time, the development of a higher level of racial consciousness and a sense of civic responsibility would have to compete with more mundane considerations such as personal elevation in social status and nonessential news. In Chicago, the *Conservator*, and the other papers widely circulated in the downtown area and the emerging Dearborn Corridor—the *Western Appeal*,

Salt Lake City's *Broad Ax*, and the *Indianapolis Freeman*—left much to be desired. They relied on national news of general interest of the boilerplate variety. Items involving Great Britain's Queen Victoria and other non-blacks filled at least one page of every issue of the smaller newspapers.

Hale G. Parker would later see fit to comment that while the white *Chicago Inter Ocean*, which contained Albion W. Tourgee's "Bystander's Notes" column, was more than satisfactory, nothing in the same vein held true for the black press. He proposed to Tourgee the idea of converting a new publication, the *Basis*, into a sheet that contained a full page devoted to the interests of the city's African American population.[286] While nothing substantial developed from the idea, Parker felt that "the acorn must precede the oak." In addition, from time to time, the *Chicago Daily News* sought out Robert Mitchell to inform the greater community on the dynamics and occurrences of the black community.[287]

C. Bonding along Martial Lines

Veterans of Illinois's Twenty-ninth Infantry Regiment and of other units during the Civil War era retained loyalty to one another a generation after the end of the conflict. Camaraderie of this sort, which was almost familial, confirmed the intensity and intimacy of emotions among soldiers who had bonded as members of the same regiment or smaller units. Captain Luis F. Emilio of the Fifty-fourth Massachusetts depicted this feature of military life as normal and exemplary as he wrote of the Civil War two decades later: "It has been written that 'the regiment is the family.' To the soldier his true commander is a father; his superiors, elder brothers to be deferred to and obeyed; the recruits, his younger kinsmen whom he cares for and supports by example. He cherishes and proudly recounts the traditions of glorious deeds and dangerous enterprises."[288]

They often kept in touch because of a similarity in work experiences. In addition, with the close physical proximity of their housing, which also facilitated the unity of their circle, the men were frequently called upon by federal pension officials to corroborate details of injury and disease while previously on active duty. Exemplifying this process was William Collins of Company B, who seemed the gregarious type, knowing and being known by a considerable number of his fellow soldiers. He was acquainted with Louis Clary in Chicago immediately before enlistment, served with Clary during the war, and lived several doors away on the same street for a period before his early death in civilian life.[289] Sergeant James H. Brown of Company C, who lived on the lakefront several blocks east of the Dearborn Street

Corridor, also attracted the interest of his men after the war and held their loyalty as he operated an employment bureau and provided sometimes questionable, corroborating information for their pension claims.

Other army veterans, who had shared the ordeal of armed struggle followed by the exhilaration of victory, lived their lives in a climate ranging from celebrity to anonymity until they organized and chartered John Brown Post No. 50 in September 1880. This post was formed as part of the massive Union veterans' organization, the Grand Army of the Republic, which was established in the aftermath of Union triumph. Part charitable organization, part political lobby, the GAR helped define the character of the nation in the postwar period. Continuous attention to the veterans' financial needs was met through successful pension legislation passed by the U.S. Congress. In what was proclaimed to be the largest black post in the nation, Chicago's racially separate unit conformed to the national pattern set in motion with the GAR founding. The Brown post deviated from the national practice of staggering induction, and thereby continually increased its membership by practicing immediate investiture of new members. In building its membership, the post attracted black veterans from diverse units of the USCT, including some members of the Twenty-ninth Illinois.[290]

Belonging to the post and participating in veterans' activities developed into an expressive acknowledgment of the value of their very existence. For these "old soldiers," death, or illness, always loomed on the horizon. A large number of veterans seem to have died during this period as they grew older or succumbed to the illnesses and infirmities of aging. So for decades after the combat experience, out of necessity and personal concern, the soldiers kept in contact through monthly activities and the post's provision of charitable services for comrades in need.[291] Importantly, martial bonding carried a collective value in that women and children were not ignored but formed part of a national auxiliary, the Women's Relief Corps, No. 14.[292] Veterans enjoyed themselves in various ways, with the post planning a "camp fire" for Friday, December 31, 1886, at Battery D. The public was invited with the hearty invitation of "Do not fail to be there" for the price of one dollar. One newspaper announcement read: "Young men, old men, ladies, and all are invited to come and enjoy themselves with those old soldiers and their families and friends. We will give the only entertainment that takes in the entire American people. Prof. Henderson with his orchestra of 25 musicians will be on hand[,] so you may look for other music than the 'Mikado.'"[293]

Participation in local picnics served as a buildup to the Grand Encampments (a version of a national convention) of Civil War veterans in 1889 and other years. At these regional and national events, the value of these black soldiers' service to the causes of Union and to Emancipation would be collectively revisited through shared camp victuals, speeches, old war songs, stories, and other gestures extolling martial honor. The social clustering by mature veterans of the Civil War quite possibly provided the model that spurred additional associational activities along military lines.

A newer generation now picked up the baton of military ardor. The importance of black Chicago and other Illinoisans establishing a military presence cannot be underestimated at a time when Social Darwinism heralded the age of bellicosity as an integral element in the global march of Western civilization. The quasi-military Hannibal Guard still existed as a militia unit but was headed by a new division commander, B. G. Johnson, a native of Boston, who had come to Chicago in 1880.[294] By May 1890, interested men held a series of meetings in the northern end of the Black Belt at Central Hall, at Twenty-second Street and Wabash Avenue. The idea emerged for laying the foundation of a larger unit of battalion strength by organizing multiple companies. The Ninth Battalion was thus born. Once accepted, two companies of one hundred men each grew to several companies and eventually six in Chicago alone. One of its most important purposes was to "reflect [favorably] upon the Colored people of Illinois as well as Chicago."[295] The process was replicated downstate within several counties in Illinois's southern tier. With this step, these men demonstrated an acute awareness that military deportment was always well received by the entire public as a measure of group maturity and stability.

B. G. Johnson served as captain of the Ninth, and the up-and-coming John R. Marshall held the rank of second lieutenant while heading Company A. The link between the new military leadership and the Civil War and postwar soldiery continued through three men who became officers and therefore shared invaluable soldiering experience. Among their ranks were James H. Johnson, later a lieutenant colonel, who had spent five years in the Ninth Cavalry Regiment (the famed "Buffalo Soldiers") on the western plains. John McDonald, known as the "Old Soldier," and who was later a second lieutenant, had seen ten years of service in the Twenty-fourth Infantry, which also had served the nation in the western states and territories. One other member of the Ninth Battalion claimed to have lived the Civil War battlefield experience. From the city's so-called elite, only the names of physicians appeared with Drs. Daniel Hale Williams and A. M. Curtis serving as medical affiliates. Meanwhile, in downstate Illinois, likeminded African Americans organized simultaneously while maintaining contact with their racial kinsmen in Chicago.

• • •

D. Provident Hospital

African Americans solved the problem of discriminatory health care and nurses' training when they organized Provident Hospital in 1891, although the project also required substantial financial support from liberal whites. Despite its need as a training and health care facility, the concept of organizing an all-black medical facility institution was anathema to certain segments within the African American community. The controversy that ensued was not an ideological conflict between institutional separatists and abolitionist-integrationists, but rather a monumental dispute among assimilationists within the refined and respectable classes over the tactical value of supporting a separate institution. Overall, the acceptance or rejection of ideas and plans for separate development depended on the point of racial origination. If white liberals, or conservatives, or racists, or for that matter, Caucasians of whatever persuasion made a suggestion affecting black life, such as the proposition in 1889 to build an all-black branch of the YMCA, near-hysterical controversy ensued.[296] Had the idea emanated from the ranks of African Americans and was clearly designed to work for the benefit of the black community, such as the plan to open an all-black kindergarten in 1898, vigorous discussion, but not rancor and aggressive opposition, would have occurred. As a sign of the times, a coterie of educated community activists emerged, including attorney John G. Jones and teacher Lettie Trent, who also added to heated discourse on matters of this type.

While Jones indignantly opposed the opening of the hospital facility, he proved to be just one of many voices condemning the venture as a surrender to segregation and second-class status. At one meeting, he exclaimed "I'd let Colored people die in the streets and be eaten by flies before I'd put them in a separate hospital."[297] Ignoring these controversies that had arisen along racial lines, Dr. Daniel Hale Williams and Rev. Louis H. Reynolds of the West Side's St. Stephen A.M.E. Church relentlessly pursued the endeavor, which was aimed at improving health care and opportunities in medical training. Just as an ethnically and religiously conscious Jewish community founded Michael Reese Hospital in 1881 as a medical center, nursing training school, and charitable institution to meet its communal needs, so African Americans acted similarly. The need for a general hospital was great because, overall, "prior to the 1900s, medical care was delivered in the home by physician visits and public health or private duty nurses. . . . Nurses provided vital services through visiting nurse associations and hospital nursing corps" and "with most gratifying results."[298] Most importantly, many of the patients that Provident would serve would be able to avail themselves of quality medical care for the first time when they needed it. According to

Kletzing and Crogman, with the exception of the Freedmen's Hospital in Washington, D.C., Provident Hospital was "the only institution [nationally] engaged in special work in behalf of the Colored people. It [was] unique in its character, and those for whom its benefits [were] more specially intended [were] grateful for and appreciative of its advantages."[299] As the African Methodists increased their support, primarily from the powerful Board of Bishops of the A.M.E. Church, the project proceeded forward.[300]

Provident's founding began in 1889, when aspiring nurse Emma Reynolds faced discrimination at the Cook County Nursing School because of her race. She appealed to her brother, Rev. Louis H. Reynolds, for assistance, and Reynolds organized an effort to resolve the problem. He met with black West Siders and South Siders, along with the city's leading African American physician, Dr. Daniel Hale Williams, to develop an ameliorative course of action. With Dr. Williams now at the head of the effort, and with the support of influential African Americans and even more influential whites, the drive to establish Provident Hospital moved forward.

The major problem facing African Americans at this juncture was fundraising. Some community support already existed because a hospital would improve health care among a segment of the city's population desperately in need of such a facility. Ambitious health-care advocates who wanted to enter the field of nursing to serve humanity obviously backed it. From the West Side, Robert M. Hancock, who had risen to the rank of foreman at the industrial giant Allis Chalmers, assisted Reynolds in fund-raising. On the South Side, Lloyd G. Wheeler, Fannie Barrier Williams, Edward H. Wright, and others helped Dr. Daniel Hale Williams corral donors. The city's white elite proved why it deserved its claim to civic leadership in the level of its philanthropy. It contributed in enormous sums; for example, the meatpacker Philip Armour, who seasonally lived one and a half miles to the northeast on Prairie Avenue's Millionaire's Row, donated heavily because Rev. Jenkin Lloyd Jones of All Souls Unitarian Church convinced him of the worthiness of the cause.[301] George M. Pullman's daughter, restaurateur H. H. Kohlsaat, and Dr. F. C. Greene contributed two hundred dollars apiece; and, under the influence of Rabbi Emil Hirsch, the Young Men's Hebrew Association gave a hundred dollars. According to Buckler, "the rest was collected bit by bit. . . . The Sunday School of the Third Presbyterian Church [which serviced the wealthy Prairie Avenue mansions] gave $41.41; Bethel Church took up a special collection of $7 and there was a Christmas collection of $11.25. In such small amounts and even smaller was the total of $2,114.03 finally achieved."[302] As for the African American elite, it contributed in sums commensurate with its wealth, which proved to be somewhat insubstantial. Finally, in 1891, the three-story brick building destined to be Provident

Hospital and Nurses Training School opened its door; it would provide its services for another century.

E. Literary Societies and an Interest in Ideas and Letters

Several literary societies met the intellectual needs of a select segment of African Americans. The most prominent was the Prudence Crandall Club, named after a white abolitionist schoolteacher who suffered for her belief in the innate ability of the African to learn, and at a pace of intellectual inquiry equal to whites. Culturally, the twenty-five member Prudence Crandall Study Club typified the kind of organization that nurtured the elite when it committed itself to intellectual enlightenment and perfecting social decorum. Designated areas of discussions centered around the sciences, literature, philosophy, music, and art. The group was organized in 1887 under the urging of Fannie and S. Laing Williams, and with the support of Mrs. Mary Richardson Jones; historian Willard Gatewood has described it as the first in a succession of high-status social organizations, and one that was inclusive of most of the first families of black Chicago.[303] If any group proved amenable to an appreciation of the theoretical possibility of true racial equality as manifested in unfettered opportunity and freedom of personal association, it was the intellectually inclined, and they would be drawn early in the twentieth century to the magnetism of an organized crusade for equality led by the NAACP.[304] Families with refined tastes also belonged to the Fellowship Club, the Autumn Club, and the Lotus Social Club on the South Side, and the Garden City Literary Club on the West Side. These clubs and literary groups usually formed under the auspices of the older African Methodist churches such as Quinn Chapel and Bethel. White as well as black lecturers spoke regularly to Sunday crowds after church services on topics as diverse as the human intellect could conceive and understand. Once women's clubs started, they also sponsored weekday lectures on various topics. The white progressive friend and philanthropist Herman Kohlsaat assisted in this effort to free the mind from inanity and the mundane by helping to found and finance the Colored Men's Library Association in 1887.

Further, on an individual basis, several African Americans planned, but evidently never finished, books on topics such as Reconstruction politics and education, voting rights in antebellum America, and a history of African Americans. What was especially notable about the last topic was the identity of its author—politician James Ellis Bish—who was destined to be the fourth African American to be elected to the Illinois General Assembly. He wrote *Past, Present, and the Future of the Negro*.[305]

VI. POLITICS AND INTERRACIAL LINKAGE

African American participation in the political process increased in Chicago during the 1880s, in direct contrast to the South, where racial interaction began its slide into various modes of segregation and exclusion, political and otherwise. Voting privileges allowed the mass of the male population to participate in politics, and they continued to use this right to their advantage. Through this phase of political involvement, and before massive political machines beckoned to adventurous African Americans, office holding represented *the* great symbol for a people denied recognition in so many areas of American life. The *Conservator* recommended that blacks seek to increase office holding in "high and distinguished offices in which the power of appointment and control would bring rewards and [status] to many Negroes commensurate to the offices held by white politicians."[306] However, office holding was only a secondary gauge of political effectiveness exhibited by a growing, politically savvy black electorate. Patronage employment, or job holding, ranked as being just as important, since making a living through gainful employment provided the workingman and his family their daily sustenance. Pride in office holding raised the emotions, but employment kept households intact as breadwinners received steady paychecks.

The partisan political preference of three thousand black male voters conformed to the city's pattern, which exhibited different tendencies in national and local elections. The African Americans' national allegiance was Republican; however, in local elections, African Americans often voted Democratic, breaking the hold that Frederick Douglass and other black Republicans had over the northern electorate.[307] Civil War veterans with membership in the GAR could be counted on to vote their consciences as well as for their economic interests, since the issue of pensions dominated political discussion and Congressional legislation. An easing of the requirements for pension applicants after 1890 proved an especially alluring reason to support the Republican party.[308]

Patronage employment and office holding as two beneficial elements of political participation jointly had another use in that they provided grist for contentious political campaigning. On the eve of the presidential election of 1884, one Republican broadside warned of exchanging political support for limited Democratic appointed positions. The popularity and political magnetism of Democratic Mayor Carter H. Harrison (1879–1887; 1893), former Kentuckian and erstwhile slave owner, was attacked for disloyalty during the Civil War period. "Colored men! Men of reason, I know you are!" the publication exhorted. "Can we be bought by a few well timed positions before the election? Which is better, sweet Liberty to six millions of colored people, or a few positions of honor, profit and trust, to catch the votes of the masses? Colored men are not for sale now! It is the same dodge of the slave traders and importers who for a little red flannel, a few brass trinkets, bought hundreds of slaves from the Kings of Africa, brought them to this country and sold them into bondage for money!" Yet the old Kentuckian relied comfortably on his record of alleged fairness and liberality toward blacks.[309] One white newspaperman reflectively described the mayor in these terms: "He ordinarily desired nothing better than to rule Chicago, somewhat as if it were a Kentucky plantation and he its 'old marster.'"[310] To his credit, Harrison brought financial solvency to the city, so that the municipal payroll was met on time. In addition, the problem of epidemics was broached, especially that of typhoid, which claimed a high percentage of the 19.26-per-1,000 deaths in 1883.

When Democrat R. C. Sullivan, clerk of the probate court, appointed the highly skilled African American William G. Anderson as his stenographer and typewriter, African Americans learned that voting a split ticket in local elections could bring a hefty dividend. This was counterbalanced by one of the more visible Republican political appointments of the decade, that of Joseph W. Moore, who held the distinction of being the first South Town clerk. South Town extended from Thirty-ninth Street on the north, to the Chicago River on the west, to the lake at the east, and to undeveloped areas to the south. B. G. Johnson, the commander of the Hannibal Guard, found employment as a messenger at the U.S. Custom House when he arrived in Chicago in 1880. Within eight years he had risen to the rank of inspector, a position he was to hold for over four decades.[311]

Interestingly enough, other politically connected municipal workers were listed in the contemporary history of the Eighth Regiment, an indicator of how important the political-fraternal-military bond had become. They also held memberships in various fraternal and military orders, as did John Buckler, who served as an assistant of sorts to the collector of the Port of Chicago and who later became a customs inspector. In addition, Robert Jackson had entered the postal service in 1888 as a mail stamper and would rise to become a foreman. Franklin A. Denison won appointment as an assistant prosecuting attorney for the City of Chicago in 1891 under Mayor Washburne. William B. Akins worked for seventeen months as a discount clerk at the Department of Water and later performed as an inspector at the World's Columbian Exposition. He held the distinction in political circles as being "the recognized political leader among the North Side Colored voters."[312]

Patronage under single-term mayors John A. Roche (Republican, 1887–1889) and DeWitt C. Cregier (Democrat, 1889–1891) featured limited patronage. The extent of the employment advances made under Republican Mayor Hempstead Washburne (1891–1893) are unknown, except for his appointment of the attorney Franklin Denison and a library clerk. Even with limitations, a medical professional could benefit from having forged a political link. Before he gained renown as a physician, the Republican Daniel Hale Williams held membership in the Hamilton Club, which opened the door for him to obtain a political plum in 1889 with his appointment to the Illinois State Board of Health.[313] Winning working-class and pinstripe patronage and favors noticeably represented another measure of political effectiveness.

Exclusion from local office-holding in major positions did not prevent African Americans from continuing to seek state-level berths, especially the position of state representative. The first African American member of the General Assembly, John W. E. Thomas, served his second set of consecutive terms beginning in 1883 and ending in 1905. Joining him in Springfield were former Kentuckians George F. Ecton, who served one term (1887–1889), and Edward H. Morris, who served two sets of nonconsecutive two-year terms (1891–1893 and 1903–1905). Ecton, who had moved to Chicago in 1873 and worked as a maître d'hôtel, is reported to have promoted the cause of civil rights, especially protection from abduction from Illinois to the Southern states for prosecution. Morris enjoyed a solid reputation, and his popularity led a *Chicago Defender* reporter to write both biblically and posthumously that "his entrance into [the General Assembly] was the morning star of our efforts in intelligent political action and achievements." Supposedly, and most likely during his latter term, Morris was viewed as "one of the ablest of the House, so much so that he soon became a political power, and his aid was sought after by those who had bills of importance to be passed."[314] Another individual gaining state office was Ninth Battalion officer James Ellis Bish, who was "one of the most prominent and influential Colored men in Chicago and prime mover in all municipal elections."[315] Although in terms of overall significance office-holding proved mainly symbolic, it did demonstrate to African Americans that the door to political participation was open. Importantly, the fact of their presence in Springfield had its greatest effect on the lives of African Americans in Illinois.

Black detractors sometimes saw these office holders as persons who could not achieve in the competitive sphere of entrepreneurship and business, where the true mettle of worth was being measured. The *Illinois Record* of Springfield noted, "For whatever may be said of the old ones[,] they were men not creatures without a visible means of support, except the salary they drew from holding public office." These politicians, or political operatives, were not men of great accomplishment, nor were they men around whom legends spring (with the exception of Edward H. Morris), but they did represent the prototype of men on the move, whose greatest success and acceptance would come in the next century.[316]

Last, the political sphere also presented interracial contact at a level where cooperation reached its zenith. Only in the philanthropic sphere were similar relationships evolving, and those found African Americans acting as recipients of white benevolence.

The death in 1879 of John Jones, the original antebellum and Reconstruction-era "Everyman," coincided with the advent of a new era of more dynamic economic, institutional, civic, and political growth. While Jones had embodied a particular type of civic and political leadership consistent with his times, younger professionals in medicine, law, and journalism, both Chicago-bred and migrant, emerged to replace him. Notable were Edward H. Morris, Ferdinand L. Barnett, Fannie Barrier Williams, Charles E. Bentley, and Hale G. Parker. Representing the new generation of post-abolitionist role models, they dreamed of and imagined themselves as bona fide citizens of a modernizing nation, one that had proven on battlefields that backwardness in racial policies deserved elimination.

Relations with whites could continue on an amicable basis, and as historian James M. McPherson has described, there were still white friends to aid in the cause of African American advancement.[317] But the racial progress in its new form revolved around the enjoyment of rights and the opening of opportunities at a level never imagined previously by most whites and blacks. Simultaneously, a rising racial and group consciousness evidenced a greater level of human agency than any previous generation of African Americans had envisioned, let alone experienced. In this new arrangement, blacks shed dependency for results brought about through their own efforts for the most part. Within the African American community, a social gap remained and broadened. Literally, elite African Americans were separated from working-class blacks through both social and physical distance, making it quite understandable that in the absence of regular contact, neither group knew a great deal about the other, and neither group influenced the other. As to civic leadership, rank-and-file citizens adhered to laws and rules passed at the bequest of the city's white elite, not the black one. In the social sphere, multiple agendas produced disparate groups. More and more political activities occurred within the purview of the two major parties, which had their own avaricious, self-absorbed leaderships. Most importantly, the varied lifestyles and interests of African Americans demonstrated that they had arrived in every aspect as bona fide Chicagoans. As Drake and Cayton pointed out, it was during this era that African Americans molded themselves, becoming their own heroes; though they suffered under poverty, they also reveled in the Gilded Age's prosperity and competed as Chicagoans, much to their own satisfaction.

Chapter 5

Fair and War, 1893–1900

No one who has not seen it, can form any idea of the immensity and grandeur of the exposition; nor can I give any adequate description of it. It has been very fitly called "The White City" and one standing under the Peristyle and looking down the Court of Honor . . . might easily imagine himself in a fairy city.

— JAMES WELDON JOHNSON, 1893

If we fail [in military operations in Cuba] the whole race will have to shoulder the burden.

— COLONEL JOHN R. MARSHALL,
Eighth Illinois National Guard, U.S. Volunteers, 1898

The relationship of the Negro community to this event [the world's fair] throws some light on Negro-white relations and the strength of Negro institutions during the nineties.

— ST. CLAIR DRAKE, 1940

A MAJOR RECONFIGURATION of the African American community was readily observable between the opening of the World's Columbian Exposition of 1893 and the immediate aftermath of the Spanish-American War, a period during which Chicago laid claim to being the nation's "Second City." This transformation kept pace as best it could with the city's growth and development, and a discernible class structure was becoming recognizable, but now class structure rested on the accumulation of wealth rather than cultural attainment and status. At the same time, black Chicago's institutional base expanded, with far more diversification and covering more varied interests than ever before. Interracial relations mainly still rested on amiability, demonstrating that fluidity existed in a city committed to individualized competition and civil order throughout the greater community.

While the world's fair of 1893 represented Chicago's affirmation of its Phoenix-like ability to rise from physical disaster to world-class municipal status, based on its technological progress in architecture, transportation, merchandising, and major areas of industrial production, African Americans claimed and won a meaningful role as workers, patrons, lecturers, performers, artists, and visitors despite a widespread historical misperception suggesting their exclusion.[1] Persons from throughout the African world who arrived in Chicago as visitors included Nubians, New Yorkers, Zulu from South Africa, and energetic and curious "New Negroes" from elsewhere in the Midwest, the eastern seaboard, and the American South. As white America looked forward, Frederick Douglass's black America could never forget slavery, so it also looked backward to a period of national shame, hoping that white America would respond with contrition. To many blacks, the fair held the symbolic promise of being an important ritual of possible white racial redemption and black acceptance into the nation's body politic and social fabric.

Five years later, war afforded Chicago and the nation an opportunity to demonstrate their readiness for global involvement in trade, diplomacy, and empire. Conflict with an effete Spanish Empire moreover afforded African American males their first opportunity since the Civil War to demonstrate their manhood on the field of battle. While not all African Americans agreed with the nation's latest imperial foray, this conflict allowed blacks the chance to reestablish the black martial tradition and confirm a powerful claim to citizenship rights. Once again, African Americans demanded the right to get involved as full-fledged citizens, this time as frontline combatants at the beginning of the conflict.

The foundation was laid for another century's realization of a dream of inclusion as the fair triggered an increase in migration of the talented and confident. Community corridors of opportunity and success emerged, from the South Side along State and Dearborn streets to the West Side along Lake Street and into pockets of settlement in between. Within these enclaves, cultural and ideological transformation accompanied social reconfiguration and marked the character of this generation of "New Negroes"—able, optimistic, unrelenting, and successful.

I. DEMOGRAPHY: THE ARRIVAL OF THE MASSES
AND THE TALENTED TENTH

The migration to Chicago of the masses and of a refined element that would become known as the Talented Tenth continued, spurred in part by economic opportunity and by the stories of the fabled "White City," the world's fair of 1893, officially named the World's Columbian Exposition. St. Clair Drake found "the great influx of Negroes coming to the World's Columbian Exposition served to introduce the Negro community of Chicago to Negroes in other areas, resulted in some persons staying in the city, and increased the interest in church and associational life. The trends originating during this period found their full expression in the [new century] which followed."[2]

Monroe Nathan Work fixed the size of the black population in 1896 at 22,742 out of the city's total of 1,626,635 persons based on a recent school census. Fellow researcher Richard R. Wright Jr. reported that the population of 1900 experienced an increase of 2,000 persons in two months because of violence in New Orleans that induced their flight. As to the relevance of the young within this population, African American children constituted only a small proportion of this mass of laboring-class persons. When Work examined the 1900 census and focused on the emerging Black Belt's Third Ward, he found very few children and an average family size of two to four persons in approximately 60 percent of the households. Two-headed families continued to dominate the community landscape. Single-parent families were present, but they constituted a small minority of all black families and tended to be incorporated within extended family networks and headed by middle-aged women who usually were widowed, separated, or divorced.[3]

As dynamic as the migrants of past times had been, additional adult newcomers brought with them an even higher level of human dynamism to the benefit of black Chicago and the city in general. Most notable were civic activist Ida B. Wells and the activist A.M.E. ministers Reverdy Ransom and Archibald Carey. Wells made Chicago her permanent home in 1895, Ransom arrived in 1896, and Carey in 1897. Other notable arrivals were Robert Sengstacke Abbott, Julius F. Taylor, and Jesse Binga. Abbott visited the city during the fair, sang on the fairgrounds in 1893 as part of the Hampton Quartet, and fell in love with Chicago. He returned for a permanent residence in 1897. Two years later, Taylor, an acerbic newspaper publisher from Salt Lake City, returned east and settled permanently in the city. In the process, he brought with him political ambition and the tool for its realization, his newspaper, the Broad Ax. Binga came to Chicago with ideas and a hunger for wealth. Never a person to relent in his personal quest to

achieve a goal, he soon would own extensive plots of real estate and implement a plan to own his own bank.

The city, no doubt, also gained reciprocally from the brief presence of a
young Mary McLeod Bethune in 1894. Her early interest and commitment
to humanity led her through the doors and into the classrooms of the
Moody Bible Institute, where she studied various aspects of home and foreign missionary work. Another southerner of rising prominence, Booker T.
Washington, attended the world's fair and returned to visit frequently at the
end of the decade just as Frederick Douglass had done until his death in
1895.

II. THE CHANGING CITY LANDSCAPE

The physical and human landscape of black Chicago continued to undergo
dramatic changes during the decade that significantly molded its social and
economic configuration for generations to come. Fortunately, this transformation and framing were documented contemporaneously by an African
American researcher, Monroe Nathan Work, who inaugurated a social science approach that included examining the city's black population with
microscopic precision. Operating from the campus of the fledgling University of Chicago during the early 1900s, Work, in his role as participant-
observer, conducted street-level surveys that had him examining each of the
three major sides of town—North, West, and South—rather than just focusing on the most densely populated section south of Twenty-second Street
that was to become the famed Black Belt (Figure 45).

The pattern of settlement assumed a complexity of its own, and the
"ghetto" of historical and sociological construction did not exist at this
point in Chicago's history. The work of Allan H. Spear is especially useful
at this point because his pioneering work separated legendary housing patterns from documented, census-based patterns.[4] His *Black Chicago: The
Making of a Negro Ghetto, 1890–1920* was primarily concerned with the
point when the African American population became concentrated enough
to establish its presence and possible control over housing and designated
public space within the city, and what that demographic hegemony meant
to the quality of life of the population involved. The historical pivot in his
study, and others like it in Harlem, Detroit, Cleveland, Milwaukee, and
Buffalo, was the "Great Migration" of 1915–1918, which attracted 50,000
new workers to Chicago amid the 500,000 it drew to the entirety of the
North.[5] Although a major issue for examination, it is beyond the purview
of what is to be covered in volume one of this study.

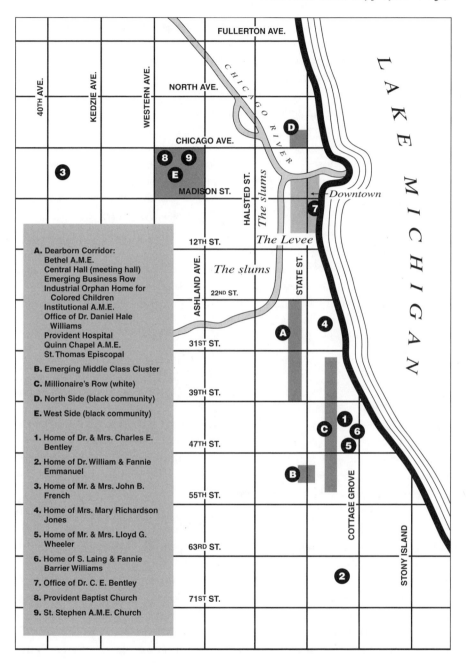

Fig. 45. Black Chicago, 1900

The distribution of the African American population over the city's landscape in post-annexation Chicago (after 1889) found many African Americans living in high concentration in the midst of their own group, such as along the Dearborn Street Corridor. Others were isolated from this heavy concentration in predominantly white communities, such as those found on the West Side and North Side. Then there were African Americans residing in small clusters of what were statistically—but not in actuality—socially racially mixed areas such as Englewood, Hyde Park, and the far South Side's Morgan Park neighborhood. Home-owning rose dramatically in these areas as manifestations of claims to higher social status and the economic protection of property investment.[6]

On the West and North sides of the city, the smaller enclaves produced a distinct experience for African Americans. There was social isolation at times, if the community was predominantly white and offered only limited social acceptance. If the neighborhood or cluster was predominantly black, there was social camaraderie among fellow blacks and also some social acceptance from and mingling with whites. Importantly, there was a semblance of racial peace. The dispersion of the African American population throughout the city represented the natural demographic contours expected in an area when restrictive housing agreements were nonexistent and exclusionary racial policies lacked the strength of custom.

On the West Side, despite the image usually conjured of its vast working class, there also resided families representative of various other segments of the African American population. The Johnson-Hudson and Cherry families belonged to the growing cluster of entrepreneurs and businessmen. Jesse Johnson left Tennessee, where he had been born after slavery, and journeyed to Chicago in 1900 with his family. He distinguished himself as a master carpenter; quickly putting his skills to work, he built nine houses over several years.[7] James Hudson was another Tennessean; he was born in 1889 and arrived in Chicago as a child in 1892. Once he reached adulthood, Hudson would marry the Johnsons' daughter, Willie Dee, and the couple would make Providence Baptist their church home.

Another entrepreneurial family was that of patrician father Wiley Cherry, who arrived in Chicago from Colrain, North Carolina, in 1893. His wife, Margaret, and their daughters, Mattie and Lovie, soon followed. While it is unknown whether their coming to the city was linked directly to the World's Columbian Exposition of 1893 and the opportunities it clearly offered to the adventurous and enterprising, the entrepreneurial spirit of the age inspired Mr. Cherry in a city that catered to the independent-minded individual. The business chronicler Isaac Harris had described the acquisitive mood of many African Americans, and Wiley Cherry proved an example of this character. He soon started a grocery, which within a short time had given way to a masonry and plastering business on Lake Street where, through the years, the Cherrys prospered financially. Earlier, after the birth of Wiley and Margaret Cherry's first son, Jim, in 1895, the family rented or owned a frame home at 442 South Western Avenue. Living on Western Avenue, the city's westernmost boundary until 1869, placed the Cherrys on the city's West Side, which was home to 200,000 people of mixed ethnic and racial backgrounds in 1890. Most were newly arrived immigrants from southern and central Europe who were joining Germans and the Irish from previous decades, who, in turn, were pressing on the heels of wealthier native white Americans. Racial pride and a sense of racial solidarity led the Cherry family to seek cultural affinity among fellow African Americans. The Cherrys quickly affiliated with the expanding African American community found along a mixed residential and commercial corridor on either side of Lake Street. This family also established membership at the Providence Baptist Church.

Meanwhile, the history of the Lewis family gives some insight into typical family life among the professional class.[8] Previous to Dr. John W. Lewis Sr.'s entering the medical profession during the second decade of the twentieth century, he had opened a pharmacy along the Lake Street business corridor. He had arrived in Chicago in the late 1890s from Oskaloosa, Iowa, where he had worked as a pharmacist's assistant. Then he pursued medical training at Rush Medical School. Dr. Lewis's wife arrived in Chicago from Virginia in the 1900s. Their son, John Jr., followed in his father's footsteps into medicine later in the century. The West Side also had its members of the city's black elite, with the Frenches and the Hancocks retaining the status they had established in the previous decade.[9]

Life for young Lovelynn Miller Evans unfolded on the far North Side of the city. Born on March 9, 1893, in Chicago's Lakeview community, she grew up in a biracial household in a racially mixed neighborhood where she recalled fondly how she enjoyed her childhood. As a child in the era before the dominance of the internal-combustion engine, she enjoyed riding her pony-drawn cart along the lakefront with an air of complete freedom. Her African American father had arrived from Louisiana in 1888, and shortly after his daughter's birth, Joseph Miller and his German American wife, Elizabeth, were on the verge of seeing the fruits of their labor blossom, as his moving and storage business seemed well on the way to success. Lovelynn Miller Evans attended the Horace Greeley Elementary School, where one of her classmates was the future journalist Westbrook Pegler. She concluded her education with graduation from Lakeview High School.[10]

An older Charles Liggett reached Chicago before the dawn of the new century and headed far north near the lakefront, where he quickly found housing among whites. A son of slaves who had spent his childhood in Mobile, Alabama, also among whites, Liggett, once in Chicago, replaced segregation with social acceptance and remained a North Sider late into his retirement years. His neighborhood was sparsely settled and was reached by horse-drawn cars, offering serenity and peace, and finally, a boon to physical mobility in cable cars. The few African Americans who lived in the area shopped where they lived, but when they sought a traditional African American religious experience, they found themselves heading to the South Side.[11]

Native-born Chicagoan Gertrude Davis was another North Sider and the fifth of twelve children born to a former slave father of unmixed racial ancestry and a free mother with a triple heritage of Native American, West African, and Irish bloodlines. At the time of her birth on November 12, 1873, the family lived along the "Plank Road" (now known as Milwaukee Avenue). They were among the first settlers in the area, their arrival predating that of most whites. As she recalled during her mature years, when her father "settled over on the northwest side of Chicago there were no white families at all, only a few Colored families, but by the time I was able to remember white people began to come into this section of Chicago. All of the Negro families were well established. The white immigrants would ask for shelter, food and work and my father, like other settlers, would house the white men in his barn and hire them out as farm hands for their board and keep. . . . This section of the city at that time was known as Avondale. . . . It was not until I married that I came to know the South Side of Chicago."[12]

For the younger Martha Dawson, life began in 1899 in the North Side house her father built in the sparsely settled northwest section of the newly annexed Jefferson Park Township. Her parents were early settlers in the area during the post–Civil War period and enjoyed the company of their white neighbors. Her life continued to revolve around this area, even when she reached her mature years, as she accommodated herself to life apart from the cultural and social orbit of African Americans.[13]

In the meantime, almost twenty thousand persons concentrated along racial lines near the heart of the city, and the Black Belt was assuming its legendary form. It was here, along the Dearborn Street Corridor, that the population increase among African Americans assumed its most impressive dimensions, encompassing a small number of businesses along State Street and many family-owned homes along Dearborn, Armour, Clark, and Butterfield streets. Life along the Dearborn Street Corridor assumed a unique rhythm for the bulk of the city's respectables as well as for most of the refined element. The area represented an expanding African American racial enclave that seemed to be in the thick of everything of importance in the city. It was situated in close proximity to the downtown section; to the famed

Millionaire's Row on the South Side's Grand Boulevard, where the homes of the wealthier Chicagoans lay directly to the east; to the notorious vice district known as the "Levee," which overlapped its northern boundary; and even to the fairgrounds of the World's Columbian Exposition when it opened on May 1, 1893. Transportation abounded; major thoroughfares traversed the area as well as running nearby, with north-south streetcars available on State Street and Wentworth Avenue. Accessible by streetcar and elevated trains, carriage traffic, or by foot, this community sat about two miles south of the heart of the central business district and five miles north of Jackson Park, the site of the world's fair.

The corridor anchored an expanding African American community extending from Twenty-second Street roughly southward to Thirty-ninth, and from Wentworth Avenue on the west to State Street (and later Wabash Avenue) on the east. Importantly, it was home to about one-fourth of the city's twenty thousand African Americans and was the location of the bulk of its biggest and most influential churches and the black-operated Provident Hospital. The area's impressive growth meant that building a successful commercial strip along State Street, one block east of Dearborn Street, entered the realm of the probable as African Americans expanded their economic options. While professionals such as Dr. Charles C. Bentley practiced in downtown offices by the 1890s, his close friend and confidant Dr. Daniel Hale Williams maintained offices on Thirty-first Street, as did many others. Williams's offices were actually located at the edge of the corridor in "neutral" racial territory. There, he shared space in a magnificent building that housed white and black professionals on the northwest corner of Michigan Boulevard and Thirty-first Street. The district included both poorer homes and better residences along its streets. A substantial portion of home ownership was found here, so this area qualified as the locus of social influence, cultural expression, and economic stability for the Black Belt. Yet many African Americans sought to invest permanently in housing found outside its perimeters.[14]

While this diverse section witnessed the construction of some new edifices, overall they paled in comparison with more substantial white and black housing immediately to the south and east. Basically, the construction of approximately thirty-seven hundred residential structures within the corridor had reached a point of completion and saturation by 1895.[15] One- and two-story structures dominated; most were made of brick but some were wood framed. Many homes were substantial, but there were no mansions.

Contemporary descriptions told the story in all its complexity. When newspapers such as the Broad Ax, the Appeal, and the Indianapolis Freeman reported on the activities of "society," the addresses cited were more often than not near Dearborn and Armour Avenue. Attorney and Mrs. Edward

H. Morris resided at 2712 Dearborn, indicating that status was based on more than just "where you lived"; also important was the manner in which you lived. In the case of the Morrises, they lived well, as manifested in their summer itinerary of 1899, which had them returning home from a grand Eastern tour of Boston, Newport, New York, and Philadelphia.[16] Along with Morris's rarefied status among black lawyers, Mrs. Morris's socialite mother, Mrs. Montgomery, added prestige to the family and its presence in the community. The elder socialite was remembered as "a stately woman of pale [smooth] complexion who wore a gray coiffure that had a close resemblance to that of Mrs. Potter Palmer."[17]

Dr. Austin Maurice Curtis and his wife lived at 3543 Dearborn, seven blocks from his office at 2942 Armour. In the same locale, but representing another time and a newer generation, the newborn Annetta, the child of Charles and Mildred Taylor, entered the world on March 1, 1899. She would call this area home until almost the end of her 101 years.[18]

Rev. Reverdy Ransom, a Social Gospel community activist, saw the area through a different set of spectacles. He understood its varied rhythms and would write that African Americans were "housed for the most part in flimsy, frame houses on Dearborn Street, Armour Avenue, and adjoining streets extending to the Chicago River."[19] The condition of the streets was appalling; Rev. Richard R. Wright Jr. remarked in a similar vein that "only a few of these streets are paved, 33rd street being the only one with asphalt and cedar block paving."[20]

Yet misery and deprivation in the midst of splendor and elegance was nothing new in urban living. Many of the veterans of the Civil War, along with their families, friends, and acquaintances who resided in the area, inhabited some of the least desirable housing units.[21] By virtue of their occupations and income, they struggled daily as part of the lower end of black Chicago's respectable element. Among the veterans, residential mobility reached alarming rates, with some individuals or families moving every year as they fought to make ends meet.

Many became "lodgers," non-family-related renters who moved into a household until they could get established and acclimated to big-city living, and thus afford independent rental or self-purchased housing. That Chicago's laboring-class black population included lodgers in housing and family life was not an unusual factor, and it was not necessarily negative. Single persons who came to the North and settled on the West Side were absorbed into the households in which they lived, becoming honorary members of those families. Dr. Daniel Hale Williams arrived in Chicago and immediately joined the household of Mrs. Mary Richardson Jones until he became solidly established.[22] Unattached persons, as well as childless, recently married couples, lived with families both because of a shortage in housing and because of the institutional protection this arrangement provided. These people shared not only the rent or mortgage payment, but also a valuable social and family life—and this was an arrangement enjoyed by European immigrant groups as well. There can be no doubt that the bane of the urban family was bad housing. By the same token, because opportunities for African Americans to secure decent housing for rental purposes or purchase were limited, securing the scarce funds needed to survive loomed as paramount also. The city's worst housing and acknowledged slum, "Packingtown," was located significantly to the west of the Dearborn Corridor and was inhabited by European immigrants.[23]

As a locus of creativity, the Dearborn Corridor was becoming the geographical and cultural core of the Chicago African American community. So it should not have been surprising to find that the excitement and bonding of 1893—the activities on the fairgrounds, and the stimulating discussions and meetings held inside the fair's boundaries and at the Art Palace at the downtown Art Institute of Chicago—expanded beyond the perimeters of these venues. They resumed or were replicated in parallel activities taking place continuously in Chicago's African American churches throughout the duration of the fair, of which more will be said later.

The residential landscape south of the Dearborn Corridor revealed that a number of the more prominent and socially rising African American families made their homes in racially mixed areas of the South Side. These were located in near proximity to heavily black settlements such as those found usually south of Fifty-first Street and parallel to State Street. The Gibbs family, including their daughter Grace, who was a recent Howard University graduate, lived at 5023 Armour. Clubwoman Mrs. L. A. Davis, who was vacationing in the summer of 1899 at Mackinac Island, lived at 5017 Armour Avenue. She planned to return to the city in time for the annual convention of the National Association of Colored Women, where she would deliver the welcoming opening address.[24]

Far southward of the Dearborn Corridor lay the diverse, predominantly white neighborhoods, where numerous other African American families lived. When Richard R. Wright Jr., University of Chicago student and son of the president of Georgia State Industrial School, reached the city, he resided with Rev. D. W. Jones, who lived at 5520 Ingleside Avenue in the Hyde Park community.[25] A mile southward, Professor William and Mrs. Fannie Emanuel made their home at 6352 Rhodes Avenue in the Washington Park subdivision of the Woodlawn community. The story was similar in other residential pockets in Englewood, Lilydale, Morgan Park, and the steel-producing Southeast Side.

A world apart from these experiences were those of the socially dispossessed African Americans who lived immediately north and northwest of the Dearborn Corridor. Monroe N. Work identified twin cores of slum life where the bulk of them established their homes. One extended between Lake Michigan to the east, the Chicago River and Clark Street to the west, Twenty-second Street to the south, and Van Buren to the north, lying within the boundaries of the infamous Levee district, which housed the city's vice amid slums. It was the area and the population that Rev. William T. Stead examined for his work on degenerate behavior, *If Christ Came to Chicago*. A portion of the area was sometimes called "darkest Africa,"[26] derisively named by whites and by African Americans living to the south of the area.

Across the river rose the western version of these slums. Its boundaries were Grand Avenue to the north, Madison to the south, Jefferson Street to the east, and Ann (Racine) Street to the west. While the Levee was home to 4,900 African Americans, 800 lived in the Western Division.[27] Unfortunately, the former was home to too many Civil War veterans and their families. The first in war had become the last to receive the benefits of society in peacetime. A federal pension examiner observed the conditions under which one veteran lived in this area: "He lives in a dive which is almost worth a man's life if I go into it. So I didn't."[28] Their presence in these economically depressed areas indicated, moreover, that all of the residents of these enclaves possessed different lifestyles, so no wholesale classification for them as criminally inclined is reasonable. In addition to their economic needs being denied, there were no major churches located in these areas to serve the spiritual needs of these Chicagoans, only missions and storefront religious activities. Nationally, these slum dwellers represented the largest concentration of poverty in any of the larger cities, including New York, Philadelphia, or Baltimore.[29]

III. THE ECONOMIC FABRIC

Chicago's African American laboring force knew labor intimately and had a tradition of hard work that was recognized by *Scribner's Magazine* early in the decade.[30] Without a whimper, but with resolution, they conformed to a labor pattern that produced wealth and needed services for others while being misrepresented nationally as ne'er-do-wells.[31] While in 1900 they represented 1.8 percent of the total population, the males constituted 2.3 percent of all breadwinners and the women 3.3 percent.[32] They also continued to find themselves relegated to the service sector, which, despite its limitations, provided them with uninterrupted work along with survival-level wages.

At the beginning of the decade, possible employment at the world's fair held out the promise of better conditions, if only on a temporary basis. By the middle of the decade, a combination of economic and racial influences stifled opportunity for the mass of workers for decades to come. Part of this economic saga was recounted by two African American journalists whose lives were to be forever intertwined after their professional collaboration in Chicago in 1893. In the most famous of Columbian literary pieces written by African Americans, *The Reason Why the Colored American Is Not in the World's Columbian Exposition*, Ida B. Wells and Ferdinand L. Barnett rendered some economic observations that linked the historical basis for African American impoverishment and underemployment with the somewhat present favorable conditions whites encountered. Wells wrote, "The labor of one-half of this country has always been, and is still being done by [the African Americans]. The first credit this country had in its commerce with foreign nations was created by production resulting from their labor. The wealth created by their industry has afforded to the white people of this country the leisure essential to their group progress in education, art, science, industry, and invention."[33]

Ferdinand L. Barnett noticed a problem when he analyzed world's fair employment, which had a pattern of clear intent to harm African Americans. To his credit, Barnett rejected in absolute terms a continued African American horizontal monopoly of jobs in menial and service positions. He instead demanded a vertical integration of the workforce, with African Americans sharing positions along the pyramid of work, from the base to its apex. Barnett's advantage over his future wife's views came with his intimate knowledge of the Chicago scene and his contemporary perspective. However, he displayed a blind spot in reaching conclusions prior to his assessment of what actually transpired during the fair. In rushing to meet a deadline for publication of *The Reason Why the Colored American Is Not in the World's Columbian Exposition*, he penned his views first, before the event's opening in May 1893, and he then allowed his precast ideological bent to determine a wrong before he had completed a comprehensive observation of the situation. He wrote: "In this wonderful hive of national industry, representing an outlay of thirty million dollars, and numbering its employees by the thousands, only two colored persons could be found whose occupations were of a higher grade than that of a janitor, laborer and porter, and these two only clerkships. Only as a menial is the Colored American to be seen—the Nation's deliberate and cowardly tribute to the southern demand 'to keep the Negro in his place.'"[34] However, for the black working class in a nation on the verge of a major depression, work of any kind was cherished. No doubt Barnett also perceived the ominous constriction of the white, skilled portion of the labor force, which had benefited directly from the adoption of racist notions of hiring as part of Social Darwinian practice.

Meanwhile, on-the-scene observations of conditions at the fairgrounds at the south end of the city sometimes presented more enthusiasm about the possibilities of work opportunities. Two visitors to Chicago, both destined for greatness in the realm of letters, reported on their experiences. A young Paul Lawrence Dunbar of Dayton, Ohio, arrived in Chicago in the spring of 1893 with plans to write a world's fair column for his hometown *Dayton Herald*. Once in the city, he joined thousands of other men seeking but not necessarily finding work. His biographer wrote, "out on the fairgrounds he tramped from building to building, but no workers were needed. Finally he got a job, cleaning one of the big domes. That lasted only a few days. His next job was in a basement shipping room, uncrating exhibit specimens. Here dampness soon brought on a racking cough. The cough got worse, and Paul quit to look for work out of doors, or at least where there was good air."[35]

James Weldon Johnson also arrived about the same time from Atlanta, but he had easier access to work in carpentry and a guarantee of work as a chair boy, assisting fairgoers unable to walk the entirety of the fairgrounds. Thus his work experience offered another dimension to the world of work for the skilled black man. When he wrote home to Atlanta University, he described how "by reason of our industrial training in Atlanta University, fifteen of us were employed to do work at the grounds as carpenters, at $3.25 per day of eight hours, and the other was employed as a plasterer at $4.50. There is more work here than men can be employed to do. Any price is being paid for workmen."[36]

As to which experience was more common is worth examination, especially in light of the charges made in *The Reason Why the Colored American Is Not in the World's Columbian Exposition*. An analysis of photographs and pencil sketches of the work site suggests the existence of a cosmopolitan workforce, but by no means could a shaded face indicate with certainty that a worker was of African descent. Most trades, such as designing, glaziering, surveying, painting, sculpting, and molding, were off limits to certain groups, particularly African Americans, and many immigrants possessed swarthy hues that could be mistaken for the mixed hues of African Americans from a distance; some apparently dark faces in the old pictures might simply have resulted from a faint pen mark.

While work on the fairgrounds for African Americans was finite, their presence could hardly have been called invisible. The official World's Columbian Exposition photographs of the various staffs included African Americans along with their colleagues. The photograph of the director of works, Daniel H. Burnham, and his staff included E. Jackson, head janitor, along with his coworkers. Each man was dressed appropriately for the occasion. Chief Buchanan and his staff are pictured outside the Agricultural Building, with J. Shreeves dressed dapperly. Manufacturers and staff from the Hide and Leather Building posed for their place in history; included was an unidentified African American in the top row. The operation of the famous circular, steel-framed wheel of William Ferris relied on A. S. Johnson to perform his duties as official office guard.

Washingtonian Louis B. Anderson landed "the job of exchange reader in his department of Publicity and Promotion. Among the archives of the Exposition the scrap-books containing all newspaper references to the Fair throughout the world represent his work in that department."[37] The importance of the matter is found in the fact that despite some prevalent racism, these employees could have been excluded or hidden, but they were not. They are featured as integral parts of organizations, appearing dignified and neither representing themselves nor their race in a derogatory fashion. However, in at least one exhibit depicting slave-plantation Louisiana, the latter did occur.

Deliberate, calculated racial exclusion proved the rule for hiring men for the Columbian Guard, the elite, quasi-military escort, police, and fire protective unit of the fair. Very early, hiring for the Columbian Guard unfolded in a depressing, obviously racist, Machiavellian scenario. Exclusion of African Americans became the rule as two thousand openings were filled. When William J. Crawford, a seven-year resident in the city, applied for a position, the staff physician deliberately misread a chest measurement to make Crawford fall one inch short of a required expanded chest size of thirty-six inches. Even Crawford's immediate reexamination by another white doctor failed to satisfy the Columbian Guard's leadership. Two subsequent letters of reconsideration fell on closed eyes. The Guard remained lily-white for the duration of the fair. Ferdinand L. Barnett was especially vociferous in denouncing this practice, which saw able-bodied, educated, capable African Americans exempted from this group purportedly because of weight, height, and other deficiencies.[38] Never the elite police force that its commander U. S. Colonel Rice envisioned, its stature could only have been enhanced by men such as Crawford. Although the Guard proved itself valorous by its acts of bravery and the human losses it suffered during the horrendous Cold Storage Building fire during the summer of 1893, fairgoers commonly complained about the guards' brusqueness, ignorance of directions, and stiff, ineffective deportment.[39]

In contrast, the fair's custodial staff, which included African Americans, served as a unit falling under the jurisdiction of the Guard's leadership (until a week before the fair opened, when it became part of the responsi-

Fig. 46. Custodial workers, part of Columbian Guard,
at World's Columbian Exposition.
Chicago Historical Society, ICHi-29970.

bility of the superintendent of buildings). Photographs depict these workers
immaculately dressed; one custodian is seen walking across the fairgrounds
in conversation, and two others are shown in a work-related situation (Figures 46, 47). It is easy to imagine that their role exceeded their occupation
as described. A common practice in the South was to refuse to dignify African American endeavors with the proper designations and titles; the same
probably occurred in this instance. The interests and needs of the mass of
African American fairgoers were no doubt met by this compromise version
of the Guard. This arrangement would have also reduced the fears of white
Southerners that they might experience some version of racial equality

Fig. 47. Scene from the Chicago world's fair;
note African American worker at bottom center.
Special Collections and Preservation Division, Chicago Public Library.

while in the North. Since janitorial duties were relegated to another segment of the workforce, this explanation gains in currency. One other point
is relevant: photographic evidence from the family files of Civil War veteran
Andrew Peter Jackson shows his sons on or near the fairgrounds, and they
are dressed in police uniforms. This evidence lends another puzzling piece
of history to the story of the world's fair.

An additional portion of the workforce found anywhere from 1,017 to
2,000 janitors on nightly duty; they had the responsibility of cleaning up the
fairgrounds and buildings after closing. Some African Americans were hired
as "washroom caretakers." Demanding on his time, but not deleterious to his
dignity, Paul Lawrence Dunbar took such work at a pay scale of $10.50 per
week, with Tuesday being payday.[40] The persons who engaged in the various
types of work described to this point constituted that segment of society
referred to as the respectables.

Students from Atlanta University and elsewhere at white institutions
earned money as attendants who would roll moving chairs throughout the
fairgrounds at seventy-five cents per hour, of which they received a percentage. These student "chair boys" could expect to earn up to forty dollars a

week. The miles of fairgrounds and the countless exhibits to be viewed made this conveyance service important to the average fairgoer. "The rolling-chairs that run about the grounds and through the buildings are the salvation of many a fainting spirit. To thousands of human beings with nothing but a human back and human legs the fair would be a failure without them. They are a support for the weary, strength for the weak."[41] In all, more than one thousand young workers were hired, and at least fifty of them were presumably African American. According to James Weldon Johnson, writing for his college newsletter, the *Bulletin of Atlanta University*, he and his classmates experienced anxiety and anticipation at having the opportunity to visit the nation's second-largest city, along with availing themselves of the opportunity to earn money toward their school expenses. Whether this opportunity was available to the adult males of the city's African American community is unknown.

One of the more dramatic incidents the chair boys experienced involved a strike protesting a drop in earnings. While the white chair boys faced the issue with an air of labor consciousness, the blacks remained aloof deliberately, considering themselves favored to be earning what they did as well as fortunate to be at the Chicago world's fair. In their collective consciousness, they realized they were students temporarily acting as workers. As they saw the situation, their permanent affiliation with the academy would allow them to grasp the knowledge that allowed men to rule the world. What this division over challenging management wrought is unknown, but it could not have enhanced relations between the summer workers. This incident would have served to reenforce in the white mind the validity of the end-of-the-century caricature of the black worker as strikebreaker, or, in this case, a reluctant supporter of the just cause of labor against oppressive capital.

There were also instances in which racism spoiled what appeared on the surface to be amiable relations between the college men. James Weldon Johnson noted that usually anything derogatory said about the members of his race were voiced beyond earshot. As to relations with other whites who would ride in their "gospel chariots," it might have been captured accurately on an occasion or two by this assessment of human contact: "There is sometimes a contrast in manners and education between the occupant of the chair and the man behind that is not in the favor of the former. When one sees what is evidently a citizen with far more money than brains, and without the faintest appreciation of the beauties that encompass him, wheeled about at seventy-five cents an hour by a youth so far his superior that any comparison is impossible, it causes one to realize Fortune is indeed an irresponsible flirt, who is never so happy as when doing the wrong thing."[42]

Particular exhibits, such as those of private businesses, used company workers. Another challenge to maintain the dignity of labor took place during the summer months of 1893, when the Pullman Company placed its famous Palace Cars on stationary display at the world's fair at the imposing Transportation Building. An officious Pullman employee named Mr. Fritsch provided regular status reports to his "honored Mr. Pullman" on the number of visitors inspecting the cars, the number of important dignitaries who viewed the cars with a prospect of adding them to their railroads or personal travel accouterments, and the efficiency of his retinue of porters, who kept the cars spotless. On one occasion, Fritsch proudly wrote to Pullman, "we had a fine train to show today. It was cleaned well inside and outside, as I had made it pretty lively for the [work] force yesterday and am determined to return a well-kept train to Pullman [the town] Oct. 31."[43] Porters on the actual rolling trains worked just as hard as this crew on the stationary exhibit, yet the prospects of decent wages never materialized for any of them, a feature sadly typical for all employees of the Pullman Company.

The small number of African American musicians in the city and from around the nation who secured work in Chicago before the fair played in isolated settings, such as in the Levee district. On the fairgrounds, however, they faced complete exclusion. An overwhelming number of the organized bands in the city were white, so they dominated the musical scene. When the Haitians celebrated their designated day at the fair in July, the highly regarded and all-white Iowa State Band provided the music. Even the eagerly anticipated Colored American Day in August featured the music of the all-white Gilmore's band. The many visiting African American musicians, such as pianist Scott Joplin of Sedalia, Missouri, were left to find employment where they could—in his case on the periphery of the fairgrounds, where many visitors retired after their exhaustive strolls. In fact, he might have headed a band.

Despite the restraints on black performers and their music, some probably played immediately outside the fairgrounds along Stony Island Avenue or near the Midway. Singing groups such as the Fisk Jubilee Singers and the Hampton Quartet sang extensively at African American functions both on and off the fairgrounds and were well received by both races. Another group, the Standard Quartet, performed at a musical concert in July 1893, singing "Negro spiritual songs while others contributed patriotic songs."[44]

Significantly, the only authentic African-based music played on the fairgrounds occurred at the Dahomey Village, and it was apparently enjoyed by as many as it might have annoyed with incessant rhythmic and counter-rhythmic drumming.[45] Equally important, Will Marion Cook stated that ragtime was born in 1893, at the occasion of the fair. According to Cook, "About 1898 marked the starting and quick growth of the so-called 'ragtime.' As far back as 1875[,] Negroes in questionable resorts along the Mississippi had commenced to evolve this musical figure, but at the World's Fair in Chicago 'ragtime' got a running start and swept the Americas, next Europe, and to-day the craze has not diminished."[46]

The question of long-term work throughout the city loomed far more important than employment at the fair, which was temporary in nature (1891–1893). For the city's unemployed, their plight could not be denied forever, although that appeared to be the case at times. The African American laboring class suffered through the depression of 1893 just like their white fellow citizens. The fifth of the nineteenth century's major national economic depressions affected the Chicago economy (after the previous dislocations of 1819, 1837, 1857, and 1873) with a devastating impact. In its intensity, it lasted at least until 1897, and while blacks did not resort to violence as white workers did at the Pullman Works in 1894, they endured the same economic deprivation. They also suffered from the slap of exclusion that found the American Railway Union endorsing a racial clause in its constitution that denied them membership in 1894. In an episode reminiscent of the Haymarket Riot, racism once again denied African Americans a part to play in a major industrial confrontation. Decried as only good enough to act as strikebreakers, some blacks angrily acted out that role as part of an "Anti-Strikers Railroad Union."[47]

The longevity of work for black laborers depended on countervailing forces—the tenacity of the regular white labor force to hold out for its demands, the successful manipulations of the packinghouse owners to exploit a low-paid and therefore cheap labor force, and, in the eyes of some, the benevolence of the packers. Utilized as workers in the Union Stockyards on a very limited basis between 1881 and 1894, African Americans strove to acquire jobs in this better-paying work environment. In organization, the stockyards represented a labor-intensive workplace where large numbers of unskilled and skilled laborers performed such duties as killing livestock and then hauling, carrying, stuffing as well as skillfully carving carcasses.[48] By July 1894, with the introduction of some southern-born strikebreakers into the stockyards to replace white sympathizers to the American Railway Union's strike, an invidious combination of labor and racial antipathy built against black workers. Within another month the strike had ended, leaving in its wake the permanent label of "scab" on black workers in the white mind.[49] Surprisingly, in the following years, with their exceedingly low numbers, they were able to continue working without incurring the wrath of the newest wave of foreign-born white workers, whose numbers dominated this workplace after they had displaced German and Irish workers.[50]

Among the packinghouse magnates, Philip D. Armour, who died in 1900, was remembered on the occasion of his death as a friend to African American labor and an important contributor to black charitable efforts. Fannie Barrier Williams memorialized him in early 1901 thus:

> The death of Philip D. Armour, the millionaire packer and philan-thropist, has deprived the Colored people of a friend who did more than is generally recognized for their advancement. Mr. Armour's helpful-ness was of a practical kind and went to the heart of our difficulties—the lack of opportunities to earn a living in the great hives of industry built upon by American capital and genius. The Colored people have a just complaint against nearly all the great employers of skilled and unskilled labor in the North in that they are mainly indifferent and even contemptuous to the demands of Colored men and women for a chance to earn a livelihood. . . . Not so with Mr. Armour. His heart was large enough to recognize the demands and needs [of African American workers]. . . . His instructions were that "all must be treated alike." . . . His confidence in the Colored man as a worker has been justified in the fact that the number of Colored employees has increased from year to year.[51]

Williams also found words to praise the other packers and thereby laid out a challenge for researchers to reevaluate the pre–Great Migration role of black workers in the meatpacking industry through the analysis of hard data.

In a different turn of events during the summer of 1900, black strike-breakers in general labor succumbed to white entreaties to leave the down-town construction site of the Mandel Brothers Department Store, honoring the concept of workers' solidarity.[52] This act, however, did little in the long run to improve black job chances or improve race relations. On this occa-sion, journalist Fannie Barrier Williams concluded that "a race that can be systematically deprived of one occupation after another becomes an easy vic-tim to all kinds of injustice. When they can be reduced to a position to be pitied, they will cease to be respected."[53]

Economic progress in Chicago was more evident in the business sector. According to Franklin and Moss, "it was only natural that African Ameri-cans observing the success of various individuals during the age of heroic business enterprise, should enter the fields of business and industry. Frus-trated in their efforts to participate in the businesses of whites, they embarked on a program of 'Negro business enterprise.'" This proved to be so much the case that when the socially conscious Rev. Reverdy Ransom surveyed the economic landscape, he observed optimistically that there was success in abundance among the African American population. He talked with pride and awe about businessmen such as Theodore Jones and could expand his view of economic accomplishments to include Edward H. Morris, Edward H. Wright, Ferdinand Barnett, S. Laing Williams, along with Drs. Daniel H. Williams, George C. Hall, and Charles C. Bentley. All enjoyed success in a competitive, biracial market. Five years after the dawn of the new century, an estimated 566 black businesses were operating, with 180 located in the retail sector and with 374 providing services in a variety of areas.[54]

Professionals such as Dr. Daniel Hale Williams and Dr. Charles E. Bentley prospered in their fields, providing services to white as well as permanent black patients. As top medical practitioners, they earned far in excess of the remaining twenty physicians, who realized lesser amounts of $1,500 to $5,000 annually. Attorneys (excluding Edward H. Morris) earned much less than the doctors, averaging less than $2,000 per year. Most African Americans either had little money to pay these professionals or little use of their services. To supplement their earnings, the lawyers turned to politics.[55] The later image of the totally inclusive social hierarchy that accommodated domestic and service personnel was rendered mythical.

Both viscerally and cerebrally, a significant segment of Chicago's African Americans acknowledged that Chicago and the nation were in the midst of a financial, technological, and machine revolution. African Americans participated as builders off the fairgrounds as they constructed or opened new residences and places of trade. The *Indianapolis Freeman* reported that Adam G. Smith was erecting "a large hotel at 2713 South Dearborn" and that he was one of the wealthiest Negroes in Illinois. When Joseph S. Miller, a native of Louisiana, reached the city in 1888, he arrived as a man with a dream. Within five years, he realized it, opening Miller's Buena Park Express on the far North Side of the city. The newspaper announced that the "saloon business, of course, has gone way up" and that S. J. Manning and W. M. Grant were the proprietors of a "mammoth grocery house." But when Hampton Institute graduate Robert Sengstacke Abbott of Savannah, Georgia, sought work as a printer, a trade for which he was well qualified, he faced racial rejection repeatedly. He turned to law instead and was graduated from the Kent School of Law.[56]

For one group of professionals, public school teachers, the picture was mixed. Lettie A. Trent, the schoolteacher whose name figured prominently in protest at the fair, was one of perhaps a half dozen African American teachers in the city; the number rose to thirteen by 1900.[57] Almost the entirety of Chicago's teaching corps of 5,100 in 1895, excluding its 300 college-trained teachers at the secondary level, carried the burden of being considered a mediocre mass of politically connected, high school–trained clericals.[58] Their earnings by 1900 ranged from $850 to $1,500 per year, further reflecting Chicago's shameful neglect of the educational process. Schoolteachers, therefore, lacked the professional status and liberal training in the 1890s to be considered part of the refined cluster.

The onslaught of the depression in 1893 was devastating, and only gained momentum as time passed. Massive unemployment affected all of the city's workers, with one hundred black workers on the recently constructed elevated lines (the famous "El") being discharged "without ceremony" so that whites could be hired.[59] Labor strife was common among white workers, and their demands for consideration in this instance took precedence over fairness. For African Americans, another deleterious feature of American life emerged to exacerbate conditions. The racism associated with the tenets of Social Darwinism resulted in a negative reaction from whites, who either patronized black service providers or used their labor.[60] Fannie Barrier Williams identified the period of economic change as being around 1895. She noted erosion in so many fields that "nadir" seems the only accurate description of the situation. Barbers began to lose their monopoly in the downtown area, where they had traditionally cut the hair of the white middle and upper classes. Janitors started to lose their jobs to Swedish men. In the wait service, whites, both men and women, were replacing black men in "nearly all the first-class hotels and restaurants." Greek workers took over shoe polishing.[61]

In transportation, the number of African American men working as teamsters, express drivers, and coach drivers also started to decline in the business districts. Coachmen suffered from changes in fashion that saw the wealthy choosing among the Irish, Swedes, and African Americans as though they were items in a shop window instead of human beings. Members of Chicago's reigning royalty, the Pullmans, helped set the stage for this practice as they dismissed their black coachman of eighteen years as part of this new fashion. One coachman described his situation: "The lady of the house [said], 'I am going to New York to buy a rig, something new, and I am going to bring my driver back with me,' and so she [did]. . . . You see, Chicago copies New York and New York copies Europe and every time the black man gets the worst of it."[62]

IV. THE WORLD'S COLUMBIAN EXPOSITION

The significance of the World's Columbian Exposition, or as it was popularly known and remembered, the world's fair of 1893, led to its being accorded the third star among four in Chicago's future municipal flag. Of international, national, and local importance, the exposition's real, symbolic, and recollective power was felt in global economics and empire-building, diplomacy and race relations, and importantly for this study, the continuous transformation of the African American community in Chicago. After studying the impact it had on its contemporary world, Drake assessed it as "throw[ing] some light on Negro-white relations and the strength of Negro institutions during the nineties." The world's fair illuminated much more than the fairgrounds along the south lakefront; the event permanently implanted into the black psyche the idea and image of Chicago as a city, where even if the playing field was not level, it was at least accessible for competitive entry.[63] The old adage applied: "If you can't make it in Chicago, you can't make it anywhere." Perceived as a haven of economic opportunity, it became a magnet for African Americans who had lived in the East and the South. Its effect on the demographic composition of black Chicago was just as dramatic. The exposition attracted the talented, the productive, and the restless in a manner no other occurrence had before. To the city's benefit, many were destined to become permanent residents as a result of their attraction to Chicago.

As Chicago acted as the host for the nation's second world's fair during the late spring, the summer, and into the early fall of 1893, the stage was set for a historic moment to transpire. Understandably, the world's fair represented both an awe-inspiring event and a once-in-a-lifetime experience to millions of fairgoers of all races and ethnicities. Just as prominent white Chicagoans felt pride in their city's accomplishment in successfully hosting the exposition, so did blacks, even if their role was restricted because of race and their limited wealth and social status. As proud Chicagoans, they relished the experience of the world's fair, and its influence constituted another element in African American thought despite the fact that they were not directly involved in decision making over such matters as finance, administration, and operations. The idea of the fair assumed a central role in the "Old Settler" thinking of the early twentieth century precisely because of its remarkable success. It led these older African Americans to impose near-proprietary control over the memory of the event based on their real-life participation in 1893.

If the World's Columbian Exposition appeared as a godsend to the working class because of the employment opportunities it afforded on the eve of a major economic depression, it presented an even different image to educated and professional persons, both in Chicago and in the nation. Seen as a prism, it refracted light at many different angles that almost appeared incongruous in nature because of the disparate interests of various African American groups. Only twenty-eight years after the end of slavery, to certain African Americans concerned and conscious about their social status, the event represented a signal opportunity to show the white world the extent to which African Americans had progressed beyond their distressed conditions in 1865. Whatever their backgrounds or interests, African Americans wanted to participate to the fullest extent that they could, given the racism of the period. In Chicago and throughout the nation, groups of African Americans forged an ambitious strategy and implemented plans to attain their goals of respectful recognition and full inclusion.[64] Complicated yet earnestly conceived, this strategy unfolded as African Americans used the fair as a benchmark for racial progress, or a lack of it. As they pursued high-level administrative involvement, they hoped to mold their image for the world and nation. In exhibits, they envisioned a grand display of their collective abilities. In regard to Jim Crow, African Americans prepared for the worst, but often they encountered the best in American society, as their high level of involvement and participation revealed.

Beyond their special, although important, interests, rank-and-file black visitors wanted a grand tour of the fairgrounds—in essence, to see the entire world up close. Visitors also wanted a glimpse of how well the black community was doing in the nation's second-largest city. This meant a trip to the Dearborn Street Corridor, with its many churches and homes, as well as to State Street and its entertainments. African Americans who witnessed the grandeur of the fair described it in detail. By analyzing their descriptions and interpretations of the event, a semblance of the thinking of black Americans of the period can be fathomed. This was especially important in determining the effect of the fair on black Chicagoans and how they saw their city and the world. A Hampton Institute correspondent wrote, "I was, as perhaps most people are, more impressed by the grounds and buildings themselves than by any of the exhibits. The picture of the Court of Honor, as I saw it on two evenings, encircled by the brilliantly lighted buildings, with the shining lagoon in the midst, the constantly changing electric fountains, the great search lights seeking out first one point and then another, the golden statue of Columbus standing guard over the whole, and the glimpses of the blue lake here and there between the majestic columns of the Peristyle, is one that will live long in my memory. I hope never to lose it." James Weldon Johnson shared his amazement of the White City, called by that name because of the white-painted imitation marble buildings and their columns. Sharing his views with his fellow students at Atlanta University, he wrote: "No one who has not seen it, can form any idea of the immensity and grandeur of the exposition; nor can I give any adequate description of it. It has been very fitly called 'The White City,' and one standing under the Peristyle and looking down the Court of Honor . . . might easily imagine himself in a fairy city." Then, Robert Sengstacke Abbott, the future founder and publisher of the *Chicago Defender* in 1905, seemed "undoubtedly impressed by the display Negroes made of their progress in Chicago."[65] All had seen the power and potential of global humanity, felt a kinship, and deduced that African Americans could harness that same energy to advance their interests.

The refrain often heard on the fairgrounds—"all the world is here!"— proved itself a truism. The experience of the African diaspora unfolded in grand fashion as Old World Africans and their New World counterparts had an opportunity to interact. African Americans were joined by Africans from the continent and by various diasporans from throughout the Caribbean. The visitors arrived from Dahomey in West Africa, from South Africa, from Nubia and the Sudan, and from the North African littoral. These persons interacted with millions of people at the fair, and it truly became a world's fair. At the Dahomey Village, the Fon people exhibited their craft production, demonstrated their dances, inspiring a higher level of appreciation of syncopation in Western musicologists, and dazzled the small number of friendlier citizens of America with their genuineness and warmth. Frederick Douglass met them and was embarrassed. A.M.E. church member James Alston traveled to the fair from the East to witness it as a spectacular event, but also to greet these kinsmen from afar.[66] As the Fon marched almost daily in parades, among the other international contingents, they acted as goodwill ambassadors from Africa. At the exhibitions dispersed throughout the fairgrounds at the Agriculture, Liberal Arts, and Mining Buildings, diasporan and continental African progress was on display. From African American to Caribbean to Brazilian to Liberian exhibitions, the presence, spirit, and dynamic of the black world resounded.

Although there were no Chicagoans at the fair who could match the reputations and achievements found among the nationally prominent ranks of Frederick Douglass, A.M.E. Bishops Benjamin Tanner and Henry McNeal Turner, Rev. Alexander Crummell, Booker T. Washington, and Ida B. Wells, some Chicagoans did emerge as significant participants. Once on the fairgrounds, Fannie Barrier Williams, attorneys Ferdinand L. Barnett and Edward H. Morris, and Drs. Charles E. Bentley and Daniel Hale Williams— and others—lectured, observed, and played host to visiting African Americans from throughout the nation. In their homes, churches, clubhouses, and businesses they provided a level of hospitality sorely needed in a nation where civility and amiability could never be taken for granted.

On the local scene, Lettie Trent, Fannie Barrier Williams, Ferdinand L. Barnett, Revs. John T. Jenifer and Augustin Tolton, and others protested over the character of black representation in exhibits and administration at the fair as well as the lack of opportunities for becoming involved as lecturers and guides for visiting blacks. Transplanted Ohioan and Missourian Hale G. Parker performed his duties as Missouri's alternate delegate to the National

Board of Commissioners with efficiency, according to one influential local contemporary.[67] Of the few other black Chicagoans who participated fully, Fannie Barrier Williams contributed a great deal as she lectured at two major congresses. Using the Haytian Pavilion, where Frederick Douglass held court, as their headquarters, African Americans fashioned a presence rivaling that of other participating ethnic and racial groups. Chicagoans who had honored Haiti in the pavilion's opening ceremonies dropped by with visitors from time to time. Visitors Paul Lawrence Dunbar, Ida B. Wells, Will Marion Cook, and other rising stars of the Afro-American world were present almost on a daily basis. George Washington Carver and Henry Ossawa Tanner could be seen canvassing the fairgrounds and observing the fair's marvels. Dr. Charles E. Bentley reported on the activities in the field of dentistry as that profession's official observer. James Weldon Johnson, Bishop Henry McNeal Turner, and Robert Sengstacke Abbott were there, and hundreds, and probably, thousands of their racial kin joined them, experiencing exultation along with disappointments, enjoying themselves in every manner possible, benefiting from the event having happened, and leaving their imprint on American society.

Part of advancing the race involved building a network of like-minded individuals committed to their group's improvement through cooperative social, creative, and intellectual linkages. In this, African Americans accomplished one of their many goals for 1893 at this international conclave. Assuredly, in the most unequivocal of terms, there *was* a noticeable black presence at, matched by a fervent interest in, the World's Columbian Exposition of 1893.

Beyond the social acquaintances forged at the fair and the individual and associational connections being shaped among African Americans, who traveled from throughout the nation, the many intellectually stimulating encounters at more than one hundred parliaments and congresses proved equally appealing. African Americans participated in many of these major intellectual and social phases of the fair's activities, which included 1,245 sessions featuring nearly 6,000 speakers in various congresses, bringing blacks into contact with the 700,000 other participants. Of special importance to African Americans were those meetings featuring discussions on the Negro, women, labor, Africa, education, and religion. Pertinent issues were debated ranging from those nationalistic to those gender-related to those economic. The practicality of emigrating to Africa was explored at an eight-day conference titled "The Congress on Africa." The status of black women became the focus of more than six African American women speakers at the World's Parliament of Representative Women, one of the fair's most discussed conferences. At the Congress on Labor, the plight of the southern farmer, whether sharecropper, renter, or owner, captured the attention of the economically inclined mind. The scope of the world's fair extended beyond these conferences, with other less-heralded meetings that warrant examination, especially one that discussed the future of attaining civil rights.

Because of the attention the fair enjoyed nationwide during the summer of 1893, the three-year-old National Colored Men's Protective Association shifted the location of its planned convention from St. Louis to Chicago. The Protective Association aimed to fight against southern outrages such as lynchings, peonage, and disfranchisement and against discrimination and race prejudice everywhere. The agenda of this year's fair focused on implementing constitutional changes in order to revitalize the group's organizational structure. National in membership, representatives arrived from every state in the Union. Chicagoans were present but in small numbers, interspersed as they were among three hundred delegates.

Being a host group, Chicagoans asserted themselves to the extent they could with attorney Edward H. Morris, who was the national secretary of the Afro-American League; he temporarily presided over the conference. Morris balanced complaints of his heavy-handed decisions with smiles and wit, which allowed "management of some of the refractory brothers." In an important, initial contribution to the conference, Morris set the tone as he said, "we are here to try and hasten the time when all over the land the humblest, the poorest, the blackest citizen will not be obliged to beg and plead for the thing which he has the right to demand—ordinary justice and common fair play." Chicago attorney Edward H. Wright acted as secretary and read a paper entitled "The Immigration of the Negro to Africa." Acknowledging the many obstacles to enjoying full citizenship in America, Wright still argued that the most logical option for persons of African descent was to forego emigration to Africa. The spirit of Harriet Tubman and Sojourner Truth lived on as Ida B. Wells spoke forcefully about protecting the basic rights of citizenship. This line of discourse continued as Lettie Trent called for a boycott of the fair because of repeated racial slights extending back to 1891. Her militant tone disturbed so many present that they shouted her down.[68]

After three days of deliberations, the most salient results of the meetings were a commitment to return home and share new insights with local citizenry on the merits of the National Colored Men's Protective Association, and to vote on the constitution. A call to all African American organizations to support the next year's conference brought immediate support, as did the condemnation of a proposed Colored American Day, viewed as a move to separate the races. As the organization addressed its national commitment, it devised an inclusive organizational structure that included an

Iowan, George E. Taylor, as president, a Louisianan, an Arkansan, a South Carolinian, a Mississippian, and Ida B. Wells as vice presidents. Also, Wells and Lettie Trent served on the Ladies' Auxiliary Board of Directors. Edward H. Morris and Edward H. Wright joined the National Executive Committee and Committee to Address National Issues on Race, respectively.

More important, Frederick Douglass's presence at the opening session conveyed legitimacy to the organization's existence and program. When word spread that he would attend the meeting, even whites came to hear the American legend speak. Although Douglass entered the hall and initially sat inconspicuously in the rear, as soon as the conveners noted his presence they immediately asked that he speak from the podium. Douglass's speaking routinely meant he would challenge the perennial Caucasian obsession with the "Negro Problem." Douglass tore at the heart of the Anglo-Saxon's fixation on blaming the victim: "The black man was not a problem. He was a man. There was nothing problematic about the Negro. The Negro was all right," declared Douglass, who was described in the *Chicago Inter Ocean* as a figure "whose great head of white hair was very conspicuous among the darker heads of his brethren."[69] He concluded by challenging America to live up to its promise of opportunity for all as embodied in the Constitution and Declaration of Independence.

At the World's Congress of Representative Women, black women distinguished themselves along with others of the world's female luminaries. The voices of six black women shone. Two presented major addresses and four provided commentaries, but the address delivered by Chicago's Fannie Barrier Williams was certainly the most notable. In the years preceding the fair, Williams had gained acknowledgment as an accomplished speaker and, most importantly, a person of intellect. Her cerebral qualities—including her familiarity with the thought of the New England transcendentalists and facility in other intellectual matters—were balanced with her magnetic personality; she was described as "delightfully vivacious and pungent."[70] In her lecture geared for this Darwinian decade she would have to demonstrate an acuity in racial politics and race imaging as well. Whatever the depth of her presentation, she was sure to hold the mostly white assemblage's attention with her Victorian countenance, being "petite in size," and because her face was "one of rare sweetness of expression."[71] Described in the twenty-first century as a feminist pragmatist, on May 18, 1893, thirty-eight-year-old Chicago journalist Fannie Barrier Williams eruditely lectured on "The Intellectual Progress of the Colored Women of the United States since the Emancipation Proclamation."[72] Short discussions by Anna Julia Cooper of Washington, D.C., and Fannie Jackson Coppin of Philadelphia followed.

In her carefully crafted address of approximately 5,500 words, Williams analyzed the exploited status of African American women within the American political economy, their victimization by white leadership, the cruel and enduring legacy of slavery, and the hypocrisy of white liberals on the issue of social equality. Most important, black ears heard about their achievements despite seemingly insurmountable odds, along with recognition of the indomitability of black women as they protected and enhanced their virtue and sense of womanhood.

Williams's lecture perfectly fit the times, the place, and the audience. At times she exhibited prescience, but along with it she demonstrated the ability to place the contemporary status of African American women in time, both as to the significance of this event and their role in it. Fannie Barrier Williams declared: "The most important thing to be noted is the fact that the Negro people of America have reached a distinctly new era in their career so quickly that the American mind has scarcely had time to recognize the fact, and adjust itself to the new requirements of the people in all things that pertain to citizenship."[73] In the age of Social Darwinism, she spoke of progress achieved despite adversities and without outside assistance, pointedly declaring:

> There is no wish to overstate the obstacles to colored women or to picture their status as hopeless. There is no disposition to take our place in this Congress as faultfinders or suppliants for mercy. As women of common country, with common interests, and a destiny that will certainly bring us closer to each other, we come to this altar with our contribution of hopefulness as well as with our complaints.[74]

With power brokers within both the white feminist and domestic circles present, Williams sought to persuade disbelievers about the need for racial reform in America.

Further, deferential, but not obsequious to white liberals of the abolitionist stripe, she paid them compliments sometimes overlooked. She explained that the nation needed to pay attention to the special obstacles placed in the path of African American women because they were females and black. And, similar to Douglass's constant references throughout the summer to a white tardiness in extending justice to fellow citizens, Williams began in this manner:

> Less than thirty years ago the term progress as applied to colored women of African descent in the United States would have been an anomaly. The recognition of that term to-day as appropriate is a fact full of interesting significance. That the discussion of progressive wom-

anhood in this great assemblage of the representative women of the world is considered incomplete without some account of the colored women's status is a most noteworthy evidence that we have not failed to impress ourselves on the higher scale of American life.

She continued with this pronouncement of inherent and damning truth: "Less is known of our women than of any other class of Americans."[75] The reasons were obvious, but Williams reiterated them to an audience that had to feel shame for its past and current treatment of its fellow citizens, especially its women.

As to the issue over which white America most suffered amnesia, slavery, Williams lamented:

> While I duly appreciate the offensiveness of all references to American slavery, it is unavoidable to charge to that system every moral imperfection that mars the character of the colored woman. The whole life and power of slavery depended upon an enforced degradation of everything human in the slaves. The slave code recognized only animal distinctions between the sexes, and ruthlessly ignored those ordinary separations that belong to the social state.
>
> It is a great wonder that two centuries of such demoralization did not work a complete extinction of all the moral instincts. But the recuperative power of these women to regain their moral instincts and to establish a respectable relationship to American womanhood is among the earlier evidence of their moral ability to rise above their conditions.[76]
>
> [At the advent of Emancipation], yet it must be counted as one of the most wonderful things in human history how promptly and eagerly these suddenly liberated women tried to lay hold upon all that there is in human excellence. There is a touching pathos in the eagerness of these millions of new home-makers to taste the blessedness of intelligent womanhood.[77]

Williams clearly enunciated that from this sordid system of bondage, African American women had to fight for their virtue physically, their moral reputations verbally, the opportunity to work competitively, and the right to manage their households autonomously in the same manner as white women. On the related issue of social equality, she lambasted whites for using it as a shibboleth to justify discrimination and exclusion. Nonetheless, as an optimist, Williams claimed that the important strides made by diasporan women in education and religion resulted in a betterment of the entire African American condition. As a humanist and racial tactician, she advised against the harboring of any hatred against whites on the part of

African Americans, but she never deviated from her strong tone of demanding justice and equal economic opportunity. Moreover, unlike Fannie Jackson Coppin, who would laud upper-class whites while condemning the white middle and working classes, Williams would confront and attack the elites as well. Williams's appearance at this all-important conclave catapulted her into a world she had only dreamt of entering. As reported by her hometown Brockport admirers early in the next century, the positive image she evoked at a meeting of such importance and with such media glare represented true recognition of African Americans at the fair. In *The Story of Brockport*, local bias announced that her address was "considered one of the great utterances of that notable occasion." Numerous invitations to speak nationally followed her lecture, and she spoke on the means "to the uplift of the Colored race."[78] Indeed, perhaps Williams's address represented the best pronouncement on the black position at the fair, including Frederick Douglass's at Colored American Day on August 25, 1893.

At the end of the session, an invited guest, but an uninvited speaker, who was seated on the podium rose upon special invitation to address the assemblage. By his presence, demeanor, and message, the individual had to be the Sage of Anacostia, whose ubiquitous appearances became an integral part of fair activities. Frederick Douglass's stature loomed so large that he was the only male invited to speak after the opening session and before the General Congress of the woman's conclave. The response of Douglass validated Williams's demands and clearly stamped them as appropriate for the nation. Douglass's words carried such weight that a portion of his remarks must be repeated. He proudly concluded: "I have heard to night what I rarely expected to live to hear. I have heard refined, educated colored ladies addressing—and addressing successfully—one of the most intelligent white audiences that I have ever looked upon. It is the new thing under the sun, and my heart is too full to speak; my mind is too much illuminated with hope and with expectation for the race in seeing this sign. . . . Fifty years ago and more I was alone in the wilderness. . . . (Tonight I know that is no longer true and) . . . A new heaven is dawning upon us, and a new earth is ours, in which the discriminations against men and women on account of color and sex is passing away . . . the grand spirit which has proceeded from this platform will live in your memory and work in your lives always."[79] In light of his contribution to the pamphlet *The Reason Why the Colored American Is Not in the World's Columbian Exposition*, which had promulgated the idea of black exclusion, perhaps Douglass had begun to realize that the Colored American was indeed a part of the World's Columbian Exposition.

A century after her triumph, Williams inexplicably became the target of a criticism based on a misreading of historical records, reasoning as she was

Fig. 48. Lucy E. Parsons.
Charles H. Kerr Co., Chicago.

criticized both for supposed timidity in her utterances and for approaching white racial liberal Albion W. Tourgee to help refine her presentation with additional data about progress in the South.[80] Nevertheless, couched in eloquence apparent one hundred years after its utterance, the presentation helped build what has become an intellectual tradition of black feminism/womanism. In the evaluation of one twenty-first-century sociologist, Williams's presentation represented "a manifesto for women of color and for the white women who were their allies to join hands for a future built on the faltering ideals of a great land. It is little wonder that its powerful language and call to justice yielded controversy and debate."[81]

Future Chicagoan Ida B. Wells did not speak at the conference, simply because she had complied with Frederick Douglass's request to substitute for him on a scheduled antilynching speaking tour campaign throughout Great Britain.[82] This commitment kept her out of the country until after the opening of the fair. As soon as she returned from England, however, she headed immediately for Chicago, where she spoke frequently and fervently on various topics related to the African American condition. In her multifaceted pursuits, she proved herself the equal to any feminist of the day, with views encompassing the intellectual spectrum from emigration to culture to labor exploitation. Within a month of the fair's opening, Wells had her first opportunity to participate at the fair. She immediately sought out her mentor, Frederick Douglass, at the Haytian Pavilion and used that site as her head-quarters of sorts as she distributed the famed pamphlet *The Reason Why the Colored American Is Not in the World's Columbian Exposition*.

The Congress on Labor began its proceedings on August 28, 1893, against a backdrop of national depression and widespread unemployment. The Congress's relevance was manifest in the economic conditions of the day and in the very existence of the fair. Throughout Chicago, from the South Side to the lakefront and downtown, the specter of the unemployed, overwhelm-ingly white, appeared so real as to require its being hidden by city officials. Nonetheless, labor riots provided daily fare for the city's newspapers, which denounced the unemployed as ingrates, tramps, and communists and, in gen-eral, deserving of their plight. Chicago's most revolutionary black voice, Lucy E. Parsons, the widow of Haymarket martyr Albert Parsons, spoke con-stantly this year of capitalist injustices, but not on the fairgrounds, where she probably would have faced harassment or arrest.[83] A North Sider who lived in the midst of the radicalized German community as a matter of personal preference, Parsons was uncompromising in her exposure and denunciation of labor abuses, tenement housing, poor water, the exploitation of women, and other issues. A true revolutionary on the issues affecting labor, hers was a presence conspicuously missing and definitely needed to speak for north-ern black workers (Figure 48).

Henry George, the apostle of the single-tax idea and author of *Progress and Poverty* fame, spoke, as did other labor organizers, theorists, and agitators. Booker T. Washington from Tuskegee Institute journeyed north to present his speech "The Progress of Negroes as Free Laborers." He placed part of the blame for the plight of southern blacks on the backward Southern system of agricultural production and part of the Southern black's plight on his own ignorance. An unqualified Social Darwinist, Washington sincerely believed, as so-called ultra-assimilationists did, in maximizing one's efforts to succeed in a competitive world. Washington's experiences convinced him that his fellow blacks could succeed if they adopted new attitudes, especially regard-ing their need to *will* themselves to work out of their predicament.[84]

The Southern-born Ida B. Wells spoke at this conference as well, explaining how perpetual indebtedness contributed to the downward path to peonage. Chicago's contribution came as Lloyd G. Wheeler appeared and delivered a five-minute speech, presumably on the conditions encountered by the city's African Americans as they sought equality in the workplace.[85] Then Frederick Douglass vacated the chair in deference to Henry Demarest Lloyd, after reiterating his hostility to the sharecropping system. Strangely, in Douglass's departing remarks, the plight of the Northern African American working class—excluded by custom and relegated through connivance to the domestic and service trades—received no hearing. With the bulk of the African American population located in the South, Frederick Douglass could easily overlook them in his introductory remarks, saying "poverty in tenement houses in the city is nothing to the poverty of the colored farm tenant in the South." Of course, the reality of northern life in Chicago's Levee and in portions of the Dearborn Street Corridor stood as a rebuke to Douglass's oversight.

As the summer progressed, the Parliament of Religions, the fair's most anticipated convocation, began on September 11, 1893. This monument to religious tolerance was preceded and followed by a series of small denominational congresses extending from Sunday, August 27, 1893, to Sunday, October 15, 1893, which allowed for total racial inclusion. African American Protestant involvement was significant, and a delegation of African American Catholics even met as part of the Columbian Catholic Congress, giving them "a spotlight never dreamed of."[86] Headed by Chicago's Fathers Augustin Tolton of Chicago and Charles R. Uncles of Baltimore, they discussed the benefits of membership in their universal church and the encouragements evident in the rising recognition accorded African American Catholics.[87] For the larger conclave, Christians of various persuasions were joined by Hindus, Jews, Muslims, Baha'is, Taoists, and members of many other religions.

The focus as far as many blacks were concerned was on the African Methodist Episcopal Church. Bishop Benjamin Arnett spoke on "Christianity and the Negro" and Fannie Barrier Williams once again lectured. This time her topic was "What Can Religion Further Do to Advance the Condition of the American Negro?" With deep compassion, Williams called on her African American brethren among the clergy to make religion a force for good. With equal fervor she challenged America's white leadership to live up to the American Creed and extend opportunities and amenities of full citizenship to its African American citizens. "In nothing do the American people contradict the spirit of their institutions, the high sentiments of their civilization, and the maxims of their religion," she intoned, "as they do in practically denying to our colored men and women the full rights of life, liberty, and the pursuit of happiness." Religion was not to remain static in its theological mode; it should become activist in working to "unite, and not to separate, men and women according to the superficial differences of racial lines."[88]

The next important conference assumed high importance because of its provocative topics, outspoken lecturers, transcendence over oceanic boundaries, and relevance to the contemporary issues pervading African American

372 / Harbor of Opportunity, 1866-1900

life. It directly broached the question of emigration to Africa or permanent residence in America notwithstanding its ingrained racism. The Congress on Africa was unique in that it was held over an eight-day span extending from Monday, August 14, 1893, through Monday evening, August 21, 1893. The outgrowth of an idea developed by Frederick Perry Noble, the son of a Congregational pastor of a church in the racially diverse West Side of Chicago, the congress aimed from its outset to be reflective of the linkage between political democracy and humanistic religion. Noble took immense pride in his denomination's causes and could enthusiastically describe how "Congregationalism, by its freedom from any taint of complicity with human bondage and its work since 1839, has done more for the American Negro than any other church."[89] This conference encompassed the hopes and dreams of a panoply of white liberals and abolitionists along with Social Gospel advocates, as well as self-perceived humanistic imperialists, perhaps anti-imperialists, who wished to continue the tradition of bringing Africa into the orbit of industrial, Christianizing Western Europe. Interestingly, it fit into a pattern established at the Congresses of Berlin and Brussels (held respectively during the winters of 1884–1885 and 1889–1890).

However, as humanistic as the Congregationalists and other Protestants thought they were, the most compelling question before the conference had a familiar ring, given the context of the times. It involved the possibility of transforming the African, whether diasporan or continental, into a new person—an Afro-Saxon—who conformed more readily in temperament, disposition, and level of civilization to Anglo-Saxon standards. Even when attendees to the conference heard the voices of past and present nationalism in the persons of Bishop Henry McNeal Turner, Rev. Alexander Crummell, and a certain Professor Henderson of Straight University of New Orleans, theirs, too, were the voices of transformation, of making the continental African in his home a new and better African. Continental Africans thus faced a distressing transformation into the mold of Anglo-Saxonism.

Inasmuch as the Congress was being held in the United States, its scope was broadened to devote an immense amount of time to the status of the African American as subsumed under the rubric, "the Negro Problem." To many whites, this classification allowed them the opportunity to work out a problem close to home. In this sense it had great relevance to the process of urbanization and Americanization that the black population was undergoing. Of course, Frederick Douglass assessed the problem of America as a moral crisis involving inhumane treatment and requiring courageous action on the part of whites. Significantly, a conference that originated as an endeavor conceived by white American humanitarians, intellectuals, and foreign policy advocates to examine, validate, and perpetuate the most humane features of Great Power hegemony over the African continent, along with finding ways of eliminating the worst features of American racism, was to a great extent (and to their amazement) dominated rhetorically by the diasporan and continental Africans themselves. This marvel occurred partially because of the dynamism inherent in the invited African American participants. In their ranks were both assertive, educated Chicagoans such as Ferdinand L. Barnett, Ida B. Wells, Edward H. Wright, Rev. John T. Jenifer, and others, who joined visitors Frederick Douglass, Bishop Henry McNeal Turner, Rev. Alexander Crummell, John Mercer Langston, Bishop Benjamin J. Arnett, Henry Ossawa Tanner, Professor William Crogman, Hallie Q. Brown, and an impressive young member of Vai royalty from Liberia, Prince Monolu Massaqiou.

As the opening formalities ended, and the presentations proceeded, it was left to the iconoclastic Bishop Henry McNeal Turner of the A.M.E. church to create a "sensation." Following the reading of the paper on black continental progress prepared by a "Johnson of Nigeria," Turner rose to cover the same topic, though written on African American progress, while he explored the progress and contributions made by Africans of the diaspora in manufacturing and the trades. As was to be expected, he also touted the genius and resourcefulness of his group despite the obstacles imposed on African progress by an outwardly racist South and a smug, latently racist North.

Then Turner launched into a peroration on the African origin of humankind, the subsequent debt owed Africa, and the need for a new understanding between the races based on the two previous gifts:

> Revolting as the theory may appear to some present, I believe that all humanity started black—that black was the original color of mankind. That all of these white people present descended from black ancestors, however remotely in antiquity they may have existed. If theoretical geology is entitled to any consideration whatever, the time was when the poles of the earth and the now icebound arctics were so warm that the fjords of the now tropic zones grew there luxuriantly, and the same animals that now live at the equator roamed abroad in that ancient forest. This has been verified by the bones which have been found there of the animals now restricted to the tropical regions. So as I see it, instead of black being an abnormal color, an execrated color, a color to be despised and made the badge of degradation and infamy to the extent that it involves the humanity of those who are black, if it is any color at all it is the primordial, most ancient and original color of mankind.
>
> I have reached this conclusion after years of meditation with such lights as revelation affords to my understanding, aided by the stylus of geology and the archaeological collections found in the British Museum.

Yet my interpretations may be greatly at fault and my conclusions wholly absurd, but scientific analyses undoubtedly makes black the base of all color and the black man is, therefore, a primitive man.

The drift of nature, whether interpreted speculatively or historically, would, therefore, appear to be whiteward. Primitive man who doubtless has existed for ages longer than our chronology fixes it, in my opinion was black and is the father of the white races of the earth; and, the same black, primitive man gave to the intermediate color or red Egyptian civilization learning, sciences, and philosophy; including skilled labor in its highest form, and this red race has transmitted to the white races letters, poetry, logic mechanism, and all the fundamentalities that the white races have embellished, refined, and improved upon, until it has reached the grandeur of this world-famed Chicago exposition.

Without the black man, Christianity itself would lack a purpose. For while the white man gives it system, logic and abstractions the black man is necessary to impart feeling, sanctified emotion, heart throbs and ecstasy. Thus God and nature need the black man for without him there would be an aching void in earth and heaven. The universe would be in want of a balance wheel, and the God of eternity would again give to light the forgers of creation and perform another day's work before the morning stars would sing together and the sons of God shout for joy.[90]

The immediate response from the African Americans in attendance was enthusiastic and ecstatic. "His address [was] . . . something of a revelation to many of those present . . . [and] he concluded amid loud applause," read one of newspaper account.[91] At one point in the program, occurring shortly after an especially stirring rendition of one of the traditional "Sorrow Songs" by one of the original Fisk Jubilee Singers, the magisterial Bishop Anderson of South Carolina arose from his seat on the platform, raised his right hand and proclaimed, "Bishop Turner is right!"[92]

Turner's allusions to African genius from the days of antiquity struck a responsive chord among many African Americans. Their growing sense of specialness, of human agency, rather than a loathing of their very being, was pervasively evident in the city, as well as throughout the nation. Recognition of a special quality inherent in blacks was found everywhere in African American society but especially in Chicago among the refined and the respectables. For the refined, their belief in a specialness in African Americans manifested itself in their ability to compete and achieve in a hostile Anglo-Saxon world so rapidly after citizenship status was conferred. This constituted their reason for demanding equal footing in planning and managing the world's fair. Even though their efforts proved basically fruitless, it was not because of their lack of desire and preparation. For the masses of African

Fig. 49. Ida B. Wells-Barnett.
Special Collections Research Center,
University of Chicago Library.

American peasants found in the South and domestic and service-sector workers located in the North, they believed in their messianic mission to redeem America through their past and current sufferings and deprivations. Even the lower stratum of the undesirables knew enough about Anglo-Saxon foibles; seeing whites wallow in vice and corruption along the Levee, these blacks knew that there was nothing morally or physically special about being cloaked in a white skin.

If Turner's ending was thought-provoking and "sensational" at a fair ostensibly committed to proving Nordic, or Anglo-Saxon, supremacy world-wide, his expected presentation on the topic assigned was just as significant. He extolled black achievement, mentioning to an enthusiastic audience that it was Frederick Turner of Atlanta who had invented an air traction engine likely "to revolutionize" locomotion; that Stephen Smith of Philadelphia successfully turned a fifteen-dollar start-up amount in the coal business into an endeavor capitalized at $350,000 at his death; that a Mr. Jackson in Bermuda had established the largest dry goods store on that island; and that

William "Bill" Fisher of Columbia and Charleston, South Carolina, used his genius and skills to gain recognition as "the greatest architect in his day."

The joy ringing in the ears of some Chicago blacks resounded in the city's general press. Chicago's newspapers faithfully carried portions of Turner's postulation under such headings as "Black Adam in Eden," "Was Adam a Negro?" and "Negroes, Not Apes." Reaction to the bishop's utterances was respectful, with significant portions recalled without sinister or malicious comment. Moreover, he was described in daily newspapers as "one of the most learned and eloquent colored clergy in America."[93] It is uncertain what the *Conservator* and the *Appeal* wrote about his presentation, even though it would have fit into their pattern of extolling all things black.[94] Ida B. Wells, who had just written a piece somewhat favorable to African emigration after Bishop Turner's return to America from Africa, however, was not impressed in this instance. The irascible Ida B. Wells found Turner's manner uncouth and his presentation inelegant (Figure 49).[95]

Beyond Turner's praise for African American advancement, the program featured well-conceived scholarly papers on a variety of topics. One paper discussed "Diseases and Medicine in Africa" and was written by Dr. R. W. Falkin, a former resident of Uganda, now of the University of Edinburgh's School of Medicine. His presentation was followed by Chicago Provident Hospital's Dr. Daniel Hale Williams, who spoke on "American Negroes as Surgeons and Nurses." Williams's contribution cannot be overstated. At this point in his career he became the first surgeon to successfully complete suturing on the human heart, in which the patient survived. From his work at Provident and other Chicago hospitals, he built a reputation as an institution builder and was to leave for Washington, D.C., to head the Freedmen's Hospital and develop a framework from which other black hospitals would originate.

Finally, the eagerly awaited debate over African emigration commenced. To the white abolitionists and liberals of the 1890s, the mere mention of, let alone a debate on, emigrationism caused disappointment, embarrassment, and consternation. The voluntary departure of African Americans from the country would have clearly indicated that the nation had failed to live up to its avowed principles as embodied in the Declaration of Independence and the Constitution. Seeking to keep faith in the ability of their fellow Americans to respect both the spirit and the intent of the law in a nation of laws, these liberal whites sought affirmation from interracial gatherings such as this congress. As they interacted with diasporan Africans as fellow human beings, governed under the same rules as themselves, they aspired to convince them of white sincerity. To black Chicagoans with a half century of familiarity with the debate, the outcome proved revealing.

By the time Professor Henderson of Straight University read his paper in defense of leaving the United States, Bishop Turner had already more than adequately spread the gospel of emigration wherever he went in the city. Turner was correctly described as "having no faith in the future of his race in the United States, as he believe[d] the ignoble status of the colored people in the South and their scullion employment in the North [were] sources of degradation and nothing but nationalization [would] work out the elevation of the race and he holds that Africa is the field for that." Henderson began his address with a scenario familiar to students of this nation's history:

> Let there be formed a joint stock company such as those under which Virginia and Massachusetts were colonized, and let distinguished philanthropists without regard to race be asked to assist. Let a commission of experts be selected and sent to Africa to find a place for settlement. . . . Let 10,000 . . . persons be selected, such as artisans, bricklayers, machinists, doctors, lawyers, preachers, and teachers, every trade and profession necessary for the establishment of a civilized society. I have no doubt such a plan would be feasible. Our race would respond to such an appeal.[96]

Attorney Ferdinand L. Barnett of Chicago ably presented his side in rebuttal as he read absent New Yorker T. Thomas Fortune's paper, entitled "Should Negroes Colonize Africa?" It aimed to demonstrate why African Americans should keep faith in American's promise. The strength of Fortune's argument lay in the recognized failure of recent emigrationist projects, one of which less than a year before had left hundreds of departing diasporan Africans stranded in New York. Fortune's basic challenge rested in this question: "Why did the Germans or Irish not go back to their native land? What advantages does Africa offer the Negroes that are superior to those of the United States?" The *Inter Ocean*, the racially progressive white newspaper with a predilection to favor the anti-emigrationist, abolitionist position, reported, perhaps accurately, that "ringing applause . . . followed that left no mistake as to the answer."[97] However, it was Barnett's own personal comments, challenging the emigrationist position through ridicule, that supposedly neutralized it. Along with Edward H. Morris's earlier pronouncements on emigration at the Colored Protective Men's Association conference, the voices of the city's black elite rejected the notion of leaving America. The reaction of the city's respectables, the rank and file, is unknown, but this was not the end to the issue. For nationalistically inclined African Americans, the Congress on Africa and the presence of continental Africans at the fair stimulated an increased interest in Africa.[98]

The exposition's most controversial gathering, and the one that angered and infuriated more African Americans locally and nationally than any other, was Colored American Day, held on August 25, 1893. It originated as a result of concerted, nationally based African American protest about exclusion at the fair. Thus challenged by this charge of unfair treatment, the fair's managers set aside a special day for African Americans, much in the manner of the fair's Irish Day or Illinois Day. Colored American Day, in spurring intense national debate both pro and con, became one of the most publicized events held at the fair. Yet a scrupulous overview of the disparate activities of the fair in which African Americans participated indicated that Colored American Day was perhaps of tertiary importance among all the hustle and bustle on and off the fairgrounds. Ranking ahead of this solitary day's limited activities was the eight-day Congress on Africa that concluded triumphantly several days immediately preceding Colored American Day. Further, Haytian Day and the daily activities at the Haytian Pavilion ranked higher in importance. Yet Colored American Day earned unwarranted recognition because of the controversy surrounding it contemporarily and the interest it garnered subsequently through a misreading of the past.

The *Chicago Inter Ocean,* filled with pride because of the intellectual deportment of its black friends in holding substantive discussions during the Congress on Africa the previous week, chided African Americans that they had a racial obligation to insure that Colored American Day maintained a comparative level of decorum, and to "make it a day that will give other visitors as good an impression of the colored race as did the discussion and the attendance at the African congress last week."[99] As for Colored American Day, Frederick Douglass's involvement in planning the celebration pleased the racially progressive *Chicago Inter Ocean* immensely. Rightly so, because at the moment Douglass assumed the presidency of the committee planning the event, he began to envision it as a springboard from which to expose a standing criticism of the nation's treachery toward African Americans and to present a living exhibition of black accomplishment before an international audience. Douglass knew his acceptance of the position and association with the event opened him to criticism of accepting the "half loaf" when ideological consistency required rejection of a dubious honor. Nonetheless, the opportunity to demonstrate race achievement proved too attractive to dismiss this chance.

Local clergy led the formidable opposition to the event. Chicago's Quinn Chapel A.M.E. minister, Rev. John T. Jenifer, despised the rising popularity of the cakewalk and feared its possible appearance as part of the world's fair activities. Lecturing in 1892 before a multitude of eager listeners assembled at the church, Jenifer told the huge audience that "there are two ways in which a race may become distinguished. First, through its intelligence, its industry, progress and God-fearing good citizenship; second, through its ignorance, depravity, indolence, and antagonism to the genius of good government and the spirit of progress. I am pained to notice by the newspapers that some of our people are becoming distinguished by the latter method." As to the cakewalk, he referred particularly to this dance craze as a form of "Race luggage" better left behind. "We must abandon all these grotesque features that serve to remind others of our former degraded condition in life, and cherish the best that is at our command. We are in the midst of a journey from a past condition to a better [one]. Improvement has been made, but 'race luggage' still hampers some of us, holding back the entire race." The impending fair offered both an opportunity to demonstrate advancement and a pitfall to confirm backwardness, and a curious America would ask which image was more accurate. Jenifer concluded that "we may soon be called upon for the answer in the approaching world's fair."[100]

At Olivet Baptist, the mother church of the city's Baptists, Dr. J. F. Thomas also condemned the event. At a later date, Quinn Chapel's Dr. G. C. Booth, who replaced Jenifer, along with his fellow A.M.E. colleague, Dr. D. A. Graham at Bethel, opposed the special day. The same situation held true at St. Stephen on the city's West Side. Rev. J. E. Thompson of St. Thomas Episcopal spoke out because "he did not see the fitness of it." As hundreds of members of their congregations listened, the clergy preached the correctness of a boycott. As an alternative activity for Chicagoans and visitors, they scheduled a massive picnic for the following day far off the fairgrounds in a public park.

So, the refined element legitimately feared that Colored American Day might just as easily deteriorate into a "Jubilee Day," during which the most objectionable features of black folk culture and expression (in the eyes of the elite) might be exposed to white view. This last factor explained why the chasm between the elite and the respectables continued to widen. The latter could never fathom the depth of in-group resentment held by these parvenu African American racial leaders toward what they saw in their own eyes as worthy and legitimate cultural expressions. After all, the respectables had embraced European aesthetics as part of their holistic appreciation of culture from around the entire Atlantic rim, in the spheres of the beaux arts and in African-influenced indigenous forms.

Thus Friday, August 25, 1893, was a historic day, as African Americans gained the recognition they sought to present their story to the world. Socially prominent whites attended, pleasing Douglass and the others greatly. Their presence confirmed the arrival of blacks as equals in American society, if only for several hours on a solitary afternoon. Isabella Beecher Hooker, sister to

Harriet Beecher Stowe and Rev. Henry Ward Beecher, accompanied Frederick Douglass to the stage, to the thunderous applause of the twenty-five hundred persons who filled Festival Hall. Accompanying her were her two nieces, daughters of a Beecher who commanded the first black regiment in Civil War South Carolina. Hooker embodied the abolitionist spirit that historian James M. McPherson described as still vital in liberal circles in the nation.

The more assimilationist-minded among the elite were not the only African Americans who needed the affirmation that the presence of elite whites brought. Others seemed to believe white involvement confirmed the humanity of blacks in a white-dominated world. The attendance of approximately eight hundred whites—nearly one-third of the assemblage—further attested to the possibility of racial harmony. Phoebe Couzins, who had befriended African American interests during the period before the fair as a member of the Board of Lady Managers, attended. So did Baltimore Catholic priest Rev. John R. Slattery, who shared his plans for building a three-hundred-thousand-dollar facility to train African Americans for the priesthood.

However, some prominent African Americans failed to appear, such as the featured opera singer, coloratura soprano Sissieretta Jones, known as the Black Patti. Ida B. Wells stayed away from the celebration but retroactively reversed her assessment both of the propriety of staging the event and of its value to racial progress. Originally motivated by a whimsical impulse, she apparently responded to favorable white newspaper accounts of the event, especially in the *Inter Ocean*, by later seeking out Douglass at the Haytian Pavilion. There, she apologized to the "grand old man" for placing her youthful exuberance before the qualities of racial leadership he had displayed in deciding to participate. A.M.E. Bishops Arnett and Turner absented themselves from the event, and two of the committee's vice presidents also avoided the event. Former U.S. Representative John Mercer Langston skipped the event after having urged Chicago audiences previously that they should follow his lead.

First and foremost, the oratory of Frederick Douglass dominated the event and subsequently served as the standard for any evaluation of Colored American Day. Douglass's speech evoked great emotion and mesmerized an audience of the faithful. "Shaking his white mane and trembling with the vehemence of his eloquence the old man for more than half an hour held 2,500 persons under a spell," the *Chicago Tribune* reported.[101] Short addresses by whites composed another portion of the program. Musical selections of a classical nature represented an important segment. Last, musical selections and recitations from established and rising African Americans provided entertainment and enlightenment. So, in one sense, Colored American Day proved a total success as African Americans consummated their newly acquired absorption of high culture. Their mastery of European musical and literary endeavors could surely impress the white friends of the race who might spread the word that a "New Negro had evolved," one far removed in mental bent from his or her servile days in intellectual and physical shackles.

Nearly four decades later, Dr. J. A. Majors of Chicago, serving as one of several vice presidents on the committee, fondly reflected on the event as a shining moment for his race. Majors's reflections in 1929 on the eve of planning the 1933 world's fair provided a contrasting version to the tone of earlier African American denunciations of near-total racial exclusion.[102] The white press's treatment presented the celebration as a triumph for African Americans, especially in that they showed decorum in their dress and demeanor. The *Chicago Herald* commented that the "better type of Colored people" was present, represented by schoolteachers and ministers. The tone of the *Tribune*'s reporting indicated satisfaction both with the appearance of "prominent colored men" on the stage and with the appearance of the socially prominent Beecher family. The *Inter Ocean* featured the event with first-page treatment, led by the headline, "Honor to Their Race: Colored American Day at the Exposition a Success." Aware of dissent throughout black ranks, the newspaper aired the facts as they existed and immediately legitimized the staging of the event with its opening paragraph, which read: "Colored Americans day at The Fair, and the dignified manner of the observance, did honor to the race. Even in the face of opposition in their own ranks, with which those in charge had to contend, the celebration was everything that grand old statesman and sage, Frederick Douglass, had hoped for."[103]

The elite knew that the event's successes had to be pleasing to white eyes and ears; however, the criticism from the black press also carried immense weight. The *Cleveland Gazette* disappointed them by labeling the festivity "a farce."[104] Meanwhile, the *Indianapolis Freeman* reported on Chicago events to Chicagoans and to the nation as though it was the voice of Chicago, recently labeled the "Windy City." It assessed the event, with the exception of the oratorical and musical portions, as a great failure. Relying on misinformation before the event, the *Freeman* incorrectly reported that there would be no event at all. Once the event took place, the paper clumsily reported on it with some enthusiasm, emphasizing the program portion, which featured Douglass's memorable, resounding oratory. The *Freeman*'s assessment of failure finally relied on the low attendance at the event as well as on the fairgrounds. In its conclusion, the *Freeman* stated "the 'Negro Jubilee Day' has gone glimmering."[105]

When the gates of the World's Columbian Exposition closed permanently on October 30, 1893, the world had borne witness to anything but an unsubstantial African American presence at this event. No visitor to the fair could have overlooked the involvement of the African American and continental African. The congregation of the Quinn Chapel A.M.E. Church concluded the black connection to the fair by purchasing some of the salable goods left on the fairgrounds. They bought a beautiful German organ, one of the items of pride of that great nation's exhibit; the instrument is still in use to this date.

V. THE SOCIAL FABRIC

Contrary to both popular belief and even scholarly acknowledgment, segmentation existed within the complex social fabric of black Chicago. Rather than it being a homogeneous mass, there was an elite, along with an immense body of church-going, respectable working people, and the denizens of the netherworld who interacted, competed with, and ignored each other in this city of one million souls. Without clear-cut evidence of heightened stratification based on income, education, professional status, cultural affiliation, and physiognomy, especially complexion, St. Clair Drake's framework of a complex social world encompassing the refined, the respectables, and the riffraff still seems relevant. It therefore remains usable as an instrument to understand most aspects of life until a normative class system based primarily on economic position appeared.

A. The Elite

From our viewpoint today, A.M.E. minister Reverdy Ransom's reflections on the social structure seem complementary and telling. The well-traveled and college-trained clergyman assessed the composition of black leaders in this manner: "Among the Colored men, Theodore Jones was the most prominent in business. He had a fleet of trucks nearly a half mile long. Edward H. Morris stood at the head of the Negro lawyers in the city, while Edward H. Wright, Ferdinand Barnett, and S. Laing Williams were coming into prominence at the Chicago bar and in politics. In the medical profession, Drs. Dan Williams and George C. Hall were the most prominent, and in dentistry Dr. Charles C. Bentley enjoyed a large practice among whites as well as colored people."[106]

Offering hope to women seeking professional advancement, Chicago had its first (or second) black female physician sometime before 1893 in Dr. Carrie Golden.[107] She had the distinction of performing as a staff member of the "Emergency Hospital at the World's Fair and [also] read a paper on

Fig. 50. Ida Platt.
From Progress of a Race.

'Rheumatism' at the Congress of Eclectic Physicians and Surgeons."[108] In 1896, dentist Ida Gray Nelson opened her practice,[109] and Chicago-born Ida Platt, born to free parents in 1863, became the first African American woman admitted into legal practice before the Illinois bar in 1894 (Figure 50). Platt's admittance evoked a telling historical response from one of the judges: "We have done today what we have never done before, admitted a Colored woman to the bar, and it may now be *truly* said that persons are now admitted to the Illinois bar without regard to race, sex or color."[110]

Ransom's recollections are quite different from the memories of the anonymous physician who served as a source for E. Franklin Frazier in his oft-cited *Negro Family in Chicago*. Frazier's newcomer to the city recalled a city view as seen from the bottom up: "The leading business among the colored people was railroading. The headwaiters were at the top of society. They almost dictated social customs. A man prided himself that he was Mr. So and So's valet. Next to the headwaiters were the porters and then came the barbers. I have seen that whole thing change. First there were four colored doctors. Very few colored people employed a colored physician, they didn't believe in it. There was great rivalry between the home people and the strangers. I was known as an interloper."[111]

The "home people" that the physician mentioned were maturing in their role of being molders of the dynamics of urban life, whether economic, civic, political, social, or recreational. Early in the next decade and century, they would organize the Old Settlers Club. Contemporarily, Rev. Abram T. Hall's son, Charles Edward Hall, formulated his assessment of high society from his vantage point in the state capital. Editor of the *Springfield Illinois Record,* he possessed the perfect medium and social background from which to deride Chicago African American society as being composed of "shams, monte banks, empirics, and clowns," while extolling the virtues of the first generation of antebellum days.[112]

Conflicting observations notwithstanding, the refined constituted Chicago's elite, its aristocracy, its socially prominent persons who represented black Chicago's version of white New York's privileged "400." In Du Bois's writings after the fair, the refined held the status he ascribed to a "Talented Tenth." As to African American Chicago possessing an aristocracy, or "400," that depended on accepting that little more than several dozen individuals were the equivalent of 400, and that their lack of wealth and prominence was inconsequential in modern capitalist America. Nonetheless, in the racially segmented world of Anglo-Saxonism, they did constitute a recognizable cultural and color elite among African Americans and had every right to claim reality to be whatever they wished. In 1896, the *Chicago Daily News* described this group as the city's African "400." In an article entitled "Colored Belles to Come: Chicago's African '400' Agog over Prospective Visit," the newspaper reported that "the members of Chicago's Colored '400' are getting ready to entertain four young women who are recognized as the leaders of Colored society in the United States. These young women, who have long scoffed at the idea of the existence, among the representatives of their race, of 'society' in Chicago, have sent out an olive branch, and, to emphasize the acknowledgment of their error, will be here about the middle of May."[113]

While remaining socially polite, these visiting maidens could not have found the society to which they were accustomed in Washington, D.C. ("considered the very top of the Negro world"), New Orleans, and Charleston in existence in Chicago in 1896. The young women were described in the following manner: "Miss Summerville is petite, plump, good-looking and shows little trace of the African. . . . Miss Pinchback is tall and dignified and has frequently been mistaken for a white woman. . . . Miss Griffin is an accomplished young woman of the Creole type. She has expressive eyes and is a clever conversationist."[114]

The views of this elite on racial identity revolved primarily around the question of how closely its members would align with or distance themselves from the sentiments associated with the mass of persons of African descent. The elite eschewed by choice the derivative African- and southern-based cultural practices and heritage that composed the Afro-American subculture.

Like many persons of color in color-conscious America, the elite's concern with skin color bordered on the obsessive. While it was routine for white America to denounce a dark complexion as ugly and belonging to an Amazon, from either America or Africa, and to extol the virtues of a fair complexion, the same was true for many Afro-Saxons.[115] When he visited the city for the world's fair, Paul Lawrence Dunbar, a favorite of cultured northern whites, was touted by them as a pure Negro, showing their awareness of the difference.[116] Similarly, they could chide mulatto Frederick Douglass because of his African bloodline and features.[117] Repeated references to Douglass's "mane" being reminiscent of a lion's is telling since it also carried a connotation as to color.

Whether this tension over skin color existed in Chicago to the same extreme as it did on the East coast, and in the South, in cities such as Charleston, New Orleans, and Washington, D.C., is conjectural.[118] However, awareness of color distinctions pervaded all of the corners of Afro-Saxon America and working-class Afro-America. Robert Sengstacke Abbott's early experiences in Chicago after 1897 convinced him that an internal color line existed, as he was dissuaded from pursuing a career in law by Edward H. Morris because of his dark complexion.[119] As Chicago prepared for the next century, continuous demographic growth and occupational differentiation produced a discernible socioeconomic change in previous sociocultural categories that did result in clear-cut class distinctions. If there had been an aristocracy with justifiable numbers in the aggregate, Fannie Barrier Williams would have headed it, along with her husband, the Bentleys, and the Wheelers.

The foremost historian on the "Negro 400," Willard Gatewood, described the characteristics of an aristocracy of color where, consistent with St. Clair Drake's assessment, the attainment and method of attainment of wealth played a limited role in determining "standing." As in New York, the elite in Chicago were a class delineated partially by their own self-definition. According to Ottley and Weatherby, in both cities, "unnoticed by the white world, a Negro upper class which lived in the manner of typical *middle-class* white families had come into being."[120] The elite in Chicago were expected to participate in the civic sphere open to persons of abundant resources and options, a world of self-sacrifice, as opposed to the world inhabited by ordinary citizenry, which was marked by an emphasis on personal enjoyment and self-aggrandizement. White aristocrats had options, but rarely did Chicago's "Colored 400" seek additional vestiges of respectability by adoption of the elements of civic virtue. They did display an appreciation of what whites considered high cultural attainment, however. Social skills related to recreation held a lower importance; cultural interests counted more heavily. Sophistication, attainment of cultural traits and preferences for the finer items of life, and education, represented the components making this "class."

Significantly, when a host family offered appropriate lodgings to Frederick Douglass at the time he returned for the formal opening of the fair in the spring of 1893, the S. Laing Williamses greeted him at their door—located far from the Dearborn Corridor—to greet him. Home life for the Williamses was "unusually charming and happy. The[ir] choice of pictures and an ample library give an air of refinement and culture" to their residence.[121] More often than not, dinner outside the Williamses' home meant that the Lloyd G. Wheelers were the host and hostess.[122] Dr. and Mrs. Charles E. Bentley were not to be overlooked, however, as they hosted W. E. B. Du Bois as an extended guest in August 1899. By this time, the couple was comfortably residing in new housing at 383 East Forty-fourth Street in the wealthier Grand Boulevard neighborhood.[123] No doubt it was into this circle that Richard R. Wright Jr. was invited when he arrived to study at the University of Chicago. As the son of the president of Georgia State Industrial College, located near Savannah, he was "frequently invited to the homes of many colored people in the upper intellectual and economic brackets."[124]

A social figure highlighted in Frederick H. H. Robb's *The Negro in Chicago* (1927), but apparently unrecognized as part of the elite, was George Kelly of the 3500 block of Federal Street. A former steward at the Wellington Hotel, Kelly owned "Kelly's Mansion" at 3531 Federal, referred to as "the center of social life in its day . . . [and] the mecca of the intellectual as well as the wealthy." During the world's fair, "such notables from far and near as Frederick Douglass, Paul Lawrence Dunbar, the Haytian ambassador," and others met and dined at the mansion.[125] The extent to which Kelly gained permanent acceptance into the circle he entertained has not been determined. However, the basic obscurity attached to his name and status no doubt answers the question.

Individual advancement found Fannie Barrier Williams reaching the apogee of civic leadership as she was accepted into membership at the Chicago Woman's Club in 1895. In and of itself, this one notable exception to racist exclusion in social advancement qualified Williams as a member of Chicago's civic establishment. Meanwhile, Mary Richardson Jones was being supplanted as the leader of refined society as Mrs. Fannie Emanuel, the wife of Dr. William Emanuel, moved up. A far South Sider, Mrs. Emanuel "had the genius for organizing entertainment on the standard of New York's Fifth Avenue . . . [importantly] under her, lily whiteism vanished. Professional achievement instead was the standard of her circle. The lawyers and doctors flocked to the leadership of the Emanuels."[126] One example of the Emanuels' love of festivity took place in the warmth of a Chicago summer evening as they "entertained a large company on a trolley party"

Fig. 51. Mary Richardson Jones.
*Vivian G. Harsh Research Collection of Afro-American
History and Literature, Chicago Public Library.*

that wound its way from the middle South Side, at Sixty-third Street and South Park Avenue, southward to the outer suburban ring (Figure 51).[127]

The acquisition and accumulation of wealth did not automatically confer elite status, as evidenced by the apparent lack of elite status afforded to several high-profile persons upon their deaths. For example, the politician John W. E. Thomas died extremely wealthy by African American standards, with an estate of $100,000, yet he was apparently not considered a member of the elite. In addition, Daniel "Uncle Dan" Scott had amassed a small fortune of $100,000 from saloon keeping and the cartage business at the time of his death in 1895; he too seems not to have been accepted into the elite.[128]

This assessment proved true within the broader social sphere that existed simultaneously with the staid world of imagined civic virtue and cultural refinement inhabited by the refined element. The blame for obscuring this meaning to posterity rests with twentieth-century sociologist E. Franklin Frazier, who set into motion an acceptance of a skewed view of the city's inner social dynamics. He embraced the parochial recollections of a newcomer to the city as an indicator of an extant, general pattern of social mobility and status. The interviewee was a migrant of the 1890s who joined the ranks of the physicians in the early twentieth century but spoke retrospectively of "good times" and a social world dominated by Pullman porters and domestic personnel with close contact to wealthy whites.[129] Within this milieu, social skills in language were important, and valet, porter, and waiter were transformed into the raconteur, the conversationalist, and the hunter and "sporting man" at home in the Dearborn Street Corridor.[130]

In the aftermath of the fair, and with social change apparent, the appearance of a new "Ward McAllister" from outside the ranks of the refined was not unexpected. One generation removed, Drake and Cayton explained the process in the twentieth century that allowed someone like Julius Avendorph to emerge: "The upper class admits to its circles many whose incomes are far less than theirs, but who possess other valued attributes, such as advanced education or high standards of public decorum."[131] Julius Avendorph, who was a private messenger to the white real estate magnate and civic leader Ferdinand W. Peck, found his niche at this time and supposedly succeeded businessman Lloyd G. Wheeler as black society's chief social arbiter, or standard setter. He bolted dramatically onto the social scene as a social organizer and master of ballroom decorum through the pages of the *Western Appeal* in 1891. While Wheeler was described in 1893 as being a man with "considerable money and [who] increases his opportunities as social dictator by liberal expenditure," Avendorph could match his alleged predecessor in neither expended income nor social prominence. As for the myth that Pullman porters, or other occupational groups who produced leaders, *dominated* black society, it could have occurred only within their own social domains. Daniel Hale Williams's comments from about 1888 rang much truer.

In any event, after 1893, it is reasonable to assume that Avendorph now stood as decorum master over many major social functions, which featured the same cuisines and wardrobe styles associated with higher-status whites. Avendorph grew in popularity, but he was always careful to avoid involvement in any of the issues of the day, such as the racial strategies that formed an integral part of the world of civic affairs.[132] In 1891, during the major civic dialogue of the day on whether African Americans should found a black hospital and training school for African Americans, his name was not mentioned. And when the influential white Unitarian minister Rev. Celia Parker Woolley established the Frederick Douglass Center early in the new century to afford the refined element an opportunity to mingle with their white counterparts, the name of this social arbiter never appeared. Even more indicative of his overall status, he never joined the aristocratic ranks of African Americans composing one half of the leadership of the Chicago branch of the National Association for the Advancement of Colored People (NAACP), which began in 1910, as S. Laing Williams, George Cleveland Hall, and Charles E. Bentley did. Membership in this organization carried the ultimate status attached to Afro-Saxon arrival in the American mainstream and therefore represented a litmus test for *civic leadership* for generations of blacks.[133]

Comparatively, other northern cities presented a variety of scenarios, showing the uniqueness at times of African Americans as they adjusted to local conditions and exigent circumstances. The composition of the highest social leadership in Chicago stood in stark contrast to a more inclusive grouping in Philadelphia, which included caterers, clerks, teachers, professional men, and small merchants.[134] Among these Philadelphians were families with lineages that stretched over generations, along with those of more recent wealth and educational achievement. Importantly, Philadelphia was home to the Boulé, an ultra-exclusive club. In Washington, D.C., the criteria for membership in the elite were stringent: "[E]lite blacks based their social status on their ties with prominent whites, their skin color, and their family backgrounds." Historian Jacqueline M. Moore continued: "They were obsessed with being seen as distinct from the race and therefore acceptable to the white community. Their principal concern was their own assimilation."[135] The situation in Chicago could not have been more different, for it lacked an aristocracy, familial and social ties to socially positioned whites, and an obsession about complexion. Erstwhile frontier, white Chicago measured status by the successful pursuit of wealth and a supposed upward social movement based on the meritorious acquisition of wealth. This explains why black Chicagoans, as bona fide Chicagoans, entered into the race for wealth through the ownership of businesses and professional endeavors. Edward H. Wright and Robert S. Abbott represented notable examples of success in Chicago.

In Cleveland, Kenneth M. Kusmer found that its small black populations in 1890 and 1900 of 3,035 (1.2 percent of the city's total) and 5,988 (1.6 percent), respectively, were "dominated by a small upper class composed mostly of merchants and small entrepreneurs, skilled craftsmen, barbers who owned their own shops, headwaiters in exclusive establishments, and a few doctors, lawyers and other professionals." Gatewood informs us that George A. Myers of Cleveland was a barber, but not an ordinary one. "He was a substantial entrepreneur, and his Hollenden House Barbershop was an elaborate establishment with a sizable staff. Its clientele included the most influential white men in Cleveland . . . [and Myers] was also an important political figure in the Republican organization of Senator Marcus A. Hanna."[136] In New York City, Brooklyn, and Boston, pedigrees dating back to Dutch settlement as well as to the Revolutionary War marked an early standard of acceptability. Employment of white servants also marked their status.[137] Ivy League education and "blue veins" further substantiated top-ten status, as black status faded while white standards of status soared.

B. THE RESPECTABLES PERSEVERE

The ranks of the respectables increased, consistent with the growth of the general population, for they represented the bulk of the African American citizenry. Their positive self-perception, which matched the externally held view of them, was based on their hard work, commendable public deportment, church affiliations and voluntarism, and acquisition of property. This was the group that allowed Booker T. Washington to extol the virtues, strengths, and successes of African Americans to influential whites in the North as he sought their economic and moral support. His salutary description, in fact, paralleled that made in *Scribner's Magazine* several years earlier. "When, even in the North, the shop, the factory, the trades have closed against us, have we not patiently, faithfully gone on taking advantage of our disadvantages, and through it all have we not continued to rise, to increase in numbers and prosperity?"[138]

Until a more formalized class structure developed, which would happen within a decade, the respectables would serve as a middling group in this socioeconomic setting. As the twentieth century approached, newly arrived professionals who were not yet socially established (such as E. Franklin Frazier's "anonymous physician") were counted among the respectables, as were federal and municipal employees and service-sector workers receiving varying and higher rates of pay and with diverse work responsibilities. Their role historically would be to contribute to a new phase in Chicago's development in which the most disparate black society ever appeared. But for the present, their sociocultural moorings overshadowed the growing economic differences between them and other African Americans.

The public deportment of these younger men and women among the respectables led the community moralists, both in the pulpit and in the press, to express shock and disappointment. To the white world and to the older generation of African Americans, these young beneficiaries of the sacrifice and successes of the early postwar generation seemed to be letting their race down. The complaints centered on the excessive amount of time spent by both sexes at the racetracks in Garfield and Washington Parks, as well as the wasteful activity of the young men in loitering around downtown saloons and ogling women.[139]

C. Life among the Economically and Socially Depressed

As interesting as the successes and lifestyles of the more affluent and average residents were, an even larger number of Chicagoans barely eked out a living. The economically depressed were adrift in a sea of humanity; clearly, a true underclass was beginning to exist. Monroe N. Work's canvases of the African American community convinced him of an interrelationship between churches and nonreligious populations, a scarcity of work, and an increase in the crimes of larceny, burglary, and robbery. He found that, as the century ended, the growth of a criminal class conformed to a decrease in economic opportunity: "there [were] a large amount of unemployed Negroes in the city, numbering several hundreds"; Work surmised that "could a census of this class be taken, it would no doubt be found into the thousands. From this class the ranks of the criminals are recruited."[140]

D. Interracial Relations

The notion of achieving racial equality in all dimensions of the social sphere still awaited its mature appreciation by the post–World War II population as a possibility rather than a theory.[141] And there was another important component to the dualism of egalitarianism. Richard R. Wright Jr., who traveled from his native Georgia to study at the newly founded University of Chicago, sought to meet a challenge that even tested the unproven concept of equality of opportunity: "The main thing that intrigued me was that I would go to school with white men and women and have an opportunity to test my ability with theirs. I had faith that I would be equal to the task. I had never sat in a class with whites, never debated them, never tested my prowess against them in anything; never even worshipped with them in church. I was most anxious for contact on what I thought would be fairly equal grounds—in the North. The thought of social equality never entered my mind—it was intellectual equality that thrilled me."[142]

While one would assume that members of the elite—such as S. Laing and Fannie Barrier Williams, Hale G. Parker, the Lloyd Wheelers, Ferdinand Barnett and Ida B. Wells-Barnett, and the Charles E. Bentleys—would be alone in seeking their earned rights through the channel of equal opportunity, those at the other end of the social spectrum, with so little at stake in society, nevertheless became equals in their shared misery. This feature became another variant in racial adjustment. Simply put, impoverishment produced interracial commiseration. Many of the city's poor overcame racial considerations and learned to live together harmoniously.[143]

The ability of so many African Americans among the respectables to participate in the same type of activities open to other Chicagoans who shared
their economic status brought some satisfaction to their lives. What African
Americans wanted, though, was an unfettered opportunity to pursue happiness as they defined it. Some racially condescending utterances of Mayor
Carter Harrison at the world's fair only served to show how far America and
Chicago had to advance in their attitudes. For the racially naive, who
thought that antebellum attitudes had disappeared with the Union's military victory in 1865, an address by the mayor of Chicago, Carter G.
Harrison, at a black conference on civil rights during the world's fair corrected that misperception. As he welcomed the delegates, he resorted to a
combination of his stock political antics mixed with southern paternalism
to deliver a most unusual address. The liberal, former Kentuckian quickly
reminded the delegates that they were wise to remain ambivalent about the
nation's abilities to keep its promises of equal protection and opportunity
for all as it worked its way to a color-blind solution to national problems.
The mayor's racial paternalism emerged just as quickly as he talked of faithful African Americans in his home state who still referred to him as "Massa
Cartah." He continued his insults through references to African American
women. "I am one who thinks the nut-brown skin capable of higher beauty
than that of the Caucasian skin," the *Chicago Evening Post* reported, as it
whimsically noted that the mayor could not resist such insensitive remarks
as "the influence of the blarney stone soon asserted itself." Harrison continued, "I have seen black men whose forms were as handsome as an Apollo
of ebony. But there is a prejudice against you. It will take time to eradicate
it. Don't try to do it in a day. Don't try to break down such prejudices. Live
with them with honest earnest conduct."[144]

Since no Chicago politician could conclude a meeting without self-con-
gratulation, the mayor's peroration included references to the political
progress he had engineered through his African American appointments.
Most notably they included police and fire departments' hirees, along with
a second female employed in the Chicago Public Library. Fortunately, the
dignified and forceful presence of Frederick Douglass at the fair, and particularly his stirring oration on Colored American Day, acted to neutralize the
mayor, who had truly been the embodiment of the Blarney stone.

Racial differences influenced the search for equality in living. The question of whether African Americans saw themselves in this last decade of the
century as part of a "problem" (as Du Bois was to define racial relations in
his *Souls of Black Folk*) presents a problem in itself. Hale G. Parker did not
view himself as part of a problem, as evidenced by his pursuit of inclusion
in the world's fair as an administrator, a position he sought and won. His

comments in 1892 clearly illustrated that he saw an American imperfection, but not a black one. The same position was enunciated by Frederick Douglass during the fair's inaugural ceremonies held in October 1892 and at Colored American Day in August 1893.[145] The nation, not black Americans, had a serious problem, and one that it had to resolve without projecting it onto the backs of a specific group.

The city's downtown jewel, the Loop, attracted all citizens and experienced limited instances of racial discrimination. While African American access to housing in many neighborhoods as well as some downtown theaters and community recreational venues was slowly becoming restricted, many downtown hotels, such as the Palmer House, Sherman Hotel, and the Auditorium Building complex, welcomed them.[146] African Americans who proposed to hold a benefit for orphans in the Loop at Central Hall in February 1893 met no opposition and concluded this charitable event with success.

The protocol of race as it was practiced in Chicago under optimum conditions had to be proven to an apprehensive Ida B. Wells-Barnett by her mentor, Frederick Douglass. What the latter assumed from decades of experience in the racially fluid North, Wells-Barnett had to experience herself. In a world's fair experience at the Boston Oyster House, a popular white restaurant, she grew to appreciate the idea that full privileges of worth, status, and service in America could extend to African Americans, even if only the privileged ones. Although she was "cocked and primed for a fight if necessary," Douglass was relaxed and chided her about her apprehensions.[147]

Once Wells-Barnett established permanent residency in Chicago and began interacting with whites, she became aware of many nuances to the problem of establishing harmonious race relations and cultivating friends among the city's powerful and influential whites. Simply put, notwithstanding the presence of a social "400," African Americans lacked the financial and political power to protect themselves and their rights without outside assistance. When in 1900 the Chicago Tribune floated a proposal for racially separate schools in Chicago for the first time in its history, and the paper's southern-born and -raised editor displayed little interest in social justice in the matter, Wells-Barnett felt compelled to take the matter to a proven friend, Jane Addams.[148] The result was victory over overt racism.

A visitor to Chicago from England, Rev. Charles F. Aked, whose acquaintance with Wells began with her tours in behalf of eliminating the scourge of lynching, showed her the importance "in giving a real lesson in democracy to our [white] American friends." Since northern whites, in particular, knew so little about African Americans through social contact, Aked felt that it was imperative that the refined element seek to inform them about another side of black life. "He thought that when we could do so without sacrificing self-respect, we should make it a point to be seen at lectures, concerts, and other gatherings of public nature and thus accustom white people to seeing another type of the race as well as their waiters and cooks, seamstresses and bootblacks."[149]

This was similar to advice given by Judge Albion Tourgee, who admonished Ferdinand L. Barnett to persuade African Americans to attend events organized to support the cause of racial justice. "I have never complained of [a] lack of appreciation from your people," he wrote, "because I saw the reasons of their failure to manifest approval, but I have been forced to take note of it by what I saw was its effect on others. I [have] known many thousands of your people [who] have the same feeling towards me which you express, but I should never guess it from their conduct." Tourgee would lecture, and almost no blacks would attend, leaving the whites who responded wondering as to what their real intentions were. Meanwhile, at the University of Chicago, black students were welcomed and fully participated in academic and extracurricular activities.[150]

Among persons of both races who labored with their hands, the artificial boundaries of skin color often broke down more quickly than they did elsewhere. The increasing frequency of interracial statutory marriage, common-law marriage, and casual courtship proved this, as did the existence of Chicago's Manasseh Society, a club consisting of more than a hundred mixed-race married couples. So despite the contemporary popularity of Social Darwinian racial tenets, America avoided a caste system.

Egalitarianism suffered in the city during the world's fair as some of the more unsavory sentiments of white Chicago, along with southern visitors, covertly or overtly espoused and practiced racism. Most notable was the spate of bias, misinformation, and falsehood produced by the media of the period—journals, magazines, souvenir books, novels, and newspapers. Most egregious were many of the souvenir books and photographic collections, of which there were more than 600. But even with their biases, *Scribner's, Independent, Atlantic Monthly, Cosmopolitan,* and *Frank Leslie's Illustrated Weekly* did inform their readerships. *World's Fair Puck* announced early on that it intended to ridicule anything or anyone that it found to be silly or weak, so throughout the fair it operated as an equal-opportunity offender.

Ferdinand L. Barnett was astutely aware of the depth of the race problem, and this affected his view of the World's Columbian Exposition. Just as Frederick Douglass did, he applied the litmus test of racial justice to the high point of American accomplishment at the end of the century. When he did, what he found left him disappointed, and he wrote about it in *The Reason Why the Colored American Is Not in the World's Columbian Exposition.* In this major contemporary document on race relations, Barnett wrote that "theoret-

ically open to all Americans, the Exposition practically is, literally and figuratively, a 'White City,' in the building of which the Colored American was
allowed no helping hand, and in its glorious success he has no share."[151] Wells
and his coauthors created an exceptional statement of the hopes, fears,
achievements, disappointments, and grievances of many African Americans;
the book illustrated the nature of the complications to be overcome as well
as the complexities of the historical circumstances to be understood. As a
protest tome, it was compelling. Polished and detailed, it represented a new
level of rejection of American racism. However, as it denounced the nation's
failed attempts to keep its promises, the pamphlet's early judgments on the
fair did not allow time for the fair's events to unfold, including what in truth
were many shining examples of African American brilliance; black agency
certainly grasped the opportunity to achieve a small portion of its racial agenda.

In Chicago, the absence of massive assaults or race riots showed that overt
racial antagonism was kept to a minimal level, partially because of the progressive municipal and civic attitude opposing racial violence as well as due
to the defiant, rather than passive, character of African Americans, which
was known to all potential antagonists. In 1896, when striking Italian workers attacked and killed strikebreaking southern blacks en masse in downstate
Spring Valley, the response from Major Buckner of the Ninth Battalion was
to organize armed men and proceed southward to protect fellow blacks. He
was dissuaded from this militant response by the more determined, conservative elements within the African American community. Meanwhile,
North Side labor agitator Lucy Parsons had previously encouraged the
Italian workers in their resistance who, from her anarchist perspective, were
the aggrieved parties in this contest between government-backed capital and
downtrodden labor.[152]

In the educational sphere, when vigilance and courage were needed the
most in 1900, Ida B. Wells-Barnett led a crusade to derail a campaign by the
Chicago Tribune to determine if white Chicagoans wanted to implement a
system of segregation in the schools.[153] Chicagoans, of course, did not.

VI. THE CULTURAL FABRIC

The major cultural and technological event of the late nineteenth century,
the World's Columbian Exposition, introduced the black Chicago population to aesthetic expression's most dynamic element, that of cultural inter-
change and sharing. Scott Joplin developed the rudiments of ragtime. The
young poet from Dayton, Paul Lawrence Dunbar, worked at the Haytian
Pavilion, impressing Frederick Douglass immensely; Henry Ossawa Tanner

(displaying his painting *First Lesson on the Bagpipe*) presented his paper "The American Negro in Art"; and a youthful George Washington Carver, still deciding between careers in painting or agricultural chemistry, won first prize for his drawing of *Yucca gloriosa*. The vocal arts of elocution and singing were represented as well; Tuskegee's dean of women Hallie Q. Brown stirred her audience as she explained that black women needed education, "time, and an equal chance in the race of life"; and the powerful and accomplished soprano Sissieretta Jones captivated her listeners with her rich operatic voice, as did the baritone Harry T. Burleigh, then studying at the National Conservatory of Music in New York. The contingent of Fon people from Dahomey, more than one hundred strong, broadened America's appreciation of syncopated music through drumming and other instrumental playing. Interestingly enough, at the Haytian Pavilion, Frederick Douglass barred Fon drumming, which was heard nightly in Haiti as the music of Vodun. The Great Sage threw his lot in completely with the beaux arts and thereby continued to demonstrate his disdain for any part of African-based popular culture. His day came on August 25, 1893, with Colored American Day, which featured classical and operatic renderings, including his grandson, Joseph Douglass, on the violin, and Paul Lawrence Dunbar reading an original poem, "The Colored American," as well as from his soon-to-be-famous collection, *Oak and Ivy*. Overall, the success of Colored American Day rested primarily on effective presentation of the audible word—read, spoken, and sung, along with the musical chord.

Significantly, black interest and support for the arts—both beaux arts, or what we know as the fine arts or grand culture, and mass culture—preceded the appearance of a socioeconomic differentiation relegating aesthetic interests to particular segments within the population. Sociologists have explained that culture is organic and a process and therefore no one group's special preserve. Hi̶s̶t̶ . . . ̶evine placed nineteenth-century appreciation of t . . . stence of "culture on a vertical plane." This long . . . :d a scenario in America during which a broad-bas . . . ıre and opera developed. Various elements within A . . . ledged their appreciation of the language, moral v̶a . . . : in the case of the former, and the intrinsic beaut . . . d to exaggerate the ubiquity of operatic music in n . . . ica," Levine wrote. E. Franklin Frazier's amazement . . . sherwomen and maids appreciating classical perfor . . . rican masters of various genres at Chicago's Orchest . . . s lack of understanding of the traditions of black Chicago and of the ability of all forms of cultural expression to inspire admiration for their intrinsic value among all people.[154]

As the century waned and a new one waxed, differences in cultural tastes—from budding and major to only slight—existed between no more than one hundred highly assimilated Afro-Saxons and fifteen thousand less-acculturated Afro-Americans. Between the refined element that was highly educated and sufficiently impressed by what passed for white standards of behavior and tastes, an affinity naturally grew. The rank and file, which contained few educated persons, had many members who were also willing to savor the white world's refinements while simultaneously cultivating an appreciation of their own race's aesthetic productions in music, dance, and literature. Persons of unmixed African descent at the mass level identified themselves primarily by the construct of race and cultural affinity for the perpetuation of their African-based way of life. Not to be overlooked, in their own way, the socially dispossessed contributed to African American mass culture in their haunts of iniquity, exemplified by the rise of jazz and jazz clubs.[155] As time passed, with successive waves of migration bringing more persons intimately associated with the Afro-American subculture as their primary communal focus into the city, the influence of the subculture over the once-broad aesthetic tastes of the community increased.

Both the elite and ordinary folk came forward late in the nineteenth century to embrace the fine arts in music during the World's Columbian Exposition of 1893. Years before that event, the expanding South Side community engaged in activities that recurred weekly. The music of choice revealed another dimension of black cultural transformation under way since Emancipation. Not unexpectedly, when the fund-raising committee of the Masonic Orphans and Old Folks' Home, located at the south end of the Dearborn Corridor at Thirty-sixth and Armour streets, planned its first major benefit to aid its building fund, it decided on a venue and program suited to both its purpose and aesthetic tastes in music. African American mezzo-soprano Flora Batson, billed as the "Queen of Song," was scheduled to sing at the Central Music Hall in downtown Chicago on February 15, 1893. The program included Batson along with two of the city's aspiring sopranos and two of its tenors in a concert that promised to satisfy the shared musical appetites of both the refined and respectable elements. But consistent with the times, the program also included other fare, in this case Miss Octavia Lucas, whose lineage included Irish forebears, which she showed as she rendered her presentation in that European dialect.

As a civic venture the Masonic program was consistent with the emerging character of the respectables as they grew to appreciate various genres of music usually assumed too aesthetically advanced for their tastes. Revealingly, Ferdinand L. Barnett's name appeared as the only recognizable member of the refined among its board of directors. So, in reality, it was reflective of the respectables' ability to appreciate the most exemplary of American culture in the beaux arts while transcending the worst features of American racism in everyday life. Rather than succumbing to negative aspersions about the African physiognomy, a careful examination of the promotional flyer shows no attempt to hide the singer's racial features as it extols her artistic abilities. So, not unexpectedly, the plethora of summer concerts held during the world's fair were noticeable for their depth of variety, artistic quality, strong popular support, and racially uplifting emphases.

Meanwhile, within the major African American area of settlement, churches along the Dearborn Street Corridor between Twenty-sixth and Thirty-first streets continued an African American tradition of providing a salutary venue along with ambience, status, and an audience for African American events and cultural development (Figure 52). As to this audience, its potential came from a church membership representing perhaps 60 percent of the population.[156] Newspaper accounts highlighted Bethel A.M.E. as the source of most of these fair-related activities, with collateral events taking place at Quinn Chapel A.M.E., Olivet Baptist, and Grace Presbyterian. Intellectual, cultural, and social activities revolved around an attempt at status transformation. The secular choices reflected the congregation and pastor's appreciation of the operatic and the classical. Using the instruments, voices, and selections associated with these genres, concert performances consummated a summer of both cultural elevation and creative enjoyment. Violins and pianos proved the major instruments of choice. The range of voices was balanced, including coloratura and mezzo-sopranos, contraltos, baritones, and tenors. Well-known performers of operatic pieces with experience in major operatic venues appeared before appreciative church throngs. Female singers, such as Maria Selika, Deseria Plato, Maggie Porter-Cole, and Sissieretta Jones, and other concert-stage artists, including well-known baritone Harry Burleigh and tenor Sidney Woodward, from the National Conservatory of Music, performed for admiring audiences. Will Marion Cook and Joseph Douglass delighted audiences with their virtuoso violin performances.

Musical selections included the "German Conqueror's March," a part of "From Craig to Sea"; "A Friar of Arder's Grave"; Arditi's "Magnetic Waltz"; and selections from Romeo and Juliet, The Merchant of Venice, and Il Trovatore. Popular songs of the day leaned toward the melancholy and serious, epitomized by "O, Promise Me" and "Out in the Deep."

Elocution and recitation took their place on the stage, too, as Ohio's Hallie Q. Brown, Boston's Ednorah Nahar, and Henrietta Vinton Davis enthralled listeners with their masterful blend of word and gesticulation.

The plethora of summer concerts was notably rich in artistic quality,

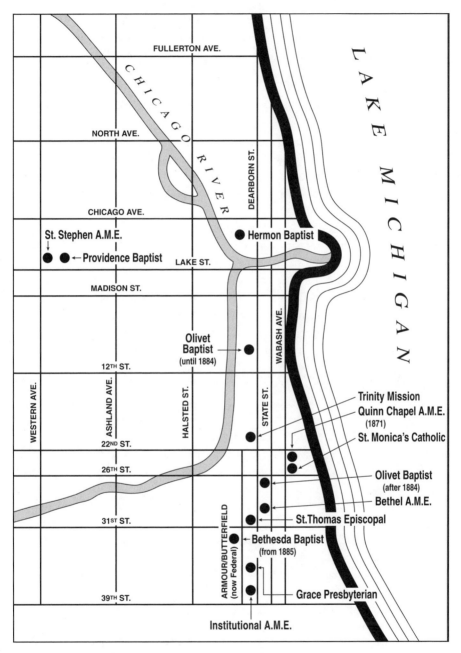

Fig. 52. Locations of Chicago's African American churches, 1880s and 1890s.

depth of variety, strong popular support, and racially uplifting emphasis. On July 25, 1893, the *Indianapolis Freeman* reported that Rachel Walker of Cleveland, a "soprano of enormous sweetness, the acknowledged prima donna of her state" would perform in a "concert of unusual magnitude" at Bethel. Joining Miss Walker on the stage were "Miss Edith D. Bushee of Aurora, Illinois, contralto and whistler, who, in company with Professor W. A. McCormack of Riverside, Illinois, the world's famous whistler, have won laurels everywhere they have appeared." Miss Valetta L. Winslow, a former Chicagoan, returned from San Francisco, "where she is the declared dels-artist of the state" to perform and visit the fair. On Tuesday evening, August 8, 1893, a special Emancipation Concert was held, again at Bethel, and featured singers, elocutionists, whistlers, violinists, and dramatic actors, who entertained to the delight of a capacity crowd.

Meanwhile, white saloons along Clark Street in the vice-ridden Levee District, and located one to two miles north of the major African American settlement, provided a venue for popular music and other forms of entertainment.[157] It was in this venue that Scott Joplin found part of his inspiration for ragtime, a strongly syncopated musical form ancestral to jazz and created within half a decade after the closing of the world's fair.[158] Joplin became the unparalleled master of the new musical form as he blended the African and the European into a new American musical idiom. Reflecting on the advent of ragtime, Cook described it thus: "The public was tired of the sing-song, samey, monotonous, mother, sister, father sentimental songs. Ragtime offered unique rhythms, curious groupings of words and melodies which gave the zest of unexpectedness."[159] Meanwhile, the popularity of songs written by blacks increased, with whites also enjoying the new music labeled derisively as "Coon Songs."[160]

Showing their appreciation of the beaux arts in the realm of formalized European-influenced painting styles, African American male and female students attended the Art Institute of Chicago in small but increasingly significant numbers from the turn of the century on.[161] To accommodate the needs of young people requiring training in acceptable mainstream dance, a private dance school taught the rules of etiquette, personal presentation, and ballroom dance movement.

Activities that were more mentally engaging occurred at the regular Thursday night meetings of Bethel A.M.E.'s Payne Literary Society. The diverse topics included "Social Distinction," "The Past, Present, and Future of the Negro," and "Bravery of the Colored Soldiers in the Wars of the Republic." At the same time, Quinn Chapel's Quinoniam Lyceum League provided nourishment for the mind by presenting its intellectual fare. Leading political and reform figures such as former Virginia congressman John Mercer

Langston, Frederick Douglass, and Ida B. Wells spoke on issues of national importance. Wells had selected this neighborhood as her home during the summer of 1893, just as she chose Chicago as her permanent place of residence after leaving New York City for a tour of the British Isles to promote her antilynching campaign in early 1893. The Men's Sunday Club of the Bethel A.M.E. Church represented perhaps the most significant gathering in which the intellectual matters of the day were discussed, including those of greatest importance as well as the mundane. Speakers, respondents, and the audience engaged in long and apparently heated discussions about lynchings, racism, Booker T. Washington, and any appropriate national and local responses.[162]

Club activities, both literary and social, grew. The Lotus Social Club, located on the West Side at 1165 Washington Street, catered to the leisure needs of all of the leading African Americans. It was described as having "a handsome club house . . . [with] the basement devoted to billiards, pool and buffet. On the first floor are the parlors and the reading and lounging rooms. The card rooms are on the second floor." Notably, at the conclusion of the fair, the newly formed Ida B. Wells Club for women and young maidens joined with the Albion Tourgee Club for men to offer both joint and gender-separate activities. The Prudence Crandall Club continued to enjoy its fine reputation for cultural presentation and intellectual enrichment. On one such occasion, at which Frederick Douglass spoke, its president Lloyd G. Wheeler opened the meeting with his customary sophistication; then Longfellow's "Psalm of Life" was sung, and Dr. Charles E. Bentley followed with a paper on "The Men of the Anti-Slavery Movement."[163]

Moreover, the scope of black, self-directed charitable efforts expanded, contrary to later beliefs that a systematic and effective approach to caring was nonexistent. In 1893, the Masonic Orphans and Old Folks' Home raised money for its operations through a fund raiser in the Loop that featured opera, popular music, dramatic readings, and Irish dialect. Two years later in 1895, Amanda Smith purchased property in the Dearborn Street Corridor and opened the Industrial Orphan Home for Colored Children. The Phyllis Wheatley Club was organized in 1896, followed by Rev. George W. Dickey's effort to salvage the lives of young women, new to the city, at the Rescue and Industrial Institute. While some madams attempted to justify their promotion of prostitution through contrived societal need and personal avarice, Dickey acted out of altruistic motivation "to do something for our young women . . . [who] come to Chicago in large numbers every year, and drift about in this great city without any guidance or friends."[164] At a cost of $10,500, he purchased a three-story structure at 2838 Dearborn, which accommodated sleeping facilities on the top floor and self-supporting skills, such as typewriting, stenography, sewing, housekeeping, and cooking, on the second.

Recognition of the moral and racial imperative to care for literal and fictive kin, along with any aging and sickly African Americans, motivated a member of Quinn Chapel A.M.E. Church, Mrs. Gabrielle Knighten Smith, to initiate an effort to provide care for this vulnerable segment of the community. Because of her "deep concern over the lack of an adequate, comfortable and cheerful place of refuge for aged Colored people," she opened her home in the Dearborn Street Corridor to five older citizens. A subsequent expansion of services led to the establishment of the Home for Aged and Infirm Colored People, which opened in 1892 and was chartered in 1898. Securing a permanent and spacious structure came from the efforts of Mrs. Smith and the benevolence of a white friend of the race, Mrs. Bena Morrison. The home consisted of eleven rooms situated in a two-story wooden frame building. Well-appointed and well-kept, it housed thirteen residents, whose ages ranged from 60 to 128 years. All were lucid, with vivid memories of "dark and dismal" days for African Americans as well as experiences since Emancipation.[165] The ubiquitous Lloyd G. Wheeler headed the board of directors, whose ranks included well-known community and political activists. With the establishment of these institutions and activities along the Dearborn Street Corridor and elsewhere, African Americans were demonstrating that they were embracing ideals and a civic commitment that showed maturity in urban adjustment.

Nationally, African American intellectual progress could be measured by the success of the American Negro Academy. Founded on March 5, 1897, under the leadership of Cambridge-trained Father Alexander Crummell of St. Luke's Episcopal Church in Washington, D.C., it strove to "promote the publication of scholarly work; [and] . . . to aid, by publications, the dissemination of the truth and the vindication of the Negro race from vicious assaults." W. E. B. Du Bois belonged, as did Professor Kelly Miller of Howard University and John. Wesley Cromwell of Boston. Black Chicago's recognized male thinkers in residence were Charles E. Bentley and S. Laing Williams. Although Williams was constantly pursued to produce scholarly materials for the academy, for some unexplained reason he failed to generate even one piece of literature, analysis, or narrative.[166] Evidently, Bentley also fell into the same category. Professional duties and the nine-hundred-mile distance between Chicago and Washington, D.C., might have prevented any active participation by either man.

The limited information that Williams shared with the academy, however, is revealing in that he understated the creativity existing around him. To him, Chicago, and apparently the Midwest, had not produced writers of any note by 1897; only George Washington Carver's painting at the 1893 world's fair had caught Williams's eye as to African American artistic merit, and scientific inquiry and creation rested solely on the shoulders of William Douglass of Chicago, who had invented an improved reaper. Two years later, Williams noted that in his estimation, the picture in Chicago was not completely bleak because the successful Sunday Men's Forum at Bethel A.M.E. served as a base for intellectual stimulation, exploration, and mental uplift of the entire community.[167] Careless in his replies for whatever reasons, perhaps professional overextension with legal matters, Williams had failed to mention the activities of his own Prudence Crandall Club, along with other important activities with which he was intimately familiar.

VII. INSTITUTIONAL DEVELOPMENT

The last few years leading up to the new century seemed to be filled with an accelerated burst of human energy accompanied by increased associational efforts. In a variety of associational and institutional efforts aimed at meeting the varied and growing needs of black Chicagoans, African Americans organized new groups and activities at a furious pace.[168] In the churches, a new pattern of worship evolved, one quite different from the usual Sunday ceremonies performed in much of the rural and small-town South. For many, emotionalism yielded to the serenity of northern, cosmopolitan African American church life. This shift in emphasis seemed at first aimed at the customary—how to celebrate the greatness of God and the influence of the church's commitment to the Creator. Notably, it also sought to purify the soul while it elevated the African American's intellectual and cultural appreciation to include mainstream America's values found in the high culture associated with higher education and the beaux arts. At the same time, other African Americans left the larger, more established churches as they transformed into more sophisticated bodies of worship. Mainly newcomers, they sought the emotional, comforting atmosphere that mission and storefront churches offered.

A. Churches

Churches, most importantly, continued their tradition of providing not only a salutary venue for spiritual salvation, but also ambience, status, and an audience for black events and cultural development. Intellectual, cultural, and social activities revolved around an attempt at behavioral transformation and, thereby, a change in status. Church governance provided males with training and experience in administration as they fulfilled their roles as deacons, trustees, and ushers, roles that, in scope of authority, went far beyond the men's mundane responsibilities. Clerical authority, and spiritual leadership over black Chicago, nevertheless rested in the hands of a learned clergy.[169] Early in the 1890s, ministers with college training pastored to the Christian faithful at three Baptist churches, Olivet, Bethesda, and Providence; three African Methodist Episcopal (A.M.E.) churches, Quinn, St. Stephen, and Bethel; St. Thomas Episcopal Church; Grace Presbyterian Church; Emmanuel Congregational Church; and St. Monica's Catholic Church. From these ten churches, along with the smaller missions, the clergy administered to the needs of religious African Americans and influenced daily behavior immensely, so powerful was the church as a social agent. The one Catholic church in this Protestant-led city was under the leadership of Father Augustin Tolton, the first African American priest in the nation.

The role of women in the church increased steadily. Historians Hine and Thompson have written about the growing influence of women in the A.M.E. church as they assumed the roles of stewardesses and even traveling evangelists, at least outside Chicago in the latter case. "At Sunday services, women were significantly in the majority, both in the pews and in the choir. The organist, or pianist, and choir director were usually women. Women were the chief fund-raisers for the church and for mission work. They were the church visitors, taking comfort to the sick and sick of heart, as well as food to the hungry. Men stood in the pulpit and sat on the church board; women did everything else."[170]

At Olivet, Rev. J. F. Thomas, pastor of the oldest black Baptist church in the city, ministered to the needs of two thousand members in a new edifice at Dearborn and Twenty-sixth Street. Thomas was described as a "pulpit orator of much power." Bethesda was led by a Rev. Dr. Birch, who was considered "one of the best educated ministers among the colored people." The A.M.E. churches shared ministers from a national pool of educated clergy. Quinn Chapel changed pastors in May 1893 as Rev. J. M. Townsend, who received his degree from Oberlin College, replaced Rev. John T. Jenifer. Townsend's résumé included a mix of scholarly training, world travel, and political office-holding in Indiana. Bethel was pastored by Rev. Dr. D. A. Graham, who was in his thirties and was an ardent prohibitionist. Grace Presbyterian, only five years old in 1893, experienced an increase in membership under the leadership of its pastor, Rev. Moses H. Jackson. Dr. James E. Thompson still presided over St. Thomas Episcopal Church. Catholics looked to Father Augustin Tolton to lead them at St. Monica's.[171]

The influence of this enclave extended far beyond this corridor to west of the Chicago River, where Providence regularly received trained clergy called through the Wood River Baptist Association and screened at Olivet. Nearby Providence was St. Stephen A.M.E., the other major denominational institution serving African Americans on the city's near West Side. Rev. D. Brown, the son of an A.M.E. bishop, earned the sobriquet of "one of the ablest of the younger men of the church."

The dynamism that marked church life throughout the century continued unabated. During late 1897 and early 1898, Monroe N. Work noted that there were twenty-four churches in existence, ten of which owned both their buildings and the land upon which they rested. The remainder were smaller mission churches, functioning in rented property such as storefronts and other buildings. One of these was Rev. Richard R. Wright Jr.'s Trinity Mission, located in the area around Eighteenth and Clark in the slum area sometimes referred to as "Darkest Africa."[172] Wright, trained at the University of Chicago, sought to bring Christ to the most economically deprived of the masses.

There were setbacks, as well: St. Monica's Roman Catholic Church, an island in a sea of Protestantism, suffered a devastating blow in 1897 when Father Tolton died; membership waned, and the church reverted to mission status for the next thirteen years.

Work estimated the combined church membership to be 6,500, which meant that the available 10,000 church seats were only partially filled. Including casual church visitors, who only attended church for funerals and cultural events, the number reached 12,000. However, this unfortunately left 10,000 nonchurchgoers outside the reach of positive organized institutional life in what Work described as "one of the greatest social factors in [African American] social life."[173]

In accordance with A.M.E. policy, Quinn Chapel rotated pastors in May 1893, as Rev. J. M. Townsend, who received his degree from Oberlin College, replaced Rev. John T. Jenifer. Within four years, Archibald Carey assumed the helm of Quinn Chapel A.M.E. Carey, a Georgian who claimed a birth and upbringing in slavery in the master's house, entered Chicago religious and political life with a boom. While pastoring in underdeveloped Florida, he ambitiously had requested an assignment in Chicago. Once he planted his feet on prairie soil, at the age of twenty-eight he immediately began to build Quinn Chapel into a solid institutional base from which to achieve his personal aspirations. His contemporary, Reverdy Ransom, described him as "intelligent, resourceful, and very ambitious for domination among men." Carey was described as "a stormy preacher. Being light in complexion, when he preached his face became as red as a beet, the veins and arteries of his neck and throat seemed ready to burst, and the people often shouted uproariously."[174]

Ransom and Carey quickly became rivals for religious and spiritual leadership over the city's African Methodists, although the former claimed he notified Carey that the city was big enough for both of them to pursue their interests. Nonetheless, the rivalry grew so intense that to insure peace Ransom acquiesced to his African Methodist colleague and allowed President McKinley to speak at Quinn Chapel instead of Bethel. Quinn Chapel easily accommodated at least nine hundred congregants and usually attracted that number regularly.[175] Still unsatiated in his quest for political power by 1900, Carey aligned himself to a rising white political star in the person of fellow Republican William Thompson, who was running for an aldermanic seat.[176]

Ransom, for his part, had taken charge of Bethel A.M.E. in September 1896 and immediately began to put in place progressive changes that were warranted by changing times and conditions.[177] He launched an excursion into combined church and social work in July 1900 with the formation of Institutional Church and Social Settlement. Reflecting the national mood of activist Protestants who provided the impetus behind the Social Gospel movement, Ransom's venture modernistically attempted to meet the needs of the new emerging urban population. This group of migrants faced problems of unemployment, juvenile delinquency, inadequate child care for working mothers, illiteracy, scarcity of wholesome recreation, and lack of proper intellectual stimulation among a myriad of ills and personal challenges. Not unaccustomed to church politics himself, Ransom was able to purchase the former abandoned Railroad Chapel at 3825 Dearborn for $34,000, after he secured financing from the well-organized national A.M.E. church body. The commodious brick building contained an auditorium that accommodated twelve hundred persons, a gymnasium, a swimming pool, a dining hall, a kitchen, and enough rooms seemingly for every idea and activity that Ransom and his wife could imagine.

Initially, Ransom was forbidden from holding morning services on Sundays by the A.M.E. bishops, who were influenced by anxious ministers at Quinn and Bethel worried about an attendance drain. Finally, Institutional A.M.E. offered Sunday morning sermons that spellbound enormous crowds every week. Ransom was charismatic and a workaholic, and his reputation grew steadily as the community increasingly appreciated the results of his social service activism. His approach, which embodied understanding, compassion, and the activist religious enthusiasm of the Social Gospel, obviously proved totally successful over time.[178] White youngsters played with black youngsters in the gymnasium. White mothers left their children with black ones at the day care center and at the kindergarten. His able ministerial assistant in this venture was Rev. Richard R. Wright Jr.

Beyond the mission of the Social Gospel, high-profile church weddings further cemented the importance of two religion-based institutions—the church, and matrimonially inaugurated family formation. Ida B. Wells claimed Chicago as her permanent home in October 1894 and, in the process, personalized her link to the community. She moved into the heart of the Dearborn Street Corridor and began a relationship with the African American community of Chicago that bloomed continually until her death in 1931. Meantime, a mutual admiration had developed between Wells and the widowed, popular attorney Ferdinand L. Barnett during the writing of the world's fair pamphlet, *The Reason Why the Colored American Is Not in the World's Columbian Exposition.* Over a short period of time, it turned to mutual affection. Ida B. Wells had found two romantic permanent sanctuaries, falling both in love with the city and with her fellow polemicist. Rev. D. A. Graham officiated on Thursday evening, June 27, 1895, as Ida B. Wells married Ferdinand L. Barnett in a standing-room-only wedding at Bethel A.M.E. Church and in what was probably one of black Chicago's most publicized social events.[179]

In her autobiography, the bride of 1895 recalled, "The interest of the public in the affair seemed to be so great that not only the church filled to overflowing, but the streets surrounding the church were so packed with humanity that it was almost impossible for the carriage bearing the bridal party to reach the church door."[180] Acting as a sign of what positive results could come from salutary interracial contact, a large number of whites from the bride's Republican party network attended the reception, which was held at 2905 Wabash Avenue, a short distance from the higher-status white areas of the city.

Another impressive public wedding occurred on December 27, 1897, at Grace Presbyterian Church, when Chicagoan Eugenia Burns and Professor John Hope of Roger Williams University in Nashville exchanged vows. According to Gatewood, the church, and thus the wedding, was aristocratic. Supposedly, the nine-year-old Grace Presbyterian "counted among its congregants many of the city's most prominent black families."[181]

Over on the West Side, along the Lake Street Corridor, Afro-American culture and the influx and influence of more migrants with a distinctive worship style led to another trend. Mass-based, emotive longings ushered in the formation of the Friendship Baptist Church in 1899. Because of its small congregation, slow growth, and related financial deficiencies, Friendship emerged initially as a mission church. It was up and running and highly attuned to the needs of a specific cluster of worshippers. It sought expressly to serve the needs of migrants and disillusioned Old Settlers who desired a form of church life steeped in the southern tradition of free expression of their faithfulness and spirituality, not of northern highbrow intellectualism.[182] At Friendship, there were no restrictions placed on congregants to conform to Anglo-Saxon and Afro-Saxon norms. From this point onward, the mix of elitism and mass impulses of the Providence and St. Stephen churches would stand in marked contrast to the mass-oriented Friendship. Following the pattern in Philadelphia that W. E. B. Du Bois observed, "each church form[ed] its own social circle, and many stray[ed] beyond its bounds."[183] Newspaper accounts highlighted Bethel A.M.E. as the source of many of the world's fair activities, with collateral events taking place at Quinn Chapel A.M.E., Olivet Baptist, and Grace Presbyterian. One might surmise that the dynamic presence of the African Methodist Episcopal Church leadership at the fair as well as the location, capacity, pastorship, and prominence of Bethel itself explained the latter's importance in the summer of 1893. As the city's third A.M.E. Church, it fit into the prominent role held by white Methodism locally and by African Methodism nationally.

In the city's premier house of worship, the membership of the Men's Sunday Club of the Bethel A.M.E. Church engaged in long, heated discussions about lynchings, racism, and the racial uplift policies of Booker T. Washington. The creation of Rev. Reverdy Ransom, the Men's Sunday Club drew in up to five hundred men to its sessions.[184] By the summer of 1899, "owing to intolerable conduct and disorder," a portion of the membership censured those accused of untoward demeanor; the latter bolted and reorganized as the new Men's Sunday Club at Quinn Chapel A.M.E. Church just a mile north. Meanwhile, the men in the rump group at Bethel reconstituted themselves and chose a new name, becoming the Men's Sunday Forum. S. Laing Williams was in the thick of the debates and claimed an active hand in restoring decorous behavior within the group. He corresponded frequently with Washington and proudly announced that the Men's Sunday Forum embraced within its ranks the men of substance of the community. The list was impressive and was "composed of men fairly representative of the best life among the colored people of the city." Included were Colonel John R. Marshall of the Eighth Infantry Regiment of Spanish-American War fame, attorneys Edward H. Morris, Hale G. Parker, Edward H. Wright, and Edward Wilson (who was the group's president), State Representative William L. Martin, Doctors Daniel Hale Williams and George Cleveland Hall and, of course, S. Laing Williams himself.[185] The group claimed that its aim was to be "practical in its usefulness," which meant that Washington's pragmatic approach had welcoming ears in Chicago. That is not to say that it was gradualist in a city known for its power to imbue dynamism. The diversity of its membership in terms of politics, social life, and ideology proved otherwise. Nor was it lacking in the intellectual power to contest any public policies and utterances that ran counter to the traditions of assertive, competitive black Chicago.

B. Fraternal Organizations and Activities

The various fraternal orders continued to grow as their appeal proved successful to an expanding community of men and women who sought beneficial and meaningful institutional affiliation. Fannie Barrier Williams described their place thus:

> Next to the Negro church in importance, as affecting the social life of the people, are the secret orders, embracing such organizations as the Masons, Odd Fellows, Knights of Pythias, True Reformers, the United Brotherhood, . . . the Ancient Order of Foresters, and the Elks. Nearly all of these secret orders have auxiliary associations composed of women. . . . The colored people believe in secret societies. I believe it safe to say that fifty per cent of the better class of Negro men are enrolled in some secret order. These affect every phase of their social life and represent the best achievements of the race in the matter of organization. In no other way is the organized Negro so reliably responsive to the requirements of his social obligations. In no other form of organization do the terms brotherhood and mutual obligations mean so much. . . . The lodge, more than any other merely social organization, is a permanent and ever-increasing force.[186]

Leaders of the units within the Masons, Elks, and other groups assumed a major role in the lives of African Americans who belonged and others who admired them from near and afar.

Nonreligious, secular activities thrived also during these enlivening times. During the summer months of 1899, Chicago was filled with various conventions. The successor to the defunct Afro-American League, the Afro-American Council, met in Chicago during August 1899 at the same time that the newly organized National Association of Colored Women's Clubs (NACW) did. Luminaries, both established and on the rise, appeared. From the ranks of national protest and gradualist circles, A.M.E. bishops Alexander Walters and Henry McNeal Turner, W. E. B. Du Bois, Booker T. Washington, along with T. Thomas Fortune from New York City arrived to confer in Bethel A.M.E.'s meeting rooms as part of the council's proceedings.

Josephine St. Pierre Ruffin came from Boston, and Mary Church Terrell—whom Ida B. Wells-Barnett considered the most educated African American woman in the nation—was the NACW's president and arrived from Washington, D.C. Local input assumed an importance as, according to sociologist Mary Jo Deegan, Fannie Barrier Williams assumed a "leading role" at the proceedings.[187]

In a preview of future contention, Booker T. Washington reached the city but avoided participating in the council's deliberations or meeting delegates. His plan was to block the new organization from criticizing the Republican party and President McKinley for its silence on widespread lynchings. He accomplished this through a secret meeting he arranged with the president of the council, Bishop Walters. The result was the development of a local version of a growing national dichotomy related to the most appropriate course of action to protest lynchings and other racial trouble. This ideological cancer was noted within the ranks of the refined especially, but it also extended into the ranks of the respectables. At the center of the contention was the ideological position claimed by Washington of Tuskegee Institute in Alabama. Since the death of Frederick Douglass and the media attention showered on Washington after his address before the Cotton States Exposition in Atlanta in 1895, white America seemed to be searching for a new black voice. Washington's fit their needs perfectly as he advocated a lessening of demands on whites, which they had grown to resent more and more, and an increase in African Americans' assuming more in the way of personal responsibility for their own uplift. Both northerner and southerner, progressive and bigot saw the sense in embracing the Tuskegeean's program of pragmatism and conciliation. When Washington spoke at the Hamilton Club in January 1896, in what was perhaps his first major address to highly influential northerners, he stressed the aforementioned factors.[188]

Contention within the law offices of Williams and Barnett seemed to exemplify the potential damage that ideological and personal differences could produce. With Ida B. Wells-Barnett now owning the *Conservator* after buying it from her husband and another owner, the paper's tone apparently assumed a more radical and demanding stance on race relations. Reflective of her experiences, no compromise seemed reasonable with the moral reprehensibleness of lynching, terrorism, and racial proscription, whether it manifested itself in North or South. S. Laing Williams appealed to the newspaper to print Washington's convoluted position on an earlier lynching in Georgia; no doubt Washington's rationale made sense to a white southern audience, but the *Conservator*'s audience was made up of black Chicagoans, who found any defense or reasonable understanding of lynching incomprehensible. In the end, Williams claimed to Washington that his explanation of the misinterpretation "did you much good and made certain people very small."[189] As the century closed, the law partners split their practice as well as their wavering friendship.

C. Spheres of Leadership

Responding to a mature, urban market in a complex, modern political economy, Chicago paved a new direction in developing noncongruent circles of leadership to preside over the affairs of its fraternal, ministerial, legal, political, military, and business organizations and establishments. Indisputably, no unilateral, or monolithic, leadership acting with a linear focus ever existed with hegemony over all of black Chicago's multifaceted interests and affairs.[190] While disparate for the most part, the various interest groups and their spokesmen often overlapped, which in turn increased their strength. Most notable is the link between the political, fraternal, and military spheres. The prominence of military service and leadership in the Civil War and Spanish-American War assumed such importance in postwar white America that President Rutherford B. Hayes preferred as his title, "General Hayes," to that usually bestowed on the nation's chief executive. Accordingly, in the emerging Black Belt, Colonel John R. Marshall, of the Eighth Regiment of the Illinois National Guard, savored not only his title and position, but also his recognized command over people to whom he provided leadership.[191] Importantly, at the time of the most intense protest against participation at the Colored American Day celebration in August 1893, the clergy assumed a leadership role over what was perceived as a major public issue, in fact, a black civic matter, involving their race's image.

At this historical juncture, no well-defined civic leadership with a clear-cut agenda for civic advancement had developed, only particular members of the elite who occasionally displayed civic righteousness along with their sense of civic duty.[192] For their part, whites basically eschewed black involvement in important civic matters, much to the chagrin of Rev. Reverdy Ransom. He complained that "when any question arises which affects the public good our white fellow-citizens rarely, if ever, call the Colored man into co-operation, but he would gladly unite to sustain civic righteousness. We are never consulted or considered except when something happens in the Black Belt." The explanation was obvious and rested in the civic powerlessness of African Americans. Ida B. Wells-Barnett once wrote in regard to another instance that "the Negro had neither numerical nor financial strength which could be used in the race's behalf."[193] There was that notable example of entry into the civic world of selflessness and commitment to the public good that included the impressive collective African American effort to organize Provident Hospital. Less notable was Ida B. Wells-Barnett's apparently singlehanded fight against suggested school segregation in 1900.

Leadership in the less glamorous areas of neighborhood affairs focused on alleviating the mundane problems associated with living in an urban setting. In matters of achieving specific, short-range goals that affected the quality of life but benefited only a small segment of the community, neighborhood or community leadership developed. In the Dearborn Street Corridor, one representative example occurred during the tenure of A.M.E. minister Reverdy A. Ransom, leader of Institutional A.M.E. Church. Arriving in Chicago immediately after the world's fair closed, Ransom embraced the role of neighborhood leader as he successfully negotiated the paving of a hole-ridden roadway with the help of a wealthy and politically connected church member and leader, in fact, of the black gambling underworld.[194]

Later, the issue of voluntary separation almost blocked the creation of a kindergarten for the emerging Black Belt community, whose working mothers needed quality day care and educational training for their children. Ida B. Wells-Barnett, as a voice for community improvement as well as for civic betterment, provided the leadership required to both initiate the plan and see to its completion. As Wells-Barnett assessed the situation, very few members of the refined class concerned themselves with those less fortunate: "none of our better class of people was doing any missionary work"[195]—or, at least none of the ones with whom she had become recently acquainted and whom she also distrusted.

There also existed an important leadership over the sphere of women in which their gender interests predominated. Two names stood prominently in this arena—Fannie Barrier Williams and Ida B. Wells-Barnett. Operating at times in the same domain, but also in separate subcircles, the two cooperated initially and then drew apart by the turn of the century. This was partially attributable to differences in regional upbringing, educational backgrounds, complexion, personality, spousal ambitions, and finally, race ideology. As their contemporary, Ransom, described them, one was "mild-mannered, of a literary turn of mind," while the other was given to "agitation."[196] Both worked with white women of prominence and influence in conformance with women's new self-defining role.

It was Wells-Barnett, however, who made the deepest imprint on the feminist/womanist movement as, first, she challenged the dictum that sharing family life and gender duty represented an apostasy. Wells-Barnett deeply valued both her marriage and motherhood, while at the same time she responded to the pressures of activism. Of the former she wrote, "what I am trying to say now is that I had become a mother before I realized what a wonderful place in the scheme of things the Creator has given woman. She it is upon whom rests the joint share of the work of creation, and I wonder if women who shirk their duties in that respect truly realize that they have not only deprived humanity of their contribution to perpetuity, but that they have robbed themselves of one of the most glorious advantages in the development of their own womanhood. I cannot begin to express how I reveled in having made this wonderful discovery for myself or how glad I was that I had not been swayed [otherwise]." Second, Wells-Barnett personally organized Chicago women among the ranks of the respectables into clubs. Her first organization was the one that took her name after she left the city at the conclusion of the world's fair, the Ida B. Wells Club. Influenced by her contacts and observations in the East, she introduced an organizational foundation for greater awareness and activism among African American women in Chicago. In a pleasant display of tact, Wells-Barnett even persuaded Mrs. Mary Richardson Jones to head the club in an honorary capacity.[197] Recognized as the template of organized women's efforts in Illinois, the Ida B. Wells Club grew in numbers and prominence.[198]

Fannie Barrier Williams contributed mightily to black women's thought and to promoting their image during this pivotal period of women's liberation from the confines of gender restrictions. Renowned even today as a major essayist, she indeed wrote as a woman for a new era. Her contribution to A New Negro for a New Century built on the triumph of her speeches at the world's fair of 1893 as she explained the revolutionary role of newly formed women's clubs nationally and in Chicago: "The club movement . . . reaches in to the sub-social condition of the entire race. Among white women clubs mean the forward movement of the best women in the interest of the best womanhood. Among the Colored women the club is the effort of the few competent in behalf of the many incompetent; that is to say that the club is only one of many means for the social uplift of a race. Among white women the club is the onward movement of the already uplifted." She continued, "The consciousness of being fully free has not yet come to the great masses of the Colored women of this country. The emancipation of the mind and spirit of the race could not be accomplished by legislation. More time, more patience, more suffering and more charity are still needed to complete the work of emancipation. The training which first enabled Colored women to organize and successfully carry on club work was originally obtained in church work. . . . The meaning of unity of effort for the common good, the development of social sympathies grew into woman's consciousness through the privileges of church work. Still another school of preparation for Colored women has been their secret societies."[199] Williams's assessment

carried a tone of caring from a distance, indicative of her intellectual inclinations and upbringing that featured limited contact with the rank and file.

Williams has recently been referred to as a "central figure in a small yet
vital group of African American women who were 'founding sisters' during
the classical era of sociology from 1890 to 1920, when it first emerged as a
distinct discipline within the academy and wider world."[200] That inclina-
tion placed her frequently in the company of Jane Addams, Sophonisba
Breckenridge, Mary McDowell, and Rev. Celia Parker Woolley, all of whom
had links to the new University of Chicago. Impressive as a women's spokesperson and tactician in her own right, based on her background, with its
particularities as to region, culture, education, and occupation, Williams
could not and did not enjoy the entrée into the domain of ordinary women
that Wells-Barnett assumed. Women's historian Wanda A. Hendricks has
referred to the Ida B. Wells Club as the state's "mother" club, and that was
because Wells-Barnett had the ability to positively nurture and embrace all
elements of womanhood and women.

Once the National Association of Colored Women's Clubs was organized, Williams wrote that the framework was in place "to give respect and
character to a race of women who had no place in the classification of progressive womanhood in America. The terms good and bad, bright, and dull,
plain and beautiful are now as applicable to Colored women as to women of
other races. There has been created such a thing as public faith in the sustained virtue and social standards of the women who have spoken and acted
so well in these representative organizations" that compose the NACW.[201]
With a voice for women by women, the presumed leadership of men over the
entire spectrum of racial thought was now directly and forever challenged.

Chicago varied greatly from the model that John Hope Franklin found for
the national black leadership. Writing that "a large number of articulate
leaders . . . were representing the views and aspirations [of African
Americans]," he concluded that "among such leaders the essayists, historians,
and the editors of the Afro-American press were almost as influential as the
religious leaders."[202] In the mighty metropolis on Lake Michigan, lawyers,
physicians, businesspersons, and military and fraternal officers joined with
highly influential churchmen to lead the elite and the masses. There were a
few essayists, to be sure, such as Fannie Barrier Williams and Ida B. Wells,
but the local black press failed to meet the levels set by African American
publications elsewhere. Frontier Chicago pioneers were living their history
and it was not to be written until these pages were printed.

National ideology and leadership often intersected. For this period, historian August Meier wrote of concomitant ideologies nationally of integration and separate development.[203] Historically, interest in the latter was all

too real in Chicago. In fact, no group-based, self-help belief system was ever anathema to assimilationists because of their willingness to employ any effective tactics at almost any time to achieve their strategic end of advancing in American society. Whether one examines the lives of Lloyd Garrison Wheeler, Ferdinand L. Barnett, or Doctors Charles E. Bentley or Daniel Hale Williams, it is clear that their actions in an urban market setting rarely followed a distinctive path of ideological consistency, because they could not. Fighting racism in America demanded that ethical and ideological relativism occupy essential places in this group's struggle. Too often practical considerations entered their thinking and any subsequent course of action. Just as doctrinally correct Puritan New England accommodated itself to a changing reality when it formulated its Half Way Covenant in 1660 to insure its spiritual survival, so black America repeatedly showed its talent for compromise and adaptation in its need to perpetuate racial advancement.

Historian Allan Spear has mistakenly described the post-Reconstruction generation of the 1880s and 1890s as being hostile to "any type of separate Negro institution [that] smacked of segregation and represented a compromise of principle." He continued, postulating, "at times, a Negro institution might be necessary as a temporary expedient, but it could never be regarded as a substitute for the ultimate goal of integration." Yet "integration," as he labeled it, or full access to America's abundant opportunities, was still considered theoretical or illusory by the overwhelming number of African Americans, including the members of the elite. Applying an accepted model covering the entirety of late-nineteenth-century northern societies, he concluded: "Before 1900, most Chicago Negro leaders accepted these doctrines as articles of faith." Spear concluded that "until after the turn of the century, [Afro-Saxons] formed a coherent elite group and set the tone of social, intellectual, and civic life of the Negro community." Of course, they did not, at least in Chicago, and the interpretation provided here of extant data does not substantiate this older analysis. Acceptance of the purported hegemony of one leadership group adhering to one particular ideological strain eliminated the possibility that any other had significant influence. Moreover, their rhetoric and action were too often inconsistent to generalize modally.[204]

The vagaries of life in a racially competitive environment demanded flexibility of thought, not ideological rigidity. The theme of Emancipation Day activities on the new year's first Sunday, January 7, 1894, provided one example of this gymnastic thinking. The tone was decidedly deferential and almost bordered on the obsequious. Dr. Charles C. Bentley earnestly asked of the crowd, "Emancipation has come and we as a people have enjoyed liberty for thirty-six years. What use have we made of it?" He continued with pride, answering, "we were left empty-handed to fight the battle of life and survive. That we have survived we have abundant evidence. That we have progressed beyond the understanding of the most is granted. In the North at least is there a movement social, political, religious, or moral in which the Negro is not sympathetically working?"[205]

Bentley was followed by Ferdinand L. Barnett, who addressed the issue of "What the Negro Has Done for Himself." In praising the courage of white abolitionists, he found it equally necessary to extol the African American virtues that exemplified self-help:

> History knows of no struggle more sublime than this. The persistent fight on civil lines, the resolute defiance of public opinion, the sacrifice made and suffered by the white men and women of that day to make the Negro free, are phases of a record which will grow brighter and brighter all the years to come. But the question of the hour is "has the Negro justified the sacrifices made for his sake?" In the utilitarian spirit of the day, "Did it pay?" If gratitude would pay the debt it would have been paid long ago. . . . The Negro appreciates all that was done for him, and the one controlling aim of the colored man is to prove worthy of the heroic sacrifice which was made for him when he was powerless to help himself. . . . Too much must not be expected of the race from a business standpoint. The man who did not own himself cannot be expected to have advanced ideas of owning anything. When the children of Israel started for the promised land they bountifully blessed themselves with all the gold, silver and precious stones they could lay their hands on and it was a rich haul. When the Colored people left the Egypt of their servitude they didn't have clothes enough to cover their good intentions, and it has been uphill work ever since. And yet the round-up for a third of a century is fair. The taxable property belonging to the race amounts to $275,000,000. Besides this our churches own nearly $25,000,000, which would give us an accumulation of about $300,000,000. . . . Under circumstances thus favorable we made our first faltering steps, and while we recognize the mistakes we have made, we still believe that the record which encourages our friends should conciliate our foes.[206]

An Englishman, Rev. William T. Stead, author of *If Christ Came to Chicago*, was in attendance and, once introduced, spent one hour thanking African Americans for their courageous example of persistence despite adversity. Two years later, Booker T. Washington arrived in the city and spoke in a similar vein. In January 1896, before the exclusive, all-white Hamilton Club (which Dr. Daniel Hale Williams would soon join), Washington echoed this standard African American refrain for the white elite:

We may, I think, safely challenge history to find a case where two races, but yesterday master and slave, today citizen and citizen, have made such marvelous progress in the adjustment of themselves to new conditions, where each has traveled so fast in the divine science of forgetting and forgiving; and yet do not misunderstand me that all is done or that there are not serious wrongs yet to be blotted out.

As he continued, he delivered a mandatory paean to Civil War sacrifice, which was followed by an extolment of black progress. The Tuskegeean intoned,

I do not, I cannot forget as an humble representative of my race the vacant seat, the empty sleeve, the lives offered up on Southern battlefields, that we might have a united country and that our flag should shelter none save freemen, nor do I forget the millions of dollars that have gone into the South from the hands of philanthropists and religious organizations. Nor are we of the black race leaving the work alone to your race in the North or your race in the South—mark what this new citizen is doing [for himself].[207]

VIII. IDEOLOGICAL CONTENTION: MILITANTS, CONSERVATIVES, AND PRAGMATISTS

The death of Frederick Douglass in February 1895 stilled more than just a symbol of an age that most Americans hoped had ended with the ratification of the Thirteenth Amendment in December 1865. Douglass's voice had further served the cause of racial understanding, which salutarily affected all Americans during the postwar decades. He calmed whites in the North with his approach and deportment, which they found acceptable given the rhetoric of a Bishop Turner, who excoriated the flag, the nation, and American moral cowardice in racial matters. In opposing emigration to Africa, Douglass reinforced in the American mind the value of the mission of this nation. Whether the mass of African American laborers in the fields, houses, docks, hotels, and factories subscribed completely to this call for reason is conjectural. Meanwhile, his partisan efforts in behalf of the Republican party bound blacks and whites together despite diminishing returns accruing to African Americans from that party's fortunes.

In his wake came a new voice of southern accommodation and acquiescence to northern industrial concern for public order throughout the nation. Booker T. Washington pursued his region's interests at the Cotton States

Exposition in September 1895, producing a widely acclaimed alternative to Douglass's more forceful manner in seeking twin acknowledgments of white contrition for slavery and contemporary national accountability for a missing commitment to social justice. As Washington's popularity grew among whites because of his rhetoric and his comforting, nonconfrontational deportment around whites, some friends and admirers of Douglass's commitment voiced their opposition to the Tuskegeean's agenda. As they saw it, it fostered an acquiescence to institutionalized racial violence through lynching, a proscribed social status, political subservience, acceptance of disfranchisement, and retrogression toward race relations that fit more into the antebellum period than the Industrial Age. In Chicago, those persons who subscribed to this position were few in number, but vocal and positioned to be heard by all segments of black and white society.

Beyond the established embodiment of protest, Edward H. Morris, the name and voice in ascendancy by 1895 was that of Ida B. Wells, who now had become Mrs. Ferdinand L. Barnett and a permanent resident of the city. Between 1895 and 1900, she bought a part ownership of the *Conservator* newspaper and wrote as a columnist on the *Chicago Inter Ocean*. Her social persona grew through her affiliation with the new national women's club movement, presidency of the Ida B. Wells Club, membership at Bethel A.M.E. Church and within the powerful A.M.E. national community, editorship of the *Conservator*, and her easily recognizable identification with the plight of the rank and file. Ida B. Wells did not lead a movement in Chicago, but neither did John Jones. It was in the same manner as Jones, nevertheless, that she acquired influence and *power of character* as she moved through her circles of equally influential whites and blacks. As an accomplished publicist and public lecturer, she had access to the major media of communications and used this access effectively. Ideologically and personally, she opposed the southern culture and experience that Booker T. Washington seemed intent on protecting. She had been violently forced from the South and remained persona non grata in that region because of her multifaceted crusade against racial inequality. In her determined crusade for legal rights and moral righteousness, much in the model of Joan of Arc, she refused to sit idly by and allow Washington to turn the clock backward on the eve of a new century and when she perceived race relations to be at the apogee of success because of Frederick Douglass's efforts. Referred to as a militant, or radical, the category left was for Washington and anyone who agreed with him to be considered a gradualist or conservative. With a demeanor shaped by her experiences in American perfidy on the issues of lynching, work, and basic human recognition of individual worth, at times she exhibited what her opponents, rivals, and friends found to be an irascible personality.

However, discrete categorization did not fit most black Chicagoans whose residence in a city where practical thinking dominated and unparalleled competition occasioned anything but an extremist stance. Fannie Barrier and S. Laing Williams, Daniel Hale Williams, Hale G. Parker, Lloyd G. Wheeler, and the bulk of Chicago's refined element lived as pragmatists in a white-dominated city in a region that had only begun to tolerate them as part of humanity. The same was true for the rank and file, whose numbers dominated the demographics of black Chicago. Significantly, they experienced a personal security that was unknown in the South. Full equality would have to wait for a more racially just climate of opinion and until both the mass of black Chicagoans and the elite more firmly established themselves economically, politically, and socially. A measured move toward equality of opportunity became their goal, and their mission was to win as many white friends as possible. These pragmatists shifted positions frequently on events, episodes, and issues, even as Wells-Barnett strongly clung to what she conceived as her life's direction.

Interestingly enough, they were all ambivalent on race relations when it came to trust and dependence on powerful whites. Again, just like John Jones, Wells-Barnett grew to depend on well-to-do English egalitarians and certain Chicagoans of note such as H. H. Kohlsaat and Jane Addams, along with Susan B. Anthony and Albion W. Tourgee of New York state, even while admitting her need to rise above distrust of whites.[208] Fannie Barrier Williams rose to the occasion and "led the appeal" for the formation of a national congress of black women to speak not only for themselves, but also for the entirety of their race.[209]

Contention—linked partially to growing personal and ideological differences among militants, conservatives, and pragmatists—rose in 1899 and 1900, when Wells-Barnett found herself at odds with both the leaders and supporters of the Afro-American Council, the successor to the Afro-American League as the premier national African American civil rights group, and the National Association of Colored Women's Clubs (NACW). In 1899, both groups met in Chicago, with the former making its headquarters at Bethel and the latter at Quinn Chapel. The contention partially surrounded Booker T. Washington's political desires to gain recognition as *the* national black Republican spokesman by currying favor with the McKinley administration by compromising on criticism of the federal government inactivity on lynchings. Wells-Barnett and others outwardly opposed his stance, but not to the extent one Chicago newspaper claimed.[210] In any event, even the *Conservator* allowed Washington to explain his position to those willing to listen.[211]

Personal considerations mixed with individual sensitivities led Wells-

Barnett to fall out with her mentor, Mary Church Terrell, president of the NACW, as well as with certain Chicagoans who were not enamored with Wells-Barnett's style and agenda. Mixed with this came ideology, as it appeared that Mrs. Booker T. Washington was carrying her husband's banner into women's circles.[212] Also involved was a jockeying for favored positions within Republican circles by the wives of all the notables of the day, including Wells-Barnett, Terrell, and Williams. Since all of the parties involved were publicists and public figures, they have left behind a paper trail that has assumed a life of its own as their activities and thinking have been accepted as that of the entire group.

Depending on the nature of particular issues, mass-level interest and thinking could range from total indifference to partial interest to fervor. Ida B. Wells-Barnett responded with frustration on several occasions over what she perceived as a lack of knowledge of self-interest. Once, she encountered this in regard to a planned kindergarten for neighborhood children living around Bethel Church. Ordinary residents opposed the project, fearing a loss of contact with a nearby white-operated facility and their children's perpetual relegation to an all-black facility. Wells-Barnett wrote: "To say that I was surprised does not begin to express my feeling. Here were people so afraid of the color line that they did not want to do anything to help supply the needs of their own people."[213]

IX. POLITICS

Traditional political participation at the local, state, and national levels continued with emphases on prestige in office holding and economic benefits with patronage. In fact, this participation increased within a political environment conducive to such involvement. Consistent with this growth, it was during this period that the black community began to gain fuller political strength.[214] The acquisition of true political power would have to wait until the next century, but an inkling of what the future could bring was manifested nonetheless in small victories. Loyalty to the Republican party remained constant, but with occasional defections locally to the Democratic cause as certain individuals sought to climb occupationally, or in those occasions when selfishness diminished, to meet some neighborhood needs. Rather than being part of a strategy for racial progress, an involvement in politics at this time primarily served as a channel for advancement for the ambitious individual.[215] The century's end would bring an absorption of ambitious individuals into a program for such persons, and in this manner paved the way for the historical phenomenon that marked authentic black political empowerment in the twentieth century. One man is associated with this transformation: the former New Yorker Edward H. Wright, who was about to earn his nickname of "the Iron Master."

Similar to events transpiring in other communities, especially within the city's ethnic enclaves, anyone who could command the direction of the Black Belt vote stood in line to receive immediate rewards. These approximately three thousand votes represented "a rich prize which rival political bosses strove to dominate and control. Any Negro politician who was strong enough to potentially control it was sure to receive a fat political job."[216] One highlight of the success of this process of early machine politics included Edward H. Wright's being elected county commissioner in 1894 and reelected in 1896. Wright seemed to be prescient for his role in black politics when in 1894 "he assisted in breaking the slate in the Republican County Convention resulting in the nomination of Theodore W. Jones for county commissioner."[217] Pushing others forward and upward only heightened Wright's power within a growing black political coterie, while strengthening his group's political influence overall. Then, in 1895, Wright was elected town clerk for South Chicago and the next year he succeeded Theodore W. Jones on the County Board.

As for Wright's climb to power, according to Robb, "during the last year of his term as County Commissioner (1900) he was elected president pro tem of the County Board with complete power of veto and removal of department heads during the president's absence." Gosnell has pointed out that this educated, assertive man (who, being from New York, was accustomed to big-city life and relations with whites on a competitive level), was swift in displaying his attributes of being "shrewd, forceful, and highly race conscious." He exercised his power when, in order to secure a position for Ferdinand L. Barnett as assistant state's attorney, he held up an appropriation sought by State's Attorney Charles Deneen's office. A clash of titans ensued: When Deneen was informed as to why his appropriation was delayed, he is alleged to have said: "I want you to understand, Mr. Wright, that I am all powerful in this office." To this Wright replied: "Yes, and I am county commissioner"—with real powers and the ability to wield them.[218]

Acting consistently to unify black political thought and activities, and attempting to acquire influence, and ultimately, power, in 1900 Edward H. Wright founded the Appomattox Club. This organization represented another milestone in developing an independent base within the independent-thinking African American community. In contrast to the typical fraternal organizations, it was led by the college-trained Wright and featured space and discussion that catered to the interests of professionals and businessmen. Its political tone was decidedly Republican and it soon became a breeding ground for the instantly ambitious and subsequently successful political types.

Meantime, the hard work, exemplary reputation, legal acumen, and obvious political approval paid off for lawyer and racial advocate Ferdinand L. Barnett late in this decade also. Popular with African Americans, allied with Wright, and recognized by his party for his effective work in the 1896 national elections, Barnett was appointed as the first black assistant state's attorney in 1897, providing black Chicago with a voice in certain high prosecutorial cases.[219]

Just as the martial and the political spheres had intersected in prior years, now religion and politics bonded loosely late during this decade. The dominant African Methodist Church exerted its influence through the pastorships of Chicago newcomers, Revs. Reverdy Ransom and Archibald Carey. The former was associated with Bethel A.M.E. (and later Institutional A.M.E.), and the latter at Quinn Chapel A.M.E. The street upon which Bethel had been built—Dearborn—was deteriorating, and the needed road work was put off by municipal government, much to the discomfort to anyone seeking an enjoyable ride on the city's roads. Governmental indifference convinced Ransom that only political pressure could provide a remedy. He challenged his indifferent alderman to act decisively and won on the issue, but only after forging an unholy alliance with Robert Motts of the State Street gambling and entertainment worlds. Although his congregation disapproved, Ransom welcomed victory and the new street.[220] The desired end had justified his embracing a religiously questionable means.

For his part, Archibald Carey's immediate quest for power, and if that was not possible, political influence, led him to embrace aldermanic candidate William Thompson in the Second Ward and to host a visit from President William McKinley. In the case of Carey's local alliance of 1900, it would enhance his stature immensely in Chicago politics over the next several decades. At the same time, he unfortunately set into motion the degradation of the church as a place of spirituality and principled civic involvement.

At the state level, office-holding with little legislative output indicated the value of participation in the Illinois General Assembly. Representatives John C. Buckner (1895–1897), James E. Bish (1895–1897), and William L. Martin (1899–1901) served basically uneventful one-term tenures in the lower house of the assembly. Buckner distinguished himself for his activities in having the Ninth Battalion recognized as a combat unit and later merged into the enlarged Eighth Regiment of the Illinois National Guard. This accomplishment of elevating a localized African American military presence to state-level involvement occurred none too soon, with war with Spain coming in 1898. Politics being filled with manipulation, Buckner did not get to enjoy his achievement, being removed by Governor Tanner before the war began.

The supposedly literary-minded James E. Bish defeated popular attorney Edward H. Morris in the election for a representative's seat in the Thirty-eighth General Assembly. When described by Morris's partisans four decades later, he "was a man of limited ability; he served one term in that body and the records do not disclose any legislative activities on his part worthy of mention."[221]

William L. Martin fared better in his assessment by Morris's partisans. He "showed ability and courage in the performance of his work. . . . He was not credited with much ability, yet he was ever alert and ready to fight for everything he thought was best for his Race."[222] Furthermore, Martin's educational credentials, intellectual savvy, and apparent social abilities won him acceptability from the elite. In reiteration and of some note, erstwhile politician John W. E. Thomas died wealthy in 1899, providing another symbol of what personal benefits political involvement could bring.

Nineteenth-century waistcoat patronage for the elite, the equivalent of the twenty-first century's pinstripe variety, was important both for the position being sought and for the need to have developed an affiliation with a political organization, primarily Republican. Dr. Daniel Hale Williams belonged to the basically white Hamilton Club, which in Republican circles guaranteed securing a desired appointment.[223] So when Williams pursued an appointment to the Illinois State Board of Health in 1899, he received it. In addition, Attorney S. Laing Williams maintained an active posture in Republican party activities during this period, participating in local, state, and national campaigns to bolster any claims to future political plums. Several years into the next century, his independent stance in belonging to his own Hyde Park Colored Republican Club instead of a recognized, regular party organization, would cost him a federal appointment.[224] Significantly, institutional development within the Black Belt had reached a level by 1900 that an African American version of the Hamilton Club could make its debut. Wright's Appomattox Club began to organize what was to become a major instrument of black empowerment in the twentieth century. The club was inclusive of politicians and businessmen, and color played no significant part in its operations.[225]

The possibilities of moving heaven and earth through political action spurred another newer Chicagoan as well as members of her gender into politics. Ida B. Wells-Barnett was active in state-level Republican politics within the women's network. No doubt partially related to her partisan activism, her husband, Ferdinand Barnett, was chosen by the National Republican party to run the Negro Bureau at the 1900 convention held in Chicago. She and her husband also forged early and close ties to the rising Ed Wright.

However, women as a group began to make their presence felt as they entered into the initial stage of black women's electoral participation. In 1894, the Illinois General Assembly voted against extending the franchise fully to women but did advance a limited use of the franchise in the election for trustees of the University of Illinois. Chicago's women as a whole participated, and the women of the Black Belt followed the leadership of Ida B. Wells and Mary McIntosh Dempsey and actively voted.[226]

Street-level as well as waistcoat politics also had their detractors because of the resulting tendency to benefit the few instead of the masses through partisanship and personal interests. The Republican-inclined *Illinois Record* commented:

> The political situation of the Negro in Chicago and Cook County is a question that has given us great study; especially as to the reason he receives so little recognition along this line. One of the great reasons he receives so little is because we fail to put men at the top to lead us who have back-bone enough to speak out for their rights. On the contrary, we put men up to lead us who can't stand the sight of a silver dollar, and will sell us out and buy us over again. If some of their white "bosses" give them a few dollars. We don't need men of that class to lead us, we need men who can stand to see millions of money and not let it turn their minds when the honor of the race is at stake.[227]

In a similar vein, the Democratic-oriented *Broad Ax* opined:

> [T]he loud mouthed, rattle-brained and empty headed Republicans always seek to keep [the Negro] in the Republican Party by appealing to his prejudices and passions. But we want to say right here, that the Negro never will amount to anything in the United States socially, politically, financially or otherwise, until he learns to think and act for himself.[228]

The successes of securing key political appointments at substantive levels of decision-making as well as the elevated military status of the Eighth Regiment clearly pointed out that African Americans in politics had moved to the next step in the process, manipulation of the system to serve desired ends for the benefit of the group rather than just an individual. Loyalty to Republicanism was not the issue; success within the political process was. This was a sign of the arrival of the "New Negro" mentality—freed from a preoccupation with the past and bondage, and bound with other Americans in their commitment to civic service and civic virtue as well as realization of group self-interest.

X. THE SPANISH-AMERICAN WAR

The black men of Chicago had fought during the Civil War, not as white men had done, to protect the integrity of the Union, but for the purpose of total liberation of themselves and their race. During this "Second American Revolution," an emphasis on liberation was a reasonable but self-serving motive. When war with Spain began in April 1898, a large portion of black Chicago now stood ready to fight just like white men for a nation they all claimed as their own. War provided the ultimate test of worthiness for citizenship, so once again, and one or two generations removed, African American men could prove to the nation that black men, women, and children deserved the supposed inalienable rights automatically accorded to all other Americans. This newer response came as the Eighth Infantry Regiment of the Illinois National Guard made its formal appearance as part of America's fighting force.

Before this historic juncture was reached, it took until 1894 for the commander of the unit, John C. Buckner, to achieve success. No clear-cut path had been trod, indicative of the racial and associated obstacles placed before African Americans. The regiment was born because of the carefully forged nexus of black masculine agency, martial ardor, impetus from the fraternal orders, and pressure-group politics. The election of the Ninth Battalion's leader, Buckner, to represent the Fifth District of the Illinois General Assembly afforded the opportunity; Major Buckner's rough-and-tumble approach provided the personal force to see the action through; Buckner's political shrewdness overcame his intellectual and educational deficiencies to supply the tactical maneuvering necessary for success. Using the dogged perseverance that marked black progress in the state since even before Emancipation, Buckner refused to accept the explanation that the Ninth Battalion could be neither funded nor inducted into the state's militia. He skillfully found his opening when he attached a rider to a military appropriations bill. Thus, the Ninth Battalion entered service as part of the First Regiment, with its wartime service scheduled as the independent Eighth Regiment.[229]

By the time the Illinois National Guard saw action overseas, Buckner had been removed from his post. A combination of falsehoods, political revenge, and personal eccentricities doomed Buckner. In 1896, when rioting between Italian immigrants and African Americans took place at Spring Valley, Illinois, Buckner was alleged to have offered armed troops to quell the disturbances, when in fact, it appeared that he had not. By disputing with two governors and showing them up with the Ninth Battalion's inclusion in the state's military arm, he had disturbed the political calm of race relations built around black acquiescence in all matters, especially those involving white manhood rights. Finally, his being upset over the unclean traveling conditions provided his troops led him to decide to withhold their participation in a military dedication of a statue of Major General John C. Logan, an Illinois Civil War hero.[230]

Meanwhile, the plight of the Cubans and Puerto Ricans living under despotic Spanish colonial rule in concentration camps and amid conditions of starvation was well known. At the time, an awareness, and in some instances, a strong affinity for these diasporans built throughout the decade.[231] Furthermore, the sense that race linked large numbers of Cubans to persons of African descent in the United States of America led to an exaggerated sensitivity to the exploits of revolutionary heroes Antonio Maceo (the "Bronze Titan"), a mulatto, and Quintin Bandera, another leader, who was of full-blooded African descent and who had carried the fight for independence from Spain to its apex. A poem written upon the Eighth's return home in 1899 conveyed this sense of racial bonding:

> Down to yon damp and molten clime,
> Crossing the dark, deep and dreary brine,
> Perhaps never to return from their weird task
> Of freeing their brother from the enemy's grasp.
> I stood and watched their steady pace
> And said within me, Ah! Noble race![232]

The sinking of the battleship USS *Maine* due to an internal explosion in Havana harbor invoked a bellicose American response. White Americans generally believed that the destruction was deliberate and external, and therefore provocative and representing a direct challenge to national honor, and yellow journalism enthusiastically and maliciously beat the drums of war. Now, with thirty African American seamen among the dead, African Americans felt an additional impetus to meet the nation's call to arms. Overall, the African American soldier's "enlistment this time called upon him to do combat for humanity's sake. And now he was equally willing to assist in the liberation of another downtrodden people who were fighting for their rights and privileges—the Cubans."[233]

There were other elements at stake for a group seeking both self-affirmation and external recognition for its humanity. Many soldiers saw themselves as working for "the betterment and elevation of the Colored race in Chicago and Illinois." Then there was the need to provide proof that blacks had reached a level of self-sufficiency as human beings and citizenship that they could do things without white help, and under the direction of their own leaders. Their cry was, "Give us a chance. We don't need white officers for our leaders, we can lead ourselves."[234] One soldier expressed the prevailing sentiment:

> When the pride and governmental honor of this great republic of ours was insulted and the stars and stripes of our nation were ruthlessly assaulted, when the 236 white American seamen and 30 brave Colored men, under the same circumstances, were blown up . . . the Negro soldier was among the first to seek revenge through the medium of the Eighth Illinois Volunteer Regiment. . . .
> . . . The 8th went to the front, enlisted with the ardor of patriots, born of the desire to fight for the country that had given them freedom and protection; to show that they, too, could fight for the cause of liberty, and finally, in aid of the suffering victims of the tyranny of Spain.[235]

During the decade, the exhibits and demonstrations of military might found at the World's Columbian Exposition and elsewhere, where the virtues of the martial were extolled as much as were scientific, philosophical, and cultural advancement, fueled an atmosphere of bellicosity. This attitude was also nurtured by the jingoistic and militant segment of the nation, which was committing itself to empire-building in the pursuit of new markets and national glory.

Among African Americans throughout America, historian Willard Gatewood noted the "widely disparate reactions within the black community." There was more than adequate antiwar sentiment to match the call to patriotic exertion. Radicals within Chicago's socialist community, such as Lucy Parsons, gave voice to the claim that the conflict shone not brightly, but dimly, as a blatant capitalist grab for power. Opposition from African nationalist leaders such as Bishop Henry McNeal Turner further raised the specter of racism as America's motivation.[236]

Even amid a climate in which American foreign involvement looked much like domestic racial imperialism transplanted abroad, military service for black men offered a perfect opportunity to prove their mettle, to gain the benefits of citizenship by offering to risk making the supreme sacrifice. Ideological considerations aside, the rank and file could follow a popular appeal contemporarily, even if it would appear out of sorts generations later. For Robert R. Jackson, born in the afterglow of Civil war triumph, and now Major Jackson in the Eighth Regiment of the Illinois National Guard, his time for glory had come. Meanwhile, excitement for full participation built in the Black Belt, with the Woman's Auxiliary of the Eighth Regiment, the churches, the politicians, and individuals such as Rev. Reverdy Ransom and Ida B. Wells-Barnett supporting the war effort.[237]

Chicago's African American soldiers were officially mustered into federal service in July 1898, and the unit's military complement was over one thousand men. Earlier, the strategic goal of these determined black men had been organizational recognition far beyond their previous battalion strength, which was only a tactical ploy. They earnestly desired a full regimental complement; so, once war was declared with Spain, the opportunity availed itself to request a unit of regimental strength that would include four to six Chicago companies along with six companies from downstate counties. Then, when the commander of a white Illinois regiment pleaded with the governor to return his regiment home to spare it from disease and guerrilla fighting, another opportunity availed itself.[238]

After the U.S. Army dispatched its four regular all-black units to Cuba, African American volunteer units prepared to follow the initial wave of troops. Against racist resistance from as high as the White House, which sought to deny African American participation,[239] the Eighth Illinois was called to action to join other black volunteer units from Alabama, North Carolina, Virginia, Indiana, Ohio, Massachusetts, and Kansas. Illinois stood alone, however, as having the only African American commanding officer over an entire regiment of black men. Two other state militias, Kansas and North Carolina, had black line officers, but the command ranks were reserved for whites.[240]

The commander of the Illinois, and black Chicago's, recognized fighting force, Colonel John R. Marshall, immediately recognized the importance of the moment. His warning rang with clarity: "I assure you that the officers and men are on the guard, because we recognize the fact that the Colored officers are on trial. The men have proven for years that they are made of all wool and a yard wide. Our success is theirs and that of the whole race. If we fail the whole race will have to shoulder the burden."[241] Governor Tanner had selected Marshall to replace the popular commander, Illinois State Representative Buckner, after the latter challenged the governor and lost the dispute. Thus Marshall carried an additional burden within his command and the black community from politically motivated contention. This friction would later surface as full-blown dissent in Cuba (Figure 53).

The stateside sendoff for the Eighth was nothing short of spectacular. Ida B. Wells-Barnett "went to Springfield with [her] children and stayed with the regiment until finally it was mustered into service, and . . . saw them entrain for Cuba."[242] At every stop heading east they were cheered by mixed crowds and honored (except in Baltimore) as they proceeded to their transport ship, the SS *Yale*.[243] Finally, they reached their destination and, to the

Fig. 53. Colonel John R. Marshall.
From Goode, "Eighth Regiment."

Fig. 54. Major Robert R. Jackson.
From Goode, "Eighth Regiment."

Fig. 55. Corporal W. T. Goode.
From Goode, "Eighth Regiment."

dismay of the soldiers of the regiment, the unit arrived in Cuba after general hostilities had ceased. Glory in battle had eluded the more bellicose among their ranks. Consequently, their orders were to take up garrison duties under the command of Colonel Marshall with his 1,195 enlisted men and forty-six officers. Marshall encountered deplorable living conditions and growing internal dissent from soldiers, who resented their being assigned garrison duty instead of frontline combat. As a peacekeeping force instead of a combat unit, the Eighth Illinois had the responsibility of managing the affairs of the towns of San Luis and Las Palmas in the absence of civilian authority.

In carrying out his orders, Colonel Marshall set up headquarters in San Luis (with six thousand inhabitants the larger of the two towns) and assigned Chicago-born Major Robert R. Jackson to assume control over the affairs of the smaller Las Palmas with two contingents of soldiers from Companies E and F (Figure 54). For Colonel Marshall, this assignment, while supposedly noncombative, still allowed the Eighth and all African American troops to prove themselves as worthy representatives of the United States. Illinois Governor Tanner wrote to Marshall, reiterating, albeit somewhat inaccurately, the importance of the regiment's assignment, telling him that "the eyes of your race and the country are upon you and your regiment. . . . I am keeping a close watch on your doings, because of the fact that yours is the only and full regiment of Afro-American soldiers ever sent to war." Marshall responded: "We are proud to be here to represent Illinois. I know our regiment is on trial and our race also. I think we will add glory to our race and honor to you who sent us."[244]

Initiating a new tradition of recorded military history, the story of the regiment was preserved for posterity through the efforts of at least two soldiers. The first was Corporal, and later Commissary Sergeant, W. T. Goode, who wrote The "Eighth Regiment" in 1899 (Figure 55). Another was written by Harry Stanton McCord, who served as the regiment's hospital steward.[245] Along with a flow of letters from the Cuban front, Chicagoans were kept abreast of their men's adjustment to heat, water, diet, disease, violence, death, and boredom. Evidence of the last appeared in the Illinois Record, which at the time was under the control of publisher Charles Edward Hall. The letters conveyed a story as old as time—men who initially thought they could identify in some aspect with a foreign culture realized firsthand how alienated they were from that culture and society, and at the same time how American they were in temperament, values, and habits. Some of the men, accustomed as they were to life in modern, urban America, immediately resented the Cuban way of life because it appeared primitive. An altercation between another unit of American troops and Cubans over a stolen pig led to a shooting and increased hostility between the Cuban people and the

Fig. 56. Corporal A. D. E. Jackson.
Special Collections and Preservation Division,
Chicago Public Library

troops, and the troops were confined to their barracks. Meanwhile, others found the circumstances tolerable and the people to their liking, and some soldiers married Cuban women.[246]

Once encamped, the troops found that their early housing was both horrendous and dangerous, and they slept with their rifles at their sides at night. Water, glistening lusciously in the sun and looking alluring from a distance, turned out to be undrinkable when examined closely. Fruits were plentiful, but "fever-like." The sweetness of the abundant sugarcane hid the germs for disease. And the diseases they encountered and from which they suffered and died ranged from dysentery to typhoid, from malaria to pneumonia, and from Bright's disease to tetanus (Figures 56, 57, 58, 59).

The letters revealed much about these conditions and another truism about war and military life—as adversity continued, resentment grew, and many of the soldiers began to despise Colonel Marshall. Charges ranged from the innocuous to the fitful, with some men writing home alleging that their commander deliberately extended their tour of duty to increase his service allotment. Internal racial division materialized, with distrust of whites transferred onto the shoulders of their commander. Marshall was assessed in this manner: "He is too near white; he is for number one; the rest can look after themselves. All the colored people of Chicago can do is pray for our safe return."[247] In January 1899, disgruntled soldiers calling themselves the Committee of Vigilance, One Hundred Privates Strong, wrote a letter home to Illinois that bordered on the mutinous about Marshall, whom they considered "the man with the white face and a black heart and hand." Individually, one man wrote the following:

> [T]he men lay awake all night and [are] up before day for they can not sleep for thinking of their loved ones at home. If it is necessary for us to stay here and die at the point of bayonet for our country's cause, we would say amen, but that the war is over and we have nothing to do but stay here and suffer this dreaded disease and heat, it is too much for us to stand. I can't say any more now but do hope the day will hasten when our boys breathe the free air of the land of their birth and realize that old song, "My Country 'Tis of Thee," for Cuba is now free and we desire to be.[248]

Supporters of the colonel found him to be "strict, but not severe," and Marshall was known to reprimand his lieutenants if he felt they were being too hard on the men.[249] With the stakes for success being so high, friction was inevitable.

Support for the men in the field came from letters and packages of food and medicine collected in Chicago. As a boost to morale, the Chicago YMCA set up a tent in Santiago to aid in writing letters and transmitting them back home. Meantime, back home, volunteers in the Black Belt collected money and medicine and sent a druggist to personally assist the troops.[250]

When the Eighth Regiment finally departed from Cuba, it left some comrades behind. Remnants of the Spanish army reconstituted as a guerrilla force in the occupied province and numbered two thousand men. So along with diseases, there were casualties from gunfire. The total number of casualties was four dead from hostile action and fourteen from disease. About six hundred men returned home on March 18, 1899, to full honors when they detrained at the Illinois Central Railroad depot in Chicago. They alighted "amid cheers of enthusiasm, tears of joy, and handshakes." Chicagoans, white as well as black, received the soldiers as heroes, reflecting well on the status of race relations. Befitting the occasion, formal military and governmental

Figs. 57 and 58. The Eighth Regiment of the Illinois National Guard.
From Goode, "Eighth Regiment."

Fig. 59. The Eighth Regiment of the Illinois National Guard.
Special Collections and Preservation Division, Chicago Public Library.

ceremonies recognized the men's service abroad. While Mayor Carter G. Harrison II delivered the city's praise, Rev. Reverdy Ransom provided a spiritual thanksgiving at a big reception that included all of the major churches, the soldiers' families, and friends in abundance.[251]

Of course, among the returning soldiers there were some who were disillusioned and heart-stricken, but most were proud to have served their country. At the conclusion of the regiment's service, the elements of redemption and group recognition took hold: "The war has proven to the satisfaction of the entire world that a once dejected, oppressed and much despised people, namely the Negro race, is capable of assisting in all human affairs."[252]

Within the world's fair city of the 1890s, social change in its fullest dimensions accompanied the external phenomenon of continuous migration from the South. In their various pursuits, African Americans experienced exhilaration and pride, disappointments, and satisfaction in their work before and during the fair. Significantly, the Colored American was *in* and *at* the World's Columbian Exposition! Participation at the fair might have been limited, but no more than the African American's inability a century later to take a full role in all of the nation's endeavors. It was nonetheless important that in the aftermath of the fair, other signal events took place and influences arose, some in continuation of what was begun at the fair, but most independent of this event and this experience.

Nationally, change was even more pervasive. Although the World's Columbian Exposition qualified as an epochal event in African American life (the same way it did in mainstream America's), externally produced forces, most times totally unrelated to the exposition, such as economic depression, court- and legislative-sanctioned segregation, debt peonage, lynchings, and disfranchisement, affected American life just as dramatically. Historically, one only has to think of the Cotton States Exposition at Atlanta in 1895 and Booker T. Washington's rise to national celebrity.

The Spanish-American War provided an opportunity to lay a firmer claim to manhood and citizen rights. Black Chicago's soldiers met the challenge but not without discomfort and death in Cuba. Meanwhile, the social configuration of black Chicago reflected rising wealth for some along with decreasing income for many more—a sure formula for socioeconomic division. The continued growth of businesses contributed mightily to this change. Growth of women's institutions and in the religious, military, fraternal, charitable, social, and political spheres also illustrated diversity and growing strength within black Chicago. Rather than dividing blacks, diversity within black Chicago fostered an institutionalized racial consciousness leading to a greater sense of independence from white direction. Increasingly, black Chicago selected from among its own members to find a group of leaders who would guide them to a better life and beyond, to the future realization of the dream of a Black Metropolis.

Epilogue

The Foundation of the Black Metropolis

[Black Chicago was] but a part of a larger, national Negro culture, its people being tied to [millions of] Negroes by innumerable bonds of kinship, associational and church membership, and a common minority status. The customs inherited by Bronzeville have been slowly growing up among American Negroes in the eighty years since slavery.

— Drake and Cayton, *Black Metropolis*

O VER THE course of the nineteenth century and on the cusp of a new era, after having experienced the ultimate vicissitudes in human transformation—moving from slavery to freedom, from constraint to choice, from dependence to independence—black Chicago reflected on its accomplishments and felt confident in anticipating an even better new century. In an almost unique pattern, a history built on maximizing the possibilities of the moment had been fashioned. Resultant progress in every aspect of life led one racial elder to reminiscence epigrammatically as to this fact: "Since 1900 the Race in Chicago has moved forward so rapidly that the world has been startled."[1]

A community life built around family and church, which first appeared during the 1840s, continued to flourish. Institutional, or associational, life reached a level where Fannie Barrier Williams totally agreed with de Tocqueville's assessment of the nation's organizing impulse among *all* of its inhabitants.[2] Blacks organized constantly, and successfully. As soon as a need was encountered, it was met with a plan of resolution. From churches to fraternal orders to social clubs to civil rights groups, as part of a "larger, national culture," associational life made life more bearable in an often-hostile setting. Spirituality reigned and initially the house-church appeared as a haven

436

nurturing a black-based religion. This stage of development of religious practice and church growth was followed by the purchase or construction of the
formal church edifice to provide a haven for hundreds of congregants who
hungered for respite from racism and various hardships. The Gilded Age
brought a proliferation of churches creating a broader denominational base
within Protestantism along with a black-led Catholic church. Within this
transformative church milieu, the mass-based church, which catered to the
needs of the more recent migrants and of the solid laboring class, challenged
the more staid, assimilationist, elite-dominated churches over both social
and spiritual relevance. What the Institutional A.M.E. Church had begun in
1900 in the way of providing social settlement services extended into a pattern of church-provided assistance, with Olivet Baptist Church taking the
lead in the 1920s.

Demographically insignificant initially, the African American population increased because of adult migration to a stage where a balanced ratio
between males and females encouraged family formation. The arrival of children and the permanence of both the nuclear family and the extended family
came with economic and social stabilization. Meanwhile, newly arrived relatives along with boarders were absorbed familially. As the city rolled out the
welcome mat to newcomers to meet its emergent labor needs in industry in
1915, a flood of fifty thousand persons arrived, somewhat reminiscent of the
post–Civil War period. The resulting population swelled to 180,000 in
1920. For the first time in nearly a century, the size of the black population
exceeded the 1-2 percent range to climb to an astounding 4 percent.
Chicago now had a sizeable African American population with which to
deal, a visible force seeking realization of its own interests. Meanwhile, the
emergence of class stratification became ever more obvious. The rise of a
handful of millionaires counterbalanced mass impoverishment and encouraged a truly viable middle class, while cosmopolitanism partially neutralized
southern, folk-based culture. The saga of the Civil War veteran continued,
even on the eve of World War I, which would see more black Chicagoans
serve their nation in war. Upon the death of a seventy-year-old *Chicago
Tribune* news dealer, who was also a veteran, his employer incurred the
wrath of crusader Ida B. Wells-Barnett by referring to him as a "newsboy"
and "aged darkey."[3]

Overall, before the onset of the Great War of 1914, black Chicago
appeared to be readying itself for the Great Migration of 1915–1918. Eventually, with the addition of this demographic asset, it would become the Black
Metropolis described by Drake and Cayton. Moreover, within four years of
the turn of the century, a sizeable segment of the African American population would culminate its decades of productive local residency with the

formation of an Old Settlers Club. Along with this sense of self-satisfaction with its presence and contributions to the development of the city, black Chicagoans also visualized an increased standing among their fellow citizens. This resulted from a positive world's fair experience, from a satisfying taste of participation in local and national affairs in politics, civic life, and defense of the nation, and by dramatic episodes of demographic and economic advancement.

Interestingly, the bonds of Chicago's Old Settler group, which were based in shared experiences of racial injustice and common hopes for salvation, heavenly if not earthly, cut across the social spectrum of class, encompassing the thinking, views, and ideas of the washerwoman, Pullman porter, businessman, and physician alike. The precondition for possessing this pattern of thinking was longevity of residence in Chicago, although the feeling appeared throughout the urban North. The Progressive-era journalist Ray Stannard Baker observed that African Americans in the North discriminated not only by skin color, but divided themselves between persons laying claim to long-term residency and those whose recent arrival relegated them to the status of newcomer: "In Philadelphia I heard of the old Philadelphia Negroes, in Indianapolis of the old Indianapolis families, in Boston a sharp distinction was drawn between the 'Boston Negroes' and the recent Southern importation. Even in Chicago, where there is nothing old, I found the same spirit. In short, it is the protest against separation, against being deprived of the advantages and opportunities of a free life."[4]

However, in Chicago the sentiment built on something more important than a protest against separation. It was celebratory of being, residing, participating, and succeeding in the ebb and flow of city life, all actions dictating how one saw herself or himself. In his preface to the Colored Men's Professional and Business Directory, Isaac C. Harris wrote:

[A]ctuated by a sensibility of race pride, and the great love and admiration which I have for the exemplary enterprise demonstrated by the colored people of Chicago, I have felt it to be an imperative duty to collect, with great care and discretion, a few facts and figures, in order to show to others of our race what the colored people in the great metropolis of the west are doing towards an honest accumulation of wealth, establishment of business, and acquiring that experience in the various professions and the branches of industry necessary to make life a grand success and the elevation of our race a true and constant aim.[5]

These linkages between tradition, mind-set, place, circumstance, and time converged in the 1920s, the decade of the flowering of the Black

Metropolis. The past civic boosterism of Ferdinand L. Barnett was matched time and time again as black Chicagoans boasted on their beloved city. Consequentially, recognition of Du Sable's eighteenth-century contribution, which translated into a nineteenth-century legacy, reached a high point in the twentieth century. It prompted Johnson and Frazier to write, respectively:

> [First,] these are its boasts . . . it points with pride to the physician who made the first successful operation on the human heart, indeed, to Jean De Baptiste, Pointe de Saible, San Domingo—a Negro, the very first settled in Chicago, to the largest number of successful young Negroes of any city in the country . . .
>
> [Second,] because Chicago has not attained the cosmopolitan character of New York and has not lost many of the features of smaller cities, she represents more nearly the pattern of Negro life at large in America. Chicago has drawn in the plantations of the lower South for her population more than New York whereas the latter has in her population a larger proportion of the eastern Seaboard. A trip on a local elevated train from the Chicago Loop will not only make visible in the types of houses along the route the different strata of the population, but those who get off at the stations are living documents of the different sections of the population they represent. Yet within this diversity there is a certain unity expressed in a community consciousness that is lacking in the cosmopolitan life of New York. In the first place, the Negro Community in Chicago has a tradition extending back to 1790 when Jean Baptiste Point de Saible, a San Domingan Negro, built a rude hut on the north bank of the Chicago River. Although no historical connection between this first settler and the present Negro group can be established, it is of paramount importance in making the community conscious of a history in the growth of the city. The recent successful struggle of the Negro group for some recognition of the first settler in the form of an appropriation by the city for a monument is significant of the increasing consciousness of its unity.[6]

It was left to Chicago scholars St. Clair Drake and Horace R. Cayton to link the cultural vortex and this very special space known today as the Black Belt, the South Side, Black Metropolis, and Bronzeville. They found the axis around which it made its progressive movement forward. It was "but a part of a larger, national Negro culture, its people being tied to [millions of] Negroes by innumerable bonds of kinship, associational and church membership, and a common minority status. The customs inherited by Bronzeville have been slowly growing up among American Negroes in the eighty years since slavery." That is, the customs developed in the period the *Chicago*

Defender had described as the point at which real history began, after Du Sable's example. As to this place's perceived image of decay and chaos, "it [was] more than the 'ghetto' revealed by statistical analysis."[7] This place was haven, home, and heaven.

Another aspect of the connection between land and spirit emerged, one that forecast the formation of even newer neighborhoods and communities. These phenomena occurred within the city's boundaries in the three major divisions—South, West, and North—with the great wave of annexations in 1889. It brought to the forefront a newer set of identities related to residence in specific sides of town—the South Side, the West Side, and the North Side.[8] Thus generic Chicago was much more than the sum of its parts. It reflected what sociologist Louis Wirth of the University of Chicago had observed during the aftermath of the nineteenth century's pattern of growth and development: "The modern metropolis is a cities of cities. It is a mosaic of little worlds, an aggregate of local communities, each one different from the others by its characteristic function in the total economy and cultural complex of city life."[9] Black Chicago and its components aptly fit into this mold.

The physical landscape produced its own social dynamics in the form of massive displays of pageantry. From Emancipation Day celebrations and operatic extravaganzas held indoors to massive church and fraternal picnics located outdoors, festivities abounded and grew in their level of community support. Larger outdoor celebrations followed in the twentieth century, with the inauguration in 1929 of the Bud Billiken Parade (now the nation's largest ethnic celebration, attracting one million people). Hundreds, then thousands upon thousands of persons celebrated life, racial pride, and the potential for a better life personified in Chicago's African American children. Joining these celebrants promenading down the city's major South Side thoroughfares on other occasions were the various fraternal orders and the military-garbed divisions of the Universal Negro Improvement Association. Racial pride sustained civic pride in being in Chicago and a part of Chicago's greatness.

The African American business community flexed its collective muscles and demonstrated emphatically the progress of which Isaac C. Harris had dreamed in 1885. Exemplified by the appearance of the Pekin Theater in 1905, the organization of the *Chicago Defender* newspaper in 1909, and the myriad business endeavors popping up elsewhere along State Street south of Twenty-second Street, African American business emerged as a real economic component in the lives of the city and of the Black Belt community. Nineteenth-century businesses had by necessity been small and oriented to a white market. Late in the century, with a population explosion accompanied by a rising sense of racial consciousness, more and more businesses catered to the residents within the Black Belt community.

The 1920s brought the blooming of the Black Metropolis, which represented the culmination of eight decades of formation, growth, and development. Highlights included the chartering of the Binga State Bank in 1921, a giant step since its inauguration as a personal banking institution in 1908. Anthony Overton expanded his business interests to extend beyond the Overton Hygienic Company he transplanted from Kansas City in 1911. His business empire now encompassed a bank to accommodate the money generated from his insurance company and advertisements in his newspaper. The Douglass National Bank, the Victory Life Insurance Company, and the *Chicago Bee* existed as testimonies to his economic acumen. In a collective sense, black Chicago boosterism took a giant step forward with national recognition of the combined holdings of the Douglass National and Binga State banks. Together, they held and controlled one-third of black America's banking assets.[10] With Robert S. Abbott's vast newspaper holdings, it was not out of the ordinary for these business giants to receive an invitation in 1929 to join greater Chicago's movers and shakers in investing in the proposed "A Century of Progress," Chicago's second world's fair.[11]

Slightly over a half century after Emancipation, black business prowess had advanced so rapidly that it was only a half century behind white Chicago in the production of its millionaire captains of commerce and industry. This remarkable feat coincided with the proliferation of scores of smaller enterprises, some well run and some marginal as to economic efficiency and profitability. Other larger enterprises that competed with them were found in insurance, transportation, and news publication, where the Supreme Liberty Life Insurance Company, Victory Life Insurance Company, and the Metropolitan Mutual Assurance Company, Your Cab Company, and the *Chicago Whip, Bee,* and *Defender* held sway. Isaac C. Harris's publication of the first business directory in 1885, coupled with business expansion, encouraged additional publications that exalted black business successes in every decade of the twentieth century.

The labor arena changed as the First World War began. While racial restrictions throughout the nineteenth century had allowed breakthroughs from the service sector into the industrial only through strikebreaking, this international conflict ironically brought expanded opportunities. Demand for war materiel peaked at a time when the ranks of labor were depleted. Corporate America found an answer by attracting black workers from other areas to Chicago, particularly from the South. Through government inducement, corporate recruiting, and family enticement to join kin in a lucrative job setting as well as a myriad other reasons, black migrants flowed into the city daily until their ranks at war's end reached fifty thousand.

The numbers of professionals continued to grow as migrant needs and the appeal of their services led to the establishment of a solid base from which a discernible middle class was soon to form. Physicians, dentists, attorneys, podiatrists, ministers, teachers, musicians, and others flocked to Chicago. Some came as part of the Great Migration; some came separately but with an awareness of its benefits; all journeyed to Chicago because of its deserved reputation as an economic engine for the middle of the continent. Importantly, few who journeyed, and arrived, ever left.

Race egalitarianism in the twentieth century marked a departure from accommodation to the status quo. Before the Civil War, African Americans relied on whites for guidance and for physical assistance for the refugees, and in preparing the way for Emancipation. An independence of mind and body soon followed, and blacks developed their own circles of leadership. Civil rights protest built to the extent that African Americans could lead the way through protective legislation and court challenges whenever discrimination was encountered. Most blacks ended the century with a reluctance to hope for too much from a society that embraced the notion of racial hierarchy as promoted through Social Darwinism. Yet black resolve was such that when they encountered a proposal for school segregation in 1903, they handily fought the idea and forced its withdrawal.[12]

Then, as the century ended, the appearance of a small yet highly influential coterie of white progressives of the neoabolitionist stripe signaled the championship of equal rights beyond parameters that rested solely on theory. By 1910, to demonstrate conclusively to African Americans that equality of opportunity and equality in interpersonal relations were real, these racial egalitarian stalwarts organized a Chicago branch of the National Association for the Advancement of Colored People, the NAACP. As white racial egalitarians and a small number of their black counterparts from the Niagara Movement merged, the dominant racial ideology of the city among African Americans faced not a total challenge, but a very real influence seeking the hearts, minds, and support of black Chicagoans.[13] At the same time, the national contention between Booker T. Washington and the growing opposition to his thinking and strategies played itself out to a limited degree in Chicago. In addition, the Chicago NAACP had to contend with an indigenous leadership that did not have to answer to a headquarters nine hundred miles away. Locally, African Americans eagerly accepted their direction in civil rights matters from their own chosen leadership found in the Appomattox Club, the Hamilton Club, the National Equal Rights League (to which Ida B. Wells-Barnett belonged), and from the desk of Robert S. Abbott at the *Chicago Defender*.

More important than the Du Bois–Washington dichotomy or the rise of the Chicago NAACP was the possibility of creating a black-led enclave, *imperium en imperio*, in the same manner that other groups were doing in Chicago. The Germans, Poles, Italians, Greeks, Jews, Irish, and Chinese had already formed enclaves that provided both them and any newcomers of their groups with a haven and incubator for their potential power. The Black Belt gave rise to the Black Metropolis, where blacks moved from mere residence to hegemony over their life's affairs. Interestingly, the dream of the Black Metropolis resided not only in the conscious strivings of African Americans who sought to better their condition in America, but also in the nationalist aspirations of many; their goals still sought culmination, and the dream was an attractive means of proving their point in microcosm. Economic and political success at the local level presaged macrocosmic triumph for all of the diasporic Africans. This was a message that Chicagoans heard repeatedly from spokesmen of the Universal Negro Improvement Association and African Communities League as well as from members of the Moorish American Science Temple, and later the Nation of Islam. Perhaps next to Harlem, no other northern city spent so much energy focusing on a life beyond the boundaries of the United States.

Last, politicians continually ran for various offices while they built a firm electoral base from which to catapult themselves into a place of prominence within local and state Republican politics. The road to true political participation as citizens had been tortuous, with inclusion through enfranchisement superceding complete exclusion by law. Greater political consciousness led to the formation of the Appomattox Club in 1900 as a black think tank. At every level of government, the black presence was more noticeable, and a strategy for racial progress was evolving in place of self-serving political participation. The leap to election of the first alderman in 1915 and the ward committeeman in 1920 would be overshadowed soon thereafter with the jump to municipal judge, state senator, and finally congressman in the 1920s.

Often overlooked was the core of activist, sometimes confrontational, black politics. It operated on a level in which agency was nurtured and disgorged; it was marked by a range of relations that ran the spectrum from accommodation to cooperation and collaboration to confrontation and hostility. Basically, it was evidenced in a unique pattern deviating from the national trend of what was termed "neo-clientage" (or racially dependent) politics by political scientist Martin L. Kilson.[14] The emerging composition of political organizations offered the basic clue: The martial spirit of the military and fraternal orders with their hungering for expressions of manhood provided its impetus. Appropriately, Edward H. Wright, the "Iron

Master," provided two examples of the combined power of rhetoric and action. His outburst in 1899, wherein he pointedly asserted the power he wielded as a county commissioner, was followed twenty-seven years later by his proclamation before a U.S. Senate Select Committee hearing in 1926: "I am the [brains behind the] group [in power]."[15] For sheer audacity, three major episodes stand out: Wright's actions in defying a decision made within his own party in 1927, William L. Dawson's congressional challenge against white incumbent Martin B. Madden in 1928, and Oscar De Priest's 1929 confrontation with racial policies in Washington, D.C. None fit the mold of supposed black complacency; all conformed to a pattern of assertiveness set in motion a century and a half previously by Jean Baptiste Pointe Du Sable.

Further, any notion of passivity among males can be quickly dismissed by recalling the stand of the Twenty-ninth Illinois, USCT, at Petersburg and their chase of Lee to Appomattox, the formation of civilians into the Hannibal Guard, Cadets, and the Ninth Battalion, and the mustering in of the Eighth Regiment, Illinois Volunteers, for duty in Cuba. The advent of the First World War found the Eighth Regiment proudly serving in combat in France. Among the women, the services that the "Big Four" furnished in behalf of the abolitionist movement were matched with the vigor that Ida B. Wells-Barnett, Irene McCoy Gaines, and others would provide for the twentieth century's early civil rights movement.

Despite the halcyon days of the 1920s with their accomplishments, successes, and triumphs galore, the dark cloud of economic depression, social dislocation, and political realignment hovered. The Great Depression of the 1930s ended the dream of the Black Metropolis but not the vitalized spirit of black Chicago. In the midst of this catastrophic human tragedy, the attributes that made life bearable and obstacles surmountable in the antebellum era still proved pervasive far into the late twentieth century. As late as 1983, Chicago's first African American mayor, Harold Washington, claimed figurative kinship with Du Sable in light of his electoral triumph.[16] However, that is a story far beyond the scope of this book and even that of the second volume (1901–1933) of Black Chicago's First Century.

Appendix A

The Illinois Black Laws

ILLINOIS STATE STATUTES
CHAPTER LXXIV.
NEGROES' AND MULATTOES.
[Approved March 3, 1845. Rev. Stat. 1845. p. 387]

(1.) Section I. No black[2] or mulatto person shall be permitted to reside in this State, until such person shall produce to the county commissioners' court where he or she is desirous of settling, a certificate of his or her freedom; which certificate shall be duly authenticated in the same manner that is required to be done in cases arising under the acts and judicial proceedings of other States. And until such person shall have given bond, with sufficient security, to the people of this State, for the use of the proper county, in the penal sum of one thousand dollars, conditioned that such person will not, at any time, become a charge to said county, or any other county of this State, as a poor person, and that such person shall, at all times, demean himself or herself, in strict conformity with the laws of this State, that now are or hereafter may be enacted; the solvency of said security shall be approved by said clerk. The clerk shall file said bond, and if said bond shall in any condition thereof be broken, the whole penalty shall become forfeited, and the clerk, on being informed thereof, shall cause the said bond to be prosecuted to effect. And it shall be the duty of such clerk to make an entry of the certificate so produced, and indorse a certificate on the original certificate, stating the time the said bond was approved and filed; and the name and description of the person producing the same; after which it shall be lawful for such free Negro or mulatto to reside in this State.

(2.) SEC. II. If any person shall harbor such Negro or mulatto as aforesaid, not having such certificate, and given bond, and taken a certificate thereof, or shall hire, or in anywise give sustenance to such Negro or mulatto, not having such certificate of freedom, and of having given bond, shall be fined in the sum of five hundred dollars, one-half thereof to the use of [words illegible] information thereof: *Provided,* This section shall not affect any Negro or mulatto who is now a resident of this State.

(3.) SEC. III. It shall be the duty of all free Negroes and mulattoes who shall come to reside in this State, having a family of his or her own, and having a certificate, as mentioned in the first section of this chapter, to give to the clerk of the county commissioners' court, at the time of making an entry of his certificate, a description, with the name and ages of his, her or their family, which shall be stated by the clerk, in the entry made by him or such certificate; and the clerk shall also state the same on the original certificate: *Provided, however,* That nothing contained in this or the preceding section of this chapter, shall be construed to prevent the overseers of the poor in any township from causing any such free Negro or mulatto to be removed, who shall come into this State contrary to the provision of the laws concerning the poor.

(4.) SEC. IV. Every black or mulatto person (slaves and persons held to service excepted,) residing in the State, shall enter his or her name, (unless they have heretofore entered the same,) together with the name or names of his or her family, with the clerk of the county commissioners' court of the county in which they reside, together with the evidence of his or her freedom, which shall be entered on record by the said clerk, together with a description of all such persons; and thereafter the clerk's certificate of such record shall be sufficient evidence for his or her freedom: *Provided,* That nothing in this chapter contained shall be construed to bar the lawful claim of any person or persons to any such Negro or mulatto.

(5.) SEC. V. Every black or mulatto person who shall be found in this State, and not having such a certificate as is required by this chapter, shall be deemed a runaway slave or servant, and it shall be lawful for any inhabitant of this State to take such black or mulatto person before some justice of the peace; and should such black or mulatto person not produce such certificate as aforesaid, it shall be the duty of such justice to cause such black or mulatto person to be committed to the custody of the sheriff or the county, who shall keep such black or mulatto person, and in three days after receiving him, shall advertise him, at the court-house door, and shall transmit a notice, and cause the same to be advertised for six weeks in some public newspaper printed nearest to the place of apprehending such black person or mulatto, stating a description of the most remarkable features of the supposed runaway; and if such person so committed shall not produce a certificate or other evidence of his freedom within the time aforesaid, it shall be the duty of the sheriff to hire him out for the best price he can get, after having given five days' previous notice thereof, from month to month, for the space of one year; and if no owner shall appear and substantiate his claim before the expiration of the year, the sheriff shall give a certificate to such black or mulatto person, who, on producing the same to the next circuit court of the county, may obtain a certificate from the court, stating the facts, and the person shall be deemed a free person, unless he shall be lawfully claimed by his proper owner or owners thereafter. And as a reward to the taker up of such Negro, there shall be paid by the owner, if any, before he shall receive him from the sheriff, ten dollars; and the owner shall pay to the sheriff, for the justice, two dollars, and reasonable costs for taking such runaway to the sheriff, and also pay the sheriff all fees for keeping such runaway, as other prisoners: *Provided, however,* That the proper owner, if any there be, shall be entitled to hire of any such runaway from the sheriff, after deducting the expenses of the same: *And provided, also,* That the taker up shall have a right to claim any reward which the owner shall have offered for the apprehension of such runaway. Should any taker up claim any such offered reward, he shall not be entitled to the allowance made by this section.

(6.) SEC. VI. If any Negro or mulatto, being the property of a citizen of the United States, residing with out this State, shall hereafter come into this State for the purpose of hiring himself or herself to labor in this State, and shall afterwards institute, or procure to be instituted, any suit or proceedings for the purpose of procuring his or her freedom, it shall be the duty of the court before which such suit or proceeding shall be instituted and pending, upon being satisfied that such Negro or mulatto had come into this State for the purpose aforesaid, to dismiss such suit or proceeding, and cause the same to be certified to the sheriff of the county, who shall immediately take possession of such Negro or mulatto, whose duty it shall be to confine such Negro or mulatto in the jail of his county, and notify the owner of such slave of the commitment aforesaid, and the said owner make immediate application for said slave; and it shall be the duty of the sheriff, on such application being made, after all reasonable costs and charges being paid, to deliver to said owner such Negro or mulatto slave.

(7.) SEC. VII. Every servant, upon the expiration of his or her time, and proof thereof made before the circuit court of the county where he or she last served, shall have his or her freedom recorded, and a certificate thereof; under the hand of the clerk, which shall be sufficient to indemnify any person for entertaining or hiring such servant; and if such certificate should happen to be torn or lost, the clerk, upon request, shall issue another, reciting therein the loss of the former.

(8.) SEC. VIII. Any person who shall hereafter bring into this State any black or mulatto person, in order to free him or her from slavery, or shall, directly or indirectly, bring into this State, or aid or assist any person in bringing any such black or mulatto person to settle or reside therein, shall be fined one hundred dollars, on conviction on indictment, or before any justice of the peace in the county where such offense shall be committed.

(9.) SEC. IX. If any slave or servant shall be found at a distance of ten miles from the tenement of his or her master, or the person with whom he or she lives, without a pass, or some letter or token, whereby it may appear that he or she is proceeding by authority from his or her master, employer or overseer, it shall and may be lawful for any person to apprehend and carry him or her before a justice of the peace, to be by his order punished with stripes, not exceeding thirty-five, at his discretion.

(10.) SEC. X. If any slave or servant shall presume to come and be upon the plantation, or at the dwelling of any person whatsoever, without leave from his or her owner, not being sent upon lawful business, it shall be lawful for the owner of such plantation, or dwelling-house, to give or order such slave or servant ten lashes on his or her bare back.

(11.) SEC. XI. Riots, routs, unlawful assemblies, trespasses and seditious speeches, by any slave or slaves, servant or servants, shall be punished with stripes, at the discretion of a justice of the peace, not exceeding thirty-nine, and he who will may apprehend and carry him, her or them before such justice.

(12.) SEC. XII. If any person or persons shall permit or suffer any slave or slaves, servant or servants of color, to the number of three or more, to assemble in his, her or their out-house, yard or shed, for the purpose of dancing or reveling, either by night or by day, the person or persons so offending shall forfeit and pay the sum of twenty dollars with costs, to any person or persons who will sue for and recover the same by action of debt or by indictment, in any court of record proper to try the same.

(13.) SEC. XIII. It shall be the duty of all coroners, sheriffs, judges and justices of the peace, who shall see or know of, or be informed of any such assemblage or slaves or servants, immediately to commit such slaves or servants to the jail of the county, and on view or proof thereof, order each and every such slave or servant to be whipped, not exceeding thirty-nine stripes, on his or her bare back, on the day next succeeding such assemblage, unless it shall happen on a Sunday, then on the Monday following; which said stripes shall be inflicted by any constable of the township, if there should be one therein, or otherwise, by any person or persons whom the said justices shall appoint, and who shall be willing so to inflict the same: *Provided, however,* That the provisions hereof shall not apply to any persons of color who may assemble for the purpose of amusement, by permission of their master, first had in writing, on condition that no disorderly conduct is made use of by them in such assemblage.

(14.) SEC. XIV. In all cases of penal laws, where free persons are punishable by fine, servants shall be punished by whipping, after the rate of twenty lashes for every eight dollars, so that no servant shall receive more than forty lashes at any one time, unless such offender can procure some person to pay the fine.

(15.) SEC. XV. No person shall buy, sell, or receive of, to or from any servant or slave, any coin or commodity, without leave or consent of the master or owner of such slave or servant, and any person so offending shall forfeit and pay to the master or owner of such slave or servant four times the value of the thing so bought, sold or received, to be recovered with costs of suit, before any court having cognizance of the same.

(16.) SEC. XVI. Any such servant being lazy, disorderly, guilty of misbehavior to his master or master's family, shall be corrected by stripes, on order from a justice of the county wherein he resides; or refusing to work, shall be compelled there to in like manner, and moreover shall serve two days for every one he shall have so refused to serve, or shall otherwise have lost, without sufficient justification. All necessary expenses incurred by any master for apprehending and bringing home any absconding servant, shall be repaid by further services, after such rates as the circuit court of the county shall direct, unless such servant shall give security, to be approved by the court, for the payment in money within six months after he shall be free from service, and shall accordingly pay the same.

(17.) SEC. XVII. All contracts between masters and servants, during the time of service, shall be void.

(18.) SEC. XVIII. The benefit of any contract of service shall be assignable by the master to any person being a citizen of this State, to whom the servant shall, in the presence of a justice of the peace, freely consent that it shall be assigned, the said justice attesting such free consent in writing; and shall also pass to the executors, administrators and legatees of the master.

(19.) SEC. XIX. No Negro, mulatto or Indian, shall at any time purchase any servant, other than of his own complexion; and if any of the persons aforesaid shall, nevertheless, presume to purchase a white servant, such servant shall immediately become free, and shall be so held, deemed and taken.

(20.) SEC. XX. Servants shall be provided by the master with wholesome and sufficient food, clothing and lodging; and at the end of their service, if they shall not have contracted for any reward, food, clothing and lodging, shall receive from him one new and complete suit of clothing, suited to the season of the year, to wit: a coat, waistcoat, pair of breeches and shoes, two pairs of stockings, two shirts, a hat and blanket.

(21.) SEC. XXI. If any servants shall at any time bring in goods or money during the time of their service, or shall, by gift or other lawful means, acquire goods or money, they shall have the property and benefit thereof for their own use; and if any servant shall be sick or lame, and so become useless or chargeable, his or her master or owner shall maintain such servant until his or her time of service shall be expired; and if any master or owner shall put away a lame or sick servant, under the pretense of freedom, and such servant becomes chargeable to the county, such master or owner shall forfeit and pay thirty dollars to the overseers of the poor of the county wherein such offense shall be committed, to the use of the poor or the county, recoverable with costs, by action of debt, in any circuit court; and, moreover, shall be liable to the action of the said overseers of the poor at the common law for damages.

(22.) SEC. XXII. The circuit court of every county shall, at all times, receive the complaints of servants, being citizens of any of the United States of America, who reside within the jurisdiction of such court, against their masters or mistresses, alleging undeserved or immoderate correction, insufficient allowances of food, raiment or lodging, or any failure in the duties of such master or mistress as prescribed in this chapter; and the said circuit court shall hear and determine complaints of masters and mistresses against their servants, for desertion without good cause, and may oblige the latter, for loss thereby occasioned, to make restitution by further services after the expiration of the time for which they had been bound.

(23.) SEC. XXIII. Any black, Colored[3] or mulatto man and white woman, and any white man and black, Colored, or mulatto woman, who shall live together in an open state of adultery or fornication, or adultery and fornication, shall be indicted, and on conviction, severally [sic] fined, in any sum not exceeding five hundred dollars, and confined in the penitentiary for a term not exceeding one year. For the second offense, the punishment shall be double; for the third, trebled, and in the same ratio for each succeeding offense.

AN ACT TO PREVENT THE IMMIGRATION OF FREE NEGROES INTO THIS STATE.
[Approved Feb. 12, 1853. Laws, 1853, p. 57]

(24.) Sec. I. Be it enacted by the People of the State of Illinois, represented in the General Assembly, That if any person or persons shall bring, or cause to be brought into this State, any Negro or mulatto slave, whether said slave is set free or not, shall be liable to an indictment, and, upon conviction thereof, be fined for every such Negro or mulatto, a sum not less than one hundred dollars, nor more than five hundred dollars, and imprisoned in the county jail not more than one year, and shall stand committed until said fine and costs are paid.

(25.) Sec. II. When an indictment shall be found against any person or persons, who are not residents of this State, it shall be the duty of the court before whom said indictment is pending, upon affidavit being made and filed in said court by the prosecuting attorney, or any other credible witness, setting forth the non-residence of said defendant, to notify the governor of this State, by causing the clerk of said court to transmit to the office of the Secretary of State a certified copy of said indictment and affidavit; and it shall be the duty of the governor, upon the receipt of said copies, to appoint some suitable person to arrest said defendant or defendants, in whatever State or county he or they may be found, and to commit him or them to the jail of the county in which said indictment is pending, there to remain and answer said indictment, and be otherwise dealt with in accordance with this act. And it shall be the duty of the governor to issue all necessary requisitions, writs and papers to the governor or other executive officer of the State, territory or province where such defendant or defendants may be found: *Provided*, That this section shall not be construed so as to affect persons, or slaves, *bona fide* traveling through this State from and to any other State in the United States.

(26.) Sec. III. If any Negro, or mulatto, bond or free, shall hereafter come into this State and remain ten days, with the evident intention of residing in the same, every such Negro or mulatto shall be deemed guilty of a high misdemeanor, and for the first offense shall be fined the sum of fifty dollars, to be recovered before any justice of the peace in the county where said Negro or mulatto may be found. Said proceedings shall be in the name of the people of the State of Illinois, and shall be tried by a jury of twelve men. The person making the information or complaint shall not be a competent witness upon said trial.

(27.) Sec IV. If said Negro or mulatto shall be found guilty, and the fine assessed be not paid forthwith to the justice of the peace before whom said proceedings were had, it shall be the duty of said justice to commit said Negro or mulatto to the custody of the sheriff of said county, or otherwise keep him, her or them in custody; and said justice shall forthwith advertise said Negro or mulatto, by posting up notices thereof in at least three of the most public places in his district, which said notices shall be posted up for ten days, and on the day and at the time and place mentioned in said advertisement, the said justice shall, at public auction, proceed to sell said Negro or mulatto to any person or persons who will pay said fine and costs, for the shortest time; and said purchaser shall have the right to compel said Negro or mulatto to work for and serve out said time, and he shall furnish said Negro or mulatto with comfortable food, clothing and lodging during said servitude.

(28.) Sec. V. If said Negro or mulatto shall not, within ten days after the expiration of his, her or their time of service as aforesaid, leave the State, he, she or they shall be liable to a second prosecution, in which the penalty to be inflicted shall be one hundred dollars, and so on for every subsequent offense the penalty shall be increased fifty dollars over and above the last penalty inflicted, and the same proceedings shall be had in each case as is provided for in the proceeding sections for the first offense.

(29.) Sec. VI. Said Negro or mulatto shall have a right to take an appeal to the circuit court of the county in which said proceedings shall have been had, within five days after the rendition of the judgment, before the justice of the peace, by giving bond and security, to be approved by the clerk of said court, to the people of the State of Illinois, and to be filed in the office of said court within said five days, in double the amount of said fine and costs, conditioned that the party appealing will personally be and appear before said court at the next term thereof, and not depart said court without leave, and will pay said fine and all costs, if the same shall be so adjudged by said court; and said security shall have the right to take said Negro or mulatto into custody, and retain the same until the order of said court is complied with. And if the judgment of the justice of the peace be affirmed in whole or in part, and said Negro or mulatto be found guilty, the said circuit court shall thereupon render judgment against said Negro or mulatto and the security of securities on said appeal bond, for the amount of fine so found by the court, and all costs of suit, and the clerk of said court shall forthwith issue an execution against said defendant and security as in other cases, and the sheriff or other officer to whom said execution is directed, shall proceed to collect the same by sale or otherwise: *Provided*, That this section shall not be so construed as to give the security on said appeal bond right to retain the custody of said Negro or mulatto for a longer time than ten days after the rendition of said judgment by said circuit court.

(30.) Sec. VII. In all cases arising under the provisions of this act, the prosecuting witness, or person making the complaint and prosecuting the same, shall be entitled to one-half of the fine so imposed and collected, and the residue of said fine shall be paid into the county treasury of the county in which said proceedings were had; and said fines, when so collected, shall be received by said county treasurer, and kept by him as a distinct and separate fund, to be called the "charity fund"; and said fund shall be used for the express and only purpose of relieving the poor of said county, and shall be paid out by said treasurer upon the order of the county court of said county, drawn upon him for that purpose.

(31.) Sec. VIII. If, after any Negro or mulatto shall have been arrested under the provisions of this act, any person or persons shall claim any such Negro or mulatto as a slave, the owner, by himself, or agent, shall have a right, by giving reasonable notice to the officer or person having the custody of said Negro or mulatto, to appear before the justice of the peace before whom said Negro or mulatto shall have been arrested, and prove his or their right to the custody of said Negro or mulatto as a slave, and if said justice of the peace shall, after hearing the evidence, be satisfied that the person or persons claiming said Negro or mulatto, is or are the owner or owners of and entitled to the custody of said Negro or mulatto, in accordance with the laws of the United States passed upon this subject, he shall, upon the owner or agent paying all costs up to the time of claiming said Negro or mulatto, and the costs of proving the same, and also the balance of the fine remaining unpaid, give to said owner a certificate of said facts, and said owner or agent so claiming, shall have a right to take and remove said slave out of this State.

(32.) Sec. IX. If any justice of the peace shall refuse to issue any writ or process necessary for the arrest and protection of any Negro or mulatto under the provisions of this act, upon complaint being made before said justice by any resident of his county, and his fees for said service being tendered him, he shall be deemed guilty of non-feasance in office, and upon conviction thereof, punished accordingly; and in all cases where the jury find for the Negro or mulatto, or that he, she or they are not guilty under the provisions of this act, the said justice of the peace shall proceed to render judgment against the prosecuting witness, or person making the complaint, and shall collect the same as other judgments: *Provided,* That said prosecuting witness, or person making said complaint, in case judgment is rendered against him, shall have a right to take an appeal to the circuit court, as is provided for in this act, in case said Negro or mulatto is found guilty.

(33.) Sec. X. Every person who shall have one-fourth Negro blood shall be deemed a mulatto.

(34.) Sec. XI. This act shall take effect and be in force from and after its passage.

PRIOR LAWS. An act respecting free Negroes, mulattoes, servants and slaves; in force March 30, 1819. Laws, 1819, p. 354; Rev. Laws, 1833, p. 457.

An act to amend an act entitled "An act respecting free Negroes, mulattoes, servants and slaves," approved March 30, 1819; in force Jan. 3, 1825. Laws, 1825, p. 50.

An act respecting free Negroes, mulattoes, servants and slaves; in force Jan. 17, 1829. Rev. Laws, 1833, p. 463.

An act to amend an act entitled "An act respecting free Negroes, mulattoes, servants and slaves," approved Jan. 17, 1829; in force Feb. 1, 1831. Rev. Laws, 1833, p. 462.

An act to amend an act entitled "An act respecting free Negroes, mulattoes, servants, and slaves," approved March 30, 1819; in force March 1, 1833. Rev Laws, 1833, p. 466.

An act in relation to free Negroes and mulattoes; in force Feb. 19, 1841. Laws, 1841, p. 189.

DECISIONS. To create the relation of master and servant, under the territorial act of Sept. 17, 1807, the indenture should be executed by both parties, before the clerk. *Cornelius v. Cohen*, Breese, 92. See *Nance v. Howard*, Breese, 83.

The act of 1807, respecting the introduction of Negroes and mulattoes into the territory, is void, it being repugnant to the 6th article of the ordinance of 1787; but indentures made under that law, are valid by the 3rd section, 6th article, of the constitution of Illinois. *Phoebe v. Jay, Breese*, 207. See *Choisser v. Hargrove*, 1 S. 317.

The children of Negroes and mulattoes, registered under the territorial laws of Indiana and Illinois, are free; and the proviso of section 3, Article 6, of the constitution of Illinois, does not render the persons therein named subject to servitude. *Beon v. Juliet*, 1 S. 258.

In the State of Illinois every person is presumed free, without regard to color, and the sale of a free person is illegal. *Bailey v. Cromwell, et al.* 3 S. 71; *Kenney v. Cook*, 3 S. 232. See also, case of *Sarah v. Borders*, 4 S. 341, in which the case of *Phoebe v. Jay*, Breese, 207, is re-affirmed.

The State of Illinois has power to prohibit the introduction of Negro slaves into the State, and to punish its citizens who introduce them. *Eells v. The People*, 4 S. 498.

The clerks of the county commissioners' courts, as successors of the clerks of the court of common pleas, and of the county courts, have the same powers and duties as their predecessors, in reference to the registering of indentured servants, under the territorial laws of Indiana and Illinois. The facts necessary to warrant the registry need not to be recited therein. The point settled in the case of *Phoebe v. Jay*, Breese, 207, is recognized in this case. *Hays v. Borders*, 1 G. 46.

A Colored person may maintain an action for services rendered, and in such action his right to freedom may be tried. The descendants of the slaves of the old French settlers, born since the ordinance of 1787, and before or since the adoption of the constitution of Illinois, cannot be held in slavery in the State. *Jarrot v. Jarrot*, 2 G. 1.

Section 5, chapter 74, Rev. Stat., 1845, is void, because it assumes to legislate on the subject of the recaption of fugitive slaves, over which subject Congress has supreme and exclusive power.

The statute in reference to Negroes and mulattoes, does not authorize the taking of a bond, until the Negro or mulatto has produced his certificate of freedom; and such Negroes and mulattoes only can reside here, who furnish evidence of their freedom and give bond under the statute. *Owens et al. v. People, Sc.*, 13 Ill. 59.

A contract made in Illinois, for the sale of a person as a slave, who is, at the time, in the State, and to a citizen of the State, is illegal and void. TRUMBULL, J. A note, taken in consideration of such a sale, will not be enforced, unless there is affirmative proof to rebut the legal presumption of freedom. CATON, J. *Hone v. Ammons*, 14 Ill. 29.

Appendix B

An Act to Repeal the "Black Laws"

AN ACT to repeal section sixteen (16) of division III, chapter XXX of the Revised Statutes, all of chapter LXXIV of said Revised Statutes, and an act entitled "An act to prevent the immigration of free Negroes into this state," commonly known as the "Black Laws."

SECTION 1. *Be it enacted by the People of the State of Illinois, represented in the General Assembly,* That section sixteen (16) division III, chapter XXX, of the Revised Statutes of this state, entitled "Criminal Jurisprudence," and chapter LXXIV of said Revised Statutes, entitled "Negroes and Mulattoes," and an act of the general assembly of this state, approved February 12, 1853, entitled "An act to prevent the immigration of free Negroes into this state," be and the same are hereby repealed; also section 23, chapter XL, Revised Statutes, entitled "Evidence and Depositions."

SECTION 2. This act to be in force from and after its passage.

APPROVED February 7, 1865.

Appendix C

An Act to Protect Colored Children in Their Rights to Attend School

AN ACT TO PROTECT COLORED CHILDREN
IN THEIR RIGHTS TO ATTEND SCHOOL.
[Approved March 24, 1874. In force July 1, 1874.]

100. NO EXCLUSIONS FOR COLOR. 1. Be it enacted by the People of the State of Illinois, represented in the General Assembly, That all directors of schools, boards of education, or other school officers whose duty it now is, or may be hereafter, to provide, in their respective jurisdictions, schools for the education of all children between the ages of six and twenty-one years, are prohibited from excluding, directly or indirectly, any such child from school on account of the color of such child.

101. PENALTY. 2. Any such school officer or officers as are mentioned in the foregoing section, or any other person, who shall exclude, or aid in the exclusion from public schools any child who is entitled to the benefits of such school, on account of such child's color, shall be fined, upon conviction, in any sum not less than 5 nor more than $100 each for every such offense.

102. INTIMIDATION OF COLORED CHILD. 3. Any person who shall, by threats, menace or intimidation, prevent any colored child entitled to attend a public school in this state from attending such school, shall, upon conviction, be fined in any sum not exceeding $25.

Appendix D

Illinois General Assembly, House Bill 45–1885

CIVIL RIGHTS
Protection to Citizens

AN ACT *to protect all citizens in their civil and legal rights and fixing a penalty for violation of the same.*

SECTION 1. *Be it enacted by the People of the State of Illinois, represented in the General Assembly:* That all persons within the jurisdiction of said State shall be entitled to the full and equal enjoyment of the accommodations, advantages, facilities and privileges of inns, restaurants, eating houses, barber shops, public conveyances on land or water, theaters, and all other places of public accommodation and amusement, subject only to the conditions and limitations established by law, and applicable alike to all citizens.

SECTION 2. That any person who shall violate any of the provisions of the foregoing section by denying to any citizen, except for reasons applicable alike to all citizens of every race and color, and regardless of color or race, the full enjoyment of any of the accommodations, advantages, facilities, or privileges in said section enumerated, or by aiding or inciting such denial, shall, for every such offense, forfeit and pay a sum not less than twenty-five (25) dollars nor more than five hundred (500) dollars to the person aggrieved thereby, to be recovered in any court of competent jurisdiction, in the county where said offense was committed; and shall also, for every such offense, be deemed guilty of a misdemeanor, and upon conviction thereof, shall be fined not to exceed five hundred (500) dollars, or shall be imprisoned not more than one year, or both: *And, provided, further,* that a judgement in favor of the party aggrieved, or punishment upon an indictment, shall be a bar to either prosecution respectively.

APPROVED June 10, 1885.

Appendix E

Data from "Jubilee"

Chicago's Black Civil War Soldiers

This study of black Chicagoans depended heavily on the federal pension records of Chicago Civil War veterans of the Twenty-ninth Infantry Regiment of the USCT (United States Colored Troops). Chicagoans as defined fell into four categories: (1) pre–Civil War residents with a residency in the city of any duration; (2) recent refugees of several months or a year's residence who reached the city during the war; (3) prospective veterans who migrated to Chicago as a result of their having been emancipated as part of the military activities of white Illinois units in both the Deep and Upper South; and (4) the immediate families and kin of the veterans. These veterans and their families had an impact on life in Chicago and in turn were influenced by the city. The meaning and scope of their lives—collectively and individually—are complex, surprising, and intriguing. The temporal and spatial dimensions of the study extended from around 1814 with an early life in captivity in the American South for Company C's fifty-year-old wagon master, William Armstrong, to the year 1939, with the death of Mrs. Amanda Jane Stewart, the widow of Company B's Private James Stewart. Both Stewarts were born in Chicago but eventually moved in a contemporary, westward, migratory pattern to the Fox River Valley on the outer rim of the Chicago area.

Of the 1,811 men carried on the regiment's roster, it was obvious that probably less than one-third were Illinoisans recruited in their own state, and among their ranks were to be found many Missourians along with persons from the bordering states of Wisconsin, Indiana, and Kentucky. Examining two key references, I gleaned a list of soldiers who designated a Chicago residency at the time of their enlistment: They were on the original, handwritten recruiting rosters of the regiment and the *Report of the Adjutant General of the State of Illinois, Volume VIII*, which contained reports on Illinois troops for the years 1861–1865. These records yielded a total of roughly two hundred potential "Chicagoans," with a highly unscientific inference putting this figure at perhaps 5 to 10 percent of the total regimental complement. Of this pool, an even smaller percentage originated from or had strong ties to Chicago. These were the one hundred men of Companies B and C in particular, but also some other companies—A, D, E, F, and G.

Characteristics of soldiers gleaned individually from federal pension records allow partial reconstruction not only of their lives as individuals and families but as a population in the aggregate. Regimental historian Miller had written that "collectively, therefore, the files allow conclusions to be drawn about soldiers' lives, which is particularly useful regarding veterans of black regiments composed mainly of illiterate men who left few other records."[1] For a history of Chicago, information had to be specific in its relation to the city for the most part, although inferential material had value also. Fortunately, my labor in the vineyards yielded savory Chicago fruit. For example, Willis and David Easley, Alexander Garrett, Moses Conley, Hardin Harris, Rodney Long, Richard Barbour, and others had federal pension records filled with ample documentation of how they lived their lives as well as how they fared in the process of obtaining a pension because of bodily disability, age, or dependency. Richard Barbour, for example, spent his formative, adolescent years in the North, in Chicago, living with his parents and working as a porter and waiter on lakebound ships, so he grew up outside the slave regimen. But even Barbour expressed uncertainty at times about his birth date, although he usually believed he knew it with certainty. Thus, he still had difficulties in proving his age to the satisfaction of federal examiners. Others were more unfortunate and failed in their efforts to determine their exact dates of birth.

The pension process, by its every nature, represented inclusion in the citizenship process for thousands of African Americans who had served in the war. Despite the persistence of racism nationally during the postwar period, African Americans applied and, in many occasions, qualified for payments from a generous, grateful, and politically savvy Republican-dominated government. Pension payment supplemented income or became, in the instances of the near destitute, the sole source of survival income. As these combat veterans participated in the process of interview, examination, and litigation, the required behavior and attitudes transformed them into bona fide citizens.

Miller has written that the final adjudication of claims was basically fair. If so, the preliminary stage was still filled with bitterness and personal, psychological conflict. The process of substantiating a claim as an invalid, aged soldier, or dependent was complex and demanding for any American citizen, but it was especially so for persons who endured combat following a lifetime of physical and emotional turmoil during bondage. Significantly, even with the legal end of slavery—an end these men had helped make possible—the rigors of pursuing claims dredged up the painful and somewhat enduring memories of their previous and best-forgotten lives in slavery. With regularity, federal examiners posed inquiries for verification of identities or conducted interviews for the purpose of completing depositions. Names of slave masters and the places of enslavement were recalled frequently, although comments about the conditions of slavery were rarely mentioned directly by whites all too willing to bury the past in the name of sectional reconciliation. This posture was also somewhat understandable given the nature of the growing bureaucracy. The officials conducting interviews and transcribing information for the signed depositions focused primarily on authenticating information directly related to vital statistics—age, birthplace, names, family ties, marriage, and so on. In the case of Private John Blakely of Company C, these poignant feelings sprang forth: "I do not know how old I am . . . . I cannot read. I have no kinfolks that I know of, except white folk related to the Lyons family who owned me before the war."[2]

The case of the widow of Private John Washington, Mrs. Violet Washington, represents the most common occurrence, in that the specter of slavery reappeared through official request. The Bureau of Pensions in Washington, D.C., contacted her with an inquiry directed through local officials to comply with a request to provide a "personal description and name of [the] former owner." Sometimes an inquiry proved unnecessary, such as in the case of Private Jordan Stewart, who died at the Battle of the Crater. Stewart's parents filed a dependent's claim in their old age and could not respond to the request to "furnish personal description of soldier, and name of former owner." Stewart's parents were Illinoisans who had married as free people in 1845, so his birthright was one of inherited liberty.[3] Evoking memory produced one of the most damning indictments of American slavery whenever the issue of marriage was mentioned. The precariousness of the slave marriage reflected slave sales and transfer of these humans as gifts of property. Significantly, the effectiveness of resistance to the slave system appeared in at least two occasions when the underground railroad was alluded to or directly mentioned.[4]

Initiating claims gradually brought these veterans, moreover, into the American mainstream as participating citizens. This set of procedures required information gathering and formed a significant portion of the social data used in the present volume. If these soldiers ever doubted their citizenship, the process affirmed their right to belong to America as part of its social fabric. Moreover, the process led to the intersection of persons with normally disparate lives. Veterans and their families were obliged to associate with individuals and groups, both black and white, with whom they might never have had contact. In the expanding African American community of Chicago, it meant that veterans had contact with leading members of that expanding group's population. The archives denote repeated linkage between them and the rising African American professional coterie as its members provided services to the veterans and their families. Physicians and attorneys already mentioned appeared prominently in documents. Institutions such as Provident Hospital and the *Conservator*, black Chicago's first newspaper, materialized also in their lives. Prominent white public figures were accessible, for example, as U.S. Representative Martin B. Madden and U.S. Senator Ruth Hanna McCormick proffered their services to constituents to assist in resolving veteran's claims.

Because race was such an influential factor in American life, a digression is in order to examine what influence it had over the lives of the prospective pensioners. Too often among the federal pension examiners, racial etiquette relied on racist assumptions and protocol. More often than not, African Americans were considered unreliable witnesses and little veracity was given to their accounts of their lives. It might have been a matter of white examiners reflecting a societal norm in treating blacks as inveterate liars, a trait associated with the latter's previous period of enslavement when the truth was what the master wanted it to be. Or, it might have resulted, in the white mind, from assuming that blacks were liars or prevaricators biologically. Deep in an examiner's subconscious, or even in the conscious mind, the lack of education on the part of interviewees probably led to a perceived notion that in terms of general intelligence, they were deficient. Overly intelligent blacks were considered manipulative of other blacks, shrewd, or uppity. Summaries of deponents often evaluated African American testimony as fair to unreliable. Rarely did the rating of "good" appear.

As though race was a determinant of veracity, special examiner J. R. Fritts used the designation "Colored" following the names of deponents who were African American.[5] Investigator examiner A. Erdman saw fit to annotate one deposition in 1896 with information that the deponent was both "colored [and] blind."[6] In his mind, it obviously bore relevance to the credibility of the person making the deposition. Examiner Read Hanna investigated the widow's claim of Mrs. Malinda Chappell that contained the potential elements for disqualification—that is, racial disqualification. He indignantly wrote:

> This matter is referred (from Washington, D.C.) to me to determine whether . . . her conduct has been such as would otherwise work a forfeiture of title to pension as his widow and particularly to ascertain whether she lived with the soldier continuously from the date of marriage to the date of his death. . . . The claimant impressed me fairly well

and about as truthful as a colored woman in her walk of life usually is. She washes and irons for a living, is fairly intelligent, perhaps above the average colored woman who washes and irons. . . . She makes her home, on a [level of] social equality with Edward Knapp and his wife, two degenerate white people. They attend a colored church and have sunk to the level of colored people.[7]

When Mrs. Chappell was deposed, she explained her devotion to her husband and her daily attending to his needs to his death. When Edward Knapp was deposed, he spoke positively of his relationship with African Americans: "My wife and I [are] engaged . . . in Mission work. I like the Colored church, Quinn Chapel, because the Colored people are a spiritual people and for this reason I belong to Quinn Chapel. . . . I was for a time assistant organist there." Special examiner J. H. Hines had these thoughts on the wife of another veteran involved in a biracial marriage: "When a girl, she was driven from pillar to post, and knows nothing about her family. That is the kind of girl that will take up with a Negro."[8]

On the other hand, special examiner J. H. Stibbs appeared conscientious, compassionate, especially meticulous, and racially enlightened in his interviewing and recording. After evaluating the claim of the family of Private Louis Clary, whose death in 1877 led to his mother filing a dependent's claim in 1892, Stibbs wrote a most telling summation. Included was the following:

> The witnesses to origin are of the best of their class, and I think it may safely be conceded that [the] soldier's death was due to disease contracted in the service. The claimant is a thoroughly honest old woman [of seventy years], who tells her story just as she remembers it. As she states, she and her family lived as the average of their class and it is difficult to say wherein she was a dependent, but the family were all workers. Soldier [was] the most important of the lot, and his steady and certain earnings were [words illegible] to meet current expenses. In an ordinary "white case" there would be no doubt as to the mother's dependence, or as I view it we must consider that claimant was a dependent under the law.[9]

Attempts at efficiency in racial designations could produce interoffice friction. One examiner was chastised for having asked a white deponent if he were white. "It is noted that in taking the testimony of three white persons, you required them to state whether they were related to the claimant. While it is a rule of practice that the relationship of claimants and witnesses be shown, it is also true that special examiners should use judgment in such matters. Hereafter you will please omit the question of relationship when the witness is white and the claimant colored."[10] One major problem in this instance was the general reluctance to admit that slavery had produced close interracial contacts, even though biracial unions began after 1619 and the racial categories were never clearly defined. In one particular case, a very important witness, the soldier's stepson, Ethelbert Graves, was the progeny of a mixed racial union.[11] In another instance, Corporal William McKenney's widow was chagrined to learn, thirty years after she had married the soldier, that he had been married previously. His earlier spouse had been a white woman who had resided both in Wisconsin and Chicago. Deposed several times (because disputed information in this claim extended over decades), the previous wife admitted her marriage to the soldier while denying that she ever knew that he was an African American. Then, as it turned out, she had been the second wife instead of the first, and the claim of the third wife was finally resolved as permanently denied in 1929.[12]

Even with the reality of interracial marriages, an examiner could dismiss a lead because of racial differences. As he investigated whether veteran William Graves had married and divorced a certain Eliza Jackson in the 1870s, examiner Read Hanna wrote,

> There is no record of divorce. I made a personal search of the chancery records of the only courts of jurisdiction and this search was verified by the Chicago Title and Trust Co., which has a complete record of all divorces granted in Cook Co., from its earliest organization. . . . I also searched the city directories. . . . In the phone directory I found Mrs. Eliza Jackson [on south Wabash Avenue] and learned she is not the party. I found Mrs. Eliza A. Jackson [on the West Side] and learned she is not identical with soldier's former wife. She is a white woman.[13]

Positive evaluations of African Americans were rare; one of the most in-depth of these, however, was by a Michigan witness, Walter Duke. In commenting on his lengthy deposition, the special examiner observed:

> Claimant bears a most excellent reputation in every way, and her statement generally may be relied on as truthful to the best of her memory—and the same may be said as to Walter Duke, who is a colored man. This Walter Duke, is a remarkable old character—he is something of a lawyer, a doctor, and a civil engineer, all of which he has picked up by observation and experience; and has been consulted in more capabilities than any man in the neighborhood, although he is a colored man. His word has never been questioned—consequently I was particular in taking

his deposition. The similarity between his testimony and that of Mrs. Potter—who is white—will be noticed, and speaks well for his entire truthfulness, as he did [not] know I had seen Mrs. Potter before I saw him.[14]

Despite the value attached to this testimony and that of others, the dependent child's claim was denied.

As to the particular value of the data contained in federal pension records, they turned out to be troves of information on life in Chicago, and each usually provided the military history of more than one soldier, since interactions with comrades were regularly cited. Material was gleaned in eight general areas: (1) vital statistics; (2) health and physical appearance; (3) sphere of work and occupation; (4) education and literacy; (5) marriage and family formation; (6) associational and organizational activities; (7) combat and wartime experience; and (8) postwar adjustment.

The first examination was of origins or vital statistics that affirmed "being," including place of, date of, and birth-status of the soldier, and any other related circumstances. Place and status at birth constituted the essential elements that the slave system stole from the African labor force to enhance its control. Proving one's date of birth involved the applicant in a sometimes grueling process. Important questions that many times could not be answered were: Did the soldier grow up within or outside of the slave regimen? Were the soldier's parents enslaved or free? What were his life's opportunities in this milieu? Was the soldier's birth recorded, either conferring or denying him a sense of belonging to humanity? Did he have a family name of his own choosing?

In general, we all have an awareness of this problem from some of the most famous voices in American life and literature. "I was born a slave on a plantation in Franklin County, Virginia. I am not quite sure of the exact place or exact date of my birth, but at any rate I suspect I must have been born somewhere and at some time." This uncertainty of existence came from Booker T. Washington. Another famous voice, that of a frequent visitor to Chicago, Frederick Douglass, repeated this lament: "The reader must not expect me to say much of my family. Genealogical trees did not flourish among slaves. A person of some consequence in civilized society, sometimes designated as father, was literally unknown to slave law and to slave practice. I never met with a slave in that part of the country who could tell me with certainty how old he was. Few at that time knew anything of the months of the year or the days of the month. They measured the ages of their children by spring-time, winter-time, harvest-time, planting-time and the like. Masters allowed no questions concerning their ages to be put to them by slaves. Such questions were regarded by the masters as evidence of an impudent curiosity. From certain events, however, the dates of which I have since learned, I suppose myself to have been born in February, 1817."[15]

Private Alexander Garrett exemplified Chicago's story. The veteran knew his birth date, or at least imagined he did with self-mesmerizing certitude. In an affidavit completed on November 14, 1907, he agreed to the accuracy of this statement: "I am unable to furnish any record of my birth as I was born during the slave period and no record was made at the time, but I do remember distinctly that my parents gave the date of my birth as Feb. 7, 1844, the family bible being burned up in 1871, but there was no record either in the Bible or otherwise."[16] On various occasions, his age indicated different dates of birth.

Garrett's widow became embroiled in a controversy over his date of birth and encountered these exacting requirements:

> He should furnish a certified copy of the public record, showing the date of his birth, if such a record exists, if not, a certified copy of the baptismal or family record.
>
> If the certified copy is furnished, the magistrate certifying the same should state in what year the Bible, or other book in which the record appears, was printed, whether the record bears any marks of erasure or alteration, and whether, from the appearance of the writing, he believes the entries to have been made about the dates given.
>
> If the claimant is unable to furnish any of the evidence indicated, he should state, with reasons, under oath.[17]

Different circumstances existed for the veteran and future Chicagoan William Graves, who was sold many times as a slave before he entered military service in 1863. Born in Kentucky to slave parents, he was sold to Missouri slave owner William Falconer, and then to a slave master in Louisiana. To prove his age, he depended on the family Bible of his Missouri master. Some controversy followed his efforts. When the illiterate former soldier was asked to explain how he knew how to contact his former master's family, he replied, "I found his residence by inquiring in Kansas City. I know the section of the city in which he lives and know all the streets by name but can not read numbers and do not know his address but I know I can find it by going there myself."[18]

James Jones was born in Terre Haute, Indiana, in 1845 but experienced as much difficulty in proving his age as anyone born under the humiliating omissions and restrictions of the southern slave system. Winning a pension based on disability, he suffered a reduction based on an age discrepancy in 1915. When he wrote to the government in 1913, his letter conveyed the feelings of a tired man. "My military descriptive roll will show that I was 18 past when I entered the service. I have no record of my birth, only as I have kept it in my head, but I feel like I was a hundred years old." When Richard Barbour's mother, Mrs. Eliza Barbour, was deposed on information about her son, her statement as to her age was uncertain: "I am about 60 years of age." Documentation available, however, showed that she was somewhere between eighty and ninety years of age. When Louis Clary's sister, Mrs. Emma Clary Bell, was deposed on information about her brother, her statement as to her age was just as uncertain: "I am about 42 years of age." Veteran John Abrams's widow, Julia Simpson Abrams, described her age in the same way: "I don't know my exact age but I think I am about 56 years of age." Her sister said, "I guess I must be about ten or fifteen years older than she is, although I don't know definitely. My mother was a slave, she lived in St. Louis, Missouri, [and] she escaped and came to Chicago during the war."[19]

Obviously, one's name was also important, whether chosen or assigned. "Masters and slaves considered slave names in the same context, although from opposite points of view. Both understood that names identified class and status and marked an appropriate degree of respect. . . . Masters sometimes gave their slaves surnames; more often, with or without their masters' consent or even knowledge, the slaves took surnames for themselves. . . . After the war slaves throughout the South took surnames or openly announced those they already had. Appropriately, they called them 'entitles.' . . . With freedom, many blacks took particular surnames for reasons other than to establish a historical link with their own family, especially since it was often difficult or impossible to do so. At the very least, they wanted the privilege of selecting a name and thereby establishing their right to make a choice. In some cases they were resorting to a ruse. 'When us black folks got set free,' explained Alice Wilkins, 'us'n change our names, so effen the white folks get together and change their minds and don't let us be free any more, then they have a hard time finding us.'"[20]

In particular, as important as date of birth was to affirming identity, one's name was just as important. In seeking to prove his identity, William Graves sought the assistance of his former master's son-in-law. His description of loss of a name and confused identity is telling: "I am acquainted with the claimant in this case, William Graves, known by me better by the name of Sanford, but I am positive that Graves and Sanford are one and the same person as I have known him for many years and when he was a slave and belonged to Mr. William Falconer formerly of Lexington Kentucky, at which time he was a young man, and it is my impression that this Graves or Sanford, as known by me, is in the neighborhood of 80 years of age. . . . I know nothing about how this soldier got the name of William Graves."[21]

Widow Malinda Chappell was known by several names—Lena, Linda, and Malinda—which caused confusion among pension officials. This prompted an inquiry from the Bureau of Pensions as to her "correct, Christian name."[22] Two surname spellings, Barbour and Barber, marked inconsistencies in the file of Richard Barbour. Another Chicagoan, Private Harry Myers, of the Eighty-eighth Infantry, USCT, and later the Third U.S. Cavalry, Heavy Artillery Unit, experienced this difficulty when he attempted to get his pension for wartime service to the Union. He explained the process by which he acquired multiple names:

> I was known to answer by the name Fleming because my father change[d] his name from Rice to Fleming after the war. At my first knowledge of the war I was captu[red] at Coldwater with my owner Joe Rice by the Illinois calvary then known as the Second Illinois Calvary [sic]. I afterward enlisted in the U.S as above stated under the name of Harry Myers. I was told by the soldiers that Rice was not my name and that my master wanted me to answer in the name of Rice because I belong to him so I change[d] my name from Rice to Myers and after discharge from the service found my father passing and answering under the name Fleming.[23]

The second feature under review concerned physical appearance and the health of veterans and their families. There were some very pertinent questions to be answered: Under what kind of circumstances was the soldier born regarding housing, medical care, food supply, and immunity to disease? What was his state of health before the war, while in the military, after service, and at the time of death?

Among the troops, the normal health complaints cited after the war were rheumatism, pleurisy, vertigo, scurvy, kidney disorders, chronic diarrhea, heart complications, and urinary problems. One recent historical account about the Twenty-ninth seems to regard pension claims made by veterans in the 1890s as imaginative for the most part.[24] In contrast, another recent book that treats the subject of wartime stress generally as it related to Civil War veterans finds another perspective to the issue, one much more favorable to the combat veteran.[25]

Extensive medical examinations preceded any decisions after awarding a pension based on wartime infirmities. Certified medical practitioners had to carefully follow a book of instructions issued by the Department of the Interior. Any disability related to alcoholism, drug use, or what was referred to as "vicious habits" were causes for disqualification. In addition to physical exams, depositions were solicited to substantiate linkages between wartime service and claims of postwar physical invalidism. Regimental musician Alexander Garrett complained of rheumatism, heart problems, and neck pains after a tree limb hit him in the back of the head sometime in 1863. After he completed his military service, he was awarded a small pension of six dollars a month in 1890. A subsequent recommendation was rendered for an increase to ten dollars a month in 1904. A physician described him at the age of sixty-one as having general debility: "looks age given, muscles are soft, relaxed and thin, hands soft, slightly stooped, he is thin and emaciated, slight arcus senilis." Richard Barbour also suffered from poor health. While in the service he complained of an injury to his head that affected his equilibrium and caused convulsions.[26] As a mature man, Barbour suffered from rheumatism and dropsy. File after file contained information on the devastating effect of war on the individual veteran.

The entire Clary family suffered from poor health while living in Chicago, no doubt a combination of ill health emanating from slavery days and the unsanitary conditions faced contemporarily by residents of the poorest areas of the city. Louis Clary contracted a coughing disorder while in the service and died on the streets of Chicago as a result of this complaint in 1875. His father, Elijah, died in 1886. During the 1870s and 1880s, other family members succumbed to health ills and diseases. Siblings Henrietta and Eliza died of consumption (tuberculosis); Mary Francis passed away from cholera; Claybourn contracted typhoid fever and died; and Mason fell victim to the measles.[27]

Third, the study focused on occupational pursuits and work patterns among veterans. Many documents contained valuable information on this subject, especially the "Declaration of Invalid Pension" forms. Employment at the time of enlistment as well as at the time of application for benefits was listed. Death certificates on file that were issued in Cook County also indicated the length of time of the decedent's last employment. By socioeconomic standing, this was a distinctively lower class, working population. Occupational paths were limited by contemporary racist employment practices, the constraints of past slave duties, and the difficulty soldiers seemed to have in adjusting to a rapidly changing economic environment that required new skills in a new age. It was obvious that the training the soldiers received was of no use in the industrial workforce. With the possible exception of Alexander Garrett of Company E, who became an elevator operator, there was almost no connection between the work that the veteran pursued and the labor demands of the modern city. As a matter of fact, for the nation's most racially and economically proscribed group, the lines of work after military service resumed the same restrictive tendencies they had before service.

Fourth, education, literacy, and training were investigated to determine to what extent the soldiers' mastery of reading and writing and knowledge about the world increased as they progressed though life. The writing skills of English-born Private Willis A. Bogart and Sergeant William McCoslin were fully demonstrated, as their prose was saved for posterity. The former wrote a letter of appreciation to the widow of Colonel Charles A. Bross for his dedicated and courageous leadership on the field of battle, and the latter kept a running account of the regiment's journey from Chicago to the eastern battlefields.[28] While obviously not representative of the literary qualities of the majority of the men, the existence of these two missives raises questions about generalizations made about this group, or any group, without a basis for extrapolation. Given opportunities, how many of the men could rise to the level of their highest competency? What intellectual potential or intelligence was hidden during slavery in the South, or quasi-freedom in the North, only to rise from the ashes of racial oblivion like a Phoenix? How many of the wives and widows would display traits that induced federal examiners to note their intelligence in official correspondence when the opposite was anticipated?

The question of the availability of early and late educational opportunities was examined. In this light, signatures might assume some significance, in that they indicate the possibility of proficiency in other areas related to literacy. They might just be an indicator of a character trait, which, for instance, might explain how John A. Enders became a detective and how Sergeant Willis Easley moved up from the ranks of Pullman porter to become a valued office aide with the Illinois Central Railroad.[29] For some, like Willis Easley, Alexander Garrett, and Richard Barbour, who had prewar residence in Chicago and the opportunity to obtain free, racially unfettered schooling, the link between this background and subsequent success might be clear-cut. Their applications on file are signed, and their signatures were ones displaying strength and determination. Most soldiers were illiterate and therefore signed their names with an X.

The fifth question regarded marriage and family formation and the dynamics of family life.[30] Major areas of inquiry included the ages of the soldier and his wife upon marriage, their marriage date, and their previous marital status during slavery. Unions made under slavery encompassed several variations. There were marriages in "the white folk's manner," that is, formal ceremonies that were conducted under the direction of a white minister of the Gospel or justice of the peace.[31] The master's approval, of course, had to have been granted. Some unions took place in plantation fashion, which were witnessed and recognized by the slave community, but may or may not have included some ministerial sanction. Then there was the forced union for the master's financial gain or social control, undertaken for the purpose of bearing children or to maintain social order on the farm or plantation.

Further, the process of marriage involved other important aspects, such as finding mates and the availability of marriageable females. The circumstances of marriage relating to age and the previous social and legal circumstances of the husband and wife were just as important. The significance of the choice of marriage over uninhibited companionship indicated a great deal about the sanctity and importance of marriage. The manner of legal marriage, whether conducted before a minister, white or black, and whether it was a civil or a church ceremony, carried many complex implications. And, very important, the bearing and rearing of children resulting from the marriage revealed whether the black community would be stable or collapse from within.

Some slaves were allowed to marry with the master's consent and sometimes encouragement. Others exercised that rarity of rarities, choice within the slave regimen. Many times the slave master acted out of Christian conscience, or in accordance with good business practice—the married male with a family was least likely to flee and was more observant of rules that spared his family punishments. However, as Mrs. Cecilia McAllister, the widow of Private Frank McAllister of Company C, recalled in explaining her martial past, choice never existed in the area where she was enslaved. On her deposition, it was noted that

> [she] was born a slave and so remained until 1861. That also it was the year 1848 [and in regard to marriage] as was the custom with slaves a Negro [from another farm or plantation] asked her master for her [hand in marriage] and that her master told her he preferred to give her to some one on his own farm. That he [the outsider] and she then bunked together for a short time until her master took him away from her and made him live with a Colored girl on his [the outsider's] own farm. That there never was a marriage ceremony ever performed between her and him and that she does not regard herself as having been his wife.[32]

Another story illustrates the lack of solemnity when marriage occurred during slavery days as contrasted with days of freedom in Chicago. One widow, Mrs. Jane Liter, responded to an inquiry about the circumstances of her marriage to her deceased soldier husband and recalled the pleasure associated with the occasion. She spoke of a large number of witnesses, the presence of a minister from "the Little Bethel Church," and the location of the wedding, which was the home of a soldier who claimed the groom saved his life on the battlefield. On the other hand, when she tapped into recollections of a previous union during the days of the slave regime, it is possible to sense her anguish even though her message was transmitted through recorded words: "I was what was called married in slave times to a slave named Patrick Hughes—I was then a slave of Foster Garner who then resided on a plantation near Concord, Kentucky. . . . There was a little ceremony, and we became man and wife. We lived together until he died about the time the war commenced."[33]

Marriages were common under circumstances in which choice prevailed, such as in Chicago and throughout the North, before, during, and after the war. This increased the chances for family formation, which led to the formation of a community. The alacrity at which soldiers of the Twenty-ninth entered into unions (as shown in Chapters 2 and 3) signaled a positive new beginning for African Americans in Chicago.

Overall, women who had formerly endured the social hardships of slavery welcomed marriage, and soldiers appeared to be attractive choices. Soldiers had proven themselves to be men in the truest sense of the nineteenth century's meaning—they had risked death, they had sacrificed, and the marriageable men had survived the hellish nature of war. E. Franklin Frazier described the situation: "These women had doubtless been schooled in self-reliance and self-sufficiency during slavery. . . . Neither economic necessity nor tradition had instilled in her the spirit of subordination to masculine authority. Emancipation only tended to confirm in many cases the spirit of self-sufficiency which slavery had taught."[34]

Often, the women had preceded the men to Chicago, as was the case with Jane Liter, who come from Kentucky to Cairo, Illinois, under the auspices of the U.S. Army. Then, it was on to Chicago, where she met and wed John Liter after the end of hostilities and after the Twenty-ninth Infantry had been mustered out of service in late fall of 1865. Julia Simpson met her husband, John Abrams, after the war, when he was an "older man" (as she described him); they married in 1890 when he was at least fifty years of age. In the case of the Clary family, the parents were united in slavery, but the family had come from northeastern Alabama, minus husband, Elijah, and son, Louis, a future U.S. army recruit.

In looking at ages at the time of marriage, two patterns emerge: same-age marriages that occurred late in adult life, and different-age marriages where the husband was quite a bit older than the wife. The union of Alexander Garrett and Victoria Queen, who married at ages forty-eight and forty-six, respectively, exemplified the pattern of late marriages of veterans to women who were in their own age range. The other pattern, that of late-age marriages that involved soldiers and women sometimes one-half their age, raises the question of motivation. These might have been cases of single persons seeking companionship in a fast-paced, socially isolated, and changing world. In the case of William Graves and his wife, Lenora, they married when he was fifty-three and she was twenty-eight. This aroused the suspicions of examiners, who wrote: "Claimant and soldier were married in 1890 when he was past middle age and she was nearly 30. She alleges no prior marriage of either and furnished evidence to that effect." In the case of Henry and Malinda Chappell, he was sixty-nine and she was thirty-three. The Bureau of Pensions ordered an investigation on these grounds: "The claimant in this case is a colored woman, still young, a resident of Chicago, Ill. She married the soldier in October, 1904, being half his age and her former husband had secured a divorce from her." Once again the search for companionship and social fulfillment might offer the most direct and tangible explanation. Perhaps future sociological research into this matter might give a more plausible answer for those questioning the power of platonic love or an attempt to fill a void of loneliness.[35]

Being honest, or dishonest, about one's past could reinforce or destroy one's case for obtaining a favorable pension decision. John Abrams had told his wife that he had never married before their union; however, when the truth of his previous undissolved marriage was brought forth, she was denied a pension.

Moreover, family life involved family dissolution, sometimes brought on by death in battle. The Battle of the Crater claimed the life of Private James Watts, who had been married for twelve years to his wife, Judy; his death left her a widow with five young children, ages seven and one-half years to 10 months, to care for. The youngest child was James Jr.; after seven years of struggle as a single mother, Mrs. Watts succumbed to societal pressures and placed her children under guardianship. Her widow's pension claim was approved immediately.[36]

Another such case occurred outside of Chicago but is of interest. It involved the four children of Moses Nelson of Company D, whose mother had such difficulty in rearing them that a white merchant tailor assumed their guardianship out of a respect for humanity. He testified that "I only consented to act as guardian of these children because the mother experienced great difficulty in getting a proper person of her own race to act who could give the required bond."[37]

Widows' claims rarely proceeded smoothly. The widow of Alexander Garrett experienced this when her marriage of 1896 missed a deadline that said that no pensions be paid to widows in their own right if their marriages took place subsequent to June 27, 1890. The government's explanation was as follows: "She is not entitled to pension in her own right under the provisions of the act of April 19, 1908, for the reason that she did nor marry the soldier until subsequent to June 27, 1890. Apparently she has no title to pension under the general law, as the soldier appears to have died of a disability which has no connection whatever with his military service."[38] As mentioned above, another widow, Julia Simpson Abrams, was also denied a pension because her soldier husband had a previous undissolved marriage she knew nothing about, and the first wife was already receiving a pension.

Among the soldiers and families, attitudes toward the institution of marriage varied. The sanctity of marriage and power of family was important to veteran Louis Clary's dependent mother, Mrs. Nancy Clary. In contrast, the marital chicanery of the Richard Barbours of the world, detailed in Chapter 4, has been explored.

The overall dynamics of family formation are important and often include sacrifice for kin. The postwar years found some Civil War soldiers caring for their dependent parents. Once settled into civilian life in Chicago following a safe escape from bondage in the South, military service, and arduous work in the North, the soldier disregarded his own thoughts of personal happiness with a wife and children. The Twenty-ninth regiment's Cato Flowers and Louis Clary personified this commitment.[39]

Sixth, the extent to which the soldiers engaged with other comrades and citizens in associational and organizational activities was important in determining the formation of a community of interested persons. To aid our understanding of the life stories of these Civil War soldiers, who became veterans after mustering out in November and December 1865, we can divide their lives into four phases. These divisions also work in terms of a collective biography of the soldiers. In early attempts at prosopography, through the vehicle of a longitudinal study, many bits and pieces of data were uncovered and interpreted, but many more were missed. The present effort represents merely a survey with a stab at cohesiveness. This provides ample incentive for future researchers to probe the Civil War records of units like the Twenty-ninth Illinois to reach scientific conclusions using more sophisticated means and models.

In the first phase, the process of recruitment and enlistment bound men of a particular mind-set together for the rest of their lives as they pursued either glory, adventure, honor, revenge, vindication, employment, or bounty. Whatever the motivations, black Chicagoans made a conscious choice about what to do with their lives as they volunteered for military service. This preference was possible only for a free man, and many of these men were free for the first time in their lives. In some instances the time could be measured in years and parts therein. In a similar vein, persons living in Chicago before

1860 experienced a level of social proscription under the Illinois Black Laws that left a damaging imprint on their ability to make choices.

But choose they did, and once in military service, these men began to share the first of several precedent-shattering experiences. Physical examination determined fitness for military service; it was totally unlike the physical evaluations of slave sales, where selection as chattel occurred. Acceptance here meant approval for advancement into manhood and membership in the nation's volunteer warriors' caste. Being declared physically able, they had to feel proud of their fitness. Involuntary selection by the slave master for work or for sale had been superceded by the personal choice of the recruit and the approval of the federal government of the soldier's fitness. Once voluntarily becoming members of a group, they moved into a state of interdependence. Physical training and drilling commenced, and with these activities, a deepened sense of belonging to a group in which sacrifice, hardship, and challenge were considered commonplace.

Whether in combat, under fire, or during the construction of fortifications, their bonds were continually reenforced. Interdependence of members of the squad, in the platoon, within the company, and as part of the regiment grew in paramountcy. The possibility of death and injury hung over all equally. Fear and apprehension became shared disappointments both in the moment and the place.

Another phase began around the beginning of the decade of the 1880s. The Gilded Age, or Industrial era, found the veterans being shunted to the sidelines of a rising metropolis by society as they reached middle age or a later stage of maturity. They were becoming more prone to war-related illnesses and injuries, along with infirmities caused by aging and the early experiences they had during slavery. Health problems established during slavery and the hardships of life in a combat situation combined, and these men were often broken by this period. The case of Hardin Harris (detailed in Chapter 4) was especially heart wrenching.

To complete a claim for a pension, veterans such as Harris had to rely on favorable medical reports from impartial physicians as well as favorable, supportive depositions from comrades who could corroborate their claims to military-related illness. For any veteran who questioned his life's meaning as he eked out a living in a fast-paced industrial society, one in which he seemed to have no place, being sought out by white federal examiners for recollections had to be an uplifting experience. As a practice promoted by the U.S. Pension Bureau, this process served to reconnect soldiers into a network of mutual dependency. Sergeants played their previously mentioned important role again in helping to locate veterans and guiding testimony in behalf of a soldier's claim.

The bonds among some comrades remained strong. One colleague from the Twenty-ninth referred to his knowing Garrett in Chicago four years previous to their enlistment in 1863.[40] The same circumstances existed with Richard Barbour. Louis Clary knew his Twenty-ninth Regiment colleagues Willis Easley, William Collins, and Henry Carson prior to enlistment, raising the question of whether a collective consciousness existed on the eve of enlistment.[41] Men from other units, such as William A. Howard of Company B of the 102nd Colored Infantry Regiment from Michigan, became acquainted with fellow veterans. Howard served as chairman of the relief committee of John Brown Post No. 50 and used to visit fellow soldiers regularly.[42]

In the last phase, which overlapped with the previous and continued into the next century, institutions such as John Brown Post No. 50 and chapters of the Grand Army of the Republic extended a safety net to assist the veteran in need.[43] As aging and often forgotten men, they were constantly being reminded of the certainty of death. Widows and dependents filed claims and appealed claims that had been denied. In doing so, they also kept the channels of communication between veterans open as corroborating information was always being sought.

The seventh feature of the longitudinal study, wartime training and combat experience, was highlighted often in depositions relating injuries and deaths as well as on medical forms. Also important were the attitudinal changes that occurred when fighting whites as equals and being armed and elevated to the status of warrior-soldier. The experience of *presence* at significant events was exhilarating to participants. Being at Petersburg at the time of the Battle of the Crater, and then at the breakout on April 3, 1865, as well as at Appomattox on April 9, 1865, the ultimate scene of triumph over General Robert E. Lee and his vaunted Army of Northern Virginia, had to have inspired the soldier.

The eighth feature of the soldier's postwar civilian adjustment demonstrated nothing of the discipline that a soldier mastered while in service. The character of postwar civilian life, including status of the application process for invalid, dependency, and age benefits, led to questions about the material quality of these men's lives. It seems commonplace that veterans lived in the poorest neighborhoods. This description fit James Jones's residences. Jones was described as "a thick headed lout of a fellow" and had not made many friends while in service, and this pattern continued in civilian life.[44] One positive relationship that he valued was that with his wartime comrade, Frank McAllister, who befriended him and gave him lodging.[45]

Various residential patterns appeared in the soldiers' lives, but Richard Barbour's was unlike a great many other veterans in that his residence in this city was as transitory as it was continuous. Another soldier, Alexander Garrett, developed a residential pattern that was filled with continuous movement. He even lived near a prominent physician, Dr. A. W. Williams, who attended him before the soldier's death in 1913. Moreover, the question of neighborhood accessibility between high- and low-status African Americans had been answered affirmatively in Garrett's case.

Nevertheless, frequent moves within an area characterized by narrowly proscribed racial and low socioeconomic income, south of Chicago's downtown, seemed to be the norm for too many veterans and their spouses. Veteran William McKenney and his wife, Mary, later his widow, registered nearly a dozen addresses between 1885 and 1928. Sometimes the area where these people lived could best be described as "a ramshackle residential district," and if this was the case, the question arises as to whether there was anything unique in this pattern, based on their socioeconomic status.

While archival research to this date has been very revealing, unfortunately, such a pattern seems not to exist, as exemplified by some difficulties that Miller has encountered in his study of the military aspects of the men of the Twenty-ninth. Importantly, analyses of the federal pension records demand neither a sympathetic nor an unsympathetic eye and heart, but definitely a deep perception of things of importance beyond the conventionally acceptable. The spirit to see the world as these men saw it was of paramount importance to enter the world in which they lived. In my life, it was aided by a forged link with my maternal great-grandfather, Private Henry Slaughter, 116th Infantry Regiment, Kentucky, USCT. So was the capacity to feel what these warriors did as they confronted the demons of their existence, whether the suffocating cruelties of slavery or the threat of a massacre on the battlefield after surrender. For those untrained in the meanings of black life in America, such struggle might seem abnormal—but it was anything but that. Understanding part of the soldier's makeup renders seemingly meaningless, undecipherable data all the more valuable and informative.

Notes

Introduction

1. James Oliver Horton, *Free People of Color: Inside the African American Community,* vii, viii; Nell Irvin Painter, *Sojourner Truth: A Life, a Symbol,* 69, 70. See also Kenneth L. Kusmer, "The Black Urban Experience in American History." In 1998, Leon F. Litwack rendered another valuable tool in understanding and writing the history of the nonliterate by emphasizing a history of the black South based on an "interior life," in *Trouble in Mind: Black Southerners in the Age of Jim Crow,* xvi. History "from the bottom up" has now gained a newer, and obviously deserved, legitimacy. Litwack writes: "Living in largely separate worlds, the two races interacted in conformity to custom, law, and 'place.' But there were limits"; African Americans proved their capacity to create "a world of their own 'behind the veil,' as W. E. B. Du Bois described it. . . . It may be found in the families [that African Americans] maintained, in the institutions they created . . . in the businesses they established, in the churches they attended, and in the voluntary associations that afforded them important outlets and support" (xvi).

2. St. Clair Drake and Horace R. Cayton, *Black Metropolis: A Study of Negro Life in a Northern City* (hereafter cited as BM). For examples of northern studies that overlooked Chicago's free blacks, see Leonard P. Curry, *The Free Black in Urban America, 1800–1850: The Shadow of the Dream;* and James Oliver Horton and Lois E. Horton, *In Hope of Liberty: Culture, Community, and Protest among Northern Free Blacks, 1700–1860.*

3. St. Clair Drake, *Churches and Voluntary Associations in the Chicago Negro Community* (hereafter cited as CVA); Allan H. Spear, *Black Chicago: The Making of a Negro Ghetto, 1890–1920.* On the need to clarify what the ghetto "was and was not," see Lawrence W. Levine, "Comment [on the state of African American history]," 125–27.

4. Whether historical occurrence as evaluated from contemporary observation carries the value of detached, latter-day reflection has been discussed by Arthur M. Schlesinger Jr. in "The Historian as Participant." In this study, his point that there is great value in the contemporary eye, or, in *Black Chicago's First Century,* the contemporary mind and memory, carries saliency.

5. "Story of Old Settlers Reads Like Fiction" (hereafter cited as SOS).

6. [Charles Edward Hall], "Chicago in 1843: A Real 'Oldtimer' on the Life of Early Colored Settlers" (hereafter cited as OT).

7. Historical insight into the lives of African American men and women of note derived from several sources. A fragmentary base exists through the correspondence and files of Ida B. Wells-Barnett and S. Laing Williams. Autobiographies by Reverdy Ransom, Ida B. Wells, and Frederick Douglass, along with the biographies of Daniel Hale Williams, Charles Edwin Bentley, Robert S. Abbott, Lucy Parsons, and others provided useful data. Likewise, miscellany, such as those items represented by letters, obituaries, newspaper articles, photographs, membership rolls, and so on, provided data on John and

Mary Richardson Jones, Abraham T. Hall, Isaac and Emma Jane Atkinson, Lewis Isbel, Henry O. Wagoner, and others.

As previously stated, the African American community of the nineteenth century exhibited a strong sense of its place in time and space. Some family records have withstood the storms of time, oppression, and neglect. Not unexpectedly, then, a pioneers club organized in 1904 in the form of the Old Settlers Social Club of Chicago. Its rosters still exist and are part of a collection that members of the Atkinson family have preserved along with recollections, photographs, and memorabilia. They are now a part of the manuscript holdings at the Chicago Historical Society and the Vivian G. Harsh Collection on Afro-American History and Literature at the Chicago Public Library. The same was true for the family records of Abraham and Elizabeth Hall, now part of the Boger-Jones Collection, which is privately held.

8. Interview with Joan[na] C. [Hudlin] Snowden, February 3, 1938, pages 1, 9, 2, in "Old Settlers" Folder 39, Box 10, Illinois Writers Project/"Negro in Illinois" Papers (hereafter known as IWP.)

9. Jeff Lyon, "Generations: A Quiet Quest to Honor a Family's Legacy," 14–20. See also the interview with Grace Mason and Michelle Madison in Chicago in August 2000. Historical documents and photographs of the Atkinson Family are held at both the Chicago Historical Society and the Vivian G. Harsh Research Collection of Afro-American History and Literature, Chicago Public Library, Carter G. Woodson Regional Library. Henderson is credited by his family with inspiring the staging of the famed American Negro Exposition of 1940 that was held at the Chicago Coliseum.

10. BM; see also CVA, 33, 307.

11. See Monroe Nathan Work, "Crime among the Negroes of Chicago"; Monroe Nathan Work, "Negro Real Estate Holders of Chicago"; Richard R. Wright Jr., "The Industrial Condition of Negroes in Chicago"; and Richard R. Wright Jr., "The Negro in Chicago."

12. For particular essays and autobiographies, see Fannie Barrier Williams, "A Northern Negro's Autobiography"; Fanny Barrier Williams, "The Club Movement among Colored Women"; Fannie Barrier Williams, "Social Bonds in the 'Black Belt' of Chicago: Negro Organizations and the New Spirit Pervading Them"; Alfreda M. Duster, ed., Crusade for Justice: The Autobiography of Ida B. Wells (for Wells-Barnett's work with the Negro Fellowship League); Reverdy C. Ransom, The Pilgrimage of Harriet Ransom's Son (for Ransom's thinking about and work in establishing the first major African American settlement house in Chicago in Institutional A.M.E. Church); and Richard R. Wright Jr., Eighty-seven Years behind the Black Curtain (for Wright's thoughts and activities in Chicago and elsewhere).

13. For a present-day sociologist's evaluation of the placement of this scholarship, see Mary Jo Deegan, ed., The New Woman of Color: The Collected Writings of Fannie Barrier Williams, 1893–1918, xxxiii–xl.

14. BM, 45; W. E. B. Du Bois, The Souls of Black Folk, 81, 110.

15. CVA, 33. There were 1,811 total African American enlistments in the Twenty-ninth Infantry, Illinois, USCT, but this does not represent all black soldiers who served from Illinois; see Chapter 2.

16. Ralph A. Austen, "The Slave Trade as History and Memory: Confrontations of Slaving Voyage Documents and Communal Traditions," 229. Austen's comments related

directly to data on slavery that are part of the groundbreaking Du Bois Institute trans-atlantic slave data set at Harvard University. The link between the civilian lives of Civil War soldiers and their pension records is well illuminated in Lisa Y. King, "Wounds That Bind: A Comparative Study of the Role Played by Civil War Veterans of African Descent in Community Formation in Massachusetts and South Carolina, 1865–1915"; and Nick Salvatore, *We All Got History: The Memory Books of Amos Webber.*

17. See Paul K. Conkin and Roland N. Stromberg, *Heritage and Challenge: The History and Theory of History,* 146–47, who wrote: "Can anyone comprehend cultural phenom-ena—the distinctly human world of symbolic communication, of purposes, ideals, and final causes—by general types of description and explanation? . . . If one could fully describe all culturally conditioned events by their more elemental and universal con-stituents and explain them by unchanging laws, then the temporal coordinates of human events would seem to have little intellectual significance. In principle, if not in fact, one could transform any history into empirically valid generalizations and laws with no cog-nitive loss and much gain in precision and scope of understanding. . . . If one looks for similarities, again guided by general knowledge, one can always find them at some level of abstractness. But if one wants, and without all the intellectual effort, one can also find the particular and the unique, and between these poles all manner of limited sameness and rare but not unique particulars."

18. Patrick Rael, *Black Identity and Black Protest in the Antebellum North.* On education, for an general overview, see Curry, *Free Black in Urban America,* 148; and Horton and Horton, *In Hope of Liberty,* 213–21; and then contrast with Mary J. Herrick, *The Chicago Schools: A Social and Political History,* 53, and Michael W. Homel, "Race and Schools in Nineteenth-Century Chicago," 40.

19. August Meier, "Negro Class Structure and Ideology in the Age of Booker T. Washington," 261n5. For perceptions of black workers, compare Heather Cox Richardson, *The Death of Reconstruction: Race, Labor, and Politics in the Post–Civil War North, 1865–1901,* which outlines the image of blacks as undesirable workers, with the contemporary account in Joseph Kirkland, "Among the Poor of Chicago," 5, as well as with the Harvard study that examined the development of this myth in Charles H. Wesley, *Negro Labor in the United States, 1850–1925: A Study in American Economic History,* vi and chapter 5, "Will the Negro Work?" 116–55; see also Perry R. Duis, *Challenging Chicago: Coping with Everyday Life, 1837–1920,* 262–70. For more on self- and racial consciousness about African Americans having their own leadership, see W. T. Goode, *The "Eighth Regiment,"* 31.

20. W. E. B. Du Bois, *The Philadelphia Negro* (hereafter cited as *PN*).

21. Joel Williamson, *New People: Mulattoes and Miscegenation in the United States,* 72 (emphasis added).

22. Gary Collison, *Shadrach Minkins: From Fugitive Slave to Citizen,* 9.

23. Mark Twain, *Adventures of Huckleberry Finn,* 279; Richardson, *Death of Reconstruction,* 183–97.

24. Ralph Ellison, *Invisible Man,* 3.

25. In 1983, at the signal American Historical Association's "Conference on the Study and Teaching of Afro-American History" held at Purdue University, historian James Oliver Horton advanced the timely notion that the character of class structure within the African American urban community needed a fresh look. He proffered: "The

topic is especially complex because of the interplay between limited occupational opportunity and the wealth on the one hand and social connections and shade of color on the other. The issue is further complicated by the importance of the internal structure of black institutions, formal and informal, and the dynamic character of black activism and leadership. It will not be possible to comprehend the meaning of class structure among blacks until we establish some method for evaluating occupations and their relationship to status in the black community." James Oliver Horton, "Comment [on the need to reexamine the character of the African American class structure]," 133.

26. Horton, *Free People of Color*, 25.

27. Another product of the university's famed "Chicago School" of sociology, Hylan Lewis, a contemporary of Drake's, provided an applicable conceptual apparatus for understanding stratification during the early twentieth century that has applicability for this earlier period when occupational opportunities and the wealth associated with them eluded African Americans in Chicago. Lewis, who studied African Americans in the middle twentieth century in a southern Piedmont community, showed that the existence of a traditional class structure is never a given:

> If a class-organized society is one in which there is a well-defined system of rank-
> ing that distinguishes cohesive, self-conscious segments marked by differences in
> social honor and power, then [the] Kent Negro society of today is not organized
> on a class basis. A clear-cut system of social ranking and basis of association or
> intimate access was not discovered. This does not mean that there is not a level
> of consciousness; it does not mean there is not a status pattern marked by dif-
> ferent measures of prestige and privilege. . . . Rather, it suggests that numerical-
> ly significant groups differentiated on a basis of intimate association or access are
> not present, and that the people themselves do not in behavior or verbalizations
> make references to or relate themselves to such prestige collectivities. . . . Insofar
> as there are status differences and insofar as the society is changing and becom-
> ing more differentiated, one might say that class is incipient, rather than full
> blown. (Hylan Lewis, *Blackways of Kent*, 223, 224)

28. CVA, 87.

29. Herbert G. Gutman, *The Black Family in Slavery and Freedom, 1750–1925*, 433; see also 465.

30. Wright, "Industrial Condition," 2:7. See also PN, 309–11. Du Bois called for a recognition of differences among African Americans, but he wrote that they "are not, to be sure, so great or so patent as those among the whites of to-day."

31. CVA, 121.

32. Edward E. Wilson, "The Line of Equality among Negroes Is Almost Imperceptible." Additional social science findings are relevant at this point of incipient class development, especially those emanating from the discipline of history. Jackson Turner Main further placed this issue of class structure in perspective when he postulated that a full century before the fair, American seaboard society had "an embryonic class structure but it was potential only" because the basic unit of wealth, land, was equally distributed and "from the bottom to the top was but a short step." Jackson Turner Main, *The Antifederalists: Critics of the Constitution, 1781–1788*, 1. Robert H. Wiebe encoun-

tered this problem of identifying class strata in his study of the roots of progressivism, explaining it as follows: "[I]n part, the new middle class was a class only by courtesy of the historian's afterthought." Robert H. Wiebe, *The Search for Order, 1877–1920*, 112.

33. E. Franklin Frazier, *The Negro Family in Chicago*, 102–4; 125–26. Frazier accepted the comments contained in an interview with a Pullman porter (125–26) as validation of the comments of a physician (102–4) and vice versa. Frazier's uneven relationship with interviewees was revealed to the author during the 1970s when resentment against him was still high, based on his comments that Chicago's African Americans lacked intellectual abilities and interests, along with a class structure from which a bona fide "society" segment could emerge. See Frazier's revealing, yet impressionable essay, "Chicago: A Cross-Section of Negro Life."

34. It was believed at one time that no social or *civic* infrastructure existed capable of producing a leadership concerned with more than the most mundane of issues until the modern Civil Rights era of the 1960s. See James Q. Wilson's introduction to Harold F. Gosnell, *Negro Politicians: The Rise of Negro Politics in Chicago*, vi, as well as a refutation by Christopher Robert Reed, "Black Chicago Civic Organization before 1935." The issue of a late-nineteenth-century *civic* leadership has been discussed by Spear, *Black Chicago*, chapter 3. Moreover, historical understanding has been significantly influenced and the leadership spectrum skewed by the reliance on E. Franklin Frazier's interpretation of black Chicago's social structure and leadership in the late nineteenth and early twentieth century.

35. Spear, *Black Chicago*, 52–53.

36. See Ira B. Berlin, *Many Thousands Gone: The First Two Centuries of Slavery in North America*, part 1, "Societies with Slaves: The Charter Generations"; Charles Flint Kellogg, *NAACP: A History of the National Association for the Advancement of Colored People, 1909–1920* (Baltimore: Johns Hopkins University Press, 1967); Barbara Joyce Ross, *J. E. Spingarn and the Rise of the NAACP, 1911–1939* (Boston: Atheneum, 1972); and Christopher Robert Reed, *The Chicago NAACP and the Rise of Black Professional Leadership, 1909–1960*.

37. St. Clair Drake, *The Redemption of Africa and Black Religion*, 19.

38. Ira B. Berlin, Marc Favreau, and Steven F. Miller, eds., *Remembering Slavery: African Americans Talk about Their Personal Experiences of Slavery*, 165, 166.

39. John Langston Gwaltney, *Drylongso: A Self-Portrait of Black America*, xxvi–xxvii.

40. "Will Not Be Ignored: Rights of Colored People Reviewed at Central Music Hall."

41. May Wright Sewall, ed., *The World's Congress of Representative Women*, 708.

42. Mary Niall Mitchell, "'Rosebloom and Pure White,' or So It Seemed." Postwar white northerners were shocked by the exposé of the South's "white" slave children who needed social placement, both because of their existence and the threat their predicament posed to all whites who claimed pure racial lineages.

43. David Levering Lewis of Rutgers University, the preeminent biographer on Du Bois's life and thinking, has proffered the explanation that Du Bois never conceived of that concept as anything other than a brief reflection, and importantly, one that he abandoned soon after enunciating it in *Souls of Black Folk*. Notes from Lewis's lecture of October 25, 2000, at the University of Chicago (in this author's possession); and David Levering Lewis, *W. E. B. Du Bois: Biography of a Race, 1868–1919*, 281, 282.

44. Christopher Robert Reed, *"All the World Is Here!" The Black Presence at White*

City, provides an examination of African American and African participation at this event, which exceeded popular perceptions, especially if one accepts the thesis of racial exclusion.

45. See Elizabeth Dale, "'Social Equality Does Not Exist among Themselves, nor among Us': *Baylies vs. Curry* and Civil Rights in Chicago, 1888."

46. *BM*, 762–64. See also Reed, *Chicago NAACP*. This book was written with Drake and Cayton's thesis on the character of black life in mind, especially their overlooked assessment of the strength of black traditions and institutions that the outside world rarely noticed.

47. "No 'Colored Y.M.C.A.' Wanted," *Western Appeal*, November 30, 1889, 2.

48. Duster, *Crusade for Justice*, 249, 250, 304.

49. Williams, "Social Bonds," 42; *PN*, 224; Lawrence W. Levine, *Black Culture and Black Consciousness: Afro-American Folk Thought from Slavery to Freedom*, 268.

50. See Dorothy Salem, "National Association of Colored Women," 842–51, in Darlene Clark Hine, ed., *Black Women in America: A Historical Encyclopedia*.

51. Howard H. Bell, "Chicago Negroes in the Reform Movement, 1847–1853," 155.

52. Anne Meis Knupfer, *Toward a Tenderer Humanity and a Nobler Womanhood: African American Women's Clubs in Turn-of-the-Century Chicago*; Wanda A. Hendricks, *Gender, Race, and Politics in the Midwest: Black Club Women in Illinois*.

53. Stuart McConnell, *Glorious Contentment: The Grand Army of the Republic, 1865–1900*, xi–xiii.

54. The African American newspapers, such as the *Appeal*, the *Freeman*, and the *Gazette*, were filled weekly with ads for the books and with requests for agents to distribute them.

55. Jim Cullen, "'I's a Man Now': Gender and African American Men," in Darlene Clark Hine and Earnestine Jenkins, eds., *A Question of Manhood: A Reader in U.S. Black Men's History and Masculinity*, vol. 1, *"Manhood Rights": The Construction of Black Male History and Manhood, 1750–1870*, 489–501.

56. Black Chicago politics has been skillfully chronicled by historian Charles R. Branham in his dissertation, "The Transformation of Black Political Leadership in Chicago, 1865–1942"; see also Branham's article "Black Chicago: Accommodationist Politics before the Great Migration."

57. Interdisciplinary contributions shaped the foundation from which a conceptual apparatus investigating the emergence of political modernization emerged. This template provided the most useful framework for understanding how African Americans began their professional entry into politics and advanced into a posture of successful race politics. See historical studies by Charles Branham (cited above); Rayford W. Logan, *The Betrayal of the Negro: From Rutherford B. Hayes to Woodrow Wilson*; and Leslie H. Fishel Jr., "The Negro in Northern Politics, 1870–1900"; along with political science studies such as Gosnell, *Negro Politicians*, and Martin L. Kilson, "Political Change in the Negro Ghetto, 1900–1940s." Of these studies, overall, Logan and Fishel found the southern experience the most important in the nation at the time but also found a rising racial consciousness that portended solidarity and success in culture, social affairs, business, and politics. Whether this was unique to Chicago is conjectural. All five scholars agreed that black political participation in Chicago was growing more substantive even though it was in a transitional stage.

58. E. Franklin Frazier, "Theoretical Structure of Sociology and Sociological Research," reprinted in G. Franklin Edwards, ed., *E. Franklin Frazier on Race Relations: Selected Writings*, 4. For an argument that the use of firsthand accounts far outweighs their deficiencies, see Schlesinger, "Historian as Participant."

59. In 1993, Professor James Oliver Horton wrote in a similar vein as he described his personal challenge of being "forced to come to grips with my own experiences growing up in [the black] community. . . . My familiarity with my world alerted me to the markers of that historic world . . . [and they] helped me in my attempt to negotiate my way into a social interior seldom visited by historians" (*Free People of Color*, vii).

60. Levine, *Black Culture*, ix; William M. Tuttle Jr., *Race Riot: Chicago in the Red Summer of 1919*, vii.

Prologue: The Birth of Black Chicago

1. "Du Sable," radio ad for WFMT-FM, July 1985, produced by Leo Burnett USA Advertising, Chicago.

2. "Diary Entry by Colonel Arent Schuyler De Peyster, 1779" and "Recollections" of Augustin Grignon, cited in A. T. Andreas, *History of Chicago*, 1:70–72 (hereafter referred to as ATA), along with Milo M. Quaife, ed., "Property of Jean Baptiste Pointe Sable: Inventory Sale of Property, Sold by Pointe Sable to Jean Lalime, 1800—Documents." What for years has been the authoritative history of Chicago, Bessie Louise Pierce, *A History of Chicago*, used these documents to further legitimize the factual basis of Du Sable's accomplishments and contributions (the latter source is hereafter cited as BLP).

3. "Our Early Schools," *Chicago Inter Ocean*, August 14, 1892, 17; "Reminiscences of Chicago," *Chicago Herald*, June 28, 1893, 12; Work, "Negro Real Estate Holders," 5; Hobart Chatfield-Taylor, *Chicago*, 12; Louis B. Anderson, "Facts to Show We Came Here First and Are Here to Stay," 16; SOS; "First Chicagoan Lived in Peoria," *Peoria Journal Transcript*, August 5, 1934, n.p.; Gosnell, *Negro Politicians*, 13, 14; Arna Bontemps and Jack Conroy, *They Seek a City*, 12–20; Hon. Ralph H. Metcalfe, "Historical Perspective," U.S. Congress; Christopher Robert Reed, "'In the Shadow of Fort Dearborn': Honoring De Saible at the Chicago World's Fair of 1933–1934"; Juliet E. K. Walker, *The History of Black Business in America: Capitalism, Race, Entrepreneurship*, 47; and Juliet E. K. Walker, ed., *Encyclopedia of African American Business History*, 153; and "Abstract Thinking," *Chicago Reader*, February 4, 2000, Section Two, 17.

4. BLP, 1:11–13.

5. One historian's earlier effort to trace Du Sable's ancestry and the black community's response to his being linked with a European lineage is Milo M. Quaife, *Checagou: From Indian Wigwam to Modern City, 1673–1835*; see also "Pointe De Saible Turns White." Recent research into this matter has revealed a Canadian birth to a black free woman and an unknown white father near Montreal; see John F. Swenson, "Jean Baptiste Point De Sable: The Founder of Modern Chicago," 389.

6. Swenson, "Jean Baptiste Point De Sable," 389.

7. See R. David Edmunds, *The Potawatomis: Keepers of the Flame*.

8. Reed, "In the Shadow of Fort Dearborn," 400, 403, 406, 409, 410.

9. Sources for these data are De Peyster's *Diary* (1779); Grignon's *Recollections* (1794);

Inventory Sale of Property (1800); and Arsenia Williams, *Jean Baptiste Pointe Du Sable: First Chicagoan*. A full description of the inventory is found in Quaife, "Property of Jean Baptiste Pointe Sable."

10. Walker, *History of Black Business*, 47.

11. The precarious status of nonslave blacks has been explored extensively in Leon F. Litwack, *North of Slavery: The Negro in the Free States, 1790–1860*; Curry, *Free Black in Urban America*; and Horton and Horton, *In Hope of Liberty*.

12. Ida B. Wells, Frederick Douglass, Irvine Garland Penn, and Ferdinand L. Barnett, *The Reason Why the Colored American Is Not in the World's Columbian Exposition: The Afro-American's Contribution to Columbian Literature*.

13. If one person of African descent learned of Du Sable during the 1830s, common, celebratory "whispering" as a form of internal group communication could have guaranteed its dissemination; see Collison, *Shadrach*, 22.

14. BLP, 1:208n184. See also *Membership Rolls of the Old Settlers Social Club, 1904*.

15. *Indianapolis Freeman*, February 2, 1893, 1, and April 29, 1893, 3.

16. Abram L. Harris, *The Negro as Capitalist: A Study of Banking and Business among American Negroes*, 49.

17. BM, 434.

Part I. Haven of Liberty for Former Chattel and Contraband, 1833–1865

1. Charles S. Johnson, "The New Frontage on American Life," 288, 289.

2. Charles S. Johnson, "These Colored United States, VII: Illinois: 'Mecca of the Migrant Mob.'"

3. SOS.

4. Tuttle, *Race Riot*, 76.

Chapter 1. Antebellum Frontier Town and "City of Refuge," 1833–1860

1. Noted abolitionist Philo Carpenter reminisced about the earliest population in "Half a Century," *Chicago Tribune* (hereafter referred to as *CT*), July 19, 1882, in Harpel's Scrapbook, "Obituaries, up to 1884: Philo Carpenter," CHS; Chicago's earliest demographic characteristics are mentioned in Charles Joseph Latrobe, *The Rambler in North America*, 152; and Drake and Cayton used the historical findings of Lawrence D. Reddick, who referred to the city by this sobriquet in *BM*, 32.

2. Finding a theoretical framework or, in its absence, developing one through an examination of and application of relevant data became a necessity in order to write this book. Extant scholarship in Curry, *Free Black in Urban America*; Horton and Horton, *In Hope of Liberty*; and Litwack, *North of Slavery* provided the foundation from which comparative analysis was possible of the general northern population of African Americans. Yet Chicago represented a setting where the colonial experience had been skipped and life evolved in a frontier setting. Dynamic change and fluidity in interpersonal and group relations became major determining factors in the lives of all of its residents. Placing these experiences into a holistic model involving demography, family and community foundation, reli-

gion, economic life, education, social organization, and quasi-politics led to the formula-
tion of a specific template for Chicago. As for a historical framework, the University of
Chicago faculty, from historians to sociologists, paved the way. Bessie Louise Pierce's three
volumes on Chicago's general history, *A History of Chicago*, with its impressive thematic
and conceptual framework and with its immense attention to specifics, and *Black Metropolis*, with its historical sketch on early African American life, stand as key references.

3. According to Leonard Curry, the urban populations in the fifteen cities with the
largest African American populations were predominantly female among slaves, and that
was also the case among the free people of color, where males had a higher mortality rate;
see Curry, *Free Black in Urban America*, 9.

4. In the Federal Pension Record of Private Cato Flowers, Company C, CWPR, the
following is found: "the said parties [the Flowers family] were runaways or refugees from
the South." In ATA, 1:323, reference is also made to "refugees from the Southern states."
Accordingly, Drake and Cayton titled a subsection of their *Black Metropolis* "Chicago:
City of Refuge."

5. Eugene D. Genovese, *Roll, Jordan, Roll: The World the Slaves Made*, 35.

6. Gary B. Nash, *Forging Freedom: The Formation of Philadelphia's Black Community,
1720–1840*, 273–79.

7. Luther Porter Jackson, *Free Negro Labor and Property Holding in Virginia, 1830–
1860*, chapter 1.

8. BLP, 1:414, appendix, 1:393.

9. Ibid., 1:415, 1:416.

10. Declaration for Pension, January 6, 1917, Federal Pension Record of James
Stewart, Company B, CWPR.

11. The following inventory as it pertains to women has them shown as they were
listed in the *Membership Rolls of the Old Settlers Social Club* in 1904, located at the
Chicago Historical Society, pages 23 and 28. The prefix *Mrs.* was used in the *Membership
Rolls*, indicating that this population valued union within the bonds of holy matrimony.
While the title *Mrs.* is omitted in this narrative, the full names they used in 1904 are
included, obviously containing their spouses' family names in some cases. Some actual
family names that they used upon arrival in the city are unknown.

12. SOS.

13. Abraham T. Hall II, *An Argonaut of Methodism*, a volume in the Hall-Boger
Family Collection; R. R. Wright, *The Centennial Encyclopedia of the African Methodist
Episcopal Church*, 103.

14. Historian Herbert G. Gutman established this pattern as national during the antebellum period, existing in both the North and the South; see *Black Family*, xx, 433. See
also Horton and Horton, *In Hope of Liberty*, 85f.

15. Miscellaneous items, Atkinson Family Collection.

16. Curry, *Free Black in Urban America*, 11, 12. See BLP, 2:5, for a model designed for
use on the dominant white population.

17. Research findings of Professor William Andrews, historian of Brockport, New
York, on Upper New York State, in the author's possession.

18. Deposition of Walter Duke, November 25, 1895, and E. B. Olmsted to Hon.
William Lochren, November 30, 1895, Federal Pension Record of James Green, Company B, CWPR.

19. Deposition of Edward Maybin, October 24, 1892, Federal Pension Record of John Liter, Company B, CWPR.

20. J. W. Norris, comp., *General Directory and Business Advertiser of the City of Chicago*, 20.

21. Caroline Kirkland, *Chicago Yesterdays: A Sheaf of Reminiscences*, 94.

22. Federal Pension Records of Private David Easley and Sergeant Willis Easley, Company C, CWPR. The Easley siblings maintained Chicago residences over varying periods. For sister Lydia, it lasted beyond 1922; for David, until the end of the century, when he left for the Soldier's Home in Danville, Illinois; and for the peripatetic railroader Willis, until 1897, when he left to live out his twilight years in San Diego, California, Jacksonville, Florida, and Port Jefferson, New York.

23. Interview with Leota Johnson in Chicago on June 15, 2001; "Obituary," CT, May 2001; and the Taylor Family Records, in the possession of Leota Johnson.

24. BLP, 1:417 and Appendix. For a map showing the boundaries, see BLP, 1:326.

25. CVA, 35. See also Kenneth L. Kusmer, *A Ghetto Takes Shape: Black Cleveland, 1870–1930*, 13, who speaks of an African American population that was "residentially segregated" based on Drake and Cayton's implications in BM, 46–47. A more recent sociological study on racial segregation in Chicago housing reflects just the opposite. See Douglas S. Massey and Nancy A. Denton, *American Apartheid: Segregation and the Making of the Underclass*, 19–22.

Before the Great Fire of 1871, the African American population was interspersed among the predominantly white citizenry in the heavily populated South Division. The 1850 census does indicate a clustering of sorts in the First Ward among young, single men who worked as waiters. While BLP, 2:11, talks of "concentration," this clustering was a natural development among kinsmen.

26. BLP, 1:417; see also Horton and Horton, *In Hope of Liberty*, 85–88.

27. For .87 percent figure, see BLP, 2:5n1. On the oppression of Southern slavery, see Frederick Douglass, *Life and Times of Frederick Douglass*, 219. See also Charles Ball, *Fifty Years in Chains*. Ball was born into slavery but escaped twice, only to be returned to slavery. His constant fear of reenslavement dominated his life until his final burst for freedom achieved his complete liberation. The same point is made in Samuel Ringgold Ward, *Autobiography of a Fugitive Negro: His Anti-Slavery Labours in the United States, Canada, and England*, 8, 9, 18, 19. For more on reenslavement, see BLP, 2:34, and Appendix A, Statute on Negroes and Mulattoes.

28. SOS (emphasis added). As useful as demography is in giving a new dimension to understanding the West Side, it yields basically an external view of life. This was the sentiment of sociologist E. Franklin Frazier in his 1932 seminal study of black family life, *The Negro Family in Chicago*, 247. Writing that statistics "covered up the wide and fundamental cultural differences in the Negro population and gave a picture 'of average conditions,'" he called for more than an examination of the black family in the aggregate while being held in a static time frame. Aware of both descriptive and analytical values of the statistical approach, he felt that it gave less than a satisfactory view of African American life with its many distinctive features.

29. The official boundaries of Chicago in 1837 were Twenty-second Street on the south, Wood Street (1900 west) on the west, and North Avenue (1600 north) on the north.

30. OT. Norris, *General Directory*, 42, shows Johnson's occupation as "carpenter" and his address as Jackson and State streets; Henson is listed as a barber and his address as

183 Lake Street (39); Mr. Artes's (or Artis's) occupation is shown as "laborer" and his address as being north of Jackson Street in the 2nd Ward (22); Dixon's occupation is shown as "barber" on Clark Street and his residence as being on Lake Street (32); and Knight's occupations are shown as "barber and hair dresser," and his address as Clark Street near the post office (43).

31. OT. In actuality, the state demanded a $1,000 bond. See Appendix A.

32. Affidavit dated November 14, 1907, Federal Pension Record of Alexander Garrett, Company B, CWPR.

33. Henry O. Wagoner (Denver) to Hon. S. H. Kerfoot (Chicago), September 27, 1884, Henry O. Wagoner Manuscript Collection. The 1845 census shows that 140 persons designated as "Colored" lived in the city.

34. OT.

35. Miscellaneous items, Atkinson Family Collection.

36. Hallie Q. Brown, *Homespun Heroines and Other Women of Distinction*, 141.

37. A. N. Fields, "Historic Glimpses of Old Chicago," *CD*, October 22, 1932, 7.

38. Reed, *"All the World,"* 86.

39. Bontemps and Conroy, *They Seek a City*, 46.

40. On expanded household structures, lodgers, and boarders, see Horton and Horton, *In Hope of Liberty*, 96; Horton, *Free People of Color*, 31, 32, 33; and Robert L. Harris Jr., "H. Ford Douglas: Afro-American Antislavery Emigrationist," 233n34.

41. May 24, 1853, *Western Citizen*, 2.

42. BLP, 1:476.

43. Work, "Negro Real Estate Holders," 2. For an example of the emphasis one contemporary African American writer and autobiographer devoted to property owning as a sign of individual and group advancement, see Judy Winch, ed., *Cyprian Clamorgan: The Colored Aristocracy of St. Louis*, 45–63.

44. Henry Justin Smith, *Chicago's Great Century, 1833–1933*, 18.

45. Frederick H. H. Robb, ed., *The Negro in Chicago, 1779–1927*, 1:236.

46. Ethel Payne, "Unearth Tale of 'Forgotten' Man," *Chicago Defender*, July 21, 1951, 13, in John Jones File.

47. Work, "Negro Real Estate Holders," 9.

48. BM, 45.

49. On broader community, see Horton, *Free People of Color*, 37, 38, who found no attempts to form separate institutions apart from the established African American groupings and community. For an idealized example, see Painter, who comments on community formation in New York City (*Sojourner Truth*, ii). See also Rael, *Black Identity*, 47–49. Rael offers an argument useful to the one presented here. Using his examination of the public utterances from the black convention movement of the 1830s through the 1850s, he advances a thesis on the importance of an effort through which the northern African American elites developed into an articulate public voice not only for themselves but also for rank-and-file African Americans. While more persuasive for the populations of older, eastern cities, the frontier environment of black Chicago lacked a substantial population, established media, and the internal social distinctions necessary for the complete development of an elite of the sort he described emerging at this time. For Chicago's incipient community, see *BM*, 393. Also, the formation, existence, and movement of the fabled South Side community to its twentieth-century home is documented in Muriel Braxton Wilson,

"Center City Origins of the South Side Black Community of Chicago, 1860–1890."

50. St. Clair Drake, *The Redemption of Africa and Black Religion*, 19; Gutman, *Black Family*; Horton and Horton, *In Hope of Liberty*, xii ("For blacks, more than for other Americans, an American identity was built on the African foundations of old continent beliefs and values" [155]); E. Franklin Frazier, *The Negro Family in the United States*, 225.

51. See Howard Holman Bell, "A Survey of the Negro Convention Movement"; *CVA*, 36; Miles Mark Fisher, "The History of the Olivet Baptist Church of Chicago," 9; and "Some Glimpses into Low Life: A Negro Dive in Full Blast" (four references to Africa appear in this one-and-one-quarter column of coverage).

52. Williamson, *New People: Mulattoes and Miscegenation in the United States*, 121, 122, discusses how social scientists of the early twentieth century deliberately avoided seeing the reality of pride in color and race among brown-skinned African Americans.

53. Berlin, Favreau, and Miller, *Remembering Slavery*, 165, 166. While Curry disregarded a discussion of a separate culture or subculture, the Hortons devoted a chapter to it (chapter 7 of *In Hope of Liberty*). See also Gutman, *Black Family*.

54. "A Negro Dive in Full Blast."

55. Juliet E. K. Walker, *Free Frank: A Black Pioneer on the Antebellum Frontier*.

56. The most complete biography of John Jones is found in Harpel's Scrapbook, "Obituaries, up to 1884: John Jones," vol. 8, CHS. Similar and useful is "Obituary: Death of Ex-County Commissioner John Jones," *CT*, May, 22, 1879, 7. The noted Chicago authors Arna Bontemps and Jack Conroy based a chapter, almost verbatim, on the *Tribune*'s lengthy account of Jones's life, service, and death in *They Seek a City*, 44, 45.

57. The issue of homogeneity, rather an acknowledgment of heterogeneity among Colored people, was challenged contemporarily in booklet form following the Dred Scott decision of 1857 by Cyprian Clamorgan of St. Louis; see Winch, *Cyprian Clamorgan*.

58. *CVA*, 34. See also Horton, *Free People of Color*, 3, 39, 205n2, and 238.

59. Frederick Douglass, "An Address to the Colored People of the United States," in *Report of the Proceedings of the Colored National Convention, . . . 1848*, in John H. Bracey Jr., August Meier, and Elliot Rudwick, eds., *Black Nationalism in America*, 54 (emphasis added).

60. Berlin, *Many Thousands Gone*, 227.

61. See Rael, *Black Identity*, 14, 19, 21–27.

62. *OT*. See also Charles B. Sellers, *The Market Revolution: Jacksonian America, 1815–1846*, 14. As Arthur M. Schlesinger Jr. pointed out, social equality on the frontier rarely, if ever, produced economic equality; see *The Age of Jackson*, 209.

63. The Joneses were not really unique in their courageous attitude and actions, for the climate of the times produced a network of persons who stood up against slavery despite the fact they personally had achieved a semblance of freedom. In Boston during the 1850s, it was Lewis Hayden, who, like John Jones, earned his wealth as a clothing merchant. Unlike the Joneses, he was a full-blooded African American, which indicated that color differences were subsumed to the cause of group unity and safety. See Collison, *Shadrach*, 72, 73 (which includes a photograph of Hayden).

64. Interview with Mary Richardson Jones, ca. 1899, in Rufus Blanchard, ed., *The Discovery and Conquests of the Northwest with the History of Chicago*, 297, 302.

65. *CD*, October 22, 1932, 7.

66. Frazier, *Negro Family in Chicago*, 238.

67. OT; Frazier, *Negro Family in Chicago*, 224.

68. Horton, *Free People of Color*, 102, 103. For more on women's roles, see Maria Diedrich, *Love across Color Lines: Ottilie Assing and Frederick Douglass*, 175–88, 135, 150, 171, and Rael, *Black Identity*, 150–155.

69. Horton, *Free People of Color*, 116, 117.

70. Ibid., 94; interview with Mary Richardson Jones, 298. See also Mrs. L. J. Lee to Caroline McIlvaine, April 21, 1905, John Jones Papers.

71. Interview with Mary Richardson Jones, 300; Theodora Lee Purnell to Friends, September 2, 1955, John Jones Papers, Chicago Historical Society.

72. Bell, "Chicago Negroes in the Reform Movement," 155.

73. Kirkland, *Chicago Yesterdays*, 94, 95.

74. Remarks by Professor Nona Burney, moderator, on February 23, 2001, at a colloquium entitled "Exploring the Lives of Black Women in Ante Bellum Chicago, 1833–1860," held at Roosevelt University, Chicago, under the auspices of *Project: First Century*, videotape in author's possession and in Hall-Boger family collection.

75. Horton, *Free People of Color*, 107.

76. Frazier, *Negro Family in Chicago*, 140.

77. Curry, *Free Black in Urban America*, chapter 2; Wesley, *Negro Labor*, 39; Tommy L. Bogger, *Free Blacks in Norfolk, Virginia, 1790–1860*, 66; OT; Harris, *Negro as Capitalist*, 11. For a survey of African American business, real estate, and trade activities throughout the North during the antebellum period, see Harris, *Negro as Capitalist*, 5–23. Chicago's accomplishments pale in comparison with those of the African American populations in New York City, Brooklyn, Philadelphia, and Cincinnati. Still in effect a frontier town, Chicago, remained mired in its incipient pattern of growth until the 1850s. See also Walker, *History of Black Business*, 116.

78. "Chicago's Noted Negroes . . . Colored Citizens as Lawyers and in Other Positions Where Talent and Energy Are Required."

79. "John Ellis Clark, Chicago's Old Town Crier," in Harpel's Scrapbook: "Obituaries, up to 1884: John Ellis Clark," 394, CHS.

80. Cited in Charles N. Zucker, "Damage and Resistance: Free Blacks in Chicago and Springfield, 1850–1860," 27, 28. Competition between free African Americans and newly arrived Irish for the right to work marked antebellum economic life in the North. The fierceness manifested itself in violence, or in massive assemblages of well-organized Irish workingmen, who were determined as a group to dominate all lower-tiered economic activities on docks, wharves, restaurants, hotels, and other venues. Even in instances where African Americans initiated control over a particular sphere of work, the determined Irish intervened and eventually wrested control. See Noel Ignatiev, *How the Irish Became White*, 92–121.

81. For business figures for 1860, see CVA, 41; for midcentury, see BLP, 2:4; for 1859, see BLP, 1:493 (see also 45, 46). See also Kenneth M. Stampp, *America in 1857: A Nation on the Brink*, 217.

82. Schlesinger, *Age of Jackson*, 209; Henry O. Wagoner to Hon. S. H. Kerfoot, September 27, 1884, Henry O. Wagoner File. See also Harris, *Negro as Capitalist*, 3.

83. Winch, *Cyprian Clamorgan*, 47, 17. See also Meier, "Negro Class Structure," 258.

84. According to Chicago chronicler Frederick Robb, "even in slavery times, there were some to see the opportunities for business of some kind, much of which formed the

foundation for most of the business among Negroes in Chicago today [the 1920s]." See Robb, *Negro in Chicago*, 1:195, and Walker, *History of Black Business*.

85. OT; on the growing businesses, see BLP, 1:201.

86. E. Franklin Frazier, *The Negro Family in the United States*, 140. Cyprian Clamorgan mentioned other frontier cattle raisers; see Winch, *Cyprian Clamorgan*, 56.

87. "Chicago, Ill.," February 25, 1888, *Western Appeal*, 4.

88. Bontemps and Conroy, *They Seek a City*, 47.

89. Edward A. Miller Jr., *The Black Civil War Soldiers of Illinois: The Story of the Twenty-ninth U.S. Colored Infantry*, 24.

90. "Is a Famous Shaver, March 28, 1897, Louis Isbell and His Razor," in Harpel's Scrapbook: "Obituaries, up to 1884: Louis Isbell," 390, 391, CHS.

91. Winch, *Cyprian Clamorgan*, 52

92. In Boston, U.S. Senator Charles Sumner often conversed intensely with his barber and other African Americans; see Horton, *Free People of Color*, 35, 36.

93. Smith, *Chicago's Great Century*, 26.

94. Buckler, *Daniel Hale Williams*, 51. See also Robb, *Negro in Chicago*, 1:123. At this time, black New York claimed as its best physician Dr. James McCune Smith, a graduate of the University of Glasgow, who claimed seventy-seven hundred dollars in property; see Edward K. Spann, *Gotham at War: New York, 1860–1865*, 124.

95. OT; Letters, Marsha Freeman Edmond to Julia Boyd, June 20, 1887, in Herma Clark, "When Chicago Was Young: The Elegant Eighties," *Chicago Sunday Tribune*, June 28, 1936, in the Atkinson Family Collection. On the state of local transportation and on Frank Parmelee, who, with his business partner, Warren Parker, operated the largest hack (taxi carriage) service in the city, see Duis, *Challenging Chicago*, 10, 16.

96. Smith, *Chicago's Great Century*, 49.

97. Robb, *Negro in Chicago*, 1:227.

98. Perry J. Stackhouse, *Chicago and the Baptists: A Century of Progress*, 40.

99. ATA, 1:185, 186.

100. Frazier explored this question nationally on the status importance attached to skin color when Emancipation was achieved, a problem that temporarily could and did divide African Americans; see Frazier, *Negro Family in the United States*, 45, 46. See also Joel Williamson, *New People: Mulattoes and Miscegenation in the United States*. For a particular locale, Boston, see James Oliver Horton and Lois E. Horton, *Black Bostonians: Family Life and Community Struggle in the Antebellum North*, 22, 23.

101. Kirkland, *Chicago Yesterdays*, 96.

102. Horton has argued that contention along color lines between mulattoes and Negroes depended on the region in which potential relationships were forged (*Free People of Color*, 124). Likewise, Genovese has argued that the purported fissure between Negroes and mulattoes is as much postbellum fiction as it was antebellum fact; see *Roll, Jordan, Roll*, 429–31.

103. Frazier, *Negro Family in Chicago*, 104.

104. Nash, *Forging Freedom*, 219.

105. Litwack, *North of Slavery*, 182. See also Rael, *Black Identity*, 28.

106. "A Negro Dive in Full Blast." For an exploration as to the genesis of "the white children of slavery" in the American population, along with the fascination they have held for white males, see Williamson, *New People: Mulattoes and Miscegenation in the United States*, 68–71. See also Genovese, *Roll, Jordan, Roll*, 417.

107. In the South, mulattoes had begun a reconciliation with persons of unmixed blood by the 1850s out of a new social reality—their rejection by whites and the need for allies against whites. See Williamson, *New People: Mulattoes and Miscegenation in the United States*, 75.

108. Litwack, *North of Slavery*, 182, 183.

109. Kenneth M. Stampp, *The Peculiar Institution: Slavery in the Antebellum South*, viii. Stampp also clearly stated that it could be said that whites were merely black men with white skins.

110. Harpel's Scrapbook, "Obituaries, up to 1884: John Jones," CHS.

111. ATA, 1:604.

112. Henry O. Wagoner (Denver) to Hon. S. H. Kerfoot (Chicago), September 27, 1884, Henry V. [O.] Wagoner Manuscript Collection, CHS (emphasis in the original).

113. Miscellaneous, Atkinson Family Collection.

114. Mary A. Livermore, *My Story of the War: A Woman's Narrative of Four Years Personal Experience as Nurse in the Union Army*, 351; Harris, "H. Ford Douglas," 228, 229.

115. OT.

116. See CVA, 34–35; Horton and Horton, *In Hope of Liberty*, 155f; Levine, *Black Culture*, 3–5; and Berlin, *Many Thousands Gone*, 252–55.

117. CVA, 105.

118. Berlin, *Many Thousands Gone*, 252

119. Curry, *Free Black in Urban America*, 174; Drake, *Redemption of Africa*.

120. BLP, 2:355. Elsewhere in the North and South, African Americans ministered to white congregations. See Ward, *Autobiography*, 23–24, for his tenure as pastor in the Congregational Church in New York state; and John W. Blassingame, *The Slave Community: Plantation Life in the Antebellum South*, vii–ix, who describes the appearance of George Bentley as a minister to white slaveholders in Tennessee.

121. Carol V. R. George, *Segregated Sabbaths: Richard Allen and the Rise of Independent Black Churches, 1760–1840*, 162, 167.

122. Robb, *Negro in Chicago*, 1:195 (emphasis added).

123. CVA, 35. See also Fisher, "History of the Olivet Baptist Church," 26, and two articles by Jerry Thomas in the *Chicago Tribune*: "Two Churches Seek to Heal Century-Old Wounds," March 31, 1991, news section, 1, and "Evanston Worshipers Begin to Heal 1870 Rift," June 3, 1991, Chicagoland section, 1. In addition, see "Historic Church Is to Be Remodelled," *Aurora Beacon News*, April 1, 1961, 1. See also "History of the Original Providence Baptist Church," 12; and "History" of Saint Stephen African Methodist Episcopal Church, 1.

124. OT.

125. "New Quinn Chapel," *Appeal*, November 22, 1890, 1; and "Abram T. Hall, Pioneer AME Clergy," Hall-Boger Family Collection.

126. *Quinn Chapel A.M.E. Church, 1847–1967: Its Story*, 23.

127. ATA, 1:323; and Fisher, "History of the Olivet Baptist Church," 9.

128. ATA, 1:323; and BLP, 2:364.

129. OT; *Chicago Daily Journal*, February 1, 1860, 3.

130. *Chicago Daily Journal*, February 1, 1860, 3. See a similar contemporary description of the physical character of activities in a New York dive in Horton and Horton, *In Hope of Liberty*, 161–62.

131. Nash, *Forging Freedom*, 219.

132. Douglass, *Life and Times*, 283.

133. BLP, 1:74. The case was the same in Boston. See Horton, *Free People of Color*, 29.

134. Horton and Horton, *In Hope of Liberty*, 126; CVA, 10. For examples of the extensiveness of mutual aid and organization in Boston, see Horton and Horton, *Black Bostonians*, 28–32. For more on Hutchinson, see BLP, 3:49; Harpel's Scrapbook, "Obituaries," CHS; Zucker, "Damage and Resistance," 24; and SOS.

135. Robb, *Negro in Chicago*, 1:196.

136. ATA, 1:605. See also Duis, *Challenging Chicago*.

137. David M. Katzman, *Before the Ghetto: Black Detroit in the Nineteenth Century*, 175f. Drastic measures in the East found the Pennsylvania legislature yielding in 1838 to popular and elite white pressure from Philadelphia and elsewhere in the state and eliminating the theoretical right of blacks to the franchise; see Judy Winch, *Philadelphia's Black Elite: Activism, Accommodation, and the Struggle for Autonomy, 1787–1848*, 134–36.

138. In *Black Identity*, Patrick Rael argues that the black elite in other northern cities used this channel and method to bridge the gap between what they and the masses needed and what whites could deliver if sufficiently persuaded through their own language, symbols, and values.

139. CT, December 28, 1853. According to Berlin, *Many Thousands Gone*, 323, some Northern blacks held solemnized marches in anticipation of the hoped-for day of Jubilee.

140. See Peter Hinks, *To Awaken My Afflicted Brethren: David Walker and the Problem of Antebellum Slave Resistance*, 91. Hinks aptly wrote: "By the late 1820s the free black communities of the North had come of age. Resting on a settled infrastructure of numerous benevolent organizations, black churches, residential proximity, and a deep-seated ethos of mutual assistance, black communities, especially in such major centers as Boston, New York City, and Philadelphia, had not only become fully aware of themselves as distinctive entities with their own specific needs, but were much more assertive in pronouncing that difference publicly and pursuing their own needs."

141. Winch, *Philadelphia's Black Elite*, 157–61.

142. Rael, *Black Identity*, 32, 51, 132, 192–93, and 205.

143. C. Peter Ripley, ed., *The Black Abolitionist Papers*, vol. 4, *The United States, 1847–1858*, 294n3.

144. CT, December 28, 1853.

145. Douglass, *Life and Times*, 454.

146. For the 1890s, he probably meant the "cakewalk" style, which was popular during this time immediately preceding the rise of ragtime music.

147. OT.

148. BLP, 2:12n, 339; Herrick, *Chicago Schools*, 53; Homel, "Race and Schools," 40.

149. BLP, 1:279.

150. Frazier, *Negro Family in Chicago*, 87.

151. Curry, *Free Black in Urban America*, chapter 10. See also Edwin G. Burrows and Mike Wallace, *Gotham: A History of New York City to 1898*, 856.

152. "Slavery in Chicago."

153. Harris, "H. Ford Douglas," 232n24, 221; Ripley, *Black Abolitionist Papers*, vol. 4, *The United States, 1847–1858*, 217n2.

154. Horton and Horton, *In Hope of Liberty*, 120.

155. OT.

156. "Slavery in Chicago"; Zucker, "Damage and Resistance," 5; BLP, 2:12. See also William W. Freehling, *The Road to Disunion: Secessionists at Bay, 1776–1854*, 43, 125–26; and Stampp, *America in 1857*, 106–7, 134.

157. Harpel's Scrapbook, "Obituaries, up to 1884: John Jones"; Charles A. Gliozzo, "John Jones: A Study of a Black Chicagoan," 178.

158. BLP, 2:12n29, cites *Daily Democratic Press*, February 2, 1854, and the *Daily Democrat*, November 18, 1848.

159. Testimonial of Zebina Eastman in Blanchard, *Discovery and Conquests*, 282.

160. Papers of Bessie Louise Pierce relating to research on *A History of Chicago*, Series I, Box 5, Folder 7 (Civil Rights), Chicago Historical Society; and ATA, 1:605.

161. "Slavery in Chicago."

162. BLP, 2:365.

163. *History of First Baptist Congregational Church* (mimeographed pamphlet), 1; Frederick Francis Cook, *Bygone Days in Chicago: Recollections of the "Garden City" of the Sixties*, 68.

164. Horton and Horton, *In Hope of Liberty*, 238.

165. Thomas D. Morris, *Free Men All: The Personal Liberty Laws of the North, 1780–1861*, xi.

166. Smith, *Chicago's Great Century*, 25.

167. Linda Jeanne Evans, "Abolitionism in the Illinois Churches, 1834–1865," 44, 45. See BLP, 2:382–86, for a *general*, different, earlier perspective on Christian churches as a whole.

168. Stackhouse, *Chicago and the Baptists*, 29–32.

169. Stampp, *America in 1857*, 39, 106–7, 135; and Horton and Horton, *In Hope of Liberty*, 163–71.

170. Ira Miltimore to Gentlemen, May 26, 1874, Correspondence, Box 1, Zebina Eastman Papers, CHS.

171. "Slavery in Chicago."

172. Douglass, *Life and Times*, 304; David W. Blight, "John Brown: Triumphant Failure," 45.

173. Bell, "Chicago Negroes in the Reform Movement," 153.

174. Smith, *Chicago's Great Century*, 51.

175. BLP, 2:54n.

176. "When Illinois Helped Slaves on the Run toward Freedom." On the discovery of several reputed, far–South Side Underground Railroad sites, see CT, January 2, 2000, metro section, 2.

177. BM, 33. See Richard C. Wade, *Slavery in the Cities: The South, 1820–1860*, 224. What might appear as a digression is germane at this point, and it concerns the Underground Railroad, an important channel contributing to the growth of the African American population. While no physical railroad existed in actuality, this means of transporting people fleeing slavery by journeying northward relied on the helping hands of individuals, families, and churches, which were likened to conductors and depots. Historian Larry Gara's contention that the Underground Railroad lacked the coherence of a true *system* is still being debated. He wrote that according to abolitionist descriptions of assistance rendered escapees showed these were haphazard activities at best, "unlike

the complex organization brought to mind by the legendary institution." Despite the complaints and perceptions of white Southerners of the vastness of the operation, from the Illinois end, one participant revealed that "there is no organization whose object is to induce slaves to escape." With white popular sentiment, both Northern and Southern, blistering with anti-Negro feelings for the enslaved and quasi-free, one might conjecture that denials of the existence of an unpopular organization by participants was the better part of valor. See Larry Gara, *The Legend of the Underground Railroad*, 90, 91.

178. Litwack, *North of Slavery*, 100–102; Horton and Horton, *In Hope of Liberty*, 243, 244; Winch, *Philadelphia's Black Elite*, 144f.

179. BM, 36.

180. Smith, *Chicago's Great Century*, 51.

181. OT.

182. Freehling's thesis in *Road to Disunion* postulated that Southern supporters of the slave system who expected slavery to die a natural death experienced the reverse, both politically and economically, by the 1850s. See Vincent Harding, *There Is a River: The Struggle for Freedom in America*, 183.

183. BLP, 2:195–97.

184. Harding, *There Is a River*, 154–71.

185. BM, 34; CVA, 46.

186. Edwin S. Redkey, *Black Exodus: Black Nationalist and Back-to-Africa Movements, 1890–1910*, 20.

187. Collison, *Shadrach*, 77.

188. Letters, Marsha Freeman Edmond to Julia Boyd.

189. Collison, *Shadrach*, 118.

190. John Moses and Joseph Kirkland, eds., *The History of Chicago*, 193. See BLP, 2:198n23, for a discrepancy in this matter.

191. "Slavery in Chicago."

192. Douglass, *Life and Times*, 297.

193. BM, 34.

194. Rael, *Black Identity*.

195. "Political Destiny of the Colored Race, on the American Continent," Proceedings of the National Emigration Convention of Colored People, . . . 1854 (Pittsburgh: A. A. Anderson, Printer, 1854), in Bracey, Meier, and Rudwick, *Black Nationalism*, 89 (emphasis in original).

196. Harris, "H. Ford Douglas," 226, 218–24. See also Harding, *There Is a River*, 172–93.

197. Harris, "H. Ford Douglas," 225–28. See also the Lincoln-Douglas debates in Michael Johnson, ed., *Abraham Lincoln, Slavery, and the Civil War: Selected Writings and Speeches*, 72–76. The full account of Lincoln's contradictory, complex, and changing positions on race and race relations is examined in Lerone Bennett Jr., *Forced into Glory: Abraham Lincoln's White Dream*. This study is a highly detailed exploration of the argument that Lincoln's historical reputation has benefited from inaccuracies regarding his positions on race relations and Emancipation. Bennett maintains that Lincoln's recalcitrance should be seen in the light of his inability to humanely grow to the hour without external pressure, something that blacks applied incessantly in their own behalf. For a rebuttal to Bennett, see Merrill D. Peterson, *Lincoln in American Memory*.

198. Moses and Kirkland, *History of Chicago*, 193.

199. Kirkland, *Chicago Yesterdays*, 95, 96.

200. Zucker, "Damage and Resistance," 343–47.

201. Harding, *There Is a River*, 187–90.

202. Harris, "H. Ford Douglas," 221. See also Rael, *Black Identity*, 256, 264, 270–71.

203. Douglass, Speech before the American Anti-Slavery Society, on May 11, 1857, reprinted in Paul Finkelman, ed., *"Dred Scott v. Sandford": A Brief History with Documents*, 172.

204. BLP, 2:223, 224.

205. Finkelman, *Dred Scott v. Sandford*, 174.

206. Ibid., 172–74; Vincent C. Hopkins, S.J., *Dred Scott's Case*, 173–74.

207. Hopkins, *Dred Scott's Case*, 171–75.

208. Gabor Boritt, "Did He Dream of a Lily-White America?" 5; CD, February 11, 1933, 17.

209. See Benjamin Quarles, *Frederick Douglass*, 123–25; William S. McFeely, *Frederick Douglass*, 83; and Diedrich, *Love across Color Lines*, 152.

210. Harris, "H. Ford Douglas," 223.

211. *Chicago Press and Tribune*, October 24, 1859, 1.

212. Letter to the *Rochester Democrat and American*, October 31, 1859, in Frederick Douglass, *The Narrative and Selected Writings*, 201–3.

213. Ibid., 202; and BLP, 2:236, 237. Douglass often reflected on violence as a means to liberation, something all Northern African Americans had reason to ponder. In an earlier address to the American Anti-Slavery Society in 1857, Douglass had recognized the need to resort to violence on the part of slaves: "The world is full of violence and fraud, and it would be strange if the slave, the constant victim of both fraud and violence, should escape the contagion. He, too, may learn to fight the devil with fire, and for one, I am in no frame of mind to pray that this may be long deferred" (Finkelman, *Dred Scott v. Sandford*, 176). After the Brown raid, Douglass wrote in a similar vein: "Men who live by robbing their fellow-men of their labor and liberty have forfeited their right to know anything of the of the thoughts, feelings, or purposes of those whom they rob and plunder. They have by the single act of slaveholding voluntarily placed themselves beyond the laws of justice and honor, and have become only fitted with companionship with thieves and pirates—the common enemies of God and of all mankind. While it shall be considered right to protect one's self against thieves, burglars, robbers, and assassins, and to slay a wild beast in the act of devouring his human prey, it can never be wrong for the imbruted and whip-scarred slaves, or their friends, to hunt, harass, and even strike down the traffickers in human flesh" (Douglass, *Narrative and Selected Writings*, 202). The *Chicago Press and Tribune* of October 24, 1859, 1, even sympathetically reprinted a *New York Evening Post* commentary that likened Brown's activities to those of the Southern filibusters who invaded Nicaragua and hoped to acquire Cuba for the purpose of expanding the Empire of Cotton. If one act aimed at ending slavery was wrong, so was one or more intended to expand its reach.

214. Ripley, introduction to *Black Abolitionist Papers*, vol. 3, *The United States, 1830–1846*, 63.

Chapter 2. The Civil War and "Jubilee," 1861–1865

1. Charles A. Beard and Mary R. Beard, *The Rise of American Civilization*, 2:52–54. Several generations removed, young students and budding historians would read again of this transformation in a full volume devoted to this signal event and the revolutionary process it entailed. See James M. McPherson, *Abraham Lincoln and the Second American Revolution*.

2. See citations from BLP, 2:34.

3. Especially helpful as a source is evidence emanating from a longitudinal research study spanning the lives of Civil War veterans of the Twenty-ninth Infantry Regiment, Illinois, USCT. Most of the soldiers and their families studied were former slaves who enlisted in Chicago or the Chicago area and settled in the city before, during, or after the war.

4. William Graves to J. L. Davenport, Pension Commissioner, September 8, 1913, Federal Pension File of William Graves, Company B, CWPR.

5. For more on Andrew Peter Jackson, see Bethel New Life, Inc., Community Records, 1870–1986, Neighborhood History Research Collection, Special Collections and Preservation Division, Harold Washington Center, Chicago Public Library; for more on the Austin community, see Chicago Fact Book Consortium, ed., *Local Community Fact Book: Chicago Metropolitan Area, 1990*, 95.

6. R[ichard] E. Moore, *History of Bethel A.M.E. Church*, 13, 14; and Miller, *Black Civil War Soldiers*, 23. The rabid anti-Negro, anti-Union *Chicago Times* became alarmed at the rate of incoming refugees, which it considered suffocating. See the issue of October 7, 1862.

7. SOS.

8. H. F. Kletzing and W. H. Crogman, *Progress of a Race; or, The Remarkable Advancement of the American Negro . . .* , 533, 534.

9. Levine, *Black Culture*, 138.

10. See Reed, *"All the World,"* chapters 3 and 5.

11. *PN*, 74. Conceptually, sometimes consulting the older works consigned to the dustheap of history reveals the relevant theoretical basis from which understanding can come. The sociological studies of W. E. B. Du Bois and E. Franklin Frazier have proven helpful, since a scholarly concern with this population is not new. Respectively, this scholarship exists in Du Bois's *The Philadelphia Negro* and *The Souls of Black Folk*, as well as in Frazier's *The Negro Family in the United States* and *The Negro Family in Chicago*. Levine, *Black Culture*, is another significant work, concerning itself with African American adjustment to life in the South both before and after Emancipation.

12. See Ward, *Autobiography*, 3, 4. Slave parents also withheld vital information from their children so that a slip of the tongue could not lead to the family's or an individual's reenslavement. See also the Federal Pension Record of John Blakely, CWPR.

13. Deposition of William Graves, July 10, 1914, Federal Pension Record of William Graves, Company B, CWPR.

14. Deposition of Nancy Clary, February 1, 1892, Chicago, Federal Pension Record of Louis Clary, Company C, CWPR.

15. Deposition of Cecilia McAllister, July 21, 1891, Federal Pension Record of Frank McAllister, Company C, CWPR; Deposition of Lucy [Simpson] Johnson, May 23, 1913, Federal Pension Record of John Abram, Company G, CWPR.

16. Miller, *Black Civil War Soldiers*, 26.

17. Summary of Material Facts, April 19, 1877, and Deposition of Jesse Hall, February 1, 1877, Federal Pension Record of Cato Flowers, Company C, CWPR.

18. Affidavit, February 25, 1908, Federal Pension Record of Logan Davis, Company C, CWPR; Deposition of Jerry M. Smith, August 15, 1889, and Federal Pension Record of Lewis T. Wood, Company B, CWPR.

19. Livermore, *My Story*, 350–52.

20. Ibid., 365, 366.

21. Cited in CVA, 130.

22. Constance McLaughlin Green, *The Secret City: A History of Race Relations in the Nation's Capital*, 61–67. Chicago, however, in its youthfulness, was so unlike Washington that it lacked any interest in social pretension as it evolved out of its frontier phase.

23. Gutman, *Black Family*, xx, 432; see also Gwaltney, *Drylongso*, xxvi.

24. Frazier, *Negro Family in the United States*, 73.

25. Blassingame, *Slave Community*, 284–86. See also Wade, *Slavery in the Cities*, chapter 6, "Beyond the Master's Eye," for more insight into the world of the slave in an urban setting.

26. See Deposition of Lucy Jones, October 9, 1911, 7, Federal Pension File of George Jones, Company F, CWPR, which indicates that Rev. Richard DeBaptiste served as pastor at Olivet Baptist Church on the occasion of Lucy's marriage to George. The linkage between black attorneys and black applicants appears in Deposition of Richard Barbour, May 3, 1889, Federal Pension File of Richard Barbour, Company B; Filing Application Folder for Alexander G. Garrett, June 20, 1892, Federal Pension File of Alexander G. Garrett, Company B; Invalid Pension Application of Logan Davis, September 10, 1896, Federal Pension File of Logan Davis, Company C; and Articles of Agreement, (child) Miss Nellie Gash, November 22, 1892, Federal Pension File of Sgt. Jefferson Gash, Company D, all in CWPR. Contact with Dr. A. W. Williams and Provident Hospital is confirmed in Physician's Affidavit, January 29, 1904, Federal Pension File of Alexander G. Garrett, Company B, CWPR. Utilization of the services of black undertaker Charles S. Jackson by Solomon Williams, the son of veteran Peter Williams, is recorded in Payment Receipt, May 12, 1915, Federal Pension File of Peter Williams, Company C, CWPR.

27. Drake and Cayton did not find a distinguishable mass-level acceptance of this theoretically attractive alternative to segregation and voluntary separation for at least three or four generations after this period, its locus being the Second World War (BM, 42).

28. Bennett, *Forced into Glory*, 344–48. Bennett offers a thorough exploration of Lincoln's ingrained resistance to equality, emancipation, employment of black troops, and labor opportunity. His image of an emancipator was completely unearned and his stance on emancipation changed externally only when he was completely forced to accept new political realities.

29. "An Outrage," CT, January 5, 1863, 4.

30. See "Emancipation Day Jubilee." As the years passed, prosperity and demographic regeneration took their course, and by the Gilded Age, unrestrained, broad-based enthusiasm gave way to diminished support for and even cynicism about the event. The well-to-do of whatever generation saw the event as an embarrassment; the young who knew of slavery only through tradition began to ignore its significance in an age of expanding

social mobility and opportunity along the eastern seaboard. "So, [over the years] Frederick Douglass and Blanche K. Bruce, dropped out, followed by the richer and more respectable among them, until the celebration was left largely to the lower classes, especially as it was not taken up to any great extent by young graduates of the public schools" (ibid.).

31. John Hope Franklin, *The Emancipation Proclamation*, 28.

32. "The Dawn of Freedom: Celebration by the Colored Citizens." See also Paul M. Angle, "Chicago and the Emancipation Proclamation," 258.

33. Franklin, *Emancipation Proclamation*, 108. See also "Dawn of Freedom."

34. Franklin, *Emancipation Proclamation*, 117, 122.

35. Douglass, *Life and Times*, 354 (emphasis added). Also, Martin R. Delany saw some promise in a change in life in America as a result of Lincoln's issuance of the document. See Victor Ullman, *Martin R. Delany: The Beginnings of Black Nationalism*, 282–83. Something similar occurred in Spanish holdings, where the expectation of emancipation was growing. According to Berlin, *Many Thousands Gone*, 221, in 1789, Spanish King Charles IV, of the House of Bourbon, issued a *cedula* (an official decree), easing pressures on slaves in the areas of occupation and education. It was immediately interpreted as a move toward general emancipation. See also Berlin, *Many Thousands Gone*, 236, in relation to the perception that U.S. Emancipation would set all African Americans free: "Often the increase [in fugitive slaves] was propelled by rumors that the emancipation had been promulgated by some legislative enactment, judicial fiat, or executive degree." More contemporarily, during the 1970s, Vincent Harding examined the issuance and relevance of the Emancipation Proclamation from a groundbreaking black radical perspective and found it insufficient for the times (*There Is a River*, 235–37). Then, two decades later, Bennett examined the issue in his full exploration of the subject, *Forced into Glory*, 532–42.

36. "Resolutions of the Illinois General Assembly," January 7, 1863, in Document 223, Opposition to the Emancipation Proclamation, in Henry Steele Commager, ed., *Documents of American History*, 421–22.

37. William J. Simmons, *Men of Mark: Eminent, Progressive, and Rising*, 353–55.

38. Moore, *History of Bethel*, 12, 13.

39. Ibid., 17.

40. Ibid., 18, 12.

41. Livermore, *My Story*, 354, 355, 259.

42. Ibid., 262, 265.

43. Ibid., 342, 345.

44. Ibid., 260, 261. See also Ball, *Fifty Years*, 220–22. Ball, a former slave, recalled that "the slaves . . . like all other people, who suffer wrong in this world, are exceedingly prone to console themselves with the delights of a future state, when the evil that has been endured in this life, will not only be abolished, and all injuries be compensated by proper rewards, bestowed upon the sufferers, but, as they have learned that wickedness is to be punished, as well as goodness compensated, they do not stop at the point of their own enjoyments and pleasures, but believe that those who have tormented here, will be most surely be tormented in their turn hereafter."

45. Original Providence Baptist Church, *Centennial Anniversary Souvenir Year Book, 1863–1963*, 12.

46. CVA, 35, 147; Ransom, *Pilgrimage*, 11, 24, 82.

47. Fisher, "History of Olivet Baptist Church," 20–22, 26, 35n6; interview with Mrs. Mabel Chrismon, the daughter of the Xenia, Ohio, native Rev. Abraham Lincoln Harris, who came to Chicago in the 1890s to head Provident Baptist Church, October 18, 1985, Chicago, Illinois, contained in Bethel New Life—Community Records.

48. "Chicago's Noted Negroes."

49. "The Hudley Family," *Proud* 7 (St. Louis, Bicentennial II: 1976), 28.

50. BLP, 2:12n30.

51. *BM*, 45.

52. See V. Jacque Voegeli, *Free but Not Equal: The Midwest and the Negro during the Civil War*.

53. BLP, 2:12.

54. Cook, *Bygone Days*, 59f.

55. "Colored Teachers," *Chicago Evening Journal*, 3. The student was Mary E. Mann.

56. "Negro Equality in Chicago," *CT*," July 15, 1862, 3; and "Mobbing Negroes," *CT*, July 15, 1864, 4.

57. For the racially progressive account by a Republican, abolitionist sheet, read "Great Excitement on Clark Street: An Outrage upon a Colored Man," *CT*, July 15, 1862, 4; the racially hostile *Chicago Times* of the same date printed a contradictory version under the headline "Negro Equality in Chicago: How a Negro Was Ejected from an Omnibus," 3.

58. "A Riot among Laborers," *CT*, August 11, 1862; Theodore J. Karamanski, *Rally 'Round the Flag: Chicago and the Civil War*, 106–8.

59. "Another Horrible Tragedy," *CT*, January 5, 1863, 4.

60. For Massachusetts, see Alan Dawley, *Class and Community: The Industrial Revolution in Lynn*, xxiii. For New York City, see Mary White Ovington, *Half a Man: The Status of the Negro in New York*, 12, 14, and Spann, *Gotham at War*, 126, 127. See also citations from BLP, 2:26; and Ignatiev, *How the Irish Became White*. On Cincinnati, see Louis Leonard Tucker, *Cincinnati during the Civil War*, 6.

61. "Mobbing Negroes," *CT*, July 15, 1864, 4.

62. Livermore, *My Story*, 662. See also the epigraph on page 361 of Gutman, *Black Family*, the commentary from a former slave: "We knowed freedom was on us, but we didn't know what was to come with it. We thought we was going to get rich like the white folks. We thought we was going to be richer than the white folks, 'cause we was stronger and knowed how to work, and the whites didn't, and they didn't have us to work for them any more. But it didn't turn out that way. We soon found out that freedom could make folks proud, but it didn't make them rich."

63. Horton and Horton, *In Hope of Liberty*, 110.

64. Deposition of Perry Lewis, February 4, 1892, Federal Pension Record of Louis Clary, Company C, CWPR. The rigorous demands of oceanic and riverine dock work is described in Horton and Horton, *In Hope of Liberty*, 110–11.

65. BLP, 2:158.

66. Ibid., 184 and 185n135. See also Lorenzo J. Greene and Carter G. Woodson, *The Negro Wage Earner*, 23.

67. "Chicago's Noted Negroes."

68. Simmons, *Men of Mark*, 406, 407.

69. Ibid., 408; Deposition of George Jones, April 15, 1898, Federal Pension Record of George Jones, Company F, CWPR.

70. Buckler, *Daniel Hale Williams*, 70.

71. *BM*, 434.

72. SOS; "Our First U.S. Surgeon," *Illinois Record*, July 16, 1898, 1.

73. John Jones, *The Black Laws of Illinois and a Few Reasons Why They Should Be Repealed;* see also Ripley, introduction to *Black Abolitionist Papers*, vol. 3, *The United States, 1830–1846*, 63.

74. James M. McPherson, *The Negro's Civil War: How American Blacks Felt and Acted during the War for the Union*, 252–53. To the contrary, Miller concluded that "the struggle for equality, having been so little assisted by the war, went on" (*Black Civil War Soldiers*, 173).

75. See the *Tribune* account in Bontemps and Conroy, *They Seek a City*, 49.

76. Ullman, *Martin R. Delany*, 256–59.

77. Mary Elizabeth Massey, *Women in the Civil War*, 268.

78. Livermore, *My Story*, 458, 459, 456, 457.

79. "The Problem," *CT*, July 23, 1862.

80. John W. Blassingame, "The Recruitment of Colored Troops in Kentucky, Maryland, and Missouri, 1863–1865," 534.

81. Harris, "H. Ford Douglas," 228–29; Harding, *There Is a River*, 237. Civil War historian James T. Wilson entered combat under the same conditions, by passing for white; see James T. Wilson, *The Black Phalanx: A History of the Negro Soldiers of the United States in the Wars of 1775–1812, 1861–1865*, 94.

82. Letter, H. Ford Douglas to Frederick Douglass, January 8, 1863, *Frederick Douglass' Monthly* (February 1863), reprinted in Edwin S. Redkey, ed., *A Grand Army of Black Men: Letters from African-American Soldiers in the Union Army, 1861–1865*, 24–25.

83. Livermore, *My Story*, 350–53.

84. "Dawn of Freedom."

85. "Roster of Illinoisans Who Joined the 54th Massachusetts"; Luis F. Emilio, *History of the Fifty-fourth Regiment of Massachusetts Volunteer Infantry, 1863–1865*.

86. Official U.S. government records contain Chicago addresses for a small number of Massachusetts soldiers. See Emilio, *History of the Fifty-fourth*; and Thomas Truxtun Moebs, *Black Soldiers—Black Sailors—Black Ink: Research Guide on African Americans in U.S. Military History, 1526–1900*, 385, 388, 394, 404 (see index entry "Residents of Chicago, Illinois").

87. For more on Delany, see Miller, *Black Civil War Soldiers*, 11; and Ullman, *Martin R. Delany*, 282–88. For more on Langston, see Dorothy L. Drinkard, *Illinois Freedom Fighters: A Civil War Saga of the 29th Infantry, United States Colored Troops*, 14.

88. "Illinois Colored Regiment," *CT*, December 23, 1863.

89. Ibid.

90. A thorough examination of books, journals, diaries, and newspapers found almost no mention at all of the existence, let alone the meaningful participation, of African Americans representing the state of Illinois in the war effort. Unfortunately, the same held true for mentions of their battlefield participation. As a matter of fact, only scant references existed, and they were to be found in *BM*, and in ATA, 2:243, which mentions only the heroic death of the Twenty-ninth's regimental commander, the Chicago abolitionist Colonel Robert Bross. There is a passing reference also in Cook, *Bygone Days*, 28. These omissions were additionally distressing because the latter two were writ-

ing histories of Chicago. Drake and Cayton's omission in BM was somewhat understandable, since they were sociologists presenting a sketch, not a full account, of a socially proscribed African American civilian life in Chicago. The sociologists mentioned the uncertain social position African Americans held in Chicago with both purported friend and foe, along with labor strife, and community development. Significantly, they never even mentioned any military involvement as they described a national period of critical warfare. Fortuitously, two historical researchers, Dorothy L. Drinkard and Edward A. Miller, have recently rescued the regiment from obscurity. The decades-long efforts to revive the history by the late lay historian Ernest A. Griffin, the grandson of Private Charles Griffin of the Twenty-ninth, deserves mention also.

91. Arna F. Bontemps placed the locus later with the formation of the famed Eighth Regiment, Illinois National Guard, but he overlooked the Twenty-ninth completely. See "Soldiers," Box 19, Folder 1, IWP. Chicago's military tradition would produce an active-duty regiment in Cuba as part of the Spanish American War as well as a decorated front-line regiment during World War I. Twenty-first-century recognition exists in a local attempt by the National African American Military Museum Committee, to which the author belongs, to establish a permanent monument through the display of military artifacts at a designated structure.

92. According to Miller, "The state received credit for 1,811 African American enlistments, but the numbers are deceptive, because three or four hundred of the men found in Maryland and Virginia had never before seen the state; on the other hand, most early Illinois enlistees in other states' African American regiments were not credited to Illinois. To further cloud the picture, a large percentage of recruits counted for the quota were recent fugitives who had never resided in Illinois" (*Black Civil War Soldiers*, 171).

93. Civil War Muster-In and Descriptive Rolls of the Twenty-ninth Volunteer (Colored) Infantry, Illinois, Archives of the State of Illinois–Springfield.

94. Federal Pension Records of Private David Easley and Sergeant Willis Easley, Company C, CWPR.

95. Drinkard, *Illinois Freedom Fighters*, 14.

96. Harding, *There Is a River*, 238–39.

97. Versalle F. Washington, *Eagles on Their Buttons: A Black Infantry Regiment in the Civil War*, 1, 5, 11; see also Blassingame, "Recruitment of Colored Troops," 544.

98. "Illinois Colored Regiment"; and Miller, *Black Civil War Soldiers*, 25.

99. Henry Richardson to H. C. Evans, May 6, 1897, Company B, Pension Record of Henry Richardson, CWPR.

100. Joseph T. Glatthaar, *Forged in Battle: The Civil War Alliance of Black Soldiers and White Officers*, 97, 98. In not-so-north Washington, D.C., some whites feared that the influence of black military involvement would produce an "uppityness" among African Americans in that city; see Green, *Secret City*, 70.

101. Karamanski, *Rally*, 183.

102. Sergeant William McCoslin, "Letter from the Front" [July 26, 1864], 107–8.

103. Thomas Wentworth Higginson, *Army Life in a Black Regiment*, 10.

104. Bruce Catton, *A Stillness at Appomattox*, 258, 259.

105. Eric T. Dean Jr., *Shook over Hell: Post-traumatic Stress, Vietnam, and the Civil War*, 46, 47.

106. Miller, *Black Civil War Soldiers*, chapter 3, "Test of Battle," 59.

107. See Surgeon's Certificate dated July 12, 1899, Federal Pension Record of Alexander G. Garrett, Company B, CWPR, which contains a reference to the afore-mentioned soldier's injury as having occurred "at battle of Wilderness."

108. He was later described by Dr. Henry M. Lyman in 1869 as "a broken down man." Pension Record of Frank McAllister, Company C, CWPR.

109. Higginson, *Army Life*, 55, 56.

110. Report from the Adjutant General's Office, March 4, 1886, Pension Record of Lewis T. Wood, Company B, CWPR.

111. McCoslin, "Letter from the Front," 109–10.

112. Victor Hicken, *Illinois in the Civil War*, 338.

113. Kenneth Mason, "Battle of the Petersburg Crater," 2–9.

114. Drinkard, *Illinois Freedom Fighters*, 36; Hicken, *Illinois in the Civil War*, 338–39.

115. Earl Schenck Miers, *The Last Campaign: Grant Saves the Union*, 149.

116. ATA, 2:243.

117. Hicken, *Illinois in the Civil War*, 340–41.

118. General Affidavit of John Bird, date indiscernible, Pension Record of John Scott, Company E, CWPR; Surgeon's Certificate, October 24, 1874, Pension Record of Rodney Long, Company B, CWPR; Affidavit by Peter Williams, June 26, 1889, Pension Record of Peter Williams, Company C, CWPR.

119. Deposition of Jefferson Gash, February 7, 1884, Pension Record of Jefferson Gash, Company D, CWPR; Deposition of Florence L. Wolridge, December 2, 1898, Pension Record of Richard Barbour, Company B, CWPR.

120. Glatthaar, *Forged in Battle*, 150. For a full account of the decisions on the use of black troops, the battle itself, and the aftermath of the engagement, see Miller, *Black Civil War Soldiers*, 66–79. Glatthaar cites the confusing figures of 450 soldiers of the Twenty-ninth entering the battle with only 128 exiting.

121. Burnside quoted in Drinkard, *Illinois Freedom Fighters*, 41 (see also 41–43); Hicken, *Illinois in the Civil War*, 341; Miller, *Black Civil War Soldiers*, 100–102.

122. Miller, *Black Civil War Soldiers*, 153.

123. Deposition of William McKenney, December 20, 1898, Pension Record of William McKenney, Company F, CWPR; Affidavit of Moses Conley, March 27, 1894, Federal Pension Record of Alexander Garrett, Company B, CWPR.

124. Surgeon quoted in Drinkard, *Illinois Freedom Fighters*, 62; Deposition of Jonathan B. Colton, December 11, 1888, Pension Record of Moses Nelson, Company D, CWPR.

125. Drinkard, *Illinois Freedom Fighters*, 63.

126. Higginson, *Army Life*, 253. On education, see Edward G. Longacre, "Black Troops in the Army of the James, 1863–65," in Hine and Jenkins, *Question of Manhood*, 1:537; and Drinkard, *Illinois Freedom Fighters*, 62, 63.

127. Emory M. Thomas, *Robert E. Lee: A Biography*, 353.

128. General Affidavit of Isaac Foster, May 16, 1888, Pension Record of Hardin Harris, Company B, CWPR.

129. General Affidavit of James H. Rosell, June 10, 1895, Federal Pension Record of Hardin Harris, Company B, CWPR.

130. Physician's Affidavit, date indiscernible, and General Affidavit of Sgt. James H. Rosell, date indiscernible, both in Federal Pension Record of William Watkins, CWPR;

General Affidavit of Thomas Scott, March 5, 1892, Federal Pension Record of Jesse Vaughn, Company C, CWPR.

131. Deposition of Jefferson Day, August 9, 1889, Pension Record of Lewis T. Wood, NA; Ferrero quoted in Drinkard, *Illinois Freedom Fighters*, 45.

132. Interestingly, in Edward G. Longacre, *Army of Amateurs: General Benjamin F. Butler and the Army of the James, 1863–1865*, the only Twenty-ninth infantry regiment mentioned (and then only briefly) is the Twenty-ninth Connecticut, an all-black unit that was not a part of the USCT, which is sometimes confused with the Twenty-ninth Illinois.

133. Thomas, *Robert E. Lee*, 356.

134. Charles P. Roland, *An American Iliad: The Story of the Civil War*, 242.

135. Deposition of William Chambers, February 26, 1872, Federal Pension Record of William Armstrong, Company C, CWPR.

136. Catton, *Stillness*, 420.

137. Ibid., 422. See also Drinkard, *Illinois Freedom Fighters*, 74.

138. Chris M. Calkins, *The Battles of Appomattox Station and Appomattox Court House, April 8–9, 1865*, 92f.

139. What some white soldiers felt is recorded by Catton, *Stillness*, 425, and it included respect for a courageous, but now fallen, foe as well as a sense of reconciliation. To have imagined the same from black troops would stretch human sensibility. No doubt, in their unrestrained and boisterous behavior, their message was one of vindication as to their race's willingness to fight for its freedom and contempt for the soldiers were fought in behalf of their oppressors. See Calkins, *Battles of Appomattox*, 153, and Chris M. Calkins, *The Appomattox Campaign*, 177–78, for an exuberant and less charitable Union reaction. For more on the mixed feelings of the Union upon victory, from the charitable Grant to jubilant throngs in the nation's capital, see James M. McPherson, *Battle Cry of Freedom: The Civil War Era*, 849–51. The author's maternal great-grandfather was in the 116th Regiment, USCT.

140. Douglass, *Life and Times*, 373; Booker T. Washington, "Early Problems of Freedom," in Howard Brotz, ed., *Negro Social and Political Thought, 1850–1920: Representative Texts*, 384.

141. Burrows and Wallace, *Gotham*, 904, 905; Merrill D. Peterson, *Lincoln in American Memory* (New York: Oxford University Press, 1994), 18.

142. Karamanski, *Rally*, 247. For the general impact on the city, see Cook, *Bygone Days*, "The Lincoln Funeral," 316–20.

143. SOS.

144. Harding, *There Is a River*, 278.

145. Frederick H. Dyer, *A Compendium of the War of the Rebellion*, 1728.

146. Paralleling the lives of Chicagoans in the Illinois Twenty-ninth Infantry (and those other units) was the life of a soldier (who served with Chicagoans) in the Fifth Massachusetts Cavalry Regiment, USCT, Sergeant Amos Webber. His story, with an emphasis on his postwar adjustment, has been captured in Salvatore, *We All Got History*, 152–57. In addition, within two, and perhaps three, generations in the future, the grandsons and great-grandsons of former slaves would transform themselves into more assertive persons as a result of the linkage between their premilitary civilian life and their World War II experience in southern and southwestern U.S. military camps and in the

Pacific Theater of war. See Robert Franklin Jefferson, "Making the Men of the Ninety-third: African American Servicemen in the Years of the Great Depression and the Second World War, 1935–1947." From time to time some of these men would make reference to their forefathers' experience in slavery as they performed undesirable, noncombat duties during the course of the war (251, 258–60, 325).

147. Letter, H. Ford Douglas to Frederick Douglass, January 8, 1863; McCoslin quoted in Calkins, *Appomattox Campaign*, 183. See also "Enthusiastic Meeting at New England Church in Aid of Colored Refugees." To assist in the thousands of African Americans fleeing the South for Kansas, rallies and fund raisers were held throughout the North. The issue of the past military service of black soldiers was mentioned and became a metaphor for proven citizenship and deserved aid.

II. Harbor of Opportunity for New Citizens, 1866–1900

1. CVA, 87.
2. BM, 45.
3. Williams, "Social Bonds," 42; Levine, *Black Culture*, 268. To Du Bois, the secret society provided two services: social intercourse and insurance. They also "furnish[ed] pastime from the monotony of work, a field for ambition and intrigue, a chance for parade, and insurance against misfortune"; see *PN*, 224.

Chapter 3. Freedom and Fire during the Reconstruction Era, 1866–1879

1. Miller, *Black Civil War Soldiers*, x.
2. See King, "Wounds That Bind."
3. BLP, 2:11, 12nn22–26.
4. Carolyn Ashbaugh, *Lucy Parsons: American Revolutionary*, 15.
5. Ibid.
6. Moore, *History of Bethel*, 19.
7. A. N. Fields, "Historic Glimpses of Old Chicago," CD, October 22, 1932, 7; "Mrs. Joanna C. Snowden, Pioneer Chicagoan, Dies," CD, October 4, 1941, 3.
8. Ralph Nelson Davis, "The Negro Newspaper in Chicago," 26.
9. Salvatore, *We All Got History*, 152–53.
10. Declaration for Pension, Charles Demond, March 3, 1911, Federal Pension Record of Charles Demond, Twenty-sixth Infantry, USCT, CWPR.
11. "Chicago's Noted Negroes."
12. Hall-Boger Family Collection.
13. Zucker, "Damage and Resistance," 10.
14. BLP, 2:286. For an examination of the bill's impact at the nation's capital, see James M. McPherson, *Ordeal by Fire: The Civil War and Reconstruction*, 558–60.
15. "Civil Rights—Address of the Colored Citizens of Chicago to the Congress of the United States." U.S. House of Representatives. 30th Congress, 1st session, May 10, 1866, 1–5.
16. Ibid. (emphasis in the original).

17. An intriguing argument on the anti-image accorded things feminine also included the elements of manhood, of which holding the franchise was one. See Ronald J. Zboray and Mary Sarcino Zboray, "Gender Slurs in Boston's Partisan Press during the 1840s."

18. BLP, 2:300. See also McPherson, *Ordeal by Fire*, 525, 536, 540–41.

19. Katzman, *Before the Ghetto*, 3f.

20. Peterson, *Lincoln in American Memory*, 171, 173.

21. "John Jones on the Colored Race," *CT*, January 2, 1874, 5.

22. Cook, *Bygone Days*, xi.

23. Conkin and Stromberg, *Heritage and Challenge*, 198.

24. Frazier, *Negro Family in Chicago*, 88.

25. Deposition of Ethelbert Graves, September 9, 1922, Federal Pension Record of William Graves, Company B, CWPR.

26. Questionnaire, dated April 17, 1915, Federal Pension Record of Willis Easley, Company C, CWPR.

27. "Chicago's Noted Negroes."

28. Moore, *History of Bethel*, 25.

29. SOS.

30. Brown, *Homespun Heroines*, 142, 143; interview with Joan[na] C. Snowden, February 3, 1938, 7, "Old Settlers" File, IWP.

31. Karen Sawislak, *Smoldering City: Chicagoans and the Great Fire, 1871–1874*, 109–19.

32. Leota Johnson (granddaughter of Mr. Taylor), interview with author, Chicago, July 2001. See also Moore, *History of Bethel*, 26, 27, and the Wolcott File.

33. Wilson, "Center City Origins," 48–57, Homer Hoyt, *One Hundred Years of Land Value in Chicago: The Relationship of the Growth of Chicago to the Rise of Its Land Values, 1830–1933*, 113; and Work, "Negro Real Estate Holders," 11.

34. BLP, 2:158, 159.

35. *PN*, 45.

36. BLP, 2:150–52.

37. *BM*, 433.

38. Sawislak, *Smoldering City*, 168, see also 202.

39. Robb, *Negro in Chicago*, 2:257.

40. A. N. Fields, "Pioneer Settler Is Maitre d'Hotel," *CD*, April 29, 1933, 16.

41. Simmons, *Men of Mark*, 358, 360.

42. Declaration of Rodney Long, February 19, 1907, Federal Pension Record of Rodney Long, Company B, CWPR; Death Certificate of Alexander Garrett, dated February 3, 1913, Federal Pension Record of Alexander Garrett, Company B, CWPR.

43. Simmons, *Men of Mark*, 240–45. The saga of a Massachusetts Civil War veteran, Sergeant Amos Webber of the Fifth Massachusetts Cavalry, USCT, presents another, different example from the industrial sphere of attitude toward and type of work in which a black man engaged. During the Civil War, Reconstruction, and post-Reconstruction periods, Webber lived and worked in Worcester, Massachusetts. His employer was the Washburn and Moen Wire Company, where he worked as a janitor, messenger, and executive carriage driver. See Salvatore, *We All Got History*, 98, 101–3, 156–57, 171–80, 236–38, 304–5.

44. BLP, 1:182, 154.

45. Robb, *Negro in Chicago*, 1:227.

46. Stibbs to Commissioner of Pensions, October 11, 1893, Federal Pension Record of Anthony, Company B, CWPR.

47. Original Invalid Claim, September 9, 1889 review date, Federal Pension Record of Willis Easley, Company C, CWPR; Wright, "Industrial Condition," 22.

48. My interest in this occupation was stimulated by the marvel that the late, distinguished attorney at law, Earl Burrus Dickerson, Esq., attached to it. Dickerson was born in Canton, Mississippi, in the 1890s and was reared by his mother, who sacrificed mightily for his future. On several occasions during interviews about his life in Chicago from the turn of the (twentieth) century to the 1980s, the benefits he derived from his mother's hard work, his attachment and debt to her, and the memories of accompanying her as she delivered her finished product to customers, still mesmerized him as well as the listener. When encountering this occupation in documents examined for this study, the need to include it because of its importance to the world of labor became obvious. As late as the 1930s, African American washerwomen numbered 1,500, or one-half of the city's in-house or take-home laundresses. Work provided at laundries provided five times that with paychecks. *BM*, 249, 250.

49. Claimant's Oath of Delilia F. Watkins, no date, Federal Pension Record of William Watkins, Company C, CWPR.

50. Tera W. Hunter, *To 'Joy My Freedom: Southern African American Women's Lives and Labors after the Civil War*, 2, 3.

51. A'Lelia Bundles, *On Her Own Ground: The Life and Times of Madam C. J. Walker*, 46.

52. Joint Deposition of Thomas Martin and Jennie De (unk.), no date, Widow's Claim of Cecilia McAllister, Federal Pension Record of Frank McAllister, Company C, CWPR.

53. Widow's claim of Malinda L. Chappell, July 6, 1917, Federal Pension Record of Henry Chappell, Company E, CWPR; Mother's Claim, February 1877, Federal Pension Record of Cato Flowers, Company C, CWPR; Deposition of Nancy Clary, February 1, 1892, Federal Pension Record of Louis Clary, Company C, CWPR.

54. Bogger, *Free Blacks in Norfolk*, 72, 73, 120.

55. SOS. See also the *Defender's* essay (OT) for conflicting information.

56. BLP, 2:311.

57. Gosnell, *Negro Politicians*, 198n4.

58. *Joseph Medill: A Biography and Tribute*, 19.

59. SOS; File on Engine Company 21, Ken Little.

60. "Little Trace Remains of 1st Black Legislator [J. W. E. Thomas] in Illinois."

61. *BM*, 433; Herma Clark, "When Chicago Was Young: The Elegant Eighties," *Chicago Sunday Tribune*, June 28, 1936, n.p., in the Atkinson Family Collection for a reference to Platt's prosperity in the lumber business.

62. See Bundles, *On Her Own Ground*, 44.

63. Deposition of Ethelbert Graves, September 9, 1922, Federal Pension Record of William Graves, Company B, CWPR.

64. For the first schoolteacher, a contradictory claim is made for Nellie Mann, in Robb, *Negro in Chicago*, "They Were the First," 1:123. For New York, see Ovington, *Half a Man*, 10.

65. Deposition of Eliza Jane Harris, May 24, 1913, Federal Pension Record of John Abrams, Company G, CWPR.

66. "Mrs. Joanna C. Snowden, Pioneer Chicagoan, Dies."

67. "Mixed Schools," Scrapbook of Ferdinand L. Barnett, Box 10, Folder 8, Ida B. Wells Papers (hereafter referred to as the Wells Papers).

68. Livermore, My Story, 261, 265.

69. "Our Future," Chicago Conservator, n.d., in Scrapbook of Ferdinand L. Barnett, Wells Papers.

70. "Chicago's Noted Negroes."

71. See Davis, "Negro Newspaper," 26. According to the more contemporary account of Irvine Garland Penn, The Afro-American Press and Its Editors, 264, Barnett surrendered the reins in late 1878.

72. Davis, "Negro Newspaper," 10.

73. Conservator, October 26, 1878, Barnett Scrapbook, Wells Papers.

74. De Baptiste quoted in Penn, Afro-American Press, 264.

75. "Mixed Schools," Scrapbook of Ferdinand L. Barnett, Wells Papers.

76. The small pension file of John Liter revealed, upon meticulous examination, a moving story containing all of the ingredients of an American saga. Liter, a former slave, met another former slave in Chicago. An obscure Civil War veteran who served in the Twenty-ninth Illinois, Company B, USCT, Liter led a life that contained the ingredients of a Shakespearean drama, especially when the trials and travails of his wife, Jane, were included. Information in the following discussion is drawn from this file.

77. For the importance attached both to assigned names and those voluntarily chosen in freedom, see Genovese, Roll, Jordan, Roll, 447, 448.

78. E. S. Little to Hon. Green B. Rann, Commissioner of Pensions, October 25, 1892, Federal Pension File of John Liter, Company B, CWPR.

79. John Hope Franklin and Loren Schweninger, Runaway Slaves: Rebels on the Plantation, 224.

80. Ibid., 212.

81. Genovese, Roll, Jordan, Roll, 500, 501.

82. See Horton and Horton, In Hope of Liberty, 178f. As late as the first quarter of the nineteenth century, memories and stories of life in Africa were still fresh in the minds of many enslaved persons of African descent. For others, memories would fade and subsequent generations would neither be aware of actual experiences nor memories of the African way of life.

83. The experience that Jane Liter missed was considerable. Among the Ashanti, for example, "no woman st[ood] alone, for behind the woman st[ood] a united family, bound by the tie of blood, which ha[d] a power and a meaning [that a Western European or Anglo-American could] hardly grasp. . . . The whole conception of 'mother-right' afford[ed] the woman a protection and a status that [was] more than an adequate safeguard against the ill-treatment by any male or group of males" (R. E. Bradbury, The Benin Kingdom and the Edo-Speaking Peoples of South-Western Nigeria, 189, 190).

Among the Edo-speaking Bini people of the state of Benin, solemnity and ceremony, traditional rites, and obligations also marked marriage and family formation. As an example of the character of marriage, polygynous unions existed, with a man supporting up to two wives in some instances, but monogamous unions seemed to have been more pervasive. "Marriage partners were . . . expected to be virtuous, industriousness, and healthy . . . [and] a marriage ceremony performed before the ancestors to solemnize marriage [could] never, according to strict custom, be revoked; a woman must wait for the death of her husband before being permitted to solemnize marriage in this way with any other man" (Melville J. Herskovits, *Dahomey: An Ancient West African Kingdom*, 1:300–351).

Among the Fon people, who constructed the famed military state of Dahomey, the status of women and the state of marriage reached unusual levels. Some of their women were known as "Amazons." They were the females who served in the Kings' army as active-duty soldiers and who never married or were forbidden to enter into sexual unions. For women outside the military sphere and who constituted the majority of the Fon population, the structure of marriage divided into two categories, which, in turn, contained a total of thirteen variations as to marital relationships and obligations. Such was the complexity of life within the sanctity of marriage outside the American slave plantation. In America, the traditional African social order broke down before the labor and sexual demands of the Southern planter. In contrast, for the Fon, chastity before marriage was prized, and quite simply represented the fresh start of the lifetime relationship. Where it did not exist, concessions could be made to accommodate this factor into the relationship, without blame, also. On the one hand, consent had to be given by a father for the marriage of a daughter, and this usually was arranged years before puberty. In another scenario, a free man could choose a woman who also had shown her approval of him. In all cases, complex institutional arrangements and relationships became the foundation of a stable, sustaining union involving families and clans rewoven into a new network of mutuality. See R. S. Rattray, *Ashanti*, 79.

84. Deposition of Edward Maybin, October 24, 1892, Federal Pension File of John Liter, Company B, CWPR.

85. Blassingame, *Slave Community*, 149; Deposition of Jane Liter, October 17, 1892, 8, Federal Pension File of John Liter, Company B, CWPR; Blassingame, *Slave Community*, 165. For veteran Stephen Brooks, his master denied him the permanency of a union with his "wife," Rhoda, because of her status as a "free woman." See Deposition of Amanda Slate, August 16, 1889, Federal Pension File of Stephen Brooks, Company C, CWPR. Widow Emma L. Morrison had experienced a situation under slavery in which she and her beloved mate "each had a temporary partner or conjugal companion." See Declaration for Widow's Pension, April 13, 1899, Federal Pension Record of James Morrison, Company B, CWPR.

86. Frazier, *Negro Family in the United States*, 19, 20.

87. Deposition of Jane Liter, October 17, 1892, 10, 11, Federal Pension File of John Liter, Company B, CWPR.

88. Frazier, *Negro Family in the United States*, 41–44.

89. Deposition of Jane Liter, October 17, 1892, 9, Federal Pension File of John Liter, Company B, CWPR.

90. Langston Hughes wrote of the vicissitudes common to life in America for African Americans in his poem, "Mother to Son," which presents a mother's loving yet pragmatic words of advice and encouragement: "Life for me ain't been no crystal stair. / It's had tacks in it, / And splinters, / And boards torn up . . ." (*The Collected Works of Langston Hughes*, vol. 1, *The Poems: 1921–1940*, 60).

91. Deposition of Jane Liter, October 17, 1892, 7, Federal Pension File of John Liter, Company B, CWPR.

92. Gerald F. Linderman, *Embattled Courage: The Experience of Combat in the American Civil War*, 236. See also Salvatore, *We All Got History*, 152; King, "Wounds That Bind," and Michael Tow, "Secrecy and Segregation: Murphysboro's Black Social Organizations, 1865–1925," 29–33.

93. Linderman, *Embattled Courage*, 216.

94. Deposition of George Jones, April 5, 1898, Federal Pension Record of George Jones, Company F, CWPR. In 1995, Robert Jefferson completed a dissertation on bonding that would elevate this process to the level of community among the men ("Making the Men of the Ninety-third").

95. Deposition of William Collins, March 31, 1888, Federal Pension Record of William Randall, Company B, CWPR; Deposition of James Jones, July 9, 1885, 9, Federal Pension Record of James Jones, Company B, CWPR.

96. Deposition of Mary Jane Randall, March 6, 1889, Federal Pension Record of William Randall, Company B, CWPR; Deposition of Mary Jane Randall, October, n.d., 1888, (date stamped November 20, 1888), Federal Pension Record of William Randall, Company B, CWPR.

97. Widow's Declaration for Pension, May 29, 1895, Federal Pension Record of Joseph Richardson #1, (died 1865), Company F, CWPR.

98. Declaration for the Increase of an Invalid Pension, July 20, 1900, Federal Pension Record of Joseph Richardson #2, (died after 1900), Company F, CWPR.

99. Affidavit of Henry Mosely, July 13, 1892, Federal Pension Record of Frank McAllister, Company C, CWPR.

100. Examining Surgeon's Certificate, May 17, 1869, Federal Pension Record of Frank McAllister, Company C, CWPR.

101. Surgeon's Certificate, October 7, 1873, Federal Pension Record of Frank McAllister, Company C, CWPR.

102. Affidavit of Henry Mosely, July 13, 1892, and Affidavit of Celia McAllister, July 11, 1892, Federal Pension Record of Frank McAllister, Company C, CWPR.

103. *Revised United States Army Regulations of 1861*, 9.

104. Miller, *Black Civil War Soldiers*, 24; Deposition of William McKenney, February 21, 1883, Pension Record of William McKenney, Company F, CWPR.

105. Dean, *Shook over Hell*, 90.

106. Katzman, *Before the Ghetto*, 3.

107. ATA, 3:590.

108. I. C. Harris, comp., *The Colored Men's Professional and Business Directory*, 36. See also CVA, 64.

109. CVA, 64, 77.

110. "Enthusiastic Meeting." See also Salvatore, *We All Got History*, 186–88, for memories of the warm reception given to the members of the Fifty-fourth Infantry, Fifty-fifth Infantry, and Fifth Massachusetts Cavalry Regiments, USCT, by the citizens of Massachusetts.

111. "Historical Highlights of Bethel A.M.E. Church, 1962," 1.

112. *PN*, 224; Williams, "Social Bonds," 42.

113. In an example of the linkage between the military and the fraternal from

Worcester, Massachusetts, veteran Amos Webber joined the GAR in spring 1868 as its first black member (with many more to come in future years), and at the same time laid the groundwork for the formation of North Star Lodge, No. 1372, of the Grand United Order of Odd Fellows in August 1868. The intent of establishing the lodge, "given the relentless denigration of black Americans by whites" was to "counter potentially debilitating images" of the race and to "be the precursor to more concerted, collective political action as well." As Salvatore described it, "The exchange of visits between the different lodges, forming as they did an intricate pattern that crisscrossed the centers of black urban life, reinforced a larger sense of collective purpose and in that exchange of information, discussion of group strategy, and the formation of friendship lay the trellis that supported a great variety of northern black activism." See Salvatore, *We All Got History*, 162–63.

114. Williams, "Social Bonds," 42.

115. "Obituary: Death of Ex-County-Commissioner John Jones," May 22, 1879, *Chicago Tribune*, 7.

116. Sawislak, *Smoldering City*, 127–36. The opposite was the case for Philadelphia, a city where corruption, violence, and indifference toward reform marked that city's political landscape; see *PN*, 40–42n24.

117. "Chicago's Noted Negroes."

118. "An Anti–John Jones Demonstration among the Colored Citizens of the South Side," *CIO*, September 22, 1875, 8.

119. CVA, 40.

120. Roi Ottley and William J. Weatherby, *The Negro in New York: An Informal Social History*, 130, 131.

121. For a detailed treatment of how his election came about, see David A. Joens, "John W. E. Thomas and the Election of the First African American to the Illinois General Assembly."

122. "Little Trace Remains."

123. Excerpted letter by John W. E. Thomas to the Republicans of the Second Senatorial District, October 8, 1878, Chicago, Illinois, Illinois State Archives.

124. "The Reform Club, *CT*, November 3, 1876, 2.

125. "Long John Wentworth," *CT*, November 3, 1876, 2. This fear was realized temporarily after election day, when the *CT* headline of November 8, 1876, read "LOST: The Country Given over to Democratic Greed and Plunder," 1.

126. Excerpted letter by John W. E. Thomas to the Republicans of the Second Senatorial District.

127. Gosnell, *Negro Politicians*, 66. See also Illinois Secretary of State Memorial to Thomas, Illinois State Archives, Springfield.

128. Kilson, "Political Change," 167–74.

129. See Branham, "Transformation," 15–20.

130. SOS.

131. "Chicago's Noted Negroes"; SOS.

132. SOS.

133. "Chicago Colored Society," *Illinois Record*, June 18, 1898, 1.

Chapter 4. Gilded Age Chicago, 1880–1892

1. Charles S. Johnson, "These Colored United States," 926, 927; Harold M. Mayer and Richard C. Wade, *Chicago: Growth of a Metropolis*, 124, 128. See also *CIO*, "The Negro Exodus," January 15, 1880. It is important to note that Mayer and Wade's description of Chicago places it in a rather unique position as being one of those locales in the nation where opportunity rather than deterioration was occurring. Supportive evidence substantiates this stance. The classic on this period, Logan, *Betrayal of the Negro*, treats this time as one of decline in the African American status. More recently, what has become the classic on the black elite, Willard B. Gatewood's *Aristocrats of Color: The Black Elite, 1880–1920*, reiterates this theme of societal decay in his preface (x) while refuting it in his text as he proves that an elite did exist. Litwack's *Trouble in Mind* presents a monumental study which explores successful coping and successes within this period.

2. See Litwack, *Trouble in Mind*, for a recent examination of the South under legal and customary racial oppression during the post-Reconstruction era.

3. *BM*, 45.

4. Ibid., 434.

5. In a creative bit of miscounting, the July 28, 1888, edition of the *Western Appeal* placed the population at 25,000, with 300 residing on the North Side, 1,571 on the West Side, and the bulk living on the South Side.

6. Gutman, *Black Family*, 433. Gutman took noted sociologist Ernest W. Burgess to task over his introduction to Frazier's *Negro Family in Chicago*, writing: "The typical Afro-American family changed its shape in the half century between 1880 and 1930. But at all times—and in all settings—the typical black household (always a lower-class household) had in it two parents and was not 'unorganized and disorganized'" (433). For statistics on schoolchildren, see BLP, 3:518.

7. Frazier, *Negro Family in Chicago*, 71.

8. Deposition of Nancy Clary, February 1, 1892, Federal Pension Record of Louis Clary, Company C, CWPR.

9. Leota Johnson interview.

10. Nelson, *The Negro Newspaper*, 26.

11. Nahum Daniel Brascher, "Pioneer Chicagoan in Hall of Fame: Col. Wm. R. Cowan, Business, Political, Civic Leader, Passes Away after Short Illness," *CD*, June 3, 1933, 17; Ransom, *Pilgrimage*, 83.

12. Darlene Clark Hine, *Speak Truth to Power: Black Professional Class in United States History*, 174, 188.

13. Buckler, *Daniel Hale Williams*, 23.

14. Kletzing and Crogman, *Progress of a Race*, 450.

15. "Dr. C. E. Bentley," *Appeal*, April 2, 1892, 1.

16. Kletzing and Crogman, *Progress of a Race*, 448.

17. This account of the early life of Fannie Barrier Williams is based on the writings of, and correspondence between the author and the historian of Brockport, Professor Emeritus William G. Andrews of the State University of New York at Brockport, February 10, 1998.

18. "Fannie B. Williams," in Jessie Carney Smith, ed., *Notable Black American*

Women, 1251–54; Rayford W. Logan and Michael R. Winston, eds., *Dictionary of American Negro Biography*, 656; Ann Massa, "Black Women in the 'White City,'" 330.

19. A new anthology of her writings has recently appeared; see Deegan, *New Woman of Color.*

20. See Louis R. Harlan, *Booker T. Washington: The Wizard of Tuskegee, 1901–1915*, 357. I have been incorrectly identified as a detractor of S. Laing Williams, based on my comments on Williams's lack of demonstrated *leadership* skills within the ranks of the Chicago NAACP during the Progressive era. I did not criticize his overall legal competence and recognized, for better or for worse, Dr. Charles E. Bentley as the prototype of black civic leadership. Rather than a detractor, I take a more sympathetic view of Williams's place in late-nineteenth- and early-twentieth-century Chicago and feel like a supporter. See Deegan, *New Woman of Color*, xxvii, and Reed, *Chicago NAACP*, 31.

21. The famed "Bronzeville" of the 1990s reflects the revived interest in the area by city developers, real estate developers, and homeowners alike. See City of Chicago, Department of Planning and Development, "Black Metropolis Historic District," March 7, 1984 (rev. December 1994).

22. Work, "Negro Real Estate Holders," 13; for more on black Chicagoans living south of the Loop, see ibid.; for more on the real estate boom, see BLP, 3:209f.

23. "South Side's Fabled Past Revisited by Bus," *Chicago Sun-Times*, November 12, 2001, 50.

24. *CT*, February 10, 1890, 7.

25. "Chicago: Doings of the Past Week in All Parts of the Great Metropolis of the West," *Western Appeal*, April 14, 1888, 1.

26. For Millionaire's Row, see Buckler, *Daniel Hale Williams*, 25. For Hyde Park, see "Chicago," *Appeal*, June 9, 1888, 1. For marriage in 1896, see SOS.

27. For more on Terry and Hancock, see Simmons, *Men of Mark*, 409, 405–9. For more on Pinchback and the Frenches, see "A Swell Event: Grand Reception Given by Mr. and Mrs. John H. French," *Appeal*, July 20, 1889, 1. For more on property ownership, see Work, "Negro Real Estate Holders," 14, 19.

28. F. L. Barnett, "National—Masonic Convention and Celebration to be held at Chicago . . . ," *Western Appeal*, July 23, 1887, 1 (emphasis added).

29. Statistical data extracted from Eleventh U.S. Census, 1890, in BLP 2:517. The increasing black population and its participation in the Chicago labor force in seen through these figures: Harris's *Colored Men's Directory* noted 9,481 as the size of the black population in 1885; the Eleventh Census indicated that the 8,080 employed persons enumerated lived in a population of 14,271; Work's "Crime" listed 13,645 workers in a population that had risen to 22,742; and the Twelfth U.S. Census, 1900, enumerated 17,986 workers out of a total group population of 30,150.

30. *BM*, 302.

31. Work, "Crime," 206.

32. William Stibbs to Commissioner of Pensions, Washington, D.C., October 3, 1885, Federal Pension Record of James Jones, Company B, CWPR.

33. Williams, "Autobiography," 92–94.

34. Deposition of John Enders, November 14, 1890, Federal Pension Record of Milton Hawkins, Company B, CWPR; for Bond, see "The Garden City," *Appeal*, May 18, 1889, 1.

35. Deposition of Catherine Ralston, January 11, 1892, Federal Pension Record of Henry Chappell, Company E, CWPR.

36. Frazier, *Negro Family in Chicago*, 223.

37. CVA, 106.

38. Kirkland, "Among the Poor," 5. In this quotation, one may interpret "industrious" to mean "performing energetically and devotedly"; "hard working" to mean "performing robotically like the immigrants"; "economical" to mean "avoiding extravagance"; and "acquisitive" to mean "seeking wealth greedily."

39. Richard Schneirov, *Labor and Urban Politics: Class Conflict and the Origins of Modern Liberalism in Chicago, 1864–97*, 306f.

40. See Richardson, *Death of Reconstruction*, chapter 6, "The Un-American Negro, 1880–1900," 183–97. This belief by white employers in black inefficiency in the workplace continued into the early twentieth century. See Grossman, *Land of Hope*, 198, 199, 242.

41. At the end of the century, collegian Richard R. Wright Jr. held the same view about white revulsion toward work, so what he witnessed as he approached the outskirts of Chicago surprised him—white men doing hard work. See Grossman, *Land of Hope*, quoting Wright on 1, 2.

42. *PN*, 129, xxxvii, and note on 129–31.

43. Schneirov, *Labor and Urban Politics*, 220, 306, 314.

44. Report of Conferences between the Board of Directors of the World's Columbian Exposition and Representatives of the Labor Organizations of Chicago, Relative to the Employment of Labor, 1891 (Chicago: Wm. C. Hollister & Bro., Printers, 1891).

45. Sterling D. Spero and Abram L. Harris, *The Black Worker: The Negro in the Labor Movement*, x, xi, 41–45; and "Paragraphs—Containing the happenings among Colored people," *Western Appeal*, July 16, 1887, 1.

46. "Opinion of the Chicago Colored Women's Club," *Chicago Inter Ocean*, March 13, 1894, cited in Philip S. Foner and Ronald L. Lewis, eds., *The Black Worker: A Documentary History from Colonial Times to the Present*, vol. 3, *The Black Worker during the Era of the Knights of Labor*, 282. These comments were also cited in Bontemps and Conroy, *They Seek a City*, 140.

47. William R. Harris, *The Harder We Run: Black Workers since the Civil War*, 20, 21. See also Frank A. Cassell, "A Confusion of Voices: Reform Movements and the World's Columbian Exposition of 1893," 66.

48. H. C. Bunner, "The Making of the White City," 417.

49. For more on Mayor Washburne, see CVA, 87; for more on Greene, see John J. Flinn, *History of the Chicago Police*, 500; for more on Davenport, see SOS, and Atkinson family story.

50. "Colored Lights in Chicago: Citizens of Dark Hue Who Are Prominent in Business and the Professions." See also Wright, *Eighty-seven Years*, 110.

51. "Geo. W. Browne," *Appeal*, June 13, 1891, 1; "Lemuel Moore," *Appeal*, June 27, 1891, 1.

52. A. N. Field, "West Side Attracts Early Chicagoan," CD, May 27, 1933, 17.

53. "Lewis W. Cummins," *Appeal*, March 15, 1890, 1, 2.

54. BLP, 3:509f; Mayer and Wade, *Chicago*, 193; and Robert Anderson Naylor, *Across the Atlantic*, 90.

55. Dean, *Shook over Hell*, 46–48.

56. Deposition from E. Lewis stamped November 20, 1888; Depositions of Mary Jane Randall, dated October, n.d., 1888, stamped November 20, 1888, and dated March 6, 1889; William Collins, dated March 31, 1888; Rodney Long, dated April 30, 1888; and Dr. H. S. Hahn, dated March 5, 1889, all in the Federal Pension Record of William Randall, Company B, CWPR.

57. Harris, *Colored Men's Directory*, 36. Harris fixed the number of workers in hotels and restaurants at between eighteen hundred and two thousand in his 1885 publication. Subtracting the porters, janitors, and other non-wait personnel, the estimate here is fifteen hundred. In "Proposed Porters' Strike," *Appeal*, July 19, 1890, 2, the figure is also fifteen hundred. Duis gives two estimates of waiters in near approximation to this figure; see *Challenging Chicago*, 261, 267.

58. Benefits and attitudes are cited in *Indianapolis Freeman*, May 6, 1893, 7, and May 20, 1893, 5.

59. Wright, "Industrial Condition," 22, 23; Duis, *Challenging Chicago*, 265; Katzman, *Before the Ghetto*, 111, 112, 115; Wright, "Industrial Condition," 21.

60. Frazier, *Negro Family in Chicago*, 106; Deposition of James H. Brown, June 17, 1880, Federal Pension Record of Lewis T. Wood, Company B, CWPR; Wright, "Industrial Condition," 22; BM, 74; Virginia Cunningham, *Paul Laurence Dunbar and His Song*, 93, 94.

61. Simmons, *Men of Mark*, 244; and Schneirov, *Labor and Urban Politics*, 220.

62. See Arvarh E. Strickland, *History of the Chicago Urban League*; and Tuttle, *Race Riot*.

63. For more on Assembly 8286, see "Paragraphs—Containing the Happenings among Colored People," *Western Appeal*, July 16, 1887, 1 (300 workers), and Duis, *Challenging Chicago*, 266 (400 workers). For more on labor organizations, see Duis, *Challenging Chicago*, 267–68. For more on the workers' victories, see these articles in the *Appeal*: "Waiters Win," May 10, 1890, 1; "Chicago," May 17, 1890, 1; and "Winning Waiters," May 24, 1890, 1, 2.

64. *Appeal*, March 28, 1891, 1.

65. CT, May 11, 1893, 6; Duis, *Challenging Chicago*, 267–68.

66. "Prominent Members of the Colored Waiters' Alliance," *Appeal*, October 8, 1892, 1. Sketches of the leadership accompanied the article and one leader, R. B. Cabell, was recognized as someone who corresponded with the still-active abolitionist Judge Albion W. Tourgee of Mayville, New York.

67. Sharon Harley, "When Your Work Is Not Who You Are: The Development of a Working-Class Consciousness among Afro-American Women," 25, 26.

68. Interview with May Anna Madison, "I Can Handle Black Men; What I Can't Handle Is This Prejudice," in Gwaltney, *Drylongso*, 172–74.

69. Robin D. G. Kelley, "'We Are Not What We Seem': Rethinking Black Working Class Opposition in the Jim Crow South," 75–112.

70. Harris, *Harder We Run*, 20.

71. Spero and Harris, *Black Worker*, 430.

72. "Proposed Porters' Strike," *Appeal*, July 19, 1890, 2.

73. "He Beat the Pullman Co.," *Appeal*, March 8, 1890, 2.

74. "Pullman Porters' Plaint," *Appeal*, February 8, 1890, 1.

75. "The Railway Porters," *Western Appeal*, July 14, 1888, 1.

76. "Proposed Porters' Strike," *Appeal*, July 19, 1890, 2.

77. For an example of what image the Pullman porter represented to African Americans as the century turned, see the prototype in action in J. A. Rogers, *From Superman to Man*. During a cross-country journey by rail, a Southern racist "superman" is challenged intellectually by Dixon, a porter, who is more than his match cerebrally, thereby affecting the transformation in the thinking of the former by the time the trip concludes. As for the attitudes some porters assumed internally after their association, albeit as subordinates, with the nation's movers and shakers, see Spero and Harris, *Black Worker*, 431. In contrast, David D. Perata wrote of white arrogance that found women undressing in front of porters as though they were inanimate objects or perhaps completely invisible (*Those Pullman Blues: An Oral History of the African American Railroad Attendant*, xix).

78. For more on Binga, see *BM*, 465; for more on Wright, see Gosnell, *Negro Politicians*, 154.

79. Patricia McKissick and Frederick McKissick, *A Long Hard Journey: The Story of the Pullman Porter*, 30, 31. While written for a youth audience and devoid of documentation, this work is extremely useful in understanding the circumstances under which the Pullman porters emerged as a working unit along with the character of their performance during the late nineteenth century.

80. Frazier, *Negro Family in Chicago*, 125.

81. Wright, "Industrial Condition," 23.

82. Williams, "Autobiography," 92–94.

83. Williams, "The Intellectual Progress of the Colored Women of the United States," in Sewall, *World's Congress*, 706.

84. Meier, "Negro Class Structure," 260; Walker, *Encyclopedia of African American Business History*, xiii.

85. *BM*, 434.

86. Harris, *Colored Men's Directory*, n.p. For more on the continuing saga of African American triumph over adversity, see Robb, *Negro in Chicago*, 2:236.

87. SOS.

88. "Notes of the Times," *Western Appeal*, April 2, 1887, 2.

89. Kletzing and Crogman, *Progress of a Race*, 532.

90. Ibid., 549; Logan, *Betrayal of the Negro*, 233, 234; see also "A Southern Romance: Strange Story of the Parentage and Career of Dr. Charles H. M. McCallister," *Appeal*, April 12, 1890, 1, 2.

91. It was a far from perfect reporting document, however. Some businesses were overlooked; see Dale, "Social Equality," 320 and 320n28. In addition, Harris, as an Odd Fellow, overlooked the Masons and others in his effusive comments on fraternal life. See CVA, 75. Recognition of Harris's *Directory* as a major historical tool used to validate the significance of the African American presence in late-nineteenth-century Chicago is seen in BLP, 3:48, 237.

92. August Meier, *Negro Thought in America, 1880–1915: Racial Ideologies in the Age of Booker T. Washington*, chapter 3, "Economics, Self-Help, and Racial Solidarity."

93. Harris, *Colored Men's Directory*, n.p.

94. *Conservator*, December 16, 1882.

95. Robb, *Negro in Chicago*, 2:236.

96. "Colored Lights in Chicago"; Letters, Martha Freeman Edmond. See also *BM*, 433.

97. Robb, *Negro in Chicago*, 2:227.

98. "Colored Lights in Chicago."

99. *Indianapolis Freeman*, May 20, 1893, 5.

100. SOS.

101. Walker, *History of Black Business*, 178. See also Spear, *Black Chicago*, 65, 111.

102. Declaration for Restoration to the Pension Rolls, April 29, 1893, Federal Pension Record of James H. Brown, Company C, CWPR.

103. Duis, *Challenging Chicago*, 244–52.

104. J. H. Stibbs to William W. Dudley, July 2, 1884, Federal Pension Record of James H. Brown, Company C, CWPR.

105. "Washington's Grim Visitor," *Chicago Daily News*, September 21, 1886, 1.

106. "Chicago," *Appeal*, May 4, 1889, 1.

107. Meier, *Negro Thought*, chapter 9; Davis, "Negro Newspaper," 17; Nell Irvin Painter, *Exodusters: Black Migration to Kansas after Reconstruction*, 49, 50; Davis, "Negro Newspaper," 17.

108. See issue of December 18, 1886.

109. Davis, "Negro Newspaper," 10.

110. Kletzing and Crogman, *Progress of a Race*, 530.

111. "Chicago: Doings of a Week in the Great Western Metropolis," *Western Appeal*, February 11, 1888, 1. Jones's skirmishes with humanity continued, and within three weeks he had a verbal altercation in a courtroom with a policeman, requiring cooler heads to intervene and prevail (ibid., March 3, 1888, 1).

112. Ibid., 112, 113. Parker assisted his father with his patents on the inventions, and in its March 12, 1892, edition, the *Indianapolis Freeman* reported another achievement for the father, the invention of a tobacco press (5).

113. "World's Fair Commissioner."

114. See Stuart Seely Sprague, ed., *John Parker, His Promised Land: The Autobiography of John P. Parker, Former Slave and Conductor on the Underground Railroad*.

115. Work, "Crime," 206–8.

116. *Indianapolis Freeman*, February 13, 1893, 6.

117. "Our Union Club," *Appeal*, July 31, 1892, 1. The brand-new structure was to have been built of Bedford stone and pressed brick and have elevators and electric power; it would tower four stories, housing seven stores at ground level, a ballroom at the second level, the Union Club headquarters on the third floor, and sleeping rooms for nonmember gentlemen on the fourth floor. It would be financed through stock sales and was supposed to be ready for the World's Columbian Exposition, but evidently it was never built.

118. *PN*, 207.

119. Lewis, *Du Bois*, 281, 282; Gwaltney, *Drylongso*, xxiii. Recently, Lewis has stated that the dilemma of duality has been overused, and in fact, misused, beyond Du Bois's original intent. So when Du Bois talked of a warring American-ness battling a Negroness in the black psyche, and manifesting itself in a racial duality, any application of its influence on the rank and file of Afro-Chicago as well as Afro-America becomes conjectural.

120. Wright, "Industrial Condition," 22 (emphasis added).

121. David W. Kellum, "Model Railroad Man Retires after 51 Years . . . ," *Chicago Defender*, December 3, 1932, 9.

122. Data on the first generation of Pullman porters are elusive to unavailable. However, see Rogers, *From Superman to Man*; McKissick and McKissick, *Long Hard Journey*; and Perata, *Those Pullman Blues*, for insight into the continuous, unchanging struggles of these railroad workers for decent pay and dignity.

123. Vincent P. Franklin, *Black Self-Determination: A Cultural History of the Faith of the Fathers*, 149–51; 153–55.

124. Rogers, *From Superman to Man*.

125. See "Laughing at the Man," 300–320, in Levine, *Black Culture*.

126. "Chicago," *Appeal*, February 14, 1891, 1.

127. Read Hanna to Hon. Commissioner of Pensions, May 29, 1913; Deposition of Julia Abrams, May 14, 1913, 9; and Deposition of Eliza Jane Harris, May 24, 1913, 30, all in Federal Pension Record of John Abrams, Company G, CWPR.

128. See "James Johnson," *Appeal*, August 30, 1890, 2; "William G. Anderson," *Appeal*, February 21, 1891, 1; and "Chicago," February 14, 1891, 1.

129. See Chapter 3, n. 64.

130. "West Side Colored People," *Western Appeal*, July 28, 1888, 1.

131. "Order at Olivet," *Western Appeal*, June 30, 1888, 1; "Reed Routed," *Western Appeal*, September 1, 1888, 1.

132. The cakewalk could be promoted as a fun event or condemned as a self-inflicted racial offense. See "Cake Walk," *Appeal*, February 15, 1890, 2, and "Grand Cake Walk," *Appeal*, February 22, 1890, 2, for the former view, and "The Renaissance of the Cake Walk," *Appeal*, March 12, 1892, 2, and "No Cake Walks," *CIO*, March 14, 1892, 1, for the latter. The issue was revisited during the year of the World's Columbian Exposition because the elite feared that Colored American Day, August 28, 1893, might become a colossal embarrassment for African Americans, replete with cake walking and watermelon eating. This is not what transpired; see Reed, *"All the World."*

133. Cunningham, *Paul Lawrence Dunbar*, 93.

134. *Illinois Record*, July 2, 1898, 1.

135. King, "Wounds That Bind," 230–32.

136. "A Pleasing Reception," *Conservator*, December 16, 1882.

137. "Personals," *Conservator*, December 16, 1882, and consecutive issues of the *Indianapolis Freeman* during the summer months of 1893.

138. "Our Horse Reporter Moralizes," *Appeal*, December 26, 1891, 2. The closing of the Garfield Park Track on the West Side allowed the more refined crowd to enjoy themselves in the park without the distraction of witnessing the undesirable conduct of both white and black horse-track enthusiasts. Mrs. Mary Richardson Jones's granddaughter, Miss Theodora Lee, then "gave a select picnic" at the park during the following summer. See "Chicago," *Appeal*, August 27, 1892, 1.

139. Gatewood, who recognized this shift in historical development, thus began his study of the elite, *Aristocrats of Color*, in 1880.

140. Frazier, *Negro Family in Chicago*, 121.

141. Gatewood, *Aristocrats of Color*, x.

142. For more on Jones, see Fenton Johnson, "Chicago Negro Aristocracy," Memorandum of June 18, 1941, 1, Box 9, Folder 14, IW; for the description of her house, see Buckler, *Daniel Hale Williams*, 25. For more on Williams's family, see ibid., 25, 26, 82.

143. Fenton, "Chicago Negro Aristocracy," 2, 3.

144. Wright, *Eighty-seven Years*, 73, 74. Nearer the twenty-first century, this shibboleth of white society was converted into the word "integration." It became the target of black political analyses as the nation involved itself in the racial reconstruction occasioned by the Civil Rights and Black Power movements. See Stokely Carmichael [Kwame Ture] and Charles V. Hamilton, *Black Power: The Politics of Liberation in America*, 37.

145. Williams quoted in Sewall, *World's Congress*, 708; Morris quoted in "Will Not Be Ignored"; and "The Race Problem," *Appeal*, February 15, 1890, 1. In her recent article "Social Equality," legal historian Elizabeth Dale examined the Afro-Saxon position in a court case involving theater discrimination in 1888. In Dale's analysis, separating race from class provided a more valid approach legally than did the course pursued by Morris, which was the traditional in being race-based.

146. "Will Not Be Ignored."

147. Fannie Barrier Williams, "A Northern Negro's Autobiography," 91, 92.

148. "Chicago," *Western Appeal*, May 26, 1888, 1.

149. "Chicago," *Western Appeal*, March 17, 1888, 1.

150. "James H. Johnson," *Appeal*, February 14, 1891, 1.

151. "Beauty Bosoms: The Story of Chicago's Great Charity Ball from the Opening to the Closing Scene," 1. Contemporarily in the twenty-first century, the account of the United Negro College Fund's "Black and White Ball" in the *Chicago Defender*, June 16, 2003, 15, seems to have brought back to life the atmosphere of the original Charity Ball of 1892.

152. Ibid., 2. Every woman of note had her evening attire described, including Mrs. Lloyd G. Wheeler, who wore "black satin moire ribbons [and] diamonds." Rising social arbiter Julius Avendorph, who lacked wealth and social status, was mildly scathed for having on "trousers [that] were creased so stiff he couldn't keep up with the music" (1).

153. See Bishop Daniel Payne's activities in behalf of eliminating emotive church activities throughout the A.M.E. church, in James T. Campbell, *Songs of Zion: The African Methodist Church in the United States and South Africa*, 39–43, 62.

154. Richard Harlan Thomas, "Jenkin Lloyd Jones: Lincoln's Soldier of Civic Righteousness," 6. See also *CT*, September 16, 1887, 2.

155. For Grover Cleveland, see *Western Appeal*, August 31, 1887, 1, and October 22, 1887, 1; for more on the welcoming committee, see "Chicago," *Western Appeal*, April 3, 1888, 1; for more on Bentley, see Reed, *"All the World,"* 102. See also "Dr. C. E. Bentley," *Appeal*, April 2, 1892, 1, which describes Bentley's becoming president of the alumni association of the Chicago College of Dental Surgery.

156. See W. E. B. Du Bois's paean to his fallen comrade in protest advocacy over the first quarter of the twentieth century in his editorial "Postscript," *Crisis* (December 1929): 423; see also the only major biography of Bentley, Clifton O. Dummett, *Charles Edwin Bentley: A Model for All Times*. It was in the early twentieth century that Bentley made his mark in organizational activities as a leader par excellence. See also Reed, *Chicago NAACP*, for a discussion of the depth of feelings about this dichotomy.

157. Wilson Jeremiah Moses, *The Wings of Ethiopia: Studies in Afro-American Life and Letters*, 65.

158. Robert W. Rydell, *All the World's a Fair: Views of Empire at American Expositions, 1876–1916*, 52. Parker refutes this image in "World's Fair Commissioner."

159. *Western Appeal*, April 30, 1887, 1.

160. "World's Fair Commissioner."

161. Hale G. Parker to the editor, "Color at the Fair," *Chicago Inter Ocean*, December 19, 1892, 13.

162. Ibid.

163. Ibid. (emphasis added).

164. See Ray Stannard Baker, *Following the Color Line: American Negro Citizenship in the Progressive Era*, 144, 145. The progressive journalist observed at the dawn of the new century the result of a growing color consciousness among African Americans was a self-imposed color line, much to his disgust.

165. Bontemps and Conroy, *They Seek a City*, 52; "Our New Club," *Appeal*, July 31, 1892, 1. See also "Mutual Improvement," *Indianapolis Freeman*, March 26,1892, 1, which gives a very different figure, the incredibly low amount of $12,000.

166. Gatewood, *Aristocrats of Color*, 119–24; see also Cunningham, *Paul Laurence Dunbar*, 96–97.

167. For more on Thomas, see "Little Trace Remains"; and letters, Marsha Freeman Edmond to Julia Boyd. For more on Bates, see Logan, *Betrayal of the Negro*, 234. If the Bates fortune, as a solitary accumulation, reached $500,000, it more than negates the *Chicago Defender's* claim of growing wealth based on Harris's reckonings in his *Directory*. "These people [in the mid–1880s] represented an aggregate of nearly half a million dollars invested" ("Old Settler Stops Jim Crow," October 8, 1932, 7).

168. Salvatore, *We All Got History*, 294–95.

169. The housing plight of the Clary family is an example of this problem: "In the year 1865 she resided on Jackson St. between Clark St. and Fourth Avenue . . . ; in 1867, she moved to No. 10 Griswold St., between Van Buren and Jackson Streets, next, in 1868, [she] moved to Lake Forest, Cook Co., Illinois; in 1869, [she] moved to No. 82 Sherman st, Chicago, Ill., where she resided for two years or until the burning of Chicago in 1871—then [her housing was] located on State St. near Eldridge Court, where she resided until May 1872, next moved to Dearborn St. between Polk and Taylor. She moved to 353 Third Avenue where she remained about one year. Next resided at [the] corner of State and Harrison, etc." (General Affidavit of Nancy Clary, [no month] 1886, Federal Pension Record of Louis Clary, Company C, CWPR.

170. General Affidavit of James H. Rosell, June 10, 1895, and Physicians' Affidavits of January 28, 1899, and December 31, 1890, Federal Pension Record of Hardin Harris, Company B, CWPR.

171. J. H. Stibbs to Hon. President of Pensions, October 3, 1885, Federal Pension Record of James Jones, Company B, CWPR.

172. Deposition of Delilia Watkins, no date discernible, Federal Pension Record of William Watkins, Company C, CWPR; F. L. Barnett to Hon. Geo. E. Adams, July 22, 1890, Pension Records of Stephan Brown, Company C, CWPR.

173. J. H. Stibbs to Hon. Commissioner of Pensions, February 29, 1892, Federal Pension Record of Louis Clary, Company C, CWPR.

174. Ibid.

175. "Chicago," *Appeal*, January 28, 1888, 1.

176. "Old Soldier Dies in a Shed," undated and unidentified newspaper article in the National Archives.

177. Barbour's story, as follows, is outlined in E. C. Tieman, Deputy Commissioner, Bureau of Pensions, Department of the Interior, to Hon. Martin B. Madden, House of Representatives, December 6, 1914, Federal Pension Record of Richard Barbour, Company B, CWPR.

178. See "The Garden City," *Appeal*, May 24, 1890, 1, and June 21, 1890, 1, for the public announcement of Barbour's ailment and the plea for friends to visit this "old soldier" and member of John Brown Post No. 50, GAR.

179. "Dull Mr. Bright," *Western Appeal*, October 3, 1888, 1.

180. Cunningham, *Paul Laurence Dunbar*, 92, 93.

181. Henry Justin Smith, "Social Chicago Fifty Years Ago," 31.

182. Harold Richard Vynne, *Chicago by Day and Night: The Pleasure Seeker's Guide to the Paris of America*, 153, 157.

183. See "Raiding the 'Levee,'" *CIO*, July 16, 1892, 3; "Great Game of Craps," *CIO*, July 15, 1892, 8; and Work, "Crime," 218–23.

184. "Blackened His Face: A Thief Arrested with a Hotel's Towels in His Possession," *Chicago Daily News*, November 27, 1886, 1.

185. Elizabeth Dale, *The Rule of Justice: The People of Chicago versus Zephyr Davis*.

186. *PN*, 312, 313; Davis, "Negro Newspaper," 18, 19.

187. "Chicago's Noted Negroes."

188. Ibid.

189. Ibid.

190. Vynne, *Chicago by Day and Night*, 155, 156.

191. Dennis B. Downey, "Rite of Passage: The World's Columbian Exposition and American Life," 182.

192. Stephen Longstreet, *Chicago, 1860–1919*, 94, 344.

193. William T. Stead, *If Christ Came to Chicago*, 247; *PN*, 313.

194. Stead, *If Christ Came*, 247, 251.

195. Ibid., 248, 250.

196. Work, "Crime," 204–6; 212f.

197. In her imaginative legal history "Social Equality," Elizabeth Dale examines the multifaceted world of race, class, and the culture of the law with emphases on its complexities, unpredictabilities, and interrelationships. Everyday life—that is, occurrences in the real world amid as many nonlegal influences as legal—affected the law as surely as its theoretical and formal structure did. This legal approach is important in its own right, but it also gives validity to the historical approach that recognized heterogeneity as it existed.

198. Frederick Douglass, *Proceedings of the Civil Rights Mass-Meeting*, held at Lincoln Hall [Washington], October 22, 1883, in John H. Bracey Jr., August Meier, and Elliott Rudwick, eds., *The Afro-Americans: Selected Documents*, 343, 344; Eric Arnesen, "The Pullman Strike and the Long Shadow of Race," *John Marshall Law Review* 33, no. 583 (2002): 612, a part of the Second Arthur J. Goldberg Conference on Labor Law Lecture, "The Pullman Strike: Yesterday, Today and Tomorrow."

199. See Henry O. Wagoner (Denver) to Hon. S. H. Kerfoot (Chicago), September 27, 1884, Henry V. [O.] Wagoner Manuscript Collection, CHS; for Morris, see SOS; for Barnett, see Davis, "Negro Newspaper," 13, 14.

200. Interview with an anonymous Old Settler in *BM*, 67.

201. For an extensive and intense look into mid–1880s black life, see "Colored Lights in Chicago."

202. Read Hanna to Hon. Commissioner of Pensions, August 23, 1917, Federal Pension Record of Henry Garrett, Company B, CWPR.

203. *Woman's Columbian Auxiliary Association—AIM and PLAN of ACTION*, Chicago, February 1891, 2, Albion W. Tourgee Papers, Chautauqua County Historical Society, Westfield, New York (hereafter AWT).

204. Claudius O. Johnson, *Carter Henry Harrison I: Political Leader*, 196. According to Davis, "Negro Newspaper," 14, the Republican *Conservator* considered Harrison to be fair and supported him.

205. Compare this nineteenth-century relationship across racial lines to the challenge issued to black America by two theorists/activists in 1967 in Carmichael and Hamilton, *Black Power*, 37, 46–49.

206. George E. Taylor to My Dear Sir, July 17, 1892, Box 21, Item 6412, AWT.

207. See "Judge Tourgee," *Appeal*, April 2, 1892, 1; Duster, *Crusade for Justice*, 120–22; and Otto H. Olsen, *Carpetbagger's Crusade: The Life of Albion Winegar Tourgee*, 276f.

208. Tourgee to Barnett, September 16, 1891, Box 20, Item 5752, AWT (emphasis in original).

209. Ferdinand L. Barnett to Hon. Albion W. Tourgee, September 12, 1891, Box 20, Item 5748, AWT. Ida B. Wells would later write in a similar vein to Mrs. Tourgee on another matter that seemingly required an apology on behalf of all African Americans; see Wells to Mrs. Tourgee, May 19, 1895 and August 26, 1895, Wells Papers.

210. Tourgee to F[erdinand] L. Barnett, August 6, 1900, Box 29, Item 9665, 1, AWT. Although this letter was composed at the cusp of the new century, it was basically a reiteration of his position of the previous three decades.

211. S. Laing Williams to Albion W. Tourgee, Esq., October 31, 1891, Box 20, Item 5775, AWT.

212. Ida B. Wells to Judge A. W. Tourgee, February 22, 1893, Box 22, Item 6645, AWT. See also Ida B. Wells to Judge A. W. Tourgee, May 15, 1897, Box 29, Item 9406, AWT, for Wells's presumptuous extension of group congratulations on Tourgee's diplomatic appointment in France.

213. F. L. Barnett to Judge Tourgee, February 23, 1893, Box 22, Item 6646, AWT.

214. F. L. Barnett to Judge Albion Tourgee, May 24, 1897, Box 10, Folder 7, Wells Papers.

215. Fannie Barrier Williams to Hon. Albion Tourgee, March 12, 1893, Box 22, Item 6735, AWT.

216. Hale G. Parker to Judge Albion W. Tourgee, June 23, 1895, Box 25, Item 8562, AWT.

217. Hale G. Parker to My Dear Sir, July 4, 1895, Box 25, Item 8593, AWT.

218. Hale G. Parker to Judge Albion Tourgee, June 23, 1895, Box 25, Item 8562, AWT.

219. Lloyd G. Wheeler to Dear Judge [Tourgee], March 4 [1893], Box 22, Item 6711, AWT.

220. J. H. Jenkins to Mr. A. W. Tourgee, June 3, 1893, Box 20, Item 5916, AWT.

221. Moore, *History of Bethel*, 32, 37–39.

222. "Motives of Miscegenation: Why White Women Marry Negroes—A Rational Explanation." Mary Church Terrell of Washington, D.C., responded in this matter in her autobiography, *A Colored Woman in a White World* (Washington, 1940), 93. A rather disparaging story about interracial marriage appeared in the *Appeal*, July 16, 1892, 1, under the heading of news about "Chicago."

223. BM, 74; Quarles, *Frederick Douglass*, 300. See also a supportive account of the marriage in *Western Appeal*, June 13, 1885, 1.

224. See Ransom, *Pilgrimage*, 91f; and Williamson, *New People: Mulattoes and Miscegenation in the United States*, 100–103.

225. Nahum Daniel Brascher, "Pioneer Chicagoan in Hall of Fame: Col. Wm. R. Cowan, Business, Political, Civic Leader, Passes Away after Short Illness," CD, June 3, 1933, 17.

226. *Chicago Broad Ax*, December, 1904; Williams, "A Northern Negro's Autobiography," 94.

227. Some of Williams's relatives evinced resentment over his physiognomy and seemingly white identification. See Buckler, *Daniel Hale Williams*, xi, xii; and *Illinois Record*, July 1898, 3. During the Spanish American War (1898), enlisted men serving under Marshall in Cuba accused the captain of being a "white man with a black head and heart" and "too near white"; see Willard B. Gatewood Jr., *"Smoked Yankees" and the Struggle for Empire: Letters from Negro Soldiers, 1898–1902*, 204, 213.

228. Spear, *Black Chicago*, 71.

229. For Ida B. Wells-Barnett's full account, see Duster, *Crusade for Justice*, 47–52, 64, 182

230. "Not a Land of Liberty," *Appeal*, April 2, 1892, 4.

231. "Judge Tourgee," *Appeal*, April 2, 1892, 1.

232. BLP, 2:470.

233. Bruce Chadwick, *When the Game Was Black and White: The Illustrated History of Baseball's Negro Leagues*, 22, 23. Ironically, at the time Anson promoted the exclusion of black players from organized competition, white players sought freedom from what they considered "chattel slavery" in their contracts and relationship with the club owners (Federated Writers' Project [Illinois], *Baseball in Old Chicago* [Chicago: A. C. McClurg, 1939], 49, 50).

234. Larry Lester, Sammy J. Miller, and Dick Clark, *Black Baseball in Chicago*, 32.

235. Mark Ribowsky, *A Complete History of the Negro Leagues, 1884–1955*, 42.

236. *Western Appeal*, September 17, 1887, 1, and September 24, 1887, 1.

237. Chadwick, *When the Game*, 31. Major discrepancies exist in the early history of black baseball in Chicago; see Ribowsky, *Complete History of the Negro Leagues*, 41–46.

238. Lester, Miller, and Clark, *Black Baseball*, 12, 14, 20–22. See also Ribowsky, *Complete History of the Negro Leagues*, 48.

239. See Appendix D.

240. Souvenir program, "Centennial Anniversary of the Admission of the First Black Lawyer to the Illinois Bar, April 20, 1969," 4 (in author's possession).

241. "Couple Still Caught in Matrix," CD, June 14, 2003, 35. The issues of race (through racial profiling), class and legal manipulation intersected in the case of an African American couple being arrested at a downtown theater after an unsupported charge of ticket theft was leveled by a white patron who subsequently vanished. One

civil rights advocate was quoted: "It's the season of disrespect to African Americans. It really matters less the class someone is in. They [whites] care less about whether you are an executive working for a major corporation or someone who sweeps streets. Both classes have to stand together. It is getting so you can't go downtown."

242. Dale, "Social Equality," 336, 337.

243. Ibid., 319–20, 321–23. For another view of the separation along class lines within the black community, see *Western Appeal*, February 4, 1888, 1; there was some skepticism that discrimination by class might lead inevitably to segregation by race.

244. Dale, "Social Equality," 330–35.

245. See Kevin Gaines, "Rethinking Race and Class," 383, who, in his critique of Dale's analysis, calls for a comprehensive view of history with an emphasis on "socio-historical change as the background for such cases and for the origins of segregation." By necessity, a comprehensive view would take heavily into account social history to evaluate the situation.

246. In St. Paul and Minneapolis, for example, African Americans celebrated the presidential issuance of the Emancipation Proclamation in September 1862. See *Western Appeal*, September 10, 1887, 1, 4; September 17, 1887, 1, 4; and September 24, 1887, 1.

247. "In Commemoration: Colored Americans Establish a Day of Thanksgiving."

248. Ibid.

249. Penn, *Afro-American Press*, 524.

250. John Hope Franklin and Alfred A. Moss Jr., *From Slavery to Freedom: A History of African Americans*, 7th ed., 2:258.

251. Emma Lou Thornbrough, *T. Thomas Fortune: Militant Journalist*, ix, x.

252. Within three years, Morris would be active with the Colored Men's National Protective Association, and in 1915 he was listed among the potential candidates for the presidency of the Chicago branch of the nationally organized Independence Equal Rights League, headed by W. M. Trotter. See Reed, *"All the World,"* 127, and *CD*, January 9, 1915, 1.

253. Thornbrough, *T. Thomas Fortune: Militant Journalist*, 113, 116.

254. Ibid., 110, 111. See also Emma Lou Thornbrough, "T. Thomas Fortune: Militant Editor in the Age of Accommodation," 28.

255. Penn, *Afro-American Press*, 528, 529.

256. Ibid., 537.

257. Thornbrough, *T. Thomas Fortune: Militant Journalist*, 116, 117. See also S. Laing Williams to Albion W. Tourgee, Esq., October 31, 1891, Box 20, Item 5775, AWT.

258. "A National Appeal," National Colored Men's Protective Association of America, July 14, 1892, 4, Item 6407, AWT.

259. F. L. Barnett to Mrs. Potter Palmer, December 20, 1891, Box 10, folder 7, Wells Papers.

260. *Woman's Columbian Auxiliary Association—AIM and PLAN of ACTION*, Chicago, February 1891, 2, AWT; Massa, "Black Women," 319. For a full exploration of the role of women in organizing during the early stages of the fair, see Massa, "Black Women," 319–37.

261. *PN*, 234.

262. Original Providence Baptist Church, *Centennial Anniversary Souvenir Year Book, 1863–1963*, 12, 13.

263. CVA, 68.

264. A History of Greater Bethesda Missionary Baptist Church, Chicago, Illinois, 1882–1982, n.p.

265. "Olivet Choir," Western Appeal, June 16, 1888, 1, "Order at Olivet, June 30, 1888, 1, "Yaller Niggers," July 21, 1888, 1.

266. "Trubble in de Church," Appeal, May 14, 1892, 1.

267. "Editorial," Western Appeal, August 4, 1888, 2; "Defied the Bishop," August 25, 1888, 1; "Reed Routed," September 1, 1888, 1.

268. CT, September 16, 1887, 2.

269. Koby Lee-Forman, "The Simple Love of Truth: The Racial Justice Activism of Celia Parker Woolley," 268–69.

270. History of Greater Bethesda Missionary Baptist Church, n.p.

271. Chicago Sun-Times, June 3, 2003, 16, and CD, June 7, 2003, 3; "Colored Lights in Chicago."

272. Clark, "When Chicago Was Young: The Elegant Eighties."

273. "History" of Saint Stephen African Methodist Episcopal Church [first unnumbered page].

274. Moore, History of Bethel, 40, 41.

275. CVA, 108.

276. Ibid., 74.

277. See "Chicago," Western Appeal, July 28, 1888, 1; and "Rev. M. H. Jackson, Founder of Grace Church, Dies," CD, January 7, 1933, 1, 4.

278. African American church information is contained in CVA, 104–6; Wright, "Industrial Condition," 12, 13; and Robb, Negro in Chicago, 1:114.

279. "City News," Conservator, December 16, 1882, 2.

280. Conservator, December 18, 1886, 2.

281. See the Atkinson Papers for detailed information on one family's burial records, Chicago Public Library, Woodson Regional Center, Harsh Collection.

282. Conservator, December 16, 1882, 2.

283. Conservator, December 18, 1886, 2; "Chicago, Ill.," Western Appeal, March 26, 1887, 1, and March 19, 1887, 1.

284. "Twenty One Hundred," Western Appeal, February 23, 1889, 1.

285. Ibid., 448.

286. Hale G. Parker to Judge Albion W. Tourgee, June 23, 1895, Item 8562, Hale G. Parker to My Dear Sir, July 4, 1895, Item 8593, and H[ale] G. Parker to Judge A. W. Tourgee, July 15, 1895, Item 8638, all in Box 25, AWT.

287. Hale G. Parker to My Dear Sir, July 4, 1895, Box 25, Item 8593, AWT; see also Mitchell's intention to inform positively on African American thought and behavior in "Motives of Miscegenation"; "Colored Lights in Chicago"; and "Chicago's Noted Negroes."

288. Emilio, History of the Fifty-fourth, 322.

289. General Affidavit of William Collins, January 27, 1891, and Deposition of Nancy Clary, February 1, 1892, Federal Pension Record of Louis Clary, Company B, CWPR.

290. See McConnell, Glorious Contentment, 30, 31; and "Garden City," Western Appeal, August 10, 1889, 1. A special appeal for a reunion of members of the Twenty-ninth

Illinois went out in the summer of 1890, but the results are unknown; see *Western Appeal*, June 18, 1890, 2.

291. See King, "Wounds That Bind," 89–90.

292. "In Chicago," *Western Appeal*, September 1, 1888, 1, and November 28, 1891, 1. See also King, "Wounds That Bind," 167.

293. "Grand Army of the Republic," *Conservator*, December 18, 1886, 2.

294. SOS.

295. Goode, *"Eighth Regiment,"* 13. See also "Chicago," *Appeal*, June 14, 1890, 2, and July 19, 1890, 1.

296. "No 'Colored' Y.M.C.A. Wanted," *Appeal*, November 30, 1889, 2.

297. Buckler, *Daniel Hale Williams*, 71, 72

298. Richard M. Krieg and Judith A. Cooksey, *Provident Hospital: A Living Legacy*, 3; Kletzing and Crogman, *Progress of a Race*, 441.

299. Kletzing and Crogman, *Progress of a Race*, 440, 441.

300. "Chicago," *Appeal*, July 11, 1891, 1.

301. Whether it was Jones's influence or not that led Armour to totally identify with Provident Hospital's mission is conjectural. At the time of Armour's death in early 1901, Fannie Barrier Williams memorialized Armour and wrote that he made regular Sunday visits to the hospital on days when he was in good health and in Chicago. See "In Memory of Philip D. Armour," in Deegan, *New Woman of Color*, 136.

302. Buckler, *Daniel Hale Williams*, 69–73.

303. "The Windy City: Doings of a Week in the Great Western Metropolis," *Western Appeal*, January 7, 1888, 1, and Gatewood, *Aristocrats of Color*, 228. The members in attendance at a meeting of January 4, 1888, held at the home of Mrs. Mary Richardson Jones of Ray Avenue, were as follows: Mr. and Mrs. S. Laing Williams, Mr. and Mrs. F[erdinand] L. Barnett, Mr. and Mrs. L[loyd] G. Wheeler, Mr. and Mrs. J[ohn] S. Madden, Mr. and Mrs. R[obert] M. Hancock, Mr. and Mrs. Eugene Hale, Dr. and Mrs. C[harles] E. Bentley, Mr. and Mrs. Fenton Harsh, Mr. and Mrs. W[illiam] H. Hurd, Mr. and Mrs. A. A. Thompson, Mr. and Mrs. Tho[ma]s Gray, Mr. and Mrs. Geo[rge] Beard, a Mr. and Mrs. Conrad, Mr. and Mrs. Geo[rge] Ecton, Mr. and Mrs. A. K. Hall, a Mr. and Mrs. Shreves, Mr. and Mrs. J. W. Beasley, Mr. and Mrs. C. Ray, a Mr. and Mrs. Dempsey, Mr. and Mrs. G. A. King, Mr. and Mrs. J[ohn] B. French, Mrs. McCary, Mrs. G. H. Hamilton, Mrs. Willis Montgomery, a Mrs. Johnson, a Mrs. Cooper, Mrs. Lavinia Lee, a Mrs. White, Miss Dora Johnson, Miss Fannie Lewis, Messrs. G. Whispetal, E. J. Jackson, a Mr. Green of Springfield, a Mr. Coleman, and the reporter and managing editor of the *Appeal* in Chicago, C. F. Adams. Perhaps eighteen of the participants held true elite standing based on occupational, educational, residential, and income status.

304. Reed, *Chicago NAACP*. The black members of the Chicago branch of the NAACP would include Dr. Charles E. Bentley, attorney S. Laing Williams, and Garnetta Gibbs.

305. See Albion W. Tourgee to Dear Sir [Hale G. Parker], probably January 1896, Box 29, Item 9190, for Reconstruction politics and education, and James E. Bish to Mr. Albion W. Tourgee, January 11, 1891, Box 19, Item 5223, for voting rights in antebellum America, both in AWT.

306. Davis, "Negro Newspaper," 16.

307. Fishel, "Negro in Northern Politics," 466. This mold was also broken elsewhere.

See the political travails of black independent Democrat James Trotter of Boston, the father of William Monroe Trotter, in Stephen R. Fox, *The Guardian of Boston: William Monroe Trotter*, 11–13. For Philadelphia, which conforms to the pattern of total allegiance to the Republican party, see *PN*, 372–84.

308. King, "Wounds That Bind," 150, 151, 160.

309. "To the Colored Voters [of] Illinois: Richard J. Oglesby For Governor," November 1, 1884, Governor's Correspondence, Richard J. Oglesby, January 1–15, 1885, Illinois State Archives. See also Johnson, *Carter Henry Harrison*, 196.

310. Smith, "Social Chicago," 30.

311. "William G. Anderson," *Appeal*, February 21, 1891, 1; SOS.

312. Goode, *"Eighth Regiment,"* 19, 20, 69, 73, 97, quotation on 98.

313. Buckler, *Daniel Hale Williams*, 62. Based on a reference to John Jones's name, Buckler surmises that Williams was helped by a connection to him, but Jones had died before the former arrived in Chicago to complete his medical training.

314. A. N. Fields, "Historic Glimpses of Old Chicago," *CD*, October 22, 1932, 7; A. N. Fields, "Noted Lawmakers of Early Chicago," *CD*, February 4, 1933, 11.

315. Goode, *"Eighth Regiment,"* 20. For an indicator of Bish's political manipulations, see "Chicago," *Appeal*, March 22, 1890, 1; on Bish's victory as a Republican during an otherwise Democratic landslide in the city, see "Happy Mr. Bish," *Appeal*, November 12, 1892, 1.

316. "Chicago Colored Society: Those Who Blazed the Way," *Illinois Record*, June 18, 1898, 1, 2; see also the short sketches of the seven state legislators of the nineteenth century in Branham, "Black Chicago," 348–54.

317. James M. McPherson, *The Abolitionist Legacy: From Reconstruction to the NAACP*.

Chapter 5. Fair and War, 1893–1900

1. See Reed, *"All the World,"* for a new interpretation of the extent to which African Americans participated in the World's Columbian Exposition. The pervasive myth of the nearly total exclusion of African Americans from the fair has persisted since the publication of the Columbian era's famed literary piece, written by Wells, Douglass, Penn, and Barnett, *The Reason Why the Colored American Is Not in the World's Columbian Exposition*, in the spring of 1893, immediately before the gates of the fair opened on May 1. The timing of the publication explains why the pamphlet did not discuss the fair. Thus, what has informed readers for over a century is a four-part exploration: a discussion of African American achievement nationally since Emancipation by Virginian Irvine Garland Penn, an essay on the horrors of Southern lynchings by New Yorker Ida B. Wells, Washingtonian Frederick Douglass's entreaty to America's conscience to owe up to its debt to African Americans because of their enslavement for two hundred years, and Chicagoan Ferdinand L. Barnett's explanation and proof as to why the pamphlet bears the title it does. Valuable as a piece of period literature, *The Reason Why* nevertheless represents inadequate and incorrect history when it deals with activities and relationships forged at the fair.

2. CVA, 106. The fair as a magnet for work is mentioned by Richard R. Wright Jr. in his research that followed the fair by less than a decade. See Wright, "Industrial

Condition," 11.

3. Work, "Crime," 305, 306; Wright, "Industrial Condition," 5, 11; Work, "Negro Real Estate Holders," 25; Frazier, *Negro Family in Chicago,* 71. For a description of the violence and rioting in New Orleans, see Litwack, *Trouble in Mind,* 404–10.

4. Spear, *Black Chicago,* 14, 15. According to Spear, "the Negro population of the city was still relatively well distributed in 1900. Nineteen of the city's thirty-five wards had a Negro population of at least .5 per cent of the total population of the ward and fourteen wards were at least 1 per cent Negro. Only two wards had a Negro population of more than 10 per cent. In 1898, just over a quarter of Chicago Negroes lived in precincts that were more than 50 per cent Negro, and over 30 per cent lived in precincts that were at least 95 per cent white."

5. See Gilbert Osofsky, *Harlem: The Making of a Ghetto; Negro New York, 1890–1930;* Katzman, *Before the Ghetto;* Kusmer, *Ghetto Takes Shape;* Joe W. Trotter, Jr., *Black Milwaukee: The Making of an Industrial Proletariat, 1915–1945;* and Lillian Serece Williams, *The Development of a Black Community: Buffalo, New York, 1910–1940.*

6. Work, "Negro Real Estate Holders," 28.

7. Interview with Elizabeth Hudson Tatum by Archie Brown, November 21, 1984, conducted as part of the Bethel New Life neighborhood project, "Looking Backward to Move Forward," Special Collections and Manuscripts, Harold Washington Center, Chicago Public Library.

8. The following information was provided by John W. Lewis Jr., M.D, interview with author, Chicago, November 3, 1985.

9. Both the Frenches and the Hancocks held memberships in the exclusive Prudence Crandall Study Club, a requisite for confirmed elite status in black Chicago. See "The Windy City: Doings of a Week in the Great Western Metropolis," *Western Appeal,* January 7, 1888, 1. Mr. and Mrs. John B. French entertained the elite in their spacious home on Walnut Street. When former Louisiana governor and putative U.S. Senator B. S. Pinchback visited the city in 1889, the Frenches hosted a major dinner in his behalf on the West Side. Attendees included Dr. and Mrs. Daniel Hale Williams and other prominent black Chicagoans. See "A Swell Event: Grand Reception Given by Mr. and Mrs. John H. French," *Appeal,* July 20, 1889, 1. Mr. and Mrs. Robert Hancock played a similar role to the Frenches in civic and social affairs. When fund-raising for Provident Hospital was under way, Robert Hancock, who was always resplendently attired on major occasions in his "plug hat, a Prince Albert coat, and shiny speckless boots," was called upon to take a leading role. See Buckler, *Daniel Hale Williams,* 70. To facilitate the flow of future members of the elite, the Garden City Literary Club was formed, and St. Stephen A.M.E. continued to expand its middle-class developmental activities.

10. Lovelynn Miller Evans, interviews with author, Chicago, May 5, 1977, and January 25, 1978; "Obituary," *CT,* October 14, 1989; and Funeral Program, October 16, 1989, Chicago.

11. Interview with Charles Liggett, May 17, 1937, "Interviews with Old Settlers," Box 10, Folder 39, IWP.

12. Interview with Gertrude Davis, January 18, 1937, "Interviews with Old Settlers," Box 10, Folder 39, IWP.

13. Interview with Martha Dawson, March 4, 1937, "Interviews with Old Settlers," Box 10, Folder 39, IWP.

14. Work, "Negro Real Estate Holders," 28.

15. Chicago Planning Commission, *Residential Chicago*, Vol. 1, *Chicago Land Use Survey*, 16, 61.

16. "Society Items," *Broad Ax*, September 23, 1899, 1. See for example, "Charming, Gay, Chicago," *Indianapolis Freeman*, July 22, 1893, 1.

17. "Chicago Negro Aristocrats," 4, 5.

18. Leota Johnson interview.

19. Ransom, *Pilgrimage*, 81.

20. Wright, "Industrial Condition," 8.

21. A random sampling of addresses contained in correspondence from the pension files of members of the Twenty-ninth Illinois indicates constant movement.

22. Buckler, *Daniel Hale Williams*, 26.

23. Dominic A. Pacyga and Ellen Skerrett, *Chicago: City of Neighborhoods*, 464–68; see also Upton Sinclair's classic *The Jungle*, which depicts life in Packingtown for the city's immigrant population.

24. "Society Items," *Broad Ax*, July 15, 1899, 1.

25. Ibid.

26. Williams, "Social Bonds," 44. See also "Perched in a Patrol," *Western Appeal*, July 28, 1888, 1. The area was referred to in this article as "South [a.k.a. Darkest] Africa."

27. Work, "Crime," 207.

28. J. H. Stibbs to Commissioner, August 17, 1889, Federal Pension Record of Hardin Harris, Company B, CWPR.

29. Work, "Crime," 208.

30. In 1892, *Scribner's Magazine* had described working-class black Chicago in terms that resonated clearly: "The colored people have done and are doing remarkably well, considering the disadvantages and discouragements under which they live," it read. "They are industrious rather than hard working," i.e., they perform energetically and devotedly, rather than robotically (like the immigrants), "and economical rather than acquisitive," avoiding extravagance rather than seeking wealth greedily. See also Kirkland, "Among the Poor," 5n. For details on the period previous to the fair, see Harris, *Colored Men's Directory*; for information covering the end of the decade, see Work, "Negro Real Estate Holders."

31. Richardson, *Death of Reconstruction*, 183–97. See also a contemporary response to this charge by Booker T. Washington in "Color Line in Labor," *Sunday Chicago Herald*, September 3, 1893, 11.

32. Wright, "Negro in Chicago," 61.

33. Wells, preface to Wells et al., *Reason Why*.

34. Ferdinand L. Barnett, "The Reason Why," in Wells et al., *Reason Why*, 80.

35. Cunningham, *Paul Laurence Dunbar*, 93.

36. James Weldon Johnson, "Atlanta University Boys at the World's Fair."

37. *Chicago Legal News*, May 29, 1897, 333.

38. Barnett, "Reason Why," 75–79.

39. Theresa Dean, *White City Chips*, 106, 204. Countering these impressionistic jibes is the *Official Report on the Columbian Guard*, housed at CHS.

40. Cunningham, *Paul Laurence Dunbar*, 94, 95.

41. J. A. Mitchell, "Types and People at the Fair," 191.

42. Ibid.

43. See the biographical sketch along with the correspondence between Fritsch to Pullman, summer 1893, in the George M. Pullman Papers at CHS.

44. *Presto*, July 13, 1893, 13; *The Bulletin of Atlanta University*, July 13, 1893, 13.

45. The African drumming performances did not escape the attention of musicologist Henry Edward Krebhiel, who spent days at a time listening, recording on notepads, and analyzing the richness of what he was hearing. He shared his experience in print through *Afro-American Folksongs*.

46. Will Marion Cook, "City Gives 'Jazz' to Musical World," *Chicago Defender*, October 29, 1932, 7; see also Monroe Nathan Work, "The Origin of 'Ragtime Music,'" 343; and Edward A. Berlin, *King of Ragtime: Scott Joplin and His Era*, 11, 12. Berlin also pinpointed ragtime's emergence from the World's Columbian Exposition: "The fair was also a signal event in ragtime history, for, according to numerous accounts during the next two decades, it was here that ragtime surfaced from its incipient stages in black communities and became known to the wider American public" (ibid.).

47. Bontemps and Conroy, *They Seek a City*, 140. See also Eric Arnesen, "The Pullman Strike and the Long Shadow of Race," 612–14.

48. Rick Halpern and Roger Horowitz, *Meatpackers: An Oral History of Black Packinghouse Workers and Their Struggle for Racial and Economic Equality*, 4, 5.

49. Tuttle, *Race Riot*, 112–13.

50. BM, 302, 303.

51. "In Memory of Philip D. Armour," in Deegan, *New Woman of Color*, 135. See also Tuttle, *Race Riot*, 153.

52. Wright, "Industrial Condition," 29.

53. Williams, "Social Bonds," 43. See also Work, "Crime," 206.

54. Franklin and Moss, *From Slavery to Freedom*, 7th ed., 2:283; BM, 420.

55. Wright, "Industrial Condition," 14.

56. Lovelynn Miller Evans, interview with author, Chicago, on May 5, 1977; *Indianapolis Freeman*, April 29, 1893, 3; Roi Ottley, *The Lonely Warrior: The Life and Times of Robert S. Abbott*, 76, 77.

57. Wright, "Industrial Condition," 13.

58. Herrick, *Chicago Schools*, 74, 81, 82.

59. *Indianapolis Freeman*, September 9, 1893, 1.

60. Meier, "Negro Class Structure," 259.

61. Williams, "Social Bonds," 43. The culmination of this retrogressive movement, with its implications for Chicago and its sad import for the future of black labor, is discussed in Greene and Woodson, *Negro Wage Earner*, 91–96.

62. Wright, "Industrial Condition," 24.

63. Emmett J. Scott, *Negro Migration during the War* (New York: Oxford University Press, 1920), 65, 102.

64. Reed, "All the World," chapter 1.

65. "The World's Fair and Bible Institute," *Southern Workman and Hampton School Record*, September 1893, 145; James Weldon Johnson, "Atlanta University Boys at the Exposition"; Ottley, *Lonely Warrior*, 74.

66. See Krebhiel, *Afro-American Folksongs*, 60, 64, 64; Reed, "All the World," 146–49, and James Alston, "A Visit to the World's Fair," *A.M.E. Review* (July 1894), 496.

67. S. Laing Williams to My Dear Mr. Washington, May 3, 1901, Special Correspondence, S. Laing Williams, *BTW.*

68. *Chicago Inter Ocean*, June 27, 1893, 1.

69. Ibid.

70. Deegan, *New Woman of Color*, xvi; Mrs. N. F. [Gertrude] Mossell, *The Work of the Afro-American Woman*, 110–11.

71. Mossell, *Work of the Afro-American Woman*, 110–11.

72. Deegan, *New Woman of Color*, xxxivf.

73. Sewall, *World's Congress*, 704.

74. Ibid., 710.

75. Ibid., 696.

76. Ibid., 703. See also Editorial, *Appeal*, April 9, 1892, 2, in which the goal of preserving the chastity of young white Southern women was supposedly accomplished by making available within the Southern household attractive, young, vulnerable African American females.

77. Sewall, *World's Congress*, 697.

78. Ibid., 708; see also Brotz, introduction to *Negro Social and Political Thought*, 18. Charlotte Elizabeth Martin, *The Story of Brockport for One-Hundred Years, 1829–1929*, 86, 87.

79. Sewall, *World's Congress*, 717, 718.

80. Criticism of Williams's lecture and presence is found in Massa, "Black Women," 334, and McFeely, *Douglass*, 367. If Wells had criticized Williams for contacting Tourgee, this is inconsistent with the relationship Wells and Tourgee enjoyed. Tourgee held the same esteem as a white among many blacks in the 1890s that Garrison and Brown did in the antebellum period. In fact, a Tourgee Club existed along the Dearborn Street Corridor in the 2900 block. See *Crusade for Justice*, 120–22.

81. Deegan, *New Woman of Color*, xxxiv.

82. See Carby, *Reconstructing Womanhood*, 107, who mentions that Wells did not appear at the Women's Congress but mentions her activities at the Haytian Pavilion in behalf of marketing *The Reason Why*, implying that this was the totality of Wells's fair experiences, which paled with the Carby's examination of Anna Julia Cooper's feminist contributions. Wells was on her way from England when the fair opened.

83. Ashbaugh, *Lucy Parsons*, 189–92. See also "Anarchy and Reason," *Chicago Journal*, August 21, 1893.

84. Washington's reliance on personal will power to succeed seemed appropriate for these times. Marcus Garvey arrived in America seeking Washington's counsel partially because of this Washington attribute. Needless to say, Garvey's famous challenge to oppressed African Americans and continentals, "Up You Mighty Race, You Can Accomplish What You Will!" was aimed at the same group to which Washington appealed.

85. See "Color Line in Labor," *Sunday Chicago Herald*, September 3, 1893, 11.

86. J. A. Majors, "What the Negro Contributed to the World's Fair of 1893," 52.

87. *Chicago Tribune*, September 9, 1893, 9.

88. John Henry Barrows, ed., *The World's Parliament of Religions*, 1114, 1115.

89. Frederick Perry Noble, "The Chicago Congress on Africa," 311.

90. *Chicago Inter Ocean*, August 16, 1893, 8, and *Chicago Times*, August 16, 1893, 4. In his assertions about a black origin of humanity, Turner was not saying anything too

much different from those things educated, informed white writers were. See the comments of Congress secretary Noble in "Negro Problem," *Frank Leslie's Illustrated Weekly*, September 28, 1893, 206. But most importantly, what he stated had been enunciated by Edward W. Blyden decades previously in a well-read white Methodist publication (see Blyden, "The Negro in Ancient History"). Blyden had visited Chicago several years before the world's fair and had gained a reputation for his intellectual prowess and linguistic skills. Moreover, for the popular mind, the *Appeal* had featured a story on March 1, 1890, in Chicago that was titled and subtitled, "The Negroes of Old: Were Rameses the Great and His Contemporaries of Egypt Negroes?—Dark Skinned Civilization," 1, 2.

91. *CIO*, August 16, 1893, 8.

92. *Chicago Times*, August 16, 1893, 4.

93. *Chicago Herald*, August 16, 1893, 9, 5.

94. Unfortunately, there are no extant copies of either newspaper for the world's fair year 1893. However, the March 1, 1890, edition of the *Appeal* had covered the story of blacks in antiquity in "Negroes of Old."

95. Ida B. Wells had just written a defense of free debate on this issue of emigration to Africa because of the relevance and poignancy of the issue—she had not denounced the idea. See Wells, "Afro-Americans and Africa," *A.M.E. Review*, July 1892, 40–45, reprinted in Hine, *Black Women in America*, 165–69. See also the *Indianapolis Freeman*, June 17, 1893, 9. For her criticism, see *Cleveland Gazette*, September 2, 1893, 2.

96. *CIO*, August 19, 1893, 9.

97. Ibid. Since adulthood, Barnett had evaluated the merits of emigrating to Africa and had found them lacking. To him, America was the African Americans' home. See, for example, a clipping ("A Poor Beginning") he saved in support of his beliefs from 1878 concerning the voyage to Africa of the SS *Azor*, Scrapbook of Ferdinand L. Barnett, Box 10, Folder 8, Wells Papers.

98. What the congress also made obvious was the quality and volume of intellectual inquiries being generated on African American and continental African life. Bishop Henry McNeal Turner became so enthusiastic about what he heard in Chicago that he offered to buy a collection of the papers presented. Frederick Perry Noble exuberantly talked of an *Encyclopaedia Britannica on Africa*. Further, within two years of the congress, Crummell's American Negro Academy was organized. Where emigration to Africa slacked off, migration to the North picked up, proving itself incessant. Emigrationist organizations proliferated in the South and on March 19, 1895, the small, 728-ton steamer SS *Horsa* departed Savannah with two hundred African Americans on board. The trip no doubt provided part of the inspiration for Booker T. Washington's "Cast Your Buckets" admonition to southern blacks later that year.

99. *CIO*, August 22, 1893, 6.

100. "No Cake Walks," *CIO*, March 14, 1892, 1. Jenifer described the cakewalk and his opposition to it: "In former times, for the sake of raising money for charitable purposes the prize of a cake was offered for the most graceful walker. Sometimes the cake contained a ring to enhance the interest in the affair. In time these events were carried to the extreme; they became outlandish. The best people began to hold the affairs in disrepute." Physically, it involved "parading with [a] dusky partner with gigantic and graceful stride, the buck and wing dancing, the buzzard lope, etc."

101. *CT*, August 26, 1893, 3.

102. Majors, "What the Negro Contributed," 52.

103. *Chicago Herald*, August 25, 1893, 9; *CT*, August 26, 1893, 3; and *CIO*, August 26, 1893, 1.

104. Marva Griffin Carter, "The Life and Music of Will Marion Cook," 31n2.

105. "Jubilee Day," *Indianapolis Freeman*, September 2, 1893, 1.

106. Ransom, *Pilgrimage*, 81, 82.

107. See Harris, *Colored Men's Directory*, 12, which lists a Dr. Mary E. Green, with offices at 230 Twenty-second Street and with a residence at 2637 State Street, as a practicing physician as early as 1885.

108. *Indianapolis Freeman*, September 9, 1893, 1.

109. Claude Evans Driskell, *The History of Black Dental Professionals*, 22; "Desegregating Medicine," *Chicago Sun-Times*, January 13, 2002, 22A.

110. Kletzing and Crogman, *Progress of a Race*, 533 (emphasis added).

111. Frazier, *Negro Family in Chicago*, 102.

112. "Chicago Colored Society," *Illinois Record*, June 18, 1898, 1, 2.

113. "Colored Belles to Come: Chicago's African '400' Agog over Prospective Visit of the Leaders of Colored Society," 4.

114. See also Williamson, *The New People*, 148–49.

115. See "Colored Belles to Come." One contemporary tourist guide informed the more adventurous, younger, wealthy white men seeking to satisfy their vices that they should view the African American area south of the Loop known as "Cheyenne" with caution, because there dwelled, along with male cutthroats, the dreaded "Amazons," whom even policemen feared. These women were notoriously good fighters: "Most [police] officers would rather engage in a grapple with half a dozen male desperados than with one of those formidable Negresses. They are Amazonians in physique" (Vynne, *Chicago by Day and Night*, 154–57). Furthermore, the contemporary references in the guidebooks to the women of Dahomey at the world's fair as ugly unfortunately were also too commonplace and reflect white abhorrence of them for their skin color as well as any other attributes. See also Gatewood, *Aristocrats of Color*, chapter 6, for the problem of the internal color line.

116. *CT*, October 29, 1893, 26.

117. *CT*, May 28, 1893, 27.

118. Gatewood, *Aristocrats of Color*, 219.

119. Ottley, *Lonely Warrior*, 6, 7.

120. Ottley and Weatherby, *Negro in New York*, 133 (emphasis added).

121. Mossell, *Work of the Afro-American Woman*, 112.

122. McFeely, *Douglass*, 366; see also Cunningham, *Paul Laurence Dunbar*, 96–97.

123. "Society Items," *Broad Ax*, August 26, 1899, 1.

124. See Wright, *Eighty-seven Years*, 67.

125. Robb, *Negro in Chicago*, 1:237.

126. "Chicago Negro Aristocrats," 2, 3.

127. "Society Items," *Broad Ax*, July 15, 1899, 1.

128. Duis, *Challenging Chicago*, 263.

129. Frazier, *Negro Family in Chicago*, 102–4; 125, 126.

130. Criticism of the sybaritic lifestyle of individuals who frequented saloons and racetracks as "sporting men" is more than adequately described in *Illinois Record*, *Atchinson Blade*, and *Appeal*.

131. *BM*, 515.

132. Spear, *Black Chicago*, 66.

133. See Reed, *Chicago NAACP*.

134. *PN*, 7, 316.

135. Jacqueline M. Moore, *Leading the Race: The Transformation of the Black Elite in the Nation's Capital, 1880–1890*, 3; see also 32 and 188. Black Chicago was more democratic and considered socially immature, or backward, by the "400" when compared to the eastern seaboard societies. In addition, the black elite in the District of Columbia had access to attractive federal governmental positions, teaching positions at Howard University and in all-black elementary and high schools, and Freedmen's Hospital, from which to generate a stream of physicians, dentists, and educators. According to Moore, in a new and controversial theory dealing with the intersection of social status, leadership, and ideology, the members of this elite and their children avoided societal displacement once rejected by the white world during the 1890s and 1900s by accommodating themselves to the black world and catering to its needs to hold on to community leadership (6, 214).

136. Kusmer, *Ghetto Takes Shape*, 10, 98; Gatewood, *Aristocrats of Color*, 128.

137. Ottley and Weatherby, *Negro in New York*, 134. See Lewis, *Du Bois*, 104, for more on how Boston's few dozen aristocrats, fading in significance, fit into a total African American population of six thousand and a white corporate-led society of immense wealth and influence. See also Adelaide M. Cromwell, *The Other Brahmins: Boston's Black Upper Class, 1790–1950*.

138. Booker T. Washington, "Our New Citizen," in Brotz, *Negro Social and Political Thought*, 360.

139. "Our Horse Reporter Moralizes," *Appeal*, December 26, 1891, 2; "The Man about Town," *Illinois Record*, July 30, 1898, 3.

140. Work, "Crime," 205.

141. See *BM*, 763, 267–68. See also Reed, *Chicago NAACP*, which embraced this assertion; the NAACP movement was committed wholeheartedly to the realization of social equality in its full expression and naturally subsumed equality of opportunity into its ideology and mission. The question of whether blacks in the late nineteenth century had intellectually accepted the feasibility of experiencing full equality immediately or at any time soon is answered resoundingly in the negative. Part of the resistance came from the strength of the separate black communities John Hope Franklin recognized and explored in all of his editions of *From Slavery to Freedom*. For example see the third edition (1967), pp. 566–72. The issue of integration, or obvious movement toward full equality and Americanization, is also covered in E. Franklin Frazier, *Negro in the United States*, 690, 694–99.

142. Wright, *Eighty-seven Years*, 37.

143. Wright, "Negro in Chicago," 564.

144. *Chicago Evening Post*, June 26, 1893, 2.

145. See Reed, *"All the World,"* Appendix A, for Douglass's speech at Colored American Day in its entirety.

146. Duster, *Crusade for Justice*, 261, 263.

147. Ibid., 120.

148. Ibid., 276–78.

149. Duster, *Crusade for Justice*, 248.

150. Albion W. Tourgee to F[erdinand] L. Barnett, September 16, 1891, Item 5752, AWT. For more on the University of Chicago, see Wright, *Eighty-seven Years*, 37–43.

151. Wells et al., *Reason Why*.

152. Goode, "*Eighth Regiment*," 26; Ashbaugh, *Lucy Parsons*, 190–91. For a fuller account of the violent outbreak and the conditions that produced them, see Bontemps and Conroy, *They Seek a City*, 142–44, and Tuttle, *Race Riot*, 113.

153. Duster, *Crusade for Justice*, 274–78.

154. Lawrence W. Levine, *Highbrow/Lowbrow: The Emergence of Cultural Hierarchy in America*, 30–32, 96–100, 97; Frazier, "Chicago: A Cross-Section of Negro Life," 73. New York blacks were provided with a Shakespearean experience regularly as early as the 1820s at William Henry Brown's African Theater; see Burrows and Wallace, *Gotham*, 488.

155. Dempsey J. Travis, *An Autobiography of Black Jazz*, chapters 3 and 4.

156. Work, "Crime," 207.

157. Travis, *Autobiography of Black Jazz*, 8.

158. Reid Badger, *The Great American Fair: The World's Columbian Exposition and American Culture*, 120.

159. "A City Gives 'Jazz' to the Musical World," *CD*, October 29, 1932, 7.

160. "Coon Songs and the Classics," *Presto*, September 1, 1898, 7.

161. Darlene Clark Hine and Kathleen Thompson, *A Shining Thread of Hope: The History of Black Women in America*, 228.

162. Ransom, *Pilgrimage*, 83. For the role these churches played in both increasing class contact and mitigating conflict, see *CVA*, 219.

163. *CVA*, 103, 88.

164. Kletzing and Crogman, *Progress of a Race*, 444–46.

165. "The Old Folks Home," *Broad Ax*, November 4, 1899, 1. See also *Quinn Chapel A.M.E.*, 34, 35.

166. Alfred A. Moss Jr., *The American Negro Academy: Voice of the Talented Tenth*, 1. Bentley is mentioned in Moss, *American Negro Academy*, 73, 74. Williams corresponded with the academy's secretary, John Wesley Cromwell; see S. Laing Williams to John Wesley Cromwell, on March 7, 1897, December 6, 1897, September 8, 1898, November 20, 1899, and December 8, 1899, John Wesley Cromwell Papers, in the possession of Dr. Adelaide Cromwell, Brookline, Mass. (hereafter referred to as *JWC*). For Williams's failure to produce scholarship for the institution, see Williams to Cromwell, March 7, 1897, September 8, 1898, and December 8, 1899, *JWC*.

167. Williams to Cromwell, December 6, 1897, November 20, 1899, *JWC*.

168. This is the thesis of Fannie Barrier Williams's essay "Social Bonds in the 'Black Belt' of Chicago." Her subtitle, "Negro Organizations and the New Spirit Pervading Them," explained the scope of the activities that she wished to explore. She marveled at African Americans' talent and energy for organizing, especially given "the disadvantages suggested, [as] the Colored people of Chicago have shown in their efforts for self-help and self-advancement a determination that is altogether creditable" (40).

169. Wright, "Negro in Chicago," 564.

170. Hine and Thompson, *Shining Thread*, 184. Ida B. Wells-Barnett wrote of the constant fund-raising efforts of black women among whites of means and how she was once embarrassingly mistaken for one of these church solicitors in downtown Chicago. As she began a 1900 crusade against proposed segregation in the Chicago schools, she

visited the offices of the *Tribune's* editor. "When Mr. Robert W. Patterson came in I walked up to him and stood waiting for him to finish a letter before he entered his private office. He glanced up and said, 'I have nothing for you today.' I replied that I did not understand what he meant and told who I was and why I was there. He said, 'I thought you were one of the women from one of the Colored churches coming to solicit a contribution, as they very frequently do.' I laughed and said, 'It therefore seems natural that whenever you see a Colored woman she is begging for her church. I happen to be begging, Mr. Patterson, but not for money.'" See Duster, *Crusade for Justice*, 275.

171. Here and below, African American church information is contained in CVA, 104–6; and Wright, "Industrial Condition," 12, 13.

172. Work, "Crime," 206, 207.

173. Ibid.

174. Ransom, *Pilgrimage*, 88; Wright, *Eighty-seven Years*, 90.

175. Wright, *Eighty-seven Years*, 90.

176. Gosnell, *Negro Politicians*, 49.

177. Ransom, *Pilgrimage*, 82f.

178. Ibid., chapter 8, "The Institutional Church and Social Settlement," 103–18. See also Wright, *Eighty-seven Years*, 94, 95.

179. Duster, *Crusade for Justice*, 225n1, 239. Examples of "aristocratic" weddings among important African Americans can be found in Gatewood, *Aristocrats of Color*, 5–6, 164–66, and 203–6.

180. Duster, *Crusade for Justice*, 241.

181. Gatewood, *Aristocrats of Color*, 204. Who these families and people were is unknown and since the church was housed in the inauspicious edifice of a storefront in 1888, an examination of the composition of the congregation warrants further historical exploration.

182. See "The History of Friendship Missionary Baptist Church," 5, and Franklin and Moss, *From Slavery to Freedom*, 7th ed., 2:285, who consider this schism between folk preference and urban modernism as part of a national trend.

183. *PN*, 204.

184. Ransom, *Pilgrimage*, 83.

185. S. Laing Williams to My Dear Mr. Washington, November 29, 1899, Spec. Corres., S. Laing Williams, 1896–1901, BTW.

186. Williams, "Social Bonds," 41–42.

187. Deegan, *New Woman of Color*, xxxii.

188. Booker T. Washington, "Our New Citizen."

189. S. Laing Williams to My Dear Mr. Washington, April 26, 1899, Spec. Corres., S. Laing Williams, 1896–1901, Booker T. Washington Papers, Library of Congress, Washington, D.C. (Hereafter referred to as BTW).

190. See Spear, *Black Chicago*, chapter 3, "Chicago's Negro Elite," and chapter 4, "The New Leadership." Spear wrote that "The old elite dominated Negro community life until the first decade of the twentieth century. They ran the social affairs, organized the civic ventures, and acted as spokesmen for Chicago's Negroes in matters of group concern" (71). If this had been an accurate assessment, Chicago would have been unique. See the Philadelphia example as observed by Du Bois in *PN*, 317. An interesting example in the twentieth century of how black leadership appeared in multiple layers, or in

different yet interactive spheres, is found in Carmichael and Hamilton, *Black Power*, 101–3. In their example, older militant men, middle-aged women with a recognized and respected social presence, the clergy, and educators presided over disparate spheres of influence and power, and thus provided collective leadership.

191. For an indication of how powerful a factor military service became in political life and as an indicator of leadership, see Gosnell, *Negro Politicians*, 111.

192. See James Q. Wilson's introduction to Gosnell, *Negro Politicians*, vi. In contradiction, see Reed, "Black Chicago Civic Organization."

193. Ransom, *Pilgrimage*, 132; Duster, *Crusade for Justice*, 276.

194. Ransom, *Pilgrimage*, 83, 84.

195. Duster, *Crusade for Justice*, 249, 250, 304.

196. Ransom, *Pilgrimage*, 117. The closeness of Williams to the first Mrs. Ferdinand L. (Mollie, d. 1890) Barnett might also have played a part in the drift evident between the two women as the century closed. See Deegan, *New Woman of Color*, xviii.

197. Duster, *Crusade for Justice*, 251, 252, 121, 122.

198. Hendricks, in *Gender, Race, and Politics*, writes, "Known as the mother of the women's clubs in Illinois, it placed African American women squarely in the reform movement in the Midwest and served as a model for many newly created associations" (17).

199. Williams, "Club Movement," 382–83.

200. Deegan, *New Woman of Color*, xxxiii.

201. Williams, "Club Movement," 382, 383, 402.

202. John Hope Franklin, editor's foreword to Thornbrough, *T. Thomas Fortune: Militant Journalist*, vii.

203. Meier, *Negro Thought*, 139, 146, 149.

204. Spear, *Black Chicago*, 51, 52, 56. See also Kusmer, *Ghetto Takes Shape*, 116n3; in this annotated note, Kusmer stresses the need to distinguish between the ideology and the tactics of the "old elite." One could support inclusion in American society and still choose among means, some seemingly contradictory, to accomplish that end.

205. "Not Slaves, but Men: Commemoration of the Abolition of Slavery," *CIO*, January 8, 1894, 2.

206. Ibid.

207. Booker T. Washington, "Our New Citizen," 360.

208. Duster, *Crusade for Justice*, 126, 229.

209. Hendricks, *Gender, Race, and Politics*, 18, 19.

210. Ibid., 261.

211. S. Laing Williams to My Dear Mr. Washington, April 26, 1899, Spec. Corres., S. Laing Williams, 1896–1901, BTW.

212. Duster, *Crusade for Justice*, 261.

213. Ibid., 249, 250. See also the incident involving compensation for a murdered southern postmaster (254).

214. CVA, 63.

215. See the prefatory essay to Fishel, "Negro in Northern Politics," in August Meier and Elliott Rudwick, eds., *The Making of Black America: Essays in Negro Life and History*, vol. 2, *The Black Community in Modern America*, 56.

216. Ransom, *Pilgrimage*, 82. Fellow A.M.E. churchman Richard R. Wright Jr. also saw the exploitation of the political process and the voters themselves as he described

the economically dispossessed in the voting booth: "[T]hey sell their votes and they 'repeat,' if the boss tells them so" ("Negro in Chicago," 564).

217. Robb, *Negro in Chicago*, 1:103. See also Gosnell, *Negro Politicians*, 154.

218. Robb, *Negro in Chicago*, 1:103; Gosnell, *Negro Politicians*, 154; see 155n5 for a further substantiation of the historic moment in black politics from the *Chicago Defender*.

219. Gosnell, *Negro Politicians*, 155, 206.

220. Ransom, *Pilgrimage*, 83, 84.

221. A. N. Fields, "Noted Lawmakers of Early Chicago," *CD*, February 4, 1933, 11.

222. Ibid.

223. Buckler, *Daniel Hale Williams*, 62.

224. S. Laing Williams to My Dear Mr. Washington, February 19, 1905, and John G. Jones to Sen. A. J. Hopkins, December 9, 1905, Spec. Corres., S. Laing Williams, *BTW*.

225. Joe William Trotter Jr., *The African American Experience*, vol. 2, *From Reconstruction*, 363, which includes the Appomattox Club among a group that restricted its ranks "by color as well as class." Color distinctions in Chicago could never be construed to reach the level found in older eastern and southern cities. Wright, for his part, possessed a deep brown complexion. See Gosnell, *Negro Politicians*, 153.

226. A recent dissertationist has postulated that the starting point for examination of the role of black politics is during the post-Reconstruction period in the South, and in the case of Chicago, in the 1890s. See Lisa Gail Materson, "Respectable Partisans: African American Women in Electoral Politics, 1877 to 1936."

227. "'The Man about Town'—Writes about the Political and Social Situation in Chicago . . . ," *Illinois Record*, July 30, 1898, 3.

228. "Wing and Bluster," *Broad Ax*, July 29, 1899, 1.

229. Arna Bontemps, "Soldiers"—in Illinois, 5–7, *IWP*.

230. Ibid., 7–9. See also "Military History of Old Chicago," *CD*, October 29, 1932, 7.

231. Reed, *"All the World,"* 116, 117.

232. Lunette Bassett Brady, "Welcome Home," presented March 18, 1899, in Chicago to the returning troops, in Goode, *"Eighth Regiment,"* 203–5.

233. Goode, *"Eighth Regiment,"* 32. According to Rayford W. Logan, the war "not only gave to Negroes a much needed feeling of pride, [but also gave] to some other Americans a respect for Negroes that was rarely manifested" (*Betrayal of the Negro*, 335).

234. Goode, *"Eighth Regiment,"* 15, 31.

235. Ibid., 31, 222.

236. Gatewood, *"Smoked Yankees,"* 4; Ashbaugh, *Lucy Parsons*, 207. See also William Loren Katz, "The Afro-American's Response to U.S. Imperialism," 57, 58; Herbert Aptheker, ed., *A Documentary History of the Negro People in the United States*, vol. 2, *From the Reconstruction Era to 1910*, 823–26; and Bracey, Meier, and Rudwick, *Black Nationalism*, 174–75, for criticism of the war from a racial point of view.

237. Goode, *"Eighth Regiment,"* 291; Ransom, *Pilgrimage*, 85, 86; and Duster, *Crusade for Justice*, 254.

238. Goode, *"Eighth Regiment,"* 297.

239. Ibid., 221.

240. Gatewood, *"Smoked Yankees,"* 10.

241. Goode, *"Eighth Regiment,"* 231.

242. Duster, *Crusade for Justice*, 254.

243. Goode, *"Eighth Regiment,"* 109–17.

244. Governor John Tanner to Marshall, September 22, 1893, cited in Arna Bontemps, "Soldiers"—in Illinois, 12, 13, Box 19, Folder 1, *IWP*; Letter, John R. Marshall to Illinois Governor John R. Tanner, September, n.d., 1898 printed in *Parsons Weekly Blade*, September 24, 1898, and cited in Gatewood, *"Smoked Yankees,"* 188, 189.

245. "History of the Eighth Illinois U.S. Volunteers," *Broad Ax*, October 21, 1899, 1.

246. Goode, *"Eighth Regiment,"* 206. The attractiveness of the women also caught the eye of Major Robert Jackson; see Arna Bontemps, "Soldiers"—in Illinois, 12, Box 19, Folder 1, IWP.

247. Gatewood, *"Smoked Yankees,"* 204, 205.

248. Ibid., 198.

249. Goode, *"Eighth Regiment,"* 66, 165. See also 41–43.

250. Ibid., 238, 291.

251. Ibid., 165, 292–95; Ransom, *Pilgrimage*, 86.

252. Goode, *"Eighth Regiment,"* 29.

Epilogue: The Foundation of the Black Metropolis

1. SOS.

2. Williams, "Social Bonds," 40, 41.

3. "Ida B. Wells-Barnett Scores *Tribune*—Disregards Race," *CD*, May 9, 1914, 2.

4. Baker, *Following the Color Line*, 218.

5. Harris, *Colored Men's Directory*, n.p.

6. Johnson, "These Colored United States," 927; Frazier, "Chicago: A Cross-Section of Negro Life," 70.

7. *BM*, 396, 385. As Levine wrote, "Blacks had played the game by the rules and discovered definitely that the rules simply did not apply to them. The anxiety that accompanied this discovery was marked by the dramatic rise of a series of revitalization movements: . . . [for example, in] the uninhibited growth of a series of cities within cities which were increasingly separate socially and culturally" (*Black Culture*, 269).

8. One section is described in Christopher Robert Reed, "Beyond Chicago's Black Metropolis: A History of the West Side's First Century, 1837–1940."

9. Chicago Fact Book Consortium, *Local Community Fact Book: Chicago Metropolitan Area, 1990*, xvii.

10. Harris, *Negro as Capitalist*, 163.

11. See Chairman [Rufus C. Dawes] to Robert S. Abbott, January 30, 1929, Robert S. Abbott File, as well as Dawes Memorandum, February 29, 1928, and Binga to Dawes, August 1928, Jesse Binga File, all in A Century of Progress Papers, University of Illinois at Chicago Libraries.

12. Duster, *Crusade for Justice*, 274–78.

13. See Reed, *Chicago NAACP*.

14. See Kilson, "Political Change."

15. See Gosnell, *Negro Politicians*, 154, 155n5, 159.

16. First inaugural speech of Mayor Harold Washington, April 29, 1983, in Alton Miller, comp., *Climbing a Great Mountain: The Speeches of Mayor Harold Washington*, 7.

Appendix A. The Illinois Black Laws

1. Consistent with contemporary usage, the proper title *Negro* has been capitalized throughout this document. Throughout the late nineteenth century and into the twentieth, African American newspaper editors and journalists, such as Chicago's Ferdinand L. Barnett, crusaded to have this racial name capitalized. See Ferdinand L. Barnett, "Spell It with a Capital."

2. As used in the original document.

3. Consistent with contemporary usage, the proper title *Colored* has been capitalized throughout this document.

Appendix E. Data from "Jubilee": Chicago's Black Civil War Soldiers

1. Miller, *Black Civil War Soldiers*, 175.

2. Deposition of John Blakely, July 17, 1900, Federal Pension Record of John Blakely, Company C, CWPR.

3. Request form, Bureau of Pensions, February 7, 1901, Federal Pension Record of John Washington, Company B, CWPR; Request form, January 22, 1891, Federal Pension Record of Jordan Stewart, Company B, CWPR.

4. See Deposition of Ethelbert Graves, September 9, 1922, Federal Pension Record of William Graves, Company B; and Deposition of Walter Duke, November 28, 1895, Federal Pension Record of James Green, Company B, CWPR.

5. Depositions of James H. Brown, James Knight, and William Payne, on July 17, 1889, August 1, 1889, and August 12, 1889, respectively, Federal Pension Record of Lewis T. Wood, Company B, CWPR.

6. Deposition of Isaac Smith, July 13, 1896, Federal Pension Record of William McKenney, Company F, CWPR.

7. Read Hanna to Hon. Commissioner of Pensions, August 23, 1917, Federal Pension Record of Henry Garrett, Company B, CWPR.

8. Deposition of Malinda Chappell, July 5, 1917, Pension Record of Henry Chappell, Company E, CWPR; Deposition of Edward W. Knapp, July 6, 1917, Federal Pension Record of Henry Chappell, Company E, CWPR; J. H. Hines to Hon. V. Warner, Commissioner of Pensions, August 22, 1908, Federal Pension Record of William McKenney, Company F, CWPR.

9. J. H. Stibbs to Hon. Commissioner of Pensions, February 29, 1892, Pensions Record of Louis Clary, Company C, CWPR.

10. Unnamed official to F. E. Keith, July 18, 1914, Federal Pension Record of William Graves, Company B, CWPR.

11. Deposition of Lenore Graves, April 11, 1922, Federal Pension Record of William Graves, Company B, CWPR.

12. Depositions of Mary E. McKenney, November 14, 1915, and Mary Kendall McKenney, August 17, 1908, and October 17, 1908, Federal Pension Record of William McKenney, Company F, CWPR.

13. Read Hanna to Commissioner of Pensions, January 30, 1923, Federal Pension Record of William Graves, Company B, CWPR.

14. E. B. Olmsted to Hon. William Lochren, November 30, 1895, Federal Pension Record of James Green, Company B, CWPR.

15. Booker T. Washington, *Up from Slavery*, 1; Douglass, *Life and Times*, 27.

16. Affidavit dated November 14, 1907, Federal Pension Record of Alexander Garrett, Company B, CWPR.

17. Commissioner to Hon. Martin B. Madden, October 30, 1907, Federal Pension Record of Alexander Garrett, Company B, CWPR.

18. Deposition of William Graves, February 18, 1914, Federal Pension Record of William Graves, Company B, CWPR.

19. James Jones to Commissioner of Pensions, October 23, 1913, Federal Pension Record of James Jones, Company B, CWPR; E. B. Olmstead to Hon. H. Clay Evans, January 4, 1899, and Deposition of Eliza Barber (Barbour), November 23, 1898, Federal Pension Record of Richard Barbour, Company B; Deposition of Emma Clary Bell, February 3, 1892, Federal Pension Record of Louis Clary, Company C, CWPR; Deposition of Julia Abrams, May 14, 1913, Federal Pension Record of John Abrams, Company G, CWPR; Deposition of Lucy Simpson Johnson, May 25, 1913, Federal Pension Record of John Abrams, Company G, CWPR.

20. Genovese, *Roll, Jordan, Roll*, 444–47. See also Berlin, *Many Thousands Gone*: "A new name was both a symbol of personal liberation and an act of political defiance; it reversed the enslavement process and confirmed the black person's newly won liberty, just as the loss of an African name had earlier symbolized enslavement" (239).

21. Deposition of Frank F. Todd, July 8, 1914, Federal Pension Record of William Graves, Company B, CWPR.

22. J. Davenport to John L. Manning, February 24, 1912, Federal Pension Record of Henry Chappell, Company E, CWPR.

23. Affidavit by Harry Myers, c. 1881, Federal Pension Record of Harry Myers, Eighty-eighth Infantry, and Third Cavalry, Heavy Artillery Unit, CWPR.

24. Miller, *Black Civil War Soldiers*, 175.

25. Dean, *Shook over Hell*, 4, 5.

26. Surgeon's certificate, May 11, 1904, Federal Pension Record of Alexander Garrett, Company E, CWPR; Declaration for Original Invalid Pension, July 19, 1893, Federal Pension Record of Richard Barbour, Company B, CWPR.

27. Deposition of Nancy Clary, February 1, 1892, Federal Pension Record of Louis Clary, Company C, CWPR.

28. For Bogart's letter of condolences, see Miller, *Black Civil War Soldiers*, 153. For McCoslin's narrative, see Drinkard, *Illinois Freedom Fighters*, 19, citing McCoslin, "Letter from the Front."

29. Deposition of John Enders, November 14, 1890, Federal Pension Record of Milton Hawkins, Company B, CWPR; Note card, L. J. Gosper to Dear sir, February 23, 1884, Federal Pension Record of Henry Parker, Company C, CWPR.

30. An excellent scholarly reference is Gutman, *Black Family*.

31. Miller, *Black Civil War Soldiers*, 14.

32. Deposition of Cecilia McAllister, July 20, 1891, Federal Pension Record of Frank McAllister, Company C, CWPR.

33. Deposition of Jane Liter, October 17, 1892, Federal Pension Record of John Liter, Company B, CWPR.

34. Frazier, *Negro Family in the United States*, 102.

35. Acting Chief, Board of Review to Chief, Special Examination Division, December 3, 1921, Federal Pension Record of William Graves, Company B, CWPR; Chief, Board of Review to Chief, Special Examination Division, May 21, 1917, Federal Pension Record of Henry Chappell, Company E, CWPR. Interestingly enough, recent editions of the *Chicago Tribune* have carried news items that describe the circumstances under which the nation's last surviving Civil War Confederate widows chose their spouses. In one case, a twenty-one-year-old white woman married an eighty-one-year-old Confederate veteran from Alabama in 1927. The explanation for the marital rite was simple: "He was a handsome man with a bushy mustache, a quick temper and a $50-a-month [Alabama State] military pension—a princely sum in those days for a woman stalked her whole life by poverty. He was lonely; she was needy" (February 9, 2003, sec. 1, p. 12). In another case, a nineteen-year-old Arkansas white woman married an eighty-six-year-old veteran of a Virginia regiment during the depths of the Great Depression in 1934. The soldier died at age eighty-nine. Ending poverty was once again the major factor for the union (June 16, 2004, sec. 1, p. 20).

36. Claim for Increase of Widow's Pension, May 2, 1867, Federal Pension Record of James Watts, Company B, CWPR.

37. Deposition of Samuel Fletcher, December 11, 1888, Federal Pension Record of Moses Nelson, Company D, CWPR.

38. E. C. Tieman, Deputy Commissioner, Bureau of Pensions, Department of the Interior to Hon. Martin B. Madden, House of Representatives, December 6, 1914, Federal Pension Record of Alexander Garrett, Company B, CWPR.

39. Dependent Parent Claims, Federal Pension Record of Cato Flowers, Company C, and Louis Clary, Company C, CWPR.

40. Affidavit of Moses Conley, November 23, 1895, Federal Pension Record of Moses Conley, Company C, CWPR.

41. Deposition of Nancy Clary, February 1, 1892, Federal Pension Record of Louis Clary, Company C, CWPR.

42. Deposition of William A. Howard, July 11, 1917, Federal Pension File of Henry Chappell, Company E, CWPR.

43. Ibid.

44. J. H. Stibbs to Hon. Commissioner of Pensions, October 3, 1885, Federal Pension Record of James Jones, Company B, CWPR.

45. Deposition of James Jones, July 9, 1885, Federal Pension Record of James Jones, Company B, CWPR.

Bibliography

COLLECTIONS AND PAPERS

Archives of the State of Illinois–Springfield
Civil War Muster-in and Descriptive Rolls of the Twenty-ninth Volunteer (Colored) Infantry, Illinois.
Excerpted Letter by State Representative John W. E. Thomas to Republicans of the Second Senatorial District, October 8, 1878.
Roster of Illinoisans Who Joined the Fifty-fourth Massachusetts.

Archives of the United States, Washington, D.C.
Civil War Pension Records, Case Files of Approved Veterans Who Served in the Army and Navy Mainly in the Civil War and the War with Spain ("Civil War and Later Services' Certificates"), 1861–1934.
Regimental Papers, Twenty-ninth Volunteer Infantry, Illinois, U.S.C.T.

Chautauqua County Historical Society, Mayfield, New York
Tourgee, Judge Albion Winegar, Papers.

Chicago Historical Society
Atkinson Family Papers (including the Membership Rolls of the Old Settlers Club, 1904).
Eastman, Zebrina, Papers.
Jones, John, Papers.
Harpel's Scrapbook, "Obituaries, up to 1884" (vol. 8).
Pierce, Bessie Louise, Papers (including research files for A History of Chicago).
Wagoner, Henry O., File.

Chicago Public Library
Atkinson Family Papers. The Vivian G. Harsh Collection on Afro-American History and Literature, the Carter G. Woodson Regional Center.
Bethel New Life, Inc. Community Records, 1870–1986, Neighborhood History Research Collection, Special Collections and Preservation Division, Harold Washington Center.
Illinois Writers Files. "The Negro in Illinois." The Vivian G. Harsh Collection on Afro-American History and Literature, the Carter G. Woodson Regional Center.

545

Library of Congress
Washington, Booker T., Papers.
University of Chicago Library
Wells, Ida B., Papers.
Private Holdings
Black firefighters of Chicago, research papers. Collection of Ken Little, Chicago.
Black firefighters of Chicago, research papers. Collection of DeKalb Wolcott, II, Chicago.
Cromwell, John Wesley, papers. Adelaide Cromwell, Brookline, Massachusetts, curator.
Hall, Abraham T., and Joanna Huss Hall and family, papers and memorabilia. Hall-Boger family collection, Jeanne Boger Jones, Grand Rapids, Michigan, curator.
Taylor, Charles B., and family, papers and photographs. Leota Johnson, Chicago, curator.
Williams, Fannie Barrier, research materials. Collection of William G. Andrews, State University of New York at Brockport, and official historian of Brockport, February 10, 1998.

GOVERNMENT DOCUMENTS

City of Chicago. Chicago Planning Commission. *Residential Chicago*. Vol. 1, *Chicago Land Use Survey*. Chicago: Chicago Planning Commission and Works Progress Administration, 1942.
City of Chicago. Department of Planning and Development. "Black Metropolis Historic District," March 7, 1984 (rev. December 1994).
Illinois. General Assembly. Revised Statutes. Chapter 74, Imposition of Statute on Negroes and Mulattoes, 1845 [Illinois Black Laws].
Illinois. General Assembly. An Act to Prevent the Immigration of Free Negroes into This State, 1853.
Illinois. General Assembly. Resolutions in Opposition to the Emancipation Proclamation, 1863.
Illinois. General Assembly. Revised Statutes. Repeal of Statute on Negroes and Mulattoes, 1865 [Illinois Black Laws].
Illinois. General Assembly. School Statute, 1874.
Illinois. General Assembly. Civil Rights. Protection to Citizens, 1885.
Illinois. Adjutant General's Office. Report of the Adjutant General of the State of Illinois Containing Reports for the Years 1861–1866, vol. 8, 1901.

U.S. Army. Revised United States Army Regulations of 1861. Washington: U.S. Government Printing Office, 1863.

U.S. Congress. House of Representatives. 39th Cong., 1st sess., May 10, 1866.

U.S. Congress. House of Representatives. 94th Cong., 2nd sess., August 3, 1976.

U.S. War of the Rebellion: Official Records of the Union and Confederate Armies. Washington: U.S. Government Printing Office, 1880–1901.

U.S. Supplement to the Official Records of the Union and Confederate Armies. Part 2, Record of Events. Vol. 77, ed. Janet Hewett. Wilmington, Del.: Broadfoot Publishing, 1998.

NEWSPAPERS

Chicago Broad Ax
Chicago Conservator
Chicago Daily News
Chicago Defender
Chicago Evening Journal
Chicago Inter Ocean
Chicago Tribune
Cleveland Gazette
(Springfield) Illinois Record
Indianapolis Freeman
Western Appeal (after 1888, *Appeal*)

OTHER SOURCES

Anderson, Louis B. "Facts to Show We Came Here First and Are Here to Stay." *Chicago Defender*, February 7, 1920.

Andreas, A. T. *History of Chicago*. 3 vols. Chicago: Andreas, 1884. Reprint, New York: Arno, 1975.

Angle, Paul M. "Chicago and the Emancipation Proclamation." *Chicago History* 6 (1952): 257-63.

Aptheker, Herbert, ed. *A Documentary History of the Negro People in the United States*. Vol. 2, *From the Reconstruction Era to 1910*. New York: Citadel Press, 1951.

Ashbaugh, Carolyn. *Lucy Parsons: American Revolutionary*. Chicago: Charles A. Kerr Publishing, 1976.

Austen, Ralph A. "The Slave Trade as History and Memory: Confrontations of Slaving Voyage Documents and Communal Traditions." *William and Mary Quarterly* 58 (January 2001): 229-44.

Badger, Reid. *The Great American Fair: The World's Columbian Exposition and American Culture*. Chicago: Nelson-Hall, 1979.

Baker, Ray Stannard. *Following the Color Line: American Negro Citizenship in the Progressive Era*. 1908. Reprint, New York, Harper and Row, 1964.

Ball, Charles. *Fifty Years in Chains*. 1837. Reprint, New York: Dover, 1970.

Barnett, Ferdinand L. "Spell It with a Capital." *Chicago Conservator*, October 26, 1878.

Barrows, John Henry, ed. *The World's Parliament of Religions*. Chicago: Parliament Publishing, 1893.

Beard, Charles A., and Mary R. Beard. *The Rise of American Civilization*. 2 vols. New York: MacMillan Press, 1927.

"Beauty Bosoms: The Story of Chicago's Great Charity Ball from the Opening to the Closing Scene." *Appeal*, March 5, 1892.

Bell, Howard H[olman]. "Chicago Negroes in the Reform Movement, 1847–1853." *Negro History Bulletin* 7 (April 1958): 153-55.

——— . "A Survey of the Negro Convention Movement." Ph.D. diss., Northwestern University, 1953.

Bennett, Lerone, Jr. *Forced into Glory: Abraham Lincoln's White Dream*. Chicago: Johnson Publishing, 2000.

Berlin, Edward A. *King of Ragtime: Scott Joplin and His Era*. New York: Oxford University Press, 1994.

Berlin, Ira B. *Many Thousands Gone: The First Two Centuries of Slavery in North America*. Cambridge: Harvard University Press, 1998.

Berlin, Ira B., Marc Favreau, and Steven F. Miller, eds. *Remembering Slavery: African Americans Talk about Their Personal Experiences of Slavery*. New York: New Press, 1998.

Blanchard, Rufus, ed. *The Discovery and Conquests of the Northwest with the History of Chicago*. Chicago: Blanchard, 1900.

Blassingame, John W. "The Recruitment of Colored Troops in Kentucky, Maryland, and Missouri, 1863–1865." *Historian* 39 (August 1967): 533-45.

——— . *The Slave Community: Plantation Life in the Antebellum South*. Rev. ed. New York: Oxford University Press, 1979.

Blight, David W. "John Brown: Triumphant Failure." *American Prospect*, March 13, 2000, 44-45.

Blyden, Edward W. "The Negro in Ancient History." *Methodist Quarterly Review* 4th ser., 51, no. 21 (January 1869): 71-93.

Bogger, Tommy L. *Free Blacks in Norfolk, Virginia: 1790–1860*. Charlottesville: University of Virginia Press, 1997.

Bontemps, Arna, and Jack Conroy. *They Seek a City*. Garden City, N.Y.: Doubleday, Doran, 1945. Reprint, *Anyplace but Here*, Columbia: University of Missouri Press, 1997.

Boritt, Gabor. "Did He Dream of a Lily-White America?" In Gabor Boritt, ed., *The Lincoln Enigma: The Changing Face of an American Icon*. New York: Oxford University Press, 2001.

Bracey, John H., Jr., August Meier, and Elliott Rudwick, eds. *The Afro-Americans: Selected Documents*. Boston: Allyn and Bacon, 1972.

———. *Black Nationalism in America*. Indianapolis: Bobbs-Merrill, 1970.

Bradbury, R. E. *The Benin Kingdom and the Edo-Speaking Peoples of South-Western Nigeria*. London: International African Institute, 1957.

Branham, Charles Russell. "Black Chicago: Accommodationist Politics before the Great Migration." In *Ethnic Frontiers: Essays in the History of Group Survival in Chicago and the Midwest*, ed. Melvin G. Holli and Peter d'A. Jones, 211-62. Grand Rapids, Mich.: William B. Eerdmans Publishing, 1977.

———. "The Transformation of Black Political Leadership in Chicago, 1865–1942." Ph.D. diss., University of Chicago, 1981.

Brotz, Howard, ed. *Negro Social and Political Thought, 1850–1920: Representative Texts*. New York: Basic Books, 1966.

Brown, Hallie Q. *Homespun Heroines and Other Women of Distinction*. Nashville: Fisk University Library, 1926. Reprint, Freeport, N.Y.: Books Free Library Press, 1971.

Buckler, Helen. *Daniel Hale Williams: Negro Surgeon*. New York: Pitman Publishing Corporation, 1968. First published in 1956 as *Doctor Dan* by Little, Brown.

Bundles, A'Lelia. *On Her Own Ground: The Life and Times of Madam C. J. Walker*. New York: Scribner, 2001.

Bunner, H. C. "The Making of the White City." *Scribner's Magazine*, October 1892.

Burrows, Edwin G., and Mike Wallace. *Gotham: A History of New York City to 1898*. New York: Oxford University Press, 1999.

Calkins, Chris M. *The Appomattox Campaign*. Conshohocken, Pa.: Combined Books, 1997.

———. *The Battles of Appomattox Station and Appomattox Court House, April 8-9, 1865*. Lynchburg, Va.: H. E. Howard, 1987.

Campbell, James T. *Songs of Zion: The African Methodist Church in the United States and South Africa*. New York: Oxford University Press, 1995.

Carmichael, Stokely [Kwame Ture], and Charles V. Hamilton. *Black Power: The Politics of Liberation in America*. New York: Random House, 1967.

Carter, Marva Griffin. "The Life and Music of Will Marion Cook." Ph.D.

diss., University of Illinois at Urbana, 1988.

Cassell, Frank A. "A Confusion of Voices: Reform Movements and the World's Columbian Exposition of 1893." *Mid-America* 67 (winter 1985): 66.

Catton, Bruce. *A Stillness at Appomattox.* New York: Doubleday, 1953. Reprint, New York: Pocket Books, 1964.

Chadwick, Bruce. *When the Game Was Black and White: The Illustrated History of Baseball's Negro Leagues.* New York: Abbevile Press, 1992.

Chatfield-Taylor, Hobart. *Chicago.* New York: Houghton Mifflin, 1917.

Chicago Fact Book Consortium, ed. *Local Community Fact Book: Chicago Metropolitan Area, 1990.* Chicago: Academy Press, 1995.

"Chicago's Noted Negroes . . . Colored Citizens as Lawyers and in Other Positions Where Talent and Energy Are Required." *Chicago Daily News,* March 14, 1887, 4.

Collison, Gary. *Shadrach Minkins: From Fugitive Slave to Citizen.* Cambridge: Harvard University Press, 1997.

"Colored Belles to Come: Chicago's African '400' Agog over Prospective Visit of the Leaders of Colored Society." *Chicago Daily News,* May 4, 1896.

"Colored Lights in Chicago: Citizens of Dark Hue Who Are Prominent in Business and the Professions." *Chicago Daily News,* August 6, 1885, 1.

Commager, Henry Steele, ed. *Documents of American History.* New York: Appleton-Century-Crofts, 1958.

Conkin, Paul K., and Roland N. Stromberg. *Heritage and Challenge: The History and Theory of History.* Arlington Heights, Ill.: Forum Press, 1989.

Cook, Frederick Francis. *Bygone Days in Chicago: Recollections of the "Garden City" of the Sixties.* Chicago: McClurg, 1910.

Cromwell, Adelaide M. *The Other Brahmins: Boston's Black Upper Class, 1790–1950.* Fayetteville: University of Arkansas Press, 1994.

Cunningham, Virginia. *Paul Laurence Dunbar and His Song.* New York: Dodd, Mead, 1947.

Curry, Leonard P. *The Free Black in Urban America, 1800–1850: The Shadow of the Dream.* Chicago: University of Chicago Press, 1981.

Dale, Elizabeth. *The Rule of Justice: The People of Chicago versus Zephyr Davis.* Columbus: Ohio State University Press, 2001.

———. "'Social Equality Does Not Exist among Themselves, nor among Us': *Baylies vs. Curry* and Civil Rights in Chicago, 1888." *American Historical Journal* 102 (1997): 311-39.

Danckers, Ulrich, and Jane Meredith. *A Compendium of the Early History of Chicago: To the Year 1835 When the Indians Left.* John Swenson, contributing editor, with a contribution from Helen H. Tanner. River Forest, Ill.: Early Chicago, 2000.

Davis, Ralph Nelson. "The Negro Newspaper in Chicago." Master's thesis, University of Chicago, 1939.

Dawley, Alan. *Class and Community: The Industrial Revolution in Lynn.* Cambridge: Harvard University Press, 2000.

"The Dawn of Freedom: Celebration by the Colored Citizens." *Chicago Tribune,* January 5, 1863, 4.

Dean, Eric T., Jr. *Shook over Hell: Post-traumatic Stress, Vietnam, and the Civil War.* Cambridge: Harvard University Press, 1997.

Dean, Theresa. *White City Chips.* Chicago: Warren, 1895.

Deegan, Mary Jo, ed. *The New Woman of Color: The Collected Writings of Fannie Barrier Williams, 1893–1918.* DeKalb: Northern Illinois University Press, 2002.

Diedrich, Maria. *Love across Color Lines: Ottilie Assing and Frederick Douglass.* New York: Hill and Wang, 1999.

Douglass, Frederick. *Life and Times of Frederick Douglass.* 1892. Reprint, New York: Bonanza Books, 1962.

Douglass, Frederick. *The Narrative and Selected Writings.* Ed. Michael Meyer. New York: Random House, 1984.

Downey, Dennis B. "Rite of Passage: The World's Columbian Exposition and American Life." Ph.D. diss., Marquette University, 1981.

Drake, St. Clair. *Churches and Voluntary Associations in the Chicago Negro Community.* Chicago: Works Progress Administration, 1940.

——— . *The Redemption of Africa and Black Religion.* Chicago: Third World Press, 1970.

Drake, St. Clair, and Horace R. Cayton. *Black Metropolis: A Study of Negro Life in a Northern City.* New York: Harcourt, Brace and World, 1945. Reprint, Chicago: University of Chicago Press, 1993.

Drinkard, Dorothy L. *Illinois Freedom Fighters: A Civil War Saga of the 29th Infantry, United States Colored Troops.* New York: Simon and Schuster, 1998.

Driskell, Claude Evans. *The History of Chicago Black Dental Professionals.* Chicago: Claude E. Driskell, 1982.

Du Bois, W. E. B. *The Philadelphia Negro.* 1899. Reprint, New York: Schocken Books, 1967.

——— . *The Souls of Black Folk.* New York: Alfred A. Knopf, 1993.

Duis, Perry R. *Challenging Chicago: Coping with Everyday Life, 1837–1920.* Urbana: University of Illinois Press, 1998.

Dummett, Clifton O. *Charles Edwin Bentley: A Model for All Times.* St. Paul, Minn.: North Central Publishing, 1982.

Duster, Alfreda M., ed. *Crusade for Justice: The Autobiography of Ida B. Wells*. Chicago: University of Chicago Press, 1967.

Dyer, Frederick H. *A Compendium of the War of the Rebellion*. 1909. Reprint, Dayton, Ohio: Press of the Morningside Bookstore, 1978.

Edmunds, R. David. *Potawatomis: Keepers of the Flame*. Norman: University of Oklahoma Press, 1978.

Edwards, G. Franklin. *E. Franklin Frazier on Race Relations: Selected Writings*. Chicago: University of Chicago Press, 1968.

Ellison, Ralph. *Invisible Man*. New York: Vintage Books, 1972.

"Emancipation Day Jubilee." *Indianapolis Freeman*, May 13, 1893, 2.

Emilio, Luis F. *History of the Fifty-fourth Regiment of Massachusetts Volunteer Infantry, 1863–1865*. Boston: Boston Book Company, 1891.

"Enthusiastic Meeting at New England Church in Aid of Colored Refugees." *Chicago Inter Ocean*, January 15, 1880.

Evans, Linda Jeanne. "Abolitionism in the Illinois Churches, 1834–1865." Ph.D. diss., Northwestern University, 1981.

Fields, A. N. "Chicago Yesterday, Today, and Tomorrow." 40-part series. *Chicago Defender*, October 1, 1932–June 24, 1933.

Finkelman, Paul, ed. *"Dred Scott v. Sandford": A Brief History with Documents*. Boston: Bedford Books, 1997.

Fishel, Leslie H., Jr. "The Negro in Northern Politics, 1870–1900." *Mississippi Valley Historical Review* 42 (1955): 466-89.

Fisher, Miles Mark. "The History of the Olivet Baptist Church of Chicago." Master's thesis, University of Chicago, 1922.

Flinn, John J. *History of the Chicago Police*. Chicago: Chicago Police Fund, 1887. Reprint, Montclaire, N.J.: Patterson Smith, 1973.

Foner, Philip S., and Ronald L. Lewis, eds. *The Black Worker: A Documentary History from Colonial Times to the Present*. Vol. 3, *The Black Worker during the Era of the Knights of Labor*. Philadelphia: Temple University Press, 1978.

Fox, Stephen R. *The Guardian of Boston: William Monroe Trotter*. New York: Atheneum, 1971.

Franklin, John Hope. *The Emancipation Proclamation*. Garden City, N.Y.: Doubleday, 1963. Reprint, New York: Anchor Books, 1965.

———. *From Slavery to Freedom: A History of Negro Americans*. 3d ed. New York: Alfred L. Knopf, 1967.

Franklin, John Hope, and Alfred A. Moss Jr. *From Slavery to Freedom: A History of African Americans*. 7th ed. 2 vols. Boston: McGraw Hill, 1994.

Franklin, John Hope, and August Meier, eds. *Black Leaders of the Twentieth Century*. Urbana: University of Illinois Press, 1982.

Franklin, John Hope, and Loren Schweninger. *Runaway Slaves: Rebels on the Plantation*. New York: Oxford University Press, 1999.

Franklin, Vincent P. *Black Self-Determination: A Cultural History of the Faith of the Fathers*. Westport, Conn.: Lawrence Hill, 1984.

Frazier, E. Franklin. "Chicago: A Cross-Section of Negro Life." *Opportunity* 7 (March 1929): 70-73.

——— . *The Negro Family in Chicago*. Chicago: University of Chicago Press, 1932.

——— . *The Negro Family in the United States*. Chicago: University of Chicago Press, 1939.

——— . *The Negro in the United States*. New York: MacMillan, 1957.

Freehling, William W. *The Road to Disunion: Secessionists at Bay, 1776–1854*. New York: Oxford University Press, 1990.

Gaines, Kevin. "Rethinking Race and Class." *American Historical Review* 102 (April 1997): 378-87.

Gara, Larry. *The Legend of the Underground Railroad*. Lexington: University of Kentucky Press, 1961.

Gatewood, Willard B., Jr. *Aristocrats of Color: The Black Elite, 1880–1920*. Bloomington: Indiana University Press, 1990.

——— . *"Smoked Yankees" and the Struggle for Empire: Letters from Negro Soldiers, 1898–1902*. Urbana: University of Illinois Press, 1971.

Genovese, Eugene D. *Roll, Jordan, Roll: The World the Slaves Made*. New York: Vintage Books, 1976.

George, Carol V. R. *Segregated Sabbaths: Richard Allen and the Rise of Independent Black Churches, 1760–1840*. New York: Oxford University Press, 1973.

Glatthaar, Joseph T. *Forged in Battle: The Civil War Alliance of Black Soldiers and White Officers*. New York: Free Press, 1990.

Gliozzo, Charles A. "John Jones: A Study of a Black Chicagoan." *Illinois Historical Journal* 80 (1987): 177-88.

Goode, W. T. *The "Eighth Regiment."* Chicago: Blakely Printing, 1899.

Gosnell, Harold F. *Negro Politicians: The Rise of Negro Politics in Chicago*. Chicago: University of Chicago Press, 1935.

Green, Constance McLaughlin. *The Secret City: A History of Race Relations in the Nation's Capital*. Princeton: Princeton University Press, 1967.

Greene, Lorenzo J., and Carter G. Woodson. *The Negro Wage Earner*. Washington: Association for the Study of Negro Life and History, 1930.

Gutman, Herbert G. *The Black Family in Slavery and Freedom, 1750–1925*. New York: Pantheon Books, 1976.

Gwaltney, John Langston. *Drylongso: A Self-Portrait of Black America*. New York: Random House, 1980.

[Hall, Charles Edward.] "Chicago in 1843: A Real 'Oldtimer' on the Life of Early Colored Settlers." *Illinois Record*, July 9, 1898, 1.

Halpern, Rick, and Roger Horowitz. *Meatpackers: An Oral History of Black Packinghouse Workers and Their Struggle for Racial and Economic Equality.* New York: Twayne, 1996.

Harding, Vincent. *There Is a River: The Struggle for Freedom in America.* New York: Vintage Books, 1983.

Harlan, Louis R. *Booker T. Washington: The Wizard of Tuskegee, 1901–1915.* New York: Oxford University Press, 1983.

Harley, Sharon. "When Your Work Is Not Who You Are: The Development of a Working-Class Consciousness among Afro-American Women." In *"We Specialize in the Wholly Impossible": A Reader in Black Women's History*, ed. Darlene Clark Hine, Wilma King, and Linda Reed. Brooklyn: Carlson Publishing, 1995 .

Harris, Abram L. *The Negro as Capitalist: A Study of Banking and Business among American Negroes.* 1936. Reprint, Gloucester, Mass.: Peter Smith Publishing, 1968.

Harris, I. C., comp. *The Colored Men's Professional and Business Directory of Chicago.* Chicago: I. C. Harris, 1885.

Harris, Robert L., Jr. "H. Ford Douglas: Afro-American Antislavery Emigrationist." *Journal of Negro History* 62 (1977): 217-34.

Harris, William R. *The Harder We Run: Black Workers since the Civil War.* New York: Oxford University Press, 1982.

Hendricks, Wanda A. *Gender, Race, and Politics in the Midwest: Black Club Women in Illinois.* Bloomington: Indiana University Press, 1998.

Herrick, Mary J. *The Chicago Schools: A Social and Political History.* Beverly Hills, Calif.: Sage Publications, 1971.

Herskovits, Melville J. *Dahomey: An Ancient West African Kingdom.* 1938. Reprint, 2 vols., Evanston: Northwestern University Press, 1967.

Hicken, Victor. *Illinois in the Civil War.* 2d ed. Urbana: University of Illinois Press, 1991.

Higginson, Thomas Wentworth. *Army Life in a Black Regiment.* 1869. Reprint, Boston: Beacon Press, 1962.

Hine, Darlene Clark. *Speak Truth to Power: Black Professional Class in United States History.* Brooklyn: Carlson Publishing, 1996.

Hine, Darlene Clark, and Kathleen Thompson. *A Shining Thread of Hope: The History of Black Women in America.* New York: Broadway Books, 1998.

Hine, Darlene Clark, ed. *Black Women in America: A Historical Encyclopedia.* Brooklyn: Carlson Publishing, 1993.

Hine, Darlene Clark, and Earnestine Jenkins, eds. *A Question of Manhood: A*

Reader in U.S. Black Men's History and Masculinity. Vol. 1, *"Manhood Rights": The Construction of Black Male History and Manhood, 1750–1870.* Bloomington: Indiana University Press, 1999.

Hinks, Peter P. *To Awaken My Afflicted Brethren: David Walker and the Problem of Antebellum Slave Resistance.* University Park: Pennsylvania State University Press, 1997.

"History." In *Souvenir Program, 1872–1985: 113th Anniversary.* Chicago: Saint Stephen African Methodist Episcopal Church, 1985.

"The History of Friendship Missionary Baptist Church." In *Friendship Missionary Baptist Church: 75th Anniversary History,* Chicago: n.p., 1972.

A History of Greater Bethesda Missionary Baptist Church, Chicago, Illinois, 1882–1982. Chicago: n.p., 1982.

"History of the Original Providence Baptist Church." In *Centennial Anniversary Souvenir Year Book, 1863–1963.* Chicago: n.p., 1963.

Homel, Michael W. "Race and Schools in Nineteenth-Century Chicago." *Integrated Education* 12 (1974): 39-42.

Hopkins, Vincent C., S.J. *Dred Scott's Case.* New York: Fordham University Press, 1951.

Horton, James Oliver. "Comment [on the need to reexamine the character of the African American class structure]." In *The State of Afro-American History: Past, Present, and Future,* ed. Darlene Clark Hine, 130-35. Baton Rouge: Louisiana State University Press, 1986.

———. *Free People of Color: Inside the African American Community.* Washington: Smithsonian Institution Press, 1993.

Horton, James Oliver, and Lois E. Horton. *Black Bostonians: Family Life and Community Struggle in the Antebellum North.* Rev. ed. New York: Holmes and Meier, 1999.

———. *In Hope of Liberty: Culture, Community, and Protest among Northern Free Blacks, 1700–1860.* New York: Oxford University Press, 1997.

Hoyt, Homer. *One Hundred Years of Land Value in Chicago: The Relationship of the Growth of Chicago to the Rise of Its Land Values, 1830–1933.* Chicago: University of Chicago Press, 1933.

Hughes, Langston. *The Collected Works of Langston Hughes.* Vol. 1, *The Poems: 1921–1940.* Ed. Arnold Rampersad. Columbia: University of Missouri Press, 2001.

Hunter, Tera W. *To 'Joy My Freedom: Southern African American Women's Lives and Labors after the Civil War.* Cambridge: Harvard University Press, 1997.

Ignatiev, Noel. *How the Irish Became White.* New York: Routledge, 1995.

"In Commemoration: Colored Americans Establish a Day of Thanksgiving." *Chicago Inter Ocean,* January 4, 1892, 6.

Jackson, Luther Porter. *Free Negro Labor and Property Holding in Virginia, 1830–1860*. 1942. Reprint, New York: Atheneum, 1968.

Jefferson, Robert Franklin. "Making the Men of the Ninety-third: African American Servicemen in the Years of the Great Depression and the Second World War, 1935–1947." Ph.D. diss., University of Michigan, 1995.

Joens, David A. "John W. E. Thomas and the Election of the First African American to the Illinois General Assembly." *Journal of the Illinois State Historical Society* 94 (2001): 200-216.

Johnson, Charles S. "The New Frontage on American Life." In *The New Negro*, ed. Alain Locke. New York: Albert and Charles Boni, 1925. Reprint, New York: Macmillan, 1992.

——— . "These Colored United States, VII: Illinois: 'Mecca of the Migrant Mob.'" *Messenger* 5 (December 1923): 926-28.

Johnson, Claudius O. *Carter Henry Harrison I: Political Leader*. Chicago: University of Chicago Press, 1928.

Johnson, James Weldon. "Atlanta University Boys at the Exposition." *Bulletin of Atlanta University*, May 1893, 7.

——— . "Atlanta University Boys at the World's Fair." *Bulletin of Atlanta University*, April 1893, 6.

——— . "At the World's Fair." *Bulletin of Atlanta University*, May 1893, 3.

Johnson, Michael, ed. *Abraham Lincoln, Slavery, and the Civil War: Selected Writings and Speeches*. Boston: Bedford/St. Martin's, 2001.

Jones, John. *The Black Laws of Illinois and a Few Reasons Why They Should Be Repealed*. Chicago: Tribune Book and Job Office, 1864.

Joseph Medill: A Biography and Tribute. Chicago: Chicago Tribune, 1947.

Karamanski, Theodore J. *Rally 'Round the Flag: Chicago and the Civil War*. Chicago: Nelson-Hall, 1993.

Katz, William Loren. "The Afro-American's Response to U.S. Imperialism." In *African American Sociology: A Social Study of the Pan-African Diaspora*, ed. James L. Conyers Jr. and Alva Barnett. Chicago: Nelson-Hall, 1999.

Katzman, David M. *Before the Ghetto: Black Detroit in the Nineteenth Century*. Urbana: University of Illinois Press, 1973.

Kelley, Robin D. G. "'We Are Not What We Seem': Rethinking Black Working Class Opposition in the Jim Crow South." *Journal of American History* 80 (1993): 75–112.

Kilson, Martin L. "Political Change in the Negro Ghetto, 1900–1940s." In *Key Issues in the Afro-American Experience*, vol. 2, ed. Nathan I. Huggins, Martin Kilson, and Daniel M. Fox, 167-92. New York: Harcourt, Brace Jovanovich, 1971.

King, Lisa Y. "Wounds That Bind: A Comparative Study of the Role Played by Civil War Veterans of African Descent in Community Formation in Massachusetts and South Carolina, 1865–1915." Ph.D. diss., Howard University, 1999.

Kirkland, Caroline. *Chicago Yesterdays: A Sheaf of Reminiscences.* Chicago: Daughaday, 1919.

Kirkland, Joseph. "Among the Poor of Chicago." *Scribner's Magazine,* July 1892, 3-27.

Kletzing, H. F., and W. H. Crogman. *Progress of a Race; or, The Remarkable Advancement of the American Negro . . .* 1897. Reprint, New York: Negro Universities Press, 1969.

Knupfer, Anne Meis. *Toward a Tenderer Humanity and a Nobler Womanhood: African American Women's Clubs in Turn-of-the-Century Chicago.* New York: New York University Press, 1996.

Krebhiel, Henry Edward. *Afro-American Folksongs.* 1913. Reprint, New York: Frederick Ungar, 1967.

Krieg, Richard M., and Judith A. Cooksey. *Provident Hospital: A Living Legacy.* Chicago: Provident Hospital Foundation, 1998.

Kusmer, Kenneth L. "The Black Urban Experience in American History." In *The State of Afro-American History: Past, Present, and Future,* ed. Darlene Clark Hine, 91–122. Baton Rouge: Louisiana State University Press, 1986.

———. *A Ghetto Takes Shape: Black Cleveland, 1870–1930.* Urbana: University of Illinois Press, 1978.

Latrobe, Charles Joseph. *The Rambler in North America.* New York: Harper and Brothers, 1835.

Lee-Forman, Koby. "The Simple Love of Truth: The Racial Justice Activism of Celia Parker Woolley." Ph.D. diss., Northwestern University, 1995.

Lester, Larry, Sammy J. Miller, and Dick Clark. *Black Baseball in Chicago.* Chicago: Arcadia Publishing, 2000.

Levine, Lawrence W. *Black Culture and Black Consciousness: Afro-American Folk Thought from Slavery to Freedom.* New York: Oxford University Press, 1977.

———. "Comment [on the state of African American history]." In *The State of Afro-American History: Past, Present, and Future,* ed. Darlene Clark Hine, 123-29. Baton Rouge: Louisiana State University Press, 1986.

———. *Highbrow/Lowbrow: The Emergence of Cultural Hierarchy in America.* Cambridge: Harvard University Press, 1988.

Lewis, David Levering. *W. E. B. Du Bois: Biography of a Race, 1868–1919.* New York: Henry Holt, 1991.

Lewis, Hylan. *Blackways of Kent*. Chapel Hill: University of North Carolina Press, 1976.

Linderman, Gerald F. *Embattled Courage: The Experience of Combat in the American Civil War*. New York: Free Press, 1987.

"Little Trace Remains of 1st Black Legislator [J. W. E. Thomas] in Illinois." *Chicago Tribune*, December 20, 1981, 12.

Litwack, Leon F. *North of Slavery: The Negro in the Free States, 1790–1860*. Chicago: University of Chicago Press, 1961.

———. *Trouble in Mind: Black Southerners in the Age of Jim Crow*. New York: Alfred A. Knopf, 1998.

Livermore, Mary A. *My Story of the War: A Woman's Narrative of Four Years Personal Experience as Nurse in the Union Army*. 1887. Reprint, New York: Da Capo, 1995.

Logan, Rayford W. *The Betrayal of the Negro: From Rutherford B. Hayes to Woodrow Wilson*. New York: Collier Books, 1965. [Originally published as *The Negro in American Life and Thought: The Nadir, 1877– 1901*, New York: Dial Press, 1954.]

Logan, Rayford W., and Michael R. Winston, eds. *Dictionary of American Negro Biography*. New York: W. W. Norton, 1982.

Longacre, Edward G. *Army of Amateurs: General Benjamin F. Butler and the Army of the James, 1863–1865*. Mechanicsburg, Pa.: Stackpole Books, 1997.

Longstreet, Stephen. *Chicago, 1860–1919*. New York: David McKay, 1973.

Lyon, Jeff. "Generations: A Quiet Quest to Honor a Family's Legacy." *Chicago Sunday Tribune Magazine*, June 23, 1992.

Main, Jackson Turner. *The Antifederalists: Critics of the Constitution, 1781–1788*. Chicago: Quadrangle Books, 1961.

Majors, J. A. "What the Negro Contributed to the World's Fair of 1893." In *The Negro in Chicago, 1779–1929*, ed. Frederick H. H. Robb. 2 vols. Chicago: Washington Intercollegiate Club of Chicago, 1927–1929.

Martin, Charlotte Elizabeth. *The Story of Brockport for One-Hundred Years, 1829–1929*. N.p., [1929].

Mason, Kenneth. "Battle of the Petersburg Crater." Master's thesis, Kent State University, 1982.

Massa, Ann. "Black Women in the 'White City.'" *Journal of American Studies* 8, no. 3 (December 1974): 319-37.

Massey, Douglas S., and Nancy A. Denton. *American Apartheid: Segregation and the Making of the Underclass*. Cambridge: Harvard University Press, 1993.

Massey, Mary Elizabeth. *Women in the Civil War*. New York: Knopf, 1966. Reprint, University of Nebraska Press, 1994.

Materson, Lisa Gail. "Respectable Partisans: African American Women in Electoral Politics, 1877 to 1936." Ph.D. diss., University of California at Los Angeles, 2000.

Mayer, Harold M., and Richard C. Wade. *Chicago: Growth of a Metropolis*. Chicago: University of Chicago Press, 1969.

McConnell, Stuart. *Glorious Contentment: The Grand Army of the Republic, 1865–1900*. Chapel Hill: University of North Carolina Press, 1992.

McCoslin, Sergeant William. "Letter from the Front" [July 26, 1864]. *Christian Recorder*, August 27, 1864. In *A Grand Army of Black Men: Letters from African-American Soldiers in the Union Army, 1861–1865*, ed. Edwin S. Redkey, 107–10. New York: Cambridge University Press, 1992.

McFeely, William S. *Frederick Douglass*. New York: W. W. Norton, 1991.

McKissick, Patricia, and Frederick McKissick. *A Long Hard Journey: The Story of the Pullman Porter*. New York: Walker, 1989.

McPherson, James M. *The Abolitionist Legacy: From Reconstruction to the NAACP*. Princeton: Princeton University Press, 1975.

———. *Abraham Lincoln and the Second American Revolution*. New York: Oxford University Press, 1991.

———. *Battle Cry of Freedom: The Civil War Era*. New York: Ballantine Books, 1988.

———. *The Negro's Civil War: How American Blacks Felt and Acted during the War for the Union*. 1965. Reprint, New York: Ballantine Books, 1991.

———. *Ordeal by Fire: The Civil War and Reconstruction*. 2d ed. Boston: McGraw-Hill, 1992.

Meier, August. "Negro Class Structure and Ideology in the Age of Booker T. Washington." *Phylon* 23 (3d quarter, 1963): 258-66.

———. *Negro Thought in America, 1880–1915: Racial Ideologies in the Age of Booker T. Washington*. Ann Arbor: University of Michigan Press, 1963.

Meier, August, and Elliott Rudwick, eds. *The Making of Black America: Essays in Negro Life and History*. Vol. 2, *The Black Community in Modern America*. New York: Atheneum, 1970.

Miers, Earl Schenck. *The Last Campaign: Grant Saves the Union*. Philadelphia: J. B. Lippincott, 1972.

Miller, Alton, comp. *Climbing a Great Mountain: The Speeches of Mayor Harold Washington*. Chicago: Bonus Books, 1988.

Miller, Edward A., Jr. *The Black Civil War Soldiers of Illinois: The Story of the Twenty-ninth U.S. Colored Infantry*. Columbia: University of South Carolina Press, 1998.

Mitchell, J. A. "Types and People at the Fair." *Scribner's Magazine* 12 (August 1893): 186-93.

Mitchell, Mary Niall. "'Rosebloom and Pure White,' or So It Seemed." *American Quarterly* 54 (March 2002): 369-410.

Moebs, Thomas Truxtun. *Black Soldiers—Black Sailors—Black Ink: Research Guide on African Americans in U.S. Military History, 1526–1900.* Chesapeake Bay, Va.: Moebs Publishing, 1994.

Moore, Jacqueline M. *Leading the Race: The Transformation of the Black Elite in the Nation's Capital, 1880–1890.* Charlottesville: University of Virginia Press, 1999.

Moore, R[ichard] E. *History of Bethel A.M.E. Church.* Chicago: n.p., 1925. Reprint, 1988.

Morris, Thomas D. *Free Men All: The Personal Liberty Laws of the North, 1780–1861.* Baltimore: Johns Hopkins University Press, 1981.

Moses, John, and Joseph Kirkland, eds. *The History of Chicago.* Chicago: Munsell, 1895.

Moses, Wilson Jeremiah. *The Wings of Ethiopia: Studies in Afro-American Life and Letters.* Ames: Iowa University Press, 1990.

Moss, Alfred A., Jr. *The American Negro Academy: Voice of the Talented Tenth.* Baton Rouge: Louisiana State University Press, 1981.

Mossell, N. F., Mrs. [Gertrude]. *The Work of the Afro-American Woman.* 1894. Reprint, Freeport, N.Y.: Books for Libraries, 1971.

"Motives of Miscegenation: Why White Women Marry Negroes—A Rational Explanation." *Chicago Daily News,* January 26, 1884.

Nash, Gary B. *Forging Freedom: The Formation of Philadelphia's Black Community, 1720–1840.* Cambridge: Harvard University Press, 1988.

Naylor, Robert Anderson. *Across the Atlantic.* London: Roxburghe Press, 1893.

Norris, J. W., comp. *General Directory and Business Advertiser of the City of Chicago.* Chicago: Ellis and Fergus, 1844.

Olsen, Otto H. *Carpetbagger's Crusade: The Life of Albion Winegar Tourgee.* Baltimore: Johns Hopkins University Press, 1965.

Osofsky, Gilbert. *Harlem: The Making of a Ghetto; Negro New York, 1890–1930.* New York: Harper and Row, 1963.

Osthaus, Carl F. "The Rise and Fall of Jesse Binga, Black Financier." *Journal of Negro History* 58 (1973): 39-60.

Ottley, Roi. *The Lonely Warrior: The Life and Times of Robert S. Abbott.* Chicago: Henry Regnery, 1955.

Ottley, Roi, and William J. Weatherby, eds. *The Negro in New York: An Informal Social History.* New York: New York Public Library, 1967.

Ovington, Mary White. *Half a Man: The Status of the Negro in New York.* New York: Hill and Wang, 1969.

Pacyga, Dominic A., and Ellen Skerrett. *Chicago: City of Neighborhoods.* Chicago: Loyola University Press, 1986.

Painter, Nell Irvin. *Exodusters: Black Migration to Kansas after Reconstruction*. Lawrence: University Press of Kansas, 1976.

————. *Sojourner Truth: A Life, a Symbol*. New York: W. W. Norton, 1996.

Penn, Irvine Garland. *The Afro-American Press and Its Editors*. New York: John Wiley, 1891.

Perata, David D. *Those Pullman Blues: An Oral History of the African American Railroad Attendant*. New York: Twayne, 1996.

Peterson, Merrill D. *Lincoln in American Memory*. New York: Oxford University Press, 1994.

Pierce, Bessie Louise. *A History of Chicago*. 3 vols. New York: Alfred A. Knopf, 1937, 1940, 1955.

"Pointe De Saible Turns White." *Chicago Defender*, April 22, 1933; 12.

Quaife, Milo M. *Checagou: From Indian Wigwam to Modern City, 1673–1835*. Chicago: University of Chicago Press, 1933.

Quaife, Milo M., ed. "Property of Jean Baptiste Pointe Sable: Inventory Sale of Property, Sold by Pointe Sable to Jean Lalime, 1800—Documents." *Mississippi Valley Historical Review* 15 (1928): 89-92.

Quarles, Benjamin. *Frederick Douglass*. Washington, D.C.: Associated Publishers, 1948.

Quinn Chapel A.M.E. Church, 1847–1967: Its Story. Chicago: Quinn Chapel A.M.E. Church, 1967.

Rael, Patrick. *Black Identity and Black Protest in the Antebellum North*. Chapel Hill: University of North Carolina Press, 2002.

Ransom, Reverdy C. *The Pilgrimage of Harriet Ransom's Son*. Nashville: A.M.E. Sunday School Union, 1949.

Rattray, R. S. *Ashanti*. London: Oxford University Press, 1923.

Redkey, Edwin S. *Black Exodus: Black Nationalist and Back-to-Africa Movements, 1890–1910*. New Haven: Yale University Press, 1969.

Redkey, Edwin S., ed. *A Grand Army of Black Men: Letters from African-American Soldiers in the Union Army, 1861–1865*. New York: Cambridge University Press, 1992.

Reed, Christopher Robert. *"All the World Is Here!" The Black Presence at White City*. Bloomington: Indiana University Press, 2000.

————. "Beyond Chicago's Black Metropolis: A History of the West Side's First Century, 1837–1940." *Journal of the Illinois Historical Society* 92 (summer 1999): 119-49.

————. "Black Chicago Civic Organization before 1935." *Journal of Ethnic Studies* 14 (winter 1987): 65-77.

————. *The Chicago NAACP and the Rise of Black Professional Leadership, 1909–1960*. Bloomington: Indiana University Press, 1997.

————. "'In the Shadow of Fort Dearborn': Honoring De Saible at the

Chicago World's Fair of 1933–1934." *Journal of Black Studies* 21 (1991): 398-413.

Ribowsky, Mark. *A Complete History of the Negro Leagues, 1884–1955.* New York: Kensington Publishing, 2002.

Richardson, Heather Cox. *The Death of Reconstruction: Race, Labor, and Politics in the Post–Civil War North, 1865–1901.* Cambridge: Harvard University Press, 2001.

Ripley, C. Peter, ed. *The Black Abolitionist Papers.* 5 vols. Chapel Hill: University of North Carolina Press, 1985–1992.

Robb, Frederick H. H., ed. *The Negro in Chicago, 1779–1927.* 2 vols. Chicago: Washington Intercollegiate Club of Chicago, 1927–1929.

Rogers, J. A. *From Superman to Man.* New York: J. A. Rogers, 1917. Reprint, St. Petersburg, Fla.: Helga M. Rogers, 1996.

Roland, Charles P. *An American Iliad: The Story of the Civil War.* 2d ed. Boston: McGraw-Hill, 2002.

Rydell, Robert W. *All the World's a Fair: Views of Empire at American Expositions, 1876–1916.* Chicago: University of Chicago Press, 1991.

Salvatore, Nick. *We All Got History: The Memory Books of Amos Webber.* New York: Times Books, 1996.

Sawislak, Karen. *Smoldering City: Chicagoans and the Great Fire, 1871–1874.* Chicago: University of Chicago Press, 1995.

Schlesinger, Arthur M., Jr. *The Age of Jackson.* Boston: Little, Brown, 1945.
——— . "The Historian as Participant." *Daedalus* 100 (1971): 339-58.

Schneirov, Richard. *Labor and Urban Politics: Class Conflict and the Origins of Modern Liberalism in Chicago, 1864-97.* Urbana: University of Illinois Press, 1998.

Schomburg, Arthur A. "The Negro Digs Up His Past." In *The New Negro,* ed. Alain Locke. New York: Albert and Charles Boni, 1925. Reprint, New York: Macmillan, 1992.

Sellers, Charles B. *The Market Revolution: Jacksonian America, 1815–1846.* New York: Oxford University Press, 1991.

Sewall, May Wright, ed. *The World's Congress of Representative Women.* Chicago: Rand, McNally, 1894.

Simmons, William J. *Men of Mark: Eminent, Progressive, and Rising.* 1887. Reprint, New York: Arno Press and the New York Times, 1968.

"Slavery in Chicago: The Underground Railroad Which Helped Slaves to Freedom in Canada . . . An Interesting Interview with L. C. P. Freer regarding the Anti-Slavery Movement." *Chicago Sunday Inter Ocean,* June 28, 1891, 1.

Smith, Henry Justin. *Chicago's Great Century, 1833–1933.* Chicago: Consolidated Publishers, 1933.

——— . "Social Chicago Fifty Years Ago." In *Transactions for the Year 1933 of the Illinois State Historical Society* no. 40, 27-44. Chicago: Illinois State Historical Society, 1933.

Smith, Jessie Carney, ed. *Notable Black American Women*. Detroit: Gale Research, 1992.

"Some Glimpses into Low Life: A Negro Dive in Full Blast." *Chicago Daily Journal*, February 1, 1860, 3.

Spann, Edward K. *Gotham at War: New York, 1860–1865*. Wilmington, Del.: Scholarly Resources, 2002.

Spear, Allan H. *Black Chicago: The Making of a Negro Ghetto, 1890–1920*. Chicago: University of Chicago Press, 1967.

Spero, Sterling D., and Abram L. Harris. *The Black Worker: The Negro in the Labor Movement*. New York: Columbia University Press, 1931. Reprint, New York: Atheneum, 1969.

Sprague, Stuart Seely, ed. *John Parker, His Promised Land: The Autobiography of John P. Parker, Former Slave and Conductor on the Underground Railroad*. New York: W. W. Norton, 1998.

Stackhouse, Perry J. *Chicago and the Baptists: A Century of Progress*. Chicago: University of Chicago Press, 1933.

Stampp, Kenneth M. *America in 1857: A Nation on the Brink*. New York: Oxford University Press, 1990.

——— . *The Peculiar Institution: Slavery in the Antebellum South*. New York: Random House, 1956.

Stead, William T. *If Christ Came to Chicago*. Chicago: Laird and Lee, 1894.

"Story of Old Settlers Reads Like Fiction." *Chicago Defender*, May 3, 1930, 23.

Strickland, Arvarh E. *History of the Chicago Urban League*. Urbana: University of Illinois Press, 1967. Reprint, Columbia: University of Missouri Press, 2001.

Swenson, John F. "Jean Baptiste Point De Sable: The Founder of Modern Chicago." In *A Compendium of the Early History of Chicago: To the Year 1835 When the Indians Left*, by Ulrich Danckers and Jane Meredith. River Forest, Ill.: Early Chicago, 2000.

Thomas, Emory M. *Robert E. Lee: A Biography*. New York: W. W. Norton, 1995.

Thomas, Richard Harlan. "Jenkin Lloyd Jones: Lincoln's Soldier of Civic Righteousness." Ph.D. diss., Rutgers University, 1967.

Thornbrough, Emma Lou. "T. Thomas Fortune: Militant Editor in the Age of Accommodation." In *Black Leaders of the Twentieth Century*, ed. John Hope Franklin and August Meier. Urbana: University of Illinois Press, 1982.

——— . *T. Thomas Fortune: Militant Journalist*. Chicago: University of Chicago Press, 1972.

Tow, Michael. "Secrecy and Segregation: Murphysboro's Black Social Organizations, 1865–1925." *Journal of the Illinois State Historical Society* 97 (2004): 27-40.

Travis, Dempsey J. *An Autobiography of Black Jazz.* Chicago: Urban Research Institute, 1983.

Trotter, Joe William, Jr. *The African American Experience.* Vol. 2, *From Reconstruction.* Boston: Houghton Mifflin, 2001.

Tucker, Louis Leonard. *Cincinnati during the Civil War.* Columbus: Ohio State University Press for the Ohio Historical Society, 1962.

Tuttle, William M., Jr. *Race Riot: Chicago in the Red Summer of 1919.* New York: Atheneum, 1970.

Twain, Mark. *Adventures of Huckleberry Finn.* Berkeley and Los Angeles: University of California Press, 1985.

Ullman, Victor. *Martin R. Delany: The Beginnings of Black Nationalism.* Boston: Beacon Press, 1971.

Voegeli, V. Jacque. *Free but Not Equal: The Midwest and the Negro during the Civil War.* Chicago: University of Chicago Press, 1967.

Vynne, Harold Richard. *Chicago by Day and Night: The Pleasure Seeker's Guide to the Paris of America.* Chicago: Lake City Publishing, 1892.

Wade, Richard C. *Slavery in the Cities: The South, 1820–1860.* New York: Oxford University Press, 1964.

Walker, Juliet E. K. *Free Frank: A Black Pioneer on the Antebellum Frontier.* Lexington: University of Kentucky Press, 1983.

———. *The History of Black Business in America: Capitalism, Race, Entrepreneurship.* New York: Twayne, 1998.

Walker, Juliet E. K., ed. *Encyclopedia of African American Business History.* Westport, Conn.: Greenwood Press, 1999.

Ward, Samuel Ringgold. *Autobiography of a Fugitive Negro: His Anti-Slavery Labours in the United States, Canada, and England.* 1855. Reprint, Chicago: Johnson Publishing, 1970.

Booker T. Washington, *Up from Slavery.* 1901. Reprint, New York: Norton, 1996.

Washington, Versalle F. *Eagles on Their Buttons: A Black Infantry Regiment in the Civil War.* Columbia: University of Missouri Press, 1999.

Wells, Ida B., Frederick Douglass, Irvine Garland Penn, and Ferdinand L. Barnett. *The Reason Why the Colored American Is Not in the World's Columbian Exposition: The Afro-American's Contribution to Columbian Literature.* 1893. Reprint, ed. Robert W. Rydell, Urbana: University of Illinois Press, 1999.

Wesley, Charles H. *Negro Labor in the United States, 1850–1925: A Study in American Economic History.* New York: Russell and Russell, 1927.

"When Illinois Helped Slaves on the Run toward Freedom." *Chicago Sun-Times*, June 17, 1997, 12.

Wiebe, Robert H. *The Search for Order, 1877–1920*. New York: Hill and Wang, 1967.

Williams, Arsenia. *Jean Baptiste Pointe Du Sable: First Chicagoan.* Mimeographed booklet. Chicago: Frank London Brown Historical Association, n.d.

Williams, Fannie Barrier. "The Club Movement among Colored Women in America." In *A New Negro for a New Century*, ed. Booker T. Washington. Chicago: American Publishing House, 1900.

——— . "A Northern Negro's Autobiography." *Independent*, July 14, 1904, 91-96.

——— . "Social Bonds in the 'Black Belt' of Chicago: Negro Organizations and the New Spirit Pervading Them." *Charities* 15 (October 7, 1905): 40-44.

Williams, George Washington. *A History of Negro Troops in the War of the Rebellion, 1861–1865*. New York: Harper and Brothers, 1888.

Williamson, Joel. *New People: Mulattoes and Miscegenation in the United States*. New York: Free Press, 1980.

"Will Not Be Ignored: Rights of Colored People Reviewed at Central Music Hall." *Chicago Tribune*, February 10, 1890, 6.

Wilson, Edward E. "The Line of Equality among Negroes Is Almost Imperceptible." *Chicago Broad Ax*, December 25, 1909, 1.

Wilson, James T. *The Black Phalanx: A History of the Negro Soldiers of the United States in the Wars of 1775–1812, 1861–'65*. 1888. Reprint, Hartford, Conn.: American Publishing, 1890.

Wilson, Muriel Braxton. "Center City Origins of the South Side Black Community of Chicago, 1860–1890." Master's thesis, Roosevelt University, Chicago, 1984.

Winch, Judy. *Philadelphia's Black Elite: Activism, Accommodation, and the Struggle for Autonomy, 1787–1848*. Philadelphia: Temple University Press, 1988.

Winch, Judy, ed. *Cyprian Clamorgan: The Colored Aristocracy of St. Louis.* Columbia: University of Missouri Press, 1999.

Work, Monroe Nathan. "Crime among the Negroes of Chicago." *American Journal of Sociology*, 1900.

——— . "Negro Real Estate Holders of Chicago." Master's thesis, University of Chicago, 1903.

——— . "The Origin of 'Ragtime Music.'" In *Negro Year Book: An Annual Encyclopedia of the Negro, 1925–1926*. Nashville: A.M.E. Sunday School Union, 1926.

"World's Fair Commissioner." *New York Age*, February 14, 1891.

Wright, Richard R., Jr. *The Centennial Encyclopedia of the African Methodist Episcopal Church*. Philadelphia: A.M.E. Church, 1916.

———— . *Eighty-seven Years behind the Black Curtain: An Autobiography*. Nashville: A.M.E. Sunday School Union, 1965.

———— . "The Industrial Condition of Negroes in Chicago." 2 vols. Bachelor's thesis, University of Chicago, 1901.

———— . "The Negro in Chicago." *Southern Workman* 35 (1906): 553-66.

Zboray, Ronald J., and Mary Sarcino Zboray. "Gender Slurs in Boston's Partisan Press during the 1840s." *Journal of American Studies* 34 (fall 2000): 413-46.

Zucker, Charles N. "Damage and Resistance: Free Blacks in Chicago and Springfield, 1850–1860." Paper presented at the annual meeting of the Association for the Study of Afro-American Life and History, Chicago, 1976.

Index

Page numbers in italics refer to illustrations.

lawyer, 19, 202, 264, 308–9, 358;
National Colored Men's Protective
Association and, 314, 364–65,
525n252; organizations of, 273, 408;
in politics, 264, 335, 423; prominence
of, 113, 258, 325, 336, 345–46, 382;
race relations and, 284, 295, 377; on
social equality, 228, 276–77; world's
fair and, 280, 362
Morris, Thomas D., 96
Morris, William, 98
Moses, Wilson J., 281
Moss, Alfred A., Jr., 311, 357
Motts, Robert, 422
Mount Zion Baptist Church, 85, 128–30
Murray, Rev. I. S. C., 101
Myers, George A., 389

Nahar, Ednorah, 398
Nash, Gary B., 76
National Association for the
Advancement of Colored People
(NAACP), 389, 442, 514n20,
527n304, 535n141
National Association of Colored
Women's Clubs (NACW), 22, 409–10,
414, 419
National Colored Men's Protective
Association of America, 300, 313–14,
364–65
National Equal Rights League, 442
Nation of Islam, 443
Negro Family in Chicago, The (Frazier),
269, 483n33, 488n28; criticism of
introduction to, 513n6; sources for, 7,
187, 284, 383
Negro in Chicago, 1779–1929, The (Robb),
4, 491n84
"Negro in Northern Politics, 1870–1900,
The" (Fishel), 484n57
"Negro Real Estate Holders in Chicago"
(Work), 7
Nelson, Anna, 49
Nelson, David, 231
Nelson, Ida Gray, 383
Nelson, Pvt. Moses, 159

New Negro for a New Century, A, 413
*New People: Mulattoes and Miscegenation
in the United States* (Williamson),
490n52
Ninth Battalion, 24, 174, 329, 425; plan
to defend blacks with, 395, 425–26
Nixon, Mr., 299
Noble, Frederick Perry, 372, 533n98

Observer, 326
Odd Fellows, Order of, 87, 221–22, 273,
409, 512n113
*Official Report of the Niger Valley Exploring
Party* (Delany), 142
Oglesby, Annetta, 51
Old Settlers, 40, 65, 181, 304
Old Settlers Social Club, 7, 45, 383–84,
438, 479n7
"Oldtimer," in *Illinois Record* article,
52–56, 65, 74, 78, 82, 87, 100; on
black economy, 69, 71, 258; on social
life, 91, 93; on vices, 85–86
Olivet Baptist Church, 85, 315, 318,
437; illiteracy within, 271–72; influ-
ence of, 134, 204–5; ministers of, 130,
316, 404–5; world's fair and, 398, 408
Ottley, Roi, 385
Overton, Anthony, 32–33, 441
Overton Hygienic Company, 441

Paine, Stephen, 200
Painter, Nell Irvin, 2, 263
Palmer, Bertha Honore, 314
Palmer, Potter, 249, 256, 297
Palmer House Hotel, 249, 251, 393
Parker, Hale Giddings, 265, 266, 301–2,
327, 408; influence of, 280–81, 391;
leadership by, 297, 336; on race,
280–83, 392–93, 419; at world's fair,
280–83, 362–63
Parker, Isaiah, 53
Parker, John Percival, 266, 518n112
Parker, Maria Williams, 53, 82
Parker House Sausage Company, 33
Parliament of Religions (at the world's
fair), 371